Inside
ColdFusion® MX

John Cummings
Neil Ross
Robi Sen

New Riders

www.newriders.com
201 West 103rd Street, Indianapolis, Indiana 46290
An Imprint of Pearson Education
Boston • Indianapolis • London • Munich • New York • San Francisco

Inside ColdFusion® MX

Copyright © 2003 by New Riders Publishing

FIRST EDITION: August 2002

International Standard Book Number: 0-7357-1304-9

Library of Congress Catalog Card Number: *2001096722*

07 06 05 04 03 02   7 6 5 4 3 2 1

Interpretation of the printing code: The rightmost double-digit number is the year of the book's printing; the rightmost single-digit number is the number of the book's printing. For example, the printing code 02-1 shows that the first printing of the book occurred in 2002.

Printed in the United States of America

Trademarks

Warning and Disclaimer

Publisher
David Dwyer

Associate Publisher
Stephanie Wall

Production Manager
Gina Kanouse

Managing Editor
Kristy Knoop

Acquisitions Editors
Linda Anne Bump
Elise Walter

Development Editor
Chris Zahn

Senior Marketing Manager
Tammy Detrich

Publicity Manager
Susan Nixon

Project Editor
Julia Prosser

Copy Editors
Jill Batistick
Amy Lepore

Indexer
Cheryl Lenser

Manufacturing Coordinator
Jim Conway

Book Designer
Louisa Klucznik

Cover Designer
Aren Howell

Composition
Amy Parker

Inside ColdFusion® MX

Contents At a Glance

John: This book is dedicated first and foremost to my Lord and Savior, Jesus Christ, whom I try to keep at the center of everything I do. To my wife, Laura, and my soon-to-be-born daughter, Sydney, I love you both more than words can express, and I do everything for you.

Table of Contents

About the Authors

John Cummings is a senior product support engineer working with ColdFusion for Macromedia, Inc. John began working with ColdFusion in 1998, when he started using ColdFusion to develop web-based applications. Prior to joining the Macromedia Product Support Team, John worked for Allaire's consulting group, visiting ColdFusion development shops around the country and assisting them with developing and tuning their applications.

John has written several articles on various ColdFusion topics, several of which can be found on community web sites. John also worked as a contributing author on Que's *Macromedia ColdFusion 5 Web Application Construction Kit*.

In addition to working for Macromedia, John and Laura provide periodic consulting work, and they can be contacted regarding this at www.igensolutions.com.

John lives and works in Huntington, West Virginia, with his wife, Laura, and their two cats. John and Laura are expecting their first child in September 2002. You can contact John at john@mauzy-broadway.com or by visiting his web site at www.mauzy-broadway.com.

Neil Ross is a ColdFusion application architect with Ciber, Inc. in Harrisburg, Pennsylvania. Neil has five years of web and application development experience and is a Macromedia Certified ColdFusion Developer. Neil is a former member of Allaire Consulting Services and worked with Allaire clients to improve the stability of their servers and the efficiency of their application code. While with Allaire, Neil became an Allaire Certified Instructor and conducted public and private classes throughout the United States.

At the 2000 ColdFusion Developer's Conference, Neil was a key presenter, conducting hands-on sessions on optimizing ColdFusion Server performance. He has published articles and product reviews in the *ColdFusion Developer's Journal*. He has also contributed content to various online technical publications.

Neil is active in the ColdFusion community and is a frequent speaker at CFUG meetings. He is a founding member and currently serves as the manager of the Central Pennsylvania ColdFusion User Group.

Neil, his wife, Louise, and their three children currently live in Mechanicsburg, Pennsylvania. Neil can be reached at neil@codesweeper.com or by visiting his web site at www.codesweeper.com.

Robi Sen is the Vice-President of Department13, a software consultancy focusing on e-procurement, supply chain management, enterprise application integration, and web services. Formerly, he was the Chief Information Officer and Vice President of Software Development at Granularity, Inc. Mr. Sen has been working professionally in the software development world for the last 15 years, since he was recruited at the age of 16 to develop software systems for Westinghouse Hanford Co. and the Department of Defense. Mr. Sen's chief areas of interest are in the creation of a new breed of network-based applications and the development of intelligent agents, which are software systems that can interact with humans and other machines in a thoughtful manner. These systems make context-appropriate decisions for their users, without having to receive instructions from those users. He is also interested in the development of web services. He is a sought after speaker and speaks to user groups, universities, and at major conferences all over the United States.

About the Contributors

Keen Haynes is the co-founder of MKAD, Inc., a Macromedia Solutions Provider that operates in Orange County, California. He is a Certified ColdFusion Developer and formerly a senior consultant with Macromedia. While with Macromedia Consulting Services, he worked with ColdFusion, JRun, and ClusterCATS. He also provided extension development support for Macromedia's UltraDev and Dreamweaver applications. Keen is the author of several JRun-related technical articles and has presented at the Southern California CFUG, SCCFUG 2nd ColdFusion Conference, and Comdex Chicago. His first experience with ColdFusion was developing a student registration application for the University of Maryland's University College (Asian Division) Distant Education department in 1995. Retired from the United States Marine Corps in 1999, he holds an M.S. in computer systems management. An avid surfer, he also enjoys hiking in the California mountains and deserts.

Sheldon Sargent, or Sarge, (MCSE, MMCP, and Certified ColdFusion Developer) is the former ColdFusion Practice Manager for Macromedia Consulting Services. He currently provides a consummate source for security, session-management, and LDAP information as a Senior Product Support Engineer, handling incident escalations as a member of Macromedia's Product Support - Server Division.

About the Technical Reviewers

These reviewers contributed their considerable hands-on expertise to the entire development process for *Inside ColdFusion MX*. As the book was being written, these dedicated professionals reviewed all the material for technical content, organization, and flow. Their feedback was critical to ensuring that this book fit our readers' need for the highest-quality technical information.

Benjamin Blackwell is a Macromedia Certified Advanced ColdFusion 5 Developer and is the Founder/Senior Wirehead of studio machine, where he is currently developing an enterprise management system for Apache. His education began in 1993 at the Savannah College of Art and Design, where he studied graphic arts and creative writing. He fell in love with the Internet in 1995 and has been developing web applications ever since. His hobbies include cyberpunk novels, KMFDM, Anime, and his fiancée, Maria. He currently resides in San Antonio, Texas, with his aforementioned fiancée, his cat, and a pug. He wants to be William Gibson when he grows up and hopes to someday visit Japan.

Marc Dimmick has been involved in the ColdFusion community for over 6 years. He was instrumental in the establishment of a CFUG in Victoria that has been running for over 6 years and for the newly formed CFUGs in Australia. There is now a user group in each state and territory of Australia. Marc has been involved in the ICT industry for over 20 years. His activities have included everything, such as computer sales, engineering, teaching, training, design, and development. He started in the Internet industry as a graphic designer and then progressed to development and management of development teams. He has been involved with ColdFusion since version 3. He is currently General Manager of iBase Global Pty Ltd, a small enterprise in Australia.

Jeff Howden is a native Oregonian, and the 27-year-old (`http://jeffhowden.com/`) has lived and breathed ColdFusion for nearly four years. Although there are lots of fun and cool things Jeff has built over the years, there are two things of which he's the most proud. The first is a ColdFusion development methodology that results in something he calls directory-style query strings, which make for the most search-engine-friendly sites on the planet. The second is a client e-commerce project that brought in over $1.5 million in sales in 30 days after a launch with absolutely zero ColdFusion errors. Currently employed by AlphaShop Network Services (`http://alphashop.net/`), Jeff builds web-based applications designed to make clients' lives simpler and more efficient. He likes to tell them that he spends more time in front of a monitor so that they don't have to. When he's not working on client materials, you can find him hanging out, under the moniker of .jeff, on one of the many discussion lists at evolt.org (`http://evolt.org/`). You can also find articles he's written there as well.

Brandon Harper is currently a Senior Developer for Mallfinder Network, a Denver-based ASP that provides both rapid-deployment architecture for mall web sites and retail management solutions for over 180 malls across the United States. Other relevant experience includes development of web sites and extranets for companies such as *Freeskier Magazine*, Kelty Apparel, and Bid4Vacations.com. He has also provided technology consulting for Agilent, Co|Create (an HP company), Einstein Bros Bagels, GE Access, and Musco Olives. In his spare time, Brandon can be found participating in various motorsports activities, tinkering in his garage with motorcycles and turbo-charged cars, or out enjoying the beautiful Colorado scenery. His other technology interests include Linux, FreeBSD, PHP, security and privacy issues, content management, Fusebox, and performance tuning. Brandon can be reached at `brandon@spooled.net`.

Acknowledgments

John Cummings: I would like to take a moment to thank some folks who are always there to lend me a hand when I need it. First and foremost, there is my beautiful wife, Laura, who is always there to support me regardless of what I'm into. On the ColdFusion side of things, I'd like to thank Debbie Dickerson, Stephanie Juma, Rob Panico, and Dave Stanten for never running me off when I bug them with questions, Judy Ricciarelli and Mark Sefton for letting me do this type of thing, and Sean Bordner for introducing me to ColdFusion and taking the time to teach me what he knew. Thank you to my coauthor, Neil Ross, who is a pleasure to work with. Also, thanks to the many contributors who have helped make this book a reality, Sarge, and Keen Haynes. I'd also like to thank the great folks at New Riders Publishing, specifically Linda Bump, Elise Walter, and Chris Zahn, for allowing me to work with a wonderful and professional team. Finally, I want to thank Mema and Pepa, who really deserve all the credit for me actually doing something with my life.

Neil Ross: I would like to dedicate the time and effort put into making this book a reality to my wife, Louise, and to our great kids, Megan, Katherine, and Jackson. They put up with my seemingly endless hours locked away in my office and were always there to make sure that every little break that I had was filled with hugs, laughter, and loads of support. I want to also thank John Cummings for all of his work and dedication to this project and for keeping our conversations always unpredictable. Thanks to Linda Bump for allowing John and me to get involved with this project, and to Elise Walter and Chris Zahn for helping us stay on target. Last, but not least, thanks to Keen Haynes and Sarge for their contributions to this book.

Robi Sen: I would like to first thank Elise Walter, Linda Bump, and Chris Zahn as well as all the other folks at New Riders who helped out on this book. Most people think editors are there just to keep you on task and fix your grammar, but our editors went out of their way to get us what we needed, proof our content, format it, and basically make what was a very difficult deadline to meet easier. I would also like to thank John Cummings and Neil Ross who were my coauthors and a delight to work with as well as very bright people. I would also like to thank Shlomy Gantz, David Medinets, and Mark Bronner who helped with content of the book as well as moral support. Thanks also to Doug Henderson, who helped with the examples for the CF and COM section of the book. Final thanks to my family who were supportive during the three months I worked on this book.

Tell Us What You Think

As the reader of this book, you are the most important critic and commentator. We value your opinion and want to know what we're doing right, what we could do better, what areas you'd like to see us publish in, and any other words of wisdom you're willing to pass our way.

As the Associate Publisher for New Riders Publishing, I welcome your comments. You can fax, email, or write me directly to let me know what you did or didn't like about this book—as well as what we can do to make our books stronger.

Please note that I cannot help you with technical problems related to the topic of this book, and that due to the high volume of mail I receive, I might not be able to reply to every message.

When you write, please be sure to include this book's title and author as well as your name and phone or fax number. I will carefully review your comments and share them with the author and editors who worked on the book.

Fax: 317-581-4663
Email: stephanie.wall@newriders.com
Mail: Stephanie Wall
           Associate Publisher
           New Riders Publishing
           201 West 103rd Street
           Indianapolis, IN 46290 USA

Introduction

Welcome to *Inside ColdFusion MX*! This book is intended to be a comprehensive guide for ColdFusion developers. It provides the knowledge to leverage the power of the new, J2EE-based ColdFusion Server to create dynamic web applications.

The release of ColdFusion MX constitutes a major overhaul for the ColdFusion product. ColdFusion MX is the first version of ColdFusion built to leverage the J2EE initiative, and it enhances the ColdFusion developer's ability to create applications that are scalable and portable. With ColdFusion MX, you can easily extend ColdFusion by tying your application architecture to other existing J2EE-compliant applications throughout an organization. You can also deploy ColdFusion applications across a wide range of J2EE-compliant server products. This is an exciting and necessary advance for the ColdFusion product, and it will require you to gain a unique understanding of the new ColdFusion product and how you can leverage that power.

Inside ColdFusion MX takes you through the changes that that will affect you most when moving existing ColdFusion applications from ColdFusion 4.X and ColdFusion 5 to the ColdFusion MX architecture. In addition, *Inside ColdFusion MX* provides unique guidance for creating real-world applications from the ground-up that are built exclusively to leverage the power of ColdFusion MX and its uniquely new infrastructure. As the authors of this book, we have had daily involvement with the creation, management, deployment, and support of a multitude of enterprise-level ColdFusion applications. We are not removed "from the trenches," so to speak. We spend the majority of our time facing the real-world problems that you face, and in this book, we strive to give you a complete reference where you can find solutions and support for your problems.

Who This Book Is For

Inside ColdFusion MX is aimed at the intermediate-to-advanced ColdFusion developer. While everyone who works with ColdFusion will benefit from the information contained within this book, little time is spent discussing the issues that a beginner might face, as there is neither time nor room to cover those topics in addition to the advanced topics we wish to discuss.

If you work with ColdFusion on a daily basis, you will find this book a great addition to your reference library, as we cover in great detail the differences between ColdFusion MX and its predecessors. In each chapter, we provide a brief discussion of what the chapter covers and how it relates to ColdFusion developers. Then, we immediately go into greater detail by taking a problem/solution approach to a real-world scenario. In our experience, this proves to be an incredibly effective way of disseminating the necessary information in an easy-to-understand way, and this format also lends itself easily to reference usage.

Overview

Inside ColdFusion MX includes the following coverage in each chapter:

Chapter 1, "ColdFusion Starts Here," discusses the numerous changes to the ColdFusion platform, including changes to the product infrastructure and the effects of the changes on the ColdFusion application development process and developers themselves. It also identifies additions to the ColdFusion Markup Language (CFML) language and points to later discussions of syntax changes to existing language elements. The enhancements to the methods developers can use to deploy their applications are also discussed.

Chapter 2, "Preparing Your Environment," covers installation and configuration of the server and studio products for development purposes.

Chapter 3, "Before You Begin Coding—Application Planning," discusses how attention to architectural considerations, effective planning, and sticking with a standard development methodology for your project can help you to successfully complete your application development project.

Chapter 4, "Fundamentals of ColdFusion Development," digs deeper into ColdFusion application development, including ColdFusion development concepts, basic CFML, and interaction with databases.

Chapter 5, "Reusing Code," covers the key to efficient ColdFusion development. Here we show examples of code reuse and proper syntax for interacting with other application templates and third-party elements.

Chapter 6, "ColdFusion Components," covers the new ColdFusion components (CFCs), offering both basic and advanced treatment of the topic.

Chapter 7, "Complex Data Types," shows you how to use complex data types, such as lists, arrays, structures, and queries, to greatly improve the performance and power of your applications.

Chapter 8, "Application Framework," discusses the statelessness of web applications and reviews the web application framework within ColdFusion. In addition, the ColdFusion variables are discussed. They help develop sites that can remember preferences, maintain state, and improve the overall user experience.

Chapter 9, "Error Handling," discusses common circumstances that can cause problems within your applications, and it gives you ways to avoid these pitfalls.

Chapter 10, "Regular Expressions," teaches the basic use and syntax of regular expressions and metacharacters, and how to leverage regular expressions within your ColdFusion applications.

Chapter 11, "Working with Email," shows examples of how to send email within your application and how to build an application that lets you access your email on various servers.

Chapter 12, "Working with Files," covers the interaction of ColdFusion with files and enables developers to build applications that show, copy, move, save, delete, and rename files and directories. We also discuss the scheduling of tasks and how that relates to file interaction.

Chapter 13, "CFScript," discusses ColdFusion's server-side scripting language implementation— CFSCRIPT. We'll also show how developers can build user-defined functions (UDFs) within CFSCRIPT.

Chapter 14, "Debugging," provides a good overview of the choices available as you begin to debug your applications, and it covers some quick tips and tricks that help make the most of that information.

Chapter 15, "CFML Coding: Best Practices," introduces the most fundamental elements of the ColdFusion coding language and how those elements interact with each other. This section discusses using ColdFusion graphing capabilities to extend or enhance data presentation. We'll also discuss how to extend ColdFusion's built-in graphing capabilities by configuring ColdFusion to work with a full version of Macromedia Generator.

Chapter 16, "Further Extending Your Applications," demonstrates the use of some key technologies to enhance the power and functionality of a ColdFusion application and to get the most out of your code.

Chapter 17, "Common Application Development Requirements," covers development requirements that come up repeatedly with most every new project. These requirements include application security, content management, e-commerce, and personalization.

Chapter 18, "Enhancing Application Performance with Caching," examines some common caching strategies and discusses the performance improvements you can expect to see when implementing such strategies.

In Chapter 19, "Introduction to XML and ColdFusion MX," and Chapter 20, "Advanced XML," coverage includes the tighter integration of ColdFusion MX with eXtensible Markup Language (XML) and how XML and WDDX tie into the grand scheme of web services initiatives, such as .NET and Sun ONE.

Chapter 21, "Web Services and ColdFusion," introduces you to the ease with which you can establish web services by using ColdFusion components. While the web services established through ColdFusion have some limitations, ColdFusion offers the easiest implementation of web services available.

Chapter 22, "Leveraging J2EE," addresses the shift to the J2EE platform taken with ColdFusion MX. We show you how you can work with Java Server Pages (JSP), Java Server tag libraries, Java Servlets, and various Java objects, including generic classes and Enterprise Java Beans.

Chapter 23, "Working with Databases," and Chapter 24, "Advanced Database Interaction," discuss the basic concepts of relational databases, covering terminology and key concepts related to performance and infrastructure.

Chapter 25, "Administering the ColdFusion Server," covers lots of tips and tricks on how developers, database administrators, and server administrators can enhance performance of their respective parts of the puzzle to get the most out of ColdFusion MX and application code.

Chapter 26, "Performance Optimization and Scalability Planning," discusses some of the techniques that were a mainstay for the Allaire consulting group. The methodology that we developed has not been published outside that small group of people, and here we explain it so that any developer can take advantage of the secrets.

Chapter 27, "Migration to ColdFusion MX," discusses migration of older applications to your ColdFusion MX Server and testing methodologies. Included are instructions on common syntax changes to look for when updating code to ColdFusion MX specifications and how to streamline that code to work on the infrastructure.

Chapter 28, "ColdFusion Tips and Tricks," is a goodie basket filled with tips the authors and their colleagues have compiled.

In addition, you'll find full tag and function references in Appendix A, "Tag Reference," and Appendix B, "Function Reference."

Conventions

This book follows a few typographical conventions:

- Program text, tags, functions, variables, and other "computer language" examples are set in a monospace font—for example, `alert tcp`. Placeholders in syntax descriptions are set in an italic monospace font—for example, *name of your server*.

1

ColdFusion Starts Here

IF YOU'VE PICKED UP THIS BOOK, CHANCES are that you're already familiar with what Macromedia ColdFusion is and what it enables you to do when developing web applications. For those of you unfamiliar with the product and its history, we'll run through a quick refresher course.

The History

In 1995, Allaire released the first version of ColdFusion, version 1.0. This release of ColdFusion was a distant cousin to the ColdFusion that we all know and love today. Although ColdFusion MX has evolved from ColdFusion 1.0, the changes in ColdFusion over the years have been quite dramatic.

In version 1.0, ColdFusion provided web developers with a simplified way of connecting their web sites to a database backend, enabling them to allow users of their web sites to interact with their databases. Although this seems like a basic concept today, back in 1995 the web was really just beginning to take off, and the ideas ColdFusion 1.0 brought to the market were really quite revolutionary.

With each successive release of ColdFusion, Allaire increased out-of-the-box functionality by offering extensions and enhancements to the tag and function libraries included with the server. By the time ColdFusion 4.5 was released, the development community had already offered thousands of additional user-written custom tags to enhance ColdFusion Server's capabilities.

In March 2000, Macromedia and Allaire completed a merger, and shortly afterward ColdFusion 5 was released. This was the first release of ColdFusion under the Macromedia moniker. With version 5, ColdFusion enabled the community to further extend the server by creating user-defined functions (UDFs). Version 5 also provided excellent and continued support for ColdFusion Markup Language (CFML), C++, and Java-based custom tags. Performance with version 5 was enhanced through the inclusion of the "query a query" feature, as well as by enhanced server-monitoring tools that enabled system admins on all levels to keep a closer eye on their servers.

ColdFusion MX Overview

ColdFusion MX is a "next-generation" version of ColdFusion Server. With the introduction of ColdFusion MX, ColdFusion Server enters a new and exciting phase of its life. What does this mean? It means that the engine of ColdFusion Server has been retooled (or, to be more accurate, replaced) with an engine that is J2EE-compliant. This engine enables ColdFusion MX to fit easily within the strategy of any organization adopting a J2EE standard for their server infrastructure.

If you'd like to learn more about the J2EE standard and what it means to ColdFusion, you might want to jump to Chapter 22, "Leveraging J2EE," for a complete discussion of the J2EE standard.

In addition, Macromedia has included great eXtensible Markup Language (XML), .NET, and web services support in ColdFusion MX. They enable users of the product to develop next-generation web content right away by using the power of ColdFusion MX.

Fortunately, the core CFML has not changed. You still can write ColdFusion applications just as you've done in the past. Now, however, when your code is parsed and run by the ColdFusion engine, rather than being compiled into P-code (as was the standard with previous releases of ColdFusion Server), your CFML code is compiled to bytecode and executed. This enables a much faster, more stable execution of your ColdFusion application code.

Understanding the New ColdFusion

Before we discuss the new ColdFusion Server architecture, it's important to realize that from a development standpoint, very little has changed. This cannot be stressed enough. Although it's important to understand that your applications now are compiled to and executed as bytecode, it's also important to realize that you do not need to know Java to write ColdFusion applications. This is one of the greatest benefits of using ColdFusion MX. Essentially, you are getting the power, performance, and stability of a J2EE-designed web application while retaining the speed and ease of use to which you've become accustomed in ColdFusion.

You might notice that with ColdFusion MX, you as a developer are being given more power. With the introduction in ColdFusion MX of ColdFusion components (CFCs), web services support, and Flash integration services, and the deployment of applications on a variety of Java application servers, you have more options and services than ever before.

This is an exciting release of ColdFusion, as it greatly increases the power of the language by extending where applications written in CFML can be run. It also greatly increases their stability, scalability, and performance.

New Technology Brief

As you begin to explore ColdFusion MX, it's helpful to have an understanding of the new features available to you in this release. Table 1.1 lists some of the key features and their uses. Although each new feature is discussed in complete detail later in this book, we still recommend that you review Table 1.1 to familiarize yourself with the changes.

Table 1.1   **New Features in ColdFusion MX and Their Uses**

Feature	Description
XML integration	ColdFusion MX enables you to integrate your applications with XML data easily, just as you would with any other data source, by providing you with built-in document parsing, XLST transformations, and automatic serialization of XML data.
CFCs	CFCs act very much the same way as custom tags did in the past. However, you can access these components from ColdFusion pages or Flash clients, and you can call them directly as web services.
Integration with web services	Using the CFINVOKE tag, you can call web services from within your ColdFusion applications. You can also create your own web services using the power of CFCs.

continues ▶

Table 1.1   **Continued**

Feature	Description
Enhanced chart and graph capabilities	Charting in ColdFusion MX now supports multiple data series, customizable output, and drill-down data techniques.
Flash MX integration	You can easily integrate your ColdFusion applications with Macromedia Flash MX using the Flash Remoting services provided with Macromedia ColdFusion MX.
Enhanced debugging	Using new debugging features, such as the `CFTRACE` tag, and the new dockable, extendable debugging panes, you can quickly analyze and fix problems with your application code.
Built-in UNICODE support	Built-in support for the Chinese, Japanese, and Korean languages enables you to localize your applications.
Integration with Java Server Pages (JSP)	You can import servlets into your ColdFusion pages using the `CFINCLUDE` tag. Further, you can import JSP tag libraries to be used like ColdFusion tags from within your ColdFusion application.
Server-side ActionScript	Directly within your ColdFusion application code, you can create server-side logic from Flash MX clients using ActionScript.
Application Deployment Services	You can package, archive, and deploy applications more easily using the Application Deployment Services provided in ColdFusion MX.
Java Application Server support	ColdFusion MX supports deploying your ColdFusion applications on a variety of Java Application Server platforms, including JRun, WebSphere, and Sun ONE, using the Macromedia ColdFusion MX J2EE Server edition.

Summary

With the release of ColdFusion MX, Macromedia has created a completely new, powerful ColdFusion that enhances the capabilities of past versions while eliminating previous limitations.

The new version of ColdFusion should be very familiar to those who've developed with ColdFusion in the past. Nonetheless, it's still packed with new features that enable you to extend the capabilities of your ColdFusion applications beyond what was even possible with version 5.

ColdFusion MX should prove to be an excellent step into the future of web development—and it is available to you now! Have fun exploring the new world of ColdFusion MX. It is our sincere hope that this book helps you on your journey.

2

Preparing Your Environment

I N THIS CHAPTER, WE TAKE A LOOK AT THE steps required to get ColdFusion MX up and running on your server or development machine. This is actually a fairly simple process, and it should prove very intuitive if you've ever installed ColdFusion in any of its previous incarnations.

Following an overview of the installation process, we take a look at some out-of-the-box configuration settings that you might want to consider. Chapter 26, "Performance Optimization and Scalability Planning," goes into much greater detail on the tuning of specific hardware and applications for performance.

In addition, we discuss your choices regarding your ColdFusion development environment. We cover the tool of choice for most ColdFusion developers, ColdFusion Studio 5, and the newly introduced development tool, Macromedia's Dreamweaver MX.

Installing and Configuring ColdFusion

Of course, the first step in the configuration of ColdFusion MX is a successful installation of the product. As mentioned, if you've installed ColdFusion Server before, the installation process for ColdFusion MX should seem somewhat familiar to you.

Before installing ColdFusion MX, it's important to ensure that you have hardware that meets the recommended requirements for installation.

Table 2.1 gives the system requirements for installing ColdFusion MX on Windows and UNIX. An important note for Solaris customers is that with the release of ColdFusion MX, ColdFusion can no longer be run on Solaris i86 machines. To run ColdFusion MX on Solaris, you must be running a SPARC version of the Solaris operating system (OS).

Table 2.1   **Recommended and Required Minimum System Configurations for Installing ColdFusion MX**

System Resources	For ColdFusion MX Professional	For ColdFusion MX Enterprise
Random-access memory (RAM) Recommended	256MB	512MB
Required	128MB	256MB
Free disk space Recommended	500MB	750MB
Required	300MB	500MB

Depending on the OS you are using, you can install ColdFusion MX in one of two ways. First, we examine a typical Windows installation.

Installing ColdFusion MX on Windows

To install ColdFusion MX on a Windows system, you need to be certain that the target system meets some minimum patch requirements for the installation to complete successfully.

Table 2.2 lists the patches required prior to installing ColdFusion MX on a Windows system.

Table 2.2   **Patches Required for Installation on Windows**

Windows Version	Patches Required
Windows XP	No patches required at this time
Windows NT 4.0	Service Pack 5 or higher, MDAC 2.5 SP1 or higher, and MFC/MSVC 6.0
Windows 2000	Service Pack 1, MDAC 2.5 SP1 or higher, and MFC/MSVC 6.0

After you've examined the system and patch-level requirements, you can begin the install. Installation should automatically begin when you insert the ColdFusion MX CD into the CD drive. If it doesn't, you can simply browse the CD for `coldfusionmx.exe` and double-click the executable file to kick off the installation wizard.

After ColdFusion MX is installed, it should automatically detect any web servers present on the target system. ColdFusion MX includes support for Internet Information Server (IIS), iPlanet, and Apache as standalone web servers. You are given the opportunity either to select an existing web server on the system or to use the web server that comes bundled with ColdFusion MX. If you are installing ColdFusion MX on a production system, it is strongly recommended that you choose something other than the built-in ColdFusion MX web server; this web server is provided by Macromedia strictly for development servers.

After you've selected the web server with which you would like ColdFusion MX to pair itself, the web server is automatically configured for you to respond to requests for CFM files.

Java Runtime Environment (JRE) Note

As part of the ColdFusion MX installation, a JRE is installed on your system. ColdFusion MX will use the JRE for its libraries. It is *strongly* recommended that you leave this JRE set to the defaults (instead of manipulating the installation to use a preexisting JRE) because this is the only configuration supported by Macromedia. This holds true for both Windows and UNIX systems.

Installing ColdFusion MX on UNIX Systems

Just as in a Windows-based installation, installing ColdFusion MX on a UNIX-based system requires that your system meet certain patch levels prior to attempting the installation.

Table 2.3 lists the patches required prior to installing ColdFusion MX on a UNIX system.

Table 2.3   Patches Required for Installation on UNIX

UNIX Version	Patches Required
Cobalt RAQ 3, RAQ 4, and XTR	Compat-libstdc++ RPM
HP-UX	All the latest patch bundles as available from the HP web site
Solaris 2.6	105181-17 or higher, 15591-09 or higher, 105210-25 or higher, and 105568-14 or higher
Solaris 2.7	106541-08 or higher, 106327-08 or higher, and 106980-07 or higher
SuSE 7.0	Apache.rpm

Installing ColdFusion MX on a UNIX-based system requires that you know a little about your system. You should make sure that you're logged on as root when installing. On most UNIX-based systems with ColdFusion MX, you have your choice of a regular or graphical user interface (GUI)-based installation script. In most cases, you'll enable the installation script to automatically detect your system configuration and stick with the default settings.

Unlike previous versions of ColdFusion, ColdFusion MX does not require a symbolic link from the /opt directory, so you can install ColdFusion MX to any target volume that you choose.

After you begin the installation, be aware of a common problem in UNIX-based installations. When ColdFusion MX installs, it requires room to unpack all its files prior to beginning the installation. All these files are unpacked to the default temporary directory on your system (in most cases, /tmp). If there is insufficient space in the /tmp directory (you need around 300MB free), you have to free up more space or change the location of your system default temporary directory to an area of the disk with more free space (for the duration of the installation).

As noted previously, after ColdFusion MX is installed, it should automatically detect any web servers present on the target system. You are given the opportunity to select an existing web server on the system or to use the web server that comes bundled with ColdFusion MX. If you are installing ColdFusion MX on a production system, it is strongly recommended that you choose something other than the built-in ColdFusion MX web server; this web server is provided by Macromedia strictly for development servers.

After you've selected the web server with which you would like ColdFusion MX to pair itself, the web server is automatically configured for you to respond to requests for CFM files.

Summary

Now that you've installed the ColdFusion Server, you understand a little bit about how ColdFusion works. Let's next move to your development environment.

Working with Dreamweaver MX

Macromedia has recently introduced Dreamweaver MX, their new development platform for web applications. Dreamweaver MX has visual design and editing capabilities, but also sports one of the best code-editing environments on the market—Macromedia's HomeSite. Dreamweaver MX is a slick combination of Dreamweaver, HomeSite, ColdFusion Studio, and JRun Studio.

Dreamweaver MX helps you to build robust, database-driven web applications using ColdFusion Markup Language (CFML), Active Server Pages (ASP), JavaServer Pages (JSP), and PHP.

For those of you who have always used ColdFusion Studio, Dreamweaver MX includes numerous tools to help you write code efficiently. Dreamweaver MX boasts features such as tag completion and code coloring. It also includes complete reference material on Hypertext Markup Language (HTML), CFML, JavaScript, and more. One of the nicest things about Dreamweaver MX is that it maintains your hand-written code without reformatting it as many what-you-see-is-what-you-get (WYSISYG) editors tend to do.

Dreamweaver MX features that ColdFusion developers enjoy include the following:

- CFML tag insight
- Code validator with a ColdFusion version-compatibility check
- Snippets panel for saving all your favorite bits of code
- Integrated debugging
- A remote ColdFusion Server connection for browsing datasources and files
- New wizards for creating useful ColdFusion code

Dreamweaver MX Workspace

When using Dreamweaver MX in Windows, you are given a choice of two workspace layouts. The floating layout is similar to that of Dreamweaver 4. The one that I want to concentrate on is the integrated layout, which is better-suited to ColdFusion application development.

After you've installed Dreamweaver MX on your Windows-based system, you are asked to choose a workspace layout in the Workspace Setup dialog box. The Dreamweaver MX workspace has a HomeSite/Coder-Style option that offers an integrated workspace with panel groups docked within one window. This workspace is similar to HomeSite and ColdFusion Studio, but offers access to all the latest tools to help developers create applications more quickly. Table 2.4 provides an overview of the various interface elements.

Table 2.4   **Dreamweaver MX Interface Elements**

Interface Element	What It Does
Insert bar	The Insert bar contains buttons that enable you to insert pieces of code into your template. The Insert bar contains a number of different toolbars separated by their function, such as Forms or Frames.
Document toolbar	The Document toolbar contains buttons and menus that enable you to toggle between Code and Design views for your template.
Standard toolbar	The Standard toolbar contains all the standard buttons for interacting with files: New, Open, Save, Save All, Cut, Copy, Paste, Undo, and Redo. The Standard toolbar is not visible by default. To show it, choose View, Toolbars, and then Standard.
Document window	The Document window shows the current document as you edit it. It shows your document in Design view or Code view; you can also use a split view that shows both Design view and Code view.
Property inspector	The Property inspector shows you all the properties of the current tag or text on which your cursor is located.
Tag selector	The tag selector appears near the bottom of the Document window on the status bar. It shows you the tags that surround the currently selected elements. By clicking a tag in the tag selector, you can highlight all the code that appears within the selected tag in the Design or Code views.
Panel groups	Panel groups contain several related panels. You can expand or contract and dock or undock panels from your workspace.
Site panel	You use the Site panel to manage your files and folders in your site, including those that are local and remote. You can also use the Site panel to create documents or folders and to view, open, and move files and folders.
Launcher bar	The Launcher bar provides shortcut buttons to your favorite or frequently used panels or tag inspectors. You can customize which shortcut icons appear on your Launcher bar by setting your preferences for the status bar.

Creating Sites in Dreamweaver MX

If you've used ColdFusion Studio in the past, you might know that you can manage the files that make up your ColdFusion application or web site in a project. Dreamweaver MX manages all the files used in your application. The files are referred to as assets in a site.

You can create a site in Dreamweaver MX and populate it with existing files, or you can create an empty site. Either way, before you start developing your application, you must create and specify a Dreamweaver MX site (see Figure 2.1). The site is merely a way to keep your files organized and to maintain their relationships to each other. Unlike ColdFusion Studio, Dreamweaver MX automatically tracks and maintains links and manages your files.

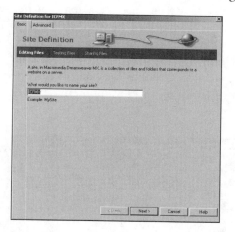

Figure 2.1   Creating a Dreamweaver MX site with the Site Definition Wizard.

To create a new site in Dreamweaver MX, select Site from the Main menu, and then select New Site. The Site Definition dialog box appears and enables you to fill out the remainder of the site configuration options by using a convenient wizard, as shown in Figure 2.1, or by selecting the Advanced tab and filling out your setting manually, as shown in Figure 2.2.

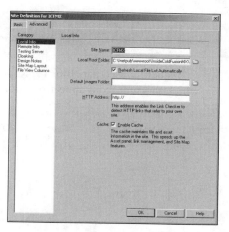

Figure 2.2   Creating a Dreamweaver MX site manually using the Advanced tab.

Connecting to Datasources in Dreamweaver MX

To connect to a ColdFusion datasource within Dreamweaver MX, you must have that datasource defined within the ColdFusion Administrator. You create a datasource within ColdFusion Administrator in the same way that you have in previous versions of ColdFusion. Dreamweaver MX provides you with tools to help you access ColdFusion Administrator.

In Dreamweaver MX, you have a Databases panel within the Application panel group. In the Databases panel, click the Modify Data Sources icon in the top-right corner. This launches the ColdFusion Adminstrator in a new browser window and enables you to create your datasource. For more information on creating ColdFusion datasources, check out Chapter 4, "Fundamentals of ColdFusion Development." Figure 2.3 shows the Database panel in Dreamweaver MX.

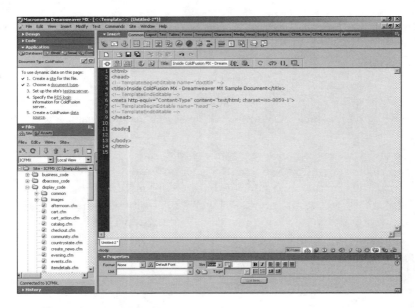

Figure 2.3   Creating a datasource connection in Dreamweaver MX.

After you've created the datasource in ColdFusion Administrator, you need to connect to it from Dreamweaver. To connect to your datasource, create a new ColdFusion template or open one that already exists inside your site.

Note

One of the nice things about Dreamweaver MX is that the tabs on the Insert bar change according to the type of document on which you're working. If you create a new HTML document, you have access to only the tabs that apply to plain HTML. If you create a new ColdFusion document, you see the tabs for CFML Basic, CFML Flow, and CFML Advanced.

After you've created your new datasource, you should see it appear in the Databases panel, although you might have to refresh the view of that panel. You then can expand your view of that particular datasource and its tables. You can even view its data as shown in Figure 2.4. If you cannot see any datasources, you can click each required step that appears within the Databases panel. These steps help you walk through the processes required to make sure that you can interact with your backend data.

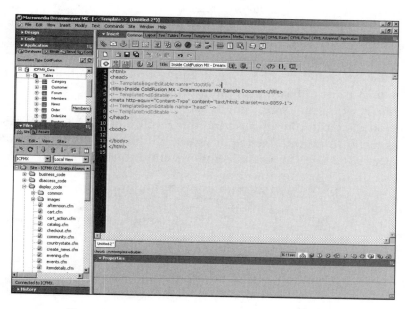

Figure 2.4   Viewing a datasource in Dreamweaver MX.

Creating Queries in Dreamweaver MX

The typical way that we looked at creating queries in ColdFusion Studio has changed a lot with Dreamweaver MX. In ColdFusion Studio, we just right-clicked a database table within our datasource and selected New Query. Up would pop the SQL/Query Builder. We'd drag and drop columns into the structured query language (SQL) statement, define our criteria, and then save our query. Then by pasting that query code into our ColdFusion template, we would create a result set. Dreamweaver MX takes a bit of a different approach.

In Dreamweaver MX, we look at all the possible sources of dynamic content. Simply put, a dynamic content source is a block of stored information that you access for evaluation or comparison processing and display within your web page or application. This includes information that is stored in the database as you might expect, but it also includes form structures with values (perhaps submitted by an HTML form), server objects, and values from JavaBeans. Any of these types of content sources can be added to Dreamweaver MX's Bindings panel.

It is probably most common that we use a database as our content source. In Dreamweaver MX, a query is referred to as a recordset. A recordset is the collection of data that is returned from the database. It might contain all the rows and columns that make up the complete database, but it can be (and should be) refined to include only the data that you need.

You can create a recordset by clicking the plus (+) button within the Bindings panel of the Application panel group. You can create your recordset without writing any SQL code in the default Simple view (see Figure 2.5), or you can write your own advanced SQL code in the Advanced view (see Figure 2.6). After you save the recordset, it is inserted into your ColdFusion template and saved to your Bindings panel for access later.

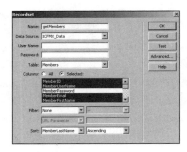

Figure 2.5 Creating a Dreamweaver MX recordset in Simple view.

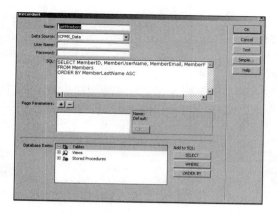

Figure 2.6   Creating a Dreamweaver MX recordset in Advanced view.

Displaying Dynamic Content

Of course, Dreamweaver MX also makes it easy for you to include dynamic content in your ColdFusion templates. You can add the dynamic content from your recordset to replace static text strings or to fill in the values for HTML or CFML attributes and more. After you've created your recordset, you can add elements of it to your application pages by simply selecting the column name from the recordset and dragging it into your code. You then drop it at the insertion point where you want the value to appear.

Once you insert a dynamic content call into your page template, the reference to that content is added to the Server Behaviors panel, which is still in the Application panel group. They are now considered server behaviors. You can edit a server behavior by double-clicking the listing within the Server Behaviors panel. When you double-click them, the same dialog box that you used to build them appears. You then can make your changes within that dialog box. When you make your change to that server behavior, it automatically is reflected within the page that you're editing. If you choose to remove one of the server behaviors in your template, you can select the code within the template and press the Delete key, or you can select the server behavior in the Server Behaviors panel and click the minus (–) button.

Dreamweaver MX lists server behaviors in the order in which they appear within the template. In the event that the same server behavior appears in a template more than once, you can distinguish between them by clicking the server behavior and checking which sections of code are highlighted.

Dreamweaver MX has several predefined server behaviors that you can use. One of them is called the Repeat Region. This creates your typical CFOUTPUT query loop. In addition to creating this code, there are other options to enable you to create a next/previous record navigation just by filling out a few optional items. For those of you who have used custom tags to take care of this in the past, you know that it is a time saver? In Figure 2.7, you can see that Dreamweaver MX includes more built-in server behaviors.

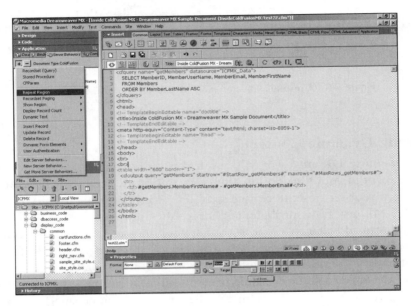

Figure 2.7 Server behaviors in Dreamweaver MX.

You can also create and edit your own custom-built server behaviors and add them to the Server Behaviors panel.

Debugging in Dreamweaver MX

You can debug your ColdFusion application code in Dreamweaver MX. If you're using Dreamweaver MX as your testing server, you can code, test, and debug the ColdFusion template without ever leaving Dreamweaver. Check out the code in Listing 2.1. You should notice that we have two CFOUTPUT closing tags.

Listing 2.1   Debugging ColdFusion Code in Dreamweaver MX

```
<cfset variables.myname="Neil Ross">
<html>
  <head>
    <title>Inside ColdFusion MX - Dreamweaver MX Debugging</title>
  </head>
  <body>
    <cfoutput>My name is #variables.fullname#</cfoutput></cfoutput>
  </body>
</html>
```

Of course, this won't work. In Figure 2.8, we can see how Dreamweaver MX handles the error.

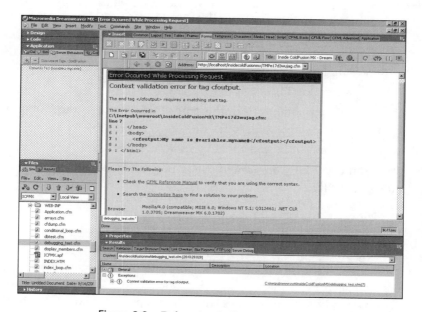

Figure 2.8   Debugging in Dreamweaver MX.

To debug a page in Dreamweaver MX, follow these simple steps:

1. Open the ColdFusion page in Dreamweaver MX.
2. Click the Server Debug icon on the Document toolbar.
3. If an Exceptions category appears in the Server Debug panel, click the plus (+) and check out the error.
4. In the Server Debug panel's Location column, click the link to open the page in Code Edit view.
5. Fix the error and save the template.

ColdFusion Components in Dreamweaver MX

One of the hottest new features of ColdFusion MX is that of ColdFusion components (CFCs). Though we do not go into a lot of detail here about CFCs (we do later in Chapter 6, "ColdFusion Components"), let us at least introduce you to them and how they can be created and accessed within Dreamweaver MX.

CFCs enable you to wrap application or business process logic into self-contained units. CFCs take encapsulation further than do ColdFusion custom tags. They yield nicely encapsulated, resuable segments of code. In addition to providing another means for code reuse, CFCs also provide a great way to create web services. CFCs are written in CFML and can encapsulate entire segments of business logic within a web application. CFCs are the preferred unit for business logic now, and ColdFusion custom tags should be used for encapsulation of presentation elements.

Dreamweaver MX enables you to create CFCs visually or by editing the CFC code directly. To create a CFC visually within Dreamweaver MX, follow these simple steps:

1. Open a new ColdFusion page.
2. Select CF Components from the drop-down menu in the Component panel.
3. Click the plus (+) button to add a new component.
4. When the Create Component dialog box opens, complete the options and click OK.

As noted, we cover the real details of CFCs in Chapter 6.

Dreamweaver enables you to view CFCs and to check out any CFC defined within your site. Dreamweaver reads, interprets, and displays information about the CFC in an easy-to-navigate tree structure within the Components panel. You can also check out each CFC's functions and arguments. In addition, you can check out the properties of any CFC function that serves as a web service. Figure 2.9 shows the Components panel and available CFCs.

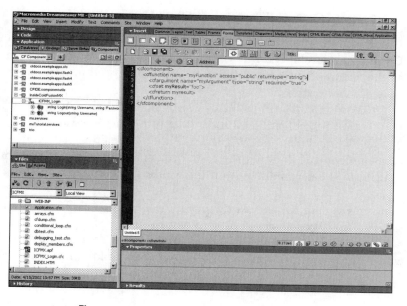

Figure 2.9   Viewing CFCs in Dreamweaver MX.

To view CFCs in Dreamweaver MX, follow these steps:

1. Open any ColdFusion page in Dreamweaver MX.
2. Select CF Components from the drop-down menu in the Components panel.
3. Click the Refresh button to view the CFCs available to the current server.
4. Click the plus (+) icons to drill down into the CFC package and individual components and functions.

You can edit a CFC in Dreamweaver MX by opening the CFC package and selecting the CFC that you want to edit. Right-click that CFC and choose Edit Code from the menu that appears. If you chose the CFC itself, the CFC template opens. If you chose to edit a particular function, the CFC template opens with the code that comprises the selected function highlighted.

Remember these tips about working with CFCs in Dreamweaver MX:

- ColdFusion MX must be running locally.
- Your testing server must be set up as Local/Network.
- The path to your local root folder must be the same as that to your testing server folder.
- The CFC must be stored on your hard drive.

Integration of ColdFusion Studio

ColdFusion Studio is the ColdFusion development tool of choice for many ColdFusion developers. One of the reasons that it is so popular is that it has all the features that most ColdFusion developers need integrated into one development platform.

ColdFusion code can be written with any text editor, from Notepad to ColdFusion Studio. It can even be written in Macromedia's Dreamweaver MX, which includes both WYSIWYG and text-editing capabilities. The development tool does not the code make. The tightness and readability of your code is determined by your knowledge of the CFML and your personal style.

In this section, we discuss the integration of the ColdFusion Studio development tool. We talk about how to best make use of ColdFusion Studio within your current development environment. We'll also show you how to customize your work area to make the most of ColdFusion Studio.

> **Note**
>
> Keep in mind that our intention is not to tell you about every tab, button, or menu that you can use, but to help you understand the interface so that you can use it more efficiently.

Getting to Know ColdFusion Studio

ColdFusion Studio is a companion application to ColdFusion Server. As mentioned, it is the development environment of choice for many ColdFusion developers. One of the reasons for this popularity is that ColdFusion Studio gives developers complete access to all the resources that they need to build a feature-rich and robust application.

ColdFusion Studio is not a WYSIWYG web page editor. It simply means that the HTML that is produced by such an editor is visual in nature and based on visual design rather than hand-coded page elements. WYSIWYG editors enable you to drag and drop elements on the page for the purposes of placement and resizing. As you add elements to the page design, the editor refreshes the design to include the new elements.

WYSIWYG editors are not, as some developers would have you believe, evil. On the other hand, they are not the answer to all your prayers either. Though these editors make quick work out of screen design and the placement of elements within the page and have become increasingly capable of creating dynamic page elements, they have less appeal to those used to coding directly in HTML and CFML.

The Studio Interface

Let's take a look at the ColdFusion Studio interface. Although we don't intend to give full coverage to every item and every feature available within Studio, we do want to draw your attention to several that are important.

The ColdFusion Studio interface is not complicated (see Figure 2.10), but there are elements that you need to know very well. Table 2.5 lists these elements and the functions that they serve within the development environment.

Table 2.5   **ColdFusion Studio Interface Elements**

Interface Element	What It Does
Main menu	This is your standard Windows-style, drop-down menu for access to all the options and functions in ColdFusion Studio.
QuickBar	This includes button-type access to many of the most commonly used tags and functions in HTML and CFML. It gives you the option of keeping one or more of the default toolbars handy or creating your own custom toolbar.
Resource window	This gives you quick access to a tab structure for file management, datasource access, projects, code snippets, online help, and the Tag Inspector.
Editor window	This is the area in which you write and edit your application code. Within this window, you can edit and view a browser rendition of your code.
Editor toolbar	This is where the developer can toggle options, such as line numbers, word wrap, the Tag Insight feature, and the Tag Completion feature.
Debugging toolbar	This enables you to debug your application pages to find errors in your code. It enables you to set breakpoints, to step through your lines of code, and to monitor variables and recordsets.
Results window	This includes tabs (to track, search, and replace operations), code validation, link verification, images, project deployment, and compilation.

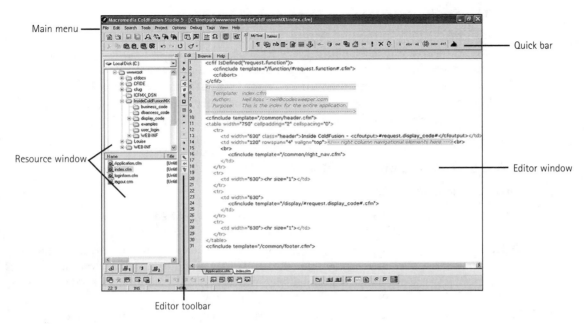

Main menu

Quick bar

Resource window

Editor window

Editor toolbar

Figure 2.10 ColdFusion Studio.

Using ColdFusion Studio

Before you start using ColdFusion Studio, you should familiarize yourself
with the key features listed in the previous section. After you are comfortable
with the ColdFusion Studio interface, you can familiarize yourself with some
of the features that you will be using quite often.

Tag Insight, Function Insight, and Tag Completion

ColdFusion Studio has some nifty functionality built in. Tag Insight and
Function Insight are features of ColdFusion Studio that provide you with
a drop-down menu of all the attributes that are associated with the tag
with which you're working.

Tag Insight (see Figure 2.11) and Function Insight are tools that enable you
to write ColdFusion code more easily and efficiently. Tag Insight helps to complete tag names, attributes, and values as you type—that is, after you've started
the tag name. For example, when you type "<cf" (without the quotation
marks), you promptly see a drop-down menu that shows you a list of all the
tags that begin with "cf". After you complete the tag name, you see a drop-
down menu that lists all the attributes available to the defined tag. Function
Insight works the same way, but it is applied to ColdFusion functions.

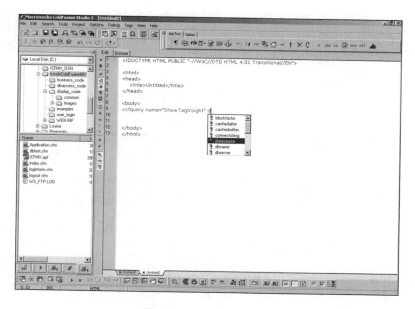

Figure 2.11   Tag Insight.

Tag Completion is a feature of ColdFusion Studio that completes many tags that you type. For instance, if you type a `CFOUTPUT` beginning tag, such as `<cfoutput>`, Tag Completion finishes the tag for you by adding the `</cfoutput>` end tag.

Expression Builder

The Expression Builder (see Figure 2.12) is a useful tool for helping you to handle the syntax of ColdFusion functions. The Expression Builder enables you to take advantage of ColdFusion functions even if you're not at all familiar with the syntax or attributes of the functions themselves. The Function Insight feature does something similar, but the Expression Builder goes way beyond that.

Function Insight requires that you are familiar with the ColdFusion function names and their use; Expression Builder enables you to browse ColdFusion functions organized by their function type. In other words, if you which to see what functions are available to be run on a ColdFusion array, open the Expression Builder, open the `Functions` folder, and then click Arrays to see a list of all array functions.

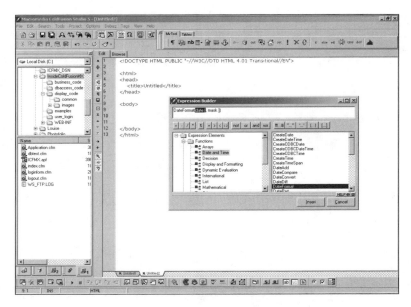

Figure 2.12 Expression Builder.

If you're stuck and need some extra hints on syntax or an actual code example, you can toggle the Help window for any component of code that you select.

Query Builder

ColdFusion Studio's Query Builder (see Figure 2.13), or SQL Builder as it is also known, is a tool that helps you to build and verify SQL statements and ColdFusion queries. It enables you to connect to your datasource and build the SQL statements that are used to drive your ColdFusion application.

The Query Builder enables you to create complex SQL statements without writing any code. Features of the Query Builder let you do the following:

- Drag and drop columns into your SQL statements
- Generate SELECT, INSERT, UPDATE, and DELETE statements
- Execute SQL statements to verify their validity
- Generate code complete with CFQUERY tags

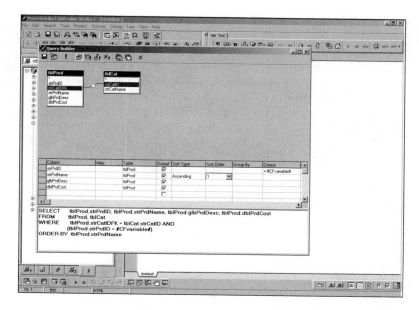

Figure 2.13   Query Builder.

SQL

SQL is an industry standard for communicating with databases. It is supported by most relational databases. SQL is discussed in-depth later in the book.

There are different ways to open the Query Builder. First, you can access it from the main menu in ColdFusion Studio by selecting Tools, SQL Builder. From there, you select a server and datasource and then drill down into the tables in that datasource. You can select queries that you've already saved or choose to create a new query. When you choose to create a new query, the Query Builder opens.

The second way to access Query Builder is through the Database tab in your Resource window. With it, you select your server and datasource and then drill down to your tables. You can customize your queries within the Query Builder to build SELECT, INSERT, UPDATE, or DELETE queries. The Query Builder also supports relational queries and table joins.

Using Code Snippets

Code snippets are a way to save small blocks of code that you use frequently. Code snippets are stored in ColdFusion Studio with a start and end portion so that you can create a snippet of code that will surround other tags or template content when inserted.

Code snippets are perfect for creating reusable blocks of code that you can use on a regular basis. Some of our favorite snippets are shown in Table 2.6.

Table 2.6 **Code Snippets**

Start Tag	End Tag

`<cfif isdefined("`	`")>`
	`<cfelse>`
	`</cfif>`

`<cfswitch expression="`	`">`
	    `<cfcase value="">`
	    `</cfcase>`
	
	`</cfswitch>`

`<cfset variables.varname="`	`">`

Code Sweepers

Code sweepers are designed to provide developers with a means to ensure that their code is formatted consistently throughout their applications. When you run a code sweeper against a code template, you can expect the code within that template to be formatted to a defined coding standard. For example, you might have some code that is written like this:

```
<HTML>
<head>
<title>Code Sweeper Test</title>
</head>
<Body>
<Table>
<tr>
<TD>Neil Ross, </TD>
<TD>neil@codesweeper.com</TD>
</TR>
</Table>
</Body>
</HTml>
```

After you run the code sweeper, your code will be nicely formatted and readable, like this:

```
<html>
<head>
    <title>Code Sweeper Test</title>
</head>
  <body>
      <table>
          <tr>
              <td>     Neil Ross,
              </td>
              <td>     neil@codesweeper.com
              </td>
          </tr>
      </table>
  </body>
</html>
```

You can easily customize any code sweeper to your coding specifications. To customize your code sweeper, press F8 to access the Studio settings. Choose CodeSweeper, and then select the code sweeper that you want to customize. Then press the Edit Profile button. You can see the CodeSweeper Settings window in Figure 2.14.

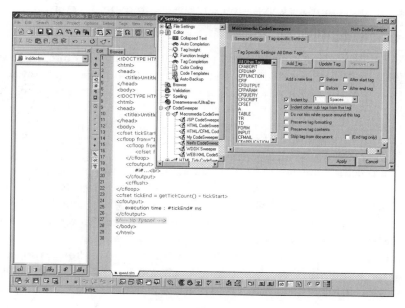

Figure 2.14   CodeSweeper Settings window.

Code sweeper settings include general settings and tag-specific settings. The general settings control the option to force all upper- or lowercase tag, attribute, and event names. It also enables you to apply attribute quoting, and it can be set for each individual tag.

Remote Development Services (RDS) and Development Mappings

ColdFusion Studio enables you to work with files on remote servers through the RDS service. RDS lets you communicate with a remote host and enables secure access to that host, while also providing the capability to browse datasources and use the SQL Builder to debug your code.

Working with files on remote servers is very much like working with them on your local or network drive. The difference is that you must first establish a connection to the remote server by adding an FTP or RDS connection through ColdFusion Studio.

To create an RDS connection, you must provide the name of the host where the files are stored. You might also need to provide a password so that ColdFusion Studio can access the resource.

Setting up development mappings ensures that you can browse the code that you are developing through the browser that is built in to ColdFusion Studio. Development mappings also enable you to use ColdFusion's debugging to debug your application code, even on remote servers.

Working with Projects

ColdFusion Studio enables you to group your templates into a collection. That collection is called a project. Project grouping is a great way to manage your files because it enables you to make changes across the project, divide smaller segments of your application into subprojects, and deploy project templates to a production server with a single upload.

Understanding Projects

A project is a collection of files that are used in your application or in your web site. A project can contain any file type. Most projects consist of application templates and HTML files as well as images, style sheets, and scripts.

You can create and access your project from the Project tab on the Resources window or through the main menu. You can manage one or more projects and access them individually with the handy Project drop-down list at the top of the Projects window. When you choose a project, you see a list of project folders and projects files in the pane just below the drop-down list.

A project lets you create a virtual file system that contains the files that you need for your project. You can add or remove files to your project from a real directory on your computer or on any computer on your network.

There are advantages to working with projects instead of with a real directory:

- Projects are easy to create and work with.
- Projects are easy to maintain and deploy.
- Projects enable you to include only the files that you need to access.
- Projects make it easy to run operations such as extended find. You can then replace or debug on only the relevant files.

Your projects will be organized into folders. There are different types of folders that you can use in a project:

- Physical folders are directly tied, or mapped, to a directory on your computer. Physical folders are either manual-inclusive or auto-inclusive:
  - Manual-inclusive folders require you to specify which files in the mapped directory should be included in the folder. The location of a manual-inclusive folder cannot be changed.
  - Auto-inclusive folders include every file in the mapped directory by definition. You can specify which file types you would like to include (for example, all the HTML files), but you cannot specify individual files to include. Auto-inclusive folders are automatically updated when you add files to or delete files from the mapped directory. Changing a folder from auto-inclusive to manual-inclusive retains all files by default.
- Virtual folders function as repositories for files that have no logical relationship to each other on a disk drive. You can think of a virtual folder as a container into which you can place whatever files you want. Virtual folders are a useful way to organize files that can be distributed across your file system.

Creating a Project

When you create a project, you must specify a folder to hold the project file. This folder must already exist somewhere on your computer. If the existing folder has files and subfolders, you can add them to the project.

After creating the initial project, you can add, edit, and delete folders in the project as necessary. You can also add and remove individual project files.

Working with Projects

Within a project, you can run all the standard file management and maintenance operations that you perform on individual files. You can also set and modify resource filters and perform a variety of other project-level tasks. Project-level tasks include operations such as verifying links throughout the project, using extended find and replace operations throughout the project, working with source control, and deploying a project.

Deploying a Project

Deployment is the process of copying all the files in your project to one or more servers. You can specify a deployment path for the entire project or for individual folders and files within that project.

Project deployment is easy and flexible. Just run the Project Deployment Wizard and it walks you through creating either a direct deployment or a scriptable deployment. By following the wizard, you can choose all the necessary options to get your project into production.

Debugging in ColdFusion Studio

You can run the debugger against your application pages to find errors in your code when RDS is enabled and a server mapping is defined. Debugging is not supported on Windows 98.

The debugger lets you perform these tasks:

- Set breakpoints and watches
- Evaluate variables and expressions
- Step through lines of code
- Investigate the code stack
- Monitor recordsets
- Observe variables in all scopes

Customizing ColdFusion Studio

There are a few small customizations that can make a world of difference for your development efforts. The key to customization is to make your development environment as comfortable as possible. When you are successful at making your development environment comfortable, shortcuts and everyday procedures can quickly become second nature. To access these customizable elements, press Shift+F8.

Custom QuickBar

ColdFusion Studio gives you the option to use button shortcuts in several default toolbars. These toolbars make up the area known as the QuickBar. These toolbars have buttons for almost every element of code that a typical application might use. I recommend that you create a customized QuickBar that includes the shortcut buttons to all the CFML and HTML tags that you use most often.

You can toggle which toolbars you want to appear in ColdFusion Studio by simply right-clicking and selecting the name of the toolbar that you want to see. The toolbar appears floating above the Studio interface. You can dock it within the QuickBar area or just about anywhere else on the screen.

To create a custom QuickBar, right-click the existing QuickBar, and then click Customize. You can also access this functionality by pressing Shift+F8 on your keyboard. Along with access to all the standard toolbar buttons, you can create custom buttons that insert customized blocks of code into your template.

Keyboard Shortcuts

Keyboard shortcuts are a great way to speed up the development process. Most developers use the same syntax and the same code conventions over and over in an application. You can customize your keyboard shortcuts to trigger the insertion of code snippets, to simulate clicking a button on your QuickBar, or to perform any of the many standard functions within ColdFusion Studio.

Keyboard shortcuts can save you a lot of time and in the long run, many headaches. Keyboard shortcuts can be created to insert your favorite code snippets and to perform standard functions.

Summary

ColdFusion Studio is the development tool of choice for many ColdFusion developers. ColdFusion Studio is rich with features that are directly tied to the development of robust ColdFusion applications. As you start to use the ColdFusion Studio development environment, get to know your surroundings. Some developers work for months or longer without knowing how to create a custom toolbar, and they waste plenty of time fumbling back and forth between one toolbar or another.

Summary

This chapter provides you with an overview of ColdFusion installation and an introduction to some of the ColdFusion development tools available to you. You can develop in ColdFusion using anything from the simplest text editor to the visual environment provided by Dreamweaver MX. We expect to see ColdFusion Studio updated in the future to include all the recent developments in ColdFusion MX. Whatever your preference for how you work, ColdFusion provides you with a comfortable development environment.

3

Before You Begin Coding—Application Planning

THE IMPORTANCE OF APPLICATION PLANNING cannot be overstated. An application plan provides a roadmap for the development process with various waypoints and milestones signaling the completion of a phase of the plan. Developers often jump straight into the development of application code without a plan. It's great that they're eager to get started, but that's not the most important thing.

Imagine you wake up one morning and decide that you're going to compete in a local 5K road race. You show up at the advertised starting point and pay your fee to register for the race. You get your number and go over and stand with a swarming crowd of people. Someone walks over and without explaining the course or giving anyone a map, fires the starter's pistol.

What's the result? Mass confusion? A couple of things are working against you. Recall that we didn't mention whether you'd prepared for this race. We only said that you woke up and decided to run it. You showed up and made your investment, but you received no instructions and had no idea of the direction that you were to run. You had no clearly defined course, rules, or a finish line.

This same type of scenario happens all too often in application development. The fact is that there is plenty of work to be completed before a developer starts to crank out application code. The work includes planning and preparing the roadmap or framework on which the application will be structured. It also includes the planning of the physical structure of the environment on which the application will function and the development of a strict methodology for the application-development process. All are essential to the successful completion of the project.

In this chapter, we discuss how attention to architectural considerations, effective planning, and sticking with a standard development methodology for your project can help you to successfully complete your application-development project. The topics of discussion in this chapter help paint a clear picture of the application-development process and can help every developer gain a better understanding of how to effectively improve his or her contribution to the process.

Application Architecture

Application architecture is an important concept to understand. The architecture of an application describes the working parts of that application, how they are defined, and how they interact with each other (see Figure 3.1).

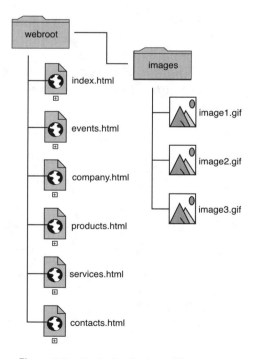

Figure 3.1 Typical web site architecture.

The application's architectural model gives developers a view of the big picture of the application rather than a close-up shot of every detail. It provides a framework that guides the interaction of various elements of the application.

The operating system (OS) or physical architecture of the server environment can influence an application's architecture. Your client's scalability requirements and their expectations in regards to the application's performance also have an effect on application architecture.

If you've ever bought something that was advertised to require "some assembly," you might be able to relate to how important it is to have a clear plan of the product and how each part interconnects and is intended to function. The instructions that are included serve much the same purpose as our application architecture. It gives you, the developer, a view of the product from several angles and from beginning to completion.

In software development, these instructions provide us with a clear vision of the organization of the application. It should detail the parts of the application and how those parts interact with other parts. It might also divide parts of the application into smaller subsystems based on their functions or behaviors. A good architecture should not stop there, however; it should also take into consideration the requirements for performance, extensibility, reuse, and presentation.

Understanding Tiered Architecture

Our discussion of application architecture now begins to take a more descriptive turn. In this next section, we take a closer look at two concepts of application architecture that define separate tiers within the application. These tiers function as a filter between logical sections of the application. The filters serve as a separator that enables the developer to group code by function and separate data from code.

Many of the concepts that we're going to talk about have a lot in common with object-oriented programming (OOP) and design principles. This is not necessarily the way that ColdFusion developers have traditionally looked at application development. As we move through the material in the next several sections, you'll see that these ideas begin to make more and more sense.

The goal of a tiered architecture is to enable the developer to separate application code into like chunks. Each tier of the application architecture contains code that has a similar purpose within the application. It is easy to take this separation of code to the extreme, but that's not what we're trying to do (nor is that very useful in most cases). Merely providing a logical division of code functionality is usually enough.

Two-Tier Architectures

We've all heard the term "client-server," right? Well, a two-tier application architecture is sometimes referred to as client-server architecture (see Figure 3.2). ColdFusion applications in their most basic form are two-tiered applications. There is code that creates an interface for the users to interact with, and there is data in the database that feeds the display. The presentation code is the first tier, or the presentation tier, and the database is the data tier.

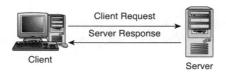

Figure 3.2   Client-server architecture.

It doesn't matter how many servers you've clustered that code across; we're not talking about physical environment architecture right now, just the functionality of the application code and how it is organized. Application architecture tiers are defined by their purpose. The following list breaks down the tiers in a two-tier architecture:

- Application tier
  - Presentation code
  - Business logic code
  - Business rule validation code
  - Component interaction code
  - Database interaction code
- Data tier
  - Storage of data

The typical two-tier application architecture is one where your application code is in one tier and your data is in another. This means that there is no separation between your presentation code, your data interface code, and your business logic code. This is typically the way that most ColdFusion developers start creating applications because typical static web sites have no need to separate code into functional groups. Check out the sample code in Listing 3.1.

Listing 3.1   **Two–Tier Application Sample Code**

```html
<html>
<head>
    <title>2-Tier Application Example</title>
</head>
<body>
<cfquery name="getCustomerEmails" datasource="ICFMX">
    SELECT CustomerName, CustomerEmail
    FROM Customers
</cfquery>
<table>
    <tr>
            <td>Customer Name</td>
        <td>Customer Email</td>
    </tr>
    <cfoutput query="getCustomerEmails">
    <tr>
        <td>#getCustomerEmails.CustomerName#</td>
        <td>#getCustomerEmails.CustomerEmail#</td>
    </tr>
    </cfoutput>
</table>
</body>
</html>
```

Of course, syntactically, there is nothing wrong with this code. It returns the needed values from the database, creates a layout for the page, and outputs the results into that layout.

The problems that you can run into with a two-tier architecture are the real killer. One of the strengths of ColdFusion is that it enables developers to easily write reusable and portable code that can be accessed from anywhere in the application. A two-tier application architecture does not play to this strength; in fact, it's only a little better than static Hypertext Markup Language (HTML). I know that you've got dynamic data coming out of the database, but if you want to change the layout of items at the top of the page or change the navigational elements of a page, you've got to touch several code templates to get this done.

What if you need to use the same query on 50 pages throughout your application? You are forced to write that query 50 times and maintain all 50 instance of that query, which can be a pain if the requirements for the query change or if the structure of your database needs to change. We later talk about code reuse in much more detail, but you should understand now that creating a well-planned architectural model enables you to avoid reworking your application down the road.

N-Tier Architectures

Applications that consist of more than two tiers are often called N-tier applications. N-tier application architectures provide a model for developers to build highly scalable and reusable applications. The N-tier architecture focuses on breaking the application into logical segments. By doing this, the developers can support each segment individually and maintain the application in sections instead of recoding the entire system as a result of minor change requests. Do you remember our code example from the typical two-tier application? Contrast what we saw in Listing 3.1 with the code shown in Listing 3.2.

Listing 3.2 **N-Tier Application Code Sample**

```
<cfinclude template="common/header.cfm">
<cfinclude template="data/getcustomeremails.cfm">
 <table>
     <tr>
          <td>Customer Name</td>
          <td>Customer Email</td>
     </tr>
     <cfoutput query="getCustomerEmails">
     <tr>
          <td>#getCustomerEmails.CustomerName#</td>
          <td>#getCustomerEmails.CustomerEmail#</td>
     </tr>
     </cfoutput>
</table>
<cfinclude template="common/footer.cfm">
```

Of course, this is just an example of one way that you could accomplish a bit more scalable application, and it's a very narrow example, but you get the picture. You now have reusable header, footer, and ColdFusion query or stored procedure templates that easily can be maintained from one place. This type of organizational structure for your code can help to alleviate numerous problems that can occur within the application-development process. When you start to think about all possible requirements that can go into the development of an enterprise application, you see that the more logically you can organize your code, the better off you are.

It seems only logical that it would be easier to support and maintain presentation code in one area that is separate from the code and that supports the business rules and business logic. Likewise, if all your data access is through stored procedures, you can keep up with that code easier and with the templates that you use to call your stored procedures as well. The N-tier architecture enables you to separate support for application components, such as databases, mail, and file servers, into their own logical areas within your application structure and within other servers as well.

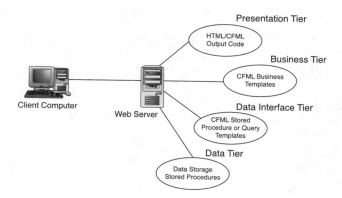

Figure 3.3   *N*-tier application architecture.

In a ColdFusion application, you often access databases that reside on the same server as the ColdFusion Markup Language (CFML) templates. With an *N*-tier architecture, you add an additional layer to your application and can separate the presentation-level code from the data in the database. This means that the code that supports what the user sees is separated from the code that makes up the pieces of business logic that run the application. The business-oriented code also is kept separate from the data that is at the heart of the application.

This type of application architecture makes much more sense and is easier to keep up with if you employ ColdFusion mappings. Take a look at Figure 3.4 to get a feel for ColdFusion mappings.

You might know that by using ColdFusion mappings, you can refer to templates using the `CFINCLUDE` tag by simply referring to that mapping. Note that the mapping is merely an alias for a physical directory to which your server has access. Don't worry if you're not familiar with how ColdFusion mappings are set up or even how they work. We discuss them thoroughly in Chapter 25, "Administering the ColdFusion Server."

For your application to perform specific functions or to conduct certain transactions, the various layers of the application interact with each other. One of the advantages of separating your application into a layered architecture is to minimize the interaction of the client or presentation layer with the backend data. The reason for this is that all your business logic code is wrapped into the business layer and only this layer interacts directly with the data. In OOP approaches, these different layers are sometimes referred to as the interface and the implementation.

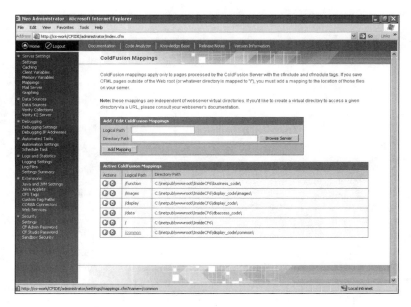

Figure 3.4 ColdFusion MX CFAS mappings.

Application Layers

Developers should take the time to understand the fundamentals of application layers to write well-organized applications that are easy to maintain. In this section, we take a look at how applications can logically be divided into layers, regardless of the physical architecture on which the application is loaded. At its most basic, the *N*-tier application architecture can be divided into the following tiers or layers:

- Presentation
- Business
- Data Interface
- Data

The layers of your application code can be separated by your physical file and directory structure. Figure 3.5 shows the ColdFusion Studio development interface. The directory structure is set up to mimic the division of application layers that we've been discussing.

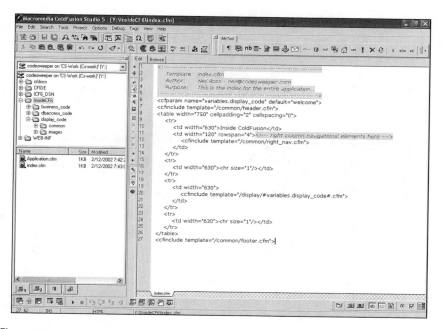

Figure 3.5 Physical directory structure of our application as seen in ColdFusion Studio 5.

The Presentation Layer

The presentation layer is made up of all elements of the application with which the user sees and interacts. This list of elements can include colors, font faces and styles, images, form controls, navigational elements, and more. These elements together are often referred to as the graphical user interface (GUI) or the user interface (UI). These elements define the look and feel of the application and their consistency and flow can determine the disposition of the user experience.

Users generally interact with ColdFusion applications through the use of a web browser. I say "generally" because ColdFusion applications are client-independent. This means that the ColdFusion Server is not concerned with the presentation-layer method or with the application logic and processing. This enables ColdFusion to output data to different types of clients, including web browsers (HTML), Personal Data Assistants (PDAs) (cHTML, XHTML), cell-phones and other wireless client browsers (WML), and even voice browsers (VoiceXML).

The UI

It seems that a new technology pops up every day to enable designers and developers to produce more feature-rich UIs. In an *N*-tier application, the presentation code for the UI should never access the database directly. Likewise, the UI code should never handle business rules or process logic. It should merely provide for screen layout. Figure 3.6 shows a simple UI.

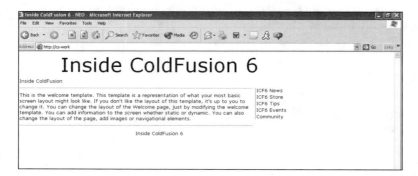

Figure 3.6   A simple UI for our application.

When discussing UI considerations, again the application architect and designer have to rely on the completeness of the requirements that have been gathered. These requirements should bring into better focus issues such as layout, colors, fonts, screen resolution, plug-ins, scripting, and browser compatibility that are necessary to deliver an application that meets the customer's needs.

Layout

I'm no artist or graphic designer and you might not be either, but paying close attention to layout of the screens throughout your application not only makes your application more aesthetically appealing to the user, but also it enhances the usability of the application itself. Consistency is one of the key elements that you need to remember about layout. You don't want your user hopping from page to page in your application and being forced to search for common elements such as navigation and form controls.

Correctly treating the unused spaces in the browser screen and having a balanced layout that utilizes all areas of the screen are important. Remember that you can say as much with a clean and professional layout as you can with lots of flashing banners, blinking text, and dancing cartoon characters.

Advertising and publishing companies employ experts in layout who provide ads with balanced and proportional layouts that mix typography, images, and text to convey a message. Each element is important to layout.

Online, layout is not quite as cut and dry. We have to worry about users' screen resolution settings and color-quality settings. Many web designers and developers use framed layouts for their sites. Some employ dynamic navigational elements. One thing is clear, however; consistency in your chosen layout method is key to making and keeping users comfortable with your application.

Colors

You should consider colors when planning the look and feel of your application. Colors can calm or can stir up emotions in users. Be careful with colors, however. Many times, designers or developers use too many colors or the wrong colors. This has the undesired effect of pulling the user's attention away from the content, and it distracts their focus.

Color on the web is quite different from color in print media. After the printed item is completed, the color cannot be changed and everyone sees the same color. It does not work this way online, however. There are many limitations to presenting color on the web. Some of the things that you should keep in mind include the following:

- Monitors that display your web site or application have a wide variety of depth settings.
- Color settings can be calibrated differently or use different gamma settings.
- OSs affect the way that color is displayed.
- Web browsers affect the way that color is displayed.

Color should be a big concern to anyone who is developing a UI. You should know that there are certain colors that are considered browser-safe. By working within the limits of those browser-safe colors, you can be more confident that your users are seeing the colors that you intended them to see.

Note

You can download the color-safe browser palette and find more tips regarding colors from Lynda Weinman's web site at www.lynda.com.

Screen Resolution

When planning your application, keep in mind the screen resolution settings of your users' video adapters. Most computers are shipped with video settings defaulted to 800×600 pixels. However, newer flat-panel monitors often have a lowest resolution setting of 1024×768.

Many developers forget that the actual usable screen real estate is less than what the resolution setting would lead you to believe. Check out the popular resolution settings and corresponding browser window sizes shown in Table 3.1 to help you keep your layout on target.

Table 3.1 **Screen Resolutions and Browser Window Sizes**

Screen Resolution Setting	Browser Window Size
640×480	600×300
800×600	760×420
1024×768	955×600

It's always a good idea to design your application so that the lowest resolution monitors can view and interact with your application without any formatting problems or excessive scrolling. Don't guess at what your users' resolution settings are. If at all possible, this information should be provided as part of your requirements-gathering process.

Fonts

We communicate user instructions with text on our screens, so, of course, we need to make sure that we pick fonts that are going to be easy for the user to read. The most commonly used fonts are Arial and Times New Roman. However, most web presentations look better with a font from the sans-serif font family. These fonts include Arial, Helvetica, or Verdana. The reason for using these standard fonts is that the user must have the specified font on his or her system, or you must push that font to the user along with your code.

By varying font sizes, styles, and colors, you can convey not only information, but also the importance of that information. Keep in mind that it's not a good idea to use more than one or two fonts in your application. In addition, remaining consistent with font sizes and styles when calling out headings or identifying notes throughout your application is an important factor in maintaining continuity.

Images

As we move through the development of our application, we are adding more and more content and are developing web graphics to support that content. As they say, a picture is worth a thousand words, and if you have the choice of reading all those words or checking out a cool graphic, I'm sure you'd choose the graphic.

There are, however, drawbacks to stuffing your application with graphics and photos. One of the largest drawbacks is the effect that overloading your web pages with references to images can cause. The reason for this is that the user must wait for all images to download before the requested page is fully viewable. Thus, if you're downloading lots of images on every page, you can slow down your page response times.

Another thing to keep in mind when you're planning your graphical presentation and considering photos, graphics, and other graphical elements (such as Flash or Shockwave files) is that the bandwidth of the end user likely is not as fast as your access to your development server (often local).

Client-Side Scripting

Many web applications use client-side scripting languages such as JavaScript and VBScript to enhance the user experience. Developers often utilize client-side scripting for form validation, user alerts and confirmation, and new windows.

VBScript is a scaled-down version of Microsoft's Visual Basic (VB) language. Support for VBScript is built in to Microsoft's Internet Explorer (IE). However, if your user is accessing your application using a Netscape or other web browser, he or she might need to download special plug-ins to support the code.

JavaScript was originally a creation of Netscape. It was called LiveScript, but the name was changed when Netscape and Sun Microsystems struck up a partnership and developed the language jointly. JavaScript shares some of the same structures and syntax with Java, but the languages are totally separate. JavaScript is most often the client-side scripting language of choice for most developers because of its cross-browser compatibility.

Browser Compatibility

Speaking of browser compatibility, developers need to be wary of problems with the compatibility of their code with various browsers. Such compatibility often affects the placement of elements on the screen.

The key to avoiding problems with browser compatibility is to find out what browser and browser version your users are using. Of course, unless your application will be viewed within a closed environment such as an intranet, this task is next to impossible. What you must do is build a profile of your typical user and build the application to support that profile.

Even after determining your typical user profile and building your application, you still have to test for compatibility. In your user's preferred browser and its nearest competitor, test your application for proper placement and alignment of screen elements. In other words, if the typical user's browser is IE 5.5, test with it, but also test with a comparable version of Netscape Navigator.

You also need to be aware that the user might have disabled support for client-side scripting languages such as JavaScript. If the user's browser does not support your code, you should plan ahead for how to handle interacting with that user.

The Business Layer

As we continue to break out the layers or tiers of *N*-tier application architectures, let's pause for a moment to get a general understanding of the business logic layer and the role it plays.

Just as every business is run on operating procedures or business rules, every application operates under a similar set of criteria. These criteria are what we call the business rules of the application. These business rules are strung together in business process logic. These business processes enable developers to create complete transactions that users will be guided through during their interaction with the application.

The business layer should provide us with an area in which we can write and store the code that interprets our business rules. It should also provide for a way to follow the logical flow of the business, or the business process logic.

Business Rules

As stated earlier, every business runs on rules, and business rules in a ColdFusion application define how the application enables users to interact with your data. For example, if a business rule states that the user must provide a valid email address to log in to the application, the application must enforce this rule. One way to enforce such a rule is to enable a user to register by providing his or her email address. We then can generate a password and email it to the email address that the user provided.

Because business rules are defined to help maintain the integrity of your data, the business rules are not defined by the application architecture. Just the opposite is true: The application architecture is defined to help support the business rules, the business processes, and the process logic.

The example that we just mentioned might use one or more specialized pieces of code to make the application adhere to the business rule that the user must provide a valid email address. One piece of code might check whether the email address provided is in the proper format. Because it is up to you how and where you enforce these rules, you might choose to enforce them using client-side scripting (using, for example, JavaScript or VBScript). This can also be accomplished using a user-defined functions (UDF) or regular expression.

Business Process Logic

Compliance with business rules usually means that your application transactions have to follow some sort of defined business-process logic. A process is an action that the user might take that requires multiple steps. Business processes enable users to move through complicated procedures in a way that breaks the process into logical steps. The user continues interacting with the application along the way until the application has gathered all the information that it needs to complete the process.

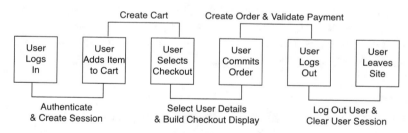

Figure 3.7   Step-by-step process logic.

Each step of a transaction should lead the user step-by-step through the process and should enforce the defined business rules along the way.

For example, many shopping cart applications require new users to register, providing personal information and ordering information along the way. They often require users to not only provide their mailing address, but also to provide billing and shipping addresses as well. A user would be overwhelmed if he or she were presented with all these requirements on the same screen.

A business process would break these requirements into chunks that are easy for the user to deal with and easy for the developer to manage. Not only do you do a service to your users, but also you do a service to your developers.

Data Interface Layer

The data interface layer provides access to the data in your backend database. It does not include any business logic or constraints on how we interact with the database. The data interface layer merely enables us to do things like SELECT, INSERT, UPDATE, and DELETE data from our database. The data interface tier should not contain code that defines any business rules or business processes, nor should it contain any code that comprises any presentation-level elements.

In your ColdFusion application, the data interface layer could be made up of templates that contain the CFSTOREDPROC calls for the stored procedures that you've written in the data layer. It could also contain CFQUERY tag calls that you've separated into functional groups or individual templates.

If you think about it, it makes sense to keep the data requests separate from the code that controls the presentation. The structure of the data itself seldom changes. The presentation-layer code, however, changes more often than anything else in the application. If you keep your CFQUERY tag calls in the same template with your presentation code, you run the risk of inadvertently messing up that code. It is better to separate the database calls into separate templates that are accessed much less frequently and that are less prone to programmers' fat fingers.

Data Layer

The data layer is responsible for the storage of your data. This is your database. The data layer is where you can tune and optimize data storage and data access and provide direct access to the data in your backend database. The data layer exists whether you employ a two-tier or *N*-tier architecture with the business logic layer as a buffer to ensure the integrity of your data through the business rules that are enforced.

The data layer is where you create stored procedures to perform queries against the data in the database. These might be very basic functions or might consist of advanced filtering and joining techniques (to be discussed later). Your stored procedures should not care about the business rules of the application, only the input and output parameters that they'll be handling. The business rules serve as a buffer to make sure that the only values that get to your stored procedures are the ones that are valid.

It is within the data layer that you optimize the performance of your database. Performance enhancements such as table indexes enable you to access data faster within the database, which speeds the query process. In turn, this improves the performance to the end user through the presentation layer.

Summary

The architectural model for any application is critical to the application's success. Whether the application is scalable, easy-to-maintain, and easy-to-extend depends on the quality of its architecture. An application's architecture is intended to give a better picture of how the entire system works. It shows how the parts work, and it enables us to see this picture from several different perspectives.

Resource Planning

A major part of the "hard" work of making your application-development efforts successful is ensuring that you've properly planned the environment in which the application is going to live. The importance of resource planning really can't be understated. To use a simple, but familiar, example, imagine that you went to work and that there was no desk for you to use, no lights for you to turn on, and no computer for you to bang out code. You'd find it pretty hard to work, wouldn't you?

Similarly, for your application to function properly, it has to have a properly designed and thought-out working environment.

In many cases, achieving success with a project implementation depends as much (if not more) on resource planning as it does on coding. How involved you are in the initial stages of project planning likely determines the amount of input that you personally have on the type and amount of hardware used. Nonetheless, being as familiar as you can with the "best-case scenarios" makes you an invaluable advisor should you find yourself in that role.

The following section attempts to familiarize you with various processes you can use to properly plan and utilize your resources while tailoring them to suit your specific applications and make the most of your fiscal resources.

Environment Considerations

Obviously, there are many times when you are tasked with application building in situations in which the architecture and environment have already been decided for you. In those cases, the best you can do as a developer is to make sure you write solid code, adhere to best practice standards, and make yourself aware of the subtleties of each specific OS/database combination where that code might be run.

Still, if you're lucky, there are times when your advice as the expert is sought in making the decisions about the platforms with which the application will live. Developers often approach these situations with a "go with what you know attitude." Although there's nothing wrong with that attitude on the surface, you'll find yourself of much more value to the client or customer if you can identify pros and cons of each platform based on the client's specific situation.

As you read on, you should gain a better understanding of how you can approach this "needs analysis" and determine the best choices for any given situation.

OSs

We're hesitant to even begin writing this section because we can hear the screams of each devoted faction ringing in our ears. Again, in many cases, you might play no role in this decision. Still, if you were asked to make a recommendation (and I'm sure you hold your own strong opinions), it would help if you were able to make that recommendation using logical analysis of the situation instead of just your personal devotion to one choice or the other.

When dealing with applications that make use of ColdFusion Server, you have three major choices in the world of OSs. Currently, versions of ColdFusion Server are available for Windows, Solaris, and Linux. Table 3.2 briefly outlines each choice and its benefits and drawbacks.

Table 3.2   Benefits and Drawbacks of OS/ColdFusion Combinations

Version	Common Benefits	Common Drawbacks
ColdFusion Windows	Ease of administration; tight integration with Internet Information Server (IIS); hardware components are generally cheaper	Slightly less overall stability; not accepted in some enterprise environments
ColdFusion Solaris	Greater overall stability of the server; often the only choice in environments that have standardized on Solaris	Increased complexity of administration; employees to manage this type of equipment are more expensive than their Windows counterparts; hardware components are generally more expensive

Version	Common Benefits	Common Drawbacks
ColdFusion Linux	The cheapest of all three choices from an OS standpoint, as many versions are free; can be run on the same, less-expensive hardware as Windows versions; can prove to be slightly more stable under certain conditions than running ColdFusion on Windows	Short product history (the first version of ColdFusion for Linux wasn't available until release 4.5); increased complexity of administration

Of course, Table 3.1 makes some broad generalizations regarding the different OS choices, and it's very brief in its discussion of the benefits and drawbacks of each choice. The intent, however, is to get you to think along those same lines as you attempt to identify the best choice for your customer (even if the customer is you!).

If you're a Linux guru already, you've eliminated one of the items I've listed in the drawbacks column. Similarly, if you already have Solaris machines that cannot be retooled to run Windows, you're on your way to a choice there as well. The key is to identify all the benefits and drawbacks of each choice, evaluate where you are and where you need to go, and then make the most informed decision possible.

The differences in stability and performance between the three versions are all pretty negligible, and the choice usually comes down to the hardware and technical resources that you or the customers have in-house.

Choosing a Database

Just as you must decide which OS you want to use for your ColdFusion Servers, you also must decide where your data is going to be stored. Just as with the OS discussion, there are many cases (especially when dealing with legacy applications) where the data is already in a database, thus eliminating the need for you to make this choice.

There are still situations, however, where the application you are building is gathering or creating the data. In those cases, it becomes necessary to decide which database you're going to use and how you want to implement it.

In general, there are two types of database systems: desktop database tools and server databases. Table 3.3 illustrates the differences between the two.

Table 3.3 **Desktop Versus Server Databases**

Characteristics	Desktop Database	Server Database
Processing of changes to the data	Occurs on the client machine, regardless of where the source file is located.	Occurs at the server, where all the hard work is done.
Availability of data	Originally designed to be used by one user at a time.	Designed with multiple simultaneous requests for data in mind.
Reliability of data	With multiple users accessing what was originally intended for one user, data integrity failures can occur.	Data stored in a database built to utilize the client-server model is extremely reliable even while being accessed and manipulated by multiple users simultaneously.
Network traffic	As most processing of the data is done client-side, the entire package must then be returned to the source machine, causing a tremendous amount of unnecessary network traffic.	Typically, the only things sent over the network in the client-server model are instructions to the database server and result sets, resulting in much less overall network traffic.

If you're serious about application performance, and you want your site to be highly available under all types of traffic load, you should ensure that you're not using a file-based database. Desktop databases were never really meant to be web-connected, and it shows.

Aside from being less reliable than their server counterparts, desktop databases are much, much slower and less secure. Because a large part of any ColdFusion application's processing time is spent waiting for result sets to return from the database, this can have a huge performance impact on your application as a whole.

You need to take a close look at the resources that are available to manage the data after it's there; in addition, make sure that you're not trying to leverage an Oracle database administrator (DBA) for Sybase work, or vice-versa. Believe it or not, the subtleties between different database management systems are often more complex than those between OSs. This makes it all the more critical to know who is available to manage the data after it's in the database.

Contrary to popular opinions, designing table layouts in SQL or Oracle doesn't make you a DBA. As you're application begins to become more heavily trafficked, you inevitably discover that you have to do some tweaking at the database level to keep things running smoothly. At this point, the DBMS you've chosen and the folks you have around you to help you support it become extremely important to you—so choose carefully.

Assessing the Needs of Your Application

What a wonderful world it would be if we were able to peer into our crystal balls and determine, well in advance, just what type of resource configuration our applications would require to function at their very best. As it is, however, we are forced to try to deliver our best estimates.

During the discovery phase of any section of a project, the first thing you usually want to do is a needs analysis. Determining an appropriate application-environment configuration is no different. Based on the requirements you've already received, as well as how you believe that the application should work in its finished state, you should be able to determine roughly how you need to configure your environment to suit your application.

Of course, to determine the actual hardware requirements of the application servers themselves, you'll want to conduct systematic load testing of the finished code. This is an absolutely necessary step and one that is covered in great detail in Chapter 26, "Performance Optimization and Scalability Planning." For now, we deal with planning the environment as a whole to suit your application.

First and foremost, you need to determine the overall architecture that you plan to implement. Depending on the needs of your application, this is where you should begin to investigate DMZs, firewalls, Network Address Translation (NAT) and Secure Socket Layer (SSL) hardware/software combinations, and so on.

Ideally, you want to expose as little of your infrastructure as possible to the outside world. The most traditional method of accomplishing this is by placing your public servers (such as the web server) on a protected subnetwork that has no access to your internal network. In this way, you can keep the public portion of your network accessible, without introducing undue security risks.

Further, you might want to make use of a firewall of some sort to restrict traffic between all computers on your network in accordance with the security policies that you or your network administrators have defined. The firewall can become an integral part of your overall design; it acts as the traffic cop, pushing traffic meant for your public servers to your predefined subnetwork and keeping unwanted intrusion from your internal systems. Figure 3.8 demonstrates this design.

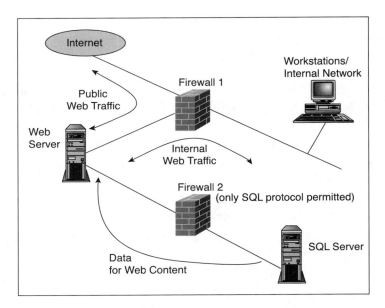

Figure 3.8 Example architecture.

After you've determined the overall design of the environment in which your application will live, you should address (as much as is within your power as the developer) the security of the public servers themselves.

Depending on the combination of OSs and web server software you have chosen, the actual methods for securing these servers differ. Still, the key things that you want to check are as follows:

- Access to public content on the servers is read-only for web users.

- The user designated as a pathway user for web clients (such as the IUSR_LocalMachine account in Windows) has only the bare minimum permissions required to gain access to material you want to make public.

- Configure your servers to limit vulnerability from denial-of-service attacks by using appropriate monitoring and filtering software, along with configuring appropriate timeouts.

- Restrict the web server itself to only server files designated within your defined web content tree.

- Disable the capability to obtain directory listings. In this way, you can help ensure that only the content you explicitly designate as public material is seen.

Of course, this is by no means a complete list, but it should help you begin to look in the right direction in thinking about securing your servers. If security is a major concern for you and your organization, there are many consultancies now offering full security audits of your architecture.

Another part of your initial security strategy should be checking vendor sites to make sure that you've installed and configured all necessary security patches. Most vendors maintain sites explicitly designed to keep their customers updated with recent security releases. After you've decided which software products you're going to use, it's a good idea to visit the vendor sites for these products and sign up for the various security alert mailing lists that are offered. These mailings typically update you as new security issues are discovered, and they tell you the actions that you need to take to protect your configuration.

Depending on the type of application that you are designing, there might be other pieces of your configuration that you need to snap in; but in almost every case, you have to start by defining a configuration and security model. After you've done the work up front, you can move on to the actual design and implementation of your application with a good understanding of the policies and limitations behind the scenes.

Planning Ahead for Scalability

When you're designing your architecture, leave yourself a path to upgrade should your application suddenly get bombarded by traffic that is much higher than you expected. When you are initially designing the architecture, you are forced to make a best-guess estimate of the amount of traffic your site will actually receive. Although this is fine as a starting point, you might find that as you gain a larger user base, you need to reevaluate how your environment is designed and expand your architecture to better suit the needs of your growing user base.

One of the easiest ways to do this is through clustering and load balancing. Clustering and load balancing enable you to have multiple servers in your environment that serve exactly the same purpose as their twins, thus splitting the work between two or more partners.

In a typical architecture, there are three places that you can cluster: at the web server, at the application server, and at the database server.

Unless you've implemented a three-tiered architecture with your application server physically separated from your web server, you likely will be performing clustering at the web/application server or at the database server.

To cluster, you need to identify where your traffic bottlenecks exist. By performing analysis on your traffic patterns and monitoring the resource usage on your application and database machines, you should be able to determine where you get the most bang for your buck.

Obviously, if your analysis shows you that your ColdFusion Servers are spending the vast majority of their time in an idle state and your database server is nearly never idle, you should consider clustering your database to spread the load.

Conversely, if the database is idle nearly 100 percent of the time and your ColdFusion Server's resources are strained, you should cluster at the ColdFusion layer.

Depending on the database that you've chosen, you should be able to find a wealth of information on your clustering options at the vendor site.

If you've determined that you need to cluster at the application-server layer, the first step in analyzing your traffic pattern is to define how many servers are necessary to service all your concurrent requests during peak load times.

Clustering ColdFusion Servers in this sense refer to having a group of web/application servers work together to service the entire site. When clustering in this way, each member of the cluster typically hosts a complete copy of the entire site so that any incoming request can be answered by any node on the cluster.

Alternatively, you might choose to centralize all web content in a single location, giving all cluster members access to this content. The content is made available on a separate physical machine on the network, typically referred to as a content or file server. The main problem with this type of configuration is that although your application servers are still clustered, the content server represents a single point of failure in that if it becomes unavailable, none of the clustered application/web servers can service any incoming requests.

One way to solve this problem is by partnering the content server and the database server, and then making each one the other's failover. In other words, although the database server's primary function in this setup is to handle incoming database requests, it would also contain copies of the content so that if the content server were to fail, the cluster nodes could look to the database server for the content. Subsequently, should the database server go offline, the content server will have a complete copy of the database that can come online to answer database requests in the event of a failure. This type of setup eliminates the need for redundant hardware, but continues to ensure high availability of all components in the cluster. Figure 3.9 demonstrates this model.

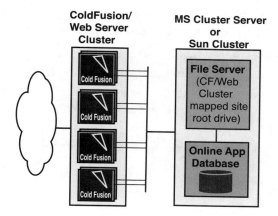

Figure 3.9   High-availability model.

Load balancing is the next major key in scalability planning. After you've decided to cluster your application servers, you need to come up with a plan for the distribution of incoming traffic between each member of the cluster.

There are many ways that you can do this, but by far the most popular choice today is through the introduction of a hardware layer. This hardware layer, typically called a load balancer, sits on the network in front of all your web-application servers. When any requests come in for your site, the load balancer answers these requests by deciding to which server on the cluster it wants to direct this traffic. The way in which it makes that decision can be controlled by the way in which you configure the load balancer itself.

Typically, if your site is located at www.somesite.com, www.somesite.com resolves to the Internet Protocol (IP) address of your load balancer. After traffic hits the load balancer, the load balancer can decide to which member of the server cluster it should translate that request. This can also give you an additional layer of security because, in this model, the load balancer itself really is the only piece of hardware that needs to have a public Internet address. After traffic has been sent there, it can usually translate the request to a private network address of a machine on the cluster for response.

After you've decided that you are going to need to cluster and implement some sort of load-balancing strategy, the next step is defining how many cluster members you actually need to handle the amount of traffic you are experiencing during peak times.

There are many different strategies and methodologies available for determining this number. We will present one that we've used successfully in the past.

First, it helps to have a general understanding of how cluster size is determined. Generally, there are a few standard factors that you need to consider:

- Expected peak requests per hour
- Expected peak simultaneous requests
- Maximum average response times that you feel are acceptable for your user base
- Specific characteristics of your application (database versus content-intensive, state management needing to maintained or not, and so on)
- Environmental characteristics (locations of firewalls, private networks, routers, and so on)

After all items have been considered, testing is required to determine the exact number of cluster members necessary to meet the expectations that you have defined.

As with any other methodology, there are many testing methods available. The one we've used successfully in the past is outlined here:

1. Determine what you think is the maximum number of requests per hour experienced by the site. You can use past data obtained from web access logs or other monitoring utilities to give you some idea of the number with which you might want to start. In addition, you need to define what you have decided is the maximum tolerable response time for your site.

    This is an important factor because it is used to determine exactly how many cluster members you need to achieve this response time.

    In addition, when you're determining your maximum tolerable response time, be sure to keep in mind that you're defining this as the "maximum allowable response time during peak periods of load."

    Although it might be desirable for you to say, "I don't want any page to take more than three seconds to return to the user," this would be a very unrealistic response time to expect under peak periods of load. The lower your maximum allowable response time, the more cluster members you likely need to keep that time down.

2. Set up a controlled test (using an enterprise-load testing tool) that stresses the site with the amount of load that you've defined in Step 1. Controlled load testing is a science all its own, and if you've never been exposed to it before, you might want to refer to Chapter 26, for more information on how to go about load testing a site in this manner.

3. Calculate the average response time of your site while you are placing it under load from the load-testing tool.

4. If the response time you saw in Step 3 is greater than the maximum tolerable response time that you defined in Step 1, you need to add another member to the cluster and start the process again at Step 2. Repeat this process until the response times you see under peak load during your testing fall within the allowable range that you defined in Step 1.

Again, you might find that you have a better way to determine your cluster needs. There is nothing wrong with developing your own methodology for determining these needs—just make sure that whatever method you use, you have some quantifiable way to measure the improvement in performance as you add members to the cluster.

Summary

In this section, we examined how to define the environment in which our application runs, as well as how to determine the specific needs of our application from an architectural standpoint. We also talked about how to expand our environment for scalability after we determine the need.

To successfully build a web application with any technology and not just ColdFusion, you have to make sure that you are properly planning and using your resources.

Making proper use of the resources you have means that you're keeping track of what they're doing and how they are doing it. This keeps everything running smoothly. The job of monitoring all components of your setup is an ongoing task throughout the life of your application, and it's a necessary step in making sure that you can identify and deal with any potential problems early on.

In addition to the number of servers you have available to you and the way that your network is architected, you also need to examine the type of hardware that you have to make sure that it's up-to-date and appropriate for the task.

You really can't over-plan your resources. It's better to have too much hardware available to you than to come up short after it's too late.

There's an old adage that the prepared companies determine the maximum amount of hardware they need for peak load and then double it just to be safe. Although that's unrealistic to expect, the core message is true. It's better to be prepared for the worst than it is to get left wishing you had.

Depending on how involved you are in the predevelopment stages of the project, you might find that most or all architecture and environment planning work has been done for you. Nevertheless, as a developer, it's important that you keep yourself well-versed in the different ways in which an application environment is planned and deployed so that you can offer expert advice based on your experiences when you are inevitably called upon to do so.

After you've completed the planning of your architecture and hardware, you then can begin thinking about how you're actually going to build the core application. Just as the architecture and hardware layer requires proper planning to ensure success, so too does the application-building process.

In the next section, we dive right into one of the first steps of this planning by beginning a discussion of the various development methodologies that are available for you to use when designing your application.

Development Methodologies

Development methodology in relation to ColdFusion application design refers to the existence of a defined set of conventions or procedures to guide you through a development project. A development methodology might define your application's physical file structure and might dictate what type of template goes into what folder. It might define naming conventions for your code templates and how those templates interact with each other.

There are many popular development methodologies floating around the ColdFusion development community. Any one of them might meet your needs and help you to design more scalable and easier-to-maintain applications. Understanding the approach of these development methodologies might even help you to define your own practice.

It is not our intention here to explain all intricacies of any development methodology. We want to help you understand the use and importance of utilizing a development methodology in your projects.

Fusebox

One of the most popular, widely known, and widely accepted development methodologies is Fusebox. Fusebox has successfully been adapted to serve as an application-development methodology for Active Server Pages (ASP), PHP, and Java Server Pages (JSP) applications. This discussion focuses on Fusebox 3, which is the latest specification. Although some of the fundamental concepts are the same, Fusebox 3 bears little resemblance to Fusebox 2. Fusebox 3 is built around the following key features:

- A nested model that supports communication between circuits. Circuits now can have a parent/child relationship, leveraging the power of inheritance. This is a departure from Fusebox 2, where circuits were independent of each other.

- A nested layout model

- Fusedocs, which provide a Program Definition Language and documentation in an eXtensible Markup Language (XML) format

- A defined set of key or core files

- Exit fuseactions (XFAs)

- A public application program interface (API)

Core Files

Fusebox 3 introduces different core files, each prefixed with FBX_:

- **FBX_Fusebox_CFxx.cfm.** The *xx* is dependent on the version of ColdFusion supported. Your Fusebox application has a separate file for each version of ColdFusion supported. The FBX_Fusebox_CFxx.cfm file replaces many of the custom tags from Fusebox 2 and should be called by the default file of your application's home circuit.

- **FBX_Settings.cfm.** This is an option file that is used to set variables. The job of the FBX_Settings.cfm file is to set up the environment in which the application runs. This replaces app_Globals.cfm, and variables specific to a circuit application are set in the app_Locals.cfm files used in Fusebox 2.

- **FBX_Circuits.cfm.** This is required in the home circuit and provides mappings of circuit aliases to physical directory paths. The circuit aliases are not required to be the same as the directory names.

- **FBX_Switch.cfm.** This is a CFSWITCH statement that contains a CFCASE for every fuseaction that the circuit handles.

- **FBX_Layouts.cfm.** This is an optional file, used to set the variable Fusebox.layoutDir, which points to the directory where layout files are kept. It also sets Fusebox.layoutFiles, which points to the layout file to be used.

Fusedocs

Unlike Fusebox 2, which used a proprietary format developed by Hal Helms, Fusebox 3 uses XML to document what a fuse does and the required input/output. The fusedoc has three elements. Responsibilities is the first and it is required.

The other two elements are properties and io. Responsibilities provide an explanation of what the fuse will do. Properties contain a number of subelements that provide information, such as history, related to the fuse. The last element, io, defines the input and output of the fuse. A more detailed explanation of these elements and their attributes can be found in the Fusebox 3 documentation.

Fusebox Basics

Fusebox helps developers build robust and scalable web applications easily, surely, and quickly—and it's surprisingly simple. A Fusebox application works by responding to requests to do something—a fuseaction, in Fusebox parlance. This request might come about as a result of a user action (a user submitting a form, for example, or clicking a link), or it might occur as a result of a system request.

When you submit the form, `index.cfm` is called. In fact, everything an application can do is done by sending a fuseaction request to `index.cfm`. This file, so central to the methodology, is called the fusebox. When a fusebox is called, a variable called fuseaction is also sent.

The fusebox's main job is to route a fuseaction request to one or more code files called fuses. These files are typically small and have well-defined roles.

The routing begins with a `CFSWITCH` statement, located in the `FBX_Switch.cfm`, that examines the value of the fuseaction. After it finds a matching value in one of the `CFCASE` statements, the code between those particular `CFCASE` tags is executed. In the Fusebox methodology, the `CFCASE` code is used to set up an environment in which one or more fuses can be called to perform whatever actions are needed to do the work requested by the variable fuseaction.

A fuse can be used to display a form, check whether a user's password and username match those found in a database, and show a menu of user options. In short, anything a web application can do can be done through the use of fuses.

Well-written fuses are very short and restrict themselves to doing only one or two things. They are easier to write (and maintain), are less buggy, and are easier to debug. They also facilitate code reuse. You seldom need a catch-all type of fuse, but you often will need fuses that handle a specific task.

Fuses have one or more *exit points*, which are areas where the action returns to the fusebox. Every link on a user menu is an exit point, just as each drill-down action to get more information is an exit point. Some exit points are visible and require user interaction, such as submitting a form or clicking a link. Other exit points are not visible. An example of an invisible exit point is a call to a CFLOCATION tag within a user-authentication template. Whether generated by user interaction or by the application itself, exit points in fuses always return to the fusebox with a fuseaction.

This is a great place to discuss the feature of XFAs. XFAs are the exit points of a fuse. In Fusebox 2, fuseactions were hard-coded into exit points:

```
<form action="index.cfm?fuseaction=verifyUser">
```

However, this impairs code reusability. If you want to reuse a fuse—whether in another application or in a different point in the same one—you now must deal with the fact that your exit fuseactions might not be the same. They might vary according to the context in which they are used. This means that you must begin introducing conditional statements in your code. Now, each time you want to reuse the fuse, you must open up the file, alter the existing code, and then save it. This introduces the very real possibility that you will introduce a bug into the code. Further, it reduces readability (and maintainability) of the code, making it just plain ugly.

Fusebox 3 enables you to use XFAs to replace the hard-coded references. This lets you create fuses that can be used anywhere, without worrying about where a form should be submitted or a link should be pointed.

```
<form action="index.cfm?fuseaction=#XFA.submitForm">
```

The value of the fuseaction is set in the FXB_Switch.cfm file:

```
<cfswitch expression="#Fusebox.fuseaction#">
    <cfcase value="verifyUser">
        <cfset XFA.submitForm="verifyUser">
        <cfinclude template="qry_verifyLogin">
    </cfcase>
    <cfcase ...
</cfswitch>
```

Fusebox Conventions

It's helpful to categorize fuses into different types. For example, some fuses display information, forms, and so on to users; others work behind the scenes to do things such as process credit cards; and still others are responsible for querying databases. Many Fusebox developers find it helpful to use a prefix when naming a fuse. Such a prefix conveys the fuse type. Examples of these are shown in Table 3.4.

Table 3.4   **Fusebox 3 Prefixes**

Fuse Name with Prefix	Explanation
dsp_ShowProductInfo.cfm	A display type fuse used to show or request information from a user
act_SaveUserInfo.cfm	An action type fuse used to perform an action without displaying information to a user
qry_GetUserInfo.cfm	A query type fuse used to interact with data-sources without displaying information to a user
url_ProcessOrder.cfm	An action type fuse used to redirect an action

These naming conventions are best thought of as suggestions. You can use the naming conventions outlined here—or not, depending on what suits you best.

If you do use them, will you use an underscore to separate the prefix from the fusename, or will you use the mixed-case spelling that many developers prefer? Personally, I like the mixed-case usage, but you might prefer something else. Whatever you choose, don't get bogged down in disputes over naming conventions; Fusebox is primarily about developing successful applications, not about naming schemes.

Encapsulation

You have seen how fuseactions are returned to the fusebox, and you have had a glimpse of the mechanism the fusebox uses to call helper fuses (a CFSWITCH statement). Fuses really do all the work in a Fusebox application. The fusebox itself acts like a manager, delegating work to one or more of these fuses.

One of the principles of modern programming is encapsulation, which states that, as much as is possible and reasonable, applications should be divided into areas of related functionality. We do this constantly in many aspects of our lives.

One of the great things about Fusebox is the flexibility it gives you as the developer. This not only lets you decide on things such as naming conventions, but also it enables Fusebox developers to experiment with new ideas without fear of running afoul of any Fusebox police. This, in turn, lets Fusebox evolve, whether to stay abreast of technology developments or simply to incorporate good ideas that weren't originally envisioned. Different developers have different goals and bring with them different techniques. Such creative diversity can only be good for the methodology.

One idea that has proven very successful in the object-oriented world is that of inheritance, a mechanism for reusing code (and surely the Holy Grail of many programmers). Having written a perfectly good circuit application, such as a user module, for one application, we surely want to use it in others and to do so without having to make wholesale changes to the code.

The original Fusebox specification doesn't make this particularly easy, so you had to muck about, changing `app_Locals.cfm` and `app_Globals.cfm`. The idea of inheritance made this process both easier and safer. Many developers welcomed the idea of nesting in Fusebox 3, which was a departure from the Fusebox 2 concept of treating each fuse or circuit as independent. Although Fusebox 3 supports a concept of inheritance that enables child circuits to be inherited from their parent circuit, circuits should have the same properties or functionalities associated with inheritance in object-oriented languages.

Summarizing Fusebox

Although we could spend all day delving deeper into the Fusebox methodology, let's wrap this discussion up by recapping what we've just discussed.

Fusebox is an application-development methodology that enables developers to create highly reusable and scalable applications by providing a framework for the application. This framework employs the use of a template that is central to the application that serves as a fusebox. It routes requests, calls includes, and sets variables.

Fusebox enables applications to be clustered or nested off the main fusebox to ensure that your application can be easily extended and enhanced. Fusebox enables developers to write code that is reusable and easy to maintain.

To learn more about Fusebox 3, visit `www.fusebox.org/`. This site contains the latest Fusebox specification and a number of excellent articles, presentations, and tutorials on Fusebox.

cfObjects

cfObjects is another popular development methodology available to ColdFusion developers. cfObjects purports to be a simple and efficient framework for building applications that can take advantage of object-oriented programming principles, including inheritance, polymorphism, and encapsulation.

Object-oriented programming enables us to better model the problem domains within our systems and designs. With an OOP methodology and framework, we can tackle very complex applications using an approach that is natural because it is similar to the way a human solves daily problems.

By combining the power and flexibility of ColdFusion with an object-oriented methodology, ColdFusion developers gain the capability to develop, share, and extend reusable class hierarchies that solve the common problems that occur in web-application design.

By making use of ColdFusion features such as exception handling, verity collections, and the request scope, you can implement OOP constructs and class libraries.

cfObjects is a collection of highly specialized custom tags, Visual Tag Markup Language (VTML) files, and Studio Wizards. At the core of the framework are different custom tags:

- CREATEOBJECT
- INVOKEMETHOD
- DECLAREMETHOD
- COLLECTGARBAGE
- CACHECLASS
- DUMPALL

These custom tags enable developers to create object-oriented class libraries or object collections. The value or the framework is in the depth of the class libraries, not the framework components. cfObjects was designed to enable any company, organization, or individual to create specialized class libraries that plug into the framework. That is, cfObjects is not a class library—it is a framework for implementing and using class libraries.

Classes

Classes are implemented as a collection of ColdFusion templates residing under a class subdirectory (one per class). The class subdirectory must exist under a directory named by a ColdFusion mapping. Within each class subdirectory, there must exist a special file named `class.cfm`. This file defines the class and superclass name. `Class.cfm` is loaded by CREATEOBJECT.

Methods

Methods are implemented as specialized custom tags that exist within the class subdirectory. Each method should contain a call to `DeclareMethod` as the first line within the CFML file.

When a method is invoked, the cfObjects framework makes all passed attributes available to the method, including the special attribute named "self," which is a reference to the object instance. This is useful for accessing the instance variables of the object.

You can download the framework for cfObjects along with all the custom tags. Remember, however, that cfObjects is not a product. It provides a framework and a development methodology for ColdFusion developers to follow. You can learn more about cfObjects at www.cfobjects.com.

SmartObjects

SmartObjects is a freely available, open-source framework that enables developers to convert a directory of CFML templates into a customizable, reusable, object-oriented component, or class. This is done by placing a class definition file, called `public.cfm`, in the directory. This template uses the `CF_CLASS` custom tag to define the directory as a class, and it makes it available to be used by other applications.

After it is defined, SmartObjects classes are not accessed directly through a web browser, but are called by—and embedded in—other templates. This is called creating an instance of, or instantiating, the class using the `CF_OBJECT` custom tag. Each instance of the class is called an object, and it is represented by a structure variable type.

Every CFML file in the class directory is called a method, and it represents any executable function such as add, edit, delete, or find. The calling application uses the `CF_CALL` custom tag to execute any of the methods that the object supports.

Classes can inherit methods from other classes, which means that they do not have to define all their own functions by themselves. Base classes provide functions that subclasses can override or extend. Using inheritance, you can simplify your applications by maximizing the amount of reusable code that you can access. You can add new methods to a class, or you can replace existing methods with new functionality. You can learn more about SmartObjects at www.smart-objects.com.

Other Established Methodologies

There's no one methodology that we can recommend that you use. We do think, however, that understanding several development methodologies helps you to better understand the application-development process. I'm sure no one has thought of every possible complication that can arise in application development. Let's take a look at a few more development methodologies.

Switch_box

Switch_box is a methodology that has definitely been influenced by other popular development methodologies. The use of the word "box" in "Switch_box" is really more coincidental to "box" in "BlackBox" or "Fusebox" than a variation on these techniques. In fact, some of the conventions of the Fusebox methodology are used in Switch_box.

The idea of classification and organization of information is as old as the human mind. It is how we understand ideas and hold on to them. It is intrinsic to our human nature. Thus, the idea for boxes and nesting of boxes is a really great way for our minds to understand the problem paradigm.

Switch_box introduced the notion of a message vector as means for directing program execution from a uniform resource locator (URL). It builds on the traditional dotted-object syntax with two important distinctions. First, it is designed to be a Hypertext Transfer Protocol (HTTP) attribute. Second, it is intended to show the clear separation of a method name from the object name.

The word "vector" means direction, and directions are calculated from coordinates. In the case of Switch_box, the axes for coordinates are the object list and the method list.

In traditional object-oriented syntax, sometimes discerning the method from the object can be a guessing game and requires beforehand-knowledge of objects and their methods. In Switch_box, the objective was to make the separation clear and unambiguous. This is the reason for putting the colon between the object tree and method tree. In Switch_box, the rule for a message vector is that any message without a colon is a method for the current box; otherwise, all message vectors must be properly formed with the object tree and method tree. In addition, in the method axis, Switch_box enables the use of a compound method tree. This feature is necessary for handling predicate noun actions and makes the process of writing program code more efficient.

Along with a message vector, the notion of a "switch operator" has also been introduced. The switch operator is merely a means to calculate the message vector path. The standard object-oriented example Books.Catalog.Adults.Inventory.Display would be in the message vector format of Books.Catalog.Adults.Inventory:Display would read as "Books switch Catalog switch Adults switch Inventory switch Display." The `CF_SWITCHBOX` custom tag handles the message-vector switch operators. To find out more about this methodology, check out Switch_box online at `www.switch-box.org`.

BlackBox

The BlackBox style of developing ColdFusion applications is based on the premise that developers like to have control over their pages. Its strengths enable developers to access the brains of an application without worrying about the predefined presentation tier.

BlackBox enables the same functionality to be used in several sections of the application, but in very different ways. It is designed so that employing this functionality creates the illusion of functions. It enables developers to easily nest applications and to create attractive URLs. BlackBox also enables developers to easily integrate multiple applications within the same web site.

BlackBox is a very simple methodology. It employs a few custom tags and functions to access individual templates and to access integrated applications. You can find out more about the BlackBox methodology by visiting `www.black-box.org`.

Developing a Personal Methodology

In the last several pages, we've looked at several development methodologies. Some of them are popular, well-publicized, and quite successful; others continue to struggle to gain acceptance in the ColdFusion development community.

I'm not going to stand up and tell you to use one or the other. I'm not going to try to point out the strongest attributes of one or the cracks in others. What I will tell you is that having a development methodology is important and that creating an established set of development guidelines helps you to maintain a minimum level of standardization in your application code.

Here are a few things to consider when you start to develop your own ideas about development methodology:

- **Coding standards.** Every application needs to have some coding standards in place. Coding standards include everything from tag case to the proper scoping of variables. Presentation-tier code calls for the combination of HTML and CFML. The presentation of your HTML and CFML code should be standardized so that it is easy for one developer to read another developer's code or to extend the application for any given point.

- **Code commenting.** I know that this could be wrapped up in a bit of information regarding coding standards. However, I'm isolating this topic because of its importance. Too many times I've seen developers write code that makes total sense to them but to anyone else, it's like reading Klingon.

Commenting should be part of your standard template. A usage comment should be included at the top of the template to provide information on the purpose of the template, its creation date, and its author. At the bottom of the template, I like to include a revision log so that developers understand the iterations that the template and the embedded presentation or functionality have gone through and the reasons that the code was added or removed.

- **Naming conventions.** The names that you give to files, links, and processes are as important as the accuracy and organization of the code that you write. It is important to employ a naming convention in your application that is easy to understand. The naming convention should help to avoid confusion in relating the process call, the template name, or the link to their functions or purposes within the application.

- **Application framework.** Of course, ColdFusion developers can take advantage of the application framework provided by the `Application.cfm` and `OnRequestEnd.cfm` templates. Remember to use these templates properly and not to call query code or employ presentation elements within these templates. They are best used for the evaluation and creation of global variables and application-level variable.

- **Business logic calls.** Business logic calls can usually be divided into functions and actions. Think of functions as specific tasks that the application processes perform. You can use a business logic template to handle the variable values that are created in a multistep process in a particular application transaction.

- **Data interface transactions.** The handling of data interface transaction should have some type of organized approach. By data interface transactions, we are referring to the templates that invoke the calls to stored procedures or that make query calls. By defining each template by its purpose and function within the application, developers can easily find and update code. This area also gives a perfect location to employ commit and rollback strategies and query caching strategies.

- **Variable standardization.** Web-based applications handle variables by passing them from template to template along the URL string or by passing them from form template to action template. The standardization of variable scopes is one of the issues that arises in any application and that gets more and more difficult to manage as your application gets more complex.

There are several custom tags out there that can help with this issue. They simplify variable testing and evaluation by converting all variables to the same scope. You can convert them to a local scope, but I suggest the request scope to avoid any conflicts with variables of the same name that are created within the template that calls the standardization implementation.

- **Exception and error handling.** ColdFusion give us the power to use its built-in, error-handling features. We have the capability to use tags, such as CFERROR, CFTRY, CFCATCH, CFTHROW, and CFRETHROW. These are error-handling methods that we can employ within our code. We can also take advantage of ColdFusion's site-wide error handling. These types of errors are things that happen while the template is being processed by ColdFusion. They are pretty predictable and enable us to define custom error-handling templates for a more user-friendly, error-message display.

  Exceptions might occur within our application at runtime. Validation and client-side scripting should take care of most of these, if not all. On the off chance that you've left out some validation or some validation does not work properly, you should have a catch-all in place to handle situations where the user supplies invalid values to the application.

Well, hopefully this gives you a good starting point and a heads-up on the things you need to consider when planning your application-development methodology. As we mentioned earlier, it helps to study the existing and established methodologies so that you can glean their strengths from them and adapt them to your needs. You also should make sure to learn from the mistakes that other developers have made in the past. Many of the existing methodologies have been refined as a result of those mistakes and are much more thorough today.

Summary

Understanding your application requirements is crucial to the planning of the infrastructure on which your application runs and to the development of an architectural plan for your application. The definition of a development methodology for your project is also important. We've seen how a methodology can simplify the interaction between logical chunks of code and can make the reuse of code easier to implement . We've also discussed a few established methodologies and some that are on the brink. Whether you choose one of these methodologies or come up with one of your own making, remember these tips:

- A methodology should serve as a framework for the development of your application.

- Your methodology should be well-defined.
- Your methodology should be well-documented.
- Your methodology should be adhered to throughout your application.
- Your methodology should be understood and employed by all developers on your project.

Summary

With a better understanding of application planning, application architecture, and development methodologies, you're ready to get into the code. The next several chapters walk you through some basic and not-so-basic aspects of CFML. Have fun!

4

Fundamentals of ColdFusion Development

NOW THAT YOU'VE BEEN INTRODUCED to ColdFusion and you've learned a bit about application development, let's begin to talk about writing ColdFusion code. Developing ColdFusion applications is easy because it's an easy-to-learn programming language. ColdFusion Markup Language (CFML) is a tag-based language, much like Hypertext Markup Language (HTML). CFML is an easy-to-understand language because it is made up of intuitively named tags.

CFML is not only made up of tags, but also includes functions. There are currently more than 100 ColdFusion tags and more than 270 ColdFusion functions. The ColdFusion tags enable developers to interact with the datasources that feed their applications. They then manipulate that data to display variable values.

By now, you know that ColdFusion is made up of the application server and CFML. One without the other does you little good. Because ColdFusion templates are interpreted by the ColdFusion Application Server, you need to make sure that you're developing code on a machine that is running a web server and the ColdFusion Application Server.

In this chapter, and those to follow, we dig deeper into ColdFusion application development. We start with a discussion of some basic ColdFusion development concepts and basic CFML. We then begin to look at writing values to the web browser and finally move on to examples and scenarios that help you master the basics of interacting with databases.

Basic CFML

ColdFusion is not a difficult language to learn. It's rather easy in fact—that's one of its many strengths. CFML is a tag-based language much like the typical HTML that we see in the majority of websites today. As the web becomes more and more interactive and dynamic, tools like ColdFusion enable developers and application users to get the most out of their web browsing experience.

CFML can be written in any text editor, such as Notepad, and can also be constructed by some WYSIWIG (what you see is what you get) tools. It is best to develop your ColdFusion code with an application that enables you to have full control over the code that you write and that does not try to "clean it up" before viewing or saving your files.

Macromedia provides several development tools that are great for writing ColdFusion code. Those tools include Macromedia's ColdFusion Studio, HomeSite, and Dreamweaver UltraDev. As of the writing of this book, the preview release of Dreamweaver MX is out, which now includes the functionality that was in Dreamweaver UltraDev. We've been told that ColdFusion Studio no longer will be sold as a separate product, but that most of the functionality will be rolled into Dreamweaver MX. It remains to be seen what functionality is left out and if Macromedia rolls out subsequent updates to the Dreamweaver MX product.

ColdFusion files are called templates. Your ColdFusion applications can be made up of one or more ColdFusion templates. ColdFusion templates, because they are viewed through a web browser, must be constructed with valid HTML. In other words, you should begin your template with an opening HTML tag and end the template with a closing HTML tag. Of course, you can include ColdFusion tags before or after those because CFML is read by the ColdFusion Server and standard HTML is returned to the web browser. The basic format of a simple HTML document is shown in Listing 4.1.

Listing 4.1   **Standard HTML Document Structure**

```
<!doctype html public "-//W3C//DTD HTML 4.01 Transitional//EN">
<html>
<head>
        <title>Example HTML</title>
</head>
<body>
   Look Mom! I'm a real web page programmer now!
</body>
</html>
```

Before we start to hammer out some code, we need to ensure that we understand some of the most fundamental concepts of ColdFusion development. First and foremost, let's discuss the ColdFusion development process.

ColdFusion Development Process

The ColdFusion development process is the process of creating and testing ColdFusion templates. This process consists of three easy steps:

1. **Code.** In this step of the process, you construct your ColdFusion template.

2. **Save.** You must now save the template before you can test it.

3. **View.** Finally, view the template in a browser to test the accuracy of the code returned from the ColdFusion Server.

I'm sure that you are thinking that the process that I've just described is a no-brainer, but you'd be surprised at how many people forget to save their templates.

ColdFusion templates, like HTML files, should be stored in a directory that is accessible to the web server. The default directory is called the root web directory, or webroot. If you're running on a Windows platform, your default webroot would be `c:\inetpub\wwwroot`.

You can create another directory to store the sample code that we walk through in this book. Let's call it `insidecfmx`. Save the code in Listing 4.1 into the `c:\inetpub\wwwroot\insidecfmx` directory. Save the template as `c:\inetpub\wwwroot\insidecfmx\4.1.htm`. Now, if you have a web server installed, you should be able to view this template at `http://127.0.0.1/insidecfmx/4.1.htm`. Of course, we've saved this as an HTML file. Next, let's save it as a CFML template.

CFML templates should always be saved with a .cfm or .cfml extension. This is how the web server knows to pass the template along to the ColdFusion Application Server. Let's save our file as `c:\inetpub\wwwroot\insidecfmx\4.1.cfm`. View the file at `http://127.0.0.1/insidecfmx/4.1.cfm`. If you are able to view this file, your ColdFusion Server is working. You have created a ColdFusion template. However, there is nothing in it that is truly dynamic. Remember that the delivery of dynamic content is one of the strengths of ColdFusion. We take advantage of this strength later on.

Tag Syntax

I mentioned earlier in the chapter that CFML tags closely resemble HTML tags. All ColdFusion tags begin with the letters "CF". Like HTML tags, most CFML tags are written with both opening and closing tags, <CF*MYTAG*> and </CF*MYTAG*>, respectively. Check out the following example of a CFQUERY tag used to query a datasource for user records.

Listing 4.2   **An Example of ColdFusion Template Syntax**

```
<!--- Get user records from the database --->
<cfquery name="q_GetUsers" datasource="ICFMX_Data">
   SELECT *
   FROM Users
</cfquery>
<!DOCTYPE HTML PUBLIC "-//W3C//DTD HTML 4.01 Transitional//EN">
<html>
<head>
      <title>ColdFusion Template Syntax</title>
</head>
<body>
<!--- Display user records in the browser --->
<table align="center" width="400">
   <tr>
      <td>Users</td>
   </tr>
<cfoutput query="q_GetUsers">
   <tr>
      <td>#q_GetUsers.FName# #q_GetUsers.LName#</td>
   </tr>
</cfoutput>
</table>
</body>
</html>
```

In Listing 4.2, we have the opening CFQUERY tag with two of the tag's attributes, a simple SQL statement, and then our closing CFQUERY tag. Notice also that the query name starts with the characters q_. Keep this in mind when we discuss naming conventions later.

Some CFML tags do not require an end tag. It has been noted that those tags can be written in a format that follows the eXtensible Markup Language (XML) format for tags that do not require end tags. Those tags could be written as <CFMYTAG/>. However, ColdFusion code is interpreted by the ColdFusion Application Server and returned to the browser as HTML, with none of the ColdFusion code visible to the browser, so it might make sense to write tags in this manner only if it is part of your overall coding standard.

Comments

You might have noticed a bit of code in Listing 4.2 that looked like this:
`<!--- CFML COMMENT --->`. This was a ColdFusion comment. Commenting code is a fundamental part of application development. Most seasoned developers make an effort to comment their code thoroughly. They know that commenting their code makes sense for a number of reasons:

- Comments help to identify a template and its purpose and can note the date that the code was created, any revisions that have been performed, and who performed the revisions.

- Comments help to break up large chunks of code into smaller, more readable sections.

- Comments help developers to understand sections of code long after development was completed.

- Comments help to explain coding standards and development processes.

ColdFusion comments are formatted much like comments in HTML. There are a few differences between HTML and CFML comments. The most noticeable difference is that HTML comments are formatted with one less dash (-) character.

`<!-- HTML COMMENT -->`

ColdFusion comments again have a very similar structure but have one additional dash as the comment opens and one extra dash when the comment closes.

`<!--- CFML COMMENT --->`

The other difference is that ColdFusion comments are not visible in the HTML code that is generated by the ColdFusion Application Server. ColdFusion comments, like all ColdFusion tags, are interpreted by the ColdFusion Server and standard HTML is returned to the browser. HTML comments, however, do show up in the HTML code that the browser displays. For this reason, use only CFML comments to make comments in your template that refer to code structure, variables, naming conventions, or anything else that your application or web site users do not need to see.

Data Types

ColdFusion is a typeless language. To ColdFusion, data has no type; however, because many applications depend on tracking the variable type of the data, ColdFusion supports several data types.

Data can be divided into two primary types, simple and complex. A simple data type can be a number or integer. A more complex data type might be a list of numbers or values (the list is actually a string), arrays of values, queries, or structures.

Let's take a closer look at the data types that ColdFusion supports (see Table 4.1).

Table 4.1 **Data Types Supported by ColdFusion**

Data Type	Description
SIMPLE DATA	
Booleans	ColdFusion uses Booleans to store logical values, TRUE or FALSE. Boolean values also equate 1 or Yes to TRUE and 0 or No to FALSE.
Date/time	Date values from 100 AD to 9999 AD and times in 24-hour clock format or a.m./p.m. Date/time values can be formatted in numerous ways.
Integers	Whole numbers without decimal points. Numbers can be noted as regular numbers or in scientific notation.
Decimal numbers	Also known as floating-point numbers. Mathematical operations can be performed on integers and decimal numbers with an accuracy of up to 12 decimal points.
Strings	Text values that must be enclosed in single or double quotes.
COMPLEX DATA	
Arrays	Values that are stored and identified by numeric indexes. Each value is called an element. Arrays can store any ColdFusion data type, including other arrays.
Lists	A string of values that are separated by some delimiter. The values can be numbers or strings. Technically, any sentence could be considered a list that is delimited by a space.
COM objects	Component objects written in component object model (COM), Common Object Request Broker Architecture (CORBA), and Java.
Queries	ColdFusion data objects that often contain a record set. You can manually create query objects or they can be constructed by ColdFusion as the result of a database query, an execution of a stored procedure, or an execution of one of several ColdFusion tags.
Structures	ColdFusion data type that stores values as key-value pairs. Can store simple or complex data types.

CFML offers numerous built-in functions to enable developers to programmatically manipulate the data types listed in Table 4.1. ColdFusion also provides functions that determine the data type of the value.

Variables

Values within a ColdFusion application are stored in variables. Variables are the constructs that hold any of the data types that we looked at in Table 4.1. There are several methods of setting variables within ColdFusion. You can use the `CFSET` or `CFPARAM` tag, or you can create the variable within a `CFSCRIPT` block. The most common of these methods is the use of the `CFSET` tag.

Unlike creating variables in some languages, ColdFusion enables us to create the variable and assign the value of the variable at the same time. Using `CFSET`, variables are created in the following manner:

```
<cfset version_name="ColdFusion MX">
```

In Table 4.1, we pointed out that strings must be enclosed by single or double quotes. The `CFSET` tag also does not have an end tag. If we set a variable whose value is numeric, the code would look like this:

```
<cfset version_number=6>
```

or like this:

```
<cfset version_number="6">
```

ColdFusion is a typeless language and does not make a distinction between strings and integers. Be careful when you set the value of one variable to another variable. For example, if we set a variable called `firstname` to `"Neil"`, we then could set another variable to that same value by referring to the first variable:

```
<cfset firstname="Neil">
<cfset myname=firstname>
```

In the second `CFSET`, the value of the variable `myname` is the first variable that we set—firstname. Had we written this:

```
<cfset myname="firstname">
```

the double quotes would have indicated to ColdFusion that `firstname` is a literal string and not a variable that we are evaluating.

There are a few rules that you must follow regarding variables:

- Start variable names with a letter and have the name contain only letters, numbers, and underscore characters.
- Do not use reserved words as variable names.
- Do not use ColdFusion variable scopes as variable names.
- Be consistent with your naming conventions and styles.

Variables can also be created using the `CFPARAM` tag. The difference between the `CFPARAM` and the `CFSET` tags is that the `CFPARAM` tag checks whether the variable already exists prior to creating it. If it does exist, the `CFPARAM` tag creates it and sets a default value. If it does exist, the `CFPARAM` tag does nothing. The `CFPARAM` tag is formed like this:

```
<cfparam name="version_name" default="ColdFusion MX">
```

For those of you who are accustomed to scripting languages, you might feel more comfortable creating variables and setting their values within a `CFSCRIPT` block. We get into a much deeper discussion of `CFSCRIPT` later in the book in Chapter 13, "CFScript." For now, however, let's take a look at the syntax for setting variables in `CFSCRIPT`:

```
<cfscript>
   version_name="ColdFusion MX";
</cfscript>
```

Inside the `CFSCRIPT` block, the variable is declared and the value is set at the same time. In addition, the operation ends with a semicolon. If you forget the semicolon or forget to put a string in quotes, you'll get a ColdFusion error.

Variable Scopes

Variable scope refers to the circumstance in which the variable can be used. It tells us facts about the variable, including where it originated, how we can use it, and where and when we can use it. Scope also describes the prefix that is appended to the variable name. This prefix helps to differentiate variables of different scopes that might have the same name.

There are different variable scopes within ColdFusion, and it is important to understand them all. ColdFusion's variable scopes include the following:

- **Local.** The variables that we have created so far are local variables. Local variables are accessible only within the template in which they were created or in any template "included" (we'll discuss includes later) into that template after the creation of the variable. Local scoped variables are referred to with the prefix `variables`. Local variable references are written as `variables.variable_name`.

    ```
    <cfset variables.today="March 1, 2002">
    ```

- **Form.** Form variables are created when a user fills out a form in a ColdFusion template and submits the form. The form can be either an HTML form or a ColdFusion form (which is actually an HTML form). Form variables are passed from the template where the form resides to another template where those variables are acted upon. That template is usually referred to as the action page. The variables are passed as key-value pairs with the key being the name of the form field and the value being the associated value. Form variables are referred to with the prefix `form`. Form variable references are written as `form.`*`form_field_name`*. There is one form variable that is sent to your action page by default; it is called `fieldnames`. It can be referred to as `form.fieldnames` and contains a comma-delimited list of all field names that were sent from the form.

- **URL.** URL variables are key-value pairs that are passed along the requested URL. These key-value pairs are referred to as URL parameters. A Hypertext Transfer Protocol (HTTP) request that contains URL parameters might look like this:

```
http://www.insidecoldfusionmx.com/index.cfm?display_code=Tips
```

When you make this request, you are requesting that `index.cfm` be loaded into the browser. You are passing a variable called `display_code` with a value of `Tips` into that template. Your `index.cfm` template would access the URL variable as `url.display_code`.

- **Query.** Query variables exist within a ColdFusion query object. Query variables are referred to as *query_name.variable_name*. In most cases, this query object is the result of a ColdFusion database query or stored procedure that returns a recordset that includes multiple columns and rows along with their values. For example, if we had a query called `getAuthors` and we wanted to get the full names and email addresses of the authors from the database, we would refer to those variables as `getAuthors.full_name` and `getAuthors.email`. (ColdFusion is not case-sensitive, so it might help to use mixed-case lettering to make your code easier to read.)

- **CGI.** The common gateway interface (CGI) scope is made up of read-only server and browser-specific variables. The exact variables that are accessible at any given time depend on the server software and browser client being used. CGI variables are available anywhere in your application. CGI variables are referred to as `cgi.`*`variable_name`*.

Checking on CGI Variables

If you want to know which CGI variables are currently accessible to you, drop the following code into your template.

```
<cfdump var="#cgi#">
```

We discuss the CFDUMP tag later in the book.

- **File.** File variables are created by ColdFusion as a result of using the CFFILE tag to upload files. File variables are read-only and can be referred to as file.*variable_name*.

- **Cookie.** Cookie variables hold the values of all the cookies that the web server retrieved from the user's browser. Cookies persist on the client machine until they expire or are deleted. Cookie variables can be referred to as cookie.*variable_name*.

- **Application.** Application variables are persistent variables that are available to any template in an application. They are commonly used to set datasource names and directory path references within an application. After they are created, application variables are available to all clients throughout the application until the ColdFusion service is restarted. Application variables can be referenced as application.*variable_name*.

  Application variables must be enabled prior to use. You enable them within the ColdFusion Administrator as well as within your application code.

- **Session.** Session variables are another kind of persistent variable. They exist, as you might expect, for the life of a single user session. All information that is stored in the session variable is specific to that single user and is destroyed when the session ends. Session variables are commonly used to store user shopping cart information and to retain user preference information after a login. Session variables can be referred to as session.*variable_name*.

  Session variables must be enabled prior to use. You enable them within the ColdFusion Administrator as well as within your application code.

- **Server.** A server variable is another persistent variable that stores data associated with the server computer on which ColdFusion is installed and running. Server variables are stored in the system memory and are available to all clients on all applications on the server. Server variables persist until the ColdFusion Server is restarted. Server variables are referenced as server.*variable_name*.

- **Client.** As another persistent variable scope, client variables store information related to a particular user. Client variables are used to maintain the client's state within the application. Client variables can persist across multiple sessions and can be stored in the server's registry, in cookies, or in a database. Client variables are referenced as client.*variable_name*.

- **Attributes.** The attributes scope is a variable scope that is unique to custom tags. They enable you to refer to values that are passed into the custom tag from the page that calls the custom tag—the calling page. Attributes are always referenced as `attributes.variable_name`.

- **Caller.** The caller scope is another variable scope that is unique to custom tags. The caller scope is similar to the attributes scope but passes values from within the custom tag back to the calling page. Caller scope variables are set as `caller.variable_name` and are referred to on the calling page as a local scoped variable.

- **Request.** The variables in the request scope are stored in a ColdFusion structure. Request variables are accessible for a single request. The request scope is accessible in nested custom tags. All request variables must be referred to with the request prefix, as in `request.variable_name`.

Sometimes, developers do not specify a scope for every variable that they create. This practice is detrimental to ColdFusion Server performance because it must search for the proper variable scope. ColdFusion searches for it in the following sequence:

1. Local variables created using `CFSET` and `CFQUERY`
2. CGI
3. File
4. URL
5. Form
6. Cookie
7. Client

Expressions

Expressions are the most basic building blocks of ColdFusion code. Very simple expressions can be variable names or values. More complex expressions might include two or more values on which you can use operators to perform calculations and comparisons. Let's take a look at a simple expression:

```
<cfset variables.firstval=12>
```

We've created a local variable called `firstval`. The expression that is its value is the number `12`:

```
<cfset variables.sum=variables.firstval+12>
<cfset variables.sum=12+12>
```

Now we've created a local variable called sum. Its value is derived by a complex expression in which we've used the operator for addition to act on the values. Both examples result in the same value.

Operators

Operators are ColdFusion constructs that enable you to perform calculations or compare expressions. There are four basic types of operators in ColdFusion:

- **Arithmetic.** Arithmetic operators perform mathematical calculations on expressions. Arithmetic operators include +, -, *, /, MOD, and ^.

- **Boolean.** Boolean operators perform local operations on expressions. They return Boolean values of TRUE or FALSE. Boolean operators include NOT, AND, OR, XOR, EQV, and IMP.

- **Comparison.** Simply compares two expressions and returns a Boolean of TRUE or FALSE. Comparison operators are also known as decision operators. Comparison operators include IS, IS NOT, CONTAINS, DOES NOT CONTAIN, GREATER THAN, LESS THAN, GREATER THAN OR EQUAL TO, and LESS THAN OR EQUAL TO.

- **String.** The string operator is used to concatenate expressions. The only string operator in ColdFusion is the ampersand (&).

Functions

ColdFusion functions enable you to perform defined sets of operations on an expression. Functions also return a value inline. ColdFusion has more than 270 built-in functions and enables developers to write their own functions, known as user-defined functions (UDFs).

Functions serve many purposes within a ColdFusion application. Some ColdFusion functions require that you provide parameter arguments on which they can perform operations. A few functions, such as the Now() function, require no parameters.

ColdFusion functions can be divided into functional groupings:

- Array functions
- Authentication functions
- Conversion functions
- Date and time functions
- Decision functions
- Display and formatting functions

- Dynamic evaluation functions
- International functions
- List functions
- Mathematical functions
- Query functions
- String functions
- Structure functions
- System functions
- XML functions
- Other functions

By way of example, let's take a look at a couple commonly used ColdFusion functions. For instance, functions are used to determine and format dates:

```
<cfset variables.todays_date=DateFormat(Now(), "mm/dd/yyyy")>
```

Functions are also used to determine data type:

```
<cfset variables.isthisanumber=IsNumeric("Hello")>
```

Summary

CFML is a language that is easy to read and understand. We're about ready to start writing code. It's important however to understand the concepts that we've covered thus far:

- Development process
- Code syntax
- Data types
- Variable scope
- Expressions
- Operators
- Functions

Bringing Data to the Browser

One of the greatest things about ColdFusion is that it can dynamically create screen content for your pages from variables. These variables can be the simple data types that we created in the last section or can be complex data types that we'll cover soon. The next thing that we need to cover is how to write these variables' values to the browser.

Outputting Values

ColdFusion uses a tag called CFOUTPUT to enable ColdFusion variables to be written to the browser. The CFOUTPUT tag requires both an open tag and a close tag:

```
<cfoutput>
    Your code goes here.
</cfoutput>
```

There really is nothing dynamic about the preceding code. Let's add a little more code, and we'll really start to see ColdFusion at work.

Listing 4.3   **Writing Data to a Page with a Simple *CFOUTPUT***

```
<!DOCTYPE HTML PUBLIC "-//W3C//DTD HTML 4.01 Transitional//EN">
<html>
<head>
        <title>More Examples</title>
</head>
<body>
   <cfset variables.myname="Neil">
   <cfset variables.booksite="http://www.insidecoldfusionmx.com">
   <cfset variables.email="neil@insidecoldfusionmx.com">
<cfoutput>
Hello, my name is #variables.myname#.
<br>
<br>
If you want to check out more examples visit #variables.booksite#, or email me at
#variables.email#
</cfoutput>
</body>
</html>
```

You'll notice in Listing 4.3 that when we output the value of a variable, we must surround our variable name with pound signs (#). This is required because ColdFusion uses the pound signs to identify which parts of the page are variables and which are literal strings. ColdFusion attempts to evaluate any expression surrounded by pound signs.

HTML uses pound signs in conjunction with hexadecimal colors. Any time that they occur within a CFOUTPUT tag as HTML, the pound signs must be escaped or ColdFusion attempts to evaluate the expression, resulting in an error. To escape the pound sign, just add an additional pound sign in front of it. Check out Listing 4.4.

Listing 4.4   **Escaping the Pound Sign**

```
<!DOCTYPE HTML PUBLIC "-//W3C//DTD HTML 4.01 Transitional//EN">

<html>
<head>
        <title>ColdFusion Template Syntax</title>
</head>
<body>
   <cfset variables.myname="Neil">
   <cfset variables.booksite="http://www.insidecoldfusionmx.com">
   <cfset variables.email="neil@insidecoldfusionmx.com">
<cfoutput>
   <table bgcolor="##EDD18F">
      <tr>
        <td>
        Hello, my name is #variables.myname#.
        <br><br>
        If you want to check out more examples visit #variables.booksite#, or email
        ➥me at #variables.email#
        </td>
      </tr>
   </table>
</cfoutput>
</body>
</html>
```

Notice that the bgcolor attribute of the table has an extra pound sign before the hexadecimal color. This is where we've escaped the original pound sign.

Looping

There are times when we need to output variables that contain more than a single value. Looping is a technique that we use in ColdFusion to output query results, lists, and other groups of values as you might have with arrays, structures, and query objects. Looping is a very powerful programming tool because it enables us you to loop through an entire set of instructions, repeating the output and any code that is contained within the loop. A simple loop might look something like this:

```
<cfloop looptype="expression">
   HTML and CFML code here ...
</cfloop>
```

Note

Let us point out here that there is no attribute within the CFLOOP tag called "LOOPTYPE"; this reference is merely to convey that the structure of the CFLOOP tag itself is the same regardless of the type of loop that you use. The differences are in the syntax of the required and optional attributes for each type of loop.

Loops can be nested, which is useful for grouping data. Nested loops must be properly formed with a closing CFLOOP tag for each nested loop. The code within the nested loop processes in its entirety with each iteration of the outer loop. Nested loops look something like this:

```
<cfloop looptype="expression">
    HTML and CFML code here ...
  <cfloop looptype="expression">
      HTML and CFML code here ...
  </cfloop>
    More HTML and CFML code here ...
</cfloop>
```

There are two ways to loop through values in ColdFusion. You can use the CFLOOP tag or you can add the query attribute to the CFOUTPUT tag. Probably the most commonly used of these two methods would be the CFOUTPUT tag, but let's look at the CFLOOP tag first because it is just as important to know how to implement a good CFLOOP.

Looping with *CFLOOP*

The CFLOOP tag is commonly used for looping through the output of lists, queries, or collections. To output values to the browser using CFLOOP, you must also use the CFOUTPUT tag within the loop. There are five types of loops:

- Index
- Conditional
- Query
- List
- Collection

Index Loop

An Index loop runs a number of iterations based on a value range set by its from and to attributes. Index loops are similar to for loops in other programming languages. An Index loop is a loop that executes the same set of code for as many times as the range between the values specified in the FROM and to attributes of the CFLOOP tag.

There are three required attributes in an Index loop:

- **index.** Sets the variable name that is used to identify the current loop number.

- **from.** Identifies the beginning of the index.

- **to.** Identifies the end of the index loop.

Consider the following example of an Index loop.

Listing 4.5   **Index Loop**

```
<cfoutput>
    <cfloop index="i" from="1" to="5">
        Current loop index value = #i#
    </cfloop>
</cfoutput>
```

When we run Listing 4.5, we get a simple output of the index values, as shown in Figure 4.1.

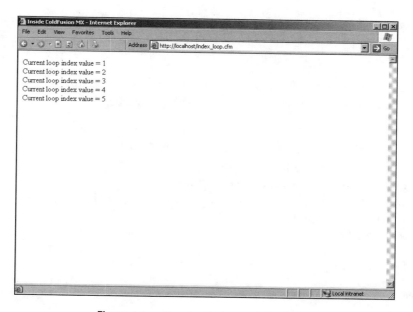

Figure 4.1   Result of using an index loop.

Conditional Loop

A Conditional loop is a loop that continues to run and execute all code within the loop until the specified condition is evaluated as FALSE. For that reason, each loop should change the value that the condition evaluates. When the condition is no longer TRUE, the loop ends and the remainder of the template is executed. The conditional loop is also known as the While loop. See Listing 4.6.

Listing 4.6   **Conditional Loop**

```
<!DOCTYPE HTML PUBLIC "-//W3C//DTD HTML 4.01 Transitional//EN">
<html>
<head>
        <title>ColdFusion Conditional Loop</title>
</head>
<body>
<cfset variables.loopcount=1>
<cfloop condition="variables.loopcount LESS THAN OR EQUAL TO 5">
        Current condition loopcount value = <cfoutput>#variables.loopcount#</cfoutput>
   <br><br>
   <cfset variables.loopcount= variables.loopcount+1>
</cfloop>
</body>
</html>
```

Listing 4.6 is a bit different from our last example in Listing 4.5, but it renders very similar results on the screen (see Figure 4.2).

Query Loop

The Query loop can be used if you have a ColdFusion query object through which to loop. A Query loop iterates for every record returned in the query result set. In this case, the CFLOOP output is the same as the CFOUTPUT with the query attribute. The Query loop enables you to loop over tags, just as with CFOUTPUT, that might not be nested within a CFOUTPUT except where you use the QUERY and group attributes within the outer CFOUTPUT tag.

Listing 4.7   **Query Loop**

```
<!DOCTYPE HTML PUBLIC "-//W3C//DTD HTML 4.01 Transitional//EN">
<html>
<head>
        <title>ColdFusion Template Syntax</title>
</head>
<body>
<!--- Get User Records --->
```

```
<cfquery name="getUsers" datasource="ICFMX">
   SELECT *
   FROM Users
</cfquery>
<!--- Get User Records --->
<cfoutput>
   <cfloop query="getUsers">
      #getUsers.UserFirstName# #getUsers.UserLastName#   - #getUsers.UserEmail#<br>
   </cfloop>
</cfoutput>
</body>
</html>
```

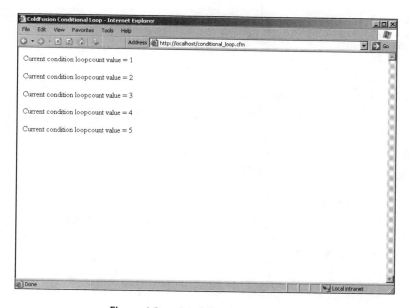

Figure 4.2   Conditional loop output.

The Query loop continues to execute for each record returned by the query and to execute all code within the loop as well. Notice that in Listing 4.7 I've properly scoped my output variables back to the getUsers query.

List Loop

We said earlier that a list is merely a string of values that are separated by some delimiter. Each value in the list is called an element. A List loop iterates through each element in a list until it evaluates each value. The List loop must have a list defined in the list attribute, by either naming a ColdFusion variable or providing a literal string. You must also specify the index attribute, which is a variable that signifies the position of each item in the list. The value of the index is the value of the current element of the list. See Listing 4.8.

Listing 4.8   **List Loop**

```
<!DOCTYPE HTML PUBLIC "-//W3C//DTD HTML 4.01 Transitional//EN">
<html>
<head>
    <title>ColdFusion Template Syntax</title>
</head>
<body>
<!--- Define my table list --->
   <cfset variables.tables="categories,customers,products">
<!--- Output my table list --->
My list contains:
   <cfloop list="#variables.tables#" index="index_var">
           <br><br>
      <cfoutput>#index_var#</cfoutput>
   </cfloop>
</body>
</html>
```

Collection Loop

A Collection loop enables you to iterate through values that are held in a ColdFusion structure or in a COM or Distributed Component Object Model (DCOM) collection object. In Listing 4.9, we loop through a simple structure to output the value of the current key.

Listing 4.9   **Looping Through a ColdFusion Structure**

```
<!DOCTYPE HTML PUBLIC "-//W3C//DTD HTML 4.01 Transitional//EN">
<html>
<head>
    <title>ColdFusion Template Syntax</title>
</head>
<body>
<!--- Create a structure and loop through its contents --->
<cfset Authors = StructNew()>
<cfset tmp = StructInsert(Authors, "FirstName", "Neil")>
<cfset tmp = StructInsert(Authors, "LastName", "Ross")>
<cfset tmp = StructInsert(Authors, "Email", "neil@codesweeper.com")>
<!--- Output the Author Data --->
<cfoutput>
<cfloop collection="#Authors#" item="AuthoInfo">
#AuthoInfo#<br>
            #StructFind(Authors, AuthoInfo)#
```

```
            <br>
            <br>
</cfloop>
</cfoutput>
</body>
</html>
```

Ending a Loop

At any point within your loop, it is easy to break the loop and continue with the processing of the remainder of the page. Place a CFBREAK tag within the loop and as soon as it is reached, the loop ends and the template code continues to process with the first line immediately following the closing CFLOOP tag.

Listing 4.10 **Index Loop**

```
<!DOCTYPE HTML PUBLIC "-//W3C//DTD HTML 4.01 Transitional//EN">
<html>
<head>
     <title>ColdFusion Template Syntax</title>
</head>
<body>
<cfset variables.lastloop=5>
<cfloop index="i" from=1 to=#variables.lastloop#>
<cfif variables.lastloop IS 3><cfbreak></cfif>
    Current loop index value = <cfoutput>#i#</cfoutput>
   <br><br>
   <cfset variables.lastloop=variables.lastloop-1>
</cfloop>
</body>
</html>
```

The code continues to process and write the values to the browser until it outputs the following:

```
Current loop index value = 1
Current loop index value = 2
```

Looping with *CFOUTPUT*

Looping with CFOUTPUT is probably the most commonly used looping method. It is used in conjunction with the ColdFusion query object. We've seen how to use the CFOUTPUT tag to output simple variables.

To enable looping with the CFOUTPUT tag, we must add the query attribute and specify an available query. See Listing 4.11.

Listing 4.11   **Outputting Multiple Records with** *CFOUTPUT*

```
<!DOCTYPE HTML PUBLIC "-//W3C//DTD HTML 4.01 Transitional//EN">
<html>
<head>
      <title>ColdFusion Template Syntax</title>
</head>
<body>
<!--- Get User Records --->
<cfquery name="getUsers" datasource="ICFMX_data">
    SELECT *
    FROM User
</cfquery>
<!--- Output Selected User Records --->
<cfoutput query="getUsers">
      #getUsers.UserFirstName# #getUsers.UserLastName# - #getUsers.UserEmail#,br>
</cfoutput>
</body>
</html>
```

By adding the query attribute to the CFOUTPUT tag, we've succeeded in doing exactly what the CFLOOP/CFOUTPUT combination would do, but with less code to write or maintain.

Conditional Processing Logic

Conditional processing logic is the decision-making process within a ColdFusion template. Conditional logic is used to evaluate and compare expressions then process code based on the results of that comparison.

ColdFusion gives us three methods of making runtime decisions within our code:

- IF statements
- SWITCH statements
- The IIf() function

IF Statements

ColdFusion uses a typical If/Else, style processing with the CFIF tag. The CFIF tag can be used to evaluate any statement that can return a Boolean value. The CFIF statement requires a closing CFIF tag. CFIF statements can include CFIF, CFELSEIF, and CFELSE tags, as well as other nested CFIF statements.

```
<cfif 1+1 IS 3>
   HTML and CFML code here ...
</cfif>
```

The CFELSEIF tag is used within a CFIF statement and offers an option if the CFIF value is determined to be FALSE. There can be any number of CFELSEIF statements within a single CFIF statement.

```
<cfif 1+1 IS 3>
   HTML and CFML code here ...
<cfelseif 1*1 IS 2>
   HTML and CFML code here ...
</cfif>
```

The CFELSE tag provides the statement a default option. After the CFIF and all CFELSEIF tags have been evaluated to FALSE, the CFELSE tag process any code between it and the closing CFIF tag.

```
<cfif 1+1 IS 3>
   HTML and CFML code here ...
<cfelseif 1*1 IS 2>
   HTML and CFML code here ...
<cfelse>
   execute this HTML and CFML code
</cfif>
```

Let's take a look at an IF statement that provides us with a better example of a CFIF statement.

Listing 4.12 **Example of *CFIF* Use**

```
<!DOCTYPE HTML PUBLIC "-//W3C//DTD HTML 4.01 Transitional//EN">
<html>
<head>
     <title>ColdFusion Template Syntax</title>
</head>
<body>
<!--- Form Action Page --->
<cfif IsDefined("form.submit_button") AND form.submit_button IS "Update User">
<!--- Update the User --->
  <cfquery datasource="ICFMX">
     UPDATE Users
     SET UserName = '#form.UserName#',
         EAddress = '#form.EAddress#'
     WHERE UserID = #form.UserID#
  </cfquery>
You've successfully updated the user information.
<cfelseif IsDefined("form.submit_button") AND form.submit_button IS "Delete User">
<!--- Delete the User --->
  <cfquery datasource="ICFMX">
     DELETE FROM Users
     WHERE UserID = #form.UserID#
  </cfquery>
You've successfully deleted the user information.
<cfelse>
```

continues ▶

Listing 4.12   **Continued**

```
You've entered this page improperly. Please press the back button on your browser.
</cfif>
</body>
</html>
```

The following rules apply to CFIF statements:

- CFIF/CFELSEIF/CFELSE statements can be nested.

- Multiple CFELSEIF statements can exist within a single CFIF statement.

- CFIF statements can evaluate more than one expression and can process multiple evaluations within one CFIF or CFELSEIF tag.

- Use a CFSWITCH/CFCASE/CFDEFAULTCASE statement if you have more than two CFELSEIF statements and you are checking for multiple values of a single variable.

SWITCH Statements

The biggest advantages of the CFSWITCH/CFCASE/CFDEFAULTCASE statements are the ease of readability and the increase in performance. The CFSWITCH/CFCASE/CFDEFAULTCASE statement should take the place of a CFIF statement with multiple CFELSEIF statements. A typical CFSWITCH/CFCASE/CFDEFAULTCASE statement looks something like Listing 4.13.

Listing 4.13   **Typical *CFSWITCH/CFCASE/CFDEFAULTCASE* Statement**

```
<!DOCTYPE HTML PUBLIC "-//W3C//DTD HTML 4.01 Transitional//EN">
<html>
<head>
    <title>ColdFusion Template Syntax</title>
</head>
<body>
<cfswitch expression="#url.product_id#">
    <cfcase value="1">
        <cfinclude template="/products/product1.cfm">
    </cfcase>
    <cfcase value="2">
        <cfinclude template="/products/product2.cfm">
    </cfcase>
    <cfcase value="3">
        <cfinclude template="/products/product3.cfm">
    </cfcase>
    <cfcase value="4">
        <cfinclude template="/products/product4.cfm">
    </cfcase>
```

```
    <cfcase value="5">
        <cfinclude template="/products/product5.cfm">
    </cfcase>
    <cfdefaultcase>
        <cfinclude template="/products/index.cfm">
    </cfdefaultcase>
</cfswitch>
</body>
</html>
```

I know—there's a much easier way to write the statement. Send an email to info@insidecoldfusionmx.com if you're not sure how to streamline it and type Listing 4.13 in the subject line.

IIf Inline Conditional Processing

The IIf() function is used as an inline IF statement. The IIf() function is primarily used to evaluate dynamic expressions and to return a Boolean value inline. You've probably seen the IIf() function used in ColdFusion training classes to create rows with alternating background colors.

The IIf() function is good for much more than setting background colors, however. It is probably a very underused ColdFusion function, primarily because developers just don't understand it.

Have you ever wanted to vary your code according to the time of day? Check out the code in Listing 4.14 using the IIf() function.

Listing 4.14 **Using the *IIf()* Function to Load Dynamic Content**

```
<!DOCTYPE HTML PUBLIC "-//W3C//DTD HTML 4.01 Transitional//EN">

<html>
<head>
    <title>IIf Dynamic Content</title>
</head>
<body topmargin="0" leftmargin="0" marginheight="0" marginwidth="0">
<table width="800" cellspacing="0" cellpadding="0">
<tr>
    <td><cfoutput><img src="/display_code/images/#IIf( Hour(Now()) GT 12,
    ➥DE("evening"), DE("morning"))#.gif"></cfoutput></td>
    <td width="10"></td>
    <td valign="top"><cfinclude template="/display_code/#IIf( Hour(Now()) GT 12,
    ➥DE("evening"), DE("morning"))#.cfm"></td>
</tr>
</table>
</body>
</html>
```

Based on whether it is before or after noon, we load an appropriate image to take up the left side of the screen and include varying content on the right. The screen would look something like Figure 4.3.

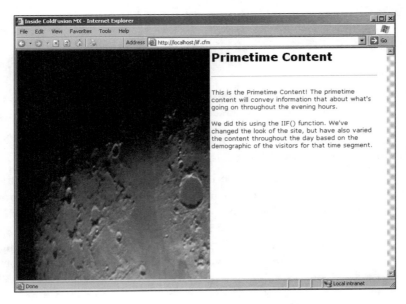

Figure 4.3   Evening content.

Summary

Displaying variable values in the browser is an easy-to-master process. A simple CFOUTPUT handles many jobs; for data types that are more complex, try looping with CFLOOP or the CFOUTPUT tag and specify the query.

Up to this point, we've learned how to set variables and write them to the screen. However, what if our variable values are sitting in a database somewhere? In the next section, we see how getting data from a database is a useful skill to have.

Interacting with Database Records

ColdFusion is known as a great tool for interacting with databases. It enables application developers to read data from and write data to local or remote databases.

In this section, we look at how to use ColdFusion to read information in the database and output that information to the browser. We'll see how ColdFusion enables us to interact with the database in the following ways:

- Selecting and displaying records
- Inserting records
- Updating records
- Deleting records

Before we begin learning how ColdFusion allows us to interact with a database, let's make sure you have an understanding of datasources.

Understanding Datasources

One of ColdFusion's strengths is its capability to work with sources of data. ColdFusion developers usually connect to a database as the source of their data. For ColdFusion to communicate with any database, you must create a connection called a datasource to point to that database. A datasource is a named connection that serves as an entry point for all database operations. You can create and configure a ColdFusion datasource in the Data Sources page of the ColdFusion Administrator.

There are a few simple rules that you should follow when establishing a datasource connection:

- Datasource names should be all one word.
- Datasource names can contain only letters, numbers, and the underscore character.
- Datasource names should not contain special characters.
- Datasource names should not be reserved words in ColdFusion.

After logging in to the ColdFusion Administrator, you should click the Data Sources link found in the left navigation bar. Upon arriving at the Data Sources page, you'll see the names of any datasources that are already connected. From this page, you can edit, verify, or delete any existing datasources connections or you can create a new one. Let's create a new datasource.

The first thing that you need to know is the type of datasource to which you're connecting. This information helps you to choose the proper database connection driver. For our purposes, let's set up a connection to a Microsoft Access database.

1. In the ColdFusion Administrator, click Data Sources under the Data & Services heading. You should see a page similar to Figure 4.4.

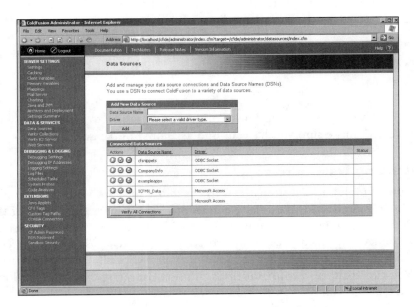

Figure 4.4 Data Sources page in ColdFusion Administrator.

2. Under Add New Data Source, enter a datasource name of **ICFMX_Data**.

3. Choose Microsoft Access as the driver.

4. Click the Add button.

5. A new form appears and you will need to fill out additional information about the datasource before the connection can be made (see Figure 4.5). The appearance of this form varies according to the driver that you chose.

6. Browse the server to find the ICFMX.mdb database file for the Database File field. If you don't have this file yet, you can download it from our web site at www.insidecoldfusionmx.com.

7. Make sure that the Use Default Username check box is checked.

8. Click the Submit button to create the datasource.

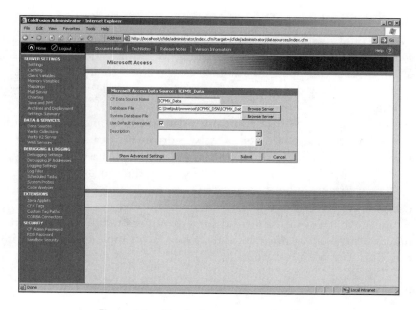

Figure 4.5   Simple datasource creation form.

ColdFusion creates the datasource and verifies that it can connect to it. We skipped over several fields because they were not required for us to set up this datasource connection. In fact, there is an entire set of advanced datasource settings that we skipped over. Again, these settings vary according to the driver type that you selected. If you need to know the details related to any datasource connection option, refer to your ColdFusion MX documentation.

You'll most commonly reference your datasource when you are making a CFQUERY tag call. Using the CFQUERY tag, you can make a call to your datasource using structured query language (SQL). The SQL that you use determines how the CFQUERY tag interacts with the datasource. Check out the following simple example of a CFQUERY call:

```
<cfquery name="getUsers" datasource="ICFMX_Data">
    SQL statements
</cfquery>
```

There are other instances where you'll reference a datasource, such as when calling stored procedures using the CFSTOREDPROC tag. We'll take a more indepth look at using SQL and at calling stored procedures in ColdFusion and interacting with databases in Chapter 23, "Working with Databases."

Selecting and Displaying Data

What would a data-driven application be without a hardy backend database? Let me say up front that we're not going to get into a lengthy discussion about SQL at this point, and neither are we going to argue the strengths and weaknesses of any database system. Let's keep it simple and take one step at a time.

The capability to select data from a database table and to display that data in the browser is the heart of a database-driven application. We've seen in a few code examples so far that we can query the database for records. In ColdFusion, we accomplish this task by using the CFQUERY tag.

The CFQUERY tag does exactly what you might think it does; it queries the database. We'll use it to select, insert, update, and delete information from the database. We'll also take a look at some ColdFusion tags that have similar functionality built in. First, let's take a look at a simple query to get information from our Members table.

Listing 4.15 **Select Query**

```
<cfquery name="getMembers" datasource="ICFMX">
   SELECT *
   FROM Members
</cfquery>
```

Pretty simple query, huh? Well, this query would be terrible to run on a table that contained thousands of records, but we'll use it for now anyway. Let's take a look at our Members table so that we know the tables with which we're working (see Figure 4.6).

When we run the query in Listing 4.16, we have a result set with all columns for each record present in the table. From the group of columns in our query, we could select any column present to output to the screen.

Listing 4.16 **Select Query with Record Output**

```
<!DOCTYPE HTML PUBLIC "-//W3C//DTD HTML 4.01 Transitional//EN">
<html>
<head>
        <title>Displaying Records</title>
</head>
<body>
<cfquery name="getMembers" datasource="ICFMX">
   SELECT *
   FROM Members
</cfquery>
<cfoutput query="getMembers">
   #getMembers.MemberFirstName# #getMembers.MemberLastName# -
```

```
#getMembers.MemberEmail#<br>
</cfoutput>
</body>
</html>
```

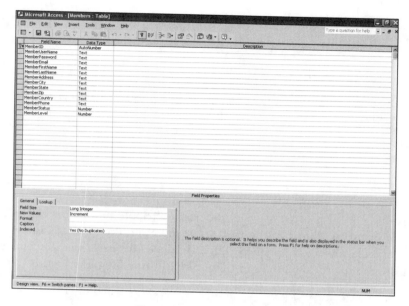

Figure 4.6 Members table.

We can also pick and choose which columns to select in our query and to ultimately output to the screen. Our modified CFQUERY might look something like this:

```
<cfquery name="getMembers" datasource="ICFMX">
   SELECT MemberFirstName, MemberLastName, MemberEmail
   FROM Members
</cfquery>
```

Because ColdFusion works so well with HTML, you might choose to display the specified column values within a table.

Listing 4.17 **Displaying Record Output in HTML Tables**

```
<!DOCTYPE HTML PUBLIC "-//W3C//DTD HTML 4.01 Transitional//EN">
<html>
<head>
        <title>Displaying Records with HTML Tables</title>
</head>
<body>
```

continues ▶

Listing 4.17 **Continued**

```
<cfquery name="getMembers" datasource="ICFMX">
   SELECT MemberFirstName, MemberLastName, MemberEmail
   FROM Members
</cfquery>
<table border="1">
      <tr>
         <td>Current Members:</td>
      </tr>
   <cfoutput query="getMembers">
      <tr>
         <td>#getMembers.MemberFirstName# #getMembers.MemberLastName# -
         ➥#getMembers.MemberEmail#<br></td>
      </tr>
   </cfoutput>
</table>
</body>
</html>
```

Remember that CFOUTPUT with the query attribute reproduces all the code
that occurs within it, just as the CFLOOP did. With the code in Listing 4.17, a
new table row and contained cells is produced for each record that is returned
from the query. The resulting output looks something like Figure 4.7.

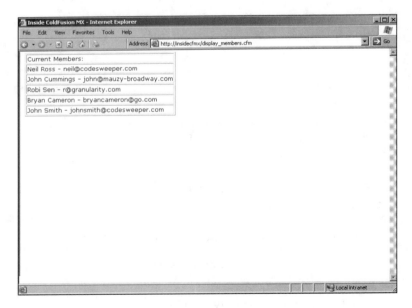

Figure 4.7 Members table output.

Notice that several rows now exist in our table.

Inserting Records—*CFINSERT*

Let's put aside the CFQUERY tag for a moment and take a look at some of the built-in tags to which ColdFusion gives us access. Interaction with the database is a two-way street, so ColdFusion helps us to insert new records into the database with the CFINSERT tag. The CFINSERT tag looks like this:

```
<cfinsert datasource="icfmx_data" tablename="Members">
```

CFINSERT is a very simple tag with a very simple purpose: to insert a single record into a single table in your database. It is a great tag for beginners who do not yet understand SQL syntax. Along with simplicity, however, comes functional and performance limitations.

The CFINSERT tag is much slower than a standard SQL INSERT statement. You can insert values into one table at a time and your form variable names must match the names of the columns in the table. If you do not want all form variables to be inserted, you must use specify which ones to insert in the FORMFIELDS attribute.

The CFINSERT tag requires that you specify two attributes: a datasource, which is the name of the datasource that contains the table into which the record is inserted; and a tablename, which is the name of the database table into which to insert the record.

The CFINSERT tag must be used in conjunction with form variables. These most often come from an HTML or CFML form. The CFINSERT tag tries to insert the values from every field in the form into the table. If a field is found in the form that does not match a field in the table, an error occurs. In Listing 4.18, we're creating the form values just above the CFINSERT tag so that you can see all the code.

Listing 4.18 **Using *CFINSERT***

```
<!DOCTYPE HTML PUBLIC "-//W3C//DTD HTML 4.01 Transitional//EN">
<html>
<head>
    <title>CFINSERT</title>
</head>
<body>
  <cfset form=StructNew()>
  <cfset form.MemberEmail="roger@codesweeper.com">
  <cfset form.MemberFirstName="Roger">
  <cfset form.MemberLastName="Ross">
  <cfinsert datasource="icfmx" tablename="Members">
    <cfquery name="getMembers" datasource="ICFMX">
```

continues ▶

Listing 4.18 **Continued**

```
        SELECT *
        FROM Members
    </cfquery>
  <table border="1">
    <tr>
        <td>Current Members:</td>
    <cfoutput query="getMembers">
    </tr>
    <tr>
        <td>#getMembers.MemberFirstName# #getMembers.MemberLastName# -
        ↪#getMembers.MemberEmail#<br></td>
    </tr>
    </cfoutput>
  </table>
</body>
</html>
```

Later in the book, we take a close look at the SQL statements needed to insert records using the CFQUERY tag. It's not difficult to do at all.

Updating Records—*CFUPDATE*

ColdFusion also provides developers with the CFUPDATE tag to help speed the process of updating values in a table. The CFUPDATE tag works much like the CFINSERT tag does and it also has the same limitations. The CFUPDATE tag requires that you specify a datasource and table name. The CFUPDATE tag updates the row that corresponds to the table's primary key value. The CFUPDATE tag looks like this:

```
<cfupdate datasource="icfmx_data" tablename="Members">
```

Deleting Records

There is not a magical ColdFusion tag for deleting records from a table. For this operation, we must use a simple SQL statement. Remember that we'll look later at more complex SQL statements.

At its most basic, the delete operation requires only that you specify the table name from which to delete records:

```
<cfquery datasource="icfmx">
    DELETE FROM Members
</cfquery>
```

This is actually very scary code. If executed, this operation would delete all records in the Members table. It is irreversible and I'm sure that some poor developer somewhere has lost a job over just such an operation.

When deleting records from a table, you should specify which records to delete. The most reliable way to do this is to specify the primary key value of the record that you want to delete. You specify this value in a WHERE clause that is positioned within the CFQUERY tag call:

```
<cfquery datasource="icfmx">
   DELETE FROM Members
   WHERE MemberID = 6
</cfquery>
```

If you need to delete multiple records, you can delete them one at a time or you can create a statement similar to the following:

```
<cfquery datasource="icfmx_data">
   DELETE FROM Members
   WHERE MemberID = 6
     OR MemberID = 5
</cfquery>
```

Summary

We've covered most of the fundamental elements of ColdFusion development in this chapter. I've found over the past several years of developing ColdFusion applications and in teaching ColdFusion courses that one of the most common mistakes that developers make is in their tag syntax. The basics that we've covered in this chapter are the key to becoming a great ColdFusion developer.

As we move into the next chapter, think about the sample code that we did for the IIf() function. It included a tag that we have yet to discuss: the CFINCLUDE tag. Chapter 5, "Reusing Code," shows us how to make the most of your code by programming for code reuse.

5

Reusing Code

THE MORE EXPERIENCED YOU BECOME WITH developing ColdFusion–based web applications, the more you realize the need for convenient, quick ways to put together your code so that it can be reused easily and frequently. Fortunately, ColdFusion gives you different choices in how you can bring prewritten ColdFusion Markup Language (CFML) code into new or existing applications.

In this chapter, we discuss the different ways in which ColdFusion enables you to create sections of code that are portable and easily reused. We also look at some examples of putting these segments of code into existing CFML applications.

CFINCLUDE

The CFINCLUDE tag will likely be your first encounter with code reuse when developing ColdFusion applications. The CFINClUDE tag enables you to embed existing ColdFusion templates into your current template by referencing the template names. Consider the following example:

```
<!---This is the code for the template PageOne.cfm--->
<HTML>
    <HEAD>
        <TITLE>Page One</TITLE>
    </HEAD>
<BODY>
<H1>This is Page One!</H1>
</BODY>
</HTML>
```

```
<!---End of PageOne.cfm--->

<!---This is the code for the template PageTwo.cfm--->
<HTML>
        <HEAD>
                <TITLE>PAGE TWO</TITLE>
        </HEAD>
<BODY>
<H1>This is Page Two!</H1>
</BODY>
</HTML>
<!---End of PageTwo.cfm--->
```

As you can see from the preceding code sample, we have two independent CFM templates. When you run the first of these pages in a web browser, you'll get output similar to that shown in Figure 5.1.

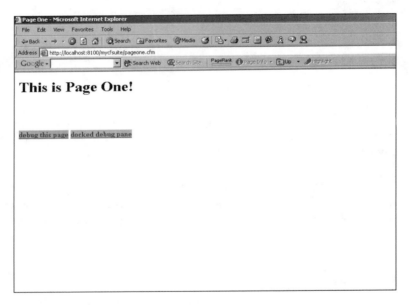

Figure 5.1   Output of `PageOne.cfm`.

Similarly, running the second of these two templates results in output similar to Figure 5.2.

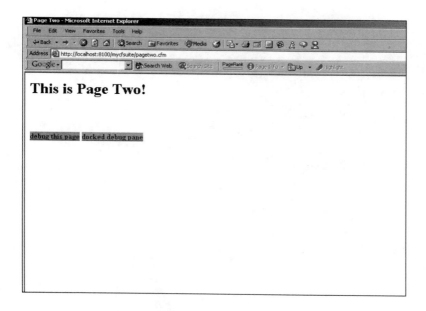

Figure 5.2 Output of PageTwo.cfm.

Suppose now that the code in PageTwo.cfm had to be included within the PageOne.cfm template exactly as it is currently written. To do this, you could simply write the code like this:

```
<!---This is the code for the template PageOne.cfm--->
<HTML>
     <HEAD>
          <TITLE>PAGE ONE</TITLE>
     </HEAD>
<BODY>
<H1>This is Page One!</H1>
<CFINCLUDE TEMPLATE="PageTwo.cfm">
</BODY>
</HTML>
<!---End of PageOne.cfm--->
```

After modifying the code for PageOne.cfm in this way, you're presented with the output shown in Figure 5.3.

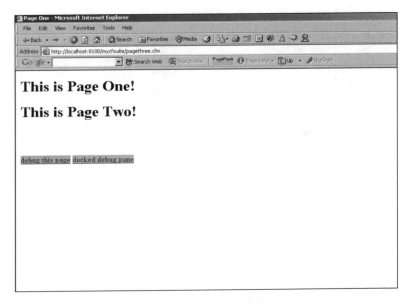

Figure 5.3   Output of modified `PageOne.cfm`.

As you can see, CFINCLUDE enables you to embed the entire content of an existing CFML template at any point in another CFML template.

You can imagine the uses for this type of functionality. Assume that you have created a header table that needs to go at the top of the page on every page within your web application. By simply creating an include to hold this table, each page that needs to display this table can "include" it. This enables you to keep the central code in one place. Thus, if the header table ever needs modification, a modification to the source file also updates all the templates that are "including" this information.

Each CFINCLUDE example to this point has "included" templates that reside in the same directory as the template into which they are included. We'll refer to these as the calling template and the included template. Because the included templates have been in the same directory, we've been able to reference them just by naming them. We have not had to worry at all about traversing the directory structure of our application or web site.

Note, however, that you might not always want to lump all the templates into one directory. Toward that end, developers often use ColdFusion mappings to create an alias for a directory where all their included templates can be stored and easily accessed from anywhere in the application. Let's look at an example of using ColdFusion mappings with the `CFINCLUDE` tag:

```
<!--- This is the code for the template PageOne.cfm --->
<HTML>
     <HEAD>
          <TITLE>PAGE ONE</TITLE>
     </HEAD>
<BODY>
<H1>This is Page One!</H1>
<CFINCLUDE TEMPLATE="/AllIncludes/PageTwo.cfm">
</BODY>
</HTML>
<!--- End of PageOne.cfm --->
```

The difference might not be readily apparent. By beginning your included template reference with a forward slash (/), ColdFusion knows to look for a ColdFusion mapping that corresponds to the alias that you provide following the forward slash. Using ColdFusion mappings, you can store included templates outside the webroot directory structure.

> **Note**
>
> In this book, you'll see many examples in which included templates are referred to by using a ColdFusion mapping. Keep your eyes open.

ColdFusion mappings are created in the ColdFusion Administrator and apply only to pages that are processed by ColdFusion Server with `CFINCLUDE` or `CFMODULE` tags. To create a ColdFusion mapping, follow these simple steps:

1. In the ColdFusion Administrator, click Mappings under the Server Settings heading (see Figure 5.4).
2. Under Add/Edit ColdFusion Mappings, enter the name of the mapping. Make sure that the name is preceded by the forward slash (/).
3. Browse to or type the full path to the directory where the includes will be stored.
4. Click the Add button.

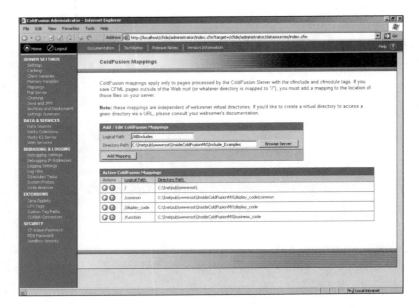

Figure 5.4 ColdFusion Mappings page in ColdFusion Administrator.

Your new mapping appears in the Active ColdFusion Mappings area at the bottom of the screen. You can now reference any template located within that mapped directory in your `CFINCLUDE` calls.

Custom Tags

One of the coolest ways in which you can create code for reuse with ColdFusion is through the use of CFML custom tags. These custom tags enable you to create snippets of code that perform a very specific function and then use that code again and again throughout your application—all without having to rewrite the source code.

At first glance, creating your own custom tags to help modularize your code might seem like a daunting task. However, after you begin to understand how ColdFusion processes these tags, you'll be amazed at how simple the entire process can be.

To demonstrate the concept, let's create a hypothetical situation. Your boss has told you that on all pages throughout your corporate intranet, she wants to see an "Updated by so and so, on such and such a date" line of text so that she can tell when pages were last modified and who made the modification.

Obviously, each member of your intranet team responsible for creating and updating content could go into the source files each time they were modified and create or edit the following line of Hypertext Markup Language (HTML) code:

```
<H3><I>Last modified by Joe User on April 26, 2002</I></H3>
```

Although this might work for a while, it might not be the best way to do things. For instance, a programmer could inadvertently damage this line of code as he or she was modifying it.

Note also that an include wouldn't be the best way to handle this problem because the name of the user modifying the page might differ from page to page, and using an include would affect the intranet globally.

Fortunately, we can create a simple CFML-based custom tag to solve our problem. Take a look at the following code example, which creates the simple customer tag CF_ModifiedBy. We'll then look at how to use this tag:

```
<!---Name: ModifiedBy.cfm
Description: Enables us to change the "modified by"
footer at the bottom of all of our intranet pages.
Author: Joe Programmer
Date: 4-26-2002
Attributes:
ModifiedBy: (Required) Specifies the name of the
person who is modifying the HTML code.
DateModified: (Required) Specifies the date that the
Document is being modified.--->
<cfparam name="attributes.modifiedby" default="">
<cfparam name="attributes.datemodified" default="">
<!---If a required parameter does not have a value passed
in, stop processing and throw an error.--->
<cfif NOT Len(attributes.modifiedby) OR NOT
Len(attributes.datemodified)>
<cfabort showerror="You must enter both your name and the
date as attributes!">
</cfif>
<cfoutput>
<h3><i>Last modified by #attributes.modifiedby#, on
#attributes.datemodified#</i></h3>
</cfoutput>
```

We've created our simple CFML custom tag. Now when someone wants to create a new CFML template that changes the modified-by line displayed at the bottom of the page, he or she can do it by adding this custom tag to the source of the CFML template, as in the following example:

```
<HTML>
    <HEAD>
        <TITLE>Sample Intranet Page</TITLE>
```

```
    </HEAD>
    <BODY>
    ----SOME CODE----
<CF_ModifiedBy ModifiedBy="Joe Programmer"
DateModified="April 26, 2002">
    </BODY>
    </HTML>
```

After this code is in the source CFML, you can see how easy it is to go back in and change the `ModifiedBy` or `DateModified` attributes. This is certainly much easier than rewriting the respective line of code for every CFML document in which it needs to appear.

Now that you understand why you'd want to use CFML custom tags and how they are written, it helps to know how ColdFusion processes these tags.

When you create a CFML custom tag, you name it as you would any other CFML template. As in the previous example, the `ModifiedBy` tag was simply called `ModifiedBy.cfm`. By the way that we call it from within our CFML code, ColdFusion knows that we intend for this file to be used as a custom tag. By appending `CF_` to the beginning of the template name, omitting the `.cfm` extension, and enclosing the name in `<>`, we are signaling to ColdFusion that we are about to invoke a custom tag.

Thus, to call a file named `ModifiedBy.cfm` as a CFML custom tag, we would place the following line of CFML in the calling template:

```
<CF_ModifiedBy>
```

After your custom tags are written, you can place them in the directory from which you are going to call them, or you can put them in a central custom tags directory. Placing custom tags in a central custom tags directory is the recommended method of storage. It provides a simple, easy-to-find repository for all your modular code. By default, this custom tag's directory is `CFUSIONMX/CustomTags`.

As you saw in our simple example, you can pass attributes into the custom tag from the calling page. After these variables are passed to the custom tag, you reference them by using the attribute's scope. This helps differentiate variables being passed into the custom tag from those that are local variables within the custom tag.

Appending any attribute/value pair to a custom tag call causes that attribute/value pair to be passed into the custom tag. As an example, if we were using the `CF_ModifiedBy` tag in a CFML template, we might call it in the following manner:

```
<cf_ModifiedBy ModifiedBy="Joe Programmer"
               DateModifed="April 26, 2002"
               FavoriteColor="Green">
```

In this case, all the following attribute/value pairs are passed into the custom tag:

```
ModifiedBy=Joe Programmer
DateModified=April 26, 2002
FavoriteColor=Green
```

Of course, our custom tag is written to make use of only the `ModifiedBy` and `DateModified` attributes, so the `FavoriteColor` attribute is ignored. Nonetheless, it is still important to know that it is present in the attributes scope.

If you want to make a specific attribute a "required" attribute, you can write logic within the custom tag to ensure that all required attributes get passed in. You can see in our `CF_ModifiedBy` example that we have done this by using `CFIF` statements to ensure that if the `ModifiedBy` and `DateModified` attributes are not present, we stop processing and present the user with an appropriate error.

CFX Custom Tags

ColdFusion Extensions (CFX) are ColdFusion custom tags that are written in Java or C++. Unlike CFML custom tags, CFX tags come in handy when you want to do something that isn't possible with traditional CFML code.

A perfect (and understandable) example of the use of ColdFusion Extensions is a custom tag that generates thumbnails of images. Obviously, with traditional CFML, you have no way of modifying the source image and generating a new, smaller representation of that image. With CFX tags, however, you can harness the power of other, robust languages (such as Java or C++) to give your ColdFusion applications all the power of those languages as well.

CFX tags are also the perfect way to incorporate functionality into a ColdFusion application that you've already written in C++ or Java. By encapsulating this functionality into a CFX tag, you enable ColdFusion developers to use this functionality at any point within a ColdFusion application by referencing it as a CFX tag.

User-Defined Functions (UDFs)

Macromedia added the concept of UDFs in ColdFusion 5.0. This was done after numerous requests from developers who wanted to create their own functions in a way that was similar to how developers created functions in other languages. With ColdFusion MX, Macromedia has added a new functionality to UDFs to make them easier to work with and more robust. They are also allowing developers to create UDFs in CFML instead of in only CFScript.

Before we move into how to create UDFs, let's go over a few reasons why we would want to use UDFs. As a developer, you often find yourself creating ColdFusion scripts that basically do the same thing over and over again. Often, these scripts have at their core simple functions or algorithms that you usually just cut and paste into your code, because creating an actual ColdFusion tag doesn't seem to be worth the time.

UDFs enable you to create ColdFusion functions that wrap or contain the frequently used snippets of code. You then can use them exactly as you would any other ColdFusion function. For instance, you can use them in tag attributes, between pound (#) signs in output, and in CFScript code. This can save you a huge amount of time and enable you to create more robust applications that require that you change only one file when changing the nature of a function. This is better than searching through countless templates that might have some custom snippet.

The uses of UDFs include the following:

- Data manipulation routines, such as a function to reverse an array
- String and date/time routines, such as a function to determine whether a string is a valid Internet Protocol (IP) address
- Mathematical calculation routines, such as standard trigonometric and statistical operations or calculating loan amortization
- Routines that call functions externally (for example, using COM or CORBA), including routines to determine the space available on a Windows File System drive

Using UDFs

You typically define a UDF on your ColdFusion page or on a page that you include. You can also define the function on one page and put it in a scope that is shared with the page that calls it. In addition, you can put commonly used functions on a single CFML page and include the page in your Application.cfm page.

You call a UDF as you would a normal ColdFusion function. One example of a UDF is a current function that calculates the current in a circuit as amperes, based on impedance and resistance (Ohm's law). You might use the function like this:

```
<cfoutput>
Current in Amps: #Current(form.resistance, form.impedance)#
</cfoutput>
```

You use the function statement to define the function in CFScript, or you can use the CFFUNCTION tag, which we cover in more detail in Chapter 6, "ColdFusion Components."

Using CFScript to create UDFs has some distinct advantages when compared to using CFML:

- The function definition syntax is more familiar to developers who use JavaScript.
- CFScript is more efficient for writing business logic, such as expressions and conditional operations.

On the other hand, CFScript has some disadvantages as well:

- CFScript function definitions cannot include CFML tags.
- CFScript's exception handling currently is not as robust and feature-rich as that of CFML tags.

So, with the information in the bulleted lists in mind, let's look at some simple examples of a CFScript function:

```
<cfscript>
function nameofthefunction(arg1, arg2, arg3, …)
{
        variable statements;
cfscript statements;
return statements;
}
</cfscript>
```

UDFs in CFScript must begin with the Function statement, although UDFs created with CFFUNCTION begin with the tag attribute name="methodname". You need to be careful when you name your UDF because UDF names cannot begin with the letters "CF" and can contain only numbers, letters, and underscores. In addition, when you are creating the name of your UDFs, you should try to create a name that is unique to the UDFs on your machine and in your application. You should do this because a UDF that has the same name as an existing CMFL function or UDF throws an error.

UDFs can also accept any numbers of parameters or have any number or variables. (For our purposes, parameters are just like UDF internal variables, but they are passed to the UDF.) Parameters can be required or optional and follow the same naming restrictions as UDFs themselves. In the example we are going to create next, we pass two required parameters to our UDF: RESISTANCE and IMPEDANCE.

Now let's create a simple UDF example. Listing 5.1 shows you such an example.

Listing 5.1   *current.cfm*

```
<cfscript>
function current(E, R)
{
  //Ohm's law
  //I = Current in amperes
  //E = Voltage in volts
  //R = Resistance in ohms
  if(NOT isNumeric(E) OR NOT isNumeric(R))
  {
    writeoutput("values for voltage or resistance must be numeric!!<br>");
    return false;
  }
  return E / R;
}
</cfscript>
<cfset volts = 100 >
<cfset resistance = 3>
<cfset curamps =  current(volts, resistance)>
<cfoutput>#curamps#: AMPS</cfoutput>
```

Let's break down this UDF. As we can see from the second line of this UDF, we have created a function called Current(), which accepts two parameters, E and R. Next we do some simple exception handling to make sure that the values passed are numbers.

We then use the reserved CFScript statement return. The return statement is required and determines what values should be returned on execution of the function. It's useful to note that UDFs can return any ColdFusion data type, including arrays, structures, and queries.

As you can see with the next lines of CFML, we set the values for volts and resistance and then called our UDF. When calling UDFs, you should give some thought to how you are going to call them. You can define your UDF in the same page (as we have done here) or you can include it as a file using CFINCLUDE. In general, you should use CFINCLUDE to access your UDFs unless you are using the same UDFs over and over again. Then you might want to use Application.cfm to load the UDF for every template.

Before we discuss UDFs further, let's take a look at developing the same UDF using CFFUNCTION and CFML tags. The general syntax for CFFUNCTION is as follows:

```
<cffunction
    name = "methodName"
    returnType = "dataType"
    roles = "securityRoles"
    access = "methodAccess"
    output = "yes" or "no"
    exceptions = "exception1, exception2, ..."
>
```

To generate the same functionality as the current.cfm UDF, we can do what is shown in Listing 5.2.

Listing 5.2 *current1.cfm*

```
<cffunction name="current1" output="yes">
<cfargument name="volts">
<cfargument name="resistance">
<cfreturn volts/resistance>
</cffunction>
<cfset volts = 100 >
<cfset resistance = 3>
<cfset curamps =  current1(volts, resistance)>
<cfoutput>#curamps#: AMPS</cfoutput>
```

CFFUNCTION enables you to use any CFML tag or CFScript construct inside the CFFUNCTION tags. Furthermore, it provides the developer with robust security and roles-based access to the function you create. In this example, we set the parameters using the CFARGUMENT tag. The CFARGUMENT tag acts just like the VAR statement in CFScript when you are creating UDFs with CFScript.

Then we use the CFRETURN tag to return the value of volts divided by resistance. Then we reference the function in exactly the same way.

It's very simple to create a UDF in CFScript as well as in CFML, so why would you want to do it using CFML and CFFUNCTION? Some reasons include the following:

- Most developers find building functions in CFML easier than in CFScript if they do not already know JavaScript or EMACS.
- You can use any CFML tag inside a CFFUNCTION tag and thus have greater flexibility in creating UDFs.
- You can use CFScript inside a function definition.

- You can control the access method to your CFFUNCTION. In addition, the specific security roles enable you to make more secure and controllable functions than you could with CFScript.

There is at least one disadvantage to using CFML and CFFUNCTION:

- In CFML, you are forced to scope your variables using the `this` statement.

In most cases, developers familiar with UDF from ColdFusion 5.0 find themselves more comfortable with developing UDFs in CFScript; most other developers find using CFFUNCTION and a choice of CFML or CFScript to be the most productive way of developing UDFs. You should choose what you find to be the most productive and comfortable for you.

Advanced UDF Concepts

Your advanced UDFs should work with an unknown amount of arguments or parameters as well as with ones that are required and ones that are not required. An example of this is your creating a UDF that sums any amount of numbers passed to it. With CFScript, you need to define the required arguments first when defining the function. For example:

```
function Sum(Arg1,Arg2)
```

This makes the arguments `arg1` and `arg2` required by default. Assume that you wrote only the following:

```
function Sum()
```

This code states there are no required parameters. The problem then becomes how you work with this unknown number of arguments. Well, with UDFs, all arguments are stored in a special `arguments` variable scope, and in the case of CFScript-based UDFs, these arguments can be accessed from the `arguments` scope as an array.

Let's look at a simple example that clarifies how to work with arguments in CFScript. In our example, we are going to create a UDF that enables us to multiply any quantity of numbers passed to it.

Listing 5.3   *MultiplyList.cfm*

```
<cfscript>
function MultiplyList()
{
  var arg_count = ArrayLen(Arguments);
  var sum = 1;
```

```
      var i = 1;
      for( i = 1 ; i LTE arg_count; i = i + 1 )
      {
        sum = sum * Arguments[i];
      }
      return sum;
    }
    </cfscript>
    <cfset val1 = 100>
    <cfset val2 = 3>
    <cfset val3 = 3>
    <cfset val4 = 6>
    <cfset theVal =  MultiplyList(val1,val2,val3,val4)>
    <cfoutput>#theVal#:</cfoutput>
```

Let's break down this code listing. In the first line, we see that we defined the function and required no arguments. Next, we do something very useful, which is to define the length of the list of arguments (that is, how many elements are in the list) that we are using.

```
var arg_count = ArrayLen(Arguments);
```

This simply sets the `arg_count` (using the array length function `ArrayLen`) to the size of the arguments list. We then create a for loop that sums the list of arguments in the list and then return the sum. Now we could just as easily redo the function line in the code to be the following:

```
function MultiplyList(Arg1, Arg2)
```

This code forces us to supply at least two numbers to multiply. The last few lines then set a series of values, which we then pass to the function to operate on.

You can play with the code and extract values or add values. You will see that it multiplies any number of values.

Let's now do the same thing using CFFUNCTION. With CFFUNCTION, we have to do things a little differently. With CFFUNCTION, we have to access our arguments as we would a structure.

Listing 5.4 *MultiplyListn.cfm*

```
<cffunction name="MultiplyListn">
  <cfset this.sum = 1>
  <cfloop collection="#Arguments#" item="argument">
    <cfset this.sum = this.sum * Arguments[argument]>
  </cfloop>
  <cfreturn this.sum>
</cffunction>
```

continues ▶

Listing 5.4 **Continued**

```
<cfset val1 = 3>
<cfset val2 = 3>
<cfset val3 = 3>
<cfset val4 = 6>
<cfset theVal = MultiplyListn(val1,val2,val3,val4)>
<cfoutput>#theVal#:</cfoutput>
```

The code should be obvious except that you should notice we are using the variable scope this. With CFFUNCTION, whenever you set a variable, it is then set to the page or request scope; thus, it is available to that page. It can be awkward if you are creating UDFs that might have variable names with the same name as other variables in your application because the UDF might overwrite those variables. In addition, the pages in which you are including your UDF might overwrite your UDFs variables. To make sure this does not happen, you should use the this scope to scope your variables to the UDF only!

A Note on this

The this scope is equivalent to local variables that you defined using the var statement in CFScript. However, unlike with CFScript, you must use the scope identifier this when you create or use the variable!

Let's try an even more complex example so that we can see a more sophisticated usage of UDF functionality. We are going to build a generic "data structure" called a stack. Simply put, data structures are systematic ways of organizing and accessing data.

We are going to build a data structure, called a stack, that is based on the principle of LIFO (last in, first out). Think of a stack as a data PEZ dispenser; instead of PUSH-ing PEZ into it, you are pushing data into it. When you want to POP out a PEZ, you are actually POP-ing out data.

Stacks are often used by applications such as your web browser. When you visit a site, a URL is PUSH-ed into the stack, and when you click the Back button, it is POP-ed out.

Let's look at the example shown in Listing 5.5.

Listing 5.5   *gStack.cfm*

```
<cfapplication name="gStack" clientmanagement="yes"  sessionmanagement="yes" >
<cffunction name="gStack">
  <!---
  This function expects a mandatory argument and a optional argument which is some
  ➡value.
  You have four actions you can perform with gStack:

  1.  PUSH - this argument tells the stack to take another number and put it to the
  top of the stack and then push any existing values 1 row down the stack.
  2.  TOP  - All this does is return the value at the very top of the stack
  3.  POP  - This return's the top value of the stack although deleteing it from the
  stack.
  4.  SIZE - Returns the size of the stack
   --->
  <cfargument name="actOption" default="PUSH">
  <cflock scope="session" type="exclusive" timeout="10" throwontimeout="No">
    <cfif NOT StructKeyExists(session, "stack")>
      <cfset session.stack = ArrayNew(1)>
    </cfif>
    <cfset size = ArrayLen(session.stack)>
    <cfswitch expression="#UCase(arguments.actOption)#">
    <cfcase value="PUSH">
      <cfif StructKeyExists(arguments, "1")>
        <cfif ArrayLen(session.stack)>
          <cfset temp = ArrayInsertAt(session.stack, 1, arguments.1)>
        <cfelse>
          <cfset session.stack[1] = arguments.1>
        </cfif>
        <cfreturn arguments.1>
      <cfelse>
        <cfreturn "error you must pass a value when you use PUSH!">
      </cfif>
    </cfcase>
    <cfcase value="TOP">
      <cfif Val(size)>
        <cfreturn session.stack[1]>
      <cfelse>
        <cfreturn "error empty array!">
      </cfif>
    </cfcase>
    <cfcase value="SIZE">
      <cfset gSize = ArrayLen(session.stack)>
      <cfreturn gSize>
    </cfcase>
    <cfcase value="POP">
      <cfif Val(size)>
        <cfif StructKeyExists(arguments, "1") AND IsNumeric(arguments.1)>
          <cfset popReturn = session.stack[arguments.1]>
          <cfset temp = ArrayDeleteAt(session.stack, arguments.1)>
          <cfreturn popReturn>
```

continues ▶

Listing 5.5 **Continued**

```
      <cfelse>
        <cfreturn "error you must pass a numeric value
when you use POP!">
        <cfabort>
      </cfif>
    <cfelse>
      <cfreturn "error empty array!">
    </cfif>
  </cfcase>
  </cfswitch>
  </cflock>
</cffunction>
```

Although this UDF is a little longer than the others on which we have worked, it's not that much different. In this one, we have turned on session variables so that we can have some persistence of data. We then define the function as well as require an argument that must be passed, which has to be PUSH, POP, TOP, or SIZE; we have also set it to a default of PUSH. The rest of the code is SWITCH and CASE statements, which handle the different options that can be chosen.

The next listing is a simple form that passes information to itself and calls the gStack function.

Listing 5.6 *test.gStack.cfm*

```
<cfinclude template="gStack.cfm">

<cfparam name="form.stkvalue" default="">
<cfparam name="form.opt" default="PUSH">
<cfparam name="variables.value" default="">

<cfscript>
  if(IsDefined('gStack'))
    if(IsCustomFunction(gStack))
      WriteOutput('gStack is a user-defined function');
    else
      WriteOutput('gStack is defined but is NOT a user-defined function');
  else
    WriteOutput('gStack is not defined');
</cfscript>
<br>
<cfoutput>
<form action="#cgi.script_name#" method="post">
  <input name="stkvalue" id="stkvalue" value="">
  <select name="opt" id="opt" size="1">
    <option value="PUSH">PUSH</option>
```

```
        <option value="POP">POP</option>
        <option value="TOP">TOP</option>
        <option value="SIZE">SIZE</option>
      </select>
      <input type="submit" value="Submit Query">
      <cfif UCase(cgi.request_method) EQ "POST">
        <p>The action performed was: #form.opt#</p>
        <cfswitch expression="#UCase(form.opt)#">
        <cfcase value="PUSH">
          <cfset t = gStack(form.opt, form.stkvalue)>
        </cfcase>
        <cfcase value="POP">
          <cfset variables.value = gStack(form.opt, form.stkvalue)>
          <p>The Value was: #variables.value#</p>
        </cfcase>
        <cfcase value="TOP,SIZE">
          <cfset variables.value = gStack(form.opt)>
          <p>The Value was: #variables.value#</p>
        </cfcase>
        </cfswitch>
      </cfif>
    </form>
</cfoutput>
```

Now the only interesting thing about this listing, besides the fact that we are interacting with our function using four variables, is the CFScript block that uses the function `IsCustomFunction`. This function enables us to check whether a UDF has been properly loaded or defined.

You often need to pass complex data types to and from your UDFs. Let's change our stack test a little bit so that it accepts a structure in the form of an order and stores it in the stack.

Listing 5.7   *test2.gStack.cfm*

```
<cfinclude template="gStack.cfm">
<cfparam name="form.ProductName" default="">
<cfparam name="form.Vendor" default="">
<cfparam name="form.Price" default="">
<cfparam name="form.quantity" default="">
<cfparam name="variables.value" default="">

<cfscript>
  if(IsDefined('gStack'))
    if(IsCustomFunction(gStack))
      WriteOutput('gStack is a user-defined function');
    else
      WriteOutput('gStack is defined but is NOT a user-defined function');
  else
```

continues ▶

Listing 5.7   **Continued**

```
    WriteOutput('gStack is not defined');
</cfscript>
<br>
<cfoutput>
  <cfif UCase(cgi.request_method) EQ "POST">
    <cfscript>
      newOrder = StructNew();
      newOrder.productName = form.ProductName;
      newOrder.Vendor = form.Vendor;
      newOrder.Price = form.Price;
      newOrder.quantity = form.quantity;

      variables.value = gStack('PUSH', newOrder);
    </cfscript>
    <cfdump var="#variables.value#">
  <cfelse>
    <form action="#cgi.script_name#" method="post">
    <table>
    <tr>
      <td>Product</td>
      <td>Vendor</td>
      <td>Price</td>
      <td>Amount</td>
    </tr>
    <tr>
      <td><input type="text" name="ProductName" id="ProductName" value=""></td>
      <td><input type="text" name="Vendor" id="Vendor" value=""></td>
      <td><input type="text" name="Price" id="Price" value=""></td>
      <td><input type="text" name="quantity" id="quantity" value=""></td>
    </tr>
    </table>
    <input type="submit" name="submit" id="submit" value="Add to Cart">
    </form>
  </cfif>
</cfoutput>
<cfdump var="#session#">
```

All we have done in this section is create a simple self-referencing form that lets us pass product information, which is then turned into a ColdFusion structure and stored using the gStack UDF. We then can see what gStack returns by using CFDUMP to see the returned structure that is now sitting at the top of the stack. You can easily pass back and forth between UDFs any ColdFusion data type, but you need to remember that they can return only one variable. Thus, if you need to return complex data, you might have to build a complex data structure, such as an array of structures or a recordset using the CFRETURN tag or statement.

If you are up for it, try creating a whole shopping cart application using gStack as a foundation. The cart should let you to add items, remove them, and so on.

Usage Considerations for UDFs

Before you start writing huge libraries of UDF functions, carefully consider who you want to use your UDFs and how you want to use them. As you have seen, you can deploy your UDFs by using a simple CFINCLUDE or by using/defining your UDF inline. In reality, though, when you are working on large applications, you most likely will be using a group of UDFs often. For example, a UDF that models a typical shopping cart might be used constantly in a certain portion of an application and you would not want to have to include the file every time on every page that you want to use. In this case, you should define your UDF in your application.cfm.

If you use dozens and dozens of UDFs, define them all on one or more templates and then include those templates in your application.cfm. This would most commonly be done if you wanted to define whole libraries of UDFs and categorize them by functional group. That way, you would have one template that defined all your security UDFs, one your Extensible Markup Language UDFs, and one your validation UDFs. Then you include these in your application.cfm so that they are available to the whole application all the time.

Summary

In this chapter, we've looked at ways in which you can develop code for modularization and reuse. We've talked about using CFINCLUDE, CFML custom tags, and CFX tags to create code that can be reused quickly and easily throughout your ColdFusion applications.

We have also explored UDFs using both CFSCRIPT and CFFUNCTION. As you have seen, UDFs let you create simple functions to very complex encapsulated algorithms for dealing with a variety of problems and situations. Proper use of UDFs can enable you to create libraries of useful functions that you can call upon to simplify your development cycle and to write cleaner and easier-to-understand code.

A great resource for more information on UDFs and UDF libraries is at www.CFLIB.org. This is a repository for ColdFusion UDFs set up by Raymond Camden and Rob Brooks-Bilson. You'll find all sorts of great UDFs that you might find useful in development or as further examples. You might even want to start submitting your own!

6

ColdFusion Components

COLDFUSION COMPONENTS (CFCs) ARE another feature that's new to ColdFusion MX. They are more than just a series of tags; they're a whole new way of creating reusable code as well as an approach to developing ColdFusion applications.

ColdFusion components bring to the language a new and exciting approach for code reuse as well as development practices that are more akin to object-oriented programming practices than previous code-reuse paradigms in ColdFusion. CFCs give ColdFusion developers an unprecedented level of functional abstraction and encapsulation as well as standardized interfaces for a variety of access methods, including SOAP-based web services.

CFCs, like ColdFusion's other code-reuse methods such as CFML tags, cfincludes, and user-defined functions (UDFs), enable developers to create functions that can be called from wherever you need them in your ColdFusion application. CFCs go a step further by adding concepts such as inheritance and introspection, allowing for a much more robust code-reuse model in large-scale applications. They also offer methods to integrate with not only other parts of your ColdFusion applications but different applications altogether through web services.

Building Your First CFC

In this section, we are going to take a look at our first ColdFusion component and call it from a ColdFusion template. ColdFusion components work like regular ColdFusion templates; you can create component files in your webroot directory or any directory under it. Unlike ColdFusion pages, you save component files with the .cfc extension, such as componentName.cfc. In addition, all ColdFusion variable scopes are available to components, including session, client, server, and application.

You use the CFCOMPONENT and CFFUNCTION tags to create ColdFusion components. By itself, the CFCOMPONENT tag does not provide functionality; rather, it provides an envelope that describes the functionality you build in CMFL and enclose in CFFUNCTION tags. Furthermore, ColdFusion components provide some behaviors that are totally new and unique to CFCs and ColdFusion MX, such as web service deployment, description, and communication via SOAP.

Let's now create a new file in ColdFusion Studio called examplequery.cfc. Enter the code in Listing 6.1 into your editor and save it to your working directory.

Listing 6.1   *testqrycfc.cfc*

```
<cfcomponent>
    <cffunction name="getEmp" returnType="query">
        <cfquery name="empQuery" datasource="ICF" dbtype="ODBC" >
            SELECT Employees.FirstName,
            Employees.LastName,
            Employees.Title,
            Employees.EmailName,
            Employees.WorkPhone,
            Employees.Extension
            FROM Employees

        </cfquery>
    <cfreturn #empQuery#>
    </cffunction>

    <cffunction name="getStartDate" returnType="query">
        <cfquery name="deptQuery" datasource="ICF" dbtype="ODBC" >
            SELECT Employees.FirstName, Employees.LastName,
            Employees.Title, Employees.DateStarted,
            Employees.Department
            FROM Employees
            ORDER BY DateStarted ASC
        </cfquery>
    <cfreturn #deptQuery#>
    </cffunction>
</cfcomponent>
```

At first this code might seem a little odd, but what we have done is create our first component with two methods or cffunctions. If you look, you will see that the code starts and ends with <cfcomponent></cfcomponent>, and nested inside it are our method calls wrapped inside <cffunction></cffunction> tags, respectively.

Next you will notice that inside the CFFUNCTION tags are rather straightforward queries that perform some operations against our ICF database.

> **Note**
>
> Any code outside a CFFUNCTION tag will execute (as well as outside a CFCOMPONENT tag) and unexpected behavior might occur; so in general, you should never have code outside your CFFUNCTION or your CFFUNCTION tag.

If you have a Java or object-oriented background, you can compare it to a very simple Java class, which in general takes the following form:

```
Public class exampleclass {
    Public static void main (string[] args) {
        System.out.println ln("example");
}
}
```

If you think about it, this simple class has a class wrapper where you define the name of the class and within that wrapper a main method. CFC also has a component wrapper, which holds inside of it various methods.

In our CFC, we have defined two methods that we can call getEmp and getStartDate both of which return query objects back to a client.

At this point, before we go further into the whys and wherefores of CFCs, let's actually call or instantiate this CFC.

Open your editor and create a file called testcfc.cfm like the one shown in Listing 6.2.

Listing 6.2 *testcfc.cfm*

```
<cfinvoke component="testqrycfc" method="getEmp" returnVariable="empResult">
<cfdump var=#empResult#>
<cfinvoke component="testqrycfc" method="getDept"  returnVariable="empResult">
<cfdump var=#empResult#>
```

Save this file and put it into your work directory. Then, using your web browser, call this template and see what the results are. They should look like those in Figure 6.1.

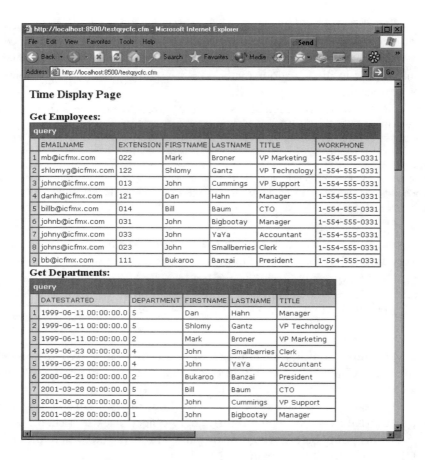

Figure 6.1 Output from `testqrycfc.cfc`.

This template enables us to "invoke" our CFC via the tag `CFINVOKE`, and it "knows" which CFC to call by providing the name of the component (`component="testqrycfc"`) and the method we want to call by (`method="getEmp"`). Finally, we then define a return variable and perform a `cfdump` operation so that we can see the output via the collection returned by our CFC.

Now, before we talk too much about how to invoke CFCs, let's go a little deeper into how to create CFCs.

Creating CFCs

Although we have touched on the very basics of CFCs, we need to cover a lot of information before you can effectively start developing them. One of the first things we need to reaffirm is that CFCs enable you to use all CFML tags, functions, variables, and constructs as well as all variable and session scopes. CFCs are best used to abstract or objectify complex code and therefore can contain complex and lengthy code inside their CFFUNCTION tags or methods.

In such a case, you can easily use cfinclude to make a more manageable and readable CFC in which each lengthy method's code is included. In Listing 6.3, we are going to create a simple CFC that will help us manage our Employees database.

Listing 6.3   *ums.cfc*

```
<cfcomponent>
    <cffunction name="createEmp" returnType="query">
        <cfquery name="createQuery" datasource="ICF" dbtype="ODBC">
    (FirstName,LastName, Title, EmailName, Extension, WorkPhone, Status,
Department, DateStarted)
        Values (
            '#arguments.FirstName#',
            '#arguments.lastName#',
            '#arguments.Title#',
            '#arguments.EmailName#',
            '#arguments.Extension#',
            '#arguments.WorkPhone#',
            #arguments.Status#,
            #arguments.Department#,
            #arguments.DateStarted#)
        </cfquery>
    <cfreturn #createQuery#>
    </cffunction>
    <cffunction name="getEmp" returnType="query">
        <cfquery name="getQuery" datasource="ICF" dbtype="ODBC" >
            SELECT Employees.FirstName, Employees.LastName,
            Employees.Title, Employees.DateStarted,
            Employees.Department
            FROM Employees
            ORDER BY DateStarted ASC
        </cfquery>
    <cfreturn #getQuery#>
    </cffunction>
        <cffunction name="deleteEmp" returnType="query">
        <cfquery name="deleteQuery" datasource="ICF" dbtype="ODBC">
            UPDATE Employees
            SET Status = 'inactive'
```

continues ▶

Listing 6.3 **Continued**

```
            Where EmployeeID = #arguments.EmployeeID#
        </cfquery>
    <cfreturn #deleteQuery#>
    </cffunction>
        <cffunction name="updateEmp" returnType="Query">
    <cfquery name="updateQuery" datasource="ICF" dbtype="ODBC">
            UPDATE Employees
            SET FirstName= '#arguments.FirstName#',LastName =
        '#arguments.lastName#', Title =
        '#arguments.Title#', EmailName =
        '#arguments.EmailName#', Extension =
        '#arguments.Extension#', WorkPhone
        '#arguments.WorkPhone#', Status
        #arguments.Status#, Department
        #arguments.Department#, DateStarted
        #arguments.DateStarted#
        Where EmployeeID = #arguments.EmployeeID#
        </cfquery>
    <cfreturn #updateQuery#>
    </cffunction>
</cfcomponent>
```

As you can see, this CFC is rather lengthy, which is not uncommon when developing ColdFusion templates that perform complex tasks. In this case, our CFC encapsulates four functions, so it needs to be long; but lengthy templates make for code that is hard to understand and to debug, support, or enhance later. We need to be able to further abstract the actual working code from our functions.

To do this, we are going to make our code easier to read and make each functional block easier to manage. For example, let's remove the CFQUERY blocks and put them into included files that will be named after their function. The createQuery block becomes createEmp.cfm (see Listing 6.4).

Listing 6.4 *ums1.cfc*

```
<cfcomponent>
    <cffunction name="createEmp" returnType="query">
        <cfinclude template="createEmp.cfm">
    <cfreturn #createQuery#>
    </cffunction>
    <cffunction name="getEmp" returnType="query">
        <cfinclude template="getEmp.cfm">
    <cfreturn #getQuery#>
    </cffunction>
    <cffunction name="deleteEmp" returnType="query">
```

```
            <cfinclude template="deleteEmp.cfm">
        <cfreturn #deleteQuery#>
        </cffunction>
        <cffunction name="updateEmp" returnType="Query">
            <cfinclude template="updateEmp.cfm">
        <cfreturn #updateQuery#>
        </cffunction>
</cfcomponent>
```

As you can see, this provides a much cleaner presentation and enables you to abstract much of the functional code from the CFC, allowing easier maintenance and testing of queries before you make them part of the CFC. For example, you can test all of your queries as they are before integrating them into a complex CFC. This enables you to do less testing on your overall CFC and during debugging. You can concentrate on issues with the CFC structure and code itself and not on the query, which you know already functions correctly.

Now let's look at how to actually use or work with CFCs that we create.

CFC Interaction

One thing you've surely noticed by now is that we have not really discussed how to pass values to and from CFCs. CFCs enable you to pass simple or very complex data in and out of them using everything from the CFINVOKE tag to URL variables, form variables, the Flash Gateway, and ColdFusion's new web services functionality.

Let's look at the different ways in which we can invoke a CFC's methods, first using the CFINVOKE tag in a simple ColdFusion template.

Using *CFINVOKE*

The CFINVOKE tag enables you to invoke the methods or functions from within ColdFusion pages or from within other components of the general form:

```
<cfinvoke
    component = "component name or reference"
    returnVariable = "variable name"
    argumentCollection = "argument collection"
    >

<cfinvoke
    method = "method name"
    returnVariable = "variable name"
    argumentCollection = "argument collection"
    >
```

Note the difference in the two forms. Although in previous examples we called both the component and the method for a specific CFC, you actually do not need to call the component argument if the CFC has already been instated. The other two arguments are optional and are needed only if you expect a return variable or need to pass a structure of arguments.

As we have already seen, invoking CFCs in this manner from a ColdFusion page is a straightforward operation. Let's look at how we can invoke a CFC using `CFOBJECT` and how you can first instantiate a CFC and then invoke the method.

First we use the `CFOBJECT` tag to instantiate the component and create a pointer to the component using a variable name. For example:

```
<cfobject name="variable name" component="the name of the CFC">
```

To invoke component methods, use the `cfinvoke` tag. The `cfinvoke` tag's `name` attribute references the variable name in the `cfobject` tag's `name` attribute. Here is an example:

```
<cfobject name="emptest" component="exmpqry1">
<cfinvoke component=exmpqry1 method="getEmp">
```

The result of running this code is shown Figure 6.2.

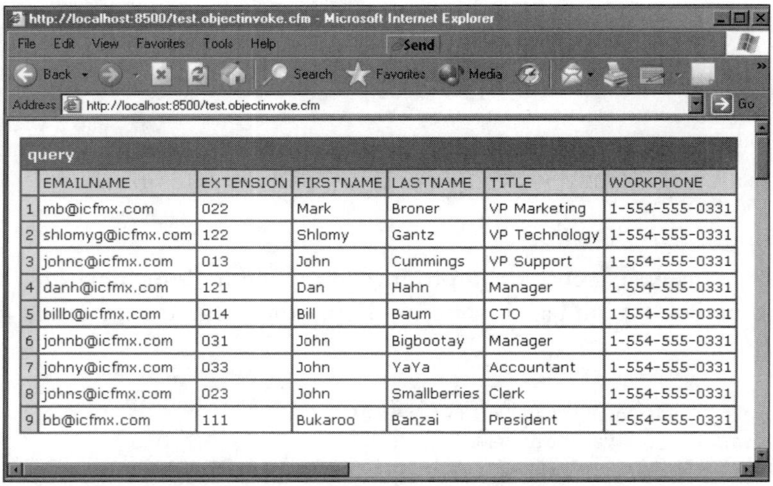

	EMAILNAME	EXTENSION	FIRSTNAME	LASTNAME	TITLE	WORKPHONE
1	mb@icfmx.com	022	Mark	Broner	VP Marketing	1-554-555-0331
2	shlomyg@icfmx.com	122	Shlomy	Gantz	VP Technology	1-554-555-0331
3	johnc@icfmx.com	013	John	Cummings	VP Support	1-554-555-0331
4	danh@icfmx.com	121	Dan	Hahn	Manager	1-554-555-0331
5	billb@icfmx.com	014	Bill	Baum	CTO	1-554-555-0331
6	johnb@icfmx.com	031	John	Bigbootay	Manager	1-554-555-0331
7	johny@icfmx.com	033	John	YaYa	Accountant	1-554-555-0331
8	johns@icfmx.com	023	John	Smallberries	Clerk	1-554-555-0331
9	bb@icfmx.com	111	Bukaroo	Banzai	President	1-554-555-0331

Figure 6.2 Calling a CFC using `CFOBJECT`.

The question then comes to mind, why would you want to first instantiate the CFC before you invoke it? Well, if you just use CFINVOKE in a template, then every time you use CFINVOKE CFMX creates a new CFC, processes your request, and then destroys your CFC. By instantiating the CFC using CFOBJECT, your CFC is created and each call using CFINVOKE from the same template does not create a new CFC, thus increasing your performance. This is especially useful when you are doing many interactions with a CFC or when you have few but complicated interactions with your CFC, and it should be used as a best practice in situations in which performance is necessary. Another time to use CFOBJECT to instantiate your CFCs is when you want to preserve data stored in the component in the same instance between different method calls.

Interacting with CFC Using Forms

Now let's look at interacting with a CFC via a form. In this next example, we are going to ask you to modify the testqrycfc.cfc file again to look like Listing 6.5.

Listing 6.5   *exmpqury1.cfc*

```
<cfcomponent>
    <cffunction name="getEmp"  returnType="query" access="remote">
        <cfquery name="empQuery" datasource="ICF" dbtype="ODBC" >
            SELECT Employees.FirstName,
            Employees.LastName,
            Employees.Title,
            Employees.EmailName,
            Employees.WorkPhone,
            Employees.Extension
            FROM Employees
        </cfquery>
            <cfdump var=#empQuery#>
    </cffunction>
    <cffunction name="getStartDate" returnType="query">
        <cfquery name="deptQuery" datasource="ICF" dbtype="ODBC">
            SELECT Employees.FirstName, Employees.LastName,
            Employees.Title, Employees.DateStarted,
            Employees.Department
            FROM Employees
            ORDER BY DateStarted ASC
        </cfquery>
<cfreturn #deptQuery#>
</cffunction>
<cffunction name="getEmpName" returnType="query" access="remote">
<cfargument name="lastName" required="true">
<cfquery name="deptQuery" datasource="ICF" dbtype="ODBC" >
```

continues ▶

Listing 6.5   **Continued**

```
        SELECT Employees.FirstName, Employees.LastName,
                    Employees.Title, Employees.DateStarted,
                    Employees.Department
                    FROM Employees
        WHERE LASTNAME LIKE '#arguments.lastName#'
        </cfquery>
        <cfreturn #deptQuery#>
        </cffunction>
        <cffunction name="createEmp" returnType="query" access="remote">
            <!--- cf arguments are needed to recive arguments as well as they act as a
first line of validation --->
            <cfargument name="FirstName" required="true">
            <cfargument name="LastName" required="true">
            <cfargument name="Title" required="false">
            <cfargument name="EmailName" required="false">
            <cfargument name="Extension" required="false">
            <cfargument name="WorkPhone" required="false">
            <cfargument name="Status" required="true">
            <cfargument name="Department" required="true">
            <cfargument name="DateStarted" required="true">
            <!--- start insert query --->
            <cfquery name="empCreate" datasource="ICF" dbtype="ODBC" >
            Insert INTO Employees
             (FirstName,LastName, Title, EmailName, Extension, WorkPhone, Status,
Department, DateStarted)

            Values (
            '#arguments.FirstName#',
            '#arguments.lastName#',
            '#arguments.Title#',
            '#arguments.EmailName#',
            '#arguments.Extension#',
            '#arguments.WorkPhone#',
            #arguments.Status#,
            #arguments.Department#,
            #arguments.DateStarted#)
            </cfquery>
            <cfoutput>Record was added</cfoutput>
        </cffunction>
</cfcomponent>
```

If you look at Listing 6.5, you will notice a few things that are different
from the other CFFUNCTION blocks. The first is the different syntax in the
CFFUNCTION block. We have added an attribute called access. For now, we are
not going to get into this in depth, but cffunction has numerous attributes
that enable you to define various things such as whether your CFC is public,
whether it's remotely accessible, whether its security settings are based on

specific roles, and other options. We will look at this in more depth in the section "Advanced ColdFusion Component Development" later in this chapter.

The next thing you will notice is a new tag called CFARGUMENT, which takes the following form:

```
<cfargument
      name="..."
      type="..."
      required="..."
      default="..."


>
```

Table 6.1 provides the various descriptions and settings for each of the possible attributes of CFARGUMENT.

Table 6.1   *cfargument* **Attributes and Descriptions**

Attribute	Required	Type	Description
name	Required	String	The argument's name.
type	Optional	Data type	The data type of the argument. Used for validating data types.
required	Optional	Boolean	Used to specify whether a parameter is required to execute a component. Values can be either true or false.
default	Optional	All types	Provides a default value when no parameter is passed.

The CFARGUMENT tag enables you to define the parameters you want to pass to a CFC within a specific component method or within a specific CFFUNCTION block. As in the preceding example, if you want to pass multiple parameters to a CFC you need to define them using multiple CFARGUMENT tags. When you want to call an argument, you call it using the standard dot notation as if you were accessing information from a ColdFusion structure.

You can also use the CFARGUMENT tag much like CFPARAM, in that you can define whether a CFARGUMENT is required or not by using the required attribute and whether it should have a default value by using the default attribute. You can use these attributes to make more robust CFCs.

Now let's actually call this CFC from a form (see Listing 6.6).

Listing 6.6 *cfcformpost.cfm*

```
<!DOCTYPE html PUBLIC "-//W3C//DTD XHTML 1.0 Strict//EN"
      "http://www.w3.org/TR/xhtml1/DTD/xhtml1-strict.dtd">

<html>
<head>
<title>Untitled</title>
</head>
<cfquery name="getDepartments" datasource="ICF" dbtype="ODBC" >
SELECT
Department.DepartmentID,
Department.DepartmentName
FROM Department
</cfquery>

<body>
<form action="exmpqry1.cfc" method="post">
<table border="0" cellspaceing="1">
<tr>
      <td>First Name</td>
      <td><input type="text" name="firstname" size="20"></td>
</tr>
<tr>
      <td>Last Name</td>
      <td><input type="text" name="lastname" size="20"></td>
</tr>
<tr>
<td>Title</td>
      <td><input type="text" name="Title" size="20"></td>
</tr>
<tr>
      <td>Email Prefix</td>
      <td><input type="text" name="EmailName" size="20"></td>
</tr>
<tr>
      <td>Extension</td>
      <td><input type="text" name="Extension" size="20"></td>
</tr>
<tr>
      <td>WorkPhone</td>
      <td><input type="text" name="WorkPhone" size="20"></td>
</tr>
<tr>
      <td>Status</td>
      <td><input type="text" name="Status" size="20"></td>
</tr>
<tr>
      <td>Department</td>
      <td><select name="department">
      <cfoutput query="getDepartments"><option
```

```
value="#DepartmentID#">#DepartmentName#</option></cfoutput>
      </td>
</tr>
<tr>
      <td>Date Started</td>
      <td><input type="text" name="DateStarted" size="20"></td>
</tr>
      <input type="Hidden" name="method" value="createEmp">
<tr>
      <td><input type="submit" value="Create Emp"></td>
</tr>
</table>
</form>
</body>
</html>
```

When you look at this code, it looks very straightforward with the minor exception of two lines. One is the following form line:

```
<form action="exmpqry1.cfc" method="post">
```

This actually invokes our CFC and passes the information via an HTTP POST method. The second one is this hidden form:

```
<input type="Hidden" name="method" value="createEmp">
```

It passes to the CFC the specific method we want to call. When accessing CFC methods via forms, you need to make sure to pass along a form variable named method whose value is the method you want to call.

Save these files and point your browser to the form (refer to Listing 6.6), fill it out, and click submit. You should get something like Figure 6.3 in your browser.

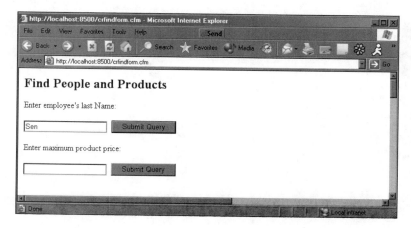

Figure 6.3 An example of calling a CFC from a form.

Now that we understand how to use forms to work with CFCs, let's look at using URLs.

CFCs Using URLs

To pass parameters to component methods using a URL, you simply need to append the parameters you want to pass to the URL in standard URL query-string, name-value-pair syntax. For example, if you wanted call the `getEmpName` method on our CFC, you would need to pass the method and last name of an employee. If you wanted to pass it from a hyperlink, it would look like this:

```
<a href="exmpqry1.cfc?method=getEmpName&lastname=hahn">
```

To pass multiple parameters using a URL, all you need to do is delimit your name-value pairs using the ampersand (&) character. Here is an example:

```
<a href="exmpqry1.cfc?method=getEmpName&lastname=hahn&firstname=dan">
```

Also as with all parameter-passing techniques that use HTTP to communicate with a CFC, you need to make the specific methods you want to communicate with accessible by adding the remote clause to the `ACCESS` attribute in the `CFFUNCTION` tag.

Using *CFScript* with CFCs

CFScript has become a very popular method for developing ColdFusion applications, and it is very useful when developing large blocks of logic, setting many variables, or creating UDFs. At times, it will be important to be able to invoke your CFCs from inside a UDF or even a standard CFScript block.

To invoke a CFC's method using CFScript you will need to use the `createObject` function. After you create a component object, you use normal function syntax to invoke component methods. Listing 16.7 provides an example.

Listing 6.7   *cfcscript.cfm*

```
<b>CFC with CFSCRIPT:</b>
<cfscript>
  exmpqrycfc=createObject("component","
    exmpqry1");
  exmpqrycfc.getEmp();
</cfscript>
<br>
```

In this example, we have a single CFSCRIPT block that assigns the exmpqrycfc variable to the exmpqry1 component using the createObject function. We then call the CFC's method as a cfscript function. That's all there is to it.

Using Component Using the Flash Gateway

One of the great new features of ColdFusion MX is the capability for developers to call ColdFusion functions—and indeed other types of objects (such as Java objects)—through the Flash MX gateway. Until now, developers had a more cumbersome approach to creating dynamic Flash applications, but Flash MX enables you to seamlessly work with programming logic that lies outside of Flash and might indeed reside on a remote server or system.

Flash MX enables you to call CFCs specifically through the Flash gateway, which then brokers the exchange and accepts a response that it then passes on to the requesting Flash client, which can then work with the information. For a basic overview, see Figure 6.4.

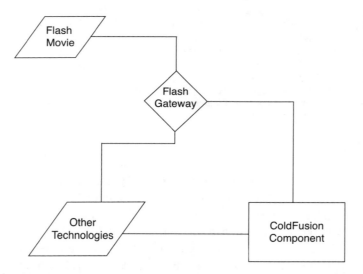

Figure 6.4   A Flash object invoking a ColdFusion component via the Flash gateway.

This allows for some very exciting development possibilities, not only being able to create data-driven Flash applications much more simply and quickly, but also allowing developers to abstract functionality away from Flash and let it reside in CFCs. If a Flash developer knows the necessary methods and parameters to pass and call into a CFC, he can independently develop his UI widgets and Flash applications without ever needing to talk with server-side developers. As we will see in the following examples, ColdFusion now enables you to create a package-like notation for creating namespaces in your CFCs. This allows code reuse and gets rid of the possibility of namespace collision or, simply put, accidentally calling objects that have the same name but different functionality.

Let's look at a simple example. In Listing 6.8, we are going to create a simple CFC that, when called by our Flash object, returns a simple message that's contained inside a ColdFusion structure.

Note

Before you begin, you must have Flash MX and the NetServices/Salsa Flash MX add-on installed; otherwise, the examples will not work.

Listing 6.8 *ObjectTest.cfc*

```
<cfcomponent name="ObjectTest">
  <cffunction name="getObject" access="remote">
    <cfargument name="foo" required="true" />
    <cfargument name="message" required="false" />
    <cfset outStruct = StructNew() />
    <cfset outStruct.foo = arguments.foo />
    <cfset outStruct.message = arguments.message />
    <cfset outStruct.from = "CF Component" />
    <cfreturn outStruct />
  </cffunction>
</cfcomponent>
```

As you can see, this is a straightforward CFC like the others we have created in this chapter. In fact, there is nothing Flash-specific about it, and you could call or invoke it with any other methods defined earlier. So now let's create our Flash script that will call the CFC.

First you will need to open your Flash MX development environment and type the code in Listing 6.9 into the ActionScript window.

Listing 6.9 *testnetservice.swf*

```
#include "NetServices.as"
#include "NetDebug.as"
Result = function()
{}
Result.prototype.onResult = function(result)
{
```

```
trace("data received from gateway");
trace("result.foo : " + result.foo);
trace("result.message : " + result.message);
trace("result.from : " + result.from);
}
Result.prototype.onStatus = function(error)
{
trace("An Error occured!");
trace("Error : " + error.description);
}
var o = new Object();
o.foo = "bar";
o.message = "This orginated from Flash";
NetServices.setDefaultGatewayUrl("http://localhost:8100/flashservices/gateway");
var gw = NetServices.createGatewayConnection();
var server = gw.getService("cf6.ObjectTest", new Result());
server.getObject(o);
```

The first thing you will notice is that the ActionScript includes two libraries that are new to Flash MX. The first is called `NetServices.as` and the other is `NetDebug.as`.

These ActionScript libraries are required for you to take advantage of the new gateway services paradigm in Flash MX, and you will also use them to create your web service objects and to debug any problems you have with the Flash remoting service.

Next we create a new ActionScript class/object called `Result`. We will use the methods in the object to catch and manipulate the data received from the server.

```
Result.prototype.onResult = function(result)
{
trace("data received from gateway");
trace("result.foo : " + result.foo);
trace("result.message : " + result.message);
trace("result.from : " + result.from);
}
```

Next we create a new function that will capture the structure returned from our CFC and output the contents of the structure. In actuality, you would want to create a loop that stepped through your structure, but here we have a very simple structure with known content, so we will just hard-code it.

In this instance, we capture data from the server when it is passed to Flash using `onResult`. To print the response from the server to the Flash output window, we use the function `trace()`.

Now we need to add some debugging, which we do with this code block:

```
Result.prototype.onStatus = function(error)
{
trace("An Error occured!");
trace("Error : " + error.description);
}
```

If for some reason our object has an error, this method will output the error so that we can debug our object.

Now we need to actually send something to our CFC. We can do that by creating a Flash object that we will send to our ObjectTest.cfc.

```
var o = new Object();
o.foo = "bar";
o.message = "This orginated from Flash";
```

Finally, we need to actually request the CFC. We can do it like this:

```
NetServices.setDefaultGatewayUrl("http://localhost:8100/flashservices/gateway");
var gw = NetServices.createGatewayConnection();
var server = gw.getService("thepathwhere.yousaved.yourcfc.ObjectTest", new Result());
server.getObject(o);
```

This code block is where we actually connect to the Flash gateway, and if you are developing on your local machine, the URL should be your local host, but it could be any URL to a Flash gateway.

The gateway will then return an object that represents a connection to the gateway. We use this connection to actually call our component (CFC) using the following:

```
var server = gw.getService("thepathwhere.yousaved.yourcfc.ObjectTest", new Result());
```

The path to which you save your CFC is referred to in dot notation instead of standard file path or URI notation. Thus, if you saved your CFC to www-root/coldfusionMX/chapter22/ObjectTest.CFC, it will become the following:

```
var server = gw.getService("coldfusionmx.chapter22.ObjectTest", new Result());
```

This dot notation allows your gateway connection to call the correct component on your targeted server, and by using unique names such as IPs, email addresses, and so on among your path, you will guarantee that you never have name collisions in your objects.

The preceding code now can call your CFC and store it in a variable called server. Next we call a method from this component using the following code:

```
server.getObject(o);
```

This also makes sure to pass our string object to the CFC's method that we invoked!

Now let's test what we have created. Go to Flash MX and use the Debug movie window. Press the Play icon and note the results in the pop-up window. You should see something like Figure 6.5.

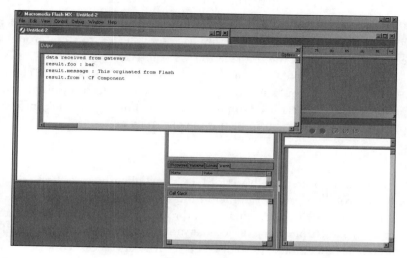

Figure 6.5   Output from our CFC via the Flash gateway!

Retrieving CFC Output

So far, we have looked at various ways of invoking and instantiating CFCs and passing parameters to them, but only to a limited extent have we looked at how to output information from CFCs or request results from a CFC operation. So far, we have ignored this in our examples and have focused on how to build CFC functions/methods and pass information to them. Now we will look at how to retrieve results from CFCs.

In general, we will return our output results from a CFC by using the CFRETRUN tag. The CFRETURN tag takes the following form:

```
<CFRETURN
     Variable name
>
```

CFRETURN only allows you to return one variable, so if you need to pass back complex information, you need to first create a structure of name-value pairs and return the structure to the calling template. In our examples, we are already returning a variety of data to the client using `CFRETURN` to not only return simple values but actual recordsets. You can return any data to the client as long as you can return it as a single variable.

In our examples, you can see that when we invoke the CFC, we also assign the return value to a temporary variable.

```
<cfinvoke component="examplequery" method="getEmp" returnVariable="empResult">
```

We then use `cfdump` to dynamically output the variable, which is a recordset, to the screen. We could just as easily have used `CFLOOP` to step through the recordset and output the information we wanted.

Also we can let the CFC just output information back to the client with `CFOUTPUT`. Usually you want to do this when you want to display a fixed message such as an error or some specific flag; but to pass back information to a calling template, you must use the `CFRETURN` tag.

Summary

We have now covered the basics of CFCs, including how to create them and how to invoke and instantiate them from forms. We also covered their direct use through `CFINVOKE` and using them through URLs and the Flash gateway. In the rest of the chapter, we will look at more advanced features of ColdFusion component models, such as roles-based security and access control.

Advanced ColdFusion Component Development

The first part of this chapter introduced the basics of ColdFusion components, but there is a lot more to ColdFusion components than meets the eye. ColdFusion components offer a series of powerful tools and functionality that has never been available to ColdFusion developers and also offer a new model by which to develop and model applications. In the rest of the chapter, we will discuss the following:

- Error handling
- Role-based security
- Component packages
- Component inheritance
- Component introspection
- Web services

Dealing with Exceptions in CFCs

As with all ColdFusion development, handling and dealing with exceptions is an important part of developing robust applications. Just like any other ColdFusion template, CFCs can use the CFCATCH and CFTRY blocks to catch and deal with exceptions. Although you are not forced to use CFCATCH and CFTRY, they can be invaluable in finding and dealing with bugs inside complex CFCs. This is especially true when you are working with many CFCs that interoperate and are dealing with unforeseen exceptions in a production environment.

So let's look at the example in Listing 6.10.

Listing 6.10 *exmpqry2.cfc*

```
<cfcomponent>
    <cffunction name="getEmp" returnType="query">
    <cftry>
        <cfquery name="empQuery" datasource="ICF" dbtype="ODBC" >
            SELECT Employees.FirstName,
            Employees.LastName,
            Employees.Title,
            Employees.EmailName,
            Employees.WorkPhone,
            Employees.Extension
            FROM Employees

        </cfquery>
    <!--- Use cfcatch to test for database errors.--->
    <!---    Print error messages. --->
    <!--- Block executes only if a Database exception is thrown. --->
        <cfcatch type="Database">
        <h1>Database Error</h1>
            <cfoutput>
<ul>
<li><b>Message:</b> #cfcatch.Message#
<li><b>Native error code:</b> #cfcatch.NativeErrorCode#
<li><b>SQLState:</b> #cfcatch.SQLState#
<li><b>Detail:</b> #cfcatch.Detail#
</ul>
            </cfoutput>
            <cfset errorCaught = "Database">
            </cfcatch>
    </cftry>
        <cfdump var=#empQuery#>
    </cffunction>
    <cffunction name="getStartDate" returnType="query">
        <cftry>
        <cfquery name="deptQuery" datasource="ICF" dbtype="ODBC" >
            SELECT Employees.FirstName, Employees.LastName,
```

continues ▶

Listing 6.10 **Continued**

```
                Employees.Title, Employees.DateStarted,
                Employees.Department
                FROM Employees
                ORDER BY DateStarted ASC
        </cfquery>
            <cfcatch type="Database">
        <h1>Database Error</h1>
                <cfoutput>
<ul>
<li><b>Message:</b> #cfcatch.Message#
<li><b>Native error code:</b> #cfcatch.NativeErrorCode#
<li><b>SQLState:</b> #cfcatch.SQLState#
<li><b>Detail:</b> #cfcatch.Detail#
</ul>
        </cfoutput>
        <cfset errorCaught = "Database">
        </cfcatch>
        </cftry>
<cfreturn #deptQuery#>
</cffunction>
<cffunction name="getEmpName" returnType="query" access="remote">
        <cfargument name="lastName" required="true">
        <cftry>
        <cfquery name="deptQuery" datasource="ICF" dbtype="ODBC" >
 SELECT Employees.FirstName, Employees.LastName,
            Employees.Title, Employees.DateStarted,
            Employees.Department
            FROM Employees
WHERE LASTNAME LIKE '#arguments.lastName#'
        </cfquery>
                        <cfcatch type="Database">
        <h1>Database Error</h1>
                <cfoutput>
<ul>
<li><b>Message:</b> #cfcatch.Message#
<li><b>Native error code:</b> #cfcatch.NativeErrorCode#
<li><b>SQLState:</b> #cfcatch.SQLState#
<li><b>Detail:</b> #cfcatch.Detail#
</ul>
        </cfoutput>
        <cfset errorCaught = "Database">
        </cfcatch>
        </cftry>
<cfreturn #deptQuery#>
</cffunction>
        <cffunction name="createEmp" returnType="query" access="remote">
        <!--- cf arguments are needed to receive arguments as well as they act as
        ➥a first line of validation --->
        <cfargument name="FirstName" required="true">
        <cfargument name="LastName" required="true">
```

```
        <cfargument name="Title" required="false">
        <cfargument name="EmailName" required="false">
        <cfargument name="Extension" required="false">
        <cfargument name="WorkPhone" required="false">
        <cfargument name="Status" required="true">
        <cfargument name="Department" required="true">
        <cfargument name="DateStarted" required="true">
        <!--- start insert query --->
        <cftry>
        <cfquery name="empCreate" datasource="ICF" dbtype="ODBC" >
        Insert INTO Employees
          (FirstName,LastName, Title, EmailName, Extension, WorkPhone, Status,
          ⮡Department, DateStarted)
        Values (
          '#arguments.FirstName#',
          '#arguments.lastName#',
          '#arguments.Title#',
          '#arguments.EmailName#',
          '#arguments.Extension#',
          '#arguments.WorkPhone#',
          #arguments.Status#,
          #arguments.Department#,
          #arguments.DateStarted#)
        </cfquery>
                        <cfcatch type="Database">
        <h1>Database Error</h1>
            <cfoutput>
<ul>
<li><b>Message:</b> #cfcatch.Message#
<li><b>Native error code:</b> #cfcatch.NativeErrorCode#
<li><b>SQLState:</b> #cfcatch.SQLState#
<li><b>Detail:</b> #cfcatch.Detail#
</ul>
        </cfoutput>
        <cfset errorCaught = "Database">
        </cfcatch>
        </cftry>
        <cfoutput>Record was added</cfoutput>
      </cffunction>
</cfcomponent>
```

In this example, we have modified Listing 6.5 to include error trapping for a database exception. This will catch any database exception and pass back a detailed error message to the client.

We could also do our error trapping as shown in Listing 6.11.

Listing 6.11 *exmpqry2.cfc* **Snippet 1**

```
<cffunction name="getEmp" returnType="query">
        <cfquery name="empQuery" datasource="ICF" dbtype="ODBC" >
                SELECT Employees.FirstName,
                Employees.LastName,
                Employees.Title,
                Employees.EmailName,
                Employees.WorkPhone,
                Employees.Extension
                FROM Employees
        </cfquery>
<cfif #empQuery.recordcount# LT 1>
 <cfthrow type="noQueryResult"
  message="No results were found. Please try again.">
<cfelse>
    <cfdump var=#empQuery#>
</cfif>
</cffunction>
```

Here we use conditional logic to see if there were any records to be found in the database and, if not, to pass back an error message that we catch on the client side (like what is shown in Listing 6.12).

Listing 6.12 *exmpqry2.cfc* **Snippet 2**

```
<h3>Time Display Page</h3>
<cftry>
<b>Get Employees:</b>
<cfinvoke component="exmpqry2" method="getEmp" returnVariable="empResult">
<cfcatch type="noQueryResult">
<p>The following error occured while processing the component
method:<br><b><cfoutput>#cfcatch.message#</cfoutput></b></p>
</cfcatch>
</cftry>
<cfdump var=#empResult#>
```

In general, any error handling method that you would normally use when writing CFML is fine. It is important to note, however, that although the ColdFusion MX Application Server usually provides helpful debugging information when developing CFML, because of the nature of CFCs, that debugging information might not be as helpful as one would like. It becomes very important to consistently use CFTRY blocks in your CFCs to catch exceptions and provide back to you specific information about what the actual problem is. Although this might not be very important if your application has only one or two CFCs, it becomes very important when you have many and are passing arguments between CFCs as well as using CFC's inheritance and other functionality (as we will see later in this chapter).

Securing Your CFCs

Nowadays, it's an unfortunate necessity to build secure applications to protect your applications from denial-of-service attacks, hackers, and data thieves. You also sometimes need to be able to restrict information to parties who have a certain access privilege. ColdFusion MX provides functionality to accomplish all of these goals.

First we are going to look at how to secure your CFCs at an access level that enables you to define exactly what can and cannot make requests or interact with your CFCs. Let's start by looking at the CFC access security levels in Table 6.2.

Table 6.2 **CFC Access Security Levels**

Security Level	Client Access
private	Accessible only to the component that declares it. This security level prevents invocation from other ColdFusion components and templates as well as other remote clients such as URLs, the Flash gateway, and web services.
package	Same as private except that components in the same package can access it.
public	Accessible to any locally executing ColdFusion page or component methods. This security level prevents invocation from remote clients such as URLs, the Flash gateway, and web services.
remote	Accessible to all client types.

If you remember from Listings 6.5 and 6.6 where we were using forms to interact with our CFCs, we modified our CFC to include the access attribute in the cfcomponent tag, as shown in Listing 6.13.

Listing 6.13 **Snippet from *exmplqury1.cfc***

```
<cffunction name="getStartDate" returnType="query" access="remote">
        <cfquery name="deptQuery" datasource="ICF" dbtype="ODBC">
            SELECT Employees.FirstName, Employees.LastName,
            Employees.Title, Employees.DateStarted,
            Employees.Department
            FROM Employees
            ORDER BY DateStarted ASC
        </cfquery>
    <cfreturn #deptQuery#>
</cffunction>
```

In Listing 6.13, we have set this function's `access` attribute to `remote`, allowing our examples that used forms, URLs, and other methods of invoking CFCs to access the CFC. For example, edit the `cffunction` line in this code and remove the `access` attribute altogether. Now we have the following:

```
<cffunction name="getEmpName" returnType="query" >
```

Then try and call this CFC via a URL:

```
<a href="exmpqry1.cfc?method=getEmpName&lastname=hahn">
```

Figure 6.6 shows you what you should see.

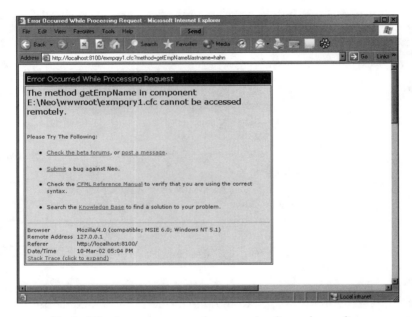

Figure 6.6   An error message thrown to the client when a client without appropriate access privilege tries to connect to a CFC.

After you have tried this, change your code back to allow remote access. Anytime you want a CFC to be accessible from a form, URL, or POST operation, you are going to have to use the `remote` access level so that ColdFusion sees all GET and POST operations as remote procedures.

Building Role-Based Component Method Security

Although it's useful to be able to define what sort of access you want to give your CFCs from remote applications or internal applications, it's also useful to be able to restrict specific CFCs by user or a user's role.

For example, if we wanted to create a CFC that deleted users from the database, we might do something like what is shown in Listing 6.14.

Listing 6.14   *deleteUser.cfc*

```
<cfcomponent>
    <cffunction name="deleteUser" returnType="query" roles="admin">
    <cfargument name="UserID" required="true">
    <cfquery name="deleteUser" datasource="ICF" dbtype="ODBC" >
     DELETE FROM USER
    WHERE User.UserID = #arguments.UserID#
    </cfquery>
    <cfreturn #deptQuery#>
    </cffunction>
</cfcomponent>
```

Obviously, we would not want just anyone to be able to delete users from tables, so here we have assigned the `roles` attribute to the administrator, (or admin). You can define multiple roles that have access to this CFC by entering multiple roles in the `roles` attribute and delimiting them with commas, as in the following:

```
<cffunction name="deleteUser" returnType="query" roles="admin, dba, etc.">
```

For more information on how to create roles and use ColdFusion MX application security, see the section "Application Security" in Chapter 17, "Common Application Development Requirements."

ColdFusion Component Packages

A useful feature of CFCs is the capability to create component packages. Component packages are any grouping of CFCs that are stored in the same directory and allow you to refer to all components in that package using a dot notation to decrease the chance of name "collisions" when sharing components. Components stored in the same directory are members of a component package much like you would have, for example, with a Java JAR file, although not exactly the same.

To create and invoke a CFC in a "package," all you have to do is move a collection of CFCs to a specific directory under your webroot and refer to the CFC from that point using dot notation as if you were referencing a file. Let's try an example.

In your web root directory, create a folder named `icf` and another folder under that one called `components`. Now move `exmplqury1.cfc` to the `components` directory.

Create a new ColdFusion page and save it in your webroot as `test.exmpqurypackage.cfm`.

Create a new CFML template like this:

```
<cfinvoke component="icf.components.exmplqury1"
method="getEmp">
```

As you can see, this is really straightforward, but let's look at the same thing in CFScript.

```
<cfscript>
helloCFC = createObject("component", "icf.components.exmplqury1");
helloCFC.getEmp();
</cfscript>
```

We can also call a packaged component from a URL as follows:

```
http://localhost/icf/components/ exmplqury1.cfc?method= getEmp
```

As you develop your own CFCs, use packages to help you create and separate your application into functional blocks. For example, if you have a series of CFCs that you use for user management, you might group them as follows:

```
Yourcompanyname/dev/usermanagment
```

You can use anything that is not only unique but helps you define the nature of the CFCs in that package.

Component Inheritance

As previously discussed, ColdFusion MX CFCs bring a whole new way of building applications to ColdFusion that developers have been trying to replicate with methodologies such as Fusebox and ObjectCF. In the preceding section, we mentioned that CFCs allow for the concept of inheritance, although developers more familiar with Java or C++ will find CFC inheritance more like file includes.

Developers often find themselves creating a simple script, program, or function that models a certain set of functionality that they need for a specific case. For example, let's create a CFC that returns all the customers in our database (see Listing 6.15).

Listing 6.15   *getCustomers.cfc*

```
<cfcomponent>
    <cffunction name="getCustomers" returnType="query" access="remote">
    <cfquery datasource="icf" name="getOrder">
    SELECT Customer.CustomerID, Customer.CustomerFirstName,
```

```
Customer.CustomerLastName, Customer.CustomerAddress, Customer.CustomerCity,
Customer.CustomerStateID, Customer.CustomerZip, Customer.CustomerPhone,
Customer.CustomerEmail, Customer.CustomerPassword, Customer.CustomerNotification
FROM Customer, State
WHERE Customer.CustomerStateID=State.StateID
      </cfquery>
      <cfreturn #getCustomers#>
      </cffunction>
</cfcomponent>
```

Now let's imagine that your manager says that he wants you to add some new functionality to the CFC, but you would rather not mess with your working code. Instead, you can just inherit the methods and functions of the other CFC and create a new CFC, as shown in Listing 6.16.

Listing 6.16 *getPreferredCustomers.cfc*

```
<cfcomponent extends="icf.getCustomers.cfc">
      <cffunction name="getPreferredCustomers" returnType="query" access="remote">
      <cfquery datasource="icf" name="getOrder">
      SELECT Customer.CustomerID AS Customer_CustomerID, Order.OrderID,
Order.CustomerID AS Order_CustomerID, Order.OrderDate, Order.OrderAddress,
Order.OrderCity, Order.OrderStateID, Order.OrderZip, Order.CreditCardID,
Order.OrderCardNumber, Order.OrderCardExpiration, Order.OrderNameOnCard,
Customer.CustomerFirstName, Customer.CustomerLastName, Customer.CustomerAddress,
Customer.CustomerCity, Customer.CustomerStateID, Customer.CustomerZip,
Customer.CustomerPhone, Customer.CustomerEmail, Customer.CustomerPassword,
Customer.CustomerNotification
FROM Customer INNER JOIN Order ON Customer.CustomerID = Order.CustomerID
Where recordset is GRT 5
      </cfquery>
      <cfreturn #getPreferredCustomers#>
      </cffunction>
</cfcomponent>
```

Now you could just cut and paste your code and fiddle with it until you have a new CFC, but this way is much easier. You cannot CFINCLUDE your CFC because, of course, the CFML parser would get confused by the CFC component tags. But with CFCs and inheritance, you can simply "borrow" the getCustomers.cfc template's functionality if it's in a CFC like this:

```
<cfcomponent extends="basecfcyouwishtoextend.cfc">
```

This enables you to inherit all of the preceding CFCs functionality while adding your new functionality for this special case.

Inheritance thus enables you to invoke the CFC exactly the same as you normally would, but you know have access to the extra functionality of the inherited CFC. For example, you could now do the following:

```
<cfinvoke component="getPreferredCustomers" method="getPreferredCustomers">
<cfinvoke component="getPreferredCustomers" method="getCustomers">
```

ColdFusion Components and Metadata

CFCs have another great and useful function that will be a boon to managers, developers, designers, and CFC user/consumers—ColdFusion calls it *introspection*. Once again, this is loosely based on the concept of introspection from object-oriented theory, but with CFC, you can think of it as a way for you to view or get metadata about a CFC. By metadata, we mean information about how the CFC functions, including information on methods, properties, parameters, and additional information. Component metadata, also known as *component introspection*, allows programs to discover the methods and properties exposed by components. Before we go into introspection in CFCs and more, let's first browse to a CFC and take a peek and see what it looks like. Open up a browser and enter in your URL the full path and name to a CFC. Try doing **localhost:8100/examplqury1.cfc** and see what you get. You should see something like Figure 6.7.

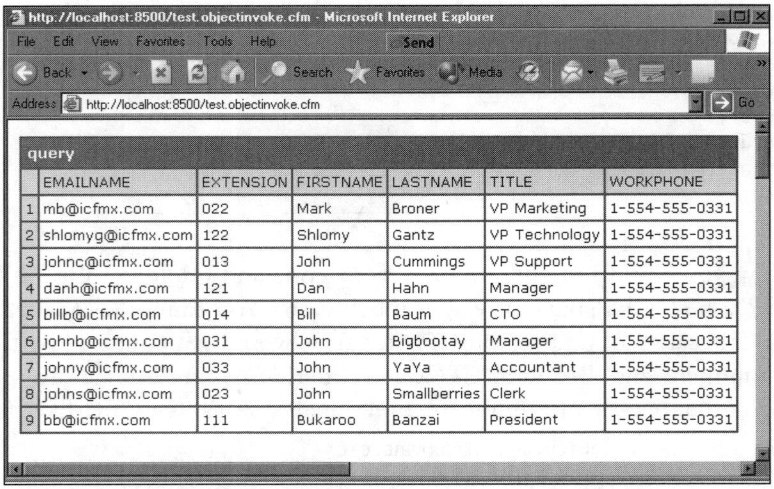

Figure 6.7 Using a browser to view metadata about a ColdFusion component.

Note that anything you might want to know about the CFC is right there for you, from CFC parameters and whether they are required or not, to methods and how they are called, as well as access privileges or information. So why is this so useful to you? Well, if you work in an organization that has several developers as well as designers, you can collaborate without constantly having to ask each other what parameters are required, what a specific method returns, or what data needs to be passed to that method before it can be invoked! In fact, you could create your CFCs, and a competent Flash designer could call them using the Flash net services and CFC introspection without ever having to talk to you!

Furthermore, CFCs provide a powerful method of providing insight into the structure of an application. Application architects, project managers, and team leaders can use the metadata to help them create and or update flow-charts, applications models in Unified Modeling Language, data diagrams, and so on without having to sit down with the developers and ask them about the CFC. Also introspection can act as a form of AutoDoc! For some applications, the information supplied by CFC introspection is all the documentation you need! So next time your manager asks you to fully document your application, at least when you work with CFCs, most of the documentation can be done via introspection.

Finally, ColdFusion MX provides three other methods to get metadata from CFCs. Table 6.3 describes each of them.

Table 6.3 **Metadata Functions**

Function	Description
cfcToMCDL	Returns component information as Macromedia description language (MCDL).
cfcToHTML	Returns component information as HTML.
cfcToWDDX	Returns component information as WDDX.

Using these functions, you can create applications that can autodiscover component functionality for a host of different uses, including CFC modeling systems, web services, work flow and process flow applications, and many others. Because you can also output CFCs as WDDX, you can even create applications in other languages that can discover component functionality via metadata using the WDDX SDK.

Introspection, inheritance, and CFCs provide powerful tools to developers and, more importantly, to IT managers and architects who are trying to apply software best practices and methodologies to web application development.

Summary

In this part of the chapter, we explored advanced features of CFC, such as how to handle exceptions, use access and roles-based security, and the features of inheritance and introspection. CFCs provide very rich functionality to help developers and architects design secure, robust, and well-designed ColdFusion applications, and CFCs should be used as a foundation for any large ColdFusion application.

Summary

This chapter covered a lot of ground, including how to create and invoke CFCs, various methods of passing information to CFCs, and how to get information back. We also looked at error trapping, securing your CFCs, inheritance, introspection, and packaging your CFCs for ease of deployment and encapsulation.

There is a lot to learn here; and although we touched on a huge amount of the functionality of CFCs, there is more to the topic than we can cover in one chapter. No matter if you are new to ColdFusion or are a long-term ColdFusion developer, you should carefully think about how CFCs can change the way you develop ColdFusion applications as a team or as an individual. If you do, you will soon start to see new possibilities for development that were never available to you before. CFCs give you an unprecedented amount of power over and flexibility in your development process while allowing you to expose only the functionality you desire to users, developers, and designers. One of the topics not covered here is CFCs and web services functionality. In Chapter 21, "Web Services and ColdFusion," we will explore this area of CFC functionality and introduce you to the power of web services!

7

Complex Data Types

W E HAVE SEEN IN PREVIOUS CHAPTERS HOW to create variables and set values for those variables within ColdFusion. There are, however, some types of variables that can hold complex values or multiple values. These are what we refer to as complex data types. In ColdFusion development you will find that you can use complex data types, such as lists, arrays, structures, and queries, to greatly improve the performance and power of your applications.

In this chapter, we take a look at complex data types and show you how to create, set values for, and evaluate the data for use in your applications.

At the end of each section, we discuss the native ColdFusion functions associated with each type of data. We show you how to use them in real code and prove to you that they can make your programming life easier.

Using *CFDUMP*

Before we get into our discussion about complex data types, we need to discuss a tool that will help you verify each test that will be run. That tool is ColdFusion's CFDUMP tag.

CFDUMP was added to ColdFusion with the release of version 5. It quickly became the best friend of many ColdFusion developers. CFDUMP was migrated into the ColdFusion tag set from Spectra, where it was known as CFA_DUMP.

CFDUMP displays the contents of both simple and complex variables. With CFDUMP, you can view the contents of a query object, a list, an array, a structure, or a Web Distributed Data eXchange (WDDX) packet. You can even access memory structures, such as the session, application, server, cookie, common gateway interface (CGI), form, and request scopes.

CFDUMP displays the values of these simple and complex data types in a table formatted in Hypertext Markup Language (HTML). Different data types have their own color borders. All structures have a blue border, while all query objects have a red border. See Table 7.1 for more information.

Table 7.1 Data Types and Their Corresponding Color Borders

Data Type	Color
Array	Green border
Array index	Light-green background
Binary/ColdFusion object	Yellow border, light-yellow background
Query	Red border
Query object column name	Light-red background
Structure	Blue border
Structure key	Light-blue background
User-defined function	Light beige
WDDX-encoded data	Black border

CFDUMP is a tag that is an indispensable tool for code debugging. You simply call the CFDUMP tag within your template and the resulting data is displayed. The syntax for this tag is the following:

```
<cfdump var="#variablename#">
```

CFDUMP is often used in conjunction with the CFABORT tag to stop the processing of a template right after the CFDUMP tag call:

```
<cfdump var="#variablename#"><cfabort>
```

Let's look at the tag in real code, as in Listing 7.1.

Listing 7.1 Using *CFDUMP* to Access the Server Memory Structure Values

```
These are the contents of my server memory structure:<br>
                    <br>
                    <cfdump var="#server#">
```

The resulting output might look something like Figure 7.1:

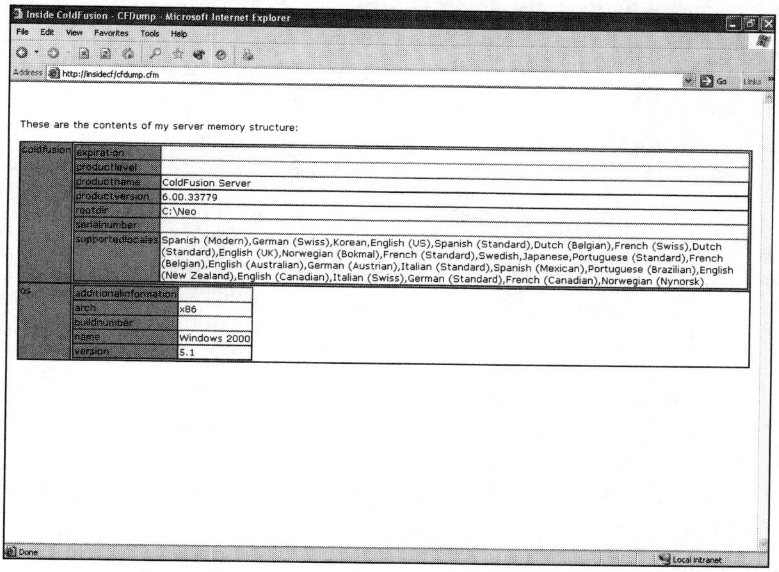

Figure 7.1   The output can be contracted by clicking the lighter-shaded structure key.

Queries

We use queries in ColdFusion to pull data out of backend databases to use within templates. A query object is a special structure within ColdFusion that holds the data in a query result set. A query object returns a row for each record in the result set. It also returns columns featuring the individual values.

There are different ways to create query objects within ColdFusion:

- You can use ColdFusion tags such as CFQUERY and CFSTOREDPROC to retrieve data from the database. This creates the query object.
- Other ColdFusion tags, such as CFDIRECTORY, CFFTP, CFLDAP, CFHTTP, CFREGISTRY (action="getall"), CFSEARCH, and CFPOP return values in a query object.
- Query objects can be created using the QueryNew() function.
- Query objects can be created as a result of some custom tag calls.

Creating Query Objects

In previous chapters, we covered how to query a data source using the CFQUERY tag. Later in this book, we discuss stored procedures in detail. A discussion of tags such as CFDIRECTORY, CFFTP, CFLDAP, and CFPOP are not appropriate at this point, so we'll save those for later as well.

We want to be able to manipulate a query object after we've created it, so let's take a look at the creation of query objects using the QueryNew() function.

The QueryNew() function creates an empty query object. When we call the QueryNew() function, we can specify a list of columns for the query object. The proper syntax is as follows:

```
<cfset GetUsers=QueryNew("FirstName,LastName,Email")>
```

This is not the full extent of it though. Not only do we need to create the query object itself, but also we have to add rows and define the contents of the individual cells. To handle these operations, we call other query functions: QueryAddRow() and QuerySetCell(). The following is a full list of query functions:

- IsQuery
- QueryNew
- QueryAddRow
- QueryAddColumn
- QuerySetCell
- QuotedValueList
- ValueList

To define how many rows are in a query object, we can use the QueryAddRow() function as follows:

```
<cfset rows=QueryAddRow(GetUsers, 3)>
```

To define the values of each cell in a row, we can use the QuerySetCell() function. The QuerySetCell() function requires that you identify the query, column, value, and row number, as shown in the following code:

```
<cfset var=QuerySetCell(GetUsers, "FirstName", "Neil", 1)>
```

Now we can take a look at the entire syntax of creating a query object. The code in Listing 7.2 sets the number of rows and sets the values of the cells in each row.

Listing 7.2 **Creating a ColdFusion Query Object**

```
<html>
<head>
        <title>Inside ColdFusion - Query Objects</title>
</head>
<body>
<table>
  <tr>
    <td>
      <!--- We first create our query object --->
      <cfset GetUsers = QueryNew("FirstName,LastName,Email")>
      <!--- Now we set our values --->
      <cfset rows=QueryAddRow(GetUsers, 3)>
        <!--- Now we set our values --->
        <cfset var=QuerySetCell(GetUsers, "FirstName", "Neil", 1)>
        <cfset var=QuerySetCell(GetUsers, "LastName", "Ross", 1)>
        <cfset var=QuerySetCell(GetUsers, "Email", "neil@codesweeper.com", 1)>
        <cfset var=QuerySetCell(GetUsers, "FirstName", "John", 2)>
        <cfset var=QuerySetCell(GetUsers, "LastName", "Cummings", 2)>
        <cfset var=QuerySetCell(GetUsers, "Email", "john@mauzy-broadway.com", 2)>
        <cfset var=QuerySetCell(GetUsers, "FirstName", "Robi", 3)>
        <cfset var=QuerySetCell(GetUsers, "LastName", "Sen", 3)>
        <cfset var=QuerySetCell(GetUsers, "Email", "r@granularity.com", 3)>
          <!--- Now we do the output --->
          My <cfif IsQuery(GetUsers)>query</cfif> data looks like this:
          <br>
          <table border="1" cellspacing="0">
            <tr><td>First Name</td><td>Last Name</td><td>Email Address</td></tr>
            <cfoutput query="GetUsers">
            <tr>
              <td>#GetUsers.FirstName#</td>
              <td>#GetUsers.LastName#</td>
              <td>#GetUsers.Email#</td>
            </tr>
            </cfoutput>
          </table>
          <br><br>
          <cfset EmailList=ValueList(GetUsers.Email)>
          The length of the list is: <cfoutput>#ListLen(EmailList)#</cfoutput>
          <br><br>
          This is the email list:<br>
          <cfoutput>#EmailList#</cfoutput>
        </td>
      </tr>
    </table>
</body>
</html>
```

Outputting Query Objects

As we've already covered using CFOUTPUT to loop through the result set of a query, we'll not go into detail here about how to do that. We will tell you, however, that this would be a really good place to start testing your CFDUMP tag.

When you run the code from Listing 7.2, you should get a result that looks a bit like Figure 7.2.

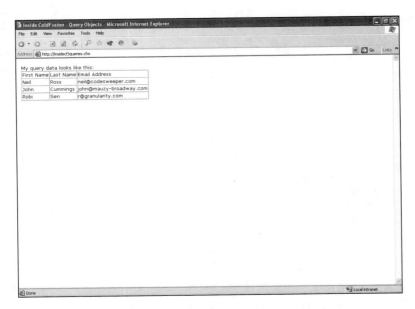

Figure 7.2 The query object content displayed.

Other query functions available to ColdFusion developers include the following:

- **IsQuery().** Returns TRUE if the specified value is a ColdFusion query object or FALSE if it is not.

    ```
    <cfif IsQuery(GetUsers)>GetUsers is a query</cfif>
    ```

- **ValueList().** Returns a comma-delimited list of values for a specified column in a query result set.

    ```
    <cfset EmailList=ValueList(GetUsers.Email)>
    ```

Query objects are some of the most frequently accessed complex variables with which you'll deal in ColdFusion development. We've shown you just how easy it is to create a list from a query result set, so why not move into lists next?

Lists

A list is a series of values arranged one after the other and separated by a delimiter. These values do not have to be in any particular order. The delimiter that separates the items in a list can be any character. Most commonly, the delimiter is a comma.

Having said that, you should know that a list is not really a complex data type. However, manipulation of lists more closely resembles the manipulation of a complex data type than that of a simple data type. ColdFusion sees the list as a string. As long as ColdFusion understands which character in the string is the delimiter, it can process each value in the list separately.

Table 7.2 gives samples of lists.

Table 7.2   **Examples of Simple Lists**

List	Description
"milk, eggs, bread, soda"	This is a list that you might see in many situations. Each item in the list is a value, and just as you can place each item from this list into a shopping cart one at a time, so too can ColdFusion act on the items individually.
"1, 2, 3, 4, 5"	A very simple list of items.

Creating a List

In ColdFusion, you can create a list just as you would any other variable. Look at the example shown in Listing 7.3.

Listing 7.3   **Creating a List Is As Easy As 1, 2, 3**

```
<html>
<head>
   <title>Inside ColdFusion MX - Lists</title>
</head>
<body>
<!--- We first create our lists --->
   <cfset newlist="1,2,3">
   <cfset othernewlist="1|2|3">
   <cfset yetothernewlist="1|2;3">
</body>
</html>
```

This is quite straightforward. Notice that in the second list, we used the |
(pipe) character as the delimiter and in the third list, we used multiple delimiters. We don't have to explain to ColdFusion at this point the character or
set of characters that we're going to use as the delimiter. When we create the
list, we just define it.

With a list, you create a variable and the list of items is viewed as the
value of that single variable. This variable can be in different scopes: local,
session, application, request, cookie, or client.

Outputting a List

To output the value of the variable, you simply call the variable within the
CFOUTPUT tag, as shown in Listing 7.4.

Listing 7.4 **Outputting the List Variable to the Screen**

```
<html>
<head>
    <title>Inside ColdFusion MX - Lists</title>
</head>
<body>
<!--- We first create our lists --->
    <cfset newlist="1,2,3">
    <cfset othernewlist="1|2|3">
    <cfset yetothernewlist="1|2;3">
<!--- Now we do the output --->
    My lists are:<br><br>
        <cfoutput>
        newlist = #newlist#<br>
            othernewlist = #othernewlist#<br>
            yetothernewlist = #yetothernewlist#
    </cfoutput>
</body>
</html>
```

A list is a variable—and a string variable at that—so we can output the variable to the page. By combining the code from Listing 7.2 and Listing 7.3, we
can produce the result in Figure 7.3.

Obviously, it is pretty easy to create a list and to output it manually.
However, what if you want to create a list and set its values on-the-fly?
Fortunately, ColdFusion can take care of that for us as well.

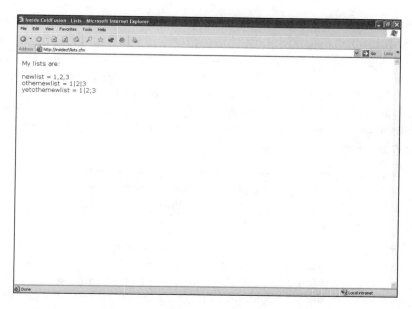

Figure 7.3   The result of the combined code from Listings 7.2 and 7.3.

List Functions

ColdFusion gives developers a number of functions to use to manipulate lists. These functions enable you to do things, such as determine the length of a list, add values to the beginning or end of the list, and even sort your list. The list functions available in ColdFusion include the following:

ArrayToList	ListFindNoCase	ListQualify
ListAppend	ListFirst	ListRest
ListChangeDelims	ListGetAt	ListSetAt
ListContains	ListInsertAt	ListSort
ListContainsNoCase	ListLast	ListToArray
ListDeleteAt	ListLen	ListValueCount
ListFind	ListPrepend	ListValueCountNoCase

In this section, we take a look at some of the most commonly used ColdFusion list functions.

Creating a List Dynamically

Lists can be created easily and dynamically in ColdFusion. Using the results of a query, you can create a list using the `ValueList()` function. You saw an example of this functionality in the last section of this chapter; let's review.

The `ValueList()` function enables you to create a list from a specific column in a query object. You can specify a delimiter for the list, but it will default to a comma. You use the following code to create the list:

```
<cfset EmailList=ValueList(GetUsers.Email)>
```

Assume that you want to know how many values are in the list. ColdFusion enables you to find this helpful little piece of information by using the `ListLen()` function, as shown in the following code snippet:

```
The length of the list is: #ListLen(EmailList)#
```

So, now you have a list of values. Let's look at outputting those values. It won't be as a single value, so let's loop through the output. You might need to perform this kind of task when you need to perform a specific job on each value in the list. ColdFusion gives you the `CFLOOP` tag for just such a task, as shown in Listing 7.5.

Listing 7.5 **Creating the Loop to Access Each Value in the List**

```
<html>
<head>
     <title>Inside ColdFusion MX - Lists</title>
</head>
<body>
<!--- We first create our query object --->
        <cfset GetUsers = QueryNew("FirstName,LastName,Email")>
<!--- Now we set our values --->
                <cfset rows=QueryAddRow(GetUsers, 3)>
<!--- Now we set our values --->
        <cfset var=QuerySetCell(GetUsers, "FirstName", "Neil", 1)>
        <cfset var=QuerySetCell(GetUsers, "LastName", "Ross", 1)>
        <cfset var=QuerySetCell(GetUsers, "Email", "neil@codesweeper.com", 1)>
        <cfset var=QuerySetCell(GetUsers, "FirstName", "John", 2)>
        <cfset var=QuerySetCell(GetUsers, "LastName", "Cummings", 2)>
        <cfset var=QuerySetCell(GetUsers, "Email", "john@mauzy-broadway.com", 2)>
        <cfset var=QuerySetCell(GetUsers, "FirstName", "Robi", 3)>
        <cfset var=QuerySetCell(GetUsers, "LastName", "Sen", 3)>
        <cfset var=QuerySetCell(GetUsers, "Email", "r@granularity.com", 3)>
<table>
     <tr>
        <td>
```

```
<!--- We first create our lists --->
                <cfset EmailList=ValueList(GetUsers.Email)>
            <cfset EmailListLen=ListLen(EmailList, ",")>
            <cfset EmailList=ListSort(EmailList, "text", "asc")>
            <cfset foundit=ListContains(EmailList, "neil")>
            <cfoutput>We found it at position number #foundit#.</cfoutput><br><br>
            <cfset EmailList=ListPrepend(EmailList, "info@insidecoldfusionmx.com")>
<!--- Now we do the output --->
            There are <cfoutput>#EmailListLen#</cfoutput> values in
EmailList.<br><br><br>
            The values of EmailList are:<br>
            <br>
            <cfset ListLoopCount=1>
            <cfloop list="#EmailList#" index="individualemail">
            <cfoutput>
                Position #ListLoopCount# = #individualemail#<br>
            </cfoutput>
            <cfset ListLoopCount=ListLoopCount+1>
            </cfloop>
            <cfset EmailListArray=ListToArray(EmailList)>
                <br><br>
            <cfdump var="#EmailListArray#">
        </td>
    </tr>
</table>
</body>
</html>
```

When the code in Listing 7.5 is executed, you can look for the output shown in Figure 7.4.

ColdFusion functions enable you to manipulate lists in a number of ways. Let's take a look at some of the commonly used list functions:

- **ListLen().** Returns the length of the list specified:

  ```
  <cfset EmailListLen=ListLen(EmailList, ",")>
  ```

- **ListSort().** Sorts the specified list:

  ```
  <cfset SortedList=ListSort(EmailList, "text", "asc")>
  ```

- **ListContains().** Returns the index of the item that matches the specified substring:

  ```
  <cfset index=ListContains(EmailList, "neil")>
  ```

- **ListAppend().** Appends a value to the end of the specified list. Returns the value of the updated list:

  ```
  <cfset EmailList=ListAppend(EmailList, "info@insidecoldfusionmx.com")>
  ```

- **ListPrepend().** Prepends a value to the beginning of the specified list. Returns the value of the updated list:

  ```
  <cfset EmailList=ListPrepend(EmailList, "info@insidecoldfusionmx.com")>
  ```

- **ListFind().** Returns the index of the first occurrence of a value within the specified list:

  ```
  <cfset position=ListFind (EmailList, "info@insidecoldfusionmx.com")>
  ```

- **ListToArray().** Converts the specified list to an array:

  ```
  <cfset EmailListArray=ListToArray(EmailList)>
  ```

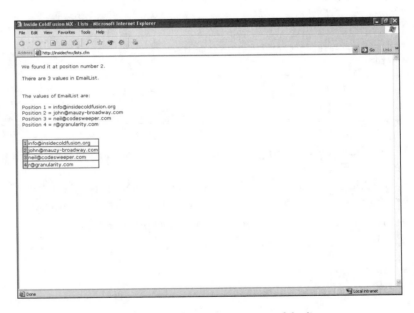

Figure 7.4 Displaying the contents of the list.

The list could, of course, go on and on, but these are the most commonly used list functions. At this point, let's move on to our next complex data type—the array.

Arrays

An array is an arrangement of memory elements in one or more planes. A ColdFusion array object stores indexed values. Each element in the array has a number assigned to it that is referred to as its index. ColdFusion arrays can have one or more dimensions or planes.

Arrays with a single dimension resemble a column of values (see Figure 7.5). Multidimensional arrays resemble a complex spreadsheet (see Figure 7.6).

Figure 7.5 One-dimensional array.

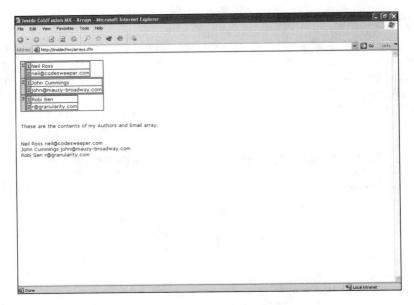

Figure 7.6 Multidimensional array.

You'll see the same kind of layout for your arrays when you use the CFDUMP tag to view their contents.

You should remember the following about ColdFusion arrays:

- ColdFusion arrays are limited to three dimensions.
- ColdFusion array indexes start at 1.
- ColdFusion array sizes can be reset after creation.
- Elements can be added or deleted from ColdFusion arrays.

Creating an Array

When you create an array within ColdFusion code, you are "initializing" the array. This is a common term in computer programming. To initialize an array in ColdFusion, you use the ArrayNew() function, as shown in the following code:

```
<cfset a_Authors=ArrayNew(1)>
```

The `ArrayNew()` function takes a single argument: a numeric value that sets the dimensions of the new array. As such, the example in the preceding code snippet would initialize a new array with a single dimension. In contrast, the following code snippets initialize two- and three-dimensional arrays, respectively:

```
<cfset a_AuthorAndEmail=ArrayNew(2)>
<cfset a_AuthorData=ArrayNew(3)>
```

Adding Elements to an Array

When you initialize your ColdFusion array, it contains no data. You must fill the array with useful bits of information. One way to add elements to an array is with the simple and familiar `CFSET` call:

```
<cfset a_Authors[1]="Neil Ross">
<cfset a_Authors[2]="John Cummings">
<cfset a_Authors[3]="Robi Sen">
```

Another way to handle the addition of elements and values to your array is to use the `ArrayAppend()` function. The `ArrayAppend()` function inserts a new value at the end of the array. The basic form of the `ArrayAppend()` function call looks like this:

```
ArrayAppend(arrayname, "new value")
```

Examine the following code:

```
<cfset tempvar=ArrayAppend(a_Authors, "Just Kidding")>
```

As we add more and more information to the array, it expands to accept the new data. You should always start filling your array with the first element—element 1—and continue without leaving gaps. ColdFusion sees gaps as undefined array elements and might throw errors in your application. In addition, you can do any sorting of the data in your array later. Adding elements to multidimensional arrays is not much different:

```
<cfset a_AuthorAndEmail[1][1]="Neil Ross">
<cfset a_AuthorAndEmail[1][2]="neil@codesweeper.com">
<cfset a_AuthorAndEmail[2][1]="John Cummings">
<cfset a_AuthorAndEmail[2][2]="john@mauzy-broadway.com">
<cfset a_AuthorAndEmail[3][1]="Robi Sen">
<cfset a_AuthorAndEmail[3][2]="r@granularity.com">
```

Note

You cannot append elements and values to a multidimensional array using the `ArrayAppend()` function.

Before we move headlong into creating output loops for array contents, take a moment to verify that the contents of your array are as you expect them to be. In addition, you should inspect the array structure by calling the CFDUMP tag, as shown in the following code:

```
<cfdump var="#a_AuthorAndEmail#">
```

Outputting an Array

You can output the values held in an array by creating a loop over each element in that array. You use, of course, the CFLOOP and CFOUTPUT tags in combination to output the called variables in a position that corresponds to each loop index.

Let's begin with an easy example. First, working with the a_Authors array, you can create a loop for each element in the array with CFLOOP. You call the CFOUTPUT tag within the CFLOOP tag itself. The result is that CFOUTPUT is performed once for each item in the array, based on the index number of the loop. In an index loop, the index of the loop represents a whole number that correlates to the loop count:

```
<cfloop index="i" from="1" to="#ArrayLen(a_Authors)#">
        <cfoutput>#a_Authors[i]#<br></cfoutput>
</cfloop>
```

Now let's take a look at the preceding code in action (see Listing 7.6).

Listing 7.6   **Create the *a_Authors* Array and the Output Loop**

```
<html>
<head>
        <title>Inside ColdFusion MX - Arrays</title>
</head>
<body>
<table>
    <tr>
        <td>
            <cfsetting enablecfoutputonly="Yes">
                <cfset a_AuthorAndEmail=ArrayNew(2)>
                <cfset a_AuthorAndEmail[1][1]="Neil Ross">
                <cfset a_AuthorAndEmail[1][2]="neil@codesweeper.com">
                <cfset a_AuthorAndEmail[2][1]="John Cummings">
                <cfset a_AuthorAndEmail[2][2]="john@mauzy-broadway.com">
                <cfset a_AuthorAndEmail[3][1]="Robi Sen">
                <cfset a_AuthorAndEmail[3][2]="r@granularity.com">
```

```
                    <cfsetting enablecfoutputonly="No">
                    These are the contents of my Authors and Email array:
                    <br>
                    <br>
                    <cfloop index="author" from="1" to="#ArrayLen(a_AuthorAndEmail)#">
                        <cfloop index="email" from="1"
to="#ArrayLen(a_AuthorAndEmail[author])#">
                            <cfoutput>#a_AuthorAndEmail[author][email]#</cfoutput>
                        </cfloop><br>
                    </cfloop>
                </td>
            </tr>
        </table>
        </body>
        </html>
```

The output should appear as shown in Figure 7.7.

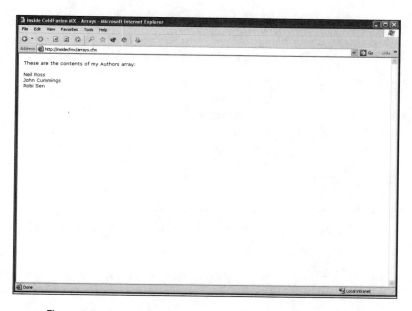

Figure 7.7   Simple display of the contents of the a_Authors array.

Outputting a two-dimensional array is a bit different, but only in respect to how the second dimension is handled. To output the elements from both dimensions, you use two CFLOOP tags. One is nested within the other and the CFOUTPUT tag is inside the inner loop. Don't let it scare you though. It's this simple:

```
<cfloop>
    <cfloop>
        <cfoutput></cfoutput>
    </cfloop>
</cfloop>
```

Of course, you can also output a three-dimensional array. The technique that we've used for the one- and two-dimensional arrays would be followed with an additional nested CFLOOP.

Array Functions

As with queries and lists, ColdFusion has different native functions that enable you to manipulate arrays—from sorting to clearing to resizing. The following array functions are available to ColdFusion developers:

ArrayAppend	ArrayIsEmpty	ArrayPrepend
ArraySwap	ArrayAvg	ArrayLen
ArrayResize	ArrayToList	ArrayClear
ArrayMax	ArraySet	IsArray
ArrayDeleteAt	ArrayMin	ArraySort
ListToArray	ArrayInsertAt	ArrayNew
ArraySum		

In addition, you should know about the following useful array functions:

- **ArrayPrepend().** Adds a value to the beginning of your array:

  ```
  <cfset tmp=ArrayPrepend(a_Authors, "Just Kidding")>
  ```

- **IsArray().** Checks whether the variable is an array and returns **Yes** or **No**:

  ```
  <cfset tmp=IsArray(a_Authors)>
  ```

- **ArrayDeleteAt().** Deletes the specified element in the array and shifts the remaining array elements to fill the deleted index:

  ```
  <cfset tmp=ArrayDeleteAt(a_Authors, 3)>
  ```

- **ArrayClear().** Removes all the data from the array:

  ```
  <cfset tmp=ArrayClear(a_Authors)>
  ```

Structures

Structures are similar to the data types that we've discussed to this point, and they are quite similar to arrays. The main difference is that a value within a structure is not identified by an index. However, it can be called by name.

ColdFusion structures utilize familiar dot notation, such as `MyStructure.Name`, to identify a structure name and key. This type of identification is much more manageable in an application setting where you need to be able to associate a variable name with its value. Believe me, you can easily get lost in the index numbers and values of an array.

One structure that is typical to ColdFusion applications is the form. When you submit a form, you pass key/value pairs to the action page. The form structure keys are represented by the form control names and the values are those associated with each form control. These values are stored in a structure called *form*. I'm sure that you're familiar with outputting variables such as *form.name*, *form.address*, and *form.email*. You might not have known it, but you were outputting values from a structure.

Creating a Structure

It's easy to create a structure in ColdFusion. Structures are created by using the `StructNew()` function. The function call does not require any additional parameters. Let's stay with our authors and email theme for a bit longer and try the following code:

```
<cfset st_AuthorData=StructNew()>
```

There's nothing more to it than that.

Adding Elements to a Structure

After you have created a structure, it remains empty until you add data to it. There are different ways to add data to a structure. These methods vary in the syntax technique that is used:

- **Dot notation syntax.** This is probably the easiest notation method to read. You simply refer to the structure name and then to the key name:

  ```
  <cfset st_AuthorData.FullName="Neil Ross">
  ```

- **Function syntax.** Using the `StructInsert()` function, you can add keys and values to the specified structure. One advantage of this method is that it does not enable you to overwrite an existing key/value pair without adding additional parameters to the function call:

  ```
  <cfset tmp=StructInsert(st_AuthorData, "Email", "neil@codesweeper.com")>
  ```

- **Associative array syntax.** ColdFusion structures are sometime referred to as associative arrays. The syntax is similar to a reference to an array, with the exception that the index number is replaced with a reference to the key name string:

```
<cfset st_AuthorData["City"]="Mechanicsburg">
```

Let's look at some real code that shows what you've learned so far about structures and that employs each method of adding data:

```
<cfset st_AuthorData=StructNew()>
<cfset st_AuthorData.FullName="Neil Ross">
<cfset tmp=StructInsert(st_AuthorData, "Email", "neil@codesweeper.com")>
<cfset st_AuthorData["City"]="Mechanicsburg">
```

Now let's dump this structure and check out how it differs from an array or query object:

```
<cfdump var="#st_AuthorData#">
```

Outputting a Structure

Outputting a structure key value is simple. You just use the dot notation that we looked at earlier to specify the structure and key:

```
Name: <cfoutput>#st_AuthorData.FullName#</cfoutput>
```

Now let's put it all together in Listing 7.7 and see what you've learned:

Listing 7.7 **Outputting *AuthorData* Structure**

```
<html>
<head>
    <title>Inside ColdFusion MX - Structures</title>
</head>
<body>
<table>
    <tr>
        <td>
        <!--- Create the structure --->
            <cfset st_AuthorData=StructNew()>
        <!--- Set structure key/value pairs --->
            <cfset st_AuthorData.FullName="Neil Ross">
            <cfset st_AuthorData.Email="neil@codesweeper.com">
            <cfset st_AuthorData.City="Mechanicsburg">
            <cfset st_AuthorData.State="Pennsylvania">
            <cfset st_AuthorData.FavoriteTeam="Arkansas Razorbacks">
        <!--- Dump the structure because we can --->
            <cfdump var="#st_AuthorData#">
```

```
                    <br>
                    <br>
            <!--- Output the structure --->
                <cfoutput>
                    The author's name is: #st_AuthorData.FullName#<br>
                    He can be reached by email at: #st_AuthorData.Email#<br>
                    He currently resides in: #st_AuthorData.City#,
#st_AuthorData.State#<br>
                        His favorite team is: #st_AuthorData.FavoriteTeam#
                </cfoutput>
            </td>
      </tr>
</table>
</body>
</html>
```

Figure 7.8 shows what the template generates in a browser.

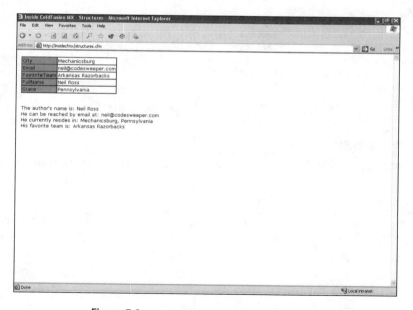

Figure 7.8   AuthorData structure in a browser.

If you need to loop through the entire structure and output all the key values, you'll want to code a collection loop. A collection loop loops over a component object model (COM) collection or a ColdFusion structure. It's similar to the simple index loop that we did for the one-dimensional array. Let's take a look at the syntax:

```
<cfloop collection="structure_name" item="key">
    <cfoutput>code code code</cfoutput>
</cfloop>
```

The collection attribute names the structure through which your code will loop. The item attribute identifies the variable that holds the values, or keys of the structure, through which you want to loop. Examine the following code, which demonstrates the use of a collection loop to output the key/value pairs in the st_AuthorData structure:

```
<cfset st_AuthorData=StructNew()>
<cfset st_AuthorData.FullName="Neil Ross">
<cfset st_AuthorData.Email="neil@codesweeper.com">
<cfset st_AuthorData.City="Mechanicsburg">
<cfloop collection="#st_AuthorData#" item="key">
    <cfoutput>
           #key# - #StructFind(st_AuthorData,key)#
    </cfoutput><br>
</cfloop>
```

Structure Functions

Once again, ColdFusion gives us a number of native functions to manipulate our structures:

StructNew	IsStruct	StructClear
Duplicate	StructCount	StructGet
StructKeyList	StructDelete	StructInsert
StructAppend	StructFind	StructIsEmpty
StructSort	StructFindKey	StructKeyArray
StructUpdate	StructCopy	StructFindValue
StructKeyExists		

Popular structure functions include the following:

- **IsStruct().** Checks whether the variable is a structure and returns **Yes** or **No**:

  ```
  <cfset tmp=IsStruct(st_AuthorData)>
  ```

- **StructClear()**. Removes all the data from the structure, but does not delete it:

  ```
  <cfset StructClear(st_AuthorData)>
  ```

- **StructDelete()**. Deletes the specified key from the specified structure. This function requires that you provide the structure name and key name:

  ```
  <cfset StructDelete(st_AuthorData, "City">
  ```

- **StructFind()**. Returns the value of the specified structure key:

  ```
  <cfset keyvalue=StructFind(st_AuthorData, "Email")>
  ```

If you're going to be using structures in your ColdFusion applications, consider all the structure functions and put together a dummy structure to run tests, as we've done in the preceding example.

Summary

To ColdFusion users who are new to application development and who don't have some type of programming background, complex data types, such as arrays and structures, can be a daunting topic to learn. Hopefully, this chapter has exposed the simplicity of these variables and has enabled you to see how you can easily incorporate them into your own applications.

Each variable type discussed has associated ColdFusion functions to enable you to create, manipulate, and delete variables. Remember that the CFDUMP tag is your friend and that you can use it liberally within your application to help with code debugging and troubleshooting.

Application Framework

8

ONE OF THE BIGGEST PROBLEMS THAT WEB APPLICATION developers face is the problem of state. State could be described as the capability of the web application to remember information, such as who is currently using the application and what he or she is doing. The application might also need to remember not only what each user was doing a few seconds ago, but also what he or she was doing a few weeks or months ago.

Developers often build their applications to remember user preferences, to analyze site traversal patterns, to analyze trends and site statistics, or to deliver customized content to each user.

To accomplish any of these things, developers need to understand the statelessness of the web. They also need to understand the features to which ColdFusion gives them access to help them conquer this problem.

In this chapter, we discuss the statelessness of web applications. We take a look at what is known as the Web Application Framework within ColdFusion. We also take a look at various types of ColdFusion variables that help us to develop sites that can remember information, maintain state, and help us to improve the overall user experience.

Web Statelessness

The problem with maintaining state is that the web is an essentially stateless environment. Each time you click a button and proceed to a new page, your request is totally separate from the previous request.

Much of the time, application developers work to build applications that "remember" things about previous user requests. A user who is still logged in to the application could produce those requests, but this "recall" could extend to previous visits to the application that took place months ago.

ColdFusion provides different variable types to help developers overcome the problem of maintaining session state.

Locking Shared Variable Access

Before entering a discussion of the variables that are used to maintain session state, let's first discuss a concept that too many developers have ignored in past versions of ColdFusion. The concept is that of locking access to shared memory variables.

When we say "shared memory variables," we are referring to application-, session-, and server-scoped variables. These variables are stored as structures in the memory of the ColdFusion Server. Because ColdFusion is a multi-threaded application server, these memory structures can be subject to multiple simultaneous requests.

These simultaneous requests access the memory structures to read the variable values or to write new values to them. When a new value is written to the memory structure, the structure might change and any other request to the same variable might experience problems. These errors might lead to memory corruption or to crashes in certain ColdFusion processes.

Memory corruption can lead to memory leaks and server instability. Watch out for the following if you suspect memory corruption in your ColdFusion Server:

- ColdFusion P-code errors
- ColdFusion Server crashes
- Unexpected variable evaluation
- Runaway ColdFusion process memory
- General operating system (OS) instability

ColdFusion gives us a method of locking access to these variables for a period of time. In effect, it enables us to single-thread-access certain variables for the purpose of reading the variable values or writing new ones.

Using *CFLOCK*

ColdFusion enables us to wrap references to shared scope variables with a call to the CFLOCK tag. The CFLOCK tag enables us to specify whether any of the shared scope variable values will be evaluated or written to.

The basic format of the CFLOCK call looks like this:

```
<cflock scope="scope" type="type" timeout="seconds">
```

Table 8.1 provides a description of the attributes used in the call.

Table 8.1 *CFLOCK* Call Attributes

Attribute	Explanation
scope	Specifies whether the scope of the variable to be locked is of the application, session, or server scope.
type	readonly is used when you are reading variable values. exclusive is used when you are setting variable values.
timeout	Number of seconds to hold the lock.

The CFLOCK tag requires an end tag. The code that you want to lock access to should be encapsulated by the CFLOCK tag call:

```
<cflock scope="session" type="readonly" timeout="10">
    <cfset variables.CurrentUser=session.CurrentUser>
</cflock>
```

Many developers are unsure of when to lock their code with a CFLOCK call. ColdFusion documentation tells us that we should use a CFLOCK tag in the following circumstances:

- Using CFLOCK around ColdFusion Markup Language (CFML) constructs that modify shared data ensures that the modifications occur sequentially, not concurrently.

- Using CFLOCK around file manipulation constructs can guarantee that file updates do not fail due to files being open for writing by other applications or ColdFusion tags.

- Using CFLOCK around CFX invocations can guarantee that CFXs that are not implemented in a thread-safe manner can be safely invoked by ColdFusion. This usually only applies to CFXs developed in C++ using CFAPI. A C++ CFX that maintains and manipulates shared (global) data structures must be made thread-safe to safely work with ColdFusion. However, writing thread-safe C++ CFXs requires advanced knowledge.

In the preceding example, we can see that the CFLOCK call wraps totally around the evaluation of the session.currentuser variable. It is more efficient to use a piece of code like this to reset the scope of the currentuser variable from session to local scope to avoid the necessity of coding CFLOCK tags every time the variable is accessed.

The scope attribute enables us to specify the variable scope to which our variable belongs. As seen in Table 8.1, the three variable scopes stored in memory are application, server, and session. When you set a lock on a variable, do not mix in variables of a different scope. This can cause errors to occur.

```
<cflock scope="application" type="readonly" timeout="10">
    <cfset variables.dsn=application.dsn>
     <cfset session.sessionuser=form.userid>
</cflock>
```

In the previous example, you can see that we are evaluating an application-scoped variable with a read-only lock; that's okay, but throwing in the set on the value of the session variable causes the code to throw an error. The best way to accomplish both operations is as follows:

```
<cflock scope="application" type="readonly" timeout="10">
   <cfset variables.dsn=application.dsn>
</cflock>

<cflock scope="session" type="exclusive" timeout="10">
   <cfset session.sessionuser=form.userid>
</cflock>
```

The two main variations on the CFLOCK tag deal with the type of lock that is created. Those variations of the type attribute are as follows:

- **Exclusive.** Single threads access the memory location of a variable for the purpose of setting the value of that variable.

- **ReadOnly.** Keeps the variable from having an exclusive lock established while enabling concurrent read access to the variable. If a user tries to establish an exclusive lock, he or she must wait for all read-only locks to expire.

As seen in Table 8.1, an exclusive lock is used for setting the value of variables. Now, let's take a look at each variation of CFLOCK:

- Application scope

  ```
  <cflock scope="application" type="readonly" timeout="10">
     <cfset variables.dsn=application.dsn>
  </cflock>
  <cflock scope="application" type="exclusive" timeout="10">
  ```

```
    <cfset application.dsn="insidecoldfusionmx_data">
</cflock>
```

- Session scope

```
<cflock scope="session" type="readonly" timeout="10">
  <cfset variables.userid=session.userid>
</cflock>
<cflock scope="session" type="exclusive" timeout="10">
  <cfset session.sessionuser=form.userid>
</cflock>
```

- Server scope

```
<cflock scope="server" type="readonly" timeout="10">
  <cfset variables.servername=server.servername>
</cflock>
<cflock scope="server" type="exclusive" timeout="10">
  <cfset server.servername="CFMXXP">
</cflock>
```

When to Lock

In short, always lock access to shared-scope variables. Too many developers have made the mistake of overlooking the necessity of locking access to these variables and have paid the price with unstable servers, crashing applications, and lost revenue. There is never an occasion when you should leave access to these variable scopes unlocked.

I know, maybe you're saying to yourself, "I only have three variables that I access in the entire application. How is this problem going to affect me? I don't have the traffic or user load required to bring down my server." Of course, all your buddies clap, "Good answer. Good answer." Well, that's your third strike and just like on *Family Feud*, you don't win the prize.

There also is no formula to when memory corruption occurs. I have seen applications that showed the first signs of instability with only one user traversing the application and others that seemed fine with more than one hundred users. However, when they crash, they all crash hard, regardless of load or how long it took to get them to the point that they crashed.

ColdFusion Lock Checking

In your ColdFusion Administrator, you have a section on locking. This section gives you the opportunity to change your lock settings for application, session, and server variable scopes. In your development environment, you should turn on the full lock checking option for each variable scope listed.

This ensures that if you have not properly locked variables, an error is returned to your browser during testing.

Application Framework

ColdFusion provides its developers with a tool that helps them tie together a group of templates into one or more applications. This tool is called the Web Application Framework.

The Web Application Framework is designed with four basic concepts in mind:

- Enabling the use of applicationwide settings and functions
- Enabling custom error handling throughout the application
- Providing for the integration of web server security
- Enabling the use of variable scopes, including application, client, server, and session

Applicationwide Settings

The Web Application Framework enables the use of applicationwide settings by enabling developers to create two special templates within the ColdFusion application. These templates make it possible for chunks of code to be "included" in each template that is requested. These settings might range from the establishment of variable values on each template to the inclusion of look and feel elements. It also enables them to include templates that contain user-defined function libraries.

The two special templates enable developers to execute common code before and after each page request. These templates are as follows:

- `Application.cfm`
- `OnRequestEnd.cfm`

It is these two templates that maintain and control the Web Application Framework.

Application.cfm

The `Application.cfm` template is a special template within ColdFusion applications. The very name of the template has special significance in a ColdFusion application and should always start with a capital "A." This is especially important on Linux or UNIX installations. The `Application.cfm` template should be placed in the root directory of your application. It is a best practice that you always capitalize the "A" in Application.cfm because it enables your code to be used in multiple environments without modification.

When any ColdFusion template is requested, ColdFusion checks the directory where that template is located for an Application.cfm template. If it finds one, it executes the Application.cfm prior to the execution of the requested template. Essentially, ColdFusion automatically processes a CFINCLUDE of the Application.cfm into the top of the requested template. If ColdFusion does not find an Application.cfm file in that directory, it begins to look up the directory tree, all the way to the root directory, until it finds an Application.cfm. If it does not find one, no error occurs. If it does find one, it includes it in the requested template as previously described.

The significance of this is that you can use one Application.cfm file throughout your application to set variables that might be needed in every template. One of the most common variables used in a ColdFusion application might be the datasource name.

It also means, of course, that you can have multiple Application.cfm templates throughout your directory structure. Templates within any given directory execute only the Application.cfm file that resides in the same directory. A very common use of this type of structure is application login. For example, you want users of your application to log in so that you can keep some record of who logs on when. Thus, you create a bit of conditional logic in your root directory Application.cfm:

```
<cflock scope="session" type="readonly" timeout="10">
   <cfif IsDefined("session.LoggedIn")>
      <cfset request.LoggedIn=session.LoggedIn>
     </cfif>
</cflock>
<cfif NOT IsDefined("request.LoggedIn")>
   <cflocation url="/login/index.cfm">
</cfif>
```

Thus, you create a login directory and a login page. Within that login directory, you create an Application.cfm template so that the code that we wrote in our root-level Application.cfm (shown previously) does not execute. If this code does execute, you experience an endless loop because the CFIF statement runs and then executes the CFLOCATION tag.

ColdFusion processes from the top of the template, down. Therefore, because the Application.cfm template executes first, any variables that you set or code execute prior to the code that resides in the requested template.

One of the original intentions for creating the Application.cfm template and its special characteristics was to enable developers to create sites and applications with a common header. However, in our discussion of

Application.cfm, we've seen how you could have an Application.cfm template in every directory throughout your directory structure. Using the Application.cfm as a "header" template totally defeats the purpose of writing reusable code. It would mean that you'd have to maintain code in each Application.cfm template throughout your application.

Use your Application.cfm templates to execute the following types of code:

- Variables
- UDF library templates
- Conditional logic

The following types of code should not be present in your Application.cfm templates:

- Database queries or stored procedure calls
- Presentation-tier code, such as Hypertext Markup Language (HTML) tables, images, or form elements

OnRequestEnd.cfm

The OnRequestEnd.cfm template serves a purpose similar to that of Application.cfm. However, when it is present, it executes at the end of each template request. The OnRequestEnd.cfm template should always have the "O", "R", and "E" capitalized. This is especially important on Linux or UNIX installations. Again, making sure that your OnRequestEnd.cfm is properly capitalized helps to ensure that you can deploy your application code in various environments.

The OnRequestEnd.cfm template must be located in the same directory as a corresponding Application.cfm and cannot execute without one. If an error occurs within a template or if a CFABORT, CFEXIT, or CFLOCATION tag is executed, the OnRequestEnd.cfm template does not execute.

Custom Error Handling

The Web Application Framework lets developers use the CFERROR tag within their applications to create custom HTML error messages when an error occurs within the application. The effect that this has on the application is that it integrates the custom look and feel of the application into the error messages themselves rather than throwing up an ugly (and sometimes cryptic) default error screen. Custom error handling also enables you to control the amount of information that the user sees about the error.

This is not the time or place for a complete discussion of custom error handling and the CFERROR tag. Refer to Chapter 9, "Error Handling," for more detailed information.

Application Security

The Web Application Framework enables developers to integrate the security of their application with that of their web server. ColdFusion Server also offers security features to control access to applications or specific pages within those applications, to a specific datasource, or to specific users. These features are accessible using the CFLOGIN, CFLOGINUSER, and CFLOGOUT tags. Refer to Chapter 17, "Common Application Development Requirements," for more detailed information.

Enabling Variable Scopes

The Web Application Framework provides ColdFusion developers with a means of enabling variable scopes that are accessible throughout the application. These scopes are the application, session, and client scopes. Before you use any of these scopes, they must be enabled by applying the CFAPPLICATION tag, which is most commonly called in the Application.cfm template.

Application Variables

Application variables are a special variable type that can be used within ColdFusion applications. Application variables could be compared with global variables in other types of application programming because after an application variable is created, it is accessible to all users of the application.

Application variables are intended to define variables and settings that remain constant throughout your entire application. It is common for datasource names to be set to the application scope.

Application variables must be referred to using the application prefix. An application variable looks like this:

```
<cflock scope="application" type="exclusive" timeout="10">
   <cfset application.DSN="ICFMX">
</cflock>
```

CFAPPLICATION Tag

To make use of application scoped variables, you must place a call to the CFAPPLICATION tag. By calling this tag, you initialize and name the application and have the capability to define other aspects of the application as well.

The CFAPPLICATION tag is typically called within the Application.cfm. It initializes the application and sets the application name. It also defines the scoping of variables within the application, enables the storage of client variables, and sets a location for the storage of those variables.

The CFAPPLICATION tag also enables the use of session variables in your ColdFusion application. Until you've enabled the use of application and session variable scopes within the CFAPPLICATION tag, you cannot use them within your application. Not only do you enable the use of application- and session-scoped variables within the CFAPPLICATION tag, but also you use it to set their timeout period.

```
<cfapplication
    name="InsideCFMX"
    sessionmanagement="Yes"
    sessiontimeout="#CreateTimeSpan("0,0,60,0")#">
```

The CreateTimeSpan() function is used to specify the timeout for the session variables within this application.

Using Application Variables

Now that you've enabled the use of application variables in your application, you can begin to use them. Because application variables are global to your application after they are set, your code should never assume that they have or have not been set. You should always test for the existence of an application variable prior to setting it. The reason is that you don't want to unnecessarily set the value of any variable that is stored in memory.

```
<cflock scope="application" type="exclusive" timeout="10">
  <cfparam name="application.dsn" default="insidecfmx">
</cflock>
```

You might have also seen the same functionality in a CFIF statement. CFPARAM is cleaner and more performance-efficient.

```
<cflock scope="application" type="exclusive" timeout="10">
    <cfif NOT IsDefined("application.dsn")>
      <cfset application.dsn="insidecfmx">
    </cfif>
</cflock>
```

Application variables, such as a datasource name, might be used over and over throughout your application. They might also be used on the same template in several places. Because application variables are shared memory variables, it makes sense to convert these variables to another variable scope prior to using them in our templates. There are two reasons for this:

- We want to avoid the practice of wrapping a CFLOCK tag around more than just a variable access.

  If we call an application-scoped variable as our datasource, we might find ourselves wrapping the CFLOCK around the entire query:

  ```
  <cflock scope="application" type="readonly" timeout="10">
  <cfquery name="AuthenticateUser" datasource=application.dsn>
  SELECT UserID
        FROM Users
        WHERE Email = '#form.email#'
                AND Password = '#form.password#'
  </cfquery>
  </cflock>
  ```

  This code is inefficient and can lead to errors if the query takes longer than the timeout on the lock.

- Creating locks over and over in a template can hurt application performance, and needed locks that are missing can lead to server instability and crashes.

  It is a better practice to set the application variables to the local scope, or better yet, the request scope:

  ```
  <cflock scope="application" type="readonly" timeout="10">
      <cfset request.dsn=application.dsn>
  </cflock>
  <cfquery name="AuthenticateUser" datasource=request.dsn>
  SELECT UserID
        FROM Users
        WHERE Email = '#form.email#'
                AND Password = '#form.password#'
  </cfquery>
  ```

The application scope is a structure. Deleting application variables is as easy as deleting any value held in a structure. You use the StructDelete() function and specify the structure name and key to be deleted:

```
<cflock scope="application" type="exclusive" timeout="10">
   <cfif NOT IsDefined("application.dsn")>
      <cfset tmp=StructDelete(application, "dsn")>
   </cfif>
</cflock>
```

As we've said, application variables are great for setting variables that stay the same throughout the application. If you want to set variables that are specific to a single user, or to a single session of that specific user, you might consider the use of session variables.

Session Variables

Session variables are persistent variables that are used to store information about a specific user session. Session variable values are stored in the ColdFusion Server memory and can therefore be accessed by any template within the ColdFusion application.

Session variables must be referred to using the session prefix. A session variable looks like this:

```
session.DSN
```

When session management is enabled within the CFAPPLICATION tag, the following session variables are created and defined uniquely for each user session:

- **Session.CFID.** Sequential numeric ID created by the ColdFusion Server for each user session
- **Session.CFToken.** A random alphanumeric string that combines with the CFID to form a unique identifier for each user session
- **Session.SessionID.** A concatenation of the application name, CFID, and the CFTOKEN, which is used to identify each user session
- **Session.URLToken.** A concatenation of CFID and CFTOKEN to be passed as a uniform resource locator (URL) parameter when the setclientcookies attribute of the CFAPPLICATION tag is set to No

Session variables are often used to hold user login information, shopping cart contents, or other session preferences. Session variables must be set with the session scope specifically defined:

```
<cflock scope="session" type="exclusive" timeout="10">
    <cfset session.UserID="U0123">
</cflock>
```

User Sessions

A user session could be defined as the requests that a single client makes to a server in the course of a visit to an application. The user session begins when he or she makes the first request and ends (theoretically) when he or she logs out of the application or when he or she closes the browser. If a user leaves the application to surf to another web site, the session has not actually ended, but it can extend until the session-identifying variables have timed out.

Session variable timeouts are set in the ColdFusion Administrator to default to 20 minutes. This means that after 20 minutes of inactivity, the user session ends. The default timeout can be overridden by creating a timeout for the session in the CFAPPLICATION tag of the Application.cfm template of the application.

New to ColdFusion MX, the ColdFusion Administrator gives us two options for session management:

- ColdFusion session management
- J2EE Servlet session management

ColdFusion session management uses two variable values to identify the session. Those variables are CFID and CFTOKEN. ColdFusion creates a space in the server's memory to hold the values of those two session variables and sets cookies on the client machine with corresponding values. It uses these to track the activity of the session. These values are combined with the application name to form a session ID.

J2EE session management uses a user/session identifier that is created for every session. That identifier is called the jsessionid. J2EE session management should be used if you will be calling CFML templates, Java Server Pages (JSP) pages, or Java Servlets within the same application.

Understanding Session Variables

Session variables, as their name implies, exist for the life of the user session. You might think that would mean that they exist until the user logs off or closes his or her browser. Well, in a perfect world that might be true, but as we know, this is not such a world.

Session variables are variables that relate to a specific user session. They are not available across sessions and are not available to other users. Session variables are great for tracking a logged-in user. They are also great for setting a simple value that identifies that he or she is logged in. It can also hold his or her user ID or email address.

Session variables are not perfect, however. They are not the answer to all your problems. One of the biggest drawbacks to session variables is that because they are stored in the memory of the server that created them, using session variables within an application that is deployed in a clustered environment often does not work.

The problem is that when a user logs in to a specific server in your cluster, the session variable is set in the server memory and a corresponding cookie is sent to the client machine. If a load gets heavy on the server into which the user logged, their subsequent requests might be moved to a server with a lesser load. This results in the loss of user information, preferences, and other session information.

The only remedy for this situation is to employ "sticky sessions" after a user logs in. This can be accomplished programmatically by specifying the server into which the user is logged in the URL for any subsequent requests. More often, however, sticky sessions are enabled within the load-balancing solution. That's a discussion for another chapter.

Enabling Session Variables

There are two basic steps to enabling the use of session variables in your application. As mentioned, the `sessionmanagement` attribute of the `CFAPPLICATION` tag must be set to `YES` to use session variables. Within the ColdFusion Administrator, you must also enable the use of session variables within the Memory Variables section. By default, session variables are enabled in ColdFusion MX.

Using Session Variables

We've already defined a user session as starting with a first request to the application. When that first request is made, ColdFusion creates several session variables. If you are using ColdFusion session management, ColdFusion creates `CFID`, `CFToken`, `SessionID`, and `URLToken`. If you have enabled J2EE session management, ColdFusion creates `SessionID` and `URLToken`.

Session variables are stored in server memory and, as such, are lost whenever that server is restarted. Therefore, it makes the most sense to use session variables to remember information pertaining to the current user session only. When that session ends, the information can be removed from the server memory without interrupting the user's visit to the application.

Let's take a look at an example of code from an application that requires a login. The code is checking for the existence of a session variable called `Session.LoggedIn`.

```
<!-------------
    Template: Login.cfm
    Author: Neil Ross (neil@codesweeper.com)
    Date: 03/01/2002
    Sample simple login page.
------------->
```

```
<form name="loginform" action="authenticate.cfm" method="post">
<table>
<cfif IsDefined("url.message")>
  <tr>
    <td colspan="2"><cfoutput>#url.message#</cfoutput></td>
  </tr>
</cfif>
  <tr>
    <td colspan="2">
      Please provide your email address and password below.
    </td>
  </tr>
  <tr>
    <td>Email: </td>
    <td><input name="email" type="text"></td>
  </tr>
  <tr>
        <td>Password: </td>
      <td><input name="password" type="password"></td>
  </tr>
  <tr>
    <td></td>
    <td><input type="submit" value="Log In"></td>
  </tr>
</table>
</form>
```

The authentication template might look something like this:

```
<!------------
      Template: Authenticate.cfm
      Author: Neil Ross (neil@codesweeper.com)
      Date: 03/01/2002
      Sample login authentication page which sets
       a session variable with a value of the email address.
-------------->
<cfif IsDefined("form.email") AND form.email IS NOT "" AND IsDefined("form.password") AND
form.password is not "">
<cfquery name="AuthenticateUser" datasource=request.dsn>
     SELECT UserID FROM Users
     WHERE Email = '#form.email#'
         AND Password = '#form.password#'
</cfquery>
     <cfif AuthenticateUser.RecordCount IS 1>
     <cflock scope="session" type="exclusive" timeout="10">
         <cfset session.CurrentUser=form.email>
     </cflock>
     <cfset variables.WelcomeMessage="Welcome to InsideColdFusionMX.com.">
     <cflocation url="/index.cfm?Message=#URLEncodedFormat(variables.WelcomeMessage)#">
<cfelse>
     <cfset variables.FailureMessage="Your username or password is incorrect. Please
try to log in again.">
```

```
        <cflocation url="login.cfm?Message=# URLEncodedFormat(variables.FailureMessage)#">
</cfif>
</cfif>
```

We can see from the example above that session variables are created using a simple CFSET call:

```
<cflock scope="session" type="exclusive" timeout="10">
  <cfset session.CurrentUser=form.email>
</cflock>
```

They can also be created using the CFPARAM tag:

```
<cflock scope="session" type="exclusive" timeout="10">
<cfparam name="session.CurrentUser" default="#form.email#">
</cflock>
```

The CFPARAM tag also effectively checks for the existence of the variable named prior to setting it and sets it only if the variable does not exist.

Similarly, a session variable can be deleted by using a simple and familiar structure call:

```
<cflock scope="Session" type="Exclusive" timeout="10">
  <cfset temp=StructDelete(Session, "CurrentUser")>
</cflock>
```

Ending a User Session

We said earlier that a user's session ends when he or she stops making requests to the application. However, it is difficult for the application to tell whether the user has finished making requests or if he or she is simply pausing. We also know that the session ends when the user has remained inactive for a period equal to or greater than the established session timeout.

If you are using J2EE session management, the session and all the associated session variables should be deleted when the user closes the browser. If you're using ColdFusion session management, the variables and their values continue to persist in the server memory until they have timed out or have been manually deleted.

You might want to end the user session programmatically. This might be through the user clicking a logout link somewhere within the application display. Try the code below to manually end the session:

```
<cflock scope="Session" type="Exclusive" timeout="10">
  <cfset temp=StructClear(Session)>
</cflock>
```

Well, this works great if the user actually clicks the link to log out. Most users, however, simply close the browser, so we have to build our applications to fit this scenario.

The session variables that identify the session are, of course, CFID and CFToken. These values are stored in the ColdFusion Server's memory. They are also set as cookies on the client machine. When ColdFusion checks the values in memory against the cookies on the client machine and does not find a match, the session is officially ended. The cookies that ColdFusion sets on the client machine do not expire when the browser is closed. They are persistent. For this reason, we often find that our session is still open even after we've closed our browser and restarted it.

To end the session when the user closes his or her browser, we must reset the expiration on the CFID and CFTOKEN cookies. The following code shows you how to do just that by setting the existing CFID and CFTOKEN values to local variables and then resetting the cookies:

```
<cfif IsDefined("cookie.CFID") AND IsDefined("cookie.CFToken">
  <cfset variables.CFID=cookie.CFID>
  <cfset variables.CFToken=cookie.CFToken>
  <cfcookie name="CFID" value=variables.CFID>
  <cfcookie name="CFToken" value=variables.CFToken>
</cfif>
```

> **Note**
>
> This is an effective solution, but only when all browsers that share those session attributes are closed. Thus, the user must close the active browser session and any child sessions that were spawned after the session variables were set.

Server Variables

Server variables are a type of persistent variable. Server variables are specific to the server on which they are created and are stored in that server's random-access memory (RAM) memory.

As with our other variables types that are stored in memory, creating or reading server variables from memory can lead to memory corruption and server instability. To access server variables, you should properly apply a CFLOCK tag around the variable access.

As mentioned, server variables are persistent, but they are also specific to the server on which they are set and exist until the ColdFusion Server is restarted, unless they are specifically deleted from the structure.

To access the server structure, use the CFDUMP tag, as follows:

```
<cfdump var="#server#">
```

There are different predefined server variables that refer to the ColdFusion installation on the server and to the server's OS. They are listed in Table 8.2.

Table 8.2 **Predefined Server Variables**

Variable Name	Description
Server.ColdFusion.Expiration	Empty if ColdFusion is a nonexpiring version. Contains an expiration date/time if it is an expiring license.
Server.ColdFusion.ProductLevel	Description of product license; Enterprise, Professional, or Developer.
Server.ColdFusion.ProductName	Name of ColdFusion product.
Server.ColdFusion.RootDir	Product installation directory.
Server.ColdFusion.SerialNumber	Serial number of the ColdFusion installation.
Server.ColdFusion.SupportedLocales	Comma-delimited list of languages supported by the current ColdFusion installation.
Server.OS.AdditionalInformation	Additional information about the OS installation.
Server.OS.Arch	OS architectural model.
Server.OS.BuildNumber	Build number of the OS installation.
Server.OS.Name	Name of the OS installation.
Server.OS.Version	OS installation version number.

Cookies

We are all familiar with the use of cookies within web sites and web applications. They are used for tasks such as identifying users when they return to use your application. In fact, a simple bug-reporting application that we recently wrote uses a cookie to remember the test user's email address and to prefill part of the login form.

Cookies are not unique to ColdFusion applications. Cookies have been around for a long time and were first introduced by Netscape for use in their Navigator web browser. Since then, not much has changed about cookies, but their integration into web browser software is all but universal.

Understanding Cookies

As we begin our discussion of the use of cookies within web applications, we should first dispel a few of the myths regarding the use of cookies. You probably remember several years ago, during the height of the cookie scare, that everyone and his brother were upset about the evil cookies that had been placed on their computers and that were exporting vital information about them and the contents of their hard drive. Many people flat-out refused to accept cookies. Some still do.

Well, cookies are not the gremlins that they were made out to be. They are neat little variables that we can create and store on the client computer to help streamline the experience of our application's users. They are not dangerous. They can, however, if used improperly, expose guarded information to potential attack.

Cookies are variables that are stored on a client computer. They can store values as strings. They are sent to the server with every page request. They are read-only by the domain that set them and are available to every requested page within that domain. You can, however, specify individual pages where the cookie is available. Cookies exist on the client machine as simple text strings. For that reason, information such as passwords and credit card numbers should never be stored in a cookie.

Using Cookies

Cookies can be set and read by ColdFusion. ColdFusion uses the CFCOOKIE tag to create cookies. The CFCOOKIE tag generally look like this:

```
<cfcookie name="Email" value="neil@codesweeper.com">
```

The only required attribute of the CFCOOKIE tag is the name attribute.

Before you decide to use cookies in your application, keep the following things in mind:

- You cannot set cookies for users who choose not to accept cookies or have cookies disabled.

- Some browsers limit the number of cookies that can be stored on a client.

- ColdFusion limits the size of a cookie to 4KB.

- You cannot use the CFCOOKIE tag to create a cookie within a template that also executes a CFLOCATION tag.

Let's work this into a bit of code that we mentioned earlier: the bug-tracking application login. I use a `CFIF` statement to test for the existence of a cookie on the client machine and, if present, prefill the email text input in the form:

```
<!-------------
    Template: Login.cfm
        Author: Neil Ross (neil@codesweeper.com)
        Date: 03/01/2002
        Sample login page with cookie evaluation
        to pre-fill the user email address.
------------->
<form name="loginform" action="authenticate.cfm" method="post">
<table>
  <tr>
    <td colspan="2">Please provide your email address and password below.</td>
  </tr>
  <tr>
    <td>Email: </td>
    <td>
      <input name="email" type="text" value="<cfif
IsDefined("cookie.email")><cfoutput>#cookie.email#</cfoutput></cfif>">
    </td>
  </tr>
<tr>
  <td>Password: </td>
  <td><input name="password" type="password"></td>
</tr>
<tr>
  <td colspan="2"><input type="submit" value="Log In"></td>
</tr>
</table>
</form>
```

Let's look at how we can make use of cookies on the authentication page:

```
<!-------------
    Template: Authenticate.cfm
        Author: Neil Ross (neil@codesweeper.com)
        Date: 03/01/2002
        Sample login authentication page which sets
        a cookie with a value of the user's email address.
------------->
<cfif IsDefined("form.email") AND form.email IS NOT "" AND IsDefined("form.password") AND
form.password is not "">
<cfquery name="AuthenticateUser" datasource=request.dsn>
    SELECT UserID
    FROM Users
    WHERE Email = '#form.email#'
        AND Password = '#form.password#'
</cfquery>
  <cfif AuthenticateUser.RecordCount IS 1>
    <cfcookie name="Email" value="#form.email#">
```

```
    Thanks for visiting, click <a href="../index.cfm">here</a> to go to the home page.
  <cfelse>
    Your username or password is incorrect. Please click <a href="login.cfm">here</a>
to try to log in again.
  </cfif>
</cfif>
```

We don't like to leave the user on this page and we've discussed the fact that you cannot execute a CFLOCATION tag in the same template that you set a cookie, so you can employ a bit of JavaScript to relocate the document. Try this:

```
<script language="JavaScript">
    document.location = "../index.cfm";
</script>
```

We could also use the CFHEADER tag to accomplish the same thing:

```
<cfset variables.redirectURL="../index.cfm">
<cfheader statuscode="302" statustext="Object Moved">
<cfheader name="location" value="#variables.redirectURL#">
```

Treat cookies just like any other variable when you evaluate them. Remember that cookies are stored on the client machine, not in your server memory; so when you access a cookie value, you do not need to use the CFLOCK tag.

Client Variables

Client variables are a great variable scope to use for persistent application variables. Client variables might be the best choice for your application. Things that you need to consider when deciding on which variable type to use for your application include the following:

- Are there any web-browser version issues or user limitations?
- Do you want to risk server stability?
- Does your application currently need to be deployed across a clustered environment or might it be in the future?

One of the greatest advantages of client variables is that they are not stored in the server memory, so we don't have to worry about memory corruption issues. Client variables can be stored in any of three places:

- In the web server's registry
- In cookies
- In a database (with or without cookies)

Understanding Client Variables

Client variables are persistent variables that you can use in your ColdFusion application to keep track of user variable values as that user moves from page to page within the application. Each user is tagged with a unique CFID/CFTOKEN combination. Depending on how you choose to implement client variables, the values of CFID and CFTOKEN might be stored and passed from page to page in different manners.

We've said that client variables can be stored in the ColdFusion Server's registry, in cookies on the client machine, or in a database. The choice of which of these methods to use for storage of the client variables can have a negative effect on application performance, but can save you some headaches in the bigger picture.

Here are a few reasons that you might want to use client variables:

- Variable values can be saved in a number of manners.

- Each method of storage has its own timeout period.

- Client variables are application-specific; so if you're running multiple applications on the same server, you can set client variables that are specific to each application.

- You don't need to worry about using CFLOCK on your client variables because their values are not stored in server memory.

Of course, client variable storage has its downside too:

- Client variables can be stored only as strings and cannot be complex data types, such as arrays and structures.

Enabling Client Variables

Prior to using client variables in your application, you must enable them. To enable client variables, you must enable them within the CFAPPLICATION tag in the Application.cfm template.

```
<cfapplication
   name="ICFMX"
   applicationtimeout="#CreateTimeSpan(0,12,0,0)#"
   sessionmanagement="Yes"
   sessiontimeout="#CreateTimeSpan(0,0,30,0)#"
    clientmanagement="Yes">
```

Storing Client Variables

We've already discussed the fact that client variables can be stored in a number of locations. By default, client variables are stored in the ColdFusion Server's registry. You can specify, however, that they be stored in cookies or in a separate database.

Table 8.3 runs down the advantages and disadvantages of storing client variables in the server's registry.

Table 8.3 **Advantages and Disadvantages of Registry-Based Client Variable Storage**

Advantages	Disadvantages
• Easy implementation	• Registry-size limitations
• Good performance	• Limited to specific server; not cluster-friendly
• Registry can be easily exported to other servers	• OS limitations
• Server-side control	

You might choose to store your client variables in simple cookies on the client machine. You need to be aware that you face the standard limitations of cookies and user preferences regarding them. Cookies perform well and are easy to implement, but you might want to consider all the pros and cons of storing client variables in cookies, as outlined in Table 8.4.

Table 8.4 **Advantages and Disadvantages of Cookie-Based Client Variable Storage**

Advantages	Disadvantages
• Easy implementation	• User preferences
• Good performance	• Limits on cookie size
• Flexible expiration	• Browser limitations on the number of cookies stored
• Client-side control	

Storing client variables in a database of their own is a great idea for a number of reasons. However, it also has its downsides. Table 8.5 presents both sides of the issue.

Table 8.5 **Considerations of Database Client Variable Storage**

Advantages	Disadvantages
■ Can use existing datasource	■ Complex to implement
■ Portable	■ Performance issues due to frequent database interaction
■ Cluster-friendly	

Using Client Variables

Of the variable scopes used to maintain user state, client variables are the one solution that could really be considered long-term. They do have their limitations, though. We mentioned earlier that client variables must be strings. They cannot be arrays, structures, query objects, eXtensible Markup Language (XML) documents, or other complex data types. You could, however, convert the complex data type to WDDX format for storage as a client variable and then convert it back to its original state prior to use.

Client variables are created just like many of the other variable scopes in ColdFusion, by using the CFSET or CFPARAM tags.

```
<cfset client.AppStyle="Patriotic">
```

or

```
<cfparam name="client.AppStyle" default="Standard">
```

After you have set the client variable, it is available for use within any page in the application for the particular client that set the variable. By using the CFPARAM tag to set a default value for the variable name, you can be assured that you can always use the variable without using a CFIF statement to evaluate the variable's existence.

Accessing client variables is easy. You don't have to refer to their storage method or anything like that; you simply call the variable name with the client scope:

```
<cfoutput>
  Show the application in the #client.AppStyle# theme.
</cfoutput>
```

If you're not sure what client variables are currently available to a client, you can always call the CFDUMP tag to output the client structure. However, this shows you all the existing client variables. If you only want to output the custom variables that have been created through the application, you can use the GetClientVariablesList() function:

```
<cfoutput>#GetClientVariablesList()#</cfoutput>
```

Because client variables are held in a structure, you can delete or manipulate client variables with any of the standard structure functions. There is, however, another method of deleting a client variable. You can use ColdFusion's `DeleteClientVariable()` function:

```
<cfset tmp=DeleteClientVariable("client.AppStyle")>
```

Only custom client variables can be deleted. This excludes the default client variables (see Table 8.6). Client variables can also be timed out. Within the ColdFusion MX Administrator, you can set default timeouts for your client variables.

If you call a `CFLOCATION` when using client variables in your application, the `CFID` and `CFTOKEN` automatically are appended to your URL when you are calling a CFM or DBM page. You can disable this feature by adding the `addtoken` attribute to your `CFLOCATION` tag and specifying the following:

```
<cflocation url="/index.cfm?display=News" Addtoken="No">
```

If you need to pass other parameters along the URL, you can run into trouble with the automatic inclusion of `CFID` and `CFTOKEN`. What happens is that the automatically included parameters are formatted as `?CFID=3&CFTOKEN=39297791`. The problem occurs when this is appended to a URL that already has URL parameters included. The resulting URL call might look like this:

```
http://www.insidecoldfusionmx.com/index.cfm?display_code=News?CFID=3&CFTOKEN=39297791
```

Errors will result.

As with many of our other variable scopes, there are a few client variables that are predefined. The client scope has six built-in, read-only variables. These are outlined in Table 8.6.

Table 8.6 **Client Scope Variables**

Variable	Description
Client.CFID	The client ID.
Client.CFToken	The client security token.
Client.URLToken	A concatenation of CFID and CFTOKEN. Stored as CFID=123&CFTOKEN=23457323. This variable is useful if the client does not support cookies and you must pass the CFID and CFTOKEN values.
Client.HitCount	The number of page requests made by the client.
Client.LastVisit	The last time the client visited the application.
Client.TimeCreated	The time at which the CFID and CFTOKEN variables of the client were created.

Summary

Application state is a complex topic and a complex problem with which to deal in web applications. It is one that web developers wrestle with in a big way. Understanding what makes it an issue, the ways to maintain session state, and the variables that we can use to manipulate sessions and to help track them gives us the upper hand.

We discussed in some detail the Web Application Framework in this chapter. We noted that it does the following things:

- Enables the use of applicationwide settings and functions
- Enables custom error handling throughout the application
- Provides for the integration of web server security
- Enables the use of variable scopes, including application, client, server, and session

We discussed the various variable scopes available to us through settings in the ColdFusion Administrator and within the Web Application Framework's `Application.cfm` template. We also discussed enabling applicationwide settings, such as session management or client management.

In the upcoming chapters, we're going to expand on this discussion and explore the use of custom error handling within a ColdFusion application, and later, the creation of applicationwide security.

9

Error Handling

OF COURSE, WE ALL LIKE TO THINK THAT we're really good developers. In a lot of cases, that's probably true. Still, like it or not, there are going to be times when the code that you write will not perform the way you expected. In those instances, it's important to make sure that you've provided a way for your application to gracefully handle those errors.

If you were to attempt to perform a function within your application and that attempt was met with failure, you'd probably be able to easily decipher from the standard error message exactly what had caused the failure to occur.

These standard error messages, while not particularly beautiful from a user interface (UI) standpoint, do provide a large amount of critical debugging information. Still, the end users of your application will likely have no need for this type of information, and they will probably feel much more comfortable when presented with an application error if it is wrapped in a neat little package. This is where error handling in ColdFusion MX comes in.

In this chapter, we discuss common circumstances that can cause problems within your applications and ways that you can avoid these pitfalls. For the instances in which errors that you couldn't, or didn't, anticipate are generated, we examine some ways that you can handle the errors to prevent application instability. We do this in a way that ensures that your end users feel as if everything is under control with your application, even when errors are occurring.

Finally, we examine some tips and tricks that enable you to hide the critical "standard" error messages from your users while still being able to look at them yourself when trying to diagnose your server problems.

Error Types

To understand why exception conditions, or critical errors, occur, you need to understand the different types of errors that you can encounter. Because error conditions can occur at various points in the parse/execution process, it's important to know the ways in which you can distinguish such errors and make provisions for their handling.

For the purposes of our discussion, you should understand the four main types of errors that you might encounter when developing/running ColdFusion MX applications:

- Runtime
- Compiler
- Input
- Template

Runtime Errors

Runtime errors occur after your ColdFusion Markup Language (CFML) code has been compiled and is executing through the ColdFusion engine. Runtime errors often result from the fact that your application is receiving an error from a third-party resource (such as a database driver or COM object, and so on) that it isn't sure how to handle.

Runtime errors can also be caused by internal server errors or other conditions that are beyond your control. Further, you can purposefully generate runtime errors with CFTHROW tags for the purposes of error handling.

To fix conditions that generate runtime errors, you can examine the templates that are generating the errors and look for specific code segments that consistently cause the error. Often, this process involves commenting out all code in a given page and then reinserting it line by line until you discover the piece of code (or third-party resource) that is causing your server to produce errors.

In the event of internal server errors, you'll often find yourself pouring over the contents of the stack traces generated by the server to determine where things went wrong. Common causes of internal server errors include server memory corruption, improper administrator settings, and insufficient server resources.

Compiler Errors

Compiler errors are errors that occur as the ColdFusion Server attempts to compile your raw CFML code into Java. If you've developed ColdFusion applications for any length of time, you're certain to have come across a compiler error. These errors can be caused by an invalid CFML tag or improper use of CFML code within the template itself.

As ColdFusion begins to parse your American Standard Code for Information Interchange (ASCII) CFML templates to turn them into Java code, it needs to make sure that there are no critical errors in the code itself. If compiler errors are being thrown, you must fix them in the development process. To do so, you'll need to examine the error message you are receiving to determine in which template the errors are occurring. You then can make sure that you've got the CFML code syntactically correct before proceeding.

Because of their nature, compiler errors cannot be trapped by try/catch routines; compiler errors occur before the try/catch routine can be executed.

Input Errors

Input errors (or data errors) occur as a result of data that an end user has sent to your application (through a form field or similar input method).

Typically, when you have form fields available for user input, you are validating that data in some way on the server. If, for example, you have a form field reserved for the age of a user, you might be checking on the server that the value entered into this field is an integer. If the data entered doesn't mesh with the "rules" that you've set up for the field, an error will occur.

Generally, input errors are errors that you expect (and want) to occur if certain criteria are not met. Because you know that there will be occasions in which these errors are thrown, you'll typically code some sort of error handling into your application for them. This error handling might be as simple as returning the user to the previous page, with a notice as to why the data he or she entered was incorrect, missing, or in the wrong format.

As mentioned, input errors are generally expected within the framework of any application that accepts user input. These types of errors will generally never cause server instability or poor performance.

Missing Template Errors

Missing template errors are slightly different from standard 404 errors that you receive from your web server. The only real difference between a missing template error and a web server 404 error is the fact that the missing template error is actually sent from ColdFusion. ColdFusion answers any request for a template with a .cfm extension, including requests for templates that don't exist.

Naturally, the best way to resolve these errors is by looking carefully at the error message to determine if the template is actually missing.

The most common causes of missing template errors on production systems are typographical errors in the name of the template being called or a bad path in a link. (A bad path is revealed when CF looks for a specific template in a directory where it doesn't exist.) Fortunately, missing template errors are usually easily corrected by carefully examining the error message being reported.

Still, there will be times in which you cannot anticipate that missing template errors might be thrown. Fortunately, there is a provision in the ColdFusion Administrator that enables you to set up a default "missing template handler" for your web application. This missing template handler is displayed in place of the default error message whenever ColdFusion encounters a request for a CFM template that doesn't appear to exist.

Figure 9.1 gives you a view of the missing template handler dialog box in the ColdFusion Administrator.

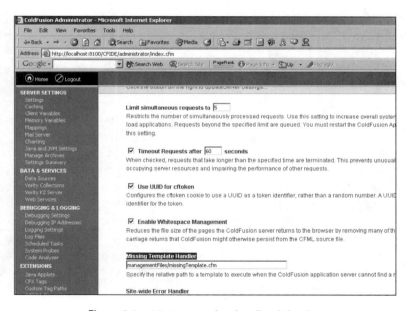

Figure 9.1 Missing template handler dialog box.

Try/Catch/Throw Routines

Within CFML, you have tags specifically designed to enable you to handle errors and to continue processing your application pages. The try/catch block is one way in which you might choose to handle an error generated within one of your ColdFusion templates. You would use try/catch blocks anywhere within your application where an error from which you could recover might occur.

Before we begin with an example of how you would use this functionality in a real-world application, let's take a quick look at the types of error handling tags available within ColdFusion MX (see Table 9.1).

Table 9.1 **ColdFusion MX Error Handling Tags**

Error	Handling Tag General Use of Tag
CFTRY	Within a CFML template, CFTRY tags are used to surround specific segments of code that can generate an error.
	When used in conjunction with the CFCATCH tag, CFTRY enables you to specify a second piece of code to run only when the code within the CFTRY block has failed to execute properly.
CFCATCH	CFCATCH is always used within a CFTRY block. You use CFCATCH to specify a piece of code that you want to run if the code contained within the CFTRY block has failed and a certain error type was generated.
	You can have multiple CFCATCH blocks with different catch types within a single CFTRY block.
	There are various catch types available to you in ColdFusion MX:

- application
- database
- template
- security
- object
- missinginclude
- expression
- lock
- custom_type
- any

continues ▶

Table 9.1 **Continued**

Error	Handling Tag General Use of Tag
	A catch type of any is always the default and is used when no other catch type is specified.
	In addition to these basic types, there are a number of extended error types that you can use with your CFCATCH blocks to obtain more granular control over your application flow. These advanced exception types are covered in detail later in this chapter.
CFTHROW	The CFTHROW tag enables you to purposefully throw an error of a specified type within your code that could consequently cause a specific catch type to run.
CFRETHROW	The CFRETHROW tag forces your error handling routine to exit the currently executing CFCATCH block and throw a new exception of the same type so that error handling can continue.
	This is useful when the specific catch block in which the error is first sent is not written specifically to deal with the type thrown.
	With the CFRETHROW tag, you can rethrow an error of the same type to enable a higher-level error handler to deal with it.
CFFINALLY	The CFFINALLY tag, new to ColdFusion MX, enables you to specify a section of code within any CFCATCH block that you want to be executed no matter what happens.
	Even if an error isn't thrown, any content in the CFFINALLY block will still execute.
	If an error is thrown and the CFCATCH block is called into use, content in the CFFINALLY block will execute after the CFCATCH tag has finished running the code contained within its block.

Try/Catch

Now that we've taken a look at all the error handling tags available to you in ColdFusion MX, let's examine how we might use some of them.

First, let's take a look at how we might want to implement a simple try/catch block in our ColdFusion code.

Suppose we want to run a database query that retrieves a list of cars from a database. The table that holds the names of the car models is called models. This should be a simple enough query, assuming that we don't do something silly like spell our table name modeels; but what if we do? That's where the try/catch block takes over to help us out.

Examine the following code, noting the fact that we are misspelling the table name models:

```
<cftry>
    <cfquery name="GetCars" datasource="request.dsn">
    SELECT *
    FROM modells
    </cfquery>
<cfcatch type="database">
There was an unfortunate database error.  Please try
again.
</cfcatch>
</cftry>
```

In code, when the database error is encountered, an error is thrown. Without the try/catch block, the error would be sent back to the user in the standard, unfriendly error format that relays either an open database connectivity (ODBC) or native driver error message.

Although this type of error message is fine (and sometimes necessary) for the developer of the application to see, it won't mean much to the end user. Generally, he or she will be much happier with the "There was an unfortunate database error" type of message.

When using CFCATCH within a CFTRY block, you will also have catch variables available to you. These variables are populated whenever a catch type is encountered, and they can be used to provide more information about the specific type of error that was encountered.

Table 9.2 examines the different variables available to you when you are using CFCATCH to trap errors.

Table 9.2 *CFCATCH* **Error Variables**

Variable Name	Description
CFCATCH.TYPE	This variable stores the exception type encountered.
	The contents of this variable will be the same as the exception type specified in the CFCATCH block.
CFCATCH.MESSAGE	This variable will contain the diagnostic message generated by the particular exception encountered.
	If there was no message associated with the encountered exception, this variable will remain as an empty string.
CFCATCH.DETAIL	This variable holds a detailed message about the encountered exception as generated by the ColdFusion engine.
	This variable can be useful if you're trying to determine at precisely which point in your code the exception was encountered.

continues ▶

Table 9.2 **Continued**

Variable Name	Description
CFCATCH.TAGCONTEXT	This variable contains stack information about the name and position of tags in the tag stack. For this variable to contain information, you must have stack tracing enabled in the ColdFusion Administrator.
CFCATCH.NATIVEERRORCODE	When you're dealing with database connections, any error will generally result in a common error code. This variable will store that error code information, provided that the catch is of type database.
	If no error code is available, the variable will read -1.
CFCATCH.SQLSTATE	The SQLState associated with the exception is reported in this variable.
	Much like the NativeErrorCode variable, this variable will exist only when the catch is of type database.
	If no SQLState is reported with the specific error code being generated, this value will report a value of -1.
CFCATCH.ERRNUMBER	This value will contain the internal expression error number associated with the error when the catch is of type expression.
CFCATCH.MISSINGFILENAME	This value is useful when the catch is of type missinginclude. The value of this variable will include the name of the missing included file.
CFCATCH.LOCKNAME	When a catch type is defined as lock and your application code generates an exception as a result of a named lock, this variable will report the name of the named lock that generated the error.
CFCATCH.LOCKOPERATION	With the catch type of lock, this value will specify the type of error encountered when trying to create a lock for a specific segment of code.

Variable Name	Description
CFCATCH.ERRORCODE	When the catch type is set to custom, this variable is used to send back a custom error string associated with the error encountered.
CFCATCH.EXTENDEDINFO	When the catch type is set to any, this variable is used to hold a custom error to be sent back to the user.

In many cases, you'll want to use these catch variables as a way to troubleshoot the actual reason for the error. The output presented to the user typically will be a generic, user-friendly, "error has occurred" type message.

In such cases, the CFCATCH variables enable you to continue to present user-friendly error messages to the end user while still getting to the root cause of the trouble by carefully examining the content of the variables.

Using *CFTHROW*

In the earlier examples in this chapter, we looked at how to make use of a simple try/catch block to catch a database error as a result of a typographical error we made when we queried a specific database table. Now, let's look at a scenario in which we might want to purposefully throw an error within our application.

Suppose that we had a CFML template that required a UserID be passed in before we allowed processing to continue. In that case, we might want to use a try/catch routine to make sure that the UserID passed in was valid; otherwise, we might want to send a specific message back to the user telling him or her that something went wrong. The following code demonstrates this concept in action:

```
<cftry>
    <cfif NOT isDefined("UserId")>
<cfthrow message="I threw an error when I checked for ID">
    </cfif>
<cfcatch type="any">
    An error occurred
</cfcatch>
```

In this code, you see that we're checking to make sure that a UserID is defined. If it's not, we want our catch block to tell our user that "An error occurred." However, we want to know that "I threw an error when I checked for ID" occurred, which is what we're using the CFTHROW tag for in this instance.

The CFTHROW tag can take various attributes, all of which are outlined in Table 9.3.

Table 9.3 **CFTHROW Attributes**

Attribute	Description
TYPE	This is an optional attribute that enables you to enter a custom throw type or to use the predefined application type.
MESSAGE	This is the message that you want to use to describe what has happened that has caused the throw section to run.
DETAIL	This is an optional attribute that enables you to specify a detailed description of the reason why you are throwing the error.
ERRORCODE	This attribute is optional and can be used to generate a custom error code that you are supplying.
EXTENDEDINFO	This attribute is optional and can be used to generate custom error information that you are supplying.

Custom Errors

In some cases, you might want to develop custom errors that control the way that error related output is presented to the end user in a given situation. In ColdFusion, you can do this by making use of the CFERROR tag. The CFERROR tag enables you to specify different types of error handling pages for various types of errors that might be encountered when working through your ColdFusion application.

CFERROR enables you to specify error pages for four specific types of errors:

- **Validation.** Validation errors occur when a user inputs something into a form field or other user-input device and the information causes problems with your applications logic flow. As an example, suppose you have a form action page that depends on knowing the age of a user. The user is supposed to have input his or her age into a form that was submitted to the action page. If for any reason the user age is not present or if the data entered is invalid, you'll want a way to control the way that the error caused by this validation failure is presented to the user.

- **Exception.** Exception errors are errors that are produced as a direct result of an application exception occurring. There are many reasons (such as memory corruption and corrupt templates) why an application exception can occur. Generally, however, these errors are unrecoverable from an application operation standpoint. This is in direct contrast to the validation error, which can easily be corrected by the user, allowing processing to continue. Because of this, you'd most likely want to have different error handling templates with different message sets for these two different types of errors.

- **Request.** Request errors act as the "catchall" error handler. Request errors handle any error that occurs that is not caught by any other portion of the error handling that you have in place. As a result of the way in which request errors occur, it's a good idea to make the error message you present to the user as a result of these errors very general in nature. It has to be general because it's unlikely that you'll be able to anticipate all the conditions that might generate a request error.

- **Monitor.** The monitor error type is a special type of custom error handler that you can use when debugging your applications. Specifying a template to run as a monitor error handler causes the contents of that template to be run prior to any other error handling processing (such as CFTRY/CFCATCH blocks within a given template). This is useful if you want to log the specifics of any errors encountered to a special log file prior to running the code through the standard CFTRY/CFCATCH blocks in your code.

Using *CFERROR*

You can use the CFERROR tag when you want to create and generate custom error messages from within your ColdFusion application code. Table 9.4 explains the attributes available for use with the CFERROR tag.

Table 9.4   *CFERROR* **Attributes**

Attribute	Description
Exception	This is a required attribute that specifies the type of exception that this particular custom error will handle. The choices available to you include validation, exception, request, and monitor. Each exception type was discussed in the previous section of this chapter.
MailTo	This optional attribute enables you to specify an email address for a person to whom you would like to have any errors mailed that were handled by this custom error template.
Template	This is a required attribute that contains the path to the template you want to use to handle this type of error.
Type	This is a required attribute that enables you to specify the type of error that this custom error template is designed to handle.

With CFERROR, you are somewhat limited in the types of errors that you can handle. With the exception of the monitor error type, all the types handled by CFERROR will be caught only when they are not explicitly handled elsewhere in your ColdFusion code. What does this mean? Examine the following example:

```
<cftry>
    <cfif NOT isDefined("UserID")>
<cfthrow message="I threw an error when I checked for ID">
    </cfif>
<cfcatch type="any">
    An error occurred
</cfcatch>
```

You can see by this example that we are using a CFTRY/CFCATCH block to check whether the UserID value is defined. If it is not, we throw an error, presumably because this value will be required later in the processing.

With the CFTRY/CFCATCH block in place, if the UserID variable doesn't exist, the try/catch error handling will let us know. We then can tell the user this message: "I threw an error when I checked for ID." This alerts the user that a required parameter is missing and that our processing has come to a halt.

Assume that the try/catch error handling block was missing from our code. When our template got to the point where our logic depended on the presence of the UserID variable and it wasn't there, the user would get a messy standard ColdFusion message about an invalid or missing expression.

With CFERROR, even if we have no try/catch code in place, our error would still be caught. Suppose in the application.cfm file of our ColdFusion application that we have added the following line of code:

```
<cferror type = "REQUEST" template = "defaultError.cfm">
```

The CFERROR type request acts as a catchall. Thus, when our application found that the UserID variable was missing, it didn't throw the ugly ColdFusion error back to our user. Instead, it presented him or her with the contents of the defaultError.cfm file, which is the template we've specified in our CFERROR statement.

When making use of the CFERROR tag, you are given some default variables that are returned if CFERROR is executed. These variables can be used to provide you or your users with more information about the error encountered. These variables can be output or appended to an email message to the administrator of your site, just like any other ColdFusion variable.

The variables that you have available to you differ depending on the error type that your CFERROR statement has been written to handle. Table 9.5 lists the variables returned by CFERROR for the exception, request, and monitor error types.

Table 9.5   **Error Variables Returned by *CFERROR* When the Error Type Is Exception, Request, or Monitor**

Variable Returned	Description of Variable
Error.Browser	This variable returns to you the variable running on the client machine when the error was returned.
Error.DateTime	This variable returns to you the date/time value associated with the time when the error was generated.
Error.Diagnostics	This variable returns detailed error information from the ColdFusion Server (if available) about the error.
Error.GeneratedContent	This variable returns the generated content of the request that failed.
Error.HTTPReferer	This variable returns the uniform resource locator (URL) of the page that the client was on prior to coming to the page where the error was generated (in other words, the referring page).
Error.MailTo	This is the email address to which this error message was reported (if one was specified in the original CFERROR statement).
Error.QueryString	This variable returns the URL query string of the request that generated the error.
Error.RemoteAddress	This variable returns the Internet Protocol (IP) address of the client machine that generated the error.
Error.Template	This variable returns the name of the template that was being executed when the error was generated.

Table 9.6 demonstrates the variables returned by CFERROR for the validation error type.

Table 9.6   **Error Variables Returned by *CFERROR* When the Error Type Is Validation**

Variable Returned	Definition of Variable
Error.InvalidFields	This variable returns a list of validation errors that occurred.
Error.ValidationHeader	This variable returns the text of the validation header.
Error.ValidationFooter	This variable returns the text of the validation footer.

Site-Wide Error Handlers

In addition to the many other ways that you can handle errors, ColdFusion MX provides you with a setting in the ColdFusion Administrator that enables you to specify a site-wide error handling page. The page you set here provides you with one last line of defense before your users are presented with standard ColdFusion error syntax.

It's a good idea to specify a site-wide error handling template in the Administrator to act as a catchall for any unintentionally unhandled error messages. Keep in mind, however, that when you specify an error template in the Administrator, the template you use needs to be somewhat generic because all ColdFusion applications on the server will use this template for any unhandled errors that they encounter.

Summary

In this chapter, we've covered how you can use ColdFusion's built-in error handling techniques to improve the performance and flow of your ColdFusion applications.

Although error handling is sometimes overlooked by inexperienced developers in their zeal for getting a project completed, it's vital to understand how important proper error handling is to the performance of an application. The benefit of ensuring that you've taken steps to eliminate any unhandled errors from your applications cannot be overstated. You would be amazed at the stability improvement that can occur simply by eliminating unhandled errors from your application.

Although it does take time and effort up front to properly handle ColdFusion errors, the benefit your application will derive from this is well worth the effort.

10

Regular Expressions

IF YOU'VE NEVER WORKED WITH REGULAR EXPRESSIONS, you might not have any idea what they are, how they work, or what a powerful weapon they are to have in your arsenal. Regular expressions might be second nature to programmers who have come to ColdFusion from other programming backgrounds. They're used extensively in languages such as Visual C++, Tcl, Java, and Perl, and they also can be used in JavaScript.

Regular expressions are used in ColdFusion to parse text, to find patterns or substrings within a string, and to replace patterns or substrings within a string. Regular expressions can be made up of letters, numbers, punctuation characters, and other special characters and metacharacters.

Metacharacters are the special characters that perform functions within a regular expression. They can also be characters within the string for which you're searching, but they must be escaped to be considered a literal character.

There are four native ColdFusion functions that enable ColdFusion programmers to utilize the power of regular expressions to help solve complex search and parsing problems. There are two functions for finding patterns within string: REFind() and REFindNoCase(). In addition, there are two more that find and replace patterns within a string: REReplace() and REReplaceNoCase(). Each function enables you to do some very powerful things with your code.

As we proceed through this chapter, you'll learn more about the basic use and syntax of regular expressions, the metacharacters that we mentioned, and how to leverage regular expressions within your ColdFusion applications.

Basic Syntax

At its simplest, a regular expression finds a literal string within another literal string. The syntax of a regular expression can be as simple as the following:

```
REFind("b", "abc")
```

Although this example is very basic, don't underestimate how powerful regular expressions can really be. How about this one:

```
REFind("time", "Now is the time for all good men")
```

The returned value is the location of the first occurrence of the regular expression within your string. The resulting value of our first example is "2," and the resulting value of our second example is "12." The value corresponds to the first occurrence of the complete search pattern within the string that you are searching. Returning a value for the occurrence of the search pattern is helpful in that it identifies a successful result. It also enables you to carry out other processing, such as splitting a single value into multiple values at the position of the occurrence of the pattern.

We'll take a look at some much more complex regular expressions in just a minute, but first, we need to discuss the use of metacharacters. They can save you a lot of time in formatting your regular expressions.

Metacharacters

To really make use of regular expressions, you must be familiar with metacharacters and their meanings within the regular expression language. They exist to perform specialized functions in relation to your search criteria. This does not mean that the use of these characters is only for those specialized functions; but if you actually want to search for a character that the regular expression will recognize as a metacharacter, you must escape it. You're already familiar with escaping characters within ColdFusion Markup Language (CFML) code because we often must escape the # character.

Here are the metacharacters with which you'll need to familiarize yourself:

- **Asterisk (*).** The asterisk matches zero or more occurrences of the character that immediately precedes it. This means that if you code [a-z]*, the regular expression evaluates true regardless of the string.

- **Backslash (\).** The backslash is used to escape metacharacters so that they can be used as literal characters within your search. For example, if you wanted to search for the backslash character itself, you'd have to escape it like this: `c:\\`.

- **Carat (^).** The carat is used to match characters that appear at the beginning of a string. For example, searching for `^Please` in a string that starts "Please hand me the…" would return a value of "1" because the regular expression does indeed appear at the beginning of the string. However, you can also use the carat to exclude characters from the match. Using our same example, `[^Pl]` would return a value of "3" because the first two characters are excluded from the search and the match begins at the third character.

- **Curly brackets ({}).** The curly brackets are used to specify a range of occurrences to which the regular expression needs to be matched within the search string. For example, later on you'll see this in a regular expression example: `([a-z]{2,3})`. This means that an alphabetic character is to be matched two or three times for the regular expression to evaluate true. By the same principle, `{1,10}` would signify a range of 1–10. You can also specify a number of occurrences rather than a range by listing only one numeric reference, as in `([a-z]{2})`.

- **Dollar sign ($).** A dollar sign matches the end-of-line character. For example, the regular expression "`rascals$`" would match the end of the string "I love to watch the little rascals" but not the string "I love to watch the little rascals." because of the period that follows the word "rascals."

- **Parentheses (()).** Parentheses are used to group segments of the regular expression, dividing the regular expression into subexpressions. Using parentheses within your regular expression can extend the functionality of the regular expression and enable you to search for multiple combinations of characters and character classes.

Parentheses also enable you to take advantage of back references, also known as remembered matches. Back references enable your regular expressions to refer back to subexpressions that have already been matched. The best use for this is when you want to use a matched pattern as part of future searches. A good example of this would be if you want to search a sentence to remove duplicated words. For example, let's say your string to be searched is "One of the best things about regular expressions is". The regular expression that you would use would look like this:

```
<cfset NoDupes=REReplaceNoCase(("One of the best things about regular
expressions is",  "([a-z]+)[]+\1", "\1", "All")>
```

- **Period (.).** A period represents any single character within a string except for the newline character. For example, the regular expression "st.p" would match the strings "step" or "stop", but not "steep".

- **Pipe (|).** A pipe enables you to match the character set specified on either side of the pipe, essentially an OR statement. For example, "d|dy" would match "bird" or "birdy".

- **Plus (+).** The plus sign represents one or more matches of a regular expression within a string. For example, [a-z]+ will match the @ in the search string "neil@codesweeper.com".

- **Question mark (?).** The question mark matches the first occurrence of the preceding pattern or string within your search string. For example, neil? will match "neil@codesweeper.com" or "neilross@codesweeper.com".

Table 10.1 covers the order of precedence for regular expression operators.

Table 10.1   **Regular Expressions Order of Precedence**

Description	Operator
Bracket symbols	[==] [::] [..]
Escaped characters	\\<*special character*>
Bracket expression	[ ]
Subexpressions/back references	\\(\\)\\n
Single character duplication	*\\{a,b\\}
Concatenation	_
Anchoring	^$

POSIX Character Classes

The Portable Operating Systems Interface (POSIX) standard defines character combinations. These combinations are available to ColdFusion developers for use within regular expressions. They help to make regular expressions easier to write, read, and maintain.

Different POSIX character classes are available to ColdFusion. The most common ones include the following:

- **alpha [:alpha:].** Matches combinations of alphabetic characters, regardless of case, (A–Za–z).

- **alnum [:alnum:].** Matches combinations of alphabetic or numeric characters, regardless of case or order, (A–Za–z, 0–9).

- **digit [:digit:].** Matches any combination of numeric characters, (0–9).

- **lower [:lower:].** Matches combinations of lowercase alphabetic characters, (a–z).

- **punct [:punct:].** Matches any punctuation mark or combination of punctuation marks. The characters covered by this character class include the following: ` ! " # $ % & ' ( ) * + , - . / : ; < = > ? [ \ ] ^ _ ` { | } ~ '.

- **space [:space:].** Matches any whitespace character.

- **upper [:upper:].** Matches combinations of uppercase alphabetic characters, (A–Z).

Other available POSIX character classes that you can use within your ColdFusion code include the following:

- **cntrl [:cntrl:].** Matches any character that is not included in one of the other POSIX character classes. The characters include carriage return, formfeed, or newline.

- **graph [:graph:].** Matches any printable character other than carriage return, formfeed, newline, space, tab, or vertical tab.

- **print [:print:].** Matches any printable character.

- **xdigit [:xdigit:].** Matches any hexadecimal digit. An example is [A–Fa–f0–9].

One rule to remember when using POSIX character classes is that they must always be contained within two pairs of square brackets. Let's start with a simple example:

```
<cfset secretmessage = REReplace("E!V!A!C!U!A!T!E! !N!O!W!", "[[:punct:]]", "",
"ALL")>
```

The preceding regular expression returns "EVACUATE NOW" when output. The [:punct:] POSIX character class matches all the ! characters in the string and replaces them with the specified string. In this case, "", which is an empty string. Now let's look at something a little more complex:

```
<cfset secretmessage =
REReplace(REReplace("I243*w22i3423l1*m2e678e21t234*y234121ou231*08313452a2343te34r",
"[[:digit:]]", "", "ALL"), "[[:punct:]]", " ", "ALL")>
```

Remember that ColdFusion functions enable recursive processing. The preceding example shows the `REReplace()` regular expression function calling itself, but each call replaces different character types. The resulting string after all iterations of the `REReplace()` function is "I will meet you later".

It's pretty easy to do what we've done in the preceding examples. We know the strings and know what needs to be replaced. However, what if we don't have that information? Let's look at some functions that can help us with that problem.

Finding Strings

When you need to know the position of an expression being searched within a string, you should use the `REFind()` or `REFindNoCase()` functions. These regular expression functions return the position and length of the first occurrence of the matched substring or pattern from the specified start position.

The difference between the two is that the `REFind()` function is case-sensitive and the `REFindNoCase()` function is not case-sensitive. These two functions share the same syntax, so you don't have to worry about learning any additional attributes from one to the other.

```
REFind(reg_expression, string [, Start ] [, returnsubexpressions ])
REFindNoCase(reg_expression, string [, Start ] [, returnsubexpressions ])
```

As mentioned, you can find an exact string within another string, or you can search for a pattern if you do not know the exact string. This can come in handy when you're looking for things like email addresses within a larger string. We'll take a look at some code that works for finding email addresses in just a minute. First, however, let's look at an example of how to find a specific string within a larger string. Let's start by creating our string:

```
<cfset string = "Now is the time for all good men">
```

Now let's search for a string within it:

```
<cfoutput>
        #REFind("time", string, "1")#
</cfoutput>
```

The value that results from the preceding code is "12" because the expression "time" occurs at the twelfth character position in the string.

I promised that we'd look at an example of how to find an email address within a string. So, let's consider the following example:

```
<cfset string = "Email me at neil@codesweeper.com">
```

Now for our regular expression:

```
<cfoutput>
    #REFind("[[:alnum:]\.\_]+@[[:alnum:].]+[[:alpha:]]", string, "1")#
</cfoutput>
```

The result of our output here is "13", identifying again the position where the match begins. There is a limitation to the code above, however. Have you realized what it is? Well, it doesn't take into account the format of international email addresses. For better coverage, try something like this:

```
<cfset string = "Email me at neil@codesweeper.com">
```

Now for our regular expression:

```
<cfoutput>
#REFindNoCase("[[:alnum:]]
\.\_+([[:alnum:]])+@[[:alnum:]]+([[:alnum:]]+)*\.(([[:alpha:]]{2,3})|(aero|coop|info¦m
useum|name))")#
</cfoutput>
```

Now look at Listing 10.1. It enables you to capture email addresses within a string and print them out:

Listing 10.1 **Find Multiple Email Addresses in a String**

```
<html>
<head>
    <title>Regular Expressions</title>
</head>
<body>
<table>
    <tr>
        <td class="codesample">
<br>
<br>
<cfset searchstring = "Please email neil@codesweeper.com, john@mauzy-broadway.com or
r@granularity.com with your questions.">
<cfset regex = "[[:alnum:]]+\@+([[:alnum:]]|[[:alnum:]]*\-
[[:alnum:]])+(\.[[:alnum:]]+)*\.(([:alpha:]]{2,3}))">
Our original search string: <br>
<cfoutput>#searchstring#</cfoutput>
<br>
<br>
    <cfset startpos = 1>
    <cfloop condition="startpos gt 0">
        <cfset match = REFindNoCase(regex, searchstring, startpos, TRUE)>
        <cfset foundvalues = Mid(searchstring, match.pos[1], match.len[1])>
            <cfoutput>
                #foundvalues#<br>
            </cfoutput>
        <cfif match.len[1] is 0><cfbreak></cfif>
```

```
            <cfset startpos=match.pos[1]+match.len[1]>
      </cfloop>
            </td>
      </tr>
</table>
</body>
</html>
```

Notice in Figure 10.1 that we have defined the regular expression outside the actual REFindNoCase() function call. We can do this with any regular expression and can even include those variables into our application to reuse the call in several places. Of course, there's a better way to handle this, but that's a discussion about user-defined functions.

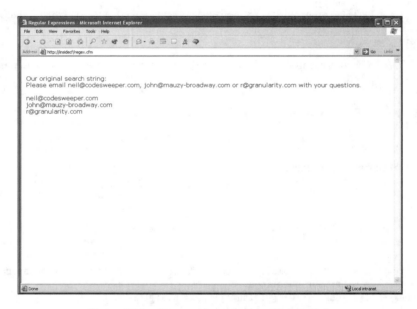

Figure 10.1 Generated output from Listing 10.1.

The resulting output shows that each email address in the string has been found and written to the page. That's a bit more complex, no doubt, but it works quite well. We could also employ the code used in Figure 10.1 along with an insert query to build an email mailing list. Want to know more about this one? Visit our site at www.insidecoldfusionmx.com.

Replacing Strings

Now let's take a look at replacing characters in a string using regular expressions. The replace functions that we have access to are `RExplace()` and `RExplaceNoCase()`. Just as with find functions, the difference between these two is simply that one is case-sensitive whereas the other is not. `RExplace()` is case-sensitive. These two functions also share the same syntax requirements with three required parameters:

```
RExplace(string, reg_expression, substring [, scope ])
RExplaceNocase(string, reg_expression, substring [, scope ])
```

The first required parameter is the string that you want to parse. You can hardcode this string (that is, enclose it in double quotes), or you can call a variable:

```
<cfset newstvar=RExplace("this is the stuff that I want to parse", "stuff", "string",
"One")>
<cfoutput>
     newstvar = #newstvar#
</cfoutput>
```

or

```
<cfset stvar="this is the stuff that I want to parse">
<cfset newstvar=RExplace(stvar, "stuff", "string", "One")>
<cfoutput>
        newstvar = #newstvar#
</cfoutput>
```

The second required parameter is the expression that you want to replace. We can see in the last example that this could be a string, but it could also be a pattern that we want to match. Look at the following example:

```
<cfset URL="http://www.insidecoldfusion.org">
<cfoutput>
   URL = #url#
   <br><br>
   #ReplaceNoCase(URL, 'http://', '')#
</cfoutput>
```

Your resulting output would look like Figure 10.2.

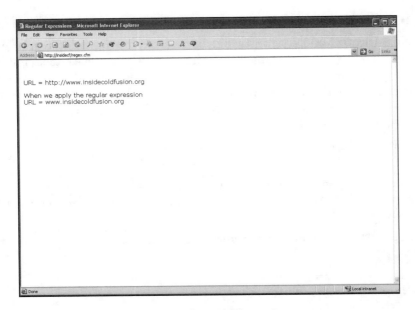

Figure 10.2 Sample regular expression output.

Let's revisit our examples from earlier in the chapter:

```
<cfset secretmessage = REReplace("E!V!A!C!U!A!T!E! !N!O!W!", "[[:punct:]]", "",
"ALL")>
```

and

```
<cfset secretmessage =
REReplace(REReplace("I243*w22i3423ll*m2e678e21t234*y234121ou231*08313452a2343te34r",
"[[:digit:]]", "", "ALL"), "[[:punct:]]", " ", "ALL")>
```

Of course, this is not an example that you'll likely use, but it illustrates a point about RERepIace() and REReplaceNoCase(). Now let's take a look as some examples of how you might use regular expressions in your ColdFusion applications:

- Replace spaces in filenames with an underscore character. This one comes in handy with any file that users are able to upload. I've had to use this one on images that users upload:

  ```
  <cfset newfile=REReplace(oldfile, "( )", "_", "All">
  ```

- Remove words that the user has doubled on input. This happens frequently when users type extended comments into a text area, but it could happen anywhere:

```
<cfset NoDupes=REReplaceNoCase(forminput, "([[:alpha:]]+)[]+\1", "\1",
"All")>
```

- Remove all hyperlinks from a string. This one comes in handy if you have a message board or forum and don't allow links to be posted:

```
<cfset newstvar=REReplaceNoCase(stvar, "<a *href[^>]+>([^(</a>)]*)</a>",
"\1", "All")>
```

Summary

Regular expressions can be a powerful tool for ColdFusion developers. They enable us to solve real problems in our code and to perform some pretty cool pattern matching and text manipulation.

To begin to understand how to make use of regular expressions in your applications, practice coding them. As we will discuss in later chapters, regular expressions come in handy when you write user-defined functions within ColdFusion.

11

Working with Email

WHEN DEVELOPING APPLICATIONS WITH COLDFUSION, you can leverage the power of email to enable you to communicate directly with your users. This can be a great enhancement to the overall power of your application, and everything you need to make it work is built in to the ColdFusion engine. This makes email functionality easy to implement in to sites built with ColdFusion.

By adding email functionality to your applications, you can streamline many processes. Email functionality enables your application to automatically respond to requests made by users, provide automated updates on account or order status, send requested files or other attachments, generate automated reminders, and provide a host of other great user-experience enhancements.

By using the tools built in to the ColdFusion engine, you can both send and receive email directly from your application.

In this chapter, we discuss the multiple ways in which you can use ColdFusion to create, read, send, receive, manage, and manipulate email messages. We also touch on some ways that you can improve the out-of-the-box performance that you typically see when using the built-in mailer components.

Preparing Your Environment

Before you begin integrating email with your applications, you'll need to make sure that you've correctly configured your environment so that ColdFusion can communicate with your selected email server.

Figure 11.1 shows you the email configuration page in the ColdFusion Administrator.

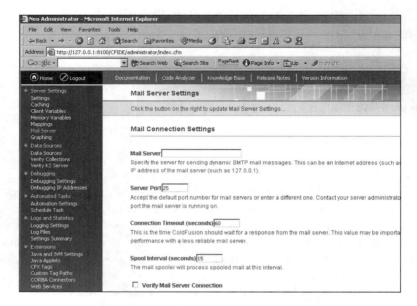

Figure 11.1   Email configuration page of the ColdFusion Administrator.

In the Mail Server text box, you enter the Internet Protocol (IP) address of the mail server that you want ColdFusion to use to send the email from your application. It's important that you understand that ColdFusion itself is not a mail server. All ColdFusion does is take the messages that your application is sending and forward them to the mail server that you have specified for processing.

In some cases, the mail server that you are using in conjunction with ColdFusion might exist on the ColdFusion Server itself. In these cases, it's correct for you to enter the IP **127.0.0.1** loopback address as the mail server address. This tells ColdFusion that the mail server you are using is on the same physical machine as ColdFusion itself.

If the mail server you are using is physically separate from ColdFusion, make sure that you enter the IP address—rather than the host name—of the mail server. This enables ColdFusion to continue processing mail from your application in the event that your network is having Domain Name System (DNS) problems.

In situations in which your mail servers are part of a cluster, you'll need to load balance the traffic sent to them. In addition, in situations in which you don't control the mail server that you are using with ColdFusion, it might be necessary to use the host name of the mail machine. Using the host name works fine, but you must be aware that if DNS problems arise, ColdFusion might be unable to send mail until the problems are resolved.

In the Server Port text box, unless your network administrator has explicitly directed you to use a specific port to communicate with your mail server, you'll want to use **25**. This is the default Simple Mail Transfer Protocol (SMTP) port.

In the Connection Timeout (seconds) field, you usually can leave the timeout set to the default (60 seconds). If you know in advance that you have either a slow connection between ColdFusion and the mail server or a mail server that takes a long time to validate connections, you might need to tweak this value accordingly.

If you leave the Spool Interval (seconds) text box with a value of 15 seconds, which is the default, you are generally fine for most applications. This interval determines how long the executive process waits between checks of the mail spool to determine if mail needs to be processed. You can save a little overhead by raising this value, but be careful not to set it too high. Doing so can cause the spool to accumulate a lot of messages waiting to be sent. Unfortunately, having too much unprocessed mail in the spool has, in the past, caused performance problems with CFMAIL.

Check the Verify Mail Server Connection check box if this is the first time that you've attempted to set up a mail server through your ColdFusion Administrator. Checking this box forces ColdFusion to attempt a handshake with the mail server after you submit the values on this page. You will be told in an onscreen message whether ColdFusion's attempt to connect with the mail server was successful.

In the event that you get a "Connection Verification Failed!" message when you submit the form, go back to the Mail Server text box and make sure that you've indeed entered the correct IP address of your mail server. If you know that the IP address you've entered is correct, attempt to verify the network connection between the ColdFusion Server and the IP address you've entered. You can do this by bringing up a command prompt or terminal window on the ColdFusion Server and pinging the IP address that you've entered for the mail server. If you get a message indicating that the IP address is unreachable, you might need to verify the IP address and network configuration again with your network administrator.

At this point, it's important to stop for a moment and discuss a scenario. Some developers write code that must exist on a ColdFusion Server that is shared by multiple applications. In many of these cases, you might not have access to the ColdFusion Administrator. Even if you do have access to the ColdFusion Administrator, you might not have the right to add or edit the mail server that ColdFusion uses by default. Fortunately, this doesn't mean that you can't make use of CFMAIL.

The developers of the ColdFusion Application Server took this into account when developing the product and have made it possible for you to specify the mail server to which you want to connect. You can also specify the port on which you want to connect, the username/password you need to use, and many other parameters. All these parameters can be specified directly from within the CFMAIL tag itself. In the event that you cannot configure the ColdFusion Administrator for the mail server you need to use, you can use the parameters of CFMAIL to specify these elements. We discuss the details of how to do so later in this chapter.

Toward the bottom of the Mail Settings page in the ColdFusion Administrator, you will notice two items under Mail Logging Settings. These two items enable you to have some control over the types of messages that ColdFusion will log about the mail that it is automatically forwarding to the mail server.

Figure 11.2 shows the Mail Logging Settings options available in the ColdFusion Administrator.

The first setting you can control is the severity of messages that are written to your log files. When you make use of CFMAIL in any of your applications, you'll want to keep track of when things don't go as expected so that you can troubleshoot and fix problems as quickly as possible.

The Error Log Severity drop-down list enables you to control the types of messages that are written to the special mail.log file. This file appears in your log directory after you begin using CFMAIL. Should your application have a problem sending email, any messages about the nature of the problem are recorded in this mail.log file. It's a good idea to check this and all log files frequently and examine and fix any errors that are reported. Generally, a healthy application should have log files that grow very slowly over time. If you begin to notice a high number of errors being recorded in any log file, that's a good indication that something unexpected has occurred and the problem needs to be investigated and solved.

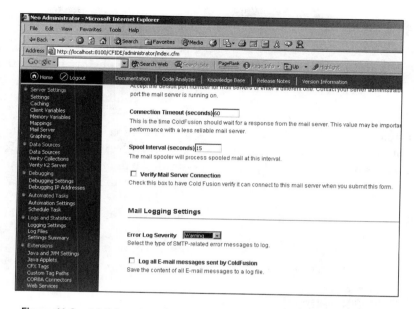

Figure 11.2 Mail Logging Settings options in the ColdFusion Administrator.

The next choice you have is whether you want ColdFusion to record the content of all messages that it sends. Usually, on production servers, this is a bad idea. It requires additional overhead to perform this task; in addition, depending on the volume of mail that your server sends daily, it may require a large amount of disk space. Unless you have a very specific reason for needing to record the content of all the messages you are sending, you'll probably want to leave this setting turned off.

If you are using ColdFusion to enable users of your system to construct web-based email messages, there might be privacy concerns that you'll need to consider before deciding to log the content of the email messages being sent. If you do make the decision to record the content of these messages and the messages were constructed by one of your users, you'll likely need to tell them that their communications are being recorded.

After you've got your environment properly configured and have verified that your ColdFusion Server can communicate with the mail server you have chosen, you can begin exploring the ways in which you can implement automated emailing in your applications.

CFMAIL

The CFMAIL tag enables you as a developer to have your web application act as an email client, creating and sending email to anyone or anything that has a valid email address.

Creating an email message inside your web application using CFMAIL isn't that much different from what you do when you create an email message manually using Outlook or Eudora. The process is essentially the same. Just as Outlook can't do anything with the email other than create it, neither can ColdFusion's CFMAIL tag do anything with the mail message other than get it ready to be sent to the mail server that you've specified.

Let's start by looking at a simple example. In this example, we want our template to send an email message to pengo@penguins.com that says "Hello Pengo!".

Assuming that we've already set up our ColdFusion Administrator to connect with our mail server, the following code accomplishes our goal:

```
<cfmail from="sender@sender.com"
        to="pengo@penguins.com"
        subject="Hello">
Hello Pengo!
</cfmail>
```

If your mail server was set up correctly in the ColdFusion Administrator, in just a few moments, pengo@penguins.com should be reading the wonderfully cheery greeting.

Now, what if you had no access to the ColdFusion Administrator, but you still wanted to send this message automatically from within one of your templates? In such a case, you'd need to make use of some of the additional parameters of the CFMAIL tag to specify the mail server that you are going to use, the port on which you'll send, and so on:

```
<cfmail from="sender@sender.com"
        to="pengo@penguins.com"
        subject="Hello"
        server="IP Address or host name of the mail server"
        port="Port on the mail server to send to">
Hello Pengo!
</cfmail>
```

Of course, this is a very simple example of how CFMAIL works, but it should clearly illustrate how the CFMAIL tag is essentially acting as another mail client for, in this case, your web application.

In most cases, you won't know in advance the email address of the person to whom you're sending the email. In most situations, you'll want to be able to automatically send email to a user in response to a request he or she has made to your site.

Let me give you a real-world example. Let's say that you have a site that requires username/password access to certain areas. You want users to be able to register with your site, specifying the email addresses and passwords they'd like to use. After they've done this, you'd like to automate the entire process of creating username/password combinations and emailing the information to them. With CFMAIL, this can be done quite easily:

1. A user visits your site and requests a username/password combination by filling out a form that asks for the email address and password he or she would like to use.

2. After the form is submitted, the email address and password is dumped into a database where you keep your users' information.

3. The same "action" page where you inserted the email address and password into the database could also automatically email the new account information back to the user by making use of the CFMAIL tag in the following manner:

```
<cfmail from="you@yoursite.com"
        to="#form.emailAddress#"
        subject="Your account has been created">
Based on your recent request for a username and password to our site, an
account has been created for you.   Your account information is as
follows:
Username: #form.emailAddress#
Password: #form.password#
</cfmail>
```

In addition to plain-text email, CFMAIL enables you to send email in Hypertext Markup Language (HTML) format and to attach files as you would with any other mail client.

When you send mail in plain-text format, the message is sent exactly as it is formatted, with all whitespace and carriage returns included.

The CFMAIL tag behaves similarly to the CFOUTPUT tag, in that any variables contained within them are evaluated and the evaluation is included in the resulting output.

Table 11.1 describes the attributes that can be used with the CFMAIL tag to control how mail is sent.

Table 11.1 **Attributes That Can Be Used with** *CFMAIL*

Attribute	Description
To	This is a required attribute that specifies to whom the email should be sent. There are three ways in which you can specify a to address. You can enter the address manually (john@mauzy-broadway.com), you can use a variable that resolves to an email address (#form.emailAddress#), or you can use the name of a query column that contains email addresses. If you use a query column variable in the to parameter, remember that a copy of the email is sent to each email address contained in the query result set.
From	This is a required attribute that lets the recipient of the email know from whom the mail is coming. Again, this address can be specified manually or by using a variable that resolves to a valid email address. When placing an address in the from field, make sure that you use an address that the mail server will accept. Many mail servers process only those messages that come from addresses that are permitted to relay through their systems. If you have questions as to whether the address you're using is allowed to relay in this way, contact your mail administrator.
Cc	This is an optional attribute that enables you to specify a recipient that you'd like to have cc'd on the message.
Bcc	This is an optional attribute that enables you to specify a recipient that you'd like to have bcc'd (blind carbon copied) on the message. This user receives a copy of the message in its entirety, but the original recipient is not aware that this person was included.
Subject	This is a required attribute that specifies the subject of the email being sent. All or any part of the subject text can be generated dynamically through use of a variable.
Type	This is an optional attribute that enables you to distinguish between plain-text email and email that you want to be displayed as HTML in the recipients' mail clients. If you specify TYPE="HTML", any HTML tags you've placed in the content or body of the message are processed for display.
Maxrows	This is an optional attribute that enables you to specify the maximum number of emails that you want this instance of CFMAIL to generate. This is an especially useful attribute if your TO field is generated from a query result set, yet you want to email only to the first 50 or 100 users in the list.

Attribute	Description
MIMEattach	This is an optional attribute that enables you to specify a local file that you want to have Multipurpose Internet Mail Extension (MIME) encoded and attached to the email that you are sending.
Query	This is an optional attribute that enables you to specify the name of a query to use when you want to send multiple email messages or you want your message content to contain information drawn from the results of a previous query.
Group	This is an optional attribute that is used in conjunction with the QUERY attribute. It enables you to group messages by any specified field contained within the query.
Groupcasesensitive	By default, when using the GROUP attribute of CFMAIL, the grouping is always case-sensitive. If you want to ignore this case sensitivity in your grouping, you need to explicitly use this attribute by setting its value to No.
Startrow	This is another of the optional attributes that can be used when you are constructing email using the results of a query. This attribute enables you to specify at which row in the query result set you want to begin processing the query.
Server	This is a required attribute and should contain the IP address or host name of the mail server that you want to use to process your mail messages. If you omit this attribute, ColdFusion defaults to attempting to use the mail server that has been defined in the ColdFusion Administrator.
Port	This is an optional attribute that enables you to specify at which port your mail server is listening for incoming SMTP requests. Usually, this will be port 25 (which is the default), but you can change that default here if you have special environmental considerations.
Mailerid	This is an optional parameter that enables you to pass in a mailer ID that will be used in the header of your mail message. The default header that is passed in reads "ColdFusion Application Server"; however, you might want to change this depending on your specific application needs.
Timeout	This is an optional parameter that enables you to specify how long you want your CFMAIL routine to wait for a connection to the mail server you've specified before timing out. If you leave this attribute blank, ColdFusion defaults to using the value contained in the ColdFusion Administrator Mail Settings page.

Attaching Files to Your Messages

In many cases, rather than just sending a flat email to your users, you'll want to send them a file, such as a document or image, in response to their request. CFMAIL provides you with two ways in which you can accomplish this task. The first is through the use of the MIMEattach parameter of the CFMAIL tag itself. By using this parameter, you can specify the file that you want appended to the message that is being sent to the user:

```
<cfmail from="sender@sender.com"
        to="#form.emailAddress#"
        subject="Here is the file you requested."
        MIMEattach="C:\Temp\file.jpg">
Hi,
Attached you will find the file that you requested when you visited my site.    Enjoy!
</cfmail>
```

Although this method of attaching files will work just fine, it doesn't give much in the way of flexibility. For example, suppose you want to attach an image, but you want to have that image appear as part of the email. With the MIMEattach parameter of CFMAIL, this isn't possible. Luckily, there is another way in which you can attach files that does give you this flexibility:

```
<cfmail from="sender@sender.com"
        to="#form.emailAddress#"
        subject="Here is the file you requested.">
Hi,

Below you will see the file you requested when you visited my site.    Enjoy!

<cfmailparam file="C:\Temp\file.jpg">
</cfmail>
```

The CFMAILPARAM tag enables you to attach either a file or additional header to an email message. For CFMAILPARAM to work, it must be nested within a CFMAIL tag as in the previous example. This is becoming the more common way to attach files with CFMAIL because of the increased flexibility in the way in which you can present the attachment to the recipient.

Table 11.2 gives you an overview of the CFMAILPARAM tag and its attributes.

Table 11.2 **Attributes of the *CFMAILPARAM* Tag**

Attribute	Description
File	There are two attributes that can be used with the CFMAILPARAM tag to tell it what you are attempting to do: file and name. If FILE is included, there is no need for name, and vice versa. However, one or the other is always required. Here, you would simply specify the path to the file that you want to attach to the message.
Name	This is a required attribute if you do not specify a FILE parameter. This enables you to name the header that you are going to insert.
Value	This is the value of the header that you want to insert. This attribute is used only when you were using CFMAILPARAM name= and not file.

Now that you have an understanding of how you can use CFMAIL to create and send email messages and attachments, we'll move our discussion to CFPOP, which enables you to use ColdFusion Server to retrieve and manage messages that already exist on a remote mail server.

CFPOP and Message Management

Previously in this chapter, we discussed how you can use CFMAIL to create and send messages to recipients directly from your ColdFusion application. This is just one of the ways that ColdFusion enables you to leverage the power of email to enhance your web applications.

Through the use of the CFPOP tag, you can enable users of your web applications to retrieve, read, and delete messages that exist on remote POP mail servers. This can be useful if you need to create a portal-type site, check a specific server for alerts, or create a host of other applications.

In the next code example, let's examine how we might connect to a remote server and download the message headers on that server to see what email we have waiting for us:

```
<cfpop server = "#server#"
       username = #UserName#
       password = #pwd#
 action = "getheaderonly"
 name = "TheMessageHeaders">

<cfoutput query = "TheMessageHeaders">
From: #From# — Subject: #Subject#<BR>
</cfoutput>
```

The preceding code example will connect to the mail server we specify, check for any messages that exist for the username we've specified, and then output a summary of those messages to us.

In the previous example, if we had specified `getall` as an attribute of `action`, as opposed to `getheaderonly`, CFPOP would have retrieved the entire message contents, rather than just the header information.

Table 11.3 gives you an overview of the valid attributes for use with the CFPOP tag.

Table 11.3 Attributes of the *<CFPOP>* Tag

Attribute	Description
Server	This is a required attribute used to specify the IP address of the POP server to which you want to connect.
Port	This is an optional parameter that enables you to specify the port on which you want to connect to the POP server. By default, this is 110, the standard POP port.
Username	Although this is an optional attribute, this is where you need to specify the username of the user for whom you are attempting to retrieve mail. If nothing is specified here, the username defaults to anonymous, though it should be noted that most mail servers will reject an attempt to connect as an anonymous user.
Password	This is an optional parameter that should correspond to the password of the user that you've specified in the `username` attribute.
Action	This is an optional parameter that enables you to specify one of three options. You can choose to retrieve only message headers by specifying `getheaderonly`, you can return all available information by specifying `getall`, or you can attempt to delete a specific message by specifying `delete`. By default, the action will be `getheaderonly` to speed up the processing of this tag.
Name	This parameter is required if you've chosen an action of `getheaderonly` or `getall`. This enables you to specify a name of the query object that is returned. This is the query in which your message information will be contained, and you'll need to refer to the `name` you specify here to output any information.

Attribute	Description
Messagenumber	This is an optional parameter that enables you to specify the message number on which you want the action performed. If you've chosen delete as your action, a message number is required. With any other action, only the message numbers specified will be retrieved.
Attachmentpath	This parameter is useful when your action=getall. This enables attachments to be retrieved and written to the specified directory.
Timeout	This is an optional parameter that specifies the time, in seconds, to wait for mail processing to complete. The default timeout value is 60 seconds; so if you know you have a large attachment to download, you may want to increase this value.
Maxrows	This is an optional parameter that enables you to specify the maximum number of messages to be retrieved from the server, starting with the startrow parameter.
Startrow	This is an optional parameter that enables you to specify the first message number that you would like to retrieve. By default, this value is set to 1.
Generateuniquefilenames	This is an optional Yes/No parameter that enables you to specify whether you want the attachments to be saved with a unique name in the event of a naming conflict.

As with tags like CFFILE and CFQUERY, CFPOP generates some unique query values depending on the action that you have specified.

Table 11.4 describes the query values that are returned for all actions completed with CFPOP.

Table 11.4   **Query Values Returned for All Actions Completed with CFPOP**

Value Returned	Description
Queryname.Recordcount	This value returns the total number of records that were returned when your CFPOP action was completed.
Queryname.Currentrow	When processing a query result set for output, there may be times in which you will want to display the row with which you are currently working. This value enables you to retrieve that number.
Queryname.ColumnList	This returns a list of all column names contained with in the query result set returned by your CFPOP action.

The following list describes the values that are returned by CFPOP when your action is equal to getheaderonly or getall:

- queryname.Date
- queryname.From
- queryname.Replyto
- queryname.Subject
- queryname.CC
- queryname.To
- queryname.Messagenumber

The following list describes the values that are returned by CFPOP when your action is getall. These values are not available when the action equals getheaderonly.

- queryname.Body
- queryname.Header
- queryname.Attachments
- queryname.Attachmentfiles

You can use any of the values returned by your CFPOP action in the output of your pages to construct an application that almost completely mimics the functionality of a mail client.

Summary

In this chapter, we've discussed how to prepare your environment to leverage the power of email in enhancing your ColdFusion applications. At a high level, you can integrate your ColdFusion Server with a single mail server by configuring the ColdFusion Administrator to connect directly to the mail server of your choosing.

Beyond that, we've discussed how to use the CFMAIL tag to construct messages, attach files, and send those messages to singular or multiple recipients. We've also discussed how to use the optional parameters available for CFMAIL to specify things like server names, ports, usernames, and passwords on an application-by-application basis.

You should also be comfortable with attaching files to your mail messages using the optional parameter of the CFMAIL tag or by using the CFMAILPARAM tag itself.

CFPOP, in contrast to CFMAIL, enables you to read, manage, and delete existing messages by providing you with an easy way to integrate your existing ColdFusion applications with POP-compliant mail servers.

By utilizing these two powerful components of the ColdFusion Markup Language, you should be able to perform automatically through your ColdFusion applications tasks that you previously had to do manually.

Just as you can easily integrate email components into your ColdFusion application, it's just as easy to integrate the server file system into your application to provide functionality for your users. This leads us right into Chapter 12, "Working with Files."

12

Working with Files

FORTUNATELY FOR US DEVELOPERS, COLDFUSION MX gives us many opportunities to leverage the file system, the network servers, and even the system registry when we need to build a certain feature into our applications.

In this chapter, we look at how we can use ColdFusion MX to read, write, edit, and manage files on our server. We'll also discover how we can use ColdFusion to gain access to other servers through the File Transfer Protocol (FTP) and the Hypertext Transfer Protocol (HTTP).

In addition, we'll look at expanding our interaction with the file system by using CFDIRECTORY, CFREGISTRY, and scheduled tasks both within the ColdFusion Administrator and within our ColdFusion Markup Language (CFML) code.

All these methods involve ColdFusion interacting in some way with your server or another server to make your application more powerful and feature-filled. In the developer's world, that's always a good thing.

CFFILE

As a ColdFusion developer who is thinking about interacting with the file system or working with files in general, you'll likely look to the CFFILE tag, and with good reason. The CFFILE tag is one of the most powerful tools you can use when you want to do just about anything to a file.

Using the CFFILE tag, you can move, rename, copy, or delete files that exist on the server. You can read text files on the server into memory, append text to them, or create new ones altogether. In addition, CFFILE enables you to upload files from the client machine to your web server through simple Hypertext Markup Language (HTML) forms.

In most cases, when you begin to look up reference information for a particular ColdFusion tag, you expect to see a table with the tag syntax and its common attributes. In the case of CFFILE, the attributes that are passed along with the CFFILE tag are dependent on the CFFILE action that you specify.

The CFFILE tag can be used with any one of nine action types. Table 12.1 lists the various action types and common examples of their various uses.

Table 12.1 *CFFILE* **Tag Action Types**

Action Type	Common Use
append	Using the CFFILE append action type enables you to append text to the end of an existing text file.
copy	Using the copy action type, you can copy any file from one location on the server to another, just like using the OS copy command.
delete	The delete action type works just as the name implies, enabling you to delete a specific file from the server.
move	The move action type moves a file from one server location to another. Unlike the COPY action type, in which, after copying, the file still exists in the original location, with the move action type, after the file is moved, it no longer exists in the first location.
	This is useful if you want to enable users to upload files to a temp directory, but then want those files copied to another location. Using the move action type in place of copy eliminates the need to go back and delete files from the temp directory.
read	The read action type enables you to read the contents of a text file into memory. After it is in memory, you can use the variable as you would any other ColdFusion variable.
readbinary	The readbinary action type works just like the READ action type, only that it enables you to read the contents of image files (or any other binary file).
rename	Using the rename action type with CFFILE enables you to rename a specific file on the server.

Action Type	Common Use
upload	The upload action type is used when you want web clients to be able to push a file up to your server. Used in conjunction with HTML forms, the upload action type saves the uploaded file to your web server.
write	The write action type enables you to use ColdFusion to write out dynamic contents to a text file.

Understanding how each action type works and when to use each helps you determine which particular action is best suited for your development situation. For the purposes of the examples in this chapter, we'll use the UPLOAD action type because it's usually the one type developers want to make work first. For a full explanation of each action type and syntax, see Appendix A, "Tag Reference."

Uploading Files to the Server

When you want to use ColdFusion to enable your users to upload files to your web server, the first step is creating an HTML form in which they can specify the file that they want to upload.

The following example demonstrates a simple upload form that enables users to submit a file to your server for upload.

```
<html>
<head>

        <title>File Upload Form</title>
</head>
<body>
<h2>Choose File</h2>
<form action="actionPage.cfm"
enctype="multipart/form-data"
method="post">
<p>Choose the file you would like to upload:
<input type="file"
name="File"
size="30">
</p>
<input    type="submit"
value"Upload">
</form>
</body>
</html>
```

As you can see from this example, all we've done is create a simple form that enables users to choose which file they'd like to post to our server. The key when creating a file upload form is to make sure you use the correct `enctype` of `"multipart/form-data"` and to make sure that you use an input type of `"file"`. This enables your HTML to be rendered with a Browse button that permits users to select a file on their local systems for upload.

The output of the form creation code is shown in Figure 12.1.

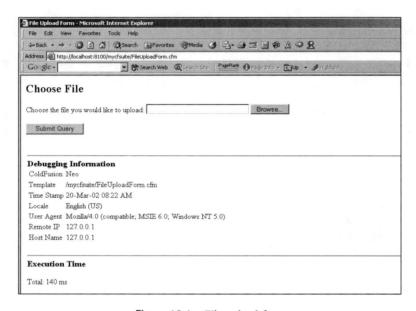

Figure 12.1   File upload form.

Now that we have our form built, we can focus on using `CFFILE` to upload the file to our server. In this case, because we want to upload the file, we'll want to use the `CFFILE` action type `UPLOAD`.

The following section of code shows you how we need to build our `actionPage.cfm` file that enables the file to be uploaded to our server:

```
<html>
<head>
  <title>File Upload Action Page</title>
</head>
<body>
  <!---Begin the file upload--->
  <cffile action="upload"
          destination="#ExpandPath(".")#/"
          nameConflict="overwrite"
          fileField="Form.File">
  <cfoutput>
```

```
  Upload of file: #cffile.serverfile# successful.
  </cfoutput>
</body>
</html>
```

With this section of code, we are actually uploading to our server the file that the client selected. Because the file uploads to the server, its contents are written into the random-access memory (RAM) on our server. After the complete file is received, the contents of the file are pulled out of RAM and actually written to a file on disk. For this reason, it's important to make sure that you have sufficient RAM on your server if you intend to allow the uploading of large files. Otherwise, you'll see an out-of-memory error, telling you that you don't have enough system resources to complete the task.

You might notice that in the output on our action page, we use some variables to tell us that the file was uploaded successfully. After a file upload is completed, you have several status variables available to you to help you determine that the upload was successful and to communicate informational messages to your users.

FileExists Function

You can use the FileExists() function to verify that a file was successfully uploaded to a server. The FileExists() function returns a simple "YES" value if the file you specify as an argument to the function is present on the server.

The FileExists() function can be used in the following manner:

```
<cfif FileExists(FullPathToYourFile)>
The file you are looking for exists in the directory specified.
</cfif>
```

Table 12.2 gives you an overview of the status variables available to you after a completed file upload. It also gives their uses.

Table 12.2   **CFFILE Upload Status Variables**

Status Variable	Use
attemptedServerFile	This variable stores the name that ColdFusion first used when attempting to write the file to your server. If there was a name conflict when uploading the file to your server, the final filename might be different.
clientDirectory	This variable tells you where the file came from on the client system. For example, if the user uploaded a file to your server from his or her C:\TEMP directory, that information would be present in this variable.

continues ▶

Table 12.2 **Continued**

Status Variable	Use
clientFile	This variable stores the full name of the file being uploaded as it was on the client file system.
clientFileName	This variable stores the name of the file as it was on the client file system, but without the file extension.
clientFileExt	This variable stores only the file extension of the file being uploaded, as it was on the client file system.
contentSubType	This variable stores the standard Multipurpose Internet Mail Extension (MIME) content subtype of the file being uploaded. For example, a value here might be GIF or JPEG.
contentType	This variable stores the broader MIME content type of the file. Here, for example, you might see image listed as the MIME type.
dateLastAccessed	This variable stores the date on which the file being uploaded was last accessed.
fileExisted	This variable returns either yes or no, telling you whether a file of the same name or extension already exists in the location to which the current file is being uploaded.
fileSize	This variable reports the size of the file being uploaded. This variable can be accessed only to get the total size of the file after the upload is complete.
fileWasAppended	This variable returns either yes or no to let you know whether ColdFusion appended the uploaded file to the end of an existing file.
fileWasOverwritten	This variable returns yes or no to let you know if a file on you server was overwritten to upload the current file.
fileWasRenamed	This variable returns either yes or no to tell you whether ColdFusion had to rename the file being uploaded to avoid a name conflict.
fileWasSaved	This variable simply tells you, yes or no, that the file was saved.
oldFileSize	This variable reports the size of the file that was overwritten (if a file was indeed overwritten) during an upload operation.

Status Variable	Use
serverDirectory	This variable reports to you the directory on the server in which the uploaded file was saved.
serverFile	This variable reports to you the name of the uploaded file after it's been saved on the server. This variable includes the complete filename, including the extension.
serverFileName	This variable gives you the name of the file as it is stored on the server after upload, excluding the file extension.
serverFileExt	This variable reports to you only the extension of the file that has been uploaded to the server.
timeCreated	This variable reports to you the date and time that the uploaded file was created on the server.
timeLastModified	This variable reports to you the date and time that the file was last modified.

You can use any of these output variables after an upload operation is complete to communicate status or to help manage the files on your server.

CFFTP

In the last section, we examined how we would use CFFILE to move files between the server and the client. Suppose we want to move files from the server to another server? That's where CFFTP comes in.

CFFTP enables ColdFusion developers to utilize FTP to move files between their ColdFusion Servers and other FTP servers.

Table 12.3 provides you with an overview of the CFFTP tag's syntax and attributes.

Table 12.3 *CFFTP* **Attributes Table**

Attribute	Description
action	This is a required attribute that determines the FTP action to be performed. Valid actions for this attribute are as follows: • open • close • changedir

continues ▶

Table 12.3 **Continued**

Attribute	Description
	▪ `createdir`
	▪ `listdir`
	▪ `removedir`
	▪ `getfile`
	▪ `putfile`
	▪ `rename`
	▪ `remove`
	▪ `getcurrentdir`
	▪ `getcurrenturl`
	▪ `existsdir`
	▪ `existsfile`
	▪ `exists`
	To perform any action on an FTP server, you must first use the `connect` action to connect to that server. An example later in this section shows you how to connect and perform a directory listing.
`username`	This is a required attribute when the action is `open`. This attribute enables you to pass in the username with which you would like to connect.
`password`	This is a required attribute when the action is `open`; this attribute specifies the password of the user whom you are connecting as.
`server`	This is a required attribute for the `open` action and enables you to specify the server to which you are connecting.
`timeout`	This is an optional attribute that enables you to specify the maximum time you want ColdFusion to wait for any FTP action to be performed. If left blank, this value defaults to 30 seconds.
`port`	This attribute enables you to specify the port to which you would like to connect on the FTP server. The default port for FTP is 21, but you might need to change this if you have configuration or firewall considerations.
`connection`	This optional attribute enables you to assign a name to this FTP connection. This attribute is useful should you want to cache this connection for later use.
`proxyserver`	This is an optional string attribute that enables you to specify the name or address of a proxy server that you want to use to connect.

Attribute	Description
retrycount	This optional attribute enables you to specify the number of times that you would like the connection to be retried should an action fail. By default, this value is 1.
stoponerror	This is an optional attribute that enables you to tell CFFTP to stop processing if an error is encountered.
	This attribute takes either a yes or no value. If set to yes, all processing is halted if an error is encountered. If this value is set to no and an error is encountered, three error variables are automatically populated so that you can diagnose the problem at a later time. These error values are as follows:
	• **cfftp.succeeded.** Returns yes or no.
	• **cfftp.errorcode.** Returns the error number associated with the error that was encountered.
	• **cfftp.errortext.** Returns a message with a short description of the error that was encountered.
passive	This optional attribute enables you to specify whether you want to allow the FTP connection to enable passive mode FTP. This attribute takes a yes or no value.

Now let's look at an example of how we would use CFFTP to connect to an FTP server and perform a simple listing on a remote directory.

```
<html>
  <head>
    <title>CFFTP Usage Example</title>
  </head>
<body>
  <!--- change these values to match an ftp account you know works --->
  <cfparam name="ftpServer" default="ftp.mauzy-broadway.com">
  <cfparam name="ftpUsername" default="anonymous">
  <cfparam name="ftpPassword" default="info@mauzy-broadway.com">
  <!--- open a connection to an ftp server --->
  <cfftp action="open"
         connection="theConnection"
         server="#ftpServer#"
         username="#ftpUsername#"
         password="#ftpPassword#"
         stopOnError="Yes">
  <!--- did we get connected? --->
  <cfoutput>#cfftp.succeeded#</cfoutput>
  <cfif cfftp.succeeded>
    <!--- perform a listing on the initial directory --->
    <cfftp action="LISTDIR"
           stopOnError="Yes"
           name="DirectoryListing"
           directory="/"
```

```
              connection="theConnection">
    <cfoutput query="DirectoryListing">
      #name#<BR>
    </cfoutput>
  </cfif>
  <!--- close the connection on the server --->
  <cfftp action="close"
         connection="theConnection"
         stopOnError="Yes">
  <!--- did the connection close ok? --->
  <cfoutput>#cfftp.succeeded#</cfoutput>
</body>
</html>
```

In addition to performing simple directory listings, you can use CFFTP to interact with the files on the FTP server just as you would using any other FTP client. This gives your ColdFusion application the power to upload/download files, manage a remote file system, and offer direct connections to file repositories for your web clients.

For a full explanation of the CFFTP syntax and its usage, see Appendix B, "Function Reference."

CFDIRECTORY

We've examined how CFFTP enables you to manage files on a remote server through the FTP protocol from within your ColdFusion applications. Earlier in this text, we also discussed how you can use CFFILE to work directly with files that exist on your ColdFusion Server. Now, suppose you want to enable your ColdFusion application to work with the directories on your server as well. With CFDIRECTORY, you can easily give your applications the ability to list, create, rename, and delete directories on your server.

Table 12.4 examines the CFDIRECTORY tag and its attributes.

Table 12.4 **CFDIRECTORY Attributes**

Attribute	Description
action	This attribute is optional, and it specifies the type of action that you'd like CFDIRECTORY to perform.
	Valid actions for the CFDIRECTORY tag are as follows:
	▪ create
	▪ delete
	▪ list
	▪ rename

Attribute	Description
	If no action is specified, the CFDIRECTORY tag defaults to list, performing a listing of the specified directory.
directory	This is a required attribute that enables you to specify the name of the directory on which you would like to perform the specified action. You should always end any directory attribute value with a slash.
filter	This is an optional attribute, which should be used when the action is set to list. The filter attribute enables you to apply a file extension filter to your directory listing so that only those files meeting the specified criteria are returned.
	As an example, if you were listing a directory of images and only wanted Graphics Interchange Format (GIF) files returned, you would use "*.gif" in the filter attribute to specify that only those files matching that criteria should be returned to you.
mode	The attribute is an optional attribute that is useful on UNIX or Linux platforms when the action is set to create. This attribute lets you set permissions on the directory that you are creating.
	Valid modes are as follows:
	▪ **644.** Sets read/write permissions for the owner and read permissions for group and other.
	▪ **666.** Sets read/write permissions for the owner, group, and other.
	▪ **777.** Sets read/write/execute permissions for all.
name	This attribute is required when the action is set to list. This attribute names your directory listing so that you know what variable to call when you want to display the output query.
	For example, if you named your directory listing MyListing, you would use <cfoutput query="MyListing"> to display the results of that directory list.
newdirectory	This attribute is required when the action is set to rename. This attribute enables you to specify the new name you want to use for the directory that you are renaming.
sort	This is an optional attribute that can be used when the action is set to list. This attribute enables you to specify the query columns on which you would like to sort, either ascending or descending.

The following example shows CFDIRECTORY performing a simple directory listing on a specified directory:

```
<html>
  <head>
    <title>Example of &lt;cfdirectory&gt; Usage</title>
  </head>
<body>
<!--- use cfdirectory to display a directory listing --->
<cfset variables.webdrive = ListFirst(ExpandPath("."),
/\")>
<cfoutput>#variables.webdrive#<br></cfoutput>
<cfdirectory directory="#variables.webdrive#/"
             name="myTempFiles"
             sort="name ASC">
<!--- output the results --->
<cfoutput query="myTempFiles">
#name#<br>
</cfoutput>
</body>
</html>
```

As with CFFTP, the example here is a simple directory listing to give you the idea of syntax and simple usage. The CFDIRECTORY tag itself, however, is much more powerful, enabling you to sort, delete, create, and rename. This opens the power of the file system to your ColdFusion application for file management purposes.

For a complete description of all CFDIRECTORY actions and syntax, refer to Appendix B.

CFREGISTRY

The CFREGISTRY tag enables you to read, write, and delete values from the system registry.

Depending on the action that you choose to perform with the CFREGISTRY tag, the attributes that the tag takes are slightly different. In this section, we quickly run down all available action options and the attributes associated with each.

ACTION="getAll"

With the CFREGISTRY action "getAll", CFREGISTRY returns all keys and values present in the specified registry branch. After they are returned, you have access to these values as you would with any other ColdFusion recordset.

Table 12.5 gives an overview of the attributes associated with the CFREGISTRY tag when the "getAll" action is specified.

Table 12.5 **Attributes for *CFREGISTRY* with the "*getAll*" Action**

Attribute	Description
branch	This is a required attribute that specifies the name of the registry branch from which you would like to retrieve values.
type	This is an optional attribute that specifies the type of data that you would like to retrieve. Valid parameters for this attribute are as follows: • string • dword • key • any
name	This is a required attribute that enables you to specify the name of the recordset in which the returned values will be stored.
sort	This is an optional attribute that enables you to sort the data returned as you would any ColdFusion recordset.

ACTION="get"

With the CFREGISTRY action "get", CFREGISTRY returns a specific registry value and stores it for you in a ColdFusion variable, as shown in the following code:

```
<html>
<head>
<title>
EXAMPLE OF CFREGISTRY USAGE
</title>
</head>
<body>
<!---USE CFREGISTRY TO DISPLAY CURRENT JRE VERSION--->
<cfregistry action="get"
    branch="HKEY_LOCAL_MACHINE\SOFTWARE\Javasoft\Java Runtime Environment"
    type="String"
    entry="CurrentVersion"
    variable="myversion">
<!---OUTPUT THE RESULTS--->
<cfoutput>
JRE Version: #myversion#<br>
</cfoutput>
<!---USE CFREGISTRY TO GET THE JRE HOME DIRECTORY FROM THE VERSION NUMBER--->
```

```
<cfregistry action="get"
    branch="HKEY_LOCAL_MACHINE\SOFTWARE\Javasoft\Java Runtime
Environment\#myversion#"
    type="String"
    entry="JavaHome"
    variable="myhome">
<!---OUTPUT THE RESULTS--->
<cfoutput>
JRE Home Directory: #myhome#<br>
</cfoutput></body>
</html>
```

Table 12.6 gives an overview of the attributes associated with the CFREGISTRY tag when the "get" action is specified.

Table 12.6 **Attributes for *CFREGISTRY* with the "*get*" Action**

Attribute	Description
branch	This is a required attribute that specifies the name of the registry branch from which you would like to retrieve values.
type	This is an optional attribute that specifies the type of data you would like to retrieve. Valid parameters for this attribute are as follows: ■ string ■ dword ■ key
entry	This is a required attribute that specifies to ColdFusion exactly which registry entry you would like to retrieve.
variable	This is a required attribute that specifies the name of the ColdFusion variable in which you would like the data that is retrieved to be stored.

ACTION="set"

With the CFREGISTRY action of "set", CFREGISTRY enables you to set the value of a registry entry or add a new entry altogether.

Table 12.7 gives an overview of the attributes associated with the CFREGISTRY tag when the "set" action is specified.

Table 12.7 **Attributes for *CFREGISTRY* with the "*set*" Action**

Attribute	Description
branch	This is a required attribute that specifies the name of the registry branch that contains (or will contain) the values that you wish to set.
type	This is an optional attribute that specifies the type of data you would like to set. Valid parameters for this attribute are as follows: ■ string ■ dword ■ key
entry	This is a required attribute that specifies to ColdFusion exactly which registry entry you would like to set.
variable	This is an optional attribute that specifies the data value to be set.

ACTION="delete"

With the CFREGISTRY action of "delete", CFREGISTRY enables you to delete a specific registry value.

Table 12.8 gives an overview of the attributes associated with the CFREGISTRY tag when the "delete" action is specified.

Table 12.8 **Attributes for *CFREGISTRY* with the "*delete*" Action**

Attribute	Description
branch	This is a required attribute and must include one of the following: ■ To delete a key, you must specify the name of the registry key to be deleted. If you want to delete an entire key, do not specify an entry. ■ To delete a value, include the name of the branch in which the value is contained and make sure to specify an entry to be deleted within that branch.
entry	This attribute is required when you want to delete a value. Enter the name of the value that you want to delete.

Summary

In this chapter, we've covered how you can use the CFFILE tag to move files between the client browser and your server. We've also examined how you can use CFFTP to manage files from server to server. Finally, we looked at how you can use the CFREGISTRY tag to interact with the system registry.

As you move forward with your application development, continually review the ways in which ColdFusion enables you to interact with both local and remote file systems to ensure that you are completing tasks efficiently and that your applications are harnessing the full power of the CFML.

13
CFScript

BECAUSE COLDFUSION IS A TAG–BASED MARKUP language, most web developers should find it relatively easy to pick up. However, developers accustomed to procedural and scripting languages often find ColdFusion's syntax ambiguous, overly simplified, or insufficient when it comes to complex or lengthy logical statements. The creators of ColdFusion realized this and tried to surmount it with the introduction of CFScript in ColdFusion 4.1. CFScript provides a method for developers who are more comfortable using scripting-based languages, such as JavaScript, to exploit their knowledge and skill. CFScript, until recently, was also the only way to create user-defined functions (UDFs). In fact, many of the examples in this chapter will be in either standard ColdFusion Markup Language (CFML) or CFScript, so the following section provides a short primer of sorts to familiarize the reader with CFScript.

CFScript can be used to set variables, loop through collections, and work with the many ColdFusion functions and expressions. One will often find that CFScript enables the author to write much clearer logic, as well as more succinct code in specific instances. Although we cannot show every instance in which CFScript should be used instead of CFML, we will provide some rules of thumb. The most important rule of thumb is to use the syntax with which you are most productive. All other considerations come after that!

CFScript is based on ECMA Script, which is essentially JavaScript, so anyone comfortable with JavaScript will find CFScript easy to learn. The European Computer Manufacturers Association (ECMA) is a European-based industry association that strives to standardize information and communication systems.

Note

For more information about ECMA Script, go to www.ecma.ch/.

Benefits

There are some distinct advantages of using CFScript over CFML tags:

- Scripting is more straightforward for working with variable assignments, controlling flow, working with expressions, and working with functions.

- Scripting programmers find this easier to read and write.

- In some cases, operations such as the setting of variables tend to be slightly faster than CFML.

For developers used to scripting languages such as PHP, Perl, ASP, and JavaScript, a CFScript block is easier to interpret than a tag-based language like CFML.

CFScript Syntax

CFScript enables the programmer to take advantage of ColdFusion's extensive scripting abilities. The general form of the CFScript tag is this:

```
<cfscript>
    Statement;
</cfscript>
```

CFScript statements are usually a single line and they must end with a semicolon. For example, the following script block assigns the value 42 to the variable foo:

```
<cfscript>
    foo = 42;
</cfscript>
```

The next block will set the variable string_foo to the string "forty two":

```
<cfscript>
    string_foo = "forty two";
</cfscript>
```

Multiple statements are done in much the same way:

```
<cfscript>
    foo = 42;
    string_foo = "forty two";
</cfscript>
```

Commenting Code

An important difference to note between ColdFusion's tag-based structure and CFScript is the formation of comments. In the tag-based structure, a comment takes the form `<!--- Comment --->`, and in CFScript, comments are denoted by a double forward slash (`//`). So, use tags like this:

```
<!--- This is a comment --->
<cfset foo = 42>
<!--- An additional comment --->
<cfset string_foo = "forty two">
```

And use CFScript like this:

```
<!--- This is a comment --->
<cfscript>
    foo = 42;
    //An additional comment
    string_foo = "forty two";
</cfscript>
```

Two forward slashes (`//`) enable the programmer to comment one line only. If a multiple line comment is desired, CFScript provides support for Java, C, and JavaScript-style comment blocks. The block begins with `/*` and ends with `*/`, as shown in the following code:

```
//This is a one-line comment
/*
This is a multiline
comment block
*/
```

Conditional Programming

Perhaps the most important aspect of programming languages is the capability to program conditional logic. The most obvious of these is the If-Then-Else statement. Take a standard ColdFusion conditional statement like the following:

```
<cfif x lt y>
    <cfset index = x>
```

```
<cfelse>
    <cfset index = y>
</cfif>
```

In CFScript, it looks very much the same:

```
<cfscript>
    if (x lt y)
        index = x;
    else
        index = y;
</cfscript>
```

Let's look at a more complex example:

```
<cfif action is "display_discount">
    <cfset display_price = price - (price * discount)>
        <cfelseif action is "display_sale">
            <cfset display_price = price - (price * sale)>
        <cfelseE>
            <cfset display_price = price>
</cfif>
```

In a script block, it would look like this:

```
<cfscript>
    if (action is "display_discount")
        display_price = price - (price * discount);
         else if (action is "display_sale")
        display_price = price - (price * sale);
    else
        display_price = price;
</cfscript>
```

For developers with formal programming backgrounds, the preceding code is a much cleaner, more succinct series of statements.

In the case of a compound statement, multiple lines are encapsulated within braces:

```
<cfscript>
    if (expression)
        Statement;
    else {
        Statement1;
        Statement2;
    }
</cfscript>
```

Working with Data Structures

CFScript also enables the programmer to simplify the construction of complex data structures. The tag-based structure of ColdFusion can easily become very tedious for this task. Let's say that we want to create a structure of customer billing information; we could do the following:

```
<cfset customer = StructNew()>
<cfset customer.ID = FORM.CUSID>
<cfset customer.name = StructNew()>
<cfset  customer.name.first = FORM.FirstName>
<cfset FSET customer.name.last = FORM.LastName>
<cfset customer.billinginfo = StructNew()>
<cfset customer.billinginfo.address = StructNew()>
<cfset customer.billinginfo.address.street = FORM.street>
<cfset customer.billinginfo.address.city = FORM.city>
<cfset customer.billinginfo.address.state = FORM.state>
<cfset customer.billinginfo.address.zipcode = FORM.zipcode>
```

In CFScript, we can avoid the use of the CFSET tag and just assign the values to the variable:

```
<cfscript>
    customer = StructNew();
    customer.ID = FORM.cusid;
    customer.name = StructNew();
    customer.name.first = FORM.firstname;
    customer.name.last = FORM.lastname;
    customer.billinginfo = StructNew();
    customer.billinginfo.address = StructNew();
    customer.billinginfo.address.street = FORM.street;
    customer.billinginfo.address.city = FORM.city;
    customer.billinginfo.address.state = FORM.state;
    customer.billinginfo.address.zipcode = FORM.zipcode;
<cfscript>
```

The construction of arrays is very similar:

```
<cfset array = ArrayNew(1)>
<cfset array[1] = "Bob">
<cfset array[2] = "Alice">
<cfset array[3] = "John">
<cfset array[4] = "Lisa">
```

In CFScript, it looks like the following:

```
<cfscript>
    array = ArrayNew(1);
    array[1] = "Bob";
    array[2] = "Alice";
    array[3] = "John";
    array[4] = "Lisa";
</cfscript>
```

Not only is this clearer, but it also saves some typing!

Looping

There are several types of loops available in also. Several of the loop types are covered in this section.

For Loop

The For loop is the CFScript form of the `CFLOOP` tag shown in the following code:

```
<cfloop INDEX="i" FROM="1" TO="10">
<cfset array[i] = i>
</cfloop>
```

This will set the values of the elements 1–10 in an array to the value of its index. In CFScript, it would look like the following:

```
<cfscript>
    for(i=1; i LTE 10; i = i + 1){
        array[i] = i;
    }
</cfscript>
```

The general form of a For loop in CFScript is as follows:

```
For (starting expression; conditional expression; incremental expression)
```

The starting expression sets the values of the index to be used within the loop (i=1 in the preceding example), and the conditional expression is the condition that must be maintained for the loop to continue. When the conditional expression is no longer true, the loop terminates. The incremental expression defines the manner in which to modify the index. This could be something like the preceding example; it could be i = i + 1, which increments the value of i every time through the loop, or something like i = i + 2 to loop over only odd or only even numbers, depending on the initial setting.

Note

Unlike ECMA Script and JavaScript, CFScript supports all the CFML expressions. This includes operators (such as +, -, =, and so on), as well as all CFML functions. You must use CFML operators, such as LT, GT, and EQ. You cannot use JavaScript operators, such as <, >, ==, or ++, so be careful.

For-In

Another application of the For loop is the ability to loop over structures. Let's create a structure of pet information:

```
<cfscript>
    pet_struct = StructNew();
    pet_ struct.cat = "Asterix";
    pet_ struct.cat = "Jenghis";
    pet_ struct.cat = "Newt";
    pet_ struct.dog = "Delilah";
    pet_ struct.bird = "Peekaboo";
</cfscript>
```

We can then loop over the pets using CFLOOP:

```
<cfloop COLLECTION="#pet_ struct #" ITEM="pet">
<cfoutput>#pet#</cfoutput></br>
</cfloop>
```

This will print the names of the pets. In CFScript, we can do the same thing:

```
<cfscript>
    for(pet in pet_ struct){
        WriteOutput("#pet#</br>");
    }
</cfscript>
```

while

Yet another type of loop is what is known as the pretest, or While, loop. What this means is that given a condition, the condition must be true before the rest of the loop will be executed. This loop is useful where a group of statements will not always need to be executed. Take for example the case of a shopping cart. If you want to loop over the contents of the cart, the following loop might be useful:

```
<cfscript>
    //Set the number of the item to display
    index = 1;
    //While loop
    while(index LTE cart_size){
        //Output the item at the specified index
        WriteOutput(shopping_cart[index]);
        //Increment index
        index = index + 1;
    }
</cfscript>
```

In the preceding example, we are using index to denote the current item to be printed. The while loop is contingent upon the index being less than the number of items in the cart, which is contained in cart_size. If the size of the cart is 0, the loop will not execute and no items will be displayed. If the cart_size is greater than 0, all items in the cart will be displayed.

do-while

The last type of loop is the post-test, or do-while, loop. This loop will execute its contents at least once; then the conditional is tested and, if true, the loop will continue until the condition is false.

For example, if we have the same problem as previously presented, but we are guaranteed to always have at least one item in the cart, we might do the following:

```
<cfscript>
    //Set the number of the item to display
    index = 1;
    //while loop
    do{
        //Output the item at the specified index
        WriteOutput(shopping_cart[index]);
        //Increment index
        index = index + 1;
    }while(index LTE cart_size)
</cfscript>
```

This will do the same thing as the regular while loop, but it will always display at least one item.

break

The break statement is used when the loop must be ended before the condition for the loop is false. In this case, the insertion of a break statement will cause the loop to end, and any code after the break that is within the loop will not be executed. For example:

```
<cfscript>
    while(condition){
        if(condition)
        break;
        else{
          statement;
          }
    }
</cfscript>
```

continue

The continue statement is used when the rest of the code in the loop does not need to be executed, but the loop must continue to run until the condition is false. In this case, the continue statement is used much like the break statement:

```
<cfscript>
    while(condition){
        if(condition)
            continue;
        else{
        statement;
        }
    }
</cfscript>
```

switch

As we saw earlier, If-Then-Else statements can be easily coded using CFScript. However, complex If structures can be difficult to code and difficult to make sense of. In this case, it might be worthwhile to use a switch statement. The tag-based version of a switch statement is the CFSWITCH tag. This tag takes a variable, and, depending on the value, will perform certain actions, or cases. For example:

```
<cfswitch expression="#somevar#">
<cfcase value="one">
    Statement
</cfcase>
</cfcase value="two">
    Statement
</cfcase>
<cfdefaultcase>
    Statement
</cfdefaultcase>
</cfswitch>
```

Here, we are switching on the value of the variable "somevar". If its value is "one", we will use the first case, and so on. If no other cases fit the value of "somevar", we will do what is contained in the CFDEFAULTCASE statements. If the default case is left out and no other case fits, no code will be executed within the switch. The CFSCRIPT version is very similar:

```
<cfscript>
    switch (somevar){
        case "one": {
    Statement;
    break;
```

```
        }
      case "two": {
  Statement;
  break;
      }
      default: {
  Statement;
  break;
        }
    }
</cfscript>
```

Note the use of the break statement at the end of each case. You should almost always put a break statement at the end of the case statement because it needs to tell ColdFusion to exit the switch statement. The break statement is optional, but if you do not use it, ColdFusion will execute all the statements in the following case statement, *even if that case is false*. This is something you more or less never want to do.

Functions

As has been evidenced by the previous examples, ColdFusion functions might be used throughout a CFScript block.

Output

Output within cfscript blocks is done using the WriteOutput function. The use of this function is the same as any other ColdFusion function: WriteOutput(*expression*).

Note

WriteOutput differs from CFOUTPUT in that you can use any expression within the WriteOutput function. For example:

```
<cfscript>
  WriteOutput(NOT Val('foo'));
</cfscript>
```

will output the following:

YES

Handling Exceptions

No matter how great a coder you are, you cannot foresee all the things that might happen when your code or application is actually used in production. For this reason, almost every programming language or scripting language has some method of exception handling to enable developers to create robust applications that gracefully handle unforeseen events or that provide *useful* and often critical debugging information so that you can find the source of the actual problem and resolve it.

At this point, you are familiar with CFML exception handling, but CFScript also has its own exception handling with its analogues to the CFTRY and CFCATCH tags. CFScript provides you the try, catch, and finally script statements, and when you develop your CFScript blocks (especially when creating UDFs), you should use them liberally!

CFScript Exception Syntax

Using exception-handling code in CFScript is very similar to using it in standard CFML. For example, let's look at the generic form of a try/catch statement in CFScript:

```
try{
    Code you wish to have handled if there is a exception}
    catch(exceptionType exceptionVariable )
    {The code you will use to deal with the exception that is characterized by
    exceptionType}
    catch(exceptionType2 exceptionVariable2 )
    {The code you will use to deal with the exception that is characterized by
    exceptionType2}
    etc...
    {The code you want to be processed in all cases, regardless of if there was an
    exception}
```

Now if you remember from CFML exception handling, a CFML CFTRY block must have CFCATCH and CFINALLY in the CFTRY block. Well, CFScript differs in this respect, so don't get caught by this. With CFScript, *you do not* place your finally statement in the try block. Instead, you place it *after* the try block.

Usually you will use a try block followed by a catch block or a series of catch blocks. Occasionally you will want to use a finally block.

In the CFScript catch block, the exceptionVariable variable contains the exception type. This variable is the equivalent of the CFCATCH tag, which is a cfcatch.Type built-in variable.

The `finally` statement and block always executes! This is something that developers often overlook. If your `catch` block catches an exception, the `finally` block executes after the `catch` block; otherwise, the `finally` block executes after the `try` block. This is really important to remember in that many developers get confused and think that a `finally` statement will not execute if there is an exception. Thus, they get some unexpected results. The `finally` statement is very useful and should be used where you have to have some code executed regardless of an exception. Some of the cases in which this would apply include alerts, logging, or the closing of a file.

Let's look at an example that we are going to use in a later chapter (Chapter 20, "Advanced XML"). One problem with ColdFusion MX's `CFXML` tag is that it does not let you validate a Document Type Definition (DTD). This can be very important when you are working with trading partners, content suppliers, or anyone else's XML that you cannot directly control.

To get around this issue, we are going to access the Apache eXtensible Markup Language (XML) parsers that ColdFusion uses directly via `CFOBJECT`. Because we are such good coders, we are going to make sure that we use exception handling! Now our code is rather well-commented, so we won't get into the specifics of it outside of how we are going to use exception handling. Our code is going to access the Java-based XML parser using the `CreateObject` function. The `catch` statement executes only if the `CreateObject` function generates an exception. The displayed information includes the exception message; the `except.Message` variable is the equivalent of calling the Java `getMessage` method on the returned Java exception object.

```
<cfscript>
    /**
    * Xerces DOM Parsing
    *
    * Note, once the DOM document is created, from the initial Xerces parse
    * of the XML document, accessing the XML elements/attributes is
    * determined by the user.
    */
    // Create a DOM Parser
    try
    {
    DOMParser = CreateObject("JAVA", "org.apache.xerces.parsers.DOMParser");
    // Create blank DOM Document to hold parsed XML
    document = CreateObject("JAVA", "org.w3c.dom.Document");
    // Set features on parser
    DOMParser.setFeature("http://apache.org/xml/features/dom/create-entity-ref-nodes",
false);
    DOMParser.setFeature("http://apache.org/xml/features/dom/include-ignorable-
whitespace", false);
    // Validate XML against a DTD
```

```
DOMParser.setFeature( "http://xml.org/sax/features/validation", true);
// Parse document
//  make sure you out in the path to your xmlDocument
// for example, parsing a document directly…
    //DOMParser.parse("http://department13.com/dev/xml/purchaseorder.xml");
DOMParser.parse(xmlDocument);
// Place parsed XML document in variable
document = DOMParser.getDocument();
// Now a DOM document containing the XML document has been created.
rootElement = CreateObject("JAVA","org.w3c.dom.Node");
rootElement = document.getDocumentElement();
WriteOutput("Our Root Node's name is: " & rootElement.getNodeName() );
 }


    catch("Any" excpt)
{
WriteOutput("The application was unable to perform a required operation.
Please try again later.<br>If this problem persists, please contact
the site Administrator and include the following information:<br>
#excpt.Message#<br>");
}</cfscript>
```

Summary

As we have shown, CFScript provides programmers with another method of developing ColdFusion MX applications. In specific situations, mostly those with long or complex logical statements, CFScript is a much cleaner and succinct method for writing code. In the next chapter, we look at developing UDFs where, more often than not, CFScript will be your method of choice.

Developers with extensive scripting or programming backgrounds will most likely warm to CFScript and find themselves more productive and comfortable using CFScript than standard tag-based CFML.

14

Debugging

ALMOST AS SOON AS YOU BEGIN WRITING COLDFUSION applications, you'll need to consider how to debug those applications when something goes wrong. Fortunately, ColdFusion MX makes debugging your applications easy by providing you with many ways to obtain lots of valuable debugging information.

After you learn how to use the different debugging tools at your disposal, you'll need to know how to interpret the information you obtain and what to do with that information after you've interpreted it. This chapter provides you with a good overview of the choices available to you as you begin to debug your applications. It also provides some quick tips and tricks that you can use to make the most of that information.

Debugging and the ColdFusion Administrator

As you begin to think about debugging your applications, one of the first places that you'll likely want to look is in the Debugging and Logging section of the ColdFusion Administrator.

In this section of the ColdFusion Administrator, you can choose the type of debugging information that you'd like to have displayed in the output of your pages. You can also choose how you'd like to have that information displayed and control who has access to it.

Debugging Settings Page

Inside ColdFusion Administrator are two sections that affect how debugging output is presented to you. The first of these pages is the Debugging Settings page. Figure 14.1 gives you an overview of this page in the Administrator.

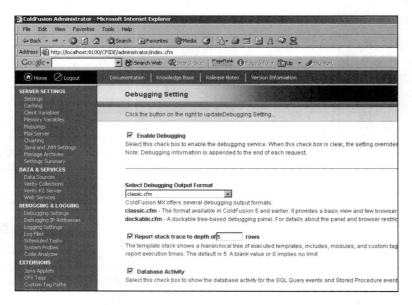

Figure 14.1 Debugging Settings page of the ColdFusion Administrator.

On this page, you can adjust the format for the debugging output that you receive, as well as what specific types of information you'd like to have displayed in your debugging output.

Table 14.1 gives you an overview of what each setting on this page will do for you and how each setting can be adjusted.

Table 14.1 **Debugging Settings Within the ColdFusion Administrator**

Debugging Setting	What Does It Do?
Enable Debugging	This is the most basic of the debugging settings included in the Administrator. This option toggles debugging information.
	When this box is checked, debugging information is displayed to all users who visit your ColdFusion Markup Language (CFML) pages, unless you've limited the debug output to a specific Internet Protocol (IP) address or group of addresses.

Debugging Setting	What Does It Do?
	This option enables you to choose the way in which you'd like to have your debugging information displayed on your output pages.
	The classic.cfm option presents all debugging information in the familiar "HTML at the bottom of the page" format that you should be used to from earlier versions of ColdFusion.
	The dockable.cfm option encapsulates all your debugging information in a Dynamic Hypertext Markup Language (DHTML) expanding tree in a separate browser window. You then can choose to have this menu float or dock itself in the current browser window.
Report Stack Trace of n Depth	Turning this option on presents a report of all ColdFusion pages that have run in response to a single Hypertext Transfer Protocol (HTTP) request.
	The execution time for all pages is also listed. The text box enables you to specify how "deep" you want the ColdFusion Server to go in reporting on templates that run.
Database Activity	Turning this option on causes debugging information related to your datasources and stored procedures to be displayed along with your other ColdFusion debugging information.
Exception Information	Checking this check box enables ColdFusion to report to you a list of any exceptions that are encountered during the processing of the ColdFusion request.
Tracing Information	When turned on and used in conjunction with the new CFTRACE tag, this feature enables tracing information for each instance of the CFTRACE tag to be reported in the debugging information of the page.
Locking Warnings	When turned on, this feature enables the ColdFusion Server to report to you any unlocked shared scope variable accesses that it encounters.
Variables	When this check box is clear, no variable information is displayed in the debugging output of the page. When turned on, you can select the types of variables for which you'd like to see debugging information.
	This feature helps you "clean up" your debugging information when you're troubleshooting specific types of errors.

Debugging IP Address Restrictions

The next section of the Administrator that deals with debugging is the Debugging IP Address Restrictions section. In this section, you control who can see the debugging information being reported by your servers.

As a general rule, on any production server, you'll want to have debugging information completely disabled so that you do not expose any sensitive information about your server to the general public—not to mention having a rather unsightly set of CFML templates.

Even in development environments, certain groups of developers might need access to debugging information that you might not want everyone working on the project to see. In those situations, you would use the Debugging IP Address Restrictions section of the ColdFusion Administrator to limit the debugging output specifically to whom you want to receive it.

Figure 14.2 gives you a look at the Debugging IP Address Restrictions page within the ColdFusion Administrator.

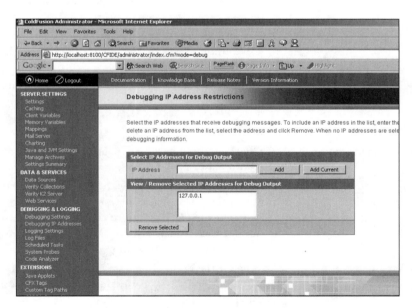

Figure 14.2   Debugging IP Address Restrictions page.

After you've enabled debugging on your development servers, you'll want to come to this page to specify those users whom you'd like to be able to view that debugging information.

By default, when debugging is enabled, only users on the server itself (the 127.0.0.1 or localhost address) can see the debugging information. To add other users to the list of people who can view the debugging information, you simply put their IP addresses in the IP Address text box on this page and click the Add button.

After you've done this, you'll notice the IP address that you've just added is now transferred to the Selected IP Addresses for Debug Output text box. To remove a user from this list, highlight his or her IP address and click the Remove Selected button at the bottom of this page.

CFTRACE

One of the new features being provided in ColdFusion MX to aid developers in the debugging of their applications is the CFTRACE tag.

With the CFTRACE tag, you can trace the execution of your application at a variety of levels. Depending on where you choose to place the CFTRACE tag within your application, you can use it to log the execution of particular pieces of code, provide timings for certain sections of CFML that you expect might be problematic, display the contents of variables at various points in the processing of your pages, examine contents of a variable prior to performing a specific function, and engage in many other useful debugging techniques. It all depends on where in your code you choose to use the tag itself.

CFTRACE enables you to peek at what the ColdFusion engine is doing as it processes your code. To demonstrate this concept, let's have a look at a simple example. Suppose we create a simple form that enables users to enter their names. After a user submits his or her name, we want our output page to say "Hello Name!" In addition, prior to displaying the name that the user entered, we are going to convert the entire string to uppercase, using the UCase() function. This is easy enough to accomplish, but it gives us a good chance to take a simple look at how you can use CFTRACE.

First, let's examine the simple code used to create the form:

```
<html>
<head>
        <title>Form Submission</title>
</head>

<body>

        <FORM ACTION="form_action.cfm" METHOD="post">
Please enter your name:<INPUT TYPE="text"
NAME="Name">
```

```
<BR>
                    <INPUT TYPE="submit"
  NAME="Submit"
                            VALUE="Submit">
        </FORM>
</body>
</html>
```

Now, if we save this code as `form.cfm` and run it, our output should look something like Figure 14.3.

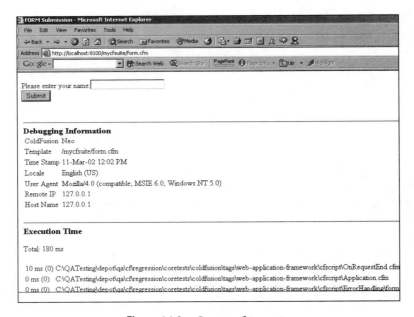

Figure 14.3   Output of `form.cfm`.

Now let's look at the code for our action page. Notice the locations in which I have placed the CFTRACE tag and the comments I've made at each trace point. They enable me to trace the logic flow as my page executes:

```
<!--- display what form variables were passed from the form.cfm page --->
<cftrace var="form" inline="yes" text="initial form tag">

<!--- change the name passed so that the whole name is uppercase --->
<cfset newname = ucase(form.name)>

<!--- use cftrace to see if my function worked --->
<cftrace var="newname" inline="yes" text="upper case conversion">
<br>
```

```
<cfoutput>
hello #newname#
</cfoutput>
```

If we save this file as `form_action.cfm` and then rerun `form.cfm`, we can see how the entire process works. I'll use the name "John" in the text box on the `form.cfm` page. After I enter my name and click Submit, the `form_action.cfm` page with my CFTRACE tags will run, and we see output like that shown in Figure 14.4.

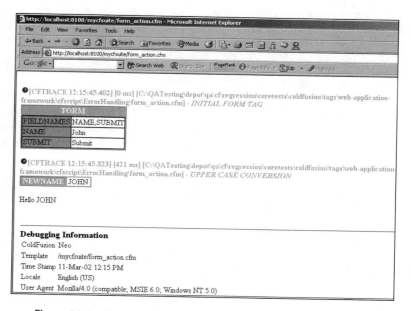

Figure 14.4   Output of `form_action.cfm` with the CFTRACE tag in use.

Looking at this output, you can see where we've examined the contents of the form variables after they were submitted. The CFTRACE tag conveniently displays for us all the variables that were sent to the action page as part of the form.

Next, we place another trace point right after the conversion of the string to uppercase. Notice how CFTRACE outputs the results of our new variable. At each point in the process, CFTRACE is providing us with timings indicating how long each piece of the page is taking to execute.

This timing and process flow information is an invaluable tool in debugging problematic applications because you can now surround any suspect pieces of code with CFTRACE points to determine exactly what is going on where and how long it's taking each section of code to complete its respective task.

The CFTRACE tag can take different attributes that help you identify the trace point with which you're working and the code that is actually executing.

Table 14.2 gives you an overview of the attributes that are available for use with the CFTRACE tag.

Table 14.2 **CFTRACE Tag Attributes**

Attribute	Description
abort	This is an optional attribute that enables you to specify whether you'd like to have page processing stop after a specific trace point.
	By default, this attribute is set to No.
category	This is an optional attribute that enables you to specify a category name for the trace point. Using the example in this section, you might place the first trace point in a "form variables" category.
	This enables you to differentiate among trace points when you're reviewing them. You can use ColdFusion variables as part of the textual names of your categories if you so choose to do so.
inline	This attribute enables you to specify whether you'd like to see trace point information in the CFML page itself. In our example, we're using inline="Yes" and are able to see the trace information on the processing pages.
	Should you fail to include this optional attribute, or should you set it to No, trace point information would still be available to you in the debugging output of the page.
text	This attribute enables you to provide a textual clue as to what this trace point is tracking.
	In the example in this section, when we traced the conversion to uppercase, we used text="upper case conversion" so that we could easily identify what the trace point was tracing based on this description.
	This text can be anything you like as long as it makes sense to you.
var	Use this attribute to specify the name of a variable that you'd like to dump at any trace point. The contents of the variable at that point in page processing is displayed.

A good thing to remember as you begin to play around with the power of the CFTRACE tag is that you can use it as much as necessary, even in code that's going to production. The overhead on this tag isn't significant, and assuming that you use the inline="No" attribute, the trace information won't be seen by anyone executing your production code unless you've specifically made that possible by allowing their IP to see debugging information through the ColdFusion Administrator on your production server.

ColdFusion MX logs all tracing output to the new log file: `cftrace.log`. This file is located in the `ColdFusionMX/logs` directory.

Summary

One of the coolest additions to ColdFusion MX is the `CFTRACE` tag. I can think of many instances in the past where having this functionality built in to the ColdFusion Server would have saved a lot of grief when trying to track down a problematic piece of code.

Although we've gone over a simple example of how you can harness the power of this tag to examine the process flow of your applications, we've by no means covered everything that you can do with this tag. Hopefully, however, as you move forward with debugging the applications you develop, you'll be encouraged to play around with ways in which you can use the built-in debugging tools of the ColdFusion engine to speed up your development time and make you a better overall programmer.

You can avoid spending too much time debugging applications by developing with accepted best practices in mind. Interestingly enough, that's what we're about to cover in Chapter 15, "CFML Coding: Best Practices," so read on!

15

CFML Coding: Best Practices

CODING COLDFUSION APPLICATIONS IS A MIXTURE of art and science. Each application has its own unique characteristics for which you must plan. This means that there often is a trade-off in the way that the code is written. It is never good to sacrifice efficiency or consistency for some weird shortcut.

This chapter discusses some of the most commonly forgotten coding best practices and code performance considerations. It is meant to be a guideline and a reminder that these things in particular should not be overlooked in the development of any ColdFusion application.

Considering Code Maintenance

To ensure that your application functions and performs as you would expect it to, you'll want to adhere to some coding practices that keep your application in top working order. The following sections touch on some simple things that you can do as a developer to make a big difference in how your application code is maintained.

Comment, Comment, Comment

Commenting code is imperative to creating an application that is easy to maintain. With proper commenting, developers can come and go, but you'll know that the proper inline documentation is there and sufficient to get them up to speed on the purpose of the template and the particulars of smaller code segments.

It is recommended that your comments include a general usage comment at the top of the template. This comment should include the template name, description of its purpose, the author's name and email address, and the date that it was created. The template should also include a revision comment at the bottom of the template that includes the dates of code revisions and the purposes of the modifications.

Of course, you'll want to include inline comments to describe where variables come from, why they are used, and any complex operations that they perform.

Use *CFSCRIPT* for Long Variable Assignment Blocks

It is always more efficient to use a CFSCRIPT block to set lots of variables rather than a long line of CFSETs. Not only are the blocks more readable and easier to maintain, but a CFSCRIPT block executes more quickly than setting the same number of variables with CFSETs.

If you must set multiple variables, you could use the following syntax:

```
<cfset variables.name = "Neil Ross">
<cfset variables.city = "Mechanicsburg">
<cfset variables.state = "Pennsylvania">
<cfset variables.email = "neil@codesweeper.com">
<cfset variables.url = "http://insidecoldfusionmx.com/">
```

However, this syntax would be more efficient:

```
<cfscript>
  variables.name = 'Neil Ross';
  variables.city = 'Mechanicsburg';
  variables.state = 'Pennsylvania';
  variables.email = 'neil@codesweeper.com';
  variables.url = 'http://insidecoldfusionmx.com/';
</cfscript>
```

Scope All Variables

Make sure that you are adding the proper scoping prefix to all your variables. Doing this makes your code much easier to read and manage. It also helps to cut down on the extra processing time required for ColdFusion to drill down through the various variable scopes. You'll want to avoid problems like this:

```
<cfscript>
  firstname = 'Neil';
```

```
    lastname = 'Ross';
    url.firstname = 'Jeff';
    url.lastname = 'Howden';
</cfscript>

<cfoutput>
My name is #firstname# #lastname#, but you can call me #url.firstname# #url.lastname#.
</cfoutput>
```

The code is a whole lot easier to read if you scope the variables properly:

```
<cfscript>
    variables.firstname = 'Neil';
    variables.lastname = 'Ross';
    url.firstname = 'Jeff';
    url.lastname = 'Howden';
</cfscript>

<cfoutput>
My name is #variables.firstname# #variables.lastname#, but you can call me
#url.firstname# #url.lastname#.
</cfoutput>
```

Coding for Performance

Performance considerations should always be on the mind of any quality developer. ColdFusion application performance often is rooted in the application code itself. In instances where code is written improperly or when necessary code elements are not included at all, performance and functionality can suffer dramatically. The following sections discuss issues that are key to improving performance in your applications.

Locking of Server, Application, and Session Variables

A commonly missed item dealing with application performance is the locking of shared scope variables. These variables should be locked in any code where server, application, or session-scoped variables are either written to or read from. Appropriate locking of server, application, and session variables must be applied or you risk degrading application performance and crashing your server.

Unless you properly implement locking, memory corruption can and will occur, which would further cause the ColdFusion Server to have threads hang when simultaneous user load is applied. To stop the inevitable memory leak, you must use the CFLOCK statement to prevent memory collision.

For writing to a scoped variable, use the `type="exclusive"` attribute:

```
<cflock scope="Application" type="exclusive" timeout="10">
    <cfset Application.myAppVar = 1>
        other Application variable statements …
</cflock>
```

For reading a scoped variable, use the `type="readonly"` attribute:

```
<cflock scope="Application" type="readonly" timeout="10">
    <cfset anyVariable = Application.myAppVar >
        other Application variable statements …
</cflock>
```

You can group multiple variables if they are all reads or all writes:

```
<cflock scope="Application" type="exclusive" timeout="10">
    <cfset Application.myAppVarX = 1>
    <cfset Application.myAppVarY = 2>
    <cfset Application.myAppVarZ = 3>
        other Application variable statements …
</cflock>
```

Also, never mix scoped variable types within a `CFLOCK` tag. Thus, the following would not be appropriate:

```
<cflock scope="Application" type="exclusive" timeout="10">
    <cfset Session.mySessionVar = 1>
    <cfset Application.myAppVar = 1>
</cflock>
```

The following also would not be appropriate:

```
<cflock scope="Application" type="exclusive" timeout="10">
    <cfset anyVariable = Application.myAppVar>
    <cfset Application.myAppVar = 1>
</cflock>
```

For more information on how to properly lock access to memory variables, refer to Chapter 8, "Application Framework."

Assigning Values to Application Variables for Each Page Request

When using the `Application.cfm` file (which is loaded with each page request) to assign application-scoped variables, be certain to encapsulate the variable assignments within a `CFIF` statement. Without doing this, the variables would be assigned for every page in the site, and thus would not be used properly. Simply test if an application-scoped variable exists. If it doesn't exist, assign all application-scoped variables. If it does exist, the assignment code is bypassed.

When setting application variables in the `Application.cfm` file, wrap the statement(s) within a `CFIF` statement:

```
<cflock type="Application" type="exclusive" timeout="10">
  <cfif NOT IsDefined("Application.ApplicationName")>
    <cfset application.applicationvar1="some value">
    <cfset application.applicationvar2="another value">
  </cfif>
</cflock>
```

It is also important to note that this same technique should be used if session scoped variables are being assigned within the `Application.cfm` template.

Overuse of *CFOUTPUT*

ColdFusion developers have heard for years that ColdFusion parses any code that lies within a `CFOUTPUT` tag. This has all too often led developers to write code which grossly overuses the `CFOUTPUT` tag and causes ColdFusion Server to work harder.

Developers should make it a goal to write clean and readable code, of course, and in regards to the `CFOUTPUT` tag, developers should have only as many of them on a single page as absolutely necessary. The following example shows overuse of the `CFOUTPUT` tag:

```
<input type="text" value="<cfoutput>#myValue1#</cfoutput>"...
<input type="text" value="<cfoutput>#myValue2#</cfoutput>"...
<input type="text" value="<cfoutput>#myValue3#</cfoutput>"...
```

Instead of the preceding code, you should wrap a single `CFOUTPUT` tag around a block of code that contains several variables to be evaluated:

```
<cfoutput>
    <input type="text" value="#myValue1#">
    <input type="text" value="#myValue2#">
    <input type="text" value="#myValue3#">
</cfoutput>
```

This code executes faster than the previous example and is easier to read and maintain.

Avoid Using Subqueries

It is a good practice to avoid using subqueries in your SELECT statements. The reason is that this causes the database engine to create an execution plan that is not or might not be the most efficient. Because the database engine does not know what the final values of the subquery might be, it must plan to look through the first table or set of tables as many times as the number of records that could be returned by the subquery.

This is an example of using a subselect:

```
<cfquery name="getEmployees" datasource="ExampleApps">
  SELECT FirstName
       , LastName
       , Email
    FROM tblEmployees
   WHERE DeptIDFK IN (SELECT DepartmentID
                        FROM tblDepartments
                       WHERE DepartmentName = 'Web Development')
</cfquery>
```

This is an example of using multiple queries:

```
<cfquery name="getDepartment" datasource="ExampleApps">
  SELECT DepartmentID
    FROM tblDepartments
   WHERE DepartmentName = 'Web Development'
</cfquery>
<cfquery name="getEmployees2" datasource="ExampleApps">
  SELECT FirstName
       , LastName
       , Email
    FROM tblEmployees
   WHERE DeptIDFK IN (#ListQualify(ValueList(getDepartment.DepartmentID), "'")#)
</cfquery>
```

Use *CFPARAM* to Set Default Values

Developers often use IF statements within their applications to test for the existence of a variable and to set default values if that variable does not exist. This can be streamlined by using the CFPARAM tag to assign default values to a variable. The following example illustrates this point:

```
<cfif NOT IsDefined("myVarName")>
    <cfset myVarname=1>
</cfif>
```

The same logic can be replicated as follows:

```
<cfparam name="myVarName" default=1>
```

Use *CFSWITCH* Instead of Multiple *CFIF* Statements

Developers should never use multiple IF statements to test for different values of the same variable. If there are more than two possible values for a single variable, you should use the CFSWITCH/CFCASE statement to enhance performance:

```
<cfif lastname = "Ross">
    <cfset myOtherVar="foo">
</cfif>
```

```
<cfif lastname = "Cummings">
      <cfset myOtherVar="bar">
</cfif>
<cfif lastname = "Sen">
      <cfset myOtherVar="foobar">
</cfif>
```

This logic works, but is not very efficient. If you use this type of code, each and every CFIF statement is evaluated for every pass through the page unnecessarily. In other words, if the first CFIF statement is true, the other CFIF statements really don't need to be evaluated—the condition has been met. Even though the first condition might be true, all the following CFIF statements are evaluated unnecessarily. To enhance performance, change this logic to use the CFSWITCH statement instead:

```
<cfswitch expression="#lastname#">
<cfcase value="Ross">
  <cfset myOtherVar="foo">
</cfcase>
<cfcase value="Cummings">
  <cfset myOtherVar="bar">
</cfcase>
<cfcase value="Sen">
  <cfset myOtherVar="foobar">
</cfcase>
</cfswitch>
```

With this logic, only the statement that evaluates to true is executed, and the other conditions are bypassed. This takes the load off the processor by not requiring it to evaluate multiple CFIF statements.

Two Function Calls to a Database to Retrieve the Unique ID of Inserted Records

Many developers commonly use two query calls to retrieve the value of a newly created record. The first query executes the insert of the new row into the table. The second query uses the MAX() function of the structured query language (SQL) to retrieve the record with the highest unique ID value.

```
<cfquery name="InsertNames" datasource="#request.dsn#">
   INSERT INTO Authors (firstname, lastname, email)
   VALUES ('#form.fname#', '#form.lname#', '#form.email#')
</cfquery>
```

This request does not return any values so it requires a second query. The next request retrieves the MAX identity field, which might or might not come from the previous INSERT query.

```
<cfquery name="getNewRecord" datasource="#request.dsn#">
    SELECT FROM Authors
         MAX(AuthorID)
</cfquery>
```

Although this method does work under a minimal load, it is possible that errors can occur when the site is put under heavier load. If multiple users attempt to run the page at the same time, there is a chance that one of the values might become orphaned, which can result in database errors within the application.

It is better to retrieve the unique ID in a single query. By doing this, you eliminate the loss of data and improve application performance. You also alleviate the need to make multiple requests to the database.

Although this approach does work, the same functionality can be achieved with the following:

```
<cfquery name="InsertNames" datasource="#request.dsn#">
   INSERT INTO Authors (firstname, lastname, email)
   VALUES ('#form.fname#', '#form.lname#', '#form.email#')
      SELECT AuthorID
</cfquery>
```

Now the single request to the database inserts the record and returns the value of the identity field of the newly created record. This method ensures that no records are orphaned—no matter how many users execute the page simultaneously. In addition, you get a performance enhancement by making only one request to the database.

Do Not Overuse the # Symbol

The # symbol is for outputting the values of ColdFusion variables to the browser. It is not needed within a ColdFusion tag such as CFSET or CFIF. You need to wrap the variable name with the # symbols only when the variable is used within an area where quotation marks are used. This concept is best explained within the following code snippet:

```
<cfif UserID EQ 33>
  <!--- ColdFusion Statements --->
</cfif>
```

Now assume you need to use the variable as part of another variable assignment:

```
<cfif UserID EQ 33>
    <cfset formAction = "updateRecord.cfm?uID=#userID#">
</cfif>
```

This time, the # symbols had to be in place to correctly assign the value of the `formAction` variable because the variable (`UserID`) is inside the quotation marks. Had the variable been outside the quotation marks, the # symbols would not have been used:

```
<cfif UserID EQ 33>
    <cfset formAction = "updateRecord.cfm?uID=" & UserID>
</cfif>
```

Both of the two previous examples give the variable `formAction` a value of `"updateRecord.cfm?uID=33"`. If the # symbol was not used and the variable was inside the quotation marks, as in the following code:

```
<cfif userID = 33>
    <cfset formAction = "updateRecord.cfm?uID=userID">
</cfif>
```

the variable `formAction` would contain the value `"updateRecord.cfm?uID=userID"`.

Replace() **Function Instead of** *CFLOOP*

Some developers use a `CFLOOP` statement to loop through a list and concatenate a variable to create the `WHERE` clause of a SQL statement. Here is an example of the `CFLOOP` logic to create the clause:

```
<cfset tempVar="">
<cfloop index="listElement" list="aList">
    <cfset tempVar = tempVar & listElement & " or ">
</cfloop>
```

This logic can easily be replicated and performance can be increased by using the `Replace()` function instead. An example of the `Replace()` function is shown in the following code:

```
<cfset tempVar = Replace(aList, ",", " or ", ALL)>
```

This one simple line of code performs the exact same functionality, but results in a large performance increase.

Use Function Calls Instead of Comparisons in *CFIF* Statements

Within CFIF statements, it makes sense to use ColdFusion functions to evaluate values rather than operators to determine the comparisons. If you put this practice into use, it results in increased application performance. Use something like the following:

```
<CFIF NOT LEN(TRIM(myFoo))>
```

rather than:

```
<CFIF myFoo IS NOT " ">
```

Reduce Whitespace with *CFSETTING, CFSILENT,* and *CFPROCESSINGDIRECTIVE*

Formatted whitespace can add weight to a ColdFusion template. To reduce whitespace that is created during the creation of variables in ColdFusion, you should call the CFSETTING with the attribute "enableCFoutputOnly" at the beginning and end of both the Application.cfm and OnRequestEnd.cfm templates. This reduces the formatted whitespace and decreases your overall file size. The result is improved processing time and higher bandwidth utilization.

In addition, you can use the CFSILENT tag to wrap code that does not require output to be sent to the browser. This keeps extraneous whitespace from being generated in the output stream by that code. A good example of CFSILENT's usage would be to wrap query statements at the beginning of a .CFM template.

Lastly, you can use the CFPROCESSINGDIRECTIVE with the attribute "SuppressWhitespace" to further eliminate the extraneous whitespace that is generated through execution of ColdFusion templates.

Request Scope

The request scope was introduced in ColdFusion 4.5. It functions pretty much just like a local variable, but can be seen within custom tags. You should make use of the request scope wherever possible in place of shared scope variables to reduce the need for locking throughout your application.

Use Functions to Resolve Criteria

It is recommended that you use function calls to resolve criteria of conditional logic. It improves performance in your application. The following is a very simple example of this concept:

```
<cfif NOT Len(foo)>
  <!--- ColdFusion Statements --->
</cfif>
```

The preceding code yields better performance than the following:

```
<cfif foo eq "">
```

Summary

Writing efficient and clean ColdFusion code is not difficult. Attention to detail and an understanding of a few of the finer points of ColdFusion Markup Language are required. An understanding of how ColdFusion tags and functions work is all but mandatory. In addition, don't forget that one of the best pieces of advice that I can give you is to properly document your code with plenty of comments.

An often-overlooked method of improving application performance is examination of the database calls that your application is making to determine if you need to restructure logic to reduce trips to the database, to replace complex database queries with stored procedures, or to involve query caching for result sets that can be reused.

More often that not, the database is a critical bottleneck in the application, so it's best not to overlook that important piece when examining application performance.

For more on database tuning and caching, be sure to review Chapter 23, "Working with Databases," and Chapter 18, "Enhancing Application Performance with Caching."

16

Further Extending Your Applications

THIS CHAPTER COVERS THREE VERY important topics: the CFHTTP and CFCONTENT tags, CFOUTPUT and the component object model (COM), and Flash integration. You might wonder what these three topics have to do with one another. Well, they all relate to integrating and working with applications and technologies outside the ColdFusion MX Server. As you run into more real-world needs in your projects, you have to develop more complex and sophisticated web applications that must integrate and work with other technologies. The technology areas covered in this chapter are areas that you are going to need to address.

Working the Web—the Power of *CFHTTP* and *CFCONTENT*

One of the most useful and powerful tags in ColdFusion's arsenal is CFHTTP. CFHTTP enables developers to perform a host of functions and operations using the GET and POST methods of Hypertext Transfer Protocol (HTTP). Some of the uses for CFHTTP are the generation of static Hypertext Markup Language (HTML), the retrieval of files, the exchanging of information with other web servers, and the polling of other applications and web servers for content such as news feeds.

Another powerful tag is the CFCONTENT tag, which enables you to set the Multipurpose Internet Mail Extension (MIME) type of content returned from a ColdFusion template as well as download files from the server to the client. By default, ColdFusion returns a MIME content type of text/html so that a web browser renders your template text as a web page.

With these two tags, you have tremendous power to create rich and sophisticated web applications that make use of the Web's underlying protocol, HTTP.

CFHTTP

The following sections cover uses of the CFHTTP tag.

Using CFHTTP to GET Information

Developers use CFHTTP to retrieve information from web sites. You use GET to retrieve files, including text and binary files, from a specified server. The retrieved data then is stored in a specific ColdFusion variable, cfhttp.filecontent. For example, let's say that we want to get a specific web site and display it in a browser. We could use the code in Listing 16.1.

Listing 16.1   *getcnn.cfm*

```
<cfhttp
method="get"
url="http://www.cnn.com"
port="80"
resolveurl="yes"
proxyport="80"
redirect="yes"
useragent="mozillia/4.5 - (WinNT; u)"
timeout="180"
throwonerror="yes">
</cfhttp>
<cfoutput>
#cfhttp.filecontent#
</cfoutput>
```

If you test this template in your browser, you see the CNN.com web site. You can try changing the uniform resource locator (URL) variable to any other web site and see what happens.

CFHTTP has many attributes. For a list of them, check out Appendix A, "Tag Reference." In our code, we define the first attribute method, which has to be GET. We then define another required attribute, URL, which is the full URL to the site we want to retrieve. Next we define the port attribute to be 80 (the standard HTTP port for web servers). Now we have set an attribute called resolveurl, which, when used in conjunction with the port attribute, appends the port value to each resolved URL. This is useful and important for dealing with URLs in the requested document. They might be relative URLs, and by setting the resolveurl attribute to Yes, it guarantees the URL contained in the requested page resolves correctly.

Another useful attribute of the CFHTTP tag is the optional redirect attribute. This attribute enables you to gracefully deal with redirect. If you set it to Yes, it enables you to follow up to five redirects. After that, it treats the redirect as if the redirect attribute were set to No, which causes it to fail on the redirect.

We can also set the useragent attribute so that the web server with which we are interacting thinks that we are using a specific web browser. In our example, we set it to mozillia/6 - (WinNT; u), which makes the web server think we were using Netscape 6. We then set the optional attribute timeout, which tells the ColdFusion Server to stop trying to resolve a URL after some specific amount of time in seconds. If you do not specify a time, CFHTTP defaults to the timeout value set in the ColdFusion Administrator page. If no timeout is set, ColdFusion indefinitely tries to resolve the URL, and because ColdFusion assigns a thread to each CFHTTP request, this can cause the server to hang. In practice, there is no reason not to set the timeout period, and it is best that you do.

Finally, we set a final optional attribute called throwonerror. This attribute, when set to Yes, lets us catch exceptions thrown by CFCATCH using a CFTRY/CFCATCH block. This is especially useful when you are testing and debugging tags that are requesting content from a variety of sites.

Another useful attribute that we can set in the CFHTTP tag is file. Using it, you can download various types of file types or directly save content from CFHTTP to a file. For example, if we want to save our CNN page to a file, we could use the code in Listing 16.2.

Listing 16.2   *savecnn.cfm*

```
<cfhttp
method="get"
url="http://www.cnn.com"
port="80"
proxyport="80"
redirect="yes"
useragent="mozillia/6 - (WinNT; u)"
timeout="180"
throwonerror="yes"
file="cnn2002029.htm"
path="c:\internet\www\mysavedcontent\"
>
</cfhttp>
```

Notice that we used another attribute here. It's called `path`, which simply tells the tag where to put the file. In addition, when you retrieve a file, ColdFusion creates another variable that you can access. It's called cfhttp.`mimetype`.

Creating a Query Object

One of the more annoying things ColdFusion developers have to deal with is extracting data from text files. Often, this is because of some legacy system that stores its data in text files instead of in a database. Although there are many ways in ColdFusion to solve the problem of extracting data from a text file, CFHTTP gives us a powerful tool for dealing with data in text files. ColdFusion and CFHTTP enable you to build query objects from a delimited text file.

For example, let's say we have a simple text file, such as the one shown in Listing 16.3.

Listing 16.3   **Order1**

```
Product,Quantity
ColdFusion MX,100,
Jrun,2
DreamWeaver,5
```

We could create a query object out of the text, as shown in Listing 16.4.

Listing 16.4   *creataquery.cfm*

```
<cfhttp
method="get"
url="http://localhost:8100/cfhttp/order1.txt"
name="testquery"
delimiter=","
textqualifier=" ">
Product||Quantity</br>
<cfoutput query="testquery">
#Product#, #Quantity#</br>
</cfoutput>
```

Using CFHTTP to build queries is pretty straightforward as you can see. Much like the earlier example, we define the method as GET and the URL points directly to where our file resides. Then we use the name attribute to identify our query, just like we would in CFQUERY. Because our text file uses commas to delimit the information in it, we use the attribute `delimiter` and give the value `delimiter=","`. Finally, we set the attribute to `" "` because there is no text qualifier. If there is a text qualifier, you must surround all field values with the text qualifier character. To include a text qualifier character in a field, use a double character. For example, if the text qualifier is `"`, you should use `""` to include a quotation mark in the field.

When you are working with your text files, you must remember that the first row of text is always interpreted as column headings; thus, that row is skipped. You can override the file's column heading names by specifying a different set of names in the `columns` attribute. You must specify a name for each column. You then use these new names in your ColdFusion Markup Language (CFML) code. In addition, if you have column headings with the same names, ColdFusion adds an underscore character to the duplicate column name to make it unique. For example, if two CustomerID columns are found, the second is renamed CustomerID_.

Posting Data

`POST` operations are the most common HTTP operations developers use to work with HTTP-based applications that expect an input and generate an output or response. CFHTTP also supports `POST` operations, as defined by HTTP 1.1. This standard enables ColdFusion developers to pass form variables, URL data, common gateway interface (CGI) variables, cookies, eXtensible Markup Language (XML), and other forms of information. For `CFHTTP POST` operations, you have to use a new tag called `cfhttpparam` for each variable you want to post.

Let's create a simple example that lets you see all the different post types at work. See Listing 16.5.

Listing 16.5 *testpost.cfm*

```
<cfhttp method="Post"
  url="http://localhost:8100/cfhttp/posttest.cfm">
  <cfhttpparam type="Cookie"
    value="8798798798"
    name="somecookie">
  <cfhttpparam type="CGI"
    value="97987987"
    name="cgivariable">
  <cfhttpparam type="URL"
    value="897987987"
    name="someurl">
  <cfhttpparam type="Formfield"
    value="Robi Sen"
    name="myname">
  <cfhttpparam type="File"
```

continues ▶

Listing 16.5   **Continued**

```
    name="afile"
    file="e:\dev\BLara.jpg">
</cfhttp>
<cfoutput>
File Content:</br>
  #cfhttp.filecontent#</br>
</br>
 Mime Type:   #cfhttp.MimeType#</br>
</cfoutput>
```

In this file, we are setting the CFHTTP method to POST as well as pointing the URL to a ColdFusion template we will create in a minute. Notice that we have created several CFHTTPPARAM tag sets. CFHTTPPARAM's general syntax is as follows:

```
<cfhttpparam
Name="variablename"
Type="transactiontype"
Value="valueofthevariable"
File="filename">
```

This tag helps specify which type of POST you want to do using the type attribute, which supports five different options:

- **URL.** Posts URL variables to applications that get parameters from information passed by means of URLs
- **FormField.** Posts form field data to applications that accept input from HTML forms
- **CGI.** Posts CGI environment variables to applications
- **COOKIE.** Posts cookies to remote applications that use them
- **FILE.** Posts files to applications

In the preceding example, we have used each CFHTTPPARAM type. Now we can create another template called posttest.cfm, as shown in Listing 16.6.

Listing 16.6   *posttest.cfm*

```
<cffile destination="e:\temp\"
  nameconflict="Overwrite"
  filefield="Form.afile"
  action="Upload"
  attributes="Normal">
<cfoutput>
  The URL variable is: #URL.someurl# <br>
```

```
  The Cookie variable is: #Cookie.somecookie# <br>
  The CGI variable is: #CGI.someurl#. <br>
  The Formfield variable is: #Form.myname#. <br>
 The file was uploaded to #File.ServerDirectory#\#File.ServerFile#.
</cfoutput>
```

This template simply validates that you did indeed pass each of the five different variable types, along with associated data. To test it, call `testpost.cfm` in your browser to confirm, remembering to change the values of the file paths to those of your own machine.

As you can see, CFHTTP provides you with a simple yet powerful way to work with HTTP.

Using *CFCONTENT*

As noted in the beginning of the chapter, the CFCONTENT tag enables you to set the MIME type of content returned from a ColdFusion template as well as download files from the server to the client. CFCONTENT proves very useful when you are trying to provide content to a number of clients or sources, such as in the case of content syndication.

In general, syndication is the supply of material for reuse and integration with other material, often through some sort of paid service subscription. The most common example of syndication is in newspapers, where such content as news, comics, columns, and so on is usually syndicated content. Newspapers receive the content from the content providers, reformat it as required, integrate it with other copy, print it, and publish it.

Content syndication is the way a great deal of information is disseminated across the web. A great example of online content syndication is Moreover.com, which supplies news and headlines from a variety of categories in a variety of formats. Currently they support JavaScript, Flash, XML, WAP, HTML, and TSV.

Using CFCONTENT, you can do much the same thing with any data you want. For example, let's say that we want to syndicate our products catalog to associate vendors and our major clients. Few of them support XML, so we have opted to supply our catalog in HTML and plain American Standard Code for Information Interchange (ASCII) text, which our less-sophisticated partners can use to update their automated purchasing solutions against our catalog (see Listing 16.7).

Listing 16.7 *catalogServer.cfm*

```
<cfquery datasource="icf" name="createCatalog" dbtype="ODBC">
SELECT Category.CategoryID AS Category_CategoryID, Category.CategoryName,
Category.CategoryDescription, Product.ProductID, Product.VendorID AS Product_VendorID,
Product.ProductDate, Product.CategoryID AS Product_CategoryID, Product.ProductName,
Product.ProductDescription, Product.ProductPricePerUnit, Product.ProductLicenseID,
Vendor.VendorID AS Vendor_VendorID, Vendor.VendorName
FROM Vendor INNER JOIN (Category INNER JOIN Product ON Category.CategoryID =
Product.CategoryID) ON Vendor.VendorID = Product.VendorID;
</cfquery>

<cfsetting enablecfoutputonly="yes" showdebugoutput="no" />
<cfif isDefined("FORM.getcatalog") or isDefined("Url.getCatalog") or
isDefined("CGI.getCatalog")>
        <cfif isDefined("FORM.getcatalog")>
        <cfif FORM.getcatalog Is "HTML">
        <cfcontent type="text/html">
        <cfsavecontent variable="tempHTML">
        <table>
<tr>
    <td>CategoryName</td>
    <td>ProductID</td>
    <td>VendorName</td>
    <td>ProductName</td>
    <td>ProductDescription</td>
    <td>ProductPricePerUnit</td>
</tr>
<cfoutput query="createCatalog">
<tr>
    <td>#CategoryName#</td>
    <td>#ProductID#</td>
    <td>#VendorName#</td>
    <td>#ProductName#</td>
    <td>#ProductDescription#</td>
    <td>#ProductPricePerUnit#</td>
</tr>
</cfoutput>
</table>
</cfsavecontent>
                <cfoutput>#tempHTML#</cfoutput>
        <cfelseif FORM.getcatalog IS "TEXT">
                <cfcontent type="text/text">
    <cfoutput query="createCatalog">
#CategoryName#,#ProductID#,#VendorName#,#ProductName#,#ProductDescription#,
➥#ProductPricePerUnit#
</cfoutput>
        <cfelse>
    Error-- You must pass either HTML,File, or Text
                </cfif>
    <cfoutput>
    #FORM.getcatalog#
```

```
     some response
     </cfoutput>
    <cfelseif isDefined("Url.getCatalog")>
         <cfif Url.getCatalog Is "HTML">
         <cfcontent type="text/html">
         <cfelseif Url.getCatalog  IS "TEXT">
             <cfcontent type="text/text">
         <cfelse>
    Error-- You must pass either HTML,File, or Text
             </cfif>
    <cfelseif isDefined("CGI.getCatalog")>
             <cfif CGI.getCatalog Is "HTML">
         <cfcontent type="text/html">
         <cfelseif CGI.getCatalog IS "TEXT">
             <cfcontent type="text/text">
         <cfelse>
    Error-- You must pass either HTML,File, or Text
             </cfif>
     </cfif>
<cfelse>
<cfcontent type="text/HTML">
no message recived
</cfif>
```

For the sake of the example, we create a file that holds our catalog in the
first part of this template; but in reality, your catalog might be dynamically
generated at the time of request, or more likely, frequently updated at specific
intervals. Next in the file, we define a simple conditional logic exposing our
catalog to requests from HTTP posts from forms, URLs, and CGI requests,
thus providing the largest possible base of subscribership. Next we use the
CFCONTENT tag to retrieve the catalog file for the requesting client and to
ensure that the MIME type is text/html. Later in the code, we change that
to text/plain, making sure that the requesting client does not resolve it
as HTML.

You can test the catalogServer.cfm template with the template shown in
Listing 16.8. It enables you to simulate various clients and post operations.

Listing 16.8 *catalogClient.cfm*

```
<cfhttp
url="http://localhost:8100/cfhttp/catalogServer.cfm"
method="POST"
resolveurl="yes">
<cfhttpparam type="FORMFIELD" name="getCatalog" value="TEXT" />
</cfhttp>
<cfoutput><pre>#CFHTTP.Header#</pre></cfoutput>
<cfoutput>#CFHTTP.FileContent#</cfoutput>
```

You can also use CFCONTENT for creating more secure web applications. For example, let's say you have content that you want users to pay for, such as your artwork, comic strips, special reports, and so on. One thing people do to circumvent paying for these types of content is to guess filenames and URLs to access the content without first paying for it. To protect against this, you could put that content in a directory not usually accessible from your web server and use CFCONTENT to access it for customers who have paid. You can also use CFCONTENT to protect your site content/downloads from being leeched from another site without users passing through your site first.

Summary

CFHTTP and CFCONTENT are very powerful tags. CFHTTP, along with simple logic, enables you to create powerful web agents that can automate the process of filling out forms, interact with remote applications through HTTP, and create queries from delimited text.

CFCONTENT enables you to change MIME types, to force a MIME type to be specified with returned ColdFusion content, and to download files from the server to a client. This enables you to create applications where the same data can be viewed from a number of applications, from typical web browsers to PDAs.

CFOBJECT and COM

As we have already seen, ColdFusion enables us to work with a variety of Java objects and components, but that's not all we are limited to. ColdFusion gives you access to COM/DCOM components and to Common Object Request Broker Architecture (CORBA) objects. In this section, we cover how you can use COM objects in your ColdFusion applications with CFOBJECT.

A Little About COM and DCOM

COM is Microsoft's attempt at building robust, portable, and reusable components with their Distributed Component Object Model distributable components, much like JavaBeans or Enterprise JavaBeans.

COM and DCOM are powerful methods that enable Windows programmers to "componentize" functionality. You can find COM objects that do everything from providing access to specific programs, such as Microsoft Office programs, to providing access to COM-based cryptography libraries.

Note

To find out more about COM, go to www.microsoft.com/com. In addition, look at www.cfcomet.com, which is a web site totally devoted to working with COM objects from ColdFusion. It's a great resource!

Working with COM Objects and ColdFusion

You can call a COM object that resides either on your local machine or anywhere on your network; but before you can do so, you need to make sure the component you are trying to call is registered. To do this, you use the regsvr32 command from a Windows command prompt, like this:

```
C:\> regsvr32 someobject.dll
```

If a COM object has been registered on your machine, you can access it from CFOBJECT using this syntax:

```
<cfobject
type="com"
name="name"
action="action"
class="progID"
context="context"
server="your server name"
```

When you connect to a COM component, you need to set the CFOBJECT type attribute to COM. The name attribute is a reference variable and is also required. It is needed, as are other CFOBJECT calls, to provide a pointer to an object's attributes and methods.

class is a required attribute and points to the COM component's program ID for the object you want to invoke. You might have trouble finding the program ID, and if so, you should check the documentation for that component, which provides you with a list of its methods as well as the ProgramID. You can also use the OLE/COM Object Viewer that comes with Visual Studio or you can download it from www.microsoft.com/com/resources/oleview.asp.

The next attribute we have to deal with is the action attribute. This is a required attribute with two possible values: Create or Connect. Create takes a COM object and instantiates it prior to invoking methods and assigning properties, while Connect enables you to link/connect to a COM object (typically an executable) that is already running on the server. An example of the use of this type of object is a background service such as Net Stat.

The context attribute is an optional attribute that enables you to specify the context under which your object is running. Table 16.1 provides the various contexts.

Table 16.1   **Context Attribute Values**

Attribute Value	Description
InProc	An in-process server object, usually a DLL, running in the same process space as ColdFusion.
local	An out-of-process server object (typically an EXE file) that is running outside the ColdFusion process space, but running locally on the same server.
remote	An out-of-process server object (typically an EXE file) that is running remotely on the network. If you specify remote, you must also use the server attribute to identify where the object resides.

The final attribute needed to call COM objects from CFOBJECT is server, which is required if the context attribute is set to remote. server simply specifics a valid server.

Properties and Methods

Any object has a series of methods and properties that you need to set and use. To set a property of a COM object, you only need to use the CFSET tag:

```
<cfset someobject.someproperty = "somevalue">
```

You can also access or get a property's value by doing this:

```
<cfset getProperty = someobject.someproperty>
```

To invoke a method with no arguments is just as simple:

```
<cfset variablename = someobject.somemethod()>
```

Methods that require arguments need to have those arguments passed by value:

```
<cfset somevar = 4>
<cfset anothervar = someobject.somemethod (somevar, someOutput)
```

You can also pass arguments by reference. Arguments passed by reference have their values modified by the COM object variable on the calling page, so the calling page can use the resulting value. To pass a variable by reference, surround the name of an existing ColdFusion variable with quotation marks. If the argument is a numeric type, assign the variable a valid number before you make the call. For example:

```
<cfset somestring="Print PI">
<cfset somenumeric=0>
<cfset result=myCOMObject.calculate(somestring, " somenumeric ")>
```

The string "Print PI" is passed to the object's calculate method as an input argument. The value of somenumeric is set by the method to a numeric value.

Let's look at a real example. Let's pretend that we want to send out bulk mailings of special offers and other mail to our customers. To do this, we automate Microsoft Office to print a form letter with each of our customers, names and pertinent information. You can look at Microsoft's COM reference for Word on MSDN at http://msdn.microsoft.com/library/default.asp?url=/library/en-us/vbawd10/html/wotocObjectModelApplication.asp.

Listing 16.9   *mailmerge.cfm*

```
<cfquery name="getCustomers" datasource="ICF" dbtype="ODBC">
SELECT Customer.CustomerID, Customer.CustomerFirstName, Customer.CustomerLastName,
Customer.CustomerAddress, Customer.CustomerCity, Customer.CustomerStateID,
Customer.CustomerZip, Customer.CustomerPhone, Customer.CustomerEmail,
Customer.CustomerPassword, Customer.CustomerNotification
FROM Customer, State
</cfquery>

<cftry>

<!--- If it exists, connect to it --->

    <cfobject
    action="Connect"
    class="Word.Application"
    name="objWord"
    type="COM">

<cfcatch>
<!--- The object doesn't exist, so create it --->
    <cftry>

    <cfobject
    action="create"
    class="Word.Application"
    name="objWord"
    type="COM">

    <cfcatch type="ANY">
    <cfabort showerror="<FONT COLOR='RED'>Cannot create Word Object<BR>Make sure Word
    is installed and that ColdFusion has permissions to use the Word COM
    objects</FONT><BR><B>Error Details:</B>  #CFCATCH.MESSAGE#">
    </cfcatch>
    </cftry>
</cfcatch>
</cftry>
```

continues ▶

Listing 16.9 **Continued**

```
<cfscript>
/* This will open Word if running locally */
objWord.Visible = true;
/* This returns the 'Documents' collection the Word Object */
objDoc = objWord.Documents;
/* Create a new document */
newDoc = objDoc.Add();
</cfscript>

<cfset strLoc = Application.DrivePath & "\temp\worddata.doc">
<!--- Delete file --->
<cfif FileExists('#Application.DrivePath#temp\worddata.doc')>
    <cftry>
    <cffile action="DELETE" FILE='#Application.DrivePath#temp\Worddata.doc'>
    <cfcatch TYPE="Any">
    </cfcatch>
    </cftry>
</cfif>
<cfscript>
/* Save the document to a location */
newDoc.SaveAs(strLoc);
 /* We specify the range of '0' -- start at the beginning of the document */
docRange = newDoc.Range(0);
</cfscript>

<cfset strtemp = "">
<!--- Loop through the query --->
<cfloop query="getCustomers">
<cfset i = getCustomers.CurrentRow>
<cfset strtemp = strtemp & "#CustomerID#" & ",">
<cfset strtemp = strtemp & "#CustomerFirstName#" & ",">
<cfset strtemp = strtemp & "#CustomerLastName#" & Chr(13) & Chr(10)>
</cfloop>

<cfscript>
/* Add text to the range */
docRange.Text = strtemp;
 /* Save the changes */
newDoc.Save();
 /* Print document
objWord.ActivePrinter = "HP LaserJet 6L on NE01:";
objWord.PrintOut();*/
 /* Close the document */
newDoc.Close();
 /* Quit Word */
objWord.Quit();
</cfscript>
```

Although this looks like a complicated template, it's really not. We connect to the Word object by specifying the class name "Word.Application". Then we use a try-catch statement to see whether an instance of the object already exists and, if so, to connect to it. If not, we create an instance of it.

We then simply use the Word document's COM objects to add text to the created Word document.

Note

Before you get excited about automating your Office applications through ColdFusion and CFOBJECT, make sure to go to http://support.microsoft.com/default.aspx?scid=kb;EN-US;q257757. There you can read about some pitfalls and Microsoft's official view of automating Office applications.

Best Practices When Using COM Objects

Although using CFOBJECT and COM to create rich ColdFusion applications is easy, it is also easy to get yourself in trouble if you do not consider what you are doing. One of the main issues with calling COM objects from ColdFusion is improper threading. You must make sure that your COM object is thread-safe. If you do not, you might experience major issues under load and bring your server to its knees. An object is thread-safe if it can be called from many programming threads simultaneously without causing errors.

Visual Basic ActiveX DLLs are typically not thread-safe. If you use such a DLL in ColdFusion, you can make it thread-safe by using the OLE/COM Object Viewer to change the object's threading model to the Apartment model.

If you are planning on storing a reference to the COM object in the application, session, or server scope, do not use the Apartment model. This threading model is intended to service only a single request. If your application requires you to store the object in any of these scopes, keep the object in the Both model, and lock all code that accesses the object.

Summary

In this section, you have learned how to work with COM objects through CFOBJECT. You are provided with an invaluable tool to extend or rapidly add rich functionality to your ColdFusion applications. You can also use COM and CFOBJECT to provide a level of application integration between your ColdFusion web applications and sophisticated applications such as PeopleSoft and SAP, which provide extensive COM support.

It's important to note that although it is very simple and easy to work with COM from ColdFusion, there are risks and you need to read all the documentation on your COM object. You need to make sure it is thread-safe, or you must force it to be thread-safe through the OLE Object View application. Then you must rigorously test it before you use it in production.

Flash Remoting with ColdFusion

Although HTML is usually enough for most web-based applications, many users expect or demand the features and power of a more typical desktop or client-server application's heavy clients. Although JavaScript, JScript, and Dynamic Hypertext Markup Language (DHTML) can provide some of the client-side logic and features users demand, many things are just not possible with those technologies. Typically, developers turn to Macromedia Flash to provide rich and powerful web-based clients; but up until now, integrating Flash with ColdFusion or other server-side applications has been a difficult and time-consuming chore. This has all changed with the development of Flash MX and Flash remoting, which we briefly touched on in Chapter 6, "ColdFusion Components." As we'll see in this section, working with Flash directly from ColdFusion has become as simple as connecting to databases using `CFQUERY`!

Flash and ColdFusion Templates

There are different ways to work with Flash from ColdFusion MX, ColdFusion components (CFCs) and web services, server-side ActionScript (AS), and CFML. Although CFCs might be many ColdFusion developers technique of choice, it's also very simple to communicate with Flash directly from CFML.

In CFML, you can communicate with Flash movies through the Flash variable scope, which is a new variable scope in ColdFusion. There are three major Flash variables in the Flash variable scope. `Flash.Params` is an array that contains the parameters passed from the Flash movie. By calling the Flash variable scope, you can access parameters passed back from Flash movies by calling the Flash parameter directly in the Flash variable scope, like this:

```
Flash.parametername
```

Depending on how you pass the values from Flash, you can refer to array values using typical array syntax or structure syntax. Only ActionScript objects can pass named parameters.

For example, if you pass the parameters as an ordered array from Flash, array[1] references the first value. If you pass the parameters as named parameters from Actionscript, you can you use structure syntax, such as params.name.

You can use most of the CFML array and structure functions on AS collections. However, the StructCopy CFML function does not work with AS collections.

Because Flash.Params is an array, it retains the order of the parameters as they were passed to the function. You use standard structure name syntax to reference the parameters, as shown in the following code:

```
<cfquery name="getCustomer" datasource="ICF" dbtype="ODBC">
SELECT Customer.CustomerID, Customer.CustomerFirstName, Customer.CustomerLastName,
Customer.CustomerAddress, Customer.CustomerCity, Customer.CustomerStateID,
Customer.CustomerZip, Customer.CustomerPhone, Customer.CustomerEmail,
Customer.CustomerPassword, Customer.CustomerNotification
FROM Customer, State
WHERE Customer.CustomerStateID='#Flash.stateID#'
</cfquery>
```

As you can see, the query returns results based on the value of the stateID passed from Flash. Now if you want to pass values as an array from Flash, you would access them like this:

```
<cfset flash.result = "Variable 1:#Flash.params[1]#, Variable 2: #Flash.params[2]#">
```

The second variable in the Flash variable scope is the result variable, which is returned to the Flash application. For example, let's create a simple ColdFusion template that passes the ColdFusion Server version information to an AS.

Listing 16.10 *getVersion.cfm*

```
<cfset tempStruct = StructNew()>
<cfset tempStruct.cfversion = #Server.ColdFusion.ProductVersion#>
<cfset tempStruct.Message = "This is your version of ColdFusion">
```

In this example, we pass a structure that contains the version information for ColdFusion as well as a simple message that is passed back to the requesting Flash application through the Flash.Result variable.

Now when you create and save this template, save it into a new folder under your webroot directory called **Flashexamples**. The reason for this is Flash and AS use the directory name that contains the ColdFusion templates as the Flash service name in AS. The actual templates contained in the directory translate to service functions in AS.

Listing 16.11 *getVersion.swf*

```
include "NetServices.as"
NetServices.setDefaultGatewayUrl("http://localhost:8500/flashservices/gateway");
gatewayConnection = NetServices.createGatewayConnection();
CFMService = gatewayConnection.getService("Flashexamples", this);
CFMService.getVersion();
```

Try testing this in your Flash MX studio. With `Flash.Return`, you can return most types of ColdFusion data to AS, as if you were working with a ColdFusion-based application, but you need to be aware of some specific data type conversions. See Table 16.2 for information on the data type conversions.

Table 16.2 **Data Type Conversion Between Flash and ColdFusion**

ActionScript Data Type	ColdFusion MX Data Type
Number (primitive data type)	Number
Boolean (primitive data type)	From ColdFusion, return to ActionScript either a 1 to indicate true or a 0 to indicate false.
String	String
AS object	Structure
AS object (passed as the only argument to a service function)	Arguments to the service function. ColdFusion pages (CFM): Flash variable scope, ColdFusion components (CFC): named arguments
Null	Null (ASC returns 0, which translates to not defined)
Undefined	Null (ASC returns 0, which translates to not defined)
Ordered array	Array
Named array	Struct
Date object	Date
XML object	XML document
Recordset	Query object

When you are working with ColdFusion and Flash, you sometimes want to limit the amount of information you return to a Flash application at one time. For example, if we do a query that returns all the products in our database, we might want to limit the amount of records returned to 10. To do this, we use the Flash variable `flash.pagesize`, which enables you to return the total record set in increments. This speeds the communication time to Flash and enables it to deal with more manageable chunks of data.

Let's do a simple example.

Listing 16.12   *getProducts.cfm*

```
<cfparam name="pagesize" default="10">
<cfif IsDefined("Flash.Params")>
  <cfset pagesize = Flash.Params[1]>
</cfif>
<cfquery name="getProducts" datasource="ICF">
 SELECT Product.ProductID, Product.ProductName, Product.ProductPricePerUnit,
Product.VendorID, Vendor.VendorID, Vendor.VendorName
FROM Product, Vendor
WHERE Product.VendorID=Vendor.VendorID
</cfquery>
<!--- set the record count to return --->
<cfset Flash.Pagesize = pagesize>
<!--- return the query --->
<cfset Flash.Result = getProducts>
```

Make sure to save this file into our `Flashexamples` directory. Now this template is pretty simple and the only thing we need to look at is `flash.pagesize`, which is new. The `flash.pagesize` variable returns the number of records it was assigned unless the total number of records was smaller than its assigned value. To test this with a simple ActionScript, go to Flash MX Studio and try this.

Listing 16.13   *getProducts.swf*

```
include "NetServices.as"
NetServices.setDefaultGatewayUrl("http://localhost:8500/flashservices/gateway");
gatewayConnection = NetServices.createGatewayConnection();
CFMService = gatewayConnection.getService("Flashexamples", this);
CFMService.getData();
```

After the initial delivery of records, the recordset ActionScript class becomes responsible for fetching records. You can configure the client-side recordset object to fetch records in various ways using the `setDeliveryMode` ActionScript function.

Summary

As you can see, all you really need to know to integrate client-side ActionScript and Flash applications with ColdFusion is two simple variables in the Flash variable scope: `flash.params` and `flash.return`. Macromedia has once again taken a complex chore like creating server-side-driven Flash applications and made it as simple as manipulating a variable scope!

Summary

In this chapter, we covered a variety of topics, including `CFOBJECT` and COM, Flash integration, `CFHTTP`, and `CFCONTENT`. Although seemingly unrelated topics, they all relate to integrating and working with applications and technologies outside the ColdFusion MX Server. As you develop more complex and sophisticated web applications that try to resolve real-world needs, integrating and working with other technologies, such as Microsoft Office through COM, becomes an inescapable requirement.

Armed with the concepts from this chapter, you can build powerful applications that take advantage of disparate applications.

17

Common Application Development Requirements

As CUTTING EDGE AS WE MIGHT WANT TO BE, there are some elements of web applications that developers find themselves writing and implementing again and again with each new web site or web application that they build. The most common development requirements include the following:

- Application security
- Content management
- E-commerce
- Personalization

Of course, there are applications out there that you can purchase to keep from having to write these application elements from scratch, but you'll probably spend as much time figuring out the code in the application as you would writing the program yourself. I'm not saying that commercial applications are not the way to go for some developers— they can give you a good idea of how to implement your own solution.

In this chapter, we give you a high-level overview of application security, content management, e-commerce, and personalization. We also show you how you can implement each in your applications.

Application Security

Some applications require that users log in before they have access to some application resources. There are two basic elements of application security:

- Authentication
- Authorization

Authentication checks whether a valid user is logged in. The authentication process usually involves user interaction with a log form and code on the backend. The authentication process queries the database to verify the username and password provided by the user in the login form and to retrieve information about that user if his or her login is validated.

For example, our InsideColdFusionMX application has many sections. Some are public and some are intended only for authenticated users. The application might let visitors view the welcome page and some other content, but it would require that a user be registered and authenticated prior to viewing the forums area.

The authorization process retrieves information about the authenticated user's rights, privileges, and roles within the application and makes decisions about what content to show the user. Authorization helps to ensure that users see and have the opportunity to interact with only those things to which they should have access.

Let's think again about the InsideColdFusionMX application. Every authenticated user might be able to see all the latest news that appears on the site, but a handful of people might also have access to edit current news items or to add new ones. By identifying the role or roles of each logged-in user, we can show selected users an icon that gives them edit access to the News section.

ColdFusion MX makes the process of implementing and managing application security much easier. This is done with several new CFML tags and functions, as shown in Table 17.1.

Table 17.1   **New ColdFusion MX Application Security Tags and Functions**

Tag or Function	Description
CFLOGIN	The CFLOGIN tag encapsulates the code that is used to authenticate users against a datasource, a Lightweight Directory Access Protocol (LDAP) directory, or another repository of user information. The CFLOGINUSER tag must be called inside the CFLOGIN tag to establish the authenticated user's identity within the ColdFusion application. This tag takes no attributes.

CFLOGINUSER	The CFLOGINUSER tag identifies the authenticated user to the ColdFusion application and optionally identifies all roles for that user. The CFLOGINUSER tag requires the name attribute and optionally takes the roles attribute. The name attribute identifies the user ID of the authenticated user. The value of the roles attribute should be a comma-delimited list of role identifiers. There should not be spaces after the commas.
CFLOGOUT	The CFLOGOUT tag logs the current user out of the application by removing his or her user ID and role from the session structure in the server memory. If the user fails to execute the CFLOGOUT tag, the user is logged out when his or her session expires. This tag takes attributes.
CFFUNCTION	The roles attribute of the CFFUNCTION tag enables the CFFUNCTION to execute only if the authenticated user's role matches with what is specified within the roles attribute of the CFFUNCTION tag.
IsUserInRole	This ColdFusion function checks whether the authenticated user is a member of any of the specified roles. If so, the function returns TRUE.
GetAuthUser	This ColdFusion function retrieves the user ID of the authenticated user. It returns the user ID value.

In the next few pages, we take a look at some of these new features in action.

User Authentication

We've stated that authentication ensures that only a valid user is logged in. ColdFusion MX has introduced the new CFLOGIN tag, which encapsulates the authentication logic. Within the body of the CFLOGIN tag, you can put all your logic that validates the username and password against the database and that differentiates between successful and unsuccessful login attempts.

If a user successfully logs in, our application should call the CFLOGINUSER tag within the body of the CFLOGIN tag. The CFLOGINUSER tag takes the ID of the logged-in user as the value of the name attribute and can optionally take the value of that user's roles as a comma-delimited list into the roles attribute.

Note

The list of values passed into the roles attribute should not contain spaces after each comma.

The most logical place to handle user authentication is in `Application.cfm`. However, there is nothing to stop us from using the older model of breaking the login procedure out into its own directory and creating separate login and authentication templates.

Application.cfm

Because `Application.cfm` runs on each template in the application, it is a perfect place within which to check for user authentication. Each time a template is requested, the application can check to make sure that the user has been authenticated. If the user is not logged in, he or she can be presented with the login form.

Let's walk through the logic of Listing 17.1. First, we check whether the `logout` form variable exists. If it does, we can call the `CFLOGOUT` tag to end the session and to delete all session variables related to this user.

Next, we check whether the `username` and `password` form variables exist. If they do not exist, we include the `loginform.cfm` template and stop further processing with the `CFABORT` tag.

If the `username` and `password` form variables do exist, we query our datasource to return the `UserID` and `Roles` for the user who is attempting to log in. If the login is validated, we use the `CFLOGINUSER` tag to set the `UserID` and `Roles` to a session variable.

If the login is not validated, we create a suitable message for the user and include the `Loginform.cfm` template again.

This is a very basic overview of the authentication and authorization process. We'll take a look at the new tags and elements in Listing 17.1 as we move through this section.

Listing 17.1 **CFLOGIN Security**

```
<cfif IsDefined("Form.logout")>
  <cflogout>
</cfif>
<cflogin>
    <cfif NOT IsDefined("Form.username") OR NOT IsDefined("Form.password")>
        <cfinclude template="loginform.cfm">
        <cfabort>
    <cfelseif  IsDefined("Form.username") AND IsDefined("Form.password")>
        <cfquery name="q_login" dataSource="#request.dsn#">
            SELECT UserID, Roles
            FROM User
            WHERE UserName = '#Form.username#'
            AND UserPassword = '#Form.password#'
            </cfquery>
        <cfif q_login.recordcount EQ "1">
```

```
                    <cfloginuser name="#q_login.UserID#" roles="#q_login.Roles#">
              <cfelse>
              <cfset loginmessage="You must provide a valid username and password.">
                    <cfinclude template="loginform.cfm">
               </cfif>
              </cfif>
</cflogin>
```

LDAP directories are also often used to store application security information. CFLOGIN can also be used to check for user authentication against an LDAP directory, to set the authenticated user ID, and to retrieve user roles (see Listing 17.2).

Listing 17.2   *CFLOGIN* **Security with LDAP**

```
<cflogin>
<!--- Setting Basic Attributes --->
<cfset root = "o=insidecoldfusionmx.com">
<cfset server="nross.insidecoldfusionmx.com">
<cfset port="399">

<!--- These attributes are used in the first search. --->
<!--- This filter  look in the objectclass for the user's ID. --->
<cfset filter = "(&(objectclass=*)(uid=#Form.UserID#))">
<!--- Need directory manager's cn and password to get the user's
    password from the directory --->
<cfset LDAP_username = "cn=directory manager">
<cfset LDAP_password = "password">

<!--- search for the user's dn information. This is used later to
    authenticate the user.
       NOTE: We do this as the Directory Manager to ensure access to the
    information --->
<cfldap action="QUERY"
    name="userSearch"
    attributes="uid,dn"
    start="#root#"
    scope="SUBTREE"
    server="#server#"
    port="#port#"
    filter="#filter#"
    username="#LDAP_username#"
    password="#LDAP_password#">

<cftry>
        <cfldap
          action="QUERY"
          name="auth"
```

continues ▶

Listing 17.2 **Continued**

```
            attributes="dn,roles"
            start="#root#"
            scope="SUBTREE"
            server="#server#"
            port="#port#"
            filter="#filter#"
            username="#userSearch.dn#"
            password="#Form.password#">     <cfcatch type="any">
  <cfif FindNoCase("Invalid credentials", cfcatch.detail)>
    <cfoutput>User ID or Password invalid for user:
#Form.UserID#
    </cfoutput>
    <cfabort>
  <cfelse>
    <cfoutput>Unknown error for user: #Form.UserID#
#cfcatch.detail#
    </cfoutput>
    <cfabort>
  </cfif>
</cfcatch>
</cftry>

<!--- the user is valid. --->
<cfif auth.recordcount>
  <cfloginuser name="#Form.UserID#" roles="#auth.roles#">
</cfif>
</cflogin>
```

In Listings 17.1 and 17.2, the code starts with the CFLOGIN tag body and then sets several of the values used as attributes in the CFLDAP tags as variables. This ensures that the same value is used in both tags, and it makes it easier to change the settings if needed.

Next we set the directory manager's username and password for the first query. The code uses the directory manager's identity to get the distinguished name (dn) for the user. If the user ID is not in the directory, the code return an empty recordset.

In the CFTRY block, we use the dn from the previous query and the user-supplied password to access the directory and get the user's roles. If either the dn or the password is invalid, the CFLDAP tag throw an error, which is caught in the CFCATCH block.

CFCATCH catches any exception that occurs. We then check whether the error information contains the string "invalid credentials", which indicates that either the dn or the password is invalid. If it does contain the text, we display an error message indicating the problem. Otherwise, we display a general error message.

If an error is caught, the CFABORT tag ends the processing of the request after displaying the error description.

If the second query returned a valid record, the user is logged in and the UserID and Roles that were returned by the query are added to the session variable. Then we close by ending the CFLOGIN tag body.

Checking for Login

The CFLOGIN tag itself takes care of checking whether the current user is logged in. Outside the CFLOGIN tag, we might need to check whether the current user has been authenticated.

I've put this check in the navigation template so that if the user is logged in, a log out button appears below the regular navigation elements. ColdFusion MX has made the task of checking for the existence of an authenticated user much easier. In applications prior to ColdFusion MX, you might have had similar functionality that looked a bit like this:

```
<cflock scope="session" type="readonly" timeout="10">
  <cfif NOT IsDefined("session.logged_in")>
    <cflocation url="login_form.cfm">
  </cfif>
</cflock>
```

In ColdFusion MX, we use the GetAuthUser() function to handle the majority of the same logic:

```
<cfif GetAuthUser() EQ "">
  <cfinclude template="login_form.cfm">
</cfif>
```

The GetAuthUser() function takes no arguments and returns the ID of the currently authenticated valid user. If the current user is not authenticated, the GetAuthUser() function does not return a value.

Loginform.cfm

Authentication requires that users identify themselves. Usually this identification happens through the input of a username and password. It really doesn't matter what values you authenticate against; for the sake of security, this process simply should not be left out.

We need to create a login form to handle the authentication tasks of the application. This form does not have to be anything fancy. It is simply a utility. However, you'll probably want to integrate the login form into the look and feel of the rest of your application. In addition, you should incorporate your application header and footer into your login template.

In `Application.cfm`, our logic determines whether the user has been authenticated. If the user has not been authenticated, the login template is executed in `Application.cfm` with a `CFINCLUDE` tag:

```
<cfinclude template="loginform.cfm">
<cfabort>
```

Note

The `CFABORT` tag is called to keep the requested template from executing.

One of the first pieces of code in our login template is the section that creates a variable for the requested URL. Many times, visitors might set a bookmark on a page within our application. Allowing that user to access the requested URL, including any URL parameters after the completion of the login, is a nice feature to build in to your application.

The code is not so complex:

```
<cfset url="http://" & cgi.server_name & ":" &cgi.server_port & cgi.script_name>
  <cfif cgi.query_string IS NOT "">
    <cfset url=url & "?#cgi.query_string#">
  </cfif>
```

In Listing 17.3, we see how this bit of conditional logic can easily be worked into our application.

Listing 17.3 **Conditional Logic for Authentication Processing**

```
<!--- Remember the Requested URL --->
<cfset url="http://" & cgi.server_name & ":" &cgi.server_port & cgi.script_name>
  <cfif cgi.query_string IS NOT "">
    <cfset url=url & "?#cgi.query_string#">
  </cfif>
<cfinclude template="/common/header.cfm">
<cfoutput>
  <form action="#url#" method="Post">
    <table align="left" width="800">
      <tr>
        <td colspan="2"><hr size="1" width="80%"></td>
      </tr>
      <tr>
        <td align="center">
      <table border="1">
          <tr>
            <td>You are not currently logged into the Inside ColdFusion MX website.
</td>
```

```
                </tr>
            <tr>
                <td align="center">
                    <table><tr>
        <td colspan="2">Please Log In:</td>
    </tr>
    <tr>
        <td align="right">User Name:</td>
        <td><input type="text" name="username" size="10"></td>
    </tr>
    <tr>
        <td align="right">Password:</td>
        <td><input type="password" name="password" size="10"></td>
    </tr>
        <td></td>
        <td align="right"><input type="submit" value=" Login "></td>
    </tr></table>
                </td>
            </tr>
    </table>
    </td>
    <td><cfinclude template="/common/right_nav.cfm"></td>
</tr>
<tr>
    <td colspan="2"><hr size="1" width="80%"></td>
    </tr>
</table>
  </form>
</cfoutput>
<cfinclude template="/common/footer.cfm">
```

The validation process takes place within Application.cfm itself. In other versions of ColdFusion, the normal method of authenticating a user was to create an authentication template and then identify that template as the target of your login form's action attribute. Because our authentication code exists within the Application.cfm template, we can point directly to the originally requested page, and authentication occurs when the request is made.

The login screen that we've built in Listings 17.1 and 17.3 should yield what is shown in Figure 17.1.

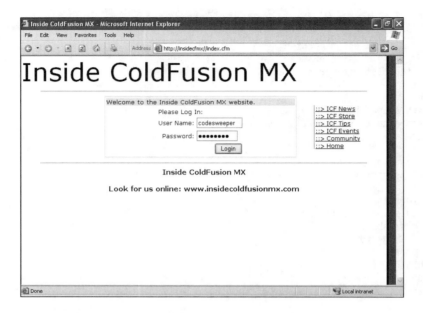

Figure 17.1 Including the login template to authenticate users.

Authorization

Authorization is the second element of application security, and it ensures that the authenticated user can view and interact with only the information for which he or she is authorized. This is just like the idea of permissions that we assign to files and shared folders on a workstation.

These permissions are usually managed by groups on our file server. In our ColdFusion MX application, these groups be referred to as roles. For example, if the authenticated user has a role assigned that enables him to add or edit content for our news section, he might see a button on his screen that enables him to access the administrative portion of the News section of our application.

The capability to enable viewers to see and interact with application content based on user roles or security privilege is a nice addition to the functionality of an application.

ColdFusion MX makes this type of functionality a lot easier with the introduction of another new tag. That tag is the CFLOGINUSER tag. The tag looks like this:

```
<cfloginuser
  name="required"
  roles="optional,comma-delimited-list">
```

The CFLOGINUSER tag identifies the authenticated user to the ColdFusion application. The name attribute holds the authenticated user's ID and the optional roles attribute identifies a comma-delimited list of user roles.

The beauty of the new login tag functionality in ColdFusion is the actual assignment of the authentication values. All the tasks that once took many lines of code are wrapped up into a neat little package (see Listing 17.4).

Listing 17.4 **Setting Authenticated User and Roles with *CFLOGINUSER***

```
<cfloginuser name="#q_login.UserID#" roles="#q_login.Roles#">
```

The preceding code creates a session structure in the ColdFusion Server memory that retains the authenticated user's ID and a list of the user's roles throughout the duration of the session.

Our earlier example mentioned that when we view the content of our news section, we see an edit button if our assigned roles enable us to do so. In Listing 17.5, let's take a look at some of the code associated with that type of functionality.

Listing 17.5 **Displaying News to Authenticated and Authorized Users**

```
<cfquery name="getNews" datasource="#application.dsn#">
    SELECT *
    FROM News
</cfquery>

<p>This is the news area for Inside ColdFusion.</p>
<cfif IsUserInRole(1)>
<table width="100%">
<cfoutput query="getNews">
<tr>
    <td>
    <table width="100%" cellspacing="0">
<tr bgcolor="f2f2f2">
    <td class="header">#getNews.NewsTitle#</td>
    <td align="right">#getNews.NewsStartDate#</td>
</tr>
<tr>
    <td colspan="2">#getNews.NewsBody#</td>
</tr>
<tr>
    <td></td>
    <td align="right">Contributor: #getNews.NewsSource#</td>
</tr>
</table>
</td>
```

continues ▶

Listing 17.5 **Continued**

```
</tr>
<tr>
    <td><hr size="1"></td>
</tr>
</cfoutput>
</table>
<cfelse>
You are not authorized to view the content on this page.
</cfif>
```

If the user is authorized to view the special features on this page, he or she sees a screen similar to what is shown in Figure 17.2.

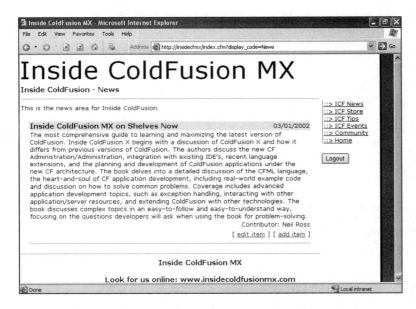

Figure 17.2 User authorized to view, edit, or add content.

If the user is not authorized to access the edit and add content functionality of this template, he or she sees a screen that looks like Figure 17.3.

We'll talk more later about authorization-based access to content and functionality when we talk about content management in the section "Content Management."

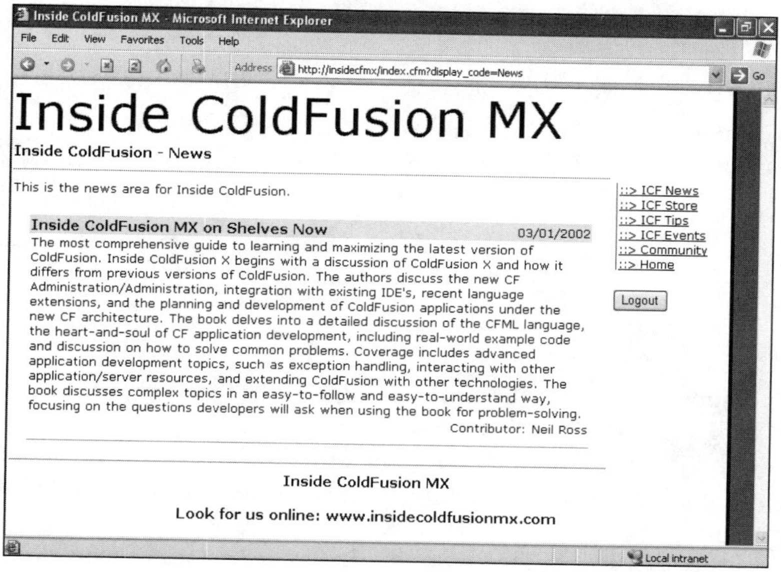

Figure 17.3 User authorized only to view content.

Logging Out

Your application should also provide some type of functionality that enables your user to log out. Failing to provide a logout mechanism is a security risk because the user session does not end until the session timeout has been reached. This means that if you log in, create a session, and then close your browser, your session remains active. The next time you open your browser (up until the session timeout), your session will still be active.

ColdFusion MX uses the new CFLOGOUT tag to complete logout transactions. CFLOGOUT takes no attributes and has no body. When CFLOGOUT is executed, it immediately kills the current user session. You might be wondering how we execute the CFLOGOUT tag. It's simple really—we just create a simple logout form or link.

The first thing that we need to know is whether the user is actually authenticated. We check for an authenticated user with the GetAuthUser() function. GetAuthUser() is a function new to ColdFusion MX. When executed, it returns the value of the user ID of the authenticated user. If there is no authenticated user ID, the function returns an empty string. Listing 17.6 shows what the code would look like.

Listing 17.6 **Including the Logout Form**

```
<cfif GetAuthUser() NEQ "">
  <cfoutput>
    <form action="index.cfm" method="Post">
     <input type="submit" Name="Logout" value="Logout">
   </form>
  </cfoutput>
</cfif>
```

Summary

Application security can be handled simply with the addition of the new tags to ColdFusion MX. Application security can be as easy as checking a username and password for authentication. Application security can add another layer of complexity when incorporating elements of authorization into the equation.

Our discussion of authorization in this sections leads us naturally into the topic of content management. This is a natural segue because the management of content is based on application authentication and a user's authorization to manipulate specific pieces or whole sections of content.

Content Management

The popularity of content-management applications has been growing for years. When the dot-com boom started, everything was about e-commerce and shopping cart this and shopping cart that. When the newness started to wane, people were left with a lot of content on their web sites, but no means to maintain the code—other than to hire a staff full of Hypertext Markup Language (HTML) jockeys to cut and paste it for them.

The goal of content management is to addresses the problem of maintaining up-to-date information in a system that enables content contribution and delivery, content deployment, and content maintenance. A good content-management solution should give real-time content updates, revision tracking, and content archiving. It should also enable users to maintain the state of their content within the context that it is displayed—without leaving the web site to visit a clunky management portal.

Well, that's a picture of an ideal world where the grass is always greener on your own side of the fence. Rather than go into too much detail about the content-management wish list, let's start with a couple of the major components of content-management systems. There are two main components to any content-management mechanism:

- Access to content
- Content workflow

Access to content describes how authenticated users are able to access content for adding, editing, or creating new content. Access to content goes hand-in-hand with our discussion of authorization in the first section of this chapter.

Content workflow describes the processes of creating, approving, and publishing content to an application. Each phase of content workflow might be made up of several steps in itself.

Building an Application for Content Management

Building a simple content-management application is pretty straightforward. Let's say that we're going to build content management into the news portion of the `InsideColdFusionMX.com` web site. Updating existing content might be as easy as creating an update template that authorized users can launch from a link on the news template. This simple link is an example of how a user gains access to content for management purposes.

The real complexity comes into play when you have multiple users who must review or approve the content before any changes are committed. However, before we go too far into the complexities of content workflow, let's start off with a very basic approach to how users can access content that they are responsible for managing.

Access to Content

We said earlier in our content-management wish list that it is always nice for users to be able to create and maintain content without being forced off to some clunky content administrator portal. Of course, a clunky content administrator portal is very practical sometimes because it enables you to create an undeniable separation between the code and logic of your web site or application and the maintenance application that supports it.

Authentication and authorization play a major part in how we model the development of our content access. Authentication, of course, assures us that only valid users can log in to the application. Authorization enables us to show special content to authenticated users who have a role that enables them to see and interact with that content. Therefore, users of certain roles can view a link to add content to our application while others cannot. Of course, the first rule of authorization is authentication.

Remember the news portion of our site from the previous section? Let's look at some practical code, as shown in Listing 17.7.

Listing 17.7 **A Simple Content-Management Implementation**

```
<cfquery name="getNews" datasource="#application.dsn#">
    SELECT *
    FROM News
</cfquery>
<p>This is the news area for Inside ColdFusion.</p>
<table width="100%">
<cfoutput query="getNews">
<tr>
    <td>
    <table width="100%" cellspacing="0">
<tr bgcolor="f2f2f2">
    <td class="header">#getNews.NewsTitle#</td>
    <td align="right">#getNews.NewsStartDate#</td>
</tr>
<tr>
    <td colspan="2">#getNews.NewsBody#</td>
</tr>
<tr>
    <td></td>
    <td align="right">Contributor: #getNews.NewsSource#</td>
</tr>
<!--- THIS IS WHERE WE ALLOW THE USER TO ACCESS THE CONTENT --->
<cfif IsUserInRole(5)>
</cfif>
<tr>
  <td colspan="2" align="right">[ <a href="/admin.cfm?function=add">add new
content</a> ] [ <a href="/admin.cfm?function=edit&item=1256">edit this content</a>
]</td>
</tr>
</table>
</td>
</tr>
<tr>
    <td><hr size="1"></td>
</tr>
</cfoutput>
</table>
```

By executing the code in Listing 17.7 we should see the options to add new content or edit the current content, as in Figure 17.4.

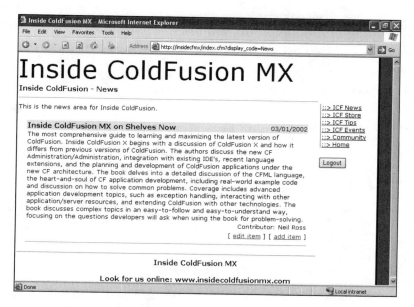

Figure 17.4 User authorized to view, edit, or add content.

The processes associated with editing the content can be simple forms where all the information is accessible and editable on a single page or screen. The editing process can consist of multiple steps. These steps are associated with each other and form what some of us call "process logic paths," a term that we acquired from our time working with Macromedia's Spectra product. Although not a front-line product anymore, Spectra employed some solid concepts related to content creation and management.

Creating Content

Creating content can be as simple as adding a single piece of information to a database table. Most of the time, however, our content tends to be much more involved. We can create content using a single form and a single action page, or we can spread our content collection across several forms, placing the values that we collect into a session structure, which is a temporary table in a database. We can also pass them all along as form variables.

Listing 17.8 is an example of a very simple screen that enables us to add data to our database. Of course, we must be authorized to see the link to add new content for this code to execute.

Listing 17.8   **Simple Content Creation Form**

```
<form action="/business_code/act_create_news.cfm" method="post">
    <table>
                    <tr>
                <td valign="top" align="right">Title:
                </td>
                <td>
                    <input type="text" name="NewsTitle" maxlength="100">
                </td>
            </tr>
            <tr>
                <td valign="top" align="right">Desciption:
                </td>
                <td>
                <textarea name="NewsDesciption" cols="50" rows="3"></textarea>
                </td>
            </tr>
            <tr>
                <td valign="top" align="right">Body:
                </td>
                <td>
                    <textarea name="NewsBody" cols="50" rows="5"></textarea>
                </td>
            </tr>
<tr>
                <td valign="top" align="right">Start Date:
                </td>
                <td>
                    <input type="text" name="NewsStartDate" maxlength="100">
                </td>
            </tr>
            <tr>
                <td valign="top" align="right">End Date:
                </td>
                <td>
                    <input type="text" name="NewsEndDate" maxlength="100">
                </td>
            </tr>
            <tr>
                <td valign="top" align="right">Source:
                </td>
                <td>
                    <input type="text" name="NewsSource" maxlength="100">
                </td>
            </tr>
            <tr>
                <td valign="top" align="right">Comments:
                </td>
                <td>
```

```
            <textarea name="NewsComments" cols="50" rows="3"></textarea>
          </td>
      </tr>
      <tr>
          <td colspan="2" align="right">
            <input type="submit" value="Create News Item">
          </td>
      </tr>
    </table>
</form>
```

When we execute the code in Listing 17.8, we see a screen similar to Figure 17.5.

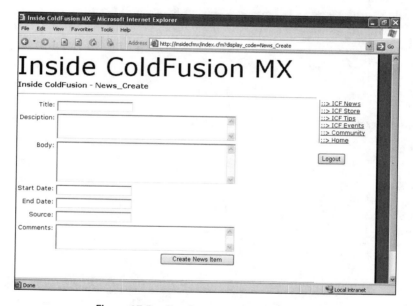

Figure 17.5   Simple content-creation form.

Some transactions are more complicated and require multiple steps in the entry process. You are required to collect values from the form input on each screen, hold them temporarily, and then commit only those values to the database upon completion of the entire process. How you handle the retention of the values that you collect is up to you. Keep in mind, however, that you don't want to do too much juggling of values, which is what you might have to do if you pass values from form page to form page.

I recommend that if you have more than two collection pages that you do not pass the values along as form variables. Keep in mind too that values stored in hidden form fields are visible when you view the source that is returned to the browser. In addition, your code can become more and more complex and less readable with each additional step in the process. You might want to place the values from your form into a session variable that you can clear at the end of the transaction. If you do pass the form values from screen to screen, you might consider passing the entire form structure as a single hidden variable.

Editing Content

The editing process is much like any editing process using HTML or ColdFusion Markup Language (CFML) forms and ColdFusion on the back-end to update and delete rows in your database tables. Figure 17.6 shows us a simple form to update the news content that we created through the code in Listing 17.9.

Listing 17.9   **Simple Content-Update Form**

```
<cfquery name="getNews" datasource="#application.dsn#">
    SELECT *
    FROM News
    WHERE NewsID = #url.News_ID#
</cfquery>

   <form action="/business_code/act_edit_news.cfm" method="post">
       <table>
            <cfoutput>
          <tr>
                  <td valign="middle" align="right">Title:
                  </td>
                  <td>
                    <input type="text" name="NewsTitle" maxlength="100"
value="#getNews.NewsTitle#" size="64">
                  </td>
             </tr>
             <tr>
                  <td valign="top" align="right">Desciption:
                  </td>
                  <td>
                  <textarea name="NewsDesciption" cols="50"
rows="3">#getNews.NewsDesciption#</textarea>
                  </td>
             </tr>
             <tr>
                  <td valign="top" align="right">Body:
                  </td>
```

```
                    <td>
                        <textarea name="NewsBody" cols="50"
rows="5">#getNews.NewsBody#</textarea>
                    </td>
            </tr>
        <tr>
                    <td valign="middle" align="right">Start Date:
                    </td>
                    <td>
                        <input type="text" name="NewsStartDate" maxlength="100"
value="#getNews.NewsStartDate#">
                    </td>
            </tr>
            <tr>
                    <td valign="middle" align="right">End Date:
                    </td>
                    <td>
                        <input type="text" name="NewsEndDate" maxlength="100"
value="#getNews.NewsEndDate#">
                    </td>
            </tr>
            <tr>
                    <td valign="middle" align="right">Source:
                    </td>
                    <td>
                        <input type="text" name="NewsSource" maxlength="100"
value="#getNews.NewsSource#">
                    </td>
            </tr>
            <tr>
                    <td valign="top" align="right">Comments:
                    </td>
                    <td>
                    <textarea name="NewsComments" cols="50"
rows="3">#getNews.NewsComments#</textarea>
                    </td>
            </tr>
        </cfoutput>
            <tr>
                    <td colspan="2" align="right">
                        <input type="submit" value="Update News Item">
                    </td>
            </tr>
        </table>
    </form>
```

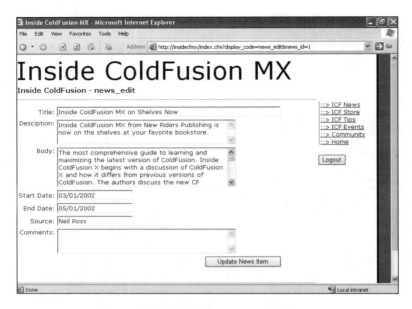

Figure 17.6   Simple content-update form.

Again, if the editing process had to be separated into more than one step, you'd need to store the form values temporarily until the entire update process had been completed.

Content Workflow

Workflow describes the business processes that take place to complete a business task. For example, if you are privy to an interesting piece of news and want to publish it to the InsideColdfusionMX.com web site, you create the news content through the web site. The web site then puts the information in the database and sends me an email. I respond to the email by reading your news item and then verifying it. I then approve the news item, schedule it to be published to the web site, and automatically send you an email upon completion of the scheduling process. Whew...there's a lot to it. That's workflow though. Workflow links individual tasks and the participants that are responsible for their completion. It also identifies which tasks must be completed before others can be started.

Workflows might sound a bit like the process logic paths that we discussed earlier, but they're really not. The difference is that a process logic path is contained within a single business process. Workflows are those business processes tied together.

Defining Workflows

Defining a workflow is a process that involves several distinct steps. How a workflow looks varies according to the tasks that it involves:

- Create a list of tasks
  - Identify contributor.
  - Contributor creates news item.
  - Editor approves or denies news item.
  - Item is published or discarded.
- Establish precedence
  - Contributor must be authenticated and authorized.
  - Contributor must create news item.
  - Editor must approve or discard news item.
  - Editor must schedule news item if approved.
- Establish notification
  - Notify editor of new news item.
  - Notify contributor of item approval or denial.

Using the authentication and authorization models that we discussed earlier, we know what roles the authenticated user can play in our workflow. In the preceding example, they can be contributors, editors, or nonparticipants.

Making Use of Existing Components

There is no sense in reinventing the wheel every time you implement a content-management solution (or any other software solution for that matter). It makes sense to make use of existing components in your content-management solution. Many existing components can be found on popular ColdFusion resource sites. One such site is the Macromedia ColdFusion Developer's Exchange at `http://devex.macromedia.com/developer/gallery/index.cfm`.

Spectra Community Source (Brief Discussion)

Macromedia Spectra is an application framework that is built on Macromedia ColdFusion. Spectra's application framework is designed to combine a set of predefined processes and visual tools that help developers define and build robust web applications. Spectra was designed to make it easy to build and manage Internet and intranet portals that employ content management, e-commerce, and personalized content.

Spectra addresses the full spectrum of participants in the application development and deployment processes. It also enables technical and nontechnical business people to manage web site content. Last, it enables developers to easily create applications that involve complex process logic and workflow. This is done through an easy-to-use visual webtop environment.

ColdFusion developers can jump right into development in the Spectra environment because Spectra is comprised of a collection of ColdFusion custom tags.

Macromedia Spectra is a community source project. Because Spectra is community source, the entire Spectra development community has the ability to contribute to the direction of the product and to the development of product improvements such as patches and code fixes. This type of interaction with the community leads to increased innovation, more frequent updates, and more frequent release cycles.

Competing Components

There are many third-party solutions out there if you do not want to build your own. Recently, the *ColdFusion Developer's Journal* released its 2001 Readers' Choice Awards. The top three content-management solutions were as follows:

- CommonSpot Content Server 2.5 from PaperThin
- soEditor 2.1 from SiteObjects
- CMS100 from Ektron

CommonSpot Content Server

PaperThin's CommonSpot Content Server is an out-of-the-box, content-management solution built for web publishing and management of dynamic content. It is designed to get everyone in your organization involved in the creation, maintenance, and publishing of web content.

CommonSpot Content Server puts business professionals in charge of the creation of valuable web content. It's easy-to-understand and intuitive features make it easy for nontechnical users to create, update, and schedule content.

CommonSpot's flexible template and data-driven architecture gives developers and administrators control of the structure and appearance of the site, while simplifying the process of maintaining the content of the site. A roles-based administration and multilevel approval workflow process gives administrators control over the content that gets published.

Because of CommonSpot's open and extensible architecture, developers can customize templates and integrate custom ColdFusion, web, e-commerce and other applications within CommonSpot's content framework.

The list of features for the CommonSpot Content Server goes on and on. Here are some of the more popular:

- Simplified web publishing
- Template-driven web pages
- Access-based roles and privileges
- Approval workflow
- Dynamic self-updating indexes and navigation
- Scheduled and personalized content
- Integrated verity search
- Seamless integration of structured data
- Extensive metadata support
- Customization of CommonSpot
- Content freshness reminders and content expiration
- Page set support
- Simple forms and datasheets
- Keywords and keyword views
- Enterprise scalability
- Dynamic page generation and static caching
- Distributed administration and security
- Cluster server

To find out more about PaperThin's CommonSpot Content Server, visit their web site at www.paperthin.com.

soEditor

SiteObjects' soEditor is not actually a content-management solution, but a ColdFusion custom tag that is built so that you can easily integrate it into a content-management solution that you have. What soEditor brings to the table is a full-featured, what-you-see-is-what-you-get (WYSISYG) editor for your content areas.

soEditor's WYSIWYG editor has word processor-like features that include the capability to insert HTML tables, images, and links. It also lets you format your text as you see fit.

soEditor's features include the following:

- Easy integration
- Simple WYSIWYG editing
- Full customization
- HTML source editing
- Spell checking
- Validation
- Word-count capabilities

In addition to these standard features, the Professional version of soEditor also offers the following:

- An image manager
- Form controls
- An integrated email form
- Style sheets
- Custom links
- A code sweeper (We like this one!)

To find out more about SiteObject's soEditor, check out their web site at www.siteobjects.com.

CMS100

Ektron's CMS100 is an entry-level content-authoring and publishing system that is built around another popular Ektron product, eWebEditPro. CMS100 enables business users to author their own web content and incorporate workflow functionality into the content approval process.

CMS100 has the following features:

- Support for CFML and Active Server Pages (ASP)
- Support for Dreamweaver/UltraDev extensions
- File uploading
- Content versioning
- Document check-in/check-out
- Content-management workflow

- Virtual staging server
- International language support
- Administration
- Microsoft structured query language (SQL) integration

For more information regarding Ektron's CMS100, visit their web site at www.ektron.com.

Summary

Whether content management is just a new buzzword or is here to stay, the concepts of content management can be employed by ColdFusion developers to help them make their world a happier place. Concepts, such as roles-based access to content and content workflow, ensure the integrity of content and that the content that is published has been approved.

Developers can easily create their own custom, content-management solutions using ColdFusion, but there are some cases where it is definitely worth not trying to reinvent the wheel. There are many third-party products out there that you can take advantage of to help make your content-management solution an award winner.

E-Commerce

When we think about e-commerce, we might think about the dot-com boom back in the late 1990s, when everyone was rushing to set up their own online stores, complete with shopping cart applications and online credit card processing. E-commerce, however, is not limited to startups that only conduct business online; it is simply the capability for any company to transact business online.

If you sell automotive decals from an online store, you need a few basic components to complete a business transaction online:

- Catalog
- Shopping cart
- Payment processing

Building a Catalog

First, you need an online catalog. Catalogs are a fairly simple type of application. They consist of some search or drill-down mechanism that enables the user to see items in the catalog based on a keyword search or category selection. The template that you create to display the resulting items probably displays several items. It might even display items in different categories.

You might also want to build a default catalog page that lists your product categories as well. Check out Figure 17.7.

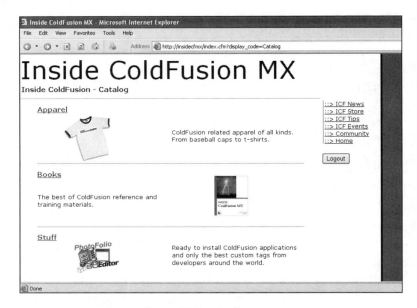

Figure 17.7 Catalog page.

When a user chooses a category or submits a search request, your catalog should return a resulting page that shows the items in the requested category or those items that meet the user's search criteria.

Listing 17.10 presents an adjective system and Figure 17.8 shows what it looks like in a browser.

Listing 17.10 **Catalog Items By Category**

```
<cfquery name="getProducts" datasource="#request.dsn#">
  SELECT  p.ProductID, p.CatID, p.ProdName, p.ProdDesc, p.ProdPrice, p.ProdSpec,
c.CategoryName
  FROM    products p, categories c
  WHERE   c.CategoryID = p.CatID
<cfif IsDefined("url.CatID")>AND c.CategoryID = #url.CatID#</cfif>
```

```
</cfquery>
<table align="left" border="0" width="100%" cellpadding="2" cellspacing="0">
  <tr>
    <td colspan="2">Welcome to the catalog. Take a look at the item available right
    ►now.</td>
  </tr>
<cfoutput query="getProducts" group="CategoryName">
  <tr>
    <td class="header"><br>#getProducts.CategoryName#</td><td align="right"><input
    ►type="button" value=" Go Back " class="button" onclick="history.go(-1);"></td>
  </tr>
<cfoutput>
  <tr>
    <td class="details" colspan="2">
      <blockquote>
        <table width="100%" cellpadding="0" cellspacing="0">
          <tr>
<td>#getProducts.ProdName#<br><blockquote>#getProducts.ProdDesc# <font style="font:
►smaller;"> - [ <a href="index.cfm?ShowContent=ItemDetails&PID=
►#getProducts.ProductID#">details</a> ]</font></blockquote></td>
          </tr>
        </table>
      </blockquote>
    </td>
  </tr>
</cfoutput>
  <tr>
    <td height="1" bgcolor="808080" colspan="2"></td>
  </tr>
</cfoutput>
</table>
```

In most cases, the catalog includes a way to show more information about each item within the catalog. This type of template is simply referred to as the details template.

Details

Any good shopping cart includes a page where the user can see the details of the item that he or she is considering purchasing. Usually, that details page includes an extended explanation of the item and its specifications. The details page often includes a link to view a larger version of the picture of the item. Listing 17.11 and Figure 17.9 provide an example of such a page.

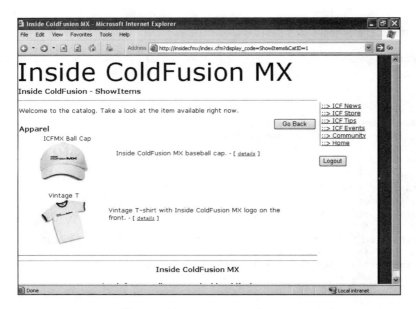

Figure 17.8 Category results page.

Listing 17.11 **Showing the Item Details**

```
<cfquery name="getProduct" datasource="#request.dsn#">
  SELECT  p.ProductID, p.CatID, p.ProdName, p.ProdDesc, p.ProdPrice, p.ProdSpec,
p.ProdThumbnail, c.CategoryName
  FROM    products p, categories c
  WHERE   c.CategoryID = p.CatID
    AND   p.ProductID = #url.PID#
</cfquery>
<table align="left" border="0" width="100%" cellpadding="2" cellspacing="0">
  <tr>
    <td colspan="2">This page would show the detailed information about the
    ➥product.</td>
  </tr>
<cfoutput>
  <tr>
    <td class="header" colspan="2"><br>#getProduct.CategoryName#</td>
  </tr>
<form action="index.cfm?ShowContent=Cart_Action" method="post">
<input type="hidden" name="item" value="#getProduct.ProductID#">
<input type="hidden" name="itemname" value="#getProduct.ProdName#">
<input type="hidden" name="price" value="#getProduct.ProdPrice#">
<input type="hidden" name="quantity" value="1">
  <tr>
    <td class="details" colspan="2" align="left"><font
    ➥class="header">#getProduct.ProdName#</font>
```

```
        <blockquote>
          <table align="right">
            <tr>
              <td valign="top" width="175" align="right">
                <img src="/images/#getProduct.ProdThumbnail#" height="159" width="159">
                <br>
                <font style="font: smaller;"><input type="submit" value=" Add to Cart "
class="button"> <input type="button" value=" Shop More " class="button"
onclick="history.go(-1);"></font>
              </td>
            </tr>
          </table>
          #getProduct.ProdDesc#<br>
          #getProduct.ProdSpec#<br>
          <font class="header">Price: #DollarFormat(getProduct.ProdPrice)#</font>
        </blockquote>
      </td>
    </tr>
  </form>
</cfoutput>
    <tr>
      <td colspan="2"><hr size="1"></td>
    </tr>
</table>
```

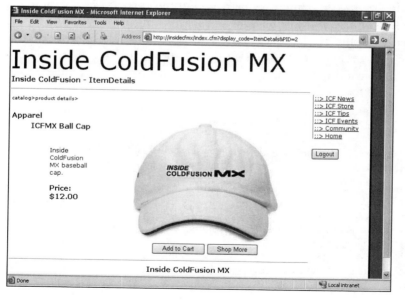

Figure 17.9   Item Details page.

Building a Shopping Cart

The shopping cart is the core functionality that lies at the heart of the e-commerce application. The shopping cart is a storage place for items that the customer is thinking about purchasing. A good shopping cart enables users to change both items and quantities.

Shopping carts store selected items for a single user. Shopping carts can store these selections for the life of the user session, or the carts can store them until they are manually removed by the user. During the planning of your shopping cart, special consideration should be given to the duration of storage for the user's selected items. This determines whether your shopping cart stores selections in session variables or stores them elsewhere.

Of course, the users must be allowed to add items to their carts. As mentioned, the users should also be allowed to update their carts by specifying new item quantities or by removing items from the cart completely.

Add to Cart/Update Cart

Every shopping cart requires an operation that enables the user to add an item or multiple items to his or her cart. The code in Listing 17.12 enables these tasks.

The code first checks whether the cart exists. The code then checks whether the shopping cart exists within the current user's session. If it does not exist, it creates the `session.MyCart` array. The code then checks for the length of the array and creates a new array item. The new array variable is actually an embedded ColdFusion structure that holds the selected item's ID, name, quantity, price, and subtotal (item price×quantity). The code uses a `CFLOCATION` tag to show the updated cart contents.

Listing 17.12 **Add Item to the Cart**

```
<cflock scope="session" type="exclusive" timeout="10">
<cfif NOT IsDefined("session.MyCart") OR ArrayIsEmpty(session.MyCart)>
    <cfset session.MyCart = ArrayNew(1)>
</cfif>
    <cfset i = ArrayLen(SESSION.MyCart) + 1>
    <cfset session.MyCart[i] = STRUCTNEW()>
    <cfset session.MyCart[i].item = form.item>
    <cfset session.MyCart[i].itemname = form.itemname>
    <cfset session.MyCart[i].quantity = form.quantity>
    <cfset session.MyCart[i].price = form.price>
    <cfset session.MyCart[i].sub_total = form.price * form.quantity>
</cflock>
<cflocation url="index.cfm?ShowContent=Cart">
```

After the item has been added to the cart, you must enable the user to view his or her cart. At this point, the user can adjust quantities, delete items from the cart, and decide whether to check out or to continue shopping. See Listing 17.13 and Figure 17.10.

Listing 17.13 **View the User's Cart**

```
<script language="JavaScript">
    function JumpToCat(){window.location="index.cfm?ShowContent=Catalog";}
    function JumpToCheckout(){window.location="index.cfm?ShowContent=Checkout";}
</script>
<cfinclude template="../common/cartfunctions.cfm">
    <table align="left" border="0" cellspacing="0" cellpadding="2" width="600">
        <tr>
            <td rowspan="3" width="250" valign="top">This is where I explain that
            ➥these are the contents of your cart.</td>
            <td width="450">
                <table width="450" border="0" cellspacing="0">
                    <tr>
                        <td class="header" valign="top">My Shopping Cart:</td>
                        <td align="right" valign="bottom"><input type="button"
                        ➥name="ClearCart" value=" Check Out Now " class="button"
                        ➥onclick="JumpToCheckout();"></td>
                    </tr>
                </table>
</td>
        </tr>
        <tr>
            <td width="450"><hr size="1"></td>
        </tr>
        <tr>
            <td>
            <table align="center" width="100%" border="1" cellspacing="0"
            ➥cellpadding="2" bordercolor="d4d4d4">
    <cfif IsDefined("session.MyCart")>
            <tr bgcolor="f2f2f2">
            <td>Item</td>
            <td>Quantity</td>
            <td>Price</td>
            <td>Sub-Total</td>
        </tr>
    <cfset total="0">
    <cfloop from="1" to = "#ArrayLen(session.MyCart)#" index="i">
            <form action="" method="post">
    <cfoutput>
        <input type="hidden" name="itemindex" value="#i#">
        <tr>
            <td>#session.mycart[i].itemname#<input type="hidden" name="item"
            ➥value="#session.mycart[i].item#"></td>
            <td><input type="text" name="quantity"
            ➥value="#session.mycart[i].quantity#" size="3" maxlength="3"
```

Listing 17.13 **Continued**

```
                     style="font: smaller;"></td>
                     <td>#DollarFormat(session.mycart[i].price)#<input type="hidden"
                     ⮑name="price" value="#session.mycart[i].price#"></td>
                     <td align="right">#DollarFormat(session.mycart[i].sub_total)#<input
                     ⮑type="hidden" name="sub_total"
                     ⮑value="#session.mycart[i].sub_total#"></td>
                </tr>
        </cfoutput>
            </cfloop>
            <cfloop from="1" to = "#ArrayLen(session.MyCart)#" index="i">
                <cfset variables.Total=#session.mycart[i].sub_total#+#total#>
            </cfloop>
            <tr>
                <td align="center"><font style="font: smaller;"><input type="submit"
                ⮑name="ClearCart" value="  Empty Cart  "
                ⮑class="button">   <input type="submit" name="UpdCart"
                ⮑value=" Update Cart " class="button"></font></td>
                <td>Total</td>
                <cfoutput><td colspan="2" align="right">#DollarFormat(variables.total)
                ⮑#</td></cfoutput>
            </tr>
</form>
</table>
      </td>
</tr>
<cfelse>
        <tr>
            <td colspan="2" align="center">Your Cart is Currently Empty!</td>
        </tr>
        </cfif>
        <tr>
            <td colspan="2" align="center"><hr size="1"></td>
        </tr>
        <tr>
            <td colspan="2" align="center"><font style="font: smaller;"><input
            ⮑type="button" name="ShopMore" value="Continue Shopping" class="button"
            ⮑onclick="JumpToCat()"></font></td>
        </tr>
    </table>
```

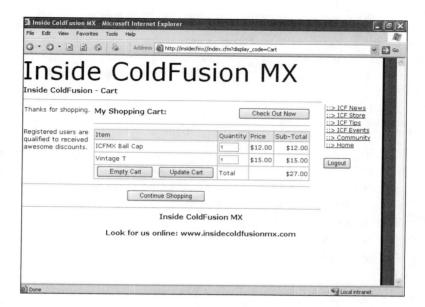

Figure 17.10 Summary of shopping cart items.

After the user has finished gathering items into the cart and adjusting the quantity of any of those items, the shopping cart application should enable the user to check out. The checkout process is the final process with which the user interacts.

Checkout and Payment Processing

The checkout process usually involves the user entering his or her name, billing and shipping information, and payment preferences. There are several ways to complete this process. You can gather all the information for a customer each time that he or she makes a purchase. However, if you expect your customers to purchase from your site again (and probably even if you don't), you should consider allowing the user to provide a password for future purchases. Even if you don't, your application could generate a password and send it to the customer for future logins.

Summary

In the preceding section, we discovered how to use ColdFusion MX to create e-commerce applications that enable our users to purchase products from our sites, to update/change shopping cart items, and to connect to a payment-processing vendor.

Although this is certainly in no way everything you need to know about developing an e-commerce site, you should now have a solid foundation on which to build as you begin to explore for yourself the ways in which you can make your site more robust and appealing to your users and potential customers.

Personalization

Personalization of web sites is a powerful tool to help generate repeat visits by customizing the site layout to the preferences of individual visitors. This enables you to present to each individual user a version of the site that he or she can tailor to his or her own personal preferences.

The theory behind this process is that by allowing users to create their own "customized spaces" on your site, you make them feel more comfortable. Thus, they might decide to use your site more frequently because it feels more "familiar" to them.

You see this technique employed to great effect by almost all the large portal sites. Whether this technique actually generates increased user visitation is up for debate. However, it's still something that you're likely to see requested by those for whom you develop.

The deeper you get into discussion of personalization techniques, the more confusing it can get. For instance, you might hear someone ask about one-to-one marketing or collaborative filtering (huh?), but the bottom line is that all these techniques strive to present site visitors with a version of the site that has been specially crafted to cater to their individual needs and preferences.

Fortunately, with ColdFusion MX, creating a personalized site is as easy as treating parts of the page that you want to change from user to user as variables.

For the sake of time, we're not going to touch on the heavier aspects of personalization (like one-to-one marketing). There are many expensive software packages designed specifically to handle that type of data matching. What we can explore, however, is how to use ColdFusion to create simple personalization for even the smallest of sites.

Simple Personalization with ColdFusion

For the purposes of this example, let's assume that we have a portal type site, in which our users come in and examine news, weather, and other types of semi-static information that we hourly update from our feed.

Because our boss saw this technique used on some portal and thought it was cool, we now have to come up with a way to enable users to get a custom welcome message and to select specific subjects that they'd like to see on their "custom" versions of our page.

So, how do we do this? Well, first we have to get the information from the user. So, we create a simple form, asking the user for his or her name, password, and the three subjects in which he or she is most interested.

We store this information in a cookie so that when the user comes back to our site, we can immediately tell who he or she is and what he or she would like to see. If our bosses are unnecessarily squeamish about cookies because of some conspiracy-theorist article that they read back in 1998, we'll store all the information in a database and make the user log in to the site so that we can retrieve it.

After we have the user's first name and the three topics in which he or she is most interested, we can begin to lay out our page, as in the following example:

```
<HTML>
    <HEAD>
    <TITLE>Our Fancy Personalization Page</TITLE>
    </HEAD>
    <BODY>
    Hello <cfoutput>#UserFirstName#</CFOUTPUT>!
    <br>
    Here are the three topics you are most interested
    in:<BR>
    <cfoutput>
    #TopicA#<BR>
    #TopicB#<BR>
    #TopicC#<BR>
    </BODY>
</HTML>
```

The previous example is about the simplest example you can imagine when it comes to personalization, but it illustrates a key point. All personalization, no matter how seemingly complex, can draw parallels to the example at which we've just looked. All you're really doing is collecting information about a user and his or her habits, and then using that information to guide him or her on your site.

In our example, we explicitly asked our user for three topics, and then we constructed a page that highlighted those three topics. However, we could have just as easily asked him or her to log in. We then could have tracked the three most-visited topics and stored this information in a database.

The next time the user comes to our site, we can automatically highlight these three topics. Keep in mind, though, that although Internet-savvy users might appreciate the technique, novices might think you're keeping too close an eye on their activities and might be scared away by this approach.

A final note on personalization: Although it might be necessary for some applications, personalization is generally used to "fluff up" sites for the user base. This is fine, but remember that it also takes server resources. Use personalization where it makes sense; but as a user, I'm not going to be too happy if it takes a page on your site an extra 10 seconds to load so that it can say "Hello Joe Schmo!"

Summary

In this section, we've examined how to use ColdFusion to create simple personalization in a web application. We've also examined some of the common uses and pitfalls of personalization in web applications.

Although some personalization might be fine to enhance the experience of visiting your site, gratuitous personalization only serves to slow down server performance, so keep this in mind when designing your applications.

Summary

This chapter covered but a few of the most commonly recurring functionality elements that ColdFusion developers would deal with in many of their applications.

Of course, there is a lot more that goes into overall application security, including considerations for making your application "unhackable."

Likewise, there is a lot more involved in content management than adding and editing text in a database column. Little things, such as content workflow and content archiving, are very important.

Who would think that a shopping cart was complete without some sort of payment processing at the end? In addition, personalization can be so much more than just saying hello to the user. Personalization could include retaining a user's shopping cart long after he or she cleared it out, even when his or her visits to the site are weeks apart. It could also include adding items to a personal home page or portal according to the user's preferences or interests. We really could go on and on.

By tying these pieces of functionality together, we've given you a starting point to explore the common application development issues. As you master the concepts here, you can move right on into more complex development scenarios.

18

Enhancing Application Performance with Caching

ASSUMING THAT THE LAUNCH OF YOUR APPLICATION is successful, you'll see traffic patterns increase over time. The more that people attempt to use your application concurrently, the more likely you are to become concerned with the overall performance of that application.

There are many ways in which you can enhance the performance of an application after it's built. You can always revisit the hardware specifications, add members to a cluster, and conduct performance testing and analysis on your code to reduce bottlenecks.

Still, one of the cheapest, quickest, and most painless ways to immediately improve your application performance is also one of the most overlooked—caching. Caching is an effective way to speed up access times on various sections of your site, reduce load on the database, and boost the throughput of your application as a whole.

ColdFusion provides you with a multitude of ways in which you can cache various portions of your application to increase performance. In this chapter, we'll examine some common caching strategies and discuss the performance improvement you can expect to see when implementing each one.

Caching Strategies

ColdFusion provides you many ways in which to cache various elements to improve performance. You have control of caching at various levels, from the caching of compiled ColdFusion Markup Language (CFML) templates to page- and query-level caching.

Understanding the types of caching available to you as a developer and the benefits and drawbacks of each is an integral part of learning how to draw the best performance out of your web applications.

Administrative Caching Options

The caching section of the ColdFusion Administrator is an appropriate place to start a discussion of caching. Figure 18.1 shows this part of the ColdFusion Administrator.

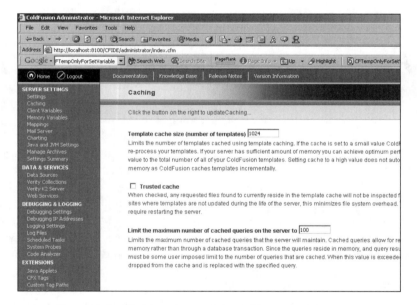

Figure 18.1 Caching section of the ColdFusion Administrator.

On this page of the ColdFusion Administrator, you see three options for configuring the way in which ColdFusion performs caching at an administrative level. We will look at each option in the following sections.

Template Cache Size

To understand the setting of the template cache size, it's important that you understand how CFML templates are processed after they're requested by a client's web browser. The process follows these steps:

1. The web server receives the request from a client browser. The web server identifies that this request is for a template with a .cfm/.cfml extension (or any extension that you have configured to be processed through the ColdFusion Server).

2. The web server knows, by the extension that the requested template has, that it needs to pass this request to the ColdFusion stub.

3. The ColdFusion stub forwards the request to the ColdFusion engine, which processes the CFM file and compiles it for execution.

4. The compiled template is run through the ColdFusion engine and processed.

5. The results of the execution are passed back to the client browser.

The Template cache size (number of templates) text box in the ColdFusion Administrator enables you to predetermine the amount of memory that you want ColdFusion to use to store compiled CFML templates.

As an example of CFML template processing, let's say that I come to your site and request your index.cfm file. If this file has already been compiled, there's really no need for me, as a client, to force the ColdFusion Server to recompile this file just for me. If there's enough room in your template cache, ColdFusion looks in there for a compiled copy of the template, checks it against what's on disk to ensure that it is the latest copy, and then executes the template.

The preceding process saves ColdFusion several steps by not forcing a recompile of templates each time a new user requests them. This might sound simple, but it can have a profound impact on your overall server performance, especially on heavily trafficked sites. If your template cache is too small, it forces ColdFusion to go through many extra steps, which creates additional processing overhead.

Luckily, in the latest version of ColdFusion, Macromedia has made it very easy for you to determine the appropriate template cache size for your server. Simply take the total number of all the CFM files on your system, and enter that number into the Template cache size (number of templates) text box.

This approach is a slight departure from the way in which you would configure the template cache size in previous versions of ColdFusion. In older versions, after CFML files were run through the engine, they were compiled into P-code (pseudocode) that was slightly larger than the size of the original templates. Because of the larger sizes, Macromedia recommended that you set this setting to 3–5 times the total size of all your CFML templates to account for expansion.

In ColdFusion MX, changing this setting is not necessary because when templates are compiled, they are actually stored as bytecode (as .class files). This makes it much easier for you, as a developer, to properly make the configuration, because you will never need to cache more than the total number of templates that you have on a given server.

Trusted Cache

The next setting over which you have control is the Trusted cache check box. Often, this setting is overlooked or just left alone because the administrators of the server don't have a good understanding of what it does.

By checking the Trusted cache check box, you achieve another significant performance boost because you're taking another step to reduce the amount of work ColdFusion Server has to perform to answer a request.

When you check the Trusted cache check box, you are essentially telling ColdFusion that you are certain that none of the source CFML has changed; thus, whatever ColdFusion has already compiled in the template cache will be fine to use.

We've already discussed how ColdFusion responds to requests for CFML templates and the way in which the engine uses the template cache to check for existing copies of compiled versions of the code. Note that ColdFusion checks the template cache to see if there's already a copy of the compiled code in there and then checks the disk for a newer version of the code. If a newer version of the code doesn't exist on disk, ColdFusion uses the compiled copy in cache, thereby eliminating the need to recompile. This saves valuable overhead.

All that the Trusted cache check box does is tell ColdFusion to eliminate the disk check from that process. In other words, after a request is made for a template, ColdFusion Server checks the template cache for a compiled copy of the code. If it's there, ColdFusion executes that compiled copy rather than checking the disk to see if a newer copy of the source is available.

Understanding this process is key to understanding why using a trusted cache in production systems is a good idea. You are saving the ColdFusion Server valuable work by not forcing it to do a disk check each and every time it finds something in the template cache that it needs.

Of course, you must understand that if your code frequently changes, and if these changes need to be seen immediately after they are made, a trusted cache isn't likely the best choice for you. The general consensus is that to flush a trusted cache, you'll need to restart the ColdFusion Server. Although this isn't technically true, the only way to flush the cache (short of a restart) is through the use of undocumented functions that might (or might not) be supported in future releases of ColdFusion.

Of course, this shouldn't be a problem on production servers where code changes occur very infrequently. If your organization already has a change cycle in place, it's usually easy to add a flush of the trusted cache to the steps involved in moving new code to production.

One of the common misconceptions I've heard about the use of a trusted cache is that developers fear that if they have dynamic content in a template, such as the results of a query, that content will be the same for all users who get a copy of the template from the trusted cache. This is simply not true. You can use a trusted cache confidently, regardless of the amount of dynamic content contained in a particular template's output. Only the compiled template is cached; it still gets executed (or run through the server) on each request so that content can be customized on a per-user basis.

Limit Maximum Number of Cached Queries

The final option that we're presented with in the caching section of the ColdFusion Administrator has to do with limiting the maximum number of cached queries that we want ColdFusion to store in random-access memory (RAM) at any given point.

By default, this option is set to 100; but contrary to what you might have heard in the past, there is no maximum limit. You can in fact choose to store as many queries in memory as you have free RAM available. Of course, you need to be aware of the size of your result sets when setting your maximum cached query value to make sure that you don't overload your free memory. Obviously, if your result sets are very large, the application memory footprint reflects this—if you're storing a large number of cached queries.

With regard to the cached queries resident on the server, one of the more common complaints has been the impression that you need to restart the ColdFusion Server to clear queries out of cache. In reality, you can effectively flush the cached queries by using the following code:

```
<cfobjectcache action="clear">
```

Running this line of code clears the entire query cache. Thus, new result sets can be stored in place of the old ones.

Summary of Administrative Caching Settings

As we've outlined, the ColdFusion Administrator provides us with three areas in which we can improve system performance by implementing caching. We're presented with a way to adjust the template cache, we're permitted to switch Trusted cache on and off, and we can specify the maximum number of cached queries that we want to store in server memory at any given time. Table 18.1 examines the benefits and drawbacks of using these options.

Table 18.1 **Pros and Cons of Administrative Caching Settings**

Administrative Caching Setting	Pros	Cons
Template cache size	Increasing the template cache size to a value equivalent to the maximum number of CFML templates present on your server ensures that the server doesn't need to recompile templates over and over for eachvisitor. Having an adequate template cache reduces overhead, enabling the ColdFusion Server to respond to all requests more quickly.	If you have a very large num ber of templates, or if your templates are excessively large, setting the template cache size to a value equivalent with the maximum number of templates eats into free memory, increas ing the overall memory foot print of ColdFusion Server. This potentially creates perfor mance problems if the server is hungry for memory.
Trusted cache	Using trusted cache enables ColdFusion Server to assume that the copy of the template already compiled and resident in the template cache is the latest copy. This reduces the need for ColdFusion to perform a disk check (which entails looking for a more recent copy of the template).	If the code on your server fre quently changes, you'll need to restart the ColdFusion Server to flush the trusted cache, unless you're willing to depend on undocumented and there fore unsupported functions to achieve this for you.
Maximum number of cached queries	By default, this value is set to 100 in the ColdFusion Administrator. If you have a high number of database queries, increasing this value enables you to serve database content to users more quickly by reading . result sets directly from server RAM rather than making another trip to the database	If your result sets are very large, or if you have an unusually high number of queries, this can potentially have a negative impact on server performance because the number of queries in RAM increases and causes ColdFusion's memory foot print to increase.

Query Caching

Query caching is an effective way to increase application performance by reducing the number of trips that ColdFusion must make to the database. When you have a query that is cached, the result set is read from server memory and immediately delivered to the user, without the need for an actual connection and data retrieval process.

One of the first steps you need to do as a developer when deciding to utilize query caching is to make intelligent decisions about the specific queries that you want to cache.

The example most commonly used when discussing query caching is one in which you are retrieving a list of U.S. states from a database to fill a drop-down list on a form. Because you're relatively certain that a new state isn't going to be added to the union in the next few days, you can feel comfortable caching this query. You know beforehand that the data returned by the query is unlikely to change from user to user, so there's no doubt that this is a good candidate for query caching.

The preceding paragraph contains a pretty good example of the types of queries it makes sense to cache, but it doesn't go quite far enough. Even if the data returned by a specific query changes hourly, you can still get a nice performance boost by caching this query as well. As a matter of fact, about the only time you really shouldn't use query caching is when the result sets will be different each and every time, for each and every user.

To cache a query, you just need to put the `cachedWithin` or `cachedAfter` parameters within the query syntax. As an example, let's assume that I want to query a database to get a list of all valid users of my web application. With no caching at all, my query might look something like this:

```
<cfquery name="qGetUsers" datasource="#request.datasource#">
    SELECT *
    FROM tbl_Users
</cfquery>
```

This is a very simple example based on a basic query. I'm sure you've done something similar in your application development.

Now let's assume that I want to cache this particular query, and I want it to remain cached for the next 3 hours. Thus, every additional user who comes to my site within the next 3 hours to retrieve this same data will be able to do so without ever having to make a trip to the database. The code would look like the following:

```
<cfquery name="qGetUsers"
    datasource="#request.datasource#"
        cachedWithin="#CreateTimeSpan(0,3,0,0)#">
        SELECT *
        FROM tbl_Users
</cfquery>
```

As you can see by the example, I've added the `cachedWithin` attribute to my `CFQUERY` syntax, and I've used the `CreateTimeSpan` function to tell ColdFusion that I'd like to have this query cached for the next 3 hours.

When using the `cachedWithin` attribute of the `CFQUERY` tag, the cached query data is used to answer all requests that come in during the time span specified. A time span is specified to the `cachedWithin` attribute through use of the `CreateTimeSpan` function.

Now let's assume that this is a production server, and I know that I'll be doing a database update on April 26, 2002. Prior to that time, I don't want the query to be cached, but for every request that comes in after that date and time, I would like the cached query results to be used.

This can be achieved easily by using the `cachedAfter` attribute of the `CFQUERY` tag, as outlined in the following example:

```
<cfquery name="qGetUsers"
        datasource="#request.datasource#"
        cachedAfter="April 26, 2002">
    SELECT *
    FROM tbl_Users
</cfquery>
```

When using the `cachedAfter` attribute of `CFQUERY`, you can pass in a date/time value after which you want the cached result set to be used. If a request is made for that particular query prior to the date/time value you've specified in the `cachedAfter` attribute, the query is run as if it were not cached at all.

It should be noted that for a cached query to be retrieved from RAM, the calling template must have the exact same structured query language (SQL) string as the query in cache. Otherwise, the query will be rerun with the new SQL string, and a new copy will be cached.

CFCACHE

In addition to compiled code and queries, there are times when you might want to cache the actual Hypertext Markup Language (HTML) output produced by a particular CFML template. With the `CFCACHE` tag, you can do just that.

The `CFCACHE` tag enables you to dramatically speed up the rendering of pages that won't contain dynamic, customized content for each user. When you use `CFCACHE` within a CFML template, ColdFusion renders a temporary file that contains the HTML output that the execution of the cached template produced.

Although you can't use CFCACHE for templates that change frequently, you can get away with using CFCACHE for templates in which the only changes are in the uniform resource locator (URL) parameters that are passed in.

For example, let's assume I have a page called doSomething.cfm. Based on the URL parameter that is passed in as a URL action, either an add, edit, or delete form is displayed.

To call the doSomething.cfm file when I want to edit the form, I might call it like this:

```
http://myserver/doSomething.cfm?Action="Edit"
```

Fortunately, I'm still able to use CFCACHE with this page because of the way in which the CFCACHE tag works.

In addition to creating temporary files containing the HTML content of the cached files, CFCACHE also creates a cache mapping file (cfcache.map). It enables me to have different copies of the cached content based on the URL parameters that I will be passing in.

To continue with the previous example, my cfcache.map file might look something like this:

```
[doSomething.cfm]
Mapping = C:\WebRoot\CF01.tmp
SourceTimeStamp = 04/26/2002 06:52:04 AM


[doSomething.cfm?Action = "Edit"]
Mapping = C:\WebRoot\CF02.tmp
SourceTimeStamp = 04/26/2002 12:42:17 AM

[doSomething.cfm?Action = "Add"]
Mapping = C:\WebRoot\CF03.tmp
SourceTimeStamp = 04/26/2002 04:23:09 AM

[doSomething.cfm?Action = "Delete"]
Mapping = C:\WebRoot\CF04.tmp
SourceTimeStamp = 04/26/2002 11:22:19 AM
```

The ColdFusion Server will use the SourceTimeStamp value located in this map file to make sure that it's using the most up-to-date copy of the source template to produce the cached results.

Invoking CFCACHE within a particular CFML template is an easy thing to do, and it is often as simple as invoking CFCACHE at the top of the template in which you want caching to occur.

For a full view of the attributes you can use with CFCACHE to gain more control over how templates are cached, refer to Appendix A, "Tag Reference."

Other Caching Methods

In addition to the caching methods that are provided for you internally by the ColdFusion Server, there are also a multitude of CFML-based custom tags that take the concept of page-based caching even further. One of the better custom tags for page-based caching is the CF_SuperCache tag that was developed by various members of the former Allaire Consulting Services team.

Using this paired custom tag, you can specify specific portions of a template that you'd like to have cached to RAM or disk. This is an alternative to caching for an entire page or not at all.

The CF_SuperCache tag is included at the official web site for this book, which is www.insidecoldfusionmx.com. In addition to this tag, you'll want to check the Macromedia Developer's Exchange at http://devex.macromedia.com/developer/gallery/, where you can find many other custom tags that address your caching needs.

Summary

In this chapter we've examined several ways in which you can utilize caching methods to improve overall application performance.

You've discovered that you have opportunities to implement a caching strategy at just about every point on the path of a typical ColdFusion request.

By setting your template cache size appropriately, you can ensure that the ColdFusion Server doesn't need to repeat compilation work on templates that have already been processed.

By turning on the Trusted cache setting, you enable the ColdFusion engine to trust the compiled copy of the CFML template that resides in template cache, without having to check on the disk to see if a more recent copy of the source code is available.

With query caching, you can remove the need for ColdFusion to make multiple trips to a database for content that isn't going to change very often. The ColdFusion Administrator provides you with a way to control the maximum number of cached queries that you can store in server memory at any given time.

Finally, you can control caching at a page-based level, by using CFCACHE and other custom tags to write out the HTML content produced by execution of CFML tags. Thus, the next time those pages are invoked, ColdFusion itself won't have to do any processing at all.

By using these strategies to improve the overall performance of your web applications, you free up valuable server resources for other tasks. With those extra resources, perhaps you might want to take time to explore how you might integrate your ColdFusion application with other technologies. This, coincidentally, is what we begin to explore in Chapter 19, "Introduction to XML and ColdFusion MX."

19

Introduction to XML and ColdFusion MX

AS WE HAVE SEEN SO FAR, ColdFusion MX has many new features and functions, but few are probably as exciting to developers as ColdFusion MX's new XML functionality. As you may or may not know, XML has rapidly become the de facto standard for information exchange between parties on the Internet, is an invaluable tool for software integration and point-to-point technologies such as Jabber, and is the foundation of web services.

Previous versions of ColdFusion have required developers to develop and deploy their own parsers or to wrap commercial or open-source XML parsers such as those from the Apache project to perform XML parsing and manipulation. This can be a daunting task even for experienced programmers. In this chapter, though, we will become familiar with the basic features of ColdFusion's XML functionality as well as the basic concepts and features of XML. After reading this chapter, you should have a good understanding of the foundational technologies and recommendations that make up XML. If you already have a solid understanding of XML and want to get to work immediately with web services, XSLT, XPath, or more advanced XML parsing, you can skip to Chapter 20, "Advanced XML."

As you might already know, ColdFusion was one of the first application servers to adopt and support XML through ColdFusion's native XML type WDDX, which was developed in 1998 by Simeon Simeonov. Since then, WDDX has helped developers integrate diverse applications, systems, and languages.

This chapter explains what XML is, how to create a Document Type Definition (DTD), what XML Schema is, how to parse XML using ColdFusion XML tags and functions, how to create a simple XML document dynamically with ColdFusion, and how to parse an XML document using ColdFusion XML tags and functions.

XML 101

The history of XML is an interesting read, but for our purposes it is not relevant. In brief, XML was developed to solve many of the problems that people were starting to have with the Hypertext Markup Language (HTML).

Specifically, the World Wide Web Consortium (W3C) developed XML so that one could maintain context with a document.

Note

You can learn more about the W3C at www.w3.org/.

Tim Berners-Lee originally created HTML as a way to accurately describe scientific abstracts and documents. Even with this humble origin, it has proven to be a fairly robust language. After 10 years and billions of web pages, HTML has evolved from its original intent and specifications. Its element names (the "tags" in an HTML document) now bear little relationship to their current meaning. For example, an HTML <div> (division) element is essentially a container for other markup; the name has lost its significance, so it can represent practically anything.

Web pages marked up in HTML lack structure, context, and semantics. Without structure, there's no effective way to develop web pages because a program requires objects with known behaviors and characteristics to work properly. In other words, without structure, you don't have much context for any piece of information within a web page. You can attempt to "screen-scrape" the contents, but this requires a lot of information about the page's visual format and relies on similar HTML structures *not* existing elsewhere in the document. Often this involves writing more or less a custom parsing program that contains rules for parsing that specific version of HTML. As any developer who has written programs to work with flat files knows, this can be a tedious and frustrating experience, especially if the target output format (which might not be a visual medium, like HTML's intended output format) changes often.

XML borrows the tag structure and container/contained relationship of formal Standard Generalized Markup Language (SGML), which is the grand-father of both XML and HTML. But XML, unlike HTML, lets you design your own tag elements, attributes, and rules. By keeping the underlying language relatively simple, this approach nicely mimics the way that most "natural" data constructs work. Consider, for example, a `shipto` block from a purchase order written as XML:

```
<shipto>
  <company>Department13</company>
  <contact>
   <title>VP</title>
   <name>Robi Sen</name>
  </contact>
  <street>122 UnterWasser</street>
  <city>Fort Collins</city>
  <state_province>Colorado</state_province>
  <zipcode>80526</zipcode>
  <country>USA</country>
 </shipto>
```

The same `shipto` structure could use a different <country> element and still be perfectly valid:

```
<shipto>
  <company>Department13</company>
  <contact>
   <title>VP</title>
   <name>Robi Sen</name>
  </contact>
  <street>122 UnterWasser</street>
  <city>Fort Collins</city>
  <state_province>Colorado</state_province>
  <zipcode>80526</zipcode>
  <country>UK</country>
 </shipto>
```

XML is generally used in one of two ways: as a method of marking up documents (its original SGML heritage), which is *document-centric*; or as data description or exchange, which is *data-centric*. As a ColdFusion application developer, you are already familiar with relational databases, so one way you can think about XML is from a database or data-centric viewpoint. For instance, to represent the preceding XML structures in a typical relational database, you might use three distinct tables: one for customer information, one for customer addresses, and perhaps another for regional codes. You might also need additional keys: primary ones for the two customer tables and a foreign key for the regional address codes. By making the structure/

schema as close to third normal form as possible, you can handle the numerous exception conditions that often plague such databases—exceptions that occur largely because most data doesn't conveniently fit into a strict table and key relational model.

> **Note**
>
> XML does not follow a relational model like most databases; so although much of how XML works is analogous to database principles, there are points where the parallels break down. Currently, many vendors of object-oriented databases are finding interest in their products in that XML can be much better modeled as objects than relation tables.

Metadata

One of the most important things about XML is its notion of *metadata*, which is a concept you will find in any data-modeling system or theory. Metadata is information about your system's data. For example, if you created a database table called Customer, you might have several different fields and data types (see Table 19.1).

Table 19.1   **The Customer Table**

Field Name	Datax
CustomerID	AutoNumber
CustomerFirstName	Text
CustomerLastName	Text
CustomerAddress	Text
CustomerCity	Text
CustomerStateID	Number
CustomerPhone	Text
CustomerEmail	Text
CustomerPassword	Text
CustomerNotification	Text

This is the same table that is in the datasource for this book.

In the case of this table, the metadata is the column names, data types, and restrictions you put on the data, such as integer range, string length, binary, date field, and so on. Metadata, as you already know, makes relational databases useful in that once you have created the schema for your database, you have a formal context and relationships for all the data you store in that database. Metadata is also what makes XML useful; however, XML accomplishes this in a couple of ways. At its simplest (and least informative), an XML document could consist of a single set of `<exampledocument>` tags, with the content being a superset of ASCII text:

```
<?xml version="1.0"?>
<hellokitty>
This XML document contains almost no real structure.
The XML parser only knows that it's an XMLdocument.
It also says Hello Kitty!
</hellokitty>
```

It is important to note that although this XML document is ridiculously simple, it is a *well-formed* XML document (unlike the other examples so far, which have been XML document fragments).

Well-Formedness

As we pointed out, the preceding document was well-formed, but what does that mean? To be well-formed, an XML document must conform to three specific rules:

- The document starts with an XML declaration: `<?xml version="1.0"?>`.
- There is a root element in which all others are contained: the `<hellokitty>` and `</hellokitty>` tags from the previous code for example,.
- All elements must be properly nested. No overlapping is permitted.

As you can see, creating a well-formed XML document is pretty straightforward. Later in this chapter we will go into more depth about well-formedness, but for now let's look at a more complex version of a XML document.

For now, imagine we have created an XML file from a database recordset containing purchase order information. (If you have used `CFFILE` to create text files, you already know most of what you need to create an XML file in ColdFusion.) Listing 19.1 presents an example of a more complex XML document.

Listing 19.1   *Pricelist.xml*

```
<?xml version="1.0" encoding="UTF-8"?>
<!DOCTYPE price-list SYSTEM=" \pricelist.dtd">
     <price-group>
          <name>ColdFusion MX</name>
          <price-element>
```

continues ▶

Listing 19.1 **Continued**

```
            <product-code>CFMX2002</product-code>
            <description>ColdFusion MX blah blah blah blah</description>
                  <license type="Server">
                        <quantity>String</quantity>
                  </license>
             <list-price>1000</list-price>
            </price-element>
      </price-group>
      <price-group>
            <name>Kojac</name>
            <price-element>
            <product-code>CFS20023</product-code>
            <description>New New New</description>
                  <license type="Server">
                        <quantity>String</quantity>
                  </license>
             <list-price>500</list-price>
            </price-element>
      </price-group>
      <price-group>
            <name>Flash MX</name>
            <price-element>
            <product-code>MACR2002F</product-code>
            <description>Macromedia Flash MX provides everything you need to create
➥and deploy rich Web content and powerful applications. Whether you are
➥designing motion graphics or building data-driven applications, Flash MX
➥has the tools you need to produce great results and deliver the best user
➥experiences across multiple platforms and devices.</description>
                  <license type="Server">
                        <quantity>String</quantity>
                  </license>
             <list-price>500</list-price>
            </price-element>
      </price-group>
      <price-group>
            <name>Jrun</name>
            <price-element>
            <product-code>MACR2002JR</product-code>
            <description>JRun Server Professional Edition is a high-performance J2EE
➥application server for deploying JSP and Servlet applications.
➥</description>
                  <license type="Server">
                        <quantity>String</quantity>
                  </license>
             <list-price>1000</list-price>
            </price-element>
      </price-group>
</price-list>
```

Just by glancing at this document, you can probably see that it's a price list and contains information on a product's product code, description, license type, list price, and what price grouping it falls into. Using our previous database analogies, you can more or less see the XML Schema (when we talk about schema in this sense, we mean like a database schema; later we will talk about an XML initiative called XML Schema that is replacing the use of DTDs, both of which are used to store further metadata for the XML document) as well as the literal values or records in the schema—something that would not be apparent from looking at a database recordset or table view. For example, Figure 19.1 shows the output of a query against a database. As you can see, all that's easily discernable is the raw data and the column names, to some extent.

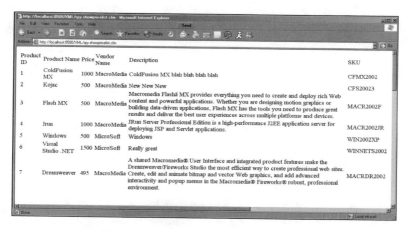

Figure 19.1   The output of a database query.

One of the great things about XML is that not only is it human readable (like HTML), it is also machine readable. This means that a computer using an XML parser can "understand" what a `shipto` tag means in the context of a document or application without having to do any special programming.

Let's break down the `Pricelist.xml` document's structure and see how it works. First, note this part of the first line:

```
<?xml version="1.0"?>
```

The first line declares that the document is an XML document (version 1.0 specifically).

The next thing we notice is the opening tag, or *root element*, for our document: `<price_list>`. If you quickly scan the document, you see that it is closed with a `</price_list>` tag. As we noted earlier, all XML tags need to have a starting tag and a closing tag. These tags are actually called *elements*, and every XML document can have only one root element.

For example, you could have this code:

```
<helloXML>
    <hello>
        <world />
        <kitty />
    </hello>
</helloXML>
```

But not this code:

```
<helloXML>
    <hello>
        <world />
        <kitty />
    </hello>
</helloXML>
<helloXML>
    <hello>
        <world />
        <kitty />
    </hello>
</helloXML>
```

You can't have the second instance because `<helloXML>` is the root element and cannot be repeated in the document. One way to think of this is that the root element is much like a table name. If it's not unique within the document, the parser does not really have a starting point with which to work. All of the other elements (called *subelements*) can be repeated as many times as you want; the only restrictions are that all elements must start with a left-angle bracket (<) and end with a right-angle bracket (>), and all beginning tags must be closed with an ending tag unless they are *empty tags*. Empty tags take the form *`<myemptytag />`*, such as `<img src="example.jpg" />` or `<br />` (the XHTML equivalents of the HTML `<img src="example.jpg">` and `<br>` tags, respectively).

So, to extend our analogy of databases to XML, the root element is much like a table name, and the subelements are like column names. In databases, though, we can assign all sorts of conditions, attributes, and logic to a column. XML also lets you assign various attributes to elements; however, our analogy starts to get a little thin here. Let's take a look at the `pricelist.xml` document again, specifically the `price-group` element:

```
<price-group>
     <name>Flash MX</name>
     <price-element>
     <product-code>MACR2002F</product-code>
     <description>Macromedia Flash MX provides everything you need to create
     ➥and deploy rich Web content and powerful applications. Whether you are
     ➥designing motion graphics or building data-driven applications, Flash MX
     ➥has the tools you need to produce great results and deliver the best user
     ➥experiences across multiple platforms and devices.</description>
          <license type="Server">
               <quantity>String</quantity>
          </license>
      <list-price>500</list-price>
     </price-element>
</price-group>
```

In this block, we see a so-called empty tag that is not empty; it has `name`, `product-code`, `license type`, `quantity`, `description`, and `list-price` attributes. To keeping pushing our database analogy, this element might look like Table 19.2 if we put it in tabular form.

Table 19.2   **Products**

Field Name	Data Type
ProductID	Number
VendorID	Number
ProductDate	Date/time
CategoryID	Number
ProductName	Text
ProductDescription	Memo
ProductPricePerUnit	Text
ProductSpecifications	Text
ProductSearchTerms	Text
ProductDemoURL	Text
ProductDocumentationURL	Text
ProductEvaluationFile	Text
ProductCommercialFile	Text
ProductLicenseID	Number

But remember that, in a database table, we can also assign table-level logic such as whether an attribute is required, needs to be of a certain length or specific data type, or can be repeated. (In some relation database servers, you can also assign complex database-level and application-level logic.) In our XML document, there is little contextual information that tells us this kind of information. However, look at the second line from Listing 19.1:

```
<!DOCTYPE price-list SYSTEM "\pricelist.dtd">
```

This line is a declaration that tells the parser that there is a DTD associated with the XML document. So, what's a DTD? For our analogy and this example, the DTD is where we store all the metadata about data-level logic and other specifics you would normally define in a database. Why can't we define that information in the XML document directly? In a database, for instance, we can define it right in a table. Well, have you ever had to change your database schema and then change all those rules? It can be a major hassle, and often after you have changed your scheme you will need to "scrub" your database's data to conform to the new data model. All in all, it takes time and specialized knowledge that is often product specific; essentially, it's why our friend the database administrator makes so much money. Instead, XML allows a document's creators to separate the document's logical structure and data (in this case, think table structure as well as records of data) from the metadata (the rules and metadata) and from the eventual target output (how the XML is eventually displayed, rendered, and produced for consumption).

Understanding Document Type Definitions

DTDs are a nice concept in that they enable developers to add and change rules about XML documents without necessarily having to change the document or the data in it. This allows for much greater flexibility.

So far, we have learned about attributes and elements but not about DTDs. Let's look at a DTD and learn how to create one. Listing 19.2 shows an example of a DTD.

Listing 19.2 **An Example of a DTD**

```
<?xml version="1.0" encoding="UTF-8"?>
<!-- ************************************************* -->
<!-- VSI Pricelist file Definition                    -->
<!-- ************************************************* -->
<!ELEMENT price-list (price-group*)>
<!ELEMENT price-group (name, price-element*)>
<!ELEMENT price-element (product-code, description, license*, list-price)>
<!ELEMENT license (quantity | unlimited)>
<!ATTLIST license
      type (Server | Clients | WebServer | FaxServer) "Server"
>
```

```
<!ELEMENT name (#PCDATA)>
<!ELEMENT product-code (#PCDATA)>
<!ELEMENT description (#PCDATA)>
<!ELEMENT list-price (#PCDATA)>
<!ELEMENT quantity (#PCDATA)>
<!ELEMENT unlimited (#PCDATA)>
```

Now that we have a DTD, let's briefly talk about how to associate DTDs with XML documents. The next sections, "Element Declaration" and "Attribute-List Declaration," dissect what goes into creating a DTD.

Because a DTD is a separate file, DTDs can be associated with an XML document in two ways: within the XML document itself (*inline*) or by a DOCTYPE reference. All inline DTDs must start with the string <!DOCTYPE. The next part of the string must be the document name, which must correspond to the document's root element. If you would like to refer to your DTD within your XML document, you can include it between the beginning and ending brackets, like this:

```
<?xml version="1.0"?>
<!DOCTYPE HelloWorld
[
<!ELEMENT HelloWorld (#PCDATA)>
]>

<HelloWorld>
    Hi how are you world
</HelloWorld>
```

You can also refer to a DTD from an external source (which is more common) via a uniform resource identifier (URI), as follows:

```
<?xml version="1.0"?>
<!DOCTYPE HelloWorld SYSTEM "HelloWorld.dtd">

<HelloWorld>

</HelloWorld>
```

This DTD declaration uses the SYSTEM parameter. This states that the DTD associated with the XML document is located somewhere on this (or another) system via the next quoted URI, such as a local file, a URL to a web server, or even an FTP site. Another way you can refer to a DTD is via the PUBLIC parameter, as follows:

```
<!DOCTYPE html
    PUBLIC "-//W3C//DTD XHTML 1.0 Transitional//EN"
    "DTD/xhtml1-transitional.dtd">
```

This is the DOCTYPE declaration for XHTML that has two quoted statements after the PUBLIC parameter. The first one is the unique name of the DTD, and the second is the URI. Public DTDs follow a specific naming convention. If you're interested in how to construct one of these, take a peek at the XML 1.0 recommendation (www.w3.org/TR/REC-xml).

Most of a DTD is made up of element declarations, which are discussed in the next section.

Element Declaration

As you probably noticed when creating a DTD, the major portion of the statements is element declarations in this form:

```
<!ELEMENT elementname content-spec>
```

Element declarations can have one of four different element content types, as shown in Table 19.3.

Table 19.3 **Element Declaration Types**

Content Type Specification	Content
Empty content	No content, an empty element
Character content	Only data or text within an element
Any content/mixed content	Can have character data, other elements, or both
Element content	Can only have subelements as specified in the element content specification

Let's try to make this a little clearer by explaining each content model specification in the following sections.

Character Data Content

One of the unique things about XML is that it specifies that all character data must be in Unicode, a superset of ASCII characters that we all know and love. Apart from the benefits this brings to cultures that use a non-Roman alphabet (Chinese, Japanese, Inuit, and so on), it forces us to call "text" something else: parsed character data (PCDATA) to be specific.

When we want to declare that an element contains nothing but text (whether numbers or ASCII characters), we can say something like this:

```
<!ELEMENT item (#PCDATA)>
Examples of our newly updated item element would be:
<item>This is an item.</item>
<item>1234</item>
```

Any (or Mixed) Content

When the ANY content identifier is used, it's typically called *mixed content* because this is the catchall definition for an element that can contain anything—either text (PCDATA) or other elements.

This type of unstructured content definition is most commonly used for complex hierarchies of elements and text or for something as simple as, say, marking up a technical book you might find on the shelves:

```
<!ELEMENT para ANY>
<para> This is a <footnote num="1"> see reference</footnote> mixed content
➥paragraph</para>
```

Empty Content

Empty content is the model for empty elements:

```
<!ELEMENT item EMPTY>
```

For example:

```
<item sku="1234" />
```

This declares that the item element is EMPTY. Although there's an attribute (sku="1234"), there's no content within the element; it's equivalent to <item sku="1234"></item>.

Element Content

The following example states that the items_ordered element must have at least one subelement item that can be repeated (signified by the plus sign):

```
<!ELEMENT items_ordered (item)+>
```

The parentheses are used to form what is called a *content particle*. Content particles can be nested within each other like this:

```
<!ELEMENT billto(company,contact,street,city,state_province,zipcode,country)>
```

This example says that the billto element must have a company element followed by a contact element, and so on. The commas are used to specify a sequence that we would like to enforce—namely that company must be followed by contact, which is followed by street, and so on. This type of construct is called a *sequence content particle*.

Furthermore, you can make specific elements repeatable, optional, or occur only once like in the items_ordered example. To do this, you must use what are called *occurrence indicators*, which are listed in Table 19.4.

Table 19.4 **Occurrence Indicators**

Indicator	Element or Content Particle Can Occur...
?	Zero or one time (optional)
*	Zero or more times (optional and repeatable)
+	One or more times (required and repeatable)

Additionally, you can use grouping and recurrence symbols to denote orders in which elements can occur:

```
<!ELEMENT component (stanza+|line)>
<!ELEMENT stanza (line+|(copyright,date))>
<!ELEMENT line (#PCDATA)>
<!ELEMENT copyright (#PCDATA)>
<!ELEMENT date (#PCDATA)>
```

This DTD describes a bare-bones poem:

- The `<poem>` element can consist of either one or more `<stanza>` elements or a single `<line>` element.
- The `<stanza>` element must consist of either a bunch of `<line>` elements. or a `<copyright>` element followed by a `<date>` element.
- The `<line>`, `<copyright>`, and `<date>` elements just contain text.

A poem converted into XML might look like the following:

```
<poem>
    <stanza>
        <line>Roses are red, Violets are blue</line>
        <line>I can write XML, and so can you!</line>
    </stanza>
    <stanza>
        <copyright>NewRiders</copyright>
        <date>2002</date>
    </stanza>
</poem>
```

Use that one on Valentine's Day!

Attribute-List Declaration

We have already covered element declarations, so now let's look at attribute-list declarations. Attributes probably look much more familiar to you as a ColdFusion developer in that they always have a name-value pairing such as in HTML:

```
<a href="http://www.w3c.org">
```

In a DTD, an attribute-list declaration always begins with the string `<!ATTLIST`, which is followed by the element name to which the attributes belong. After the element name, you can add one or more attribute declarations. Attribute declarations have three parts: the attribute name, its type, and the default declaration. The general form for an attribute declaration is as follows:

```
<!ATTLIST elemName attName attType default-decl>
```

Or from our sample DTD:

```
<!ATTLIST item
    sku CDATA #REQUIRED
    qty CDATA #REQUIRED
    description CDATA #IMPLIED
    price CDATA #IMPLIED>
```

Let's step through this example so that you can see how straightforward this really is. This attribute declaration statement says that we're talking about the attributes of the `item` element. The `item` element has four attributes: `sku`, `qty`, `description`, and `price`. All of the attributes are string data types or `CDATA` but could be one of two other data types: a set of tokenized types or an enumerated type.

Each of the attributes also has a declaration option that could be one of four types: `required`, `implied`, `fixed`, or a default `value`. The `REQUIRED` declaration means that the attribute must be present, and the `IMPLIED` declaration enables you to optionally include an attribute. The `FIXED` declaration means you must supply a value. Finally, we have the last option, `VALUE`, which enables you to define a default value that will always be used unless the user overrides it.

One of the most common complaints with the XML recommendation is the syntax for creating DTDs. For example, in an element declaration we talk about text as PCDATA, whereas in an attribute declaration it's called CDATA. Oddities like this are what sparked the XML Schema language, a rewrite of DTDs plus data typing in an XML element syntax.

Working with XML Schemas

In the preceding section, we went into great depth about what DTDs are and how to create them, but we finished up commenting on DTDs' deficiencies and discussed the creation of the XML Schema language.

In this section, we will not go into such depth and will instead suggest that you go to `www.w3.org/XML/Schema` or read New Riders' *Inside XML* by Steve Holzner to get more specific, in-depth information on XML Schemes.

What we are going to do in this section is build on your knowledge of DTDs, compare them to XML Schema, and give you enough information that you understand why and how to use XML Schemes. If you need more information, we'll show you where to go get it.

Before we get into XML Schema, let's just recap a few concepts that make DTDs difficult to use or deficient for some purposes:

- DTDs use an awkward syntax that is different from the syntax of XML documents. This requires you to learn another notation as well as XML software to have a DTD parser to validate XML.

- There is no way to specify data types and data formats that could be used to automatically map to and from programming languages.

- There is not a set of well-known basic elements to choose from.

- DTDs were inherited by XML from its predecessor, SGML, and were a good way to get XML started off quickly and to give SGML people something familiar to work with. Nevertheless, it soon became apparent that a more expressive solution was needed that used itself XML.

Defining Elements

Defining an element specifies its name and content model, meaning attributes and nested elements. In XML Schemas, the content model of elements is defined by their type. An XML document adhering to a schema can then only have elements that match the defined types. You must also distinguish between simple and complex types.

A number of simple types are predefined in the specification, such as string, integer, and decimal. A simple type cannot contain elements or attributes in its values, whereas complex types can specify nesting of elements and associations of attributes with an element.

A simple example could look like this:

```
<element name="quantity" type="positive-integer"/>
<element name="amount" type="decimal"/>
```

User-defined elements can be formed from the predefined ones using the object-oriented concepts of aggregation and inheritance. *Aggregation* groups a set of existing elements into a new one. *Inheritance* extends an already-defined element so that it can stand in for the original.

Defining values like `<value unit="Celsius">42</value>` derived from decimals would look something like this:

```
<element name="value">
<complexType base='decimal' derivedBy='extension'>
<attribute name='unit' type='string'/>
</complexType>
</element>
```

Aggregating time and value into a measurement would look like this:

```
<measurement>
<time>2000-10-08 12:00:00 GMT<time/>
<value unit="Celsius">42</value>
</measurement>
```

Here is what the resulting schema definition would look like:

```
<element name='measurement' type='measurement'/>
<complexType name='measurement'>
<element name='time' type='time'/>
<element name='value' type='value'/>
</complexType>
```

Now, if we did the same thing with a DTD, it would look something like this:

```
<!ELEMENT measurement (time, value)>
<!ELEMENT time (#PCDATA)>
<!ELEMENT value (#PCDATA)>
<!ATTLIST value (unit)>
```

One very cool thing about XML Schema is the concept of inheritance, which you will find in any object-oriented-based language such as Java (and now in CFML in CFCs!). Much like in Java, for example, you can declare a class as "abstract" to force an inherited implementation or declare a class as "final" to prevent subclassing. This way, a one-to-one mapping between an element definition and a Java (or C++ and so on) class becomes possible. This becomes important when you are trying to tie your document to actual objects or code. A specific example would be the way in which many vendors are approaching mapping web services to specific objects or code—the XML description document that descibes the services offered from a specific system even maps to the actual objects that do the work.

Expressing Cardinalities of Elements

XML Schema has more possibilities than DTD for expressing cardinalities on the elements of a document type. In DTD, you indicate that a sequence of one only (1), zero or more (*), or one or more (+) elements from a given set can occur. XML Schema uses the minOccurs and maxOccurs attributes to define cardinalities:

```
<element ref="optionalElement" minOccurs="0"/>
<element ref="twoOrMoreElements" minOccurs="2" maxOccurs="unbounded"/>
<element ref="exactlyOneElement" />
```

The default values for minOccurs and maxOccurs are 1. Another possibility is to use the choice and all elements. The element choice allows only one of its children to appear in an instance, whereas all defines that all child elements in the group can appear at most once in any order. Such constraints are very difficult and awkward to try to create in a DTD.

For example:

```
<xsd:choice>
<element ref="EitherThis"/>
<element ref="OrThat"/>
</xsd:choice>

<xsd:all>
<element ref="positive"/>
<element ref="negative"/>
</xsd:all/>
```

Namespaces

An XML Schema definition specifies one vocabulary, the target namespace, possibly using other vocabularies by including them through the use of namespaces:

```
<xsd:schema targetNamespace='http://www.physics.com/measurements'
xmlns:xsd='http://www.w3.org/1999/XMLSchema' xmlns:units=
'http://www.physics.com/units'>

<xsd:element name='units' type='units:Units'/>
<xsd:element name='measurement' type='measurement'/>
<complexType name='measurement'>
<element name='time' type='time'/>
<element name='value' type='value'/>
</complexType>
```

This mechanism offers the modularity and extensibility needed to build up a grand hierarchy of namespaces, from basic things like addresses to very specific objects in any subject matter.

Comparison

Now let's take another quick look at our DTD for a price list and then compare it to an XML Schema (see Listing 19.3).

Listing 19.3   ***Pricelist.DTD***

```
<?xml version="1.0" encoding="UTF-8"?>
<!— ******************************************************** —>
<!— VSI Pricelist file Definition                          —>
<!— ******************************************************** —>
<!ELEMENT price-list (price-group*)>
<!ELEMENT price-group (name, price-element*)>
<!ELEMENT price-element (product-code, description, license*, list-price)>
<!ELEMENT license (quantity ¦ unlimited)>
<!ATTLIST license
     type (Server ¦ Clients ¦ WebServer ¦ FaxServer) "Server"
>
<!ELEMENT name (#PCDATA)>
<!ELEMENT product-code (#PCDATA)>
<!ELEMENT description (#PCDATA)>
<!ELEMENT list-price (#PCDATA)>
<!ELEMENT quantity (#PCDATA)>
<!ELEMENT unlimited (#PCDATA)>
```

Now let's look at the same thing as an XML Schema (see Listing 19.4).

Listing 19.4   ***Pricelistschema.xsd***

```
<?xml version="1.0" encoding="UTF-8"?>
<!—W3C Schema generated by XML Spy v4.2 U (http://www.xmlspy.com)—>
<xs:schema xmlns:xs="http://www.w3.org/2001/XMLSchema" elementFormDefault="qualified">
     <xs:element name="description" type="xs:string"/>
     <xs:element name="license">
          <xs:complexType>
               <xs:choice>
                    <xs:element ref="quantity"/>
                    <xs:element ref="unlimited"/>
               </xs:choice>
               <xs:attribute name="type" default="Server">
                    <xs:simpleType>
                         <xs:restriction base="xs:NMTOKEN">
                              <xs:enumeration value="Server"/>
                              <xs:enumeration value="Clients"/>
                              <xs:enumeration value="WebServer"/>
                              <xs:enumeration value="FaxServer"/>
                         </xs:restriction>
                    </xs:simpleType>
               </xs:attribute>
          </xs:complexType>
     </xs:element>
     <xs:element name="list-price" type="xs:string"/>
     <xs:element name="name" type="xs:string"/>
     <xs:element name="price-element">
```

continues ▶

Listing 19.4   **Continued**

```
            <xs:complexType>
                <xs:sequence>
                    <xs:element ref="product-code"/>
                    <xs:element ref="description"/>
                    <xs:element ref="license" minOccurs="0"
                    ➥maxOccurs="unbounded"/>
                    <xs:element ref="list-price"/>
                </xs:sequence>
            </xs:complexType>
    </xs:element>
    <xs:element name="price-group">
            <xs:complexType>
                <xs:sequence>
                    <xs:element ref="name"/>
                    <xs:element ref="price-element" minOccurs="0"
                    ➥maxOccurs="unbounded"/>
                </xs:sequence>
            </xs:complexType>
    </xs:element>
    <xs:element name="price-list">
            <xs:complexType>
                <xs:sequence>
                    <xs:element ref="price-group" minOccurs="0"
                    ➥maxOccurs="unbounded"/>
                </xs:sequence>
            </xs:complexType>
    </xs:element>
    <xs:element name="product-code" type="xs:string"/>
    <xs:element name="quantity" type="xs:string"/>
    <xs:element name="unlimited" type="xs:string"/>
</xs:schema>
```

Wrapping Up

XML Schema offers a rich and flexible mechanism for defining XML vocabularies. It promises the next level of interoperability by describing meta-information about XML in XML. Various tools for validating and editing schemas are available from the Apache Project, IBM alphaWorks, and of course, Microsoft. It's important to reenforce that DTDs have not been replaced by XML Schema and that most XML-enabled applications use DTDs as well as most trading partners and content syndication systems that you might work with. However, XML Schema will gradually become the dominant method for creating XML metadata.

Note

ColdFusion does not support the validation of XML documents. If you want to validate your XML documents, you need to directly call an XML parser that supports validation via CFOBJECT or CFX.

XML Syntax Rules

We have covered a lot of information at this point; but as we mentioned before, XML is very simple, and there are just a few things you need to remember when working with it. Let's review some of what we've learned about creating XML:

- XML documents are composed of Unicode characters.
- XML is case-sensitive.
- Whitespace and characters such as spaces (ASCII 32), tabs (ASCII 9), carriage returns (ASCII 13), and line feeds (ASCII 10) are ignored inside of tags, but whitespace is passed on by an XML parser to its calling application. Whitespace outside of elements can be significant to the parsing application.
- XML names must begin with a letter or an underscore followed by any number of letters, digits, hyphens, underscores, or periods. For more information on characters that might need to be escaped, refer to the XML specification at `www.w3.org/TR/REC-xml`. Element names cannot contain spaces.
- Attributes must be quoted.
- XML is a reserved namespace, and XML names cannot begin with the letters "xml" in any variation, upper- or lowercase.
- XML tags must be properly nested. If an element exists inside another element, its ending tag must be before the ending element's ending tag. An empty tag is one that ends with a forward slash before the right-angle bracket. All starting tags must end with an ending tag.
- An XML document can have only one root element.

Creating XML

You now have enough knowledge about XML to write your own DTDs, XML Schemas, and XML documents, so let's actually use ColdFusion to dynamically create an XML document and parse it.

As we have seen, XML is just a type of text format, so all we will be using is `CFQUERY`, `CFFILE`, a new tag called `CFXML`, and a function called `XMLFormat()`.

Look at the code in Listing 19.5.

Listing 19.5   *createpricelistxml.cfm*

```
<cfquery datasource="ICF" name="getCatalog" dbtype="ODBC">
SELECT Product.ProductID, Product.ProductName, Product.ProductPricePerUnit,
➥Product.VendorID, Vendor.VendorID, Vendor.VendorName, Product.ProductSKU,
➥Product.ProductDescription
FROM Product, Vendor
WHERE Product.VendorID=Vendor.VendorID
</cfquery>

<cfsavecontent variable="tempxml"><?xml version="1.0" encoding="UTF-8"?>
<price-list xmlns:xsi="http://www.w3.org/2001/XMLSchema-instance" xsi:
➥noNamespaceSchemaLocation="E:\coldfusion6\workingwithXML\pricelistschema.xsd">
<cfoutput query="getCatalog">
        <price-group>
                <name>#Trim(XMLFormat(getCatalog.ProductName))#</name>
                <price-element>
                <product-code>#Trim(XMLFormat(getCatalog.ProductSKU))#</product-code>

<description>#Trim(XMLFormat(getCatalog.ProductDescription))#</description>
                        <license type="Server">
                                <quantity>String</quantity>
                        </license>
                 <list-price>#Trim(XMLFormat(getCatalog.ProductPricePerUnit))#</list-price>
                </price-element>
        </price-group>
</cfoutput>
</price-list>
</cfsavecontent>

<!-- show the XML in the HTML output -->
<cfset myXMLDocument=XmlParse(tempxml)>
 <p>This is a simple XML document that's been generated by the ColdFusion code.</p>
<cfdump var=#myXMLDocument#>

<cffile action="write"
        file="#ExpandPath(".")#/pricelist.xml"
        output="#ToString(tempxml)#">
```

All this code does is pull information from your database and store it in a
temporary variable that it then writes to a file. We could have written it to a
file, FTP'd it, sent it via HTTP or email, and so on. The only interesting
thing we are doing is making sure that all data from the database is properly
formatted for XML by trimming the whitespace and also using XMLFormat,
which was introduced in ColdFusion 4.5.

Also note that we are using a function called toString, which makes sure
that our XML data is converted to string data before we save it to a file.

Quick Tip

You might notice that we leave no whitespace between the CFSAVECONTENT tag and the opening of the XML tag. The reason for this is that ColdFusion has a tendency to add whitespace to saved content, and this can make our XML unreadable to some XML parsers.

XMLFormat escapes special XML characters so that you can put arbitrary strings safely into XML. The characters escaped by XMLFormat include the following:

- Greater than sign (>)
- Less than sign (<)
- Single quotation mark (')
- Double quotation mark (")
- Ampersand (&)

Note

Go to www.w3.org/XML/ to find more information about XML special characters and changes in XML recommendations.

Run the script in your browser and note the output. Now go to the directory and look for the file that the script generated. Drop that file into IE 5.0 or higher or Netscape 6.0. You should see something like Figure 19.2. If you have access to XML Spy or another XML tool, try opening it in that and see what you get.

Before we move on, let's build an XML document again but using a slightly different syntax. We are now going to introduce ColdFusion MX's CFXML tag, which makes working with XML very easy. The CFXML tag has the following basic structure:

```
<CFXML
    variable="xmlVarName"
    caseSensitive="yes" or "no"
>
```

CFXML creates a ColdFusion XML document object that contains the markup in the tag body. This document object is actually a ColdFusion structure that enables you to then work with your XML document as if it were a native ColdFusion variable, which it actually is once you use CFXML to convert it to an XML document object. The CFXML tag enables you to mix XML and CFML tags within its body. ColdFusion processes the CFML code in the tag body and then assigns the resulting text to an XML document object variable.

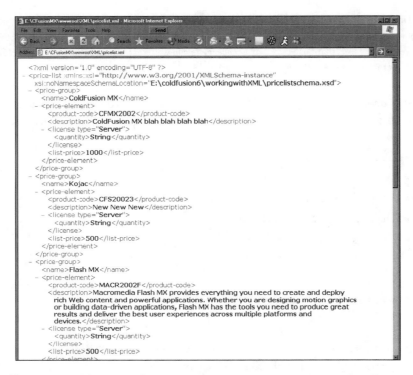

Figure 19.2 The output from `createpurchaseorder.cfm` as viewed in IE 6.0.

Let's take Listing 19.5 and change it to look like Listing 19.6.

Listing 19.6 *Creatxmlwithcfxml.cfm*

```
<cfquery datasource="ICF" name="getCatalog" dbtype="ODBC">
SELECT Product.ProductID, Product.ProductName, Product.ProductPricePerUnit,
➥Product.VendorID, Vendor.VendorID, Vendor.VendorName, Product.ProductSKU,
➥Product.ProductDescription
FROM Product, Vendor
WHERE Product.VendorID=Vendor.VendorID
</cfquery>
<cfxml variable="pricelist">
<pricelist xmlns:xsi="http://www.w3.org/2001/XMLSchema-instance" si:
➥noNamespaceSchemaLocation="E:\coldfusion6\workingwithXML\pricelistschema.xsd">
<cfoutput query="getCatalog">
    <price-group>
        <name>#Trim(XMLFormat(getCatalog.ProductName))#</name>
        <price-element>
        <product-code>#Trim(XMLFormat(getCatalog.ProductSKU))#</product-code>

<description>#Trim(XMLFormat(getCatalog.ProductDescription))#</description>
                <license type="Server">
                    <quantity>String</quantity>
```

```
            </license>
          <list-price>#Trim(XMLFormat(getCatalog.ProductPricePerUnit))#</list-price>
          </price-element>
       </price-group>
 </cfoutput>
 </pricelist>
 </cfXML>


 <!--- show the XML in the HTML output --->
  <p>This is a simple XML document that's been generated by the ColdFusion code.</p>

 <cfdump var=#pricelist#>
```

Instead of using the CFSAVECONTENT tag and saving the XML to a file, we have created a ColdFusion object that's an XML document object, which you can see by viewing this page in your browser and seeing the output of CFDUMP (see Figure 19.3).

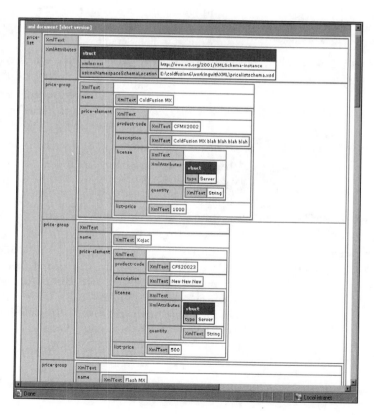

Figure 19.3   The output of the XML document object structure.

The XML document object structure is a structure that contains a set of nested XML element structures. So why even bother to use CFXML to create XML when it's just as easy to do it the other way? Well, having our XML as a native ColdFusion object will enable us to easily parse, edit, and transform our XML through ColdFusion XML functions (which would be difficult to do otherwise). Table 19.5 introduces you to some of the ColdFusion MX XML functionality.

Table 19.5 Some of ColdFusion MX's XML Functionality

Tag or Function	Description
`<cfxml variable="objectName" [caseSensitive="Boolean"]>`	Creates a new ColdFusion XML document object consisting of the markup in the tag body. The tag can include XML and CFML tags. ColdFusion processes all CFML in the tag body before converting the resulting text to an XML document object.
	If you specify the `CaseSensitive="True"` attribute, the case of element and attribute names in the document is meaningful. The default is `False`.
`XmlParse("XMLStringVar" [, caseSensitive])`	Converts an XML document that is represented as a string variable into an XML document object.
	If you specify the optional second argument as `True`, the case of element and attribute names in the document is meaningful. The default is `False`.
`XmlNew([caseSensitive])`	Returns a new, empty XML document object.
	If you specify the optional argument as `True`, the case of element and attribute names in the document is meaningful. The default is `False`.
`XmlElemNew(objectName, "elementName")`	Returns a new XML document object element with the specified name.
`XmlChildPos(element, "elementName", position)`	Returns the position (index) in an `XmlChildren` array of the *N*th child with the specified element name. For example, `XmlChildPos(mydoc.employee, "name", 2)` returns the position in `mydoc.employee.XmlChildren` of the `mydoc.employee.name[2]` element. This index can be used in the `ArrayInsertAt` and `ArrayDeleteAt` functions.

Tag or Function	Description
IsXmlDoc(objectName)	Returns True if the function argument is an XML document object.
IsXmlElem(elementName)	Returns True if the function argument is an XML document object element.
IsXMLRoot(elementName)	Returns True if the function argument is the root element of an XML document object.
ToString(objectName)	Converts an XML document object to a string representation.

So now you know how to create valid XML dynamically from ColdFusion MX! As you can see, it is very simple, but as with most things, that's the easy part. At some point, we need to be able to get data from the document, view it in another format, or have a program react or respond based on the contents of a document. To do that, we first need to be able to parse XML from ColdFusion.

Using XML with ColdFusion MX

Now that you have a working understanding of XML and how to create it, you need to know how to actually do something with it. To be able to do anything with XML, you need to be able to access or work with data in an XML document (or *stream*). ColdFusion MX enables you to do that through a series of ColdFusion tags and functions (which we will review) that allow you to parse, search, transform, edit, and so on. In this section, we are going to look at parsing XML documents we have already created.

It is possible to parse XML using ColdFusion, various functions, and regular expressions, but you would have limited capability to parse the documents and validate against a DTD. Furthermore, using ColdFusion regular expressions or some other method of parsing XML using string functions is so slow as to be unusable in most cases. Unless you only need one piece of data from a XML document, this might be an unworkable solution.

We have managed to create XML documents in the preceding listings, so let's try reading in an XML document from a file, changing it into an XML document object, and then accessing the data and doing something with it.

Let's look at the code first, as shown in Listing 19.7.

Listing 19.7 *parseXML.cfm*

```
<!DOCTYPE HTML PUBLIC "-//W3C//DTD HTML 4.01 Transitional//EN">
<html>
  <head>
    <title>Parse Price List</title>
</head>
<body>
<cffile action="read"
        file="#ExpandPath(".")#/pricelist.xml"
        variable="XMLFileText">
<!-- XMLParse function turns our text into a XML docuemnt object or ColdFusion
➥Structure --->
<cfset myXMLDocument=XmlParse(XMLFileText)>
<cfoutput>
Product name:  #myXMLDocument.XmlRoot.XmlChildren[1].XmlChildren[1].XmlText#<br>
Product SKU: #myXMLDocument.XmlRoot.XmlChildren[1].XmlChildren[2].XmlChildren
➥[1].XmlText#<br>
Product Description: #myXMLDocument.XmlRoot.XmlChildren[1].XmlChildren[2].XmlChildren
➥[2].XmlText#<br>
Product Price:  #myXMLDocument.XmlRoot.XmlChildren[1].XmlChildren[2].XmlChildren
➥[4].XmlText#<br>
</cfoutput>
</body>
</html>
```

The first thing we do in this code, as you can see, is use CFFILE to read in our XML document, and we use the new XML function XMLParse to parse the XML and convert it into an XML document object. After that, we introduce some new concepts to you that you should actually be familiar with from Chapter 7, "Complex Data Types." To extract data from a ColdFusion XML document object, we need to access the XML document object in much the same way we would access a ColdFusion structure.

As we already know, an XML document object is a series of structures, with the main structure holding one root element structure. The root element can have any number of nested element structures. Each element structure represents an XML tag (start tag/end tag set) and all its contents; it can contain additional element structures. This structure models the XML document object model (DOM), which we will talk about in much more detail in the Chapter 20, "Advanced XML."

To access the information, we just need to figure out where in the structure (from Figure 19.3) is the data we need to access (or we can look at the XML in Figure 19.2 and attempt this). One way to do this "by hand" is to count the nodes or child elements from the root element to access a specific piece of data from the structure. To get the name of the product, we need to do this:

```
<cfoutput>
#myXMLDocument.XmlRoot.XmlChildren[1].XmlChildren[1].XmlText#
</cfoutput>
```

This is one way to traverse the structure. It basically tells ColdFusion that you want to access the structure at the first child element of the first child element branch of the root element.

The output of this will then be as follows:

```
Product name: ColdFusion MX
```

This is the name of the first product in our XML document. To get access to the product's SKU/product code, you would use the following inside a cfoutput:

```
#myXMLDocument.XmlRoot.XmlChildren[1].XmlChildren[2].XmlChildren[1].XmlText#
```

This would produce the following:

```
Product SKU: CFMX2002
```

The next lines of code just change which node ColdFusion is going to access to retrieve data from. For product description, we just use the following:

```
#myXMLDocument.XmlRoot.XmlChildren[1].XmlChildren[2].XmlChildren[2].XmlText#<br>
```

For product price, we write the following:

```
#myXMLDocument.XmlRoot.XmlChildren[1].XmlChildren[2].XmlChildren[4].XmlText#<br>
```

You should be able to see by looking at the CFDUMP of pricelist how we are extracting data from each node in the DOM object. Try experimenting with this code and changing the value of the various XML childern to see what happens. For example, change Listing 19.7 to look like Listing 19.8.

Listing 19.8   *modified_parseXML.cfm*

```
<!DOCTYPE HTML PUBLIC "-//W3C//DTD HTML 4.01 Transitional//EN">
<html>
  <head>
    <title>Parse Price List</title>
</head>
<body>
<cffile action="read"
        file="#ExpandPath(".")#/pricelist.xml"
        variable="XMLFileText">
<!-- XMLParse function turns our text into a XML docuemnt object or ColdFusion
Structure -->
<cfset myXMLDocument=XmlParse(XMLFileText)>
<cfoutput>
```

continues ▶

Listing 19.8 **Continued**

```
Product name:  #myXMLDocument.XmlRoot.XmlChildren[2].XmlChildren[1].XmlText#<br>
Product SKU: #myXMLDocument.XmlRoot.XmlChildren[2].XmlChildren[2].XmlChildren
➥[1].XmlText#<br>
Product Description: #myXMLDocument.XmlRoot.XmlChildren[2].XmlChildren
➥[2].XmlChildren[2].XmlText#<br>
Product Price:  #myXMLDocument.XmlRoot.XmlChildren[2].XmlChildren[2].XmlChildren
➥[4].XmlText#<br>
</cfoutput>
</body>
</html>
```

Now execute this template. Was it what you expected? Most likely, you have an idea now how accessing DOM nodes works, but there is a lot more to it and it can be confusing. Don't worry if you are a little confused; in Chapter 20, we are going to go into great detail about how to access the DOM object. For now, though, we need to cover some more information about the basic structure of the ColdFusion XML object.

Let's look at all the different structure variables/entries that an XML document has that you can use to access an XML document object. At the top level, the XML document object has the three entries shown in Table 19.6.

Table 19.6 **Top-Level Entries for the XML Document Object**

Entry Name	Type	Description
XmlRoot	Element	The root element of the document.
XmlComment	String	A string made of the concatenation of all comments on the document. This string does not include comments inside document elements.
XmlDocType	XmlNode	The DocType attribute of the document. This entry only exists if the document specifies a DocType. This entry does not appear when cfdump displays an XML element structure.

Each XML element has the entries shown in Table 19.7.

Table 19.7 **Element Structure**

Entry Name	Type	Description
XmlName	String	The name of the element.
XmlNsPrefix	String	The prefix of the namespace.
XmlNsURI	String	The URI of the namespace.

Entry Name	Type	Description
XmlText	String	A string made up of the concatenation of all text and CDATA text in the element, but not inside any child elements.
XmlComment	String	A string made up of the concatenation of all comments inside the XML element, but not inside any child elements.
XmlAttributes	Structure	The specific element's attributes, as a structure of name-value pairs.
XmlChildren	Array	The specific element's children elements as an array.
XmlParent	XmlNode	The parent DOM node of this element. Note: XMLParent does not appear when CFDUMP displays an XML element structure.
XmlNodes	Array	An array of all the XmlNode DOM nodes contained in this element. Note: XmlNodes does not appear when cfdump displays an XML element structure.

Table 19.8 lists the contents of an XML DOM node structure.

Table 19.8 **XML DOM Node Structure**

Entry Name	Type	Description
XmlName	String	The node name. For nodes such as Element or Attribute, the node name is the element or attribute name.
XmlType	String	The node XML DOM type, such as Element or Text.
XmlValue	String	The node value. This entry is used only for Attribute, CDATA, Comment, and Text type nodes.

Table 19.9 lists the contents of the XmlName and XmlValue fields for each node type that is valid in the XmlType entry. The node types correspond to the objects types in the XML DOM hierarchy.

Table 19.9 *XmlType* **Name and Value Pairs**

Node Type	XmlName	XmlValue
Cdata	#cdata-section	Content of the CDATA section
Comment	#comment	Content of the comment
Element	Tag name	Empty string
Entityref	Name of entity referenced	Empty string
PI (processing instruction)	Target entire content excluding the target	Empty string
Text	#text	Content of the text node
Entity	Entity name	Empty string
Notation	Notation name	Empty string
Document	#document	Empty string
Fragment	#document-fragment	Empty string
Doctype	Document type name	Empty string

Note

If you need to get an element's attributes, use the element structure's XMLAttributes structure. Although XML attributes are nodes on the DOM tree, ColdFusion does not expose them as XML DOM node data structures.

Summary

Wow! We have really covered a lot in this chapter, and there is still a lot more to come in the next two chapters. Before we move on, however, let's recap what you learned in this chapter. We have covered the following:

- What XML is and how to create XML
- What a DTD is and how to create one
- What XML Schema is and how to create an XSD
- How to dynamically create XML with ColdFusion as well as XML document objects
- How to parse and extract information from an XML document using CFXML and ColdFusion MX XML functions

As you have seen, XML is a straightforward way of marking up data and is easy to create in ColdFusion. Although parsing XML and extracting valuable information is slightly more complex, it's not much harder than working with arrays and structures. The skills you have acquired in this chapter are the cornerstones to being able to create XML-enabled applications.

In the next chapter, we will explore much more complex methods of manipulating XML data, transforming XML with XSLT, and using Xpath to search or query XML.

20

Advanced XML

Chapter 19, "Introduction to XML and ColdFusion MX," talked about what XML is and how to create DTDs and schemas and introduced you to some of the basic functionality that ColdFusion supports for working with XML. In this chapter, we are going to expose you to an in-depth review of ColdFusion's XML functionality, explain exactly what goes on behind the scenes, and introduce you to a number of XML recommendations and supporting technologies such as the XML DOM, SAX, XPath, XSLT, SOAP, WSDL, and more. The technologies covered in this chapter are very complex, and we will not be able to go as in-depth as we would like on topics such as XSLT. If you need more information, we recommend New Riders' *Inside XML* by Steve Holzner as a companion to this chapter.

How ColdFusion Parses XML

In the preceding chapter, we talked briefly about how to parse XML with ColdFusion, but we did not give you much background on how ColdFusion handles XML documents internally. This section covers how ColdFusion actually works with XML behind the scenes to help you understand how to work with XML so that you can better utilize XML in ColdFusion and avoid various problems that can arise when working with XML.

ColdFusion MX currently makes use of the open-source XML parsers from the Apache Project, which can be found at `http://xml.apache.org`. ColdFusion uses the Crimson XML parser for Java. It also uses the Xalan parser for Java as the XSLT processor that it accesses using the Java XML parser API from SUN called JAXP (`http://javax.xml.parsers`) to tie it into MX.

The Crimson XML parser supports two different types of XML parsing. The first is called Simple API for XML (SAX), and the other is called document object model (DOM) parsing.

SAX and DOM were created to enable programmers to access XML without having to write a parser in their programming language of choice. Both SAX and DOM serve the same purpose, which is giving you access to the information stored in XML documents using any programming language (and a parser for that language). However, both of them take very different approaches to how the information is accessed. ColdFusion MX uses the DOM model to work with XML, but it's important to understand both models to understand not only how XML and XML parsing work but how and why ColdFusion uses the DOM model. SAX is also covered because there are certain times when you, as a developer, might need to use SAX instead of DOM.

SAX

SAX's approach to parsing documents is very different from DOM's. SAX chooses to give you access to the information in your XML document not as a tree of nodes (like we saw in Chapter 19) but as a sequence of events. Although SAX's event-based parsing makes it very fast, it also creates some problems for developers:

- You must create a custom object model.
- You must create a class that listens to SAX events and properly creates your object model.

SAX is very simple; it doesn't expect the parser to do much. All SAX requires is that the parser read in the XML document and fire a bunch of events depending on what tags it encounters in the XML document. You are responsible for interpreting these events by writing an XML document handler class, which is responsible for making sense of all the tag events and creating objects in your own object model. So you have to write the following:

- Your custom object model to "hold" all the information in your XML document

- A document handler that listens to SAX events (which are generated by the SAX parser as it's reading your XML document) and makes sense of these events to create objects in your custom object model

SAX can be really fast at runtime if your object model is simple. In most cases, it is faster than DOM because it bypasses the creation of a tree-based object model of your information. On the other hand, you do have to write a SAX document handler to interpret all the SAX events (which can be a lot of work).

SAX will fire an event for every open tag and every close tag. It also fires events for PCDATA and CDATA sections. Your document handler (which is a listener for these events) has to interpret these events in some meaningful way and create your custom object model based on them. Your document handler will have to interpret these events, and the sequence in which these events are fired is very important. SAX also fires events for processing instructions, DTDs, comments, and so on. The idea is still the same, however; your handler has to interpret these events (and the sequence of the events) and make sense out of them.

ColdFusion does not have internal support for a SAX parser, but you can either use CFOBJECT or create a CFX to work with a SAX parser. You might need to work with a SAX parser when you are working with XML documents that are many megabytes in size or when performance and speed are of absolute importance.

It's interesting to note that some DOM parser implementations are actually built using a SAX parser.

DOM

Of the two parsing methods, we are going to focus on DOM the most because ColdFusion MX uses it as a model for its XML document objects. The DOM gives you access to the information stored in your XML document as a hierarchical object model often called a tree. DOM creates a tree of nodes (based on the structure and information in your XML document), and you can access your information by interacting with this tree of nodes. The textual information in your XML document gets turned into a bunch of tree nodes. For example, let's say we have an XML document that contains a list of users from our ICF user database (see Listing 20.1).

Listing 20.1 *Users.xml*

```xml
<?xml version="1.0" encoding="UTF-8"?>
<Users>
     <sysUser Status="Active">
          <UserName>robis</UserName>
          <FirstName>Robi</FirstName>
          <LastName>Sen</LastName>
     </sysUser>
     <sysUser Status="Active">
          <UserName>lieage1</UserName>
          <FirstName>Dan</FirstName>
          <LastName>Hahn</LastName>
     </sysUser>
     <sysUser Status="Active">
          <UserName>jgull</UserName>
          <FirstName>Jenghis</FirstName>
          <LastName>Kat</LastName>
     </sysUser>
</Users>
```

The DOM would represent this data as shown in Figure 20.1.

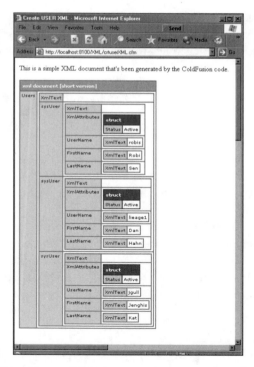

Figure 20.1 How an XML document is represented as a DOM tree.

Regardless of the kind of information in your XML document (whether it is tabular data, a list of items, binary data, or just a document), DOM creates a tree of nodes when you create a document object given the XML document. Thus, DOM forces you to use a tree model to access the information in your XML document. Because XML is hierarchical in nature, a tree model is a natural method of modeling XML.

Figure 20.1 is perhaps overly simplistic because, in DOM, each element node actually contains a list of other nodes as its children. These children nodes might contain text values or might be other element nodes. At first glance, it might seem unnecessary to access the value of an element node (for example, in <FirstName>Robi</FirstName>, Robi is the value) by looking through a list of children nodes inside of it. If each element only had one value, this would truly be unnecessary. However, elements can contain text data and other elements; this is why you have to do extra work in DOM just to get the value of an element node.

Usually when pure data is contained in your XML document, it might be appropriate to "lump" all your data in one string and have DOM return that string as the value of a given element node. This does not work so well if the data stored in your XML document is a document. In documents, the sequence of elements is very important. For pure data (like a database table), the sequence of elements does not matter, so DOM preserves the sequence of the elements it reads from XML documents because it treats everything as it if were a document. Hence, the name *document* object model.

ColdFusion actually creates an XML document object using the exact same format as the DOM tree to represent its XML document object. If we use the script in Listing 20.2 and call it from our browser (IE 5.0 or above or Netscape 6.0), we can actually view the XML document object.

Listing 20.2 **Code to View the XML Document Object**

```
<!DOCTYPE HTML PUBLIC "-//W3C//DTD HTML 4.01 Transitional//EN">
<html>
<head>
      <title>Create USER XML</title>
</head>
<body>
<cfquery datasource="icf" name="getUsers">
SELECT User.UserID, User.UserName, User.UserPassword, User.UserFirstName,
User.UserLastName, User.UserEmail, User.UserStatus, User.UserLevelID
FROM User
</cfquery>
<cfxml variable="Users"><Users><cfoutput query="getUsers">
      <sysUser Status="#Trim(XMLFormat(getUsers.UserStatus))#">
```

continues ▶

Listing 20.2 **Continued**

```
            <UserName>#Trim(XMLFormat(getUsers.UserName))#</UserName>
            <FirstName>#Trim(XMLFormat(getUsers.UserFirstName))#</FirstName>
            <LastName>#Trim(XMLFormat(getUsers.UserLastName))#</LastName>
        </sysUser>
        </cfoutput>
</Users>
</cfxml>
 <p>This is a simple XML document that's been generated by the ColdFusion code.</p>
<cfdump var=#Users#>
</body>
</html>
<cffile action="write"
  file="#ExpandPath(".")#\users.xml"
  output=#tostring(Users)#>
```

If you look at Figure 20.2, you can see how the structure outputted by
cfdump exactly models the DOM tree of the XML document.

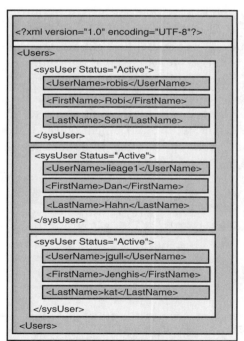
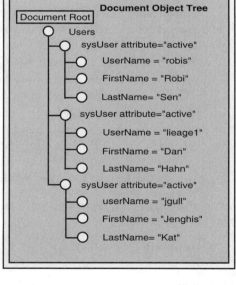

Figure 20.2 The ColdFusion XML document object.

Working with the XML Document Object

In the first section of this chapter, we actually built several XML documents and used some of ColdFusion's built-in functions to parse and access data in the XML document object created by ColdFusion without really knowing how the XML document was modeled in ColdFusion. Now that we have an understanding of the DOM and know that ColdFusion represents the DOM tree created by Crimson as a ColdFusion structure, we can use that knowledge to do some more sophisticated manipulation of XML documents in ColdFusion.

In the preceding chapter, we looked at how to extract data from a ColdFusion XML document structure, but there are more ways to do it than we showed you. Let's look at some different methods of accessing the same data in an XML document.

In the preceding chapter, we discussed how you can access a specific node in an XML document using this sort of notation:

```
myXMLDocument.XmlRoot.XmlChildren[1].XmlChildren[1].XmlText
```

This statement references the very first username in the `Users.xml` document. In ColdFusion, however, there is more than one way to get the same information. Let's look at the example in Listing 20.3.

Listing 20.3   *usersparse.cfm*

```
<!DOCTYPE HTML PUBLIC "-//W3C//DTD HTML 4.01 Transitional//EN">
<html>
<head>
      <title>Parse XML file users.xml Chapter 20:Listing 20.3</title>
</head>
<body>
<cffile action="read"
file="#ExpandPath(".")#\users.xml"
variable="XMLFileText">
<cfset myXMLDocument=XmlParse(XMLFileText)>
<cfoutput>
#myXMLDocument.XmlRoot.XmlChildren[1].XmlChildren[1].XmlText#<br>
#myXMLDocument.Users.sysUser[1].UserName.XmlText#<br>
#myXMLDocument.Users.sysUser[1]["UserName"].XmlText#<br>
#myXMLDocument["Users"].sysUser[1]["UserName"].XmlText#<br>
#myXMLDocument.XmlRoot.sysUser[1].XmlChildren[1]["XmlText"]#<br>
</cfoutput>
</body>
</html>
```

In this example, we read a file in and use the `XMLParse` function to parse the XML and turn it into a ColdFusion XML document object. We then use five different methods of accessing the username in the `Users.xml` document! ColdFusion lets you reference nodes in several different ways, as follows:

- You can use an array index to specify one of multiple elements with the same name, (for example, `#myXMLDocument.Users.UserName[1]#`, or to get the second username `#myXMLDocument.Users.UserName[2]#`).

- You can retrieve a reference of all elements of a specific name by leaving off the element identifier (array identifier or node ID). If you did `myXMLDocument.Users.UserName`, you would be returned an array of three `UserName` elements.

- You can access the `XmlChildren` array to specify an element without using its name, (for example, `myXMLDocument.XmlRoot.XmlChildren[1]`).

- Use associative array (bracket) notation to specify an element name that contains a period or colon, for example, `myotherdoc.XmlRoot["Type1.Case1"]`).

- You can also use the DOM methods in place of specific structure entry names.

You might be wondering what the best method of getting at XML document data is, but for the most part it's a matter of preference. In some specific cases in which data contains a period, for example, or a - symbol, you might have to use a specific notation to get access to your data. In most cases, the syntax we introduced in Chapter 19, in the section "XML Syntax Rules" is the best in that it will cause the fewest problems, but it can also be the least obvious syntax.

In some cases, you will need to preserve the case of an XML document. For example, you might have an XML document in which there is a tag set `<Users></Users>` and also a tag set called `<users></users>`. As we learned in the preceding chapter, this is completely valid because XML is case-sensitive. ColdFusion, though, is not, so you might need to use the `CASESENSITIVE="TRUE"` attribute in your CFML tag or specify `True` as a second argument in the `XMLNew` or `XMLParse` functions that create your ColdFusion XML document object.

Now that you understand how to access data in the XML document object, let's look at how we can modify our XML document objects.

Adding, Deleting, and Modifying XML Elements

Often when you are working with an XML document, you might want to change or edit the document in some form. You could just create a whole new document, but this is not efficient. And if you are using an XML document object to store persistent data such as global application settings, creating a whole new document would not be useful.

ColdFusion MX offers a variety of methods to enable you to manipulate XML document objects. Let's first look at some ways in which you can add data to an existing XML document using techniques you have already learned to find and/or match XML elements in a XML document object. This will utilize your knowledge of working with structures and arrays from Chapter 7, "Complex Data Types." Working with XML document objects, you will mostly use standard array and structure functions to add, edit, or delete data/elements from XML document objects. Much of the syntax and code will already be familiar to you, with the exception of the addition of XML-specific functions.

Adding Elements

Let's say we wanted to add some comments to the XML document we are working with. Let's say we want to add an XML comment to the first child in the XML document. We could do this with the following statement inside a `CFSCRIPT` block:

```
myXMLDocument.XmlRoot.XmlChildren[1].XmlComment = "This is a comment";
```

Try changing Listing 20.2 to look like the following.

```
<!DOCTYPE HTML PUBLIC "-//W3C//DTD HTML 4.01 Transitional//EN">
<html>
<head>
     <title>Create USER XML</title>
</head>
<body>
<cfquery datasource="icf" name="getUsers">
SELECT User.UserID, User.UserName, User.UserPassword, User.UserFirstName,
User.UserLastName, User.UserEmail, User.UserStatus, User.UserLevelID
FROM User
</cfquery>
<cfxml variable=" myXMLDocument "><Users><cfoutput query="getUsers">
     <sysUser Status="#Trim(XMLFormat(getUsers.UserStatus))#">
          <UserName>#Trim(XMLFormat(getUsers.UserName))#</UserName>
          <FirstName>#Trim(XMLFormat(getUsers.UserFirstName))#</FirstName>
          <LastName>#Trim(XMLFormat(getUsers.UserLastName))#</LastName>
     </sysUser>
     </cfoutput>
</Users>
```

```
</cfxml>
 <p>This is a simple XML document that's been generated by the ColdFusion code.</p>
<cfscript>
myXMLDocument.XmlRoot.XmlChildren[1].XmlComment = "This is a comment";
</cfscript>
<cfdump var=#myXMLDocument#>

</body>
</html>
<cffile action="write"
  file="#ExpandPath(".")#\users.xml"
  output=#tostring(myXMLDocument)#>
```

Notice how we added the CFSCRIPT block with the following code:

```
myXMLDocument.XmlRoot.XmlChildren[1].XmlComment = "This is a comment";
```

View it in your browser and, when you see the results of the CFDUMP, click on the "version" link to see an expanded display of the XML document object. You will notice that your XML document has been changed to include an XML comment. In fact, if you write the new XML document to a file, you will see the XML comments are now inside the file. In general, whenever you want to add new data or even elements to an XML document object, you can just follow this general form or use the same methods you have already learned to access a specific node (in our example, we used myXMLDocument.XmlRoot.XmlChildren[1]) in the XML document followed by a element structure key name (or XML property name), which in this last example was XMLComment. Then you use the function XMLElemNew to add a new element.

You must be careful, though, to make sure you point to the right node. If you leave off a numeric index like in myXMLDocument.XmlRoot.XmlChildren, for example, ColdFusion would match the expression to the first node in the list of nodes returned from XMLChildren (actually, in ColdFusion's case, the first element in the XMLChildren array) and assign your expression to it.

For example, if myXMLDocument.XmlRoot.XmlChildren[1] and myXMLDocument.XmlRoot.XmlChildren[2] exist, the following expression replaces myXMLDocument.XmlRoot.XmlChildren with a new element named neel:

```
myXMLDocument.XmlRoot.XmlChildren = XmlElemNew(myXMLDocument, "neel");
```

If you simply want to create a new element in the XML document structure, you can do something like this:

```
myXMLDocument.XmlRoot.XmlChildren[1].UserEmail =XmlElemNew(myXMLDocument,
➥"UsersEmail");
```

This will force ColdFusion to create a new element in the XML document object. The reason for this is that whenever ColdFusion encounters an expression that does not match an element, it will create a new element. You should be careful, though, because simply misspelling an element name can cause the creation of unwanted elements. If you have expressions in which the element and the element value do not match, you will get an error. Therefore, something like the following will cause an error:

```
myXMLDocument.XmlRoot.XmlChildren[1].User_Email =XmlElemNew(myXMLDocument,
➥"UsersEmail");
```

When you are adding new elements to an existing XML document object, you need to be careful not to generate errors this way.

Another nice feature when adding elements to an existing ColdFusion document is that you can have ColdFusion build parent tags for you. If you want to create an expression like the following:

```
myXMLDocument.XmlRoot.XmlChildren[1].XmlChildren[1].workphone
=XmlElemNew(myXMLDocument, "workPhone");
```

ColdFusion automatically creates the needed parent nodes and creates the child node as well.

So far, all the methods we have looked at to add or edit elements in an XML document object have used cfscript, but you can do the same thing by using functions (see Appendix B, "Function Reference") inside CFML. You do this by using array functions to insert or append elements to the XML document object. For example, if we want to add the new element userPhone to our XML document, we can use the following:

```
<cfset ArrayAppend(myXMLDocument.XmlRoot.XmlChildren [1]. userPhone,
XmlElemNew(myXMLDocument,"userPhone"))>
```

You will note that this is more or less the same as the cfscript version, if not as elegant. Now let's say we actually want to insert a new element into our XML object called securityLevel as a child of Users. We can use the following:

```
<cfset ArrayInsertAt(myXMLDocument.XmlRoot.XmlChildren, 1,
XmlElemNew(myXMLDocument,"securityLevel"))>
```

This element is inserted into the first position, which pushes Username into second, FirstName into third, and so on.

Note that the syntax in this instance is parentElement.XmlChildren. You must use this syntax when you are adding a new element to the array of elements.

If you have multiple child elements with the same name and you want to insert a new element in a specific position, use the `XmlChildPos` function to determine the location in the `XmlChildren` array where you want to insert the new element. For example, the following code determines the location of `mydoc.employee.name[1]` and inserts a new name element as the second name element:

```
<cfscript>
nameIndex = XmlChildPos(mydoc.employee, "name", 1);
ArrayInsertAt(mydoc.employee.XmlChildren, nameIndex + 1, XmlElemNew(mydoc,
        "name"));
</cfscript>
```

You can also change elements using the same techniques. Let's say we want to make the second `sysUser` element inactive; to do this, we can apply the same techniques as we would to change any data in a ColdFusion structure and use the following:

```
<cfset myXMLDocument.XmlRoot.sysUsers[2].XmlAttributes.Status="Inactive">
<cfset StructInsert(myXMLDocument.XmlRoot.sysUsers [2].XmlAttributes, "Status",
"Inactive")>
```

Or you could change the attribute's value this way:

```
<cfset myXMLDocument.XmlRoot.sysUsers [2].XmlAttributes.Status="Active">
```

This is more like a standard direct-assignment expression.

Deleting Elements

Just as there are many ways to add elements to an XML document object, there are also many approaches to deleting XML elements from an object.

For example, if we need to delete a specific element from an XML document object, we can use the `ArrayDeleteAt` function just like you would with any other array.

Let's say we want to delete the `LastName` element from our `Users.xml` object. The following line deletes the second child element in the `mydoc.employee` element:

```
<cfset ArrayDeleteAt(myXMLDocument.XmlRoot.XmlChildren, 3)>
```

Sometimes you will need to dynamically determine the position of `XmlChildren` in an array, such as in a shopping cart where people are allowed to delete specific line items. You can do this by using a function called `XmlChildPos`, which works like it sounds. It returns the index of a specific XML child position. For example, if we want to delete again the second `sysUser` element, we can do the following:

```
<cfset indexval = XmlChildPos(myXMLDocument.XmlRoot, "sysUser", 2)>
<cfset ArrayDeleteAt(myXMLDocument.XmlRoot.XmlChildren, indexval)>
```

If you want to delete multiple children all with the same name, you can use the `StructDelete` or `ArrayClear` functions with an element name. This will then delete all of the element's child elements with that name.

If you want to get rid of all your `sysUser` elements as well as their children, you can use the following:

```
<cfset StructDelete(myXMLDocument.Users, "sysUser")>
```

Or, using the array version, you can use this statement:

```
<cfset ArrayClear(myXMLDocument.Users.sysUsers)>
```

Once again, this is very similar to how you would delete data from a regular structure or array.

You can also use this same method to delete an attribute. For example:

```
<cfset StructDelete(myXMLDocument.Users.sysUsers [1].XmlAttributes, "Status")>
```

By using these same techniques, you can edit, delete, or add any data in an XML document object such as an `XMLComment` (like we did at the beginning of the section) or an attribute (which we have not shown but to which you could do same things).

Using XML–Related Technologies

In this section, we are going to look at how to work with two XML-related technologies and W3C recommendations. One is called XPath and the other is XSL/XSLT. ColdFusion MX has built-in XPath and XSLT parsers/processors, giving ColdFusion developers access to the full power of these XML-related technologies.

Using XPath

XPath is a language for finding information in an XML document. Using XPath, we can specify the locations of document structures or data in an XML document and then process the information using XSLT (which we will look at in the next section). In practice, it can be difficult to determine where XSLT stops and where XPath starts, but they were developed as two different recommendations by the W3C.

Note

Be sure to read the XPath recommendation at www.w3c.org/TR/xpath.

In many ways, XPath will seem familiar to you as a ColdFusion developer in that it has uses similar to those that SQL has for data querying. Although it is beyond the scope of this book to totally cover Xpath, we will introduce you to its basic concepts so that you can effectively use it and understand enough of it to be able to easily pick up more if needed.

Location Paths

One of the basic concepts of XPath that is fundamental to its usage (and that of XSLT) is the concept of location paths. In XPath, to specify a node or set of nodes, you use a location path that consists of one or more location steps separated by / or //, much like a file path. You can start your location path from the root node or absolute location path by using /, or you can start from a relative position based on context by using // (which starts your search at the current node you are at).

Location steps are made up of an axis, a node test, and zero or more predicates. Let's look at a quick example before we move on.

In ColdFusion MX, we can perform XPath expressions on XML document objects using the function XMLSearch, which has the following general syntax:

```
XmlSearch(xmlDoc, xPathString)
```

ColdFusion takes the XPath expression in string format and returns an array of XML document objects containing the elements that match the expression.

Let's say we want to grab all the FirstNames from our Users.xml document. Well, the XPath expression we need to perform is /Users/sysUser/FirstName, which basically tells the parser that starting from the root node, you want all the nodes that match FirstName. In ColdFusion, to execute this expression and print out the results, we do what is shown in Listing 20.4.

Listing 20.4 *xpathgetnames.cfm*

```
<cffile action="read"
  file="e:\cfusionmx\wwwroot\xml\users.xml"
  variable="myxml">
<cfscript>
  myxmldoc = XmlParse(myxml);
  selectedElements = XmlSearch(myxmldoc, "/Users/sysUser/FirstName");
  for (i = 1; i LTE ArrayLen(selectedElements); i = i + 1)
    writeoutput(selectedElements[i].XmlText & "<br>");
</cfscript>
```

If you look at this code, you can see we use the `XmlSearch` function to apply our XPath expression to our XML document object, and the results are returned as an array of elements that matches the expression. So to print them out, we loop over the array and output the results.

You should get the `FirstName` of all the `Users` in the `Users.xml` file. Looking at Figure 20.3, you can see how the XPath expression navigates the tree to return the results. It starts at the root node (which, in this case, is `Users`) and then goes to `sysUsers` and then the `FirstName` element. It returns the result and then loops through the XML file until it finds no more elements that match the expression. Let's look at XPath expressions in a little more detail.

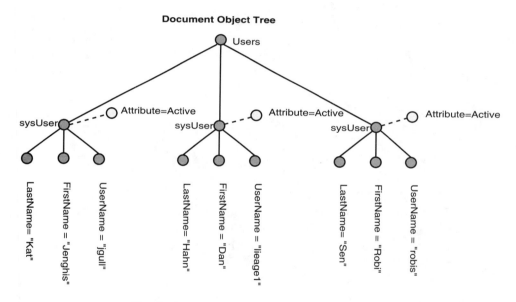

Figure 20.3 Another perspective on a DOM tree.

Path Expressions

An XPath expression is an expression used for selecting a node set by following a path or steps. Although the complete set of path expressions includes a much larger group of operators, Table 20.1 shows some of the most useful ones.

Table 20.1 **Path Expressions**

Operator	Description
element	Selects all element children of the context node.
	Example: `article`
	Selects all the child nodes of the **article** element.
/	Selects from the root node of the current document of the node in context.
	Example: `/Users`
	Selects the **Users** element, starting at the root of the document.
	Example: `x/FirstName`
	Select all **FirstName** elements that are children of **x**.
//	Selects nodes in the document from the current context that match the selection no matter where they are. When used with a context, this operator selects all descendant nodes in the context, no matter how many levels deep they are.
	Example: `//FirstName`
	Selects all **FirstName** elements no matter where they are in the document.
	Example: `x//LastName`
	Selects all **LastName** nodes that are descendant of the **x** element, no matter where they exist under the **x** element.

Before we move on, Listing 20.5 presents you with a simple script you can use to test most of your XPath expressions and examples as we move forward. It will enable you to submit an XPath expression via a form and will apply that expression to our `Users.xml` file.

Listing 20.5 *expressiontester.cfm*

```
<html>
<form action="expressiontester.cfm" method="post">
<input type="test" name="exp">
<input type="Submit" title="test Expression">
</form>
</html>
<cfif IsDefined("form.exp")>
<cfset testexp=#form.exp#>
<cffile action="read"
  file="e:\cfusionmx\wwwroot\xml\users.xml"
  variable="myxml">
<cfscript>
  myxmldoc = XmlParse(myxml);
```

```
  selectedElements = XmlSearch(myxmldoc, testexp);
  for (i = 1; i LTE ArrayLen(selectedElements); i = i + 1)
    writeoutput(selectedElements[i].XmlText & "<br>");
</cfscript>
<cfelse>
You need to define your expression!
<cfabort>
</cfif>
```

When you perform queries, note that if the XPath expression does not match anything, it will return an empty array.

XPath Axes

XPath has a special concept called an axis. An axis usually returns a list of nodes based on the context of the original node. For example, the expression /Users/sysUser/FirstName refers to the FirstName element that is a child of sysUser. sysUser, in this case, is the axis, and the list of nodes returned will be the FirstName's of the Users.

Table 20.2 shows examples of some the axis location paths.

Table 20.2   Examples of Axis Location Paths

Expression	Abbreviation	Comment
self	.	This selects the current node in the context.
ancestor		This selects a path of all parent and parent-of-parent nodes of the current node, starting from the first parent above the context node.
parent	..	This selects only the single parent of the context node.
attribute	@	This selects all the attributes of an element.
		@sysUser
		Selects the PERSONID attribute.
child		Selects all the children of the current node. This is the default in the abbreviated syntax.

Predicates

The axis helps us find nodes around the current node. To be able to find a subnode that contains a specific value, we use a predicate. It consists of a "qualifying expression" to do the query.

The syntax for the predicate uses square brackets around the expression. For example:

```
sysUser[FirstName="robi"]
```

Here are two more examples of predicates:

```
sysUser[position()=2]
```

This is syntax to find the second `sysUser` element.

```
sysUser[starts-with(name, "R")]
```

This is syntax to find all `sysUser` nodes whose name element starts with R.

XPath Expressions

XPath includes another concept called "expressions," which are basically the axis, a predicate, and some operator, such as +, =, or `mod`.

Filter patterns can consist of expressions, such as Booleans (AND, OR, and so on), substrings, and others. These expressions are found as the expression in the predicate, or they can stand on their own.

Table 20.3 shows the expressions available with XPath.

Table 20.3   **XPath Expressions**

Operator	Description
and, or	Logical and, or
=	Equal to
!=	Not equal to
>, >=	Greater than, greater than or equal to
<, <=	Less than, less than or equal to
	Remember to code the < character as the XML entity &lt when you are passing it via forms or URLs.
+, -, *, div	Addition, subtraction, multiply, divide
mod	Modular (returns the integer remainder of a division)
|	Computes (unions) two node sets

Here are some examples of the use of expressions:

```
sysUser[FirstName="Robi" and FirstName="Dan"]
```

This returns `sysUser` nodes in which the `FirstName` is `Robi` and `Dan`. It might be necessary to code the quote marks as apostrophes (single quote marks).

```
sysUser|Users
```

This returns sysUser and Users nodes using a compute (union).

There is more to XPath than we can deal with in this brief encounter, but these are the basics, and they cover the majority of XPath functionality you might use. In the next section, we will discuss XML eXstensible Stylesheet Language Transformation. We also will get to see more applications of XPath, which XSLT also uses to do pattern matching in XML documents.

XSLT with ColdFusion

The eXtensible Stylesheet Language Transformation (XSLT) is used to transform an XML document from one format to another, which may or may not be XML. XSLT is often used to convert a target XML document from XML to HTML, WML, plain text, or some other format that the requesting client needs to view the data.

XSLT is probably different from most programming languages you have worked with because it is based on template rules that specify how XML documents should be processed. Although conventional programming languages are often sequential, template rules can be based on any order because XSLT is a declarative language. The style sheet declares what output should be produced when a pattern in the XML document is matched.

For example, a style sheet could declare that when the XSLT transformation engine finds a FirstName element, it should add markup by calling the FirstName template.

Note

Once again, make sure to read the XSLT recommendation at www.w3.org/Style/XSL/.

Also note that XSLT 2.0 was in working draft during the writing of this book.

XSLT transforms an XML document by applying an eXtensible Stylesheet Language (XSL) style sheet. (When stored in a file, XSL style sheets typically have the extension .xsl.) ColdFusion provides the XmlTransform function to apply an XSL transformation to an XML document. The function takes an XML document in string format (or an XML document object and an XSL style sheet in string format) and returns the transformed document as a string.

Let's just get right into it. In the next example, we are going to use ColdFusion to change Users.xml to HTML. First let's create a CFML template to call our XSLT style sheet (see Listing 20.6).

Listing 20.6 *Test.xslsimple.cfm*

```
<cffile action="read"  file="#ExpandPath(".")#\users.xml"  variable="myxml">

<cffile action="read" file="#ExpandPath(".")#\simpleexm.xsl" variable="xslDoc">
<cfset mydocAsString=ToString(myxml)>
<cfset transformedXML = XmlTransform(mydocAsString, xslDoc)>
<cffile action="write" file="#ExpandPath(".")#\resulthtml.html"
output="#transformedXML#">

<cfoutput>#transformedXML#</cfoutput>
```

Notice that we read both the XML file and the XSL file and then convert them into strings before we hand them off to the XMLTransform function. Okay, now for the fun stuff! See Listing 20.7.

Listing 20.7 *simplexsl.xsl*

```
<?xml version="1.0" encoding="UTF-8"?>
<xsl:stylesheet version="1.0"
xmlns:xsl="http://www.w3.org/1999/XSL/Transform">
  <xsl:template match="/">
<html>
  <head>
    <title>Users</title>
  </head>
<body>
  <table border="2">
  <thead>
  <tr>
    <th>FirstName</th>
    <th>LastName</th>
    <th>User Name</th>
  </tr>
  </thead>
  <tbody>
<xsl:for-each select="Users/sysUser">
  <tr>
    <td><xsl:value-of select="FirstName"/></td>
    <td><xsl:value-of select="LastName"/></td>
    <td><xsl:value-of select="UserName"/></td>
  </tr>
</xsl:for-each>
  </tbody>
  </table>
</body>
</html>
  </xsl:template>
</xsl:stylesheet>
```

Let's step through the XSL. The first thing you will notice is that the XSL style sheet starts with the following:

```
<?xml version="1.0" encoding="UTF-8"?>
```

This means that XSL is XML, which implies something interesting. Because XSL is XML and XSL is for transforming XML, you can actually apply a style sheet to a style sheet or use a style sheet to create a new style sheet.

The second thing you will notice is this:

```
<xsl:stylesheet version="1.0" xmlns:xsl="http://www.w3.org/1999/XSL/Transform">
```

Every XSL file needs to specify the XSL namespace so that the parser knows which version of XSLT to use. The one we are using is the most current but be careful. If you have played with XSL on versions of the Microsoft parser MSXML before version 3.0, you will get an error if you try to use those same style sheets due to Microsoft's use of a temporary namespace (`www.w3.org/TR/WD-xsl" version="1.0"`). This is now outdated and doesn't conform to the latest W3C recommendation.

The namespace prefix `xsl:` is used in the rest of the XSL file to identify XSL processing statements. If a statement isn't prefixed with `xsl:`, it's simply copied to the output without being processed. This is the way to add HTML statements to the output:

```
<xsl:template match=" ... ">
```

Before processing can begin, the part of the XML document with the information to be copied to the output must be selected with an XPath expression. The selected section of the document is called a node and is normally selected with the match operator. If the entire document is to be selected, match the root node using `match="/"`. Another approach is to match the document element (the element that includes the entire document). In our example, the document element can be selected using `match="Users"`. (If you use this alternative approach, don't include `Users` in the `for-each` selection of the following code line.)

```
<xsl:for-each select=" Users/sysUser">
```

The expression `xsl:for-each` finds all `sysUser` elements in the `Users` element context using the XPath expression `Users/sysUser`. If the selected node contains all elements in the root, all of the `Users` elements will be selected. Because we want to include all `sysUser` elements in our output document, we have used this expression.

The `for-each` expression is a loop that processes the same instructions for these elements.

```
<xsl:value-of select="FirstName"/>
```

When the `xsl:for-each` expression has selected a `sysUser` element, the `xsl:value-of` expression extracts and copies to the output file the value stored in the selected element. In this case, the value stored in the `FirstName` element is copied to the output. Okay, now let's revisit XPath again as it pertains to XSLT.

Using XPath Functions in XSLT

XSLT style sheets can take advantage of a large list of functions. The following functions are just a few examples that can be used in XPath queries.

count

The `count` function takes a node set, which returns a number of the nodes present in that node set. The syntax is as follows:

```
count(nodes)
```

In Listing 20.8, we are looking for the number of times Robi and Sen are repeated in the `Users.xml`.

Listing 20.8 *countenodes.xsl*

```xml
<?xml version="1.0"?>
<xsl:stylesheet version="1.0" xmlns:xsl="http://www.w3.org/1999/XSL/Transform">
    <xsl:template match="/">
        <p>Firstname equaling Robi = <xsl:value-of
select="count(Users/sysUser[FirstName='Robi'])"/></p>
        <p>Last Name equal to Sen  = <xsl:value-of
select="count(Users/sysUser[LastName='Sen'])"/></p>
    </xsl:template>
</xsl:stylesheet>
```

You can execute this style sheet with Listing 20.9.

Listing 20.9 *countnodes.cfm*

```coldfusion
<cffile action="read"  file="#ExpandPath(".")#\users.xml"  variable="myxml">

<cffile action="read" file="#ExpandPath(".")#\countnodes.xsl" variable="xslDoc">
<cfset xslAsString=ToString(xslDoc)>
<cfset mydocAsString=ToString(myxml)>
<cfset transformedXML = XmlTransform(mydocAsString, xslAsString)>
<cfoutput>#transformedXML#</cfoutput>


which will generate The output:

Firstname equals Robi = 1
LastName equals Sen = 1
```

number

The number function converts any value to a number. If the value being parsed is a string, it will return NaN (not a number).

The following code fragment examines a node set that contains a number:

```
<p>The number is: <xsl:value-of select="number(books/book/price)"/></p>
```

The resulting output would be as follows:

```
The number is: 1900
```

position

The position function returns the position value of the element in its context. Some examples of when you might use this function include when you need to insert numbering next to a list of items or when you need to test whether the position of an element is the last one (which you would test against the last function).

If you sort your elements, it will return the position in its sorted position.

Listing 20.10 inserts the number next to the description. Note that we are using the XSLT element <xsl:number> in this example.

Listing 20.10   *getposition.xsl*

```
<?xml version="1.0"?>
<xsl:stylesheet xmlns:xsl="http://www.w3.org/1999/XSL/Transform" version="1.0">
    <xsl:template match="/">
        <xsl:for-each select="price-list/price-group">
            <p><xsl:number value="position()"/>. <xsl:value-of
select="description"/></p>
        </xsl:for-each>
    </xsl:template>
</xsl:stylesheet>
```

To test our XSLT, we are going to use Listing 20.11, which will apply our style sheet to our pricelist.xml file from Chapter 19.

Listing 20.11   *Listnodes.cfm*

```
<cffile action="read"  file="#ExpandPath(".")#\pricelist.xml"  variable="myxml">
<cffile action="read" file="#ExpandPath(".")#\getposition.xsl" variable="xslDoc">
<cfset xslAsString=ToString(xslDoc)>
<cfset mydocAsString=ToString(myxml)>
<cfset transformedXML = XmlTransform(mydocAsString, xslAsString)>
<cfoutput>#transformedXML#</cfoutput>
```

The output will look like this:

1.
2.
3.
4.
5.
6.
7.

substring

The substring function returns a part of a string based on the parameters you pass to it. The format is as follows:

```
substring(value, start)
```

```
substring(value, start, length)
```

The character position (start) begins with 1.

In Listing 20.12, we are selecting the first three letters of the product name.

Listing 20.12   *getproductname.cfm*

```
<xsl:stylesheet xmlns:xsl="http://www.w3.org/1999/XSL/Transform" version="1.0">
    <xsl:template match="/">
        <xsl:for-each select="price-list/price-group">
            <p><xsl:value-of select="substring(name, 1, 3)"/></p>
        </xsl:for-each>
    </xsl:template>
</xsl:stylesheet>
```

We can call them by using Listing 20.13.

Listing 20.13   **Code to Call First Three Letters of the Product Name**

```
<cffile action="read"  file="#ExpandPath(".")#\pricelist.xml"  variable="myxml">
<cffile action="read" file="#ExpandPath(".")#\productname.xsl" variable="xslDoc">
<cfset xslAsString=ToString(xslDoc)>
<cfset mydocAsString=ToString(myxml)>
<cfset transformedXML = XmlTransform(mydocAsString, xslAsString)>
<cfdump var="#transformedXML#">
```

This will return something like:

```
Col
Koj
Fla
Jru
Win
VisDre
```

sum

The sum function calculates totals for a node set. You need to be aware of nodes that do not contain values because this function will return NaN if one of the items is not numeric (that is, empty). You will need to do formatting of your code to overcome this, replacing empty values with a 0. The syntax is as follows:

sum(*node*)

In our XML example, if we wanted to calculate the total of all the product prices, our code would read as in Listing 20.14.

Listing 20.14 *sumprices.xsl*

```
<xsl:stylesheet
xmlns:xsl="http://www.w3.org/1999/XSL/Transform" version="1.0">
   <xsl:template match="/">
        <p>Total
Price = <xsl:value-of select="sum(//list-price)"/></p>
   </xsl:template>
</xsl:stylesheet>
```

We can test this style sheet once again with Listing 20.15.

Listing 20.15 *sumprices.cfm*

```
<cffile action="read" file="#ExpandPath(".")#\pricelist.xml" variable="myxml">
<cffile action="read" file="#ExpandPath(".")#\sumprices.xsl" variable="xslDoc">
<cfset xslAsString=ToString(xslDoc)>
<cfset mydocAsString=ToString(myxml)>
<cfset transformedXML = XmlTransform(mydocAsString, xslAsString)>
<cfoutput>#transformedXML#</cfoutput>
```

The output would yield the following:

```
Total Price = 5495
```

The preceding functions are but a few of the functions you can use in XPath and XSLT. Although we have by no means exhausted the power of XPath and XSLT, you now have the basic knowledge you need to understand these technologies and how to use them with ColdFusion.

Working with WDDX

WDDX is an XML vocabulary and technology that was developed by Allaire in 1998 for describing a complex data structure—such as an array, an associative array (that is, ColdFusion structs), or a recordset—in a generic fashion.

WDDX was developed to be an open method for exchanging complex data between a variety of applications and languages, and it is currently supported in ASP, ColdFusion, Java, Python, Perl, Flash, PHP, and Tcl/Tk!

WDDX offers developers several advantages over creating their own XML language for exchanging data: It's already well supported, is very lightweight, and is extremely easy to use. You need to have almost zero knowledge of XML to use it.

> **Note**
>
> Check out www.openwddx.org. This is the WDDX site where you can download the WDDX DTD and SDK. You can also find answers to numerous questions in its forums and email list.

WDDX supports two very basic concepts for information exchange. The first of these is *serialization* of data from its native format (that is, a query recordset) into a WDDX XML format. The second is *deserialization*, or the transformation from a WDDX XML document into a native data type such as a CFML structure or a Java associative array.

In ColdFusion, you work with WDDX via the **CFWDDX** tag, which supports the following functions

- **CFML2WDDX.** Serializes CFML into WDDX
- **WDDX2CFML.** Deserializes WDDX to CFML
- **CFML2JS.** Serializes CFML to WDDX and then automatically deserializes it into JavaScript in a single step
- **WDDX2JS.** Deserializes WDDX into JavaScript

A typical **CFWDDX** tag used to convert a CFML query object to WDDX looks like this:

```
<cfwwdx action="cfml2wddx" input="#MyQueryObject#" output="WddxTextVariable">
```

In this example, `MyQueryObject` is the name of the query object variable, and `WddxTextVariable` is the name of the variable in which to store the resulting WDDX XML.

Validating WDDX Data

The `CFWDDX` tag has a `validate` attribute that you can use when converting WDDX to CFML or JavaScript. When you set this attribute to `True`, the XML parser uses the WDDX DTD to validate the WDDX data before deserializing it. If the WDDX is not valid, ColdFusion generates an error. By default, ColdFusion does not validate WDDX data before trying to convert it to ColdFusion or JavaScript data.

The `IsWDDX` function returns `True` if a variable is a valid WDDX data packet. It returns `False` otherwise. You can use this function to validate WDDX packets before converting them to another format. For example, you can use it instead of the `CFWDDX` `validate` attribute so that invalid WDDX is handled within conditional logic instead of error-handling code. You can also use it to prevalidate data that will be deserialized by JavaScript at the browser.

Using JavaScript Objects

ColdFusion provides two JavaScript objects, `WddxSerializer` and `WddxRecordset`, that you can use in JavaScript to convert data to WDDX. These objects are defined in the file *webroot*/cfide/scripts/wddx.js.

The *CFML Reference* describes these objects and their methods in detail.

Converting CFML Data to a JavaScript Object

Let's create a simple example that takes a recordset generated from `CFQUERY` and uses WDDX to convert it to JavaScript that can be processed by our browser. Take a look at Listing 20.16.

Listing 20.16 *wddxtojs.cfm*

```
<cfquery datasource="icf" name="getUsers">
SELECT User.UserID, User.UserName, User.UserPassword, User.UserFirstName,
User.UserLastName, User.UserEmail, User.UserStatus, User.UserLevelID
FROM User
</cfquery>
<!--- Load the wddx.js file, which includes the dump function --->
<script type="text/javascript" src="/CFIDE/scripts/wddx.js"></script>
<script>
  // Use WDDX to move from CFML data to JavaScript
  <cfwddx action="cfml2js" input="#getUsers#" topLevelVariable="qj">
```

continues ▶

Listing 20.16 **Continued**

```
// Dump the recordset to show that all the data has reached
// the client successfully.
document.write(qj.dump(true));
</script>
```

Note

To see how cfwddx Action="cfml2js" works, save this code under your webroot directory (for example, in wwwroot/myapps/wddxjavascript.cfm), run the page in your browser, and select View Source in your browser.

Transferring Data from the Browser to the Server

In this section, we are going to a create a more complex example that will demonstrate how you can use WDDX to exchange information between a web browser and the application server. In Listing 20.17, we serialize form field data, post it to the server, deserialize it, and then display the data. In reality, you can create very complex and sophisticated applications that exchange a large amount of data in this same way between the browser and the server using this same approach.

Also note that our example uses the WddxSerializer JavaScript object to serialize the data and the cfwddx tag to deserialize the data.

Listing 20.17 *browsertoserver.cfm*

```
<!DOCTYPE HTML PUBLIC "-//W3C//DTD HTML 4.0 Transitional//EN">
<html>
  <head>
    <title>Transferring Data from the Browser to the Server</title>
    <script language="JavaScript" type="text/javascript"
src="/CFIDE/scripts/wddx.js"></script>
    <script language="JavaScript" type="text/javascript">
    <!--
      // Generic serialization to a form field
      function serializeData(data, formField)
      {
        if(document.personForm.firstName.value || document.personForm.lastName.value)
          doNext();
        wddxSerializer = new WddxSerializer();
        wddxPacket = wddxSerializer.serialize(data);
        if (wddxPacket != null)
          formField.value = wddxPacket;
        else
```

```
          alert('Couldn\'t serialize data');
        }

        // Person info recordset with columns firstName and lastName
        // Make sure the case of field names is preserved
        var personInfo = new WddxRecordset(new Array('firstName', 'lastName'), true);
        // Add next record to end of personInfo recordset

        function doNext()
        {
          // Extract data
          var firstName = document.personForm.firstName.value;
          var lastName = document.personForm.lastName.value;

          // User must enter at least first name or last name.
          if(!firstName && !lastName)
          {
            alert('You must enter a first name and/or last name.');
            return;
          }

          // Add names to recordset
          nRows = personInfo.getRowCount();
          personInfo.firstName[nRows] = firstName;
          personInfo.lastName[nRows] = lastName;

          // Clear input fields
          document.personForm.firstName.value = '';
          document.personForm.lastName.value = '';

          // Show added names on list
          var newName = firstName + ' ' + lastName;
          newIndex = document.personForm.names.options.length;
          document.personForm.names.options.length =
document.personForm.names.options.length + 1;
          document.personForm.names.options[newIndex].text = newName;
          document.personForm.names.options[newIndex].value = newName;
        }
      // -->
      </script>
   </head>
<cfoutput>
<!--- Data collection form --->
<form action="#cgi.script_name#" name="personForm" method="post">
  <h1>Step 1.</h1>
  <p>Add as many names as you like.</p>
  <!--- Input fields --->
  First name: <input type="text" name="firstName"><br>
  Last name: <input type="text" name="lastName"><br>
  <!--- button to add name to list --->
  <input type="button" value="Next" onclick="doNext(); this.form.firstName.focus()">
  <br><br>
```

continues ▶

Listing 20.17   **Continued**

```
<h1>Step 2.</h1>
<p>Serialize the names in to a WDDX Packet.</p>
Names added so far:<br>
<select name="names" size="5">
</select><br>
<!--- button to serialize names in to wddx packet --->
<input type="button" value="Serialize" onclick="serializeData(personInfo,
document.personForm.wddxPacket)">
<br><br>
<h1>Step 3.</h1>
<p>Send WDDX Packet to the server.</p>
<!--- This is where the WDDX packet will be stored --->
<!--- In a real application this would be a hidden input field. --->
WDDX packet display:<br>
<textarea name="wddxPacket" rows="10" cols="80" wrap="virtual"></textarea><br>
<!--- button to submit wddx packet --->
<input type="submit" value="Submit">
</form>
</cfoutput>
<!--- Server-side processing --->
<hr>
<strong>Server-side processing</strong>
<br><br>
<cfparam name="form.wddxPacket" default="">
<cfif Len(form.wddxPacket)>
  <cfif IsWDDX(form.wddxPacket)>
    <!--- Deserialize the WDDX data --->
    <cfwddx action="wddx2cfml" input="#form.wddxPacket#" output="personInfo">
    <!--- Display the query --->
    The submitted personal information is:<br>
    <cfoutput query="personInfo">
      Person #currentrow#: #firstName# #lastName#<br>
    </cfoutput>
  <cfelse>
    The client did not send a well-formed WDDX data packet!
  </cfif>
</cfif>
</body>
</html>
```

Storing Complex Data

A major use of WDDX in ColdFusion is to store complex data. The simple
example in Listing 20.18 uses WDDX to store complex data, a data structure
that contains arrays as a string in a client variable. It uses the CFDUMP tag to
display the contents of the structure before serialization and after deserializa-

tion. It uses the HTMLEditFormat function in a CFOUTPUT tag to display the contents of the client variable. The HTMLEditFormat function is required to prevent the browser from trying to interpret (and throw away) the XML tags in the variable.

Listing 20.18 *wddxStruct.cfm*

```
<cfapplication name="relatives" clientmanagement="Yes">

<cfscript>
  Order = structNew();
  Order.OrderID = 002;
  Order.OrderNum = 002;
  Order.OrderDate = "01/01/01";
  Order.ShipDate = "01/28/01";
  Order.ShipName = "Francis";
  Order.ShipAddress = "128 Maine Street";

</cfscript>
<br>
<cfdump var="#Order#"><br>
<br>
<!--- Convert data structure to string form and save it in the
      client scope --->
<cfwddx action="cfml2wddx" input="#Order#" output="Client.wddxOrder">
The contents of the Client.Order variable:<br>
<cfoutput>#HtmlEditFormat(Client.wddxOrder)#</cfoutput><br>
<br>
<!--- Now read the data from client scope into a new structure --->
<cfwddx action="wddx2cfml" input="#Client.wddxOrder#" output="OrderBack">
A dump of the wddxOrder structure <br>
generated from client.wddxOrder<br>
<br>
<cfdump var="#OrderBack#">
```

As you can see, WDDX is probably the most simple and easy-to-use XML technology out there. Using WDDX, you can create simple content and data syndication applications, e-commerce systems, internal data-storage systems, and much more. You can even use WDDX along with web services as a payload.

Summary

We have covered a lot of information in this chapter, everything from the basics of XML through XPath, XSLT, the DOM, ColdFusion XML functionality, and WDDX. Many of the topics covered in this chapter require whole books to do them justice. To become an XML guru, you will need to put in more time than just reading these chapters, but you should now have the foundation and basic understanding to solve most XML-related tasks or problems you might encounter when developing applications in ColdFusion.

In the next chapter, we are going to look at one of the newest and most exciting features of ColdFusion MX—web services.

21

Web Services and ColdFusion

IN THIS CHAPTER, YOU WILL LEARN ABOUT THE web service paradigm, how to use ColdFusion components (CFCs) to create web services, and how to invoke web services. Although ColdFusion MX web services have some limitations, they are the easiest web service implementation to use. Before we get into the implementation details, though, let's make sure we share a common understanding of what a web service is.

Web Service Basics

Web services have become a hot topic these days with vendors hyping their web service implementations and technologies, yet few people seem to be able to agree on what a web service really is. Figure 21.1 should give you some idea of what web services actually entail.

One of the major players in helping to define web services is IBM. The company defines web services in part as "… self-contained, modular business process applications, which are based on open, Internet standards. Using the technologies of WSDL (to describe), UDDI (to advertise and syndicate), and SOAP (to communicate), web services can be mixed and matched to create innovative applications, processes, and value chains" (see www-3.ibm.com/software/solutions/webservices/overview.html#webservices).

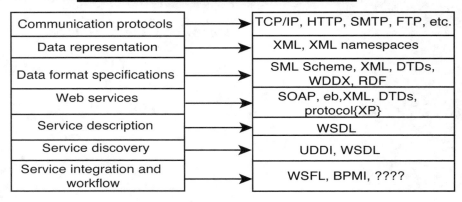

Figure 21.1 The different technologies, standards, and protocols that make up the web services paradigm.

As you can see, web services are more than just software components/objects because they can describe their own functionality and look for and dynamically interact with other web services. Web services provide a means for different organizations to connect their applications with one another to conduct dynamic e-business across a network, no matter what their application, design, or runtime environment. From a business standpoint, web services offer a new range of possibilities for how organizations and their partners develop business solutions. For years, in building applications, you had to know who was using the applications as well as how, when, where, and for what. These were the boundaries within which you used to have to create and use applications. Now, with ColdFusion MX and web services, you can build applications without having to know who the user is, where he is, or anything else about him. And as a user of these applications, you can source them as easily as you would be able to source static data on the web, only with greater freedom and little concern about the format, platform, or anything else.

Even more exciting, web services are self-integrating with other web service applications. Until now, using traditional software tools and methodologies to make two technologies work together required lots of work and planning: You had to agree on the standards to pass data (very time-consuming), the protocols, the platforms, and so on. Now, with web services, applications written to the new standards will be able to automatically integrate with each other from wherever they originate.

Currently, web services are just in the infant stage and are slowly emerging as a paradigm shift in application development—a shift akin to switching from procedural coding to object-oriented coding. ColdFusion MX is helping lead the way with its initial vision of web services. Macromedia, with ColdFusion MX, has made web services as easy as CFQUERY made database access.

Note

Here are some great web services–related links to check out:

- www.alphaworks.ibm.com
- www.webservices.org
- www.wWebservicesarchitect.com
- www.xml.com
- www.w3.org/2002/ws/
- xml.apache.org/axis/index.html

ColdFusion MX uses the Apache AXIS engine to provide its web service functionality. AXIS is by far the most popular Java-based web services implementation. ColdFusion MX currently enables you to do two of the five major functions of web services: service description and invocation. The five major functional goals of web services are as follows:

- **Service description.** ColdFusion enables you to describe your web services via WSDL.
- **Service publication.** Lets you publish your web services to a registry via UDDI.
- **Service discovery.** Automated discovery and analysis of remote services via UDDI and WSDL.
- **Service invocation.** Provides a standard-based method of invocation via SOAP and WSDL.
- **Service composing.** The capability to compose or coordinate with other web services using SOAP, WSDL, UDDI, and emerging technologies sets of web services into complex work flows and process flows.

Note

Although ColdFusion MX supports only two of the five major functional blocks of web services as defined by the W3C and various web services groups, almost no products support more than three or four functional groups. Service composition, in particular, is an emerging field in which various vendors (such as Microsoft and IBM) are pushing to have their various solutions to that area adopted by the web service community at large.

The following sections describe the components of ColdFusion MX's web service engine, as shown in Figure 21.2.

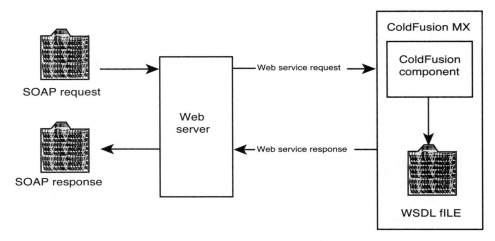

Figure 21.2 The basic architecture of ColdFusion MX's web service engine.

The Web Service Paradigm

Although most definitions of web services seem to imply that you must use SOAP, WSDL, and UDDI, this is certainly not the case. Web services are a paradigm, with .NET and AXIS being specific instances and implementations of that paradigm. Web services' main features are description, discovery, and publication, and you could use any series of technologies and protocols to accomplish this. Vendors and the web service community as a whole, though, are trying to agree on XML recommendations and to create standards for the creation of web services to guarantee maximum application interoperability.

Communication

SOAP provides a standard XML structure for sending and receiving information, much like SMTP. SOAP is often used in web services implementations to "hold" a message or data, and it often contains information in its header that describes where it is from, where it needs to go, how it needs to be handled, and so on. SOAP messages typically use HTTP as a transport layer, but you could use FTP, SMTP, JMS, or any other protocol.

In ColdFusion MX, consuming or publishing web services does not require you to be familiar with SOAP or to perform any SOAP operations. However, you should still make sure you read up on SOAP at the W3C web site (www.w3c.org).

Description and Discovery

A WSDL document is an XML file that describes a web service's purpose, where it is located, and how to access it. The WSDL document describes the operations you can invoke and their associated data types.

ColdFusion MX generates a WSDL document for a web service you create and lets you display it as a URL to provide information to potential clients. We will discuss this in greater depth later in the chapter.

Finding Web Services with UDDI

As a consumer of web services, you want to know what web services are available. As a producer of web services, you want others to be able to find information about your web services. Universal Description, Discovery, and Integration (UDDI) provides a mechanism for clients to dynamically find other web services. Using a UDDI interface, businesses can dynamically connect to services provided by external business partners. A UDDI registry is similar to a CORBA trader, or it can be thought of as a DNS service for business applications. A UDDI registry has two kinds of clients: businesses that want to publish a service (and its usage interfaces), and clients who want to obtain services of a certain kind and bind programmatically to them.

Although ColdFusion does not directly support UDDI, you can manually register or find a web service using a public UDDI registry such as the IBM UDDI Business Registry at `https://www-3.ibm.com/services/uddi/protect/registry.html`.

You can find additional information about UDDI
`http://www.uddi.org/about.html`.

Invoking a Web Service

Working with and invoking web services from ColdFusion is amazingly simple. In many ways, it's like calling a custom tag or CFC in which you pass a method, parameters, and point to a specific URI.

Let's just jump into an example, and we will explain it line by line. Take a look at Listing 21.1.

Listing 21.1 *getTemp.cfm*

```
<cfinvoke webservice="http://www.xmethods.net/sd/2001/TemperatureService.wsdl"
 method="getTemp"
 zipcode="80526"
 returnVariable="theTemp">
</cfinvoke>
<cfoutput>#theTemp#</cfoutput>
```

This listing calls a web service that provides temperature information for a specific zip code. The first thing you will notice is that we use `CFINVOKE` with an attribute called `webservice` with a value that's a URI to a WSDL file. WSDL files are XML descriptions of the API for a specific service or portion of a service, and they are published by various providers so that developers like us know how to interact with their service.

The WSDL file usually provides you with the following:

- Methods/operations of a web service
- Input parameters that you pass to each operation
- Return values from an operation

The WSDL file is very important. First, you need to have the URL to the WSDL of whatever service you want to use. Second, inside the WSDL file is important information that we need to help us figure out what parameters and methods we need to pass to the service.

First let's look at the Temperature Service WSDL file. Go ahead and use your IE browser and look at `www.xmethods.net/sd/2001/TemperatureService.wsdl`. You should see something like Listing 21.2.

Listing 21.2   *TemperatureService.wsdl*

```xml
<?xml version="1.0" ?>
 <definitions name="TemperatureService"
targetNamespace=http://www.xmethods.net/sd/TemperatureService.wsdl
xmlns:tns=http://www.xmethods.net/sd/TemperatureService.wsdl
xmlns:xsd=http://www.w3.org/2001/XMLSchema
xmlns:soap=http://schemas.xmlsoap.org/wsdl/soap/
xmlns="http://schemas.xmlsoap.org/wsdl/">
  <message name="getTempRequest">
    <part name="zipcode" type="xsd:string" />
  </message>
  <message name="getTempResponse">
    <part name="return" type="xsd:float" />
  </message>
  <portType name="TemperaturePortType">
    <operation name="getTemp">
       <input message="tns:getTempRequest" />
       <output message="tns:getTempResponse" />
    </operation>
  </portType>
  <binding name="TemperatureBinding" type="tns:TemperaturePortType">
    <soap:binding style="rpc" transport="http://schemas.xmlsoap.org/soap/http" />
    <operation name="getTemp">
     <soap:operation soapAction="" />
```

```
        <input>
            <soap:body use="encoded" namespace="urn:xmethods-Temperature"
encodingStyle="http://schemas.xmlsoap.org/soap/encoding/" />
        </input>
        <output>
            <soap:body use="encoded" namespace="urn:xmethods-Temperature"
encodingStyle="http://schemas.xmlsoap.org/soap/encoding/" />
        </output>
    </operation>
  </binding>
  <service name="TemperatureService">
    <documentation>Returns current temperature in a given U.S. zipcode</documentation>
    <port name="TemperaturePort" binding="tns:TemperatureBinding">
        <soap:address location="http://services.xmethods.net:80/soap/servlet/rpcrouter"
/>
    </port>
  </service>
</definitions>
```

At first glance, the WSDL file might be a little much to read, but it's actually very straightforward. The WSDL has several major elements with the message element being of greatest concern to us, but let's step through the file first.

The root element of the WSDL file is definitions that basically hold various namespaces to avoid naming conflicts with public services. The next major element in a WSDL file is types that define data types for the services. The next element that is of greatest importance to us is the message element. The message element defines the name and data types for the input parameters as well as the return values, and this is where we got the information for these two lines

```
method="getTemp"
zipcode="80526"
```

in our CFINVOKE tag from the WSDL file:

```
<message name="getTempRequest">
  <part name="zipcode" type="xsd:string" />
</message>
<message name="getTempResponse">
  <part name="return" type="xsd:float" />
</message>
```

This tells us that we can call a method "getTempRequest" by passing it a zip code as a string, and it will return the temperature as a floating-point number. This section is very important in that it tells you not only what to provide the web service but what to expect back and how. Oftentimes, your web service will return a data type such as an array or another complex data type that ColdFusion deals with as a structure. The conversions between ColdFusion and web service data types are shown in Table 21.1.

Table 21.1 **Data Type Relations Between ColdFusion and WSDL**

ColdFusion Data Type	WSDL Data Type
numeric	SOAP-ENC:double
boolean	SOAP-ENC:boolean
string	SOAP-ENC:string
array	SOAP-ENC:Array
binary	xsd:base64Binary
date	xsd:dateTime
struct	complex type

The next major element is the porttype, which tells us what operations are provided by this web service. After that, we have the operation element that defines the service that can be remotely called. Then we have the elements input and output that define the parameters needed for inputs and outputs.

The WSDL file might also have a fault element that defines an error message that should be thrown in the case of an exception. Next we have the element binding, which tells us what protocols we can use to access this web service. The binding element is very important in that ColdFusion can only consume web services that:

- Use RPC as the soap binding style.
- Use encoding as the encodingStyle.

If you look at the WSDL for this service, you will see that it supports both:

```
<soap:binding style="rpc" transport="http://schemas.xmlsoap.org/soap/http" />
    <operation name="getTemp">
      <soap:operation soapAction="" />
      <input>
        <soap:body use="encoded" namespace="urn:xmethods-Temperature"
encodingStyle="http://schemas.xmlsoap.org/soap/encoding/" />
      </input>
      <output>
        <soap:body use="encoded" namespace="urn:xmethods-Temperature"
encodingStyle="http://schemas.xmlsoap.org/soap/encoding/" />
      </output>
    </operation>
  </binding>
```

We also have the element service, which defines any related service and, in some cases, provides documentation for the web service. Finally, we have the element port, which defines the address for the web service. So, with this basic knowledge, you can parse a WSDL file and figure out what information you need to invoke a web service.

In general, when calling or consuming a web service, you will end up using the following general form:

```
<cfinvoke
  webservice = "URLtoWSDL"
  method = "operationName"
  inputParam1 = "val1"
  inputParam2 = "val2"
  ...
  returnVariable = "anyVariableName"
/>
```

CFINVOKE has several attributes that you need to provide when invoking a web service. The first is webservice, which specifies the URL to the WSDL file for the web service. The next attribute, method, specifies the operation of the web service to invoke, which in our example was getTemp. Next, if your webservice calls for it, you need to define parameters that need to be passed, which could be one or many. In our example, we just had zipcode="". Finally, you need to define returnVariable, which is a ColdFusion variable you define that will hold the return results from your web service if there are any.

Sometimes, if you have to pass many parameters, you will want to use the CFARGUMENT tag, which is nested inside the CFINVOKE tag as follows:

```
<cfinvoke
  webservice = "URLtoWSDL"
  method = "operationName"
  returnVariable = "anyVariableName"
/>
<cfinvokeargument name="someparam" value="1">
<cfinvokeargument name=" someparam" value="2">
</cfinvoke>
```

This is especially useful if you are creating web services that need to build the parameters dynamically. If you are trying to pass a complex array of parameters, you can do something like this:

```
<cfscript>
  stParameters = structNew();
  stParameters.parameter1 = "1";
  stParameters.parameter2 = "2";
  stParameters.parameter3 = "3";
  stParameters.parameter4 = "4";
</cfscript>
<cfinvoke
  webservice = "URL"
  method     = "methodname"
  argumentCollection = "#stParameters#"
  returnVariable = "varName"
  >
<cfoutput>#varName#</cfoutput>
```

So, as you can see with this example, we can build a structure of our parameters and pass that to the web service.

We can also consume web services using CFSCRIPT and the function CreateObject. Listing 21.3 provides an example.

Listing 21.3 *getTemp2.cfm*

```
<cfscript>
  ws = CreateObject("webservice",
      "http://www.xmethods.net/sd/2001/TemperatureService.wsdl");
  resultVar = ws.getTemp("80526");
  writeoutput(resultVar);
</cfscript>
```

In CFScript, you use the CreateObject function to connect to the web service. After connecting, you can make requests to the service. The general form for calling a web service with CFScript is as follows:

```
webServiceName = CreateObject("webservice", "URLtoWSDL")
```

After you have created the object, you can invoke the web service via dot notation:

```
webServiceName.operationName(inputVal1, inputVal2, ... )
```

The input values are the names of the parameters you want to pass. You can also name the parameters as follows:

```
ws.getTemp(zipcode="80526");
```

Or in the general form:

```
webServiceName.operationName(parametername="inputVal1", parametername="inputVal2", ... )
```

Using this name-value-pair approach is probably the better coding practice in that it's much easier to understand when inspecting the code.

To deal with the return value, you just assign the web service to a ColdFusion variable:

```
resultVar = webServiceName.operationName(inputVal1, inputVal2, ... );
```

Or you can directly deal with them by assigning them to a function, as follows:

```
writeoutput(webServiceName.operationName(inputVal1, inputVal2, ...) );
```

You might find it annoying to have to cut and paste or type the WSDL URLs, especially if you are creating a series of templates or functions that perform different requests on the same service. ColdFusion enables you to map a name to a web service in the Administrator so that you can refer to a web service by that name instead of the URL to the WSDL file. In fact, every time you invoke a web service for the first time, ColdFusion automatically registers it for you in the Administrator, and you can just go in and edit it to assign it a mapping. This enables you to change an invocation from this

```
<cfscript>
  ws = CreateObject("webservice",
       "http://www.xmethods.net/sd/2001/TemperatureService.wsdl");
  resultVar = ws.getTemp("80526");
  writeoutput(resultVar);
</cfscript>
```

to this:

```
<cfscript>
  ws = CreateObject("webservice", "TemperatureService");
  resultVar = ws.getTemp("80526");
  writeoutput(resultVar);
</cfscript>
```

Another advantage of doing things this way is that you can change the URL to the WSDL file in the ColdFusion mapping at any time without having to change all the code you've written that calls those WSDL files.

Consuming your own ColdFusion web services is actually even easier than working with web services that have not been created using ColdFusion. To call ColdFusion web services, you follow the same procedure as you would with a regular web service. Let's make one right now. First create a file called **square.cfc** and save it under your webroot, as shown in Listing 21.4.

Listing 21.4   *square.cfc*

```
<cfcomponent>
  <cffunction name="square"
              returnType="string"
              access="remote">
    <cfargument name="num1" type="string">
    <cfset sum = arguments.num1 * arguments.num1>
    <cfreturn sum>
  </cffunction>
</cfcomponent>
```

Now open up IE and type in the URL to your CFC, but after square.cfc, type **?WSDL** so that you have the following:

```
http://localhost:8100/xml/webservice/square.cfc?wsdl
```

Then view the WSDL:

```
<?xml version="1.0" encoding="UTF-8" ?>
<wsdl:definitions targetNamespace="http://webservice.xml"
xmlns:wsdl="http://schemas.xmlsoap.org/wsdl/"
xmlns:xsd="http://www.w3.org/2001/XMLSchema"
xmlns:wsdlsoap="http://schemas.xmlsoap.org/wsdl/soap/"
xmlns:intf="http://webservice.xml" xmlns:impl="http://webservice.xml-impl" xmlns:SOAP-
ENC="http://schemas.xmlsoap.org/soap/encoding/"
xmlns="http://schemas.xmlsoap.org/wsdl/">
  <wsdl:message name="CFCInvocationException" />
 <wsdl:message name="squareResponse">
  <wsdl:part name="return" type="SOAP-ENC:string" />
  </wsdl:message>
 <wsdl:message name="squareRequest">
  <wsdl:part name="num1" type="SOAP-ENC:string" />
  </wsdl:message>
 <wsdl:portType name="square">
 <wsdl:operation name="square" parameterOrder="num1">
  <wsdl:input message="intf:squareRequest" />
  <wsdl:output message="intf:squareResponse" />
  <wsdl:fault name="CFCInvocationException" message="intf:CFCInvocationException" />
  </wsdl:operation>
  </wsdl:portType>
 <wsdl:binding name="square.cfcSoapBinding" type="intf:square">
  <wsdlsoap:binding style="rpc" transport="http://schemas.xmlsoap.org/soap/http" />
 <wsdl:operation name="square">
  <wsdlsoap:operation soapAction="" />
 <wsdl:input>
  <wsdlsoap:body use="encoded"
encodingStyle="http://schemas.xmlsoap.org/soap/encoding/"
namespace="http://webservice.xml" />
  </wsdl:input>
 <wsdl:output>
  <wsdlsoap:body use="encoded"
encodingStyle="http://schemas.xmlsoap.org/soap/encoding/"
namespace="http://webservice.xml" />
  </wsdl:output>
  </wsdl:operation>
  </wsdl:binding>
 <wsdl:service name="squareService">
 <wsdl:port name="square.cfc" binding="intf:square.cfcSoapBinding">
  <wsdlsoap:address location="http://localhost:8100/xml/webservice/square.cfc" />
  </wsdl:port>
  </wsdl:service>
  </wsdl:definitions>
```

Whenever you create a CFC with the access set to remote and then request
the web service, ColdFusion automatically creates a WSDL file for you so
that you don't have to bother with it.

To call our web service, we do the same thing as before: We provide it with the URL to the WSDL file, the method (which is `square`), and a parameter (which is `NUM1`). See Listing 21.5.

Listing 21.5   *getSquare*

```
<cfinvoke webservice="http://localhost:8100/xml/webservice/square.cfc?wsdl"
  method="square"
  num1="5"
  returnVariable="var1">
</cfinvoke>
<cfdump var="#var1#">
```

If you call this service in your browser, you will get 25 as the result.

Sometimes, though, you are going to want to try to work with a web service that handles what are called "complex types of data."

```
<cfscript>
  stExch = structNew();
  stExch.currency = "DEM";
 stExch.amount = 100;
 stExch.toCurrency = "EUR";
   ws = createObject("webservice",
"http://www.shinkatech.com/interop/CurrencyConverter.wsdl");
  ws.calculateExchangeRate(stExch);
</cfscript>
```

This web service calls a service that converts currencies but expects to receive its parameters as a complex data type. If you look at the WSDL file that can be found at `http://www.shinkatech.com/interop/ CurrencyConverter.wsdl`, you will notice that the web service expects three parameters like this:

```
<complexType name="ConvertMessage">
 <all>
  <element name="currency" type="CurrencySchema:CurrencySymbol" />
  <element name="amount" type="double" />
  <element name="toCurrency" type="CurrencySchema:CurrencySymbol" />
  </all>
  </complexType>
```

In the specific case in which applications are requesting a complex data type, you can do what we have done in the example: build a ColdFusion structure that models the complex data type and then pass the structure to the web service.

Building Web Services

We actually just produced a web service and consumed it, and we did it without knowing almost anything about SOAP or WSDL. Producing web services in ColdFusion is incredibly simple, much simpler than if you tried to do it directly with Java and AXIS and even easier than building web services with .NET!

ColdFusion web services are built around CFCs, which provide a simple and elegant method for defining your web services (see Chapter 6, "ColdFusion Components").

In the preceding section, we made a CFC called square.cfc that we made remotely accessible using the access attribute and setting it to remote. If you want to use a CFC as a web service, you must set the access attribute to remote.

That's all there is to making a simple web service. Things get a little more complex, though, when you try to work with ColdFusion web services you create that use parameters of type struct or query in that they do not directly map to a WSDL data type. (If you are working with a ColdFusion application that's going to consume a web service with parameter types of query or struct, you do not need to worry in that ColdFusion correctly handles these complex data types.)

The problem with structures stems from their capability to hold an unlimited number of key-value pairs, where the values can be of any ColdFusion data type. Because of this, it cannot be directly mapped to any XML data types defined in the SOAP 1.1 encoding and XML Schema specification.

ColdFusion structures are treated as a custom type, and the complex type in the XML Schema in WSDL looks like this:

```
<complexType name="Map">
  <sequence>
    <element name="item" minOccurs="0" maxOccurs="unbounded">
      <complexType>
        <all>
          <element name="key" type="xsd:anyType" />
          <element name="value" type="xsd:anyType" />
        </all>
      </complexType>
    </element>
  </sequence>
</complexType>
```

This complex type defines a representation of a structure, where the structure keys and values can be any type.

In the WSDL mapping of a ColdFusion structure, each key-value pair in the structure points to the next element in the structure (such as a linked list) except for the final field, which contains a value.

ColdFusion queries also can cause issues, and ColdFusion publishes `query` data types as the WSDL type `QueryBean`. The `QueryBean` data type contains two elements, as illustrated here:

```
<complexType name="QueryBean">
  <all>
    <element name="data" nillable="true" type="intf:ArrayOf_SOAP-ENC_Array" />
    <element name="ColumnList" nillable="true"
type="intf:ArrayOf_SOAP-ENC_string" />
  </all>
</complexType>
```

The two elements of `QueryBean` are as follows:

- **ColumnList**. A string array that contains column names
- **data**. A two-dimensional array that contains query data

The WSDL file for a `QueryBean` defines these elements as follows:

```
<complexType name="ArrayOf_SOAP-ENC_Array">
  <complexContent>
    <restriction base="SOAP-ENC:Array">
      <attribute ref="SOAP-ENC:arrayType" wsdl:arrayType="SOAP-ENC:Array[]" />
    </restriction>
  </complexContent>
</complexType>
<complexType name="ArrayOf_SOAP-ENC_string">
  <complexContent>
  <restriction base="SOAP-ENC:Array">
    <attribute ref="SOAP-ENC:arrayType" wsdl:arrayType="xsd:string[]" />
  </restriction>
  </complexContent>
</complexType>
```

You need to be aware of these issues when you're creating your own web services that need to interoperate with other systems like .NET. One way around this potential hurdle is to just pass the record set as WDDX instead of using a complex type of query. Almost every application platform can consume WDDX, and it's a lot easier than trying to programmatically deal with the ColdFusion MX `QueryBean` complex type.

Other Web Service Options with ColdFusion

Although using CFCs and CFINVOKE is the easiest way of working with web services through ColdFusion, it's not the only way. You could also just as easily use CFHTTP to POST a SOAP message to a web service, although because CFHTTP does not let you send customer headers along with your post operation, you would be limited. With CFOBJECT and Java, though, you can perform a whole host of operations that you cannot do with ColdFusion web services by directly calling other web service products such as AXIS. For more information on working with CFOBJECT, see Chapter 22, "Leveraging J2EE."

Summary

In this chapter, we covered the basics of the web service paradigm, how to use CFCs to create web services, and how to invoke web services. Although ColdFusion MX web services have some limitations, they are the easiest web service implementation to use, and if need be, you can leverage AXIX directly or even other web service implementations by using CFOBJECT as described in Chapter 22.

22

Leveraging J2EE

As you already know, ColdFusion MX was developed in Java and runs on top of a J2EE application server. This is an exciting step for Macromedia, which has chosen to broaden the reach of ColdFusion by making it runnable on a number of new platforms and on application servers from IBM, Sun, and BEA, as well as their own JRun.

Users in the Java world will get to know the easy and rapid development possible with ColdFusion, while ColdFusion developers will get the unparalleled performance, scalability, robustness, and reliability of the mature J2EE architecture.

Another wonderful thing about Macromedia's approach to developing ColdFusion in Java and on top of J2EE application servers is its new and improved support for integrating with J2EE technologies. This enables you to develop in ColdFusion as well as Java Server Pages (JSP), Java Servlets, Java classes, and Enterprise Java Beans (EJBs); and you can seamlessly integrate with legacy and existing J2EE applications and systems.

In this chapter, we are going to show you how to work with JSP, Java Server tag libraries, Java Servlets, and various Java objects such as generic classes and Enterprise Java Beans.

We will not be providing a Java tutorial, however; so if you don't have a background in Java, you should look to the many excellent books on the subjects of J2EE and Java.

A Bit of Background on J2EE

The Java 2 Platform, Enterprise Edition (J2EE) is a Sun Microsystems standard for developing multitier enterprise applications in Java. The J2EE standard defines standardized, modular components, a set of services for those components, and the handling of many details of application behavior automatically. Vendors such as Macromedia, IBM, BEA, AGI, and many others then develop their products to conform to those standards while often adding proprietary, value-added services to differentiate their products from their competitors'.

J2EE offers all the features of the basic Java 2 platform, such as portability, the JDBC API for database access, CORBA technology for interaction with existing enterprise resources, and a security model that protects data even in Internet applications. J2EE extends this with support for Enterprise Java Beans components, the Java Servlets API, Java Server Pages, the Java Messaging Service, XML technology, and more.

ColdFusion and JSP

JSP is a tag-based language much like ColdFusion or Active Server Pages. Developers work with or create their own JSP tags in much the same way that ColdFusion developers do. ColdFusion enables you to directly invoke JSP pages, share various forms of variable scopes, pass standard HTTP data types to each other, and hyperlink to each other.

The most common situation in which you will work with JSP and ColdFusion is when calling a JSP page from a ColdFusion template or when calling a ColdFusion template from a JSP page.

For example, if you want to access a JSP page called `hello.jsp` from a ColdFusion template, you could do something like what is shown in Listing 22.1.

Listing 22.1 *getjsp.cfm*

```
<cfscript>
GetPageContext().include("hey.jsp");
</cfscript>
```

In this CFM template, we use a special function called `GetPageContext` with either the `forward` or `include` method. The methods work just like they do in JSP because ColdFusion pages are J2EE Servlet pages, and thus all ColdFusion pages have an underlying Java `PageContext` object as well. CFML includes the `GetPageContext` object that you can use with JSPs and Servlets.

If you want to pass a URL parameter to the same page, you would just do this:

```
<cfscript>
GetPageContext().include("hey.jsp?name=value");
</cfscript>
```

Your ColdFusion and JSP pages can also share data that's contained in the application, request, and session scopes. To do this, however you need to make sure you have the Use J2EE session variables option selected in your ColdFusion Administrator.

Look at the example shown in Listing 22.2.

Listing 22.2   *testvars.cfm*

```
<cfapplication name="testscope" sessionmanagement="yes">
<cflock scope="application" type="exclusive" timeout="10">
  <cfset application.appvar = "This is an Application Scoped Var">
</cflock>
<cfset request.reqvar = "This is a Request Scoped Var">
<cflock scope="session" type="exclusive" timeout="10">
  <cfset session.sessionvar = "This is a Session Scoped Var">
</cflock>
<cfscript>
  GetPageContext().include('testvars.jsp?name=Robi%20Sen');
</cfscript>
```

Now let's create a JSP page, as shown in Listing 22.3, to grab all these variables we have set.

Listing 22.3   *testvars.jsp*

```
<%@page import="java.util.*" %>
<h2>URL param passes was <%= request.getParameter("name")%>!</h2>
<br>request.myVariable: <%= request.getAttribute("reqvar")%>
<br>session.myVariable: <%=
((Map)session.getAttribute("testscope")).get("sessoinvar")%>
<br>application.myVariable: <%= application.getAttribute("application.appvar")%>
```

So, if you call the CFML template in your browser, you see that the variables have been passed.

It's just as easy to do the opposite as well. For example, to do the same thing but call a CFML template from JSP, we could follow the same pattern to do what is shown in Listing 22.4.

Listing 22.4 *cfmlvarsfromjsp.jsp*

```
<%@page import="java.util.*" %>
<% request.setAttribute("reqvar", "This is a Request Scoped Var");%>
<% ((Map)session.getAttribute("testscope")).put("sessoinvar", "This is a session
Scoped Var");%>
<% application.setAttribute("testscope.appvar", "This is a application Scoped Var");%>
<jsp:include page="getvarsfromjsp.cfm">
    <jsp:param name="name" value="Robi Sen" />
</jsp:include>
```

To get the variables from the JSP page, we would just use the code shown in Listing 22.5.

Listing 22.5 *getvarsfromjsp.cfm*

```
<cfapplication name="testscope" sessionmanagement="yes">
<cfoutput>
<h2>URL param passed from JSP is #URL.name#!</h2>
Request.myVariable: #Request.myVariable#<br>
Session.myVariable: #Session.myVariable#<br>
Application.myVariable: #Application.myVariable#<br>
</cfoutput>
```

As you can see, it's easy enough to work with JSPs, and you can use the exact same approach to working with Servlets. Finally, you have another option when trying to work with JSPs and Servlets—you can use CFHTTP to pass form or URL variables as defined in Chapter 16, "Further Extending Your Applications."

Using Tag Libraries

JSP offers developers a paradigm very similar to ColdFusion for extending the base JSP tag set. Just like ColdFusion, in JSP you can create custom tags, and JSP developers often create whole libraries that encapsulate functionality. (Check out the JRun exchange at www.macromedia.com to see downloadable JSP tag libraries.) To use JSP tag libraries in your ColdFusion applications, you can import them by putting the tag library—consisting of the taglibname.jar file and the taglibname.tld file—in the web_root/ WEB-INF/lib directory.

In the ColdFusion template where you are going to call your JSP tags, you need to specify the tag library name in a cfimport tag. For example:

```
<cfimport taglib="/WEB-INF/lib/customtags.jar" prefix="customtags">
```

Mixing JSPs and ColdFusion

In ColdFusion MX, you can actually mix JSP tags inside ColdFusion templates but not inside your CFML. For example, you can do something like this:

```
<cfimport taglib="/WEB-INF/lib/jruntags.jar" prefix="jrun" >

<jrun:sql datasrc="icf" id="product">
Select product_name from product
</jrun:sql>

<cfinclude template="helloworld.jsp" >
<cfscript>
getPageContext().include("helloworld.jsp");
</cfscript>
```

Although this provides you with access to powerful JSP tag libraries directly in your ColdFusion applications, it can become very confusing to developers who are not familiar with JSP and Java. So make sure you use JSP and Java appropriately in your development team.

Working with Java Classes and Java Beans

Ever since ColdFusion 4.5, developers have been able to call Java class files directly from CFOBJECT. Since then, Macromedia has made great strides in increasing the capability of CFOBJECT to work with Java classes and EJBs and in increasing CFOBJECT's robustness and performance.

Before you use any Java class with CFOBJECT, you have to make sure it is specified in the Java classpath in the ColdFusion Administrator. You might also have ColdFusion automatically or dynamically load your classes by putting any class you are working with in either of these directories:

- In a Java archive (.jar) file in web_root/WEB-INF/lib
- In a class (.class) file in web_root/WEB-INF/classes

> **Note**
>
> Dynamic class loading is really a feature meant to help speed up your development process and make your life easier, but it should not be used in production. This is because it causes performance issues due to ColdFusion having to check time stamps during disk I/O operations. So make sure you use just the classpath to register classes in production.

ColdFusion checks the time stamp on the file when it creates an object that is defined in either directory, even when the class is already in memory. If the file that contains the class is newer than the class in memory, ColdFusion loads the class from that directory.

If you do not want to use automatic class loading, make sure you put all classes in the JVM classpath. Classes located on the JVM classpath are loaded once per server lifetime. To reload these classes, you need to stop and restart ColdFusion Server. Custom tag libraries that have been placed in the web_root/WEB-INF/lib directory are automatically reloaded if necessary when you import the library.

To call a class that you have placed on the classpath or in one of the directories, you can use CFOBJECT like this:

```
<cfobject type="Java" class="theclassesname" name="varname">
```

This causes CFOBJECT to load the class into memory, but it does not actually make an instance of the object at that time. Only static methods and fields are accessible immediately after the call to CFOBJECT.

If you call a public method on the object without first calling the init method, there is an implicit call to the default constructor, but you do not get access to an object instance.

To call an object constructor explicitly and thereby create an instance of the object, use the special ColdFusion init method with the appropriate arguments after you use the CFOBJECT tag. For example:

```
<cfobject type="Java" class="MyClass" name="myObj">
<cfset ret=myObj.init(arg1, arg2)>
```

> **Note**
>
> ColdFusion uses a special identifier called the init method that calls the new function on the class constructor. If you have written a Java class that has an init method, a name conflict exists, and you cannot call the object's init method.
>
> To have persistent access to an object, you must use the init function because it returns a reference to an instance of the object, and CFOBJECT does not.

Let's do a quick example. Let's make a very simple Java class like the one in Listing 22.6.

Listing 22.6   *testCfobject.java*

```
class testCfobject {
    public string getString()
    return ("CFOBJECT is great");
    }
}
```

After you have compiled the code and placed it in the web_root/WEB-INF/classes directory, you can call it using CFOBJECT as in Listing 22.7.

Listing 22.7   *testcfobject.cfm*

```
<cfobject type="java" action="create" name="test" class="testCfobject">
<cfset testoutput = test.getString()>
<cfoutput>
#testoutput#
</cfoutput>
```

As you can see, this is pretty straightforward. We have a class with a single method, and we access that method by using the following:

```
<cfset testoutput = test.getString()>
```

In general, whenever we want to call a method, we use the following syntax:

```
<cfset returnmethod = obj.method()>
```

If the method has one or more arguments, you need to put the arguments inside the parentheses and separate them with commas.

```
<cfset x = 10>
<cfset retVal = obj.Method1(x, "a string")>
```

Let's try a bit more complex example. Let's say you are building a photo album application, and you need to be able to parse through a directory of images and convert all of them into thumbnails. Well, you can easily write a Java class that takes a JPEG image of some size and converts it to another, smaller JPEG thumbnail. Listing 22.8 provides an example.

Listing 22.8   *thumbnail.java*

```
//Thumbnail generator
//Usage java Thumbnail SomeJpeg.jpeg TheThumb.jpeg 50

import java.awt.Image;
import java.awt.Graphics2D;
import java.awt.geom.AffineTransform;
```

continues ▶

Listing 22.8 **Continued**

```java
import java.awt.image.BufferedImage;
import java.io.IOException;
import java.io.OutputStream;
import java.io.FileOutputStream;
import javax.swing.ImageIcon;
import com.sun.image.codec.jpeg.JPEGCodec;
import com.sun.image.codec.jpeg.JPEGImageEncoder;

class Thumbnail {
public static void main(String[] args) {
createThumbnail(args[0], args[
1], Integer.parseInt(args[2]));
}

public static void createThumbnail(
String orig, String thumb, int maxDim) {
try {
// Get the image from a file.
Image inImage = new ImageIcon(
orig).getImage();

// Determine the scale.
double scale = (double)maxDim/(
double)inImage.getHeight(null);
if (inImage.getWidth(
null) > inImage.getHeight(null)) {
scale = (double)maxDim/(
double)inImage.getWidth(null);
}

// Determine size of new image.
//One of them
// should equal maxDim.
int scaledW = (int)(
scale*inImage.getWidth(null));
int scaledH = (int)(
scale*inImage.getHeight(null));

// Create an image buffer in
//which to paint on.
BufferedImage outImage =
new BufferedImage(scaledW, scaledH,
BufferedImage.TYPE_INT_RGB);

// Set the scale.
AffineTransform tx =
new AffineTransform();
```

```
// If the image is smaller than
//the desired image size,
// don't bother scaling.
if (scale < 1.0d) {
tx.scale(scale, scale);
}

// Paint image.
Graphics2D g2d =
outImage.createGraphics();
g2d.drawImage(inImage, tx, null);
g2d.dispose();

// JPEG-encode the image
//and write to file.
OutputStream os =
new FileOutputStream(thumb);
JPEGImageEncoder encoder =
JPEGCodec.createJPEGEncoder(os);
encoder.encode(outImage);
os.close();
} catch (IOException e) {
e.printStackTrace();
}
System.exit(0);
}
}
```

To call this class, we need to provide it with several properties and call its method. We also have to make sure the data passed from ColdFusion to the Java object matches Java data types by using a special function called JavaCast.

Listing 22.9 *estthumbnail.cfm*

```
<cfobject action="create" type="java" class="Thumbnail" name="thump">
<cfset  scale=(JavaCast("int", "100"))>
<cfset myVar=thump.createThumbnail("E:\dev\largeimage.jpg", "E:\dev\newimage.jpg",
scale)>
```

As you can see, we have used the JavaCast function to set the value of the variable scale to be an integer with a value of 100. We have to do this because, although ColdFusion attempts to match Java types to ColdFusion types (as listed in Table 22.1), it often runs into issues in doing so.

Table 22.1 **ColdFusion Data Types and Corresponding Java Data Types**

ColdFusion Type	Java Type
Character	String.
Numeric	`int`/`long`/`float`/`double` (depending on `JavaCast`).
Boolean	Boolean.
Array of character	Array of string.
Array of numeric	Array of Java (`int`/`long`/`float`/`double`).
	The conversion rule depends on the Java Method Signature (`JavaCast` does not help).
Array of Java Objects	Array of Java objects.

To resolve this issue, ColdFusion provides the `JavaCast` function, which enables you to specify the Java type of a variable. The function takes two parameters: a string representing the Java data type and a variable whose type you are setting.

```
JavaCast(type, variable)
```

You can specify these Java data types: `bool`, `int`, `long`, `float`, `double`, and `String` but you cannot specify `structs` or Java date/time variables. In the case of data and time, you need to pass them as strings from ColdFusion and have the Java program convert those string values into date values.

Know that if you call your ColdFusion template in your browser after compiling and placing your Java class in your `classes` directory, you should get your JPEG image converted from a large image into a thumbnail.

Dealing with Java Exceptions

You handle Java exceptions just as you handle standard ColdFusion exceptions, with the `cftry` and `cfcatch` tags. You must specify the full class name of the Java exception class in the `cfcatch` tag that handles the exception. For example, if a Java object throws an exception named `myException`, you must specify `java.lang.exception.myException` in the `cfcatch` tag.

The following Java code defines the `testException` class that throws a sample exception. It also defines a `myException` class that extends the Java built-in `Exception` class and includes a method for getting an error message.

The `myException` class has the following code. It throws an exception with a message that is passed to it, or if no argument is passed, it throws a canned exception.

```
//class myException
public class myException extends Exception
{
  public myException2(String msg) {
    super(msg);
  }
  public myException2() {
    super("Error Message from myException");
  }
}
```

The `testException` class contains one method, `doException`, which throws a `myException` error with an error message.

```
public class testException {
  public testException ()
  {
  }
  public void doException() throws myException {
      throw new myException("Throwing an exception from testException class");
    }
}
```

Working with EJBs

To ColdFusion MX, Enterprise Java Beans are just another Java object, but there are several very specific things you must do to get ColdFusion to work with EJBs. You first need to make sure you have registered the EJB JAR file in the Administrator.

To communicate with the EJB, you need to use `CFOBJECT` to get the Java Naming and Directory Interface (JNDI) naming-context class. You will use fields from this class to define the information you use to locate the EJB. Because you only use fields, you do not initialize the object. Next you will need to load the Java `Hashtable` class to contain the context object properties via `CFOBJECT`. Initialize the `Hashtable` object using the ColdFusion `init` method. You will need to set your `Hashtable` to contain the properties required to create an initial JNDI naming context. These properties include `INITIAL_CONTEXT_FACTORY` and `PROVIDER_URL`. You might need to provide the `SECURITY_PRINCIPAL` and `SECURITY_CREDENTIALS` values as well; they might be required for secure access to the naming context.

Next load the JNDI `InitialContext` class. Call the `init` method with the `Hashtable` object values to initialize the `InitialContext` object. Call the `InitialContextext` object `lookup` method to get a reference to the `home` interface for the bean you want. Specify the JNDI name of the bean as the lookup argument. Call the `create` method of the bean's `home` object to create a new instance of the bean. If you are using Entity beans, you typically use a finder method instead. A finder method locates one or more existing entity beans.

Now you can use the bean's methods as required by your application. When finished, call the context object's `close` method to close the object.

The following code shows this process using a simple Java Entity bean. It calls the bean's `getMessage` method to obtain a message.

```
<html>
<head>
  <title>cfobject Test</title>
</head>

<body>
<H1>cfobject Test</H1>
<CFOBJECT
  action=create
  name=ctx
  type="JAVA"
  class="javax.naming.Context">
<CFOBJECT
  action=create
  name=prop type="JAVA"
  class="java.util.Hashtable">
<cfset prop.init()>
<cfset prop.put(ctx.INITIAL_CONTEXT_FACTORY, "jrun.naming.JRunContextFactory")>
<cfset prop.put(ctx.PROVIDER_URL, "localhost:2918")>
<CFOBJECT
  action=create
  name=initContext
  type="JAVA"
  class="javax.naming.InitialContext">
<cfset initContext.init(prop)>
<cfset home = initContext.lookup("Simple")>
<cfset mySimple = home.create()>
<cfset myMessage = mySimple.getMessage()>
<cfoutput>
#myMessge#<br>
</cfoutput>
<cfset initContext.close()>
</body>
</html>
```

Working with EJBs from ColdFusion is by no means an easy task; but if you can get the JNDI initial context, you are in the home stretch. If you do not have a good understanding of building, deploying, and using EJBs, you will find that you will need to consult your J2EE application server's manuals to get specific information on JNDI values and properties. Armed with that information, you should be able to call your EJB from ColdFusion.

Summary

ColdFusion MX offers amazing flexibility to developers to mix and match ColdFusion, JSP, Java Servlets, Java classes, Java Beans, and EJBs within their applications. Although you will most likely choose to develop in ColdFusion most of the time, there are specific instances in which you need the power and flexibility of Java to extend your applications or to provide services that you cannot do with CMFL.

You can also feel comfortable as a Java developer that by switching to ColdFusion to increase your development time and to rapidly create new functionality, you can still leverage your legacy Java code and applications.

23

Working with Databases

As the popularity of the Internet has increased, so have the demands and expectations of its users. Many businesses now see the Internet as a key element in their strategic plans. The Internet has evolved from a world of static Hypertext Markup Language (HTML) pages into a world of web applications that are capable of delivering dynamic content from a number of datasources. With ColdFusion, you can create applications that do more than just display dynamic data.

We can create web applications that enable a customer of an online store to do everything from searching for items to placing an order. These activities involve numerous interactions with a database. When the customer searches for a book on ColdFusion, a query is run against a database. The results of this query are returned in the form of a dynamic web page. With a series of SELECT statements, the customer could obtain a list of books on the topic of ColdFusion and details about individual books, including price, reviews, and whether the book is currently in stock. With the combination of SELECT, INSERT, and UPDATE statements, the customer can create an account and place his or her order. The power of ColdFusion and web applications does not stop with the user interface (UI). The business can leverage the web application to create shipping documents, to update inventories, to create purchase orders for distributors to replenish stock, and to generate email confirmations related to customers orders.

In Chapter 4, "Fundamentals of ColdFusion Development," we discussed the basic concepts for using ColdFusion to interact with databases. In this chapter and the next, we discuss some of the more complex interactions between ColdFusion and the database. However, before discussing topics such as stored procedures and transactions, we would be remiss if we failed to review some basic database and structured query language (SQL) concepts.

Relational Databases

Although there are a number of database models, one of the most common and the one we will discuss is the relational database. The relational database model was introduced in 1970 by an IBM employee named E.F. Codd. Codd defined a relational database as a collection of data items organized as a set of defined tables from which data can be accessed and presented in different ways without having to reorganize the database tables. Although this initially sounds a bit confusing, the relational database model is actually fairly simple when viewed as a set of basic guidelines:

- Relationships are represented by tables.
- Each row represents a unique instance of an entity.
- Columns are attributes of the entity.
- Every table has an attribute or set of attributes that when combined form a "key" that uniquely identifies each entity.
- Data is presented as a collection of relations; that is, users of the database could obtain a *view* of the database that fitted their needs.

Before we continue with more detailed discuss of relational databases, we want to take a step back and review a few of the general concepts and terms related to databases.

Understanding Databases

For the purpose of our discussion, we define data as the characteristics of people, places, things, and events. The color of your eyes, the title of this book, and the town where you live are all bits of unrelated data. A database is a structured collection of related data that is organized so that its contents (data) can be easily accessed, updated, and managed.

The database can contain one or more tables, which in turn are comprised of one or more columns. These columns contain predefined types of data. Let's look at Table 23.1. The table contains three columns: StateID, StateAbbreviation, and StateName. Each row represents a unique instance of the data contained in the columns.

Table 23.1 **The State Table**

StateID	StateAbbreviation	StateName
1	AL	Alabama
2	AK	Alaska
3	AZ	Arizona
4	AR	Arkansas
5	CA	California
6	CO	Colorado
7	CT	Connecticut
8	DE	Delaware
9	DC	District of Columbia
10	FL	Florida

Note that no two columns in a table can have the same name, and as a general rule, the column name should be meaningfully related to the data it contains. You often hear the rows commonly referred to as records, entities, or tuples. The terms "fields" and "attributes" are interchangeably used with columns.

One of our favorite visual analogies of a database is a locked file cabinet. Picture the file cabinet with a label that reads "DATABASE." The file cabinet can have one or many drawers, which are representative of the database tables. Each drawer contains files. These files are the equivalent of rows we find in the database table. Remember that we mentioned this was a locked file cabinet. To be able to access the data contained in the file cabinet, you need a key. A database management system (DBMS) is the key to a database. It is the DBMS that provides access to the data and provides the means to convert the data into meaningful information. If we send you a copy of the MDF file from a Microsoft SQL Server, it is still a database; but without the DBMS, you cannot access the data.

The concept of a database being organized and structured is a very important one. Imagine sitting in meetings all day, five days a week, taking notes on 3×5 cards. At the end of each meeting, you take all the 3×5 cards and toss them into one of five drawers in your file cabinet. After a short period, your drawers would contain a lot of 3×5 cards. Now imagine trying to retrieve a phone number you recorded in a meeting that occurred five weeks ago. Although this example might seem a bit absurd, it would be no different from creating a database table that had column names such as FirstName, PartNumber, Flavor, Publisher, and Breed. Do you find the column names a bit confusing? That is exactly the point. We want our data to be organized and structured so that the data can be useful information.

Keys

In a relational database, tables normally contain a single field or combination of fields that uniquely identifies each record or row. This is known as the primary key. Any column or combination of columns that contain a unique value can be a primary key. Many texts that deal with the topic of database development refer to these as candidate keys. You also see candidate keys that are not used as primary keys referred to as alternate keys. Primary keys that are formed by the combination of columns are known as composite primary keys.

Primary keys are important because they are how users of the database distinguish between records in a table. In some cases, you have to create an artificial primary key. This happens when the columns in a table do not lend themselves to natural uniqueness.

If we return to our previous discussion of the online bookstore, we can find a number of examples where tables might require an artificial primary key. Our database contains a table appropriately named Author. This table contains columns such as FirstName, LastName, Address1, Address2, City, StateID, and Email. Although we might initially be inclined to select the combination of columns FirstName and LastName as a primary key, what happens if we have two authors named Bob Smith? To resolve this problem, we would create an artificial key called Author_ID. In many cases, you use a mechanism such as AutoNumber (Access) or Sequencing (Oracle) to automatically create the value. This eliminates the need for the user to determine a unique value.

It is possible to create tables that do not have a primary key. The lack of a primary key creates a number of problems, including difficulties with manipulating data and preventing record duplication.

We have mentioned how tables in a relational database represent relationships. It is the primary key that helps to establish the link or relationship between tables. When the column in a table matches the primary key of another table, that column is known as a foreign key. As with primary keys, a foreign key can be a single column or multiple columns. A table can also contain foreign keys from more than one table.

Returning once more to our online bookstore, recall in our Author table that the primary key was the column Author_ID. Our database also contains the table State. The primary key in the State table is the column StateID. The StateID is also stored in the Author table. StateID is a primary key in the State table and a foreign key in the Author table. It is the foreign key that creates the relationship between the tables Author and State. This relationship is often referred to as a parent/child relationship, and the foreign key's table is called a lookup table. In our example, the State table would be the parent and lookup table, although the Author table is the child. Keep in mind that this is different from the parent/child relationship that you might have encountered in object-oriented programming (OOP).

It is a common technique to populate the options of a select list with the values from a lookup table. This gives the developer a way to ensure that the values a user attempts to enter for the column in a child table exist in the parent table. It is important to understand that there is more to this technique than simply making a UI that is friendly. If you were to create an input form to add new records to the Author table, your relational database management system (RDBMS) would check whether the value submitted for the foreign key field exists in the parent table. If a user enters a value of 99 in the field for StateID and 99 is not a value that exists in the StateID column of the State table, an error is returned.

This process of ensuring that the data in our relationship stays related is known as maintaining referential integrity. There are two rules of referential integrity. The rules apply to all databases. The first rule governs primary keys and states that primary keys cannot contain null values. If the primary key is a composite, then none of the columns that make up the composite primary key can contain null values.

The second rule of referential integrity says that the database cannot contain any unmatched foreign key values. It is this rule that prevents a user from entering the value 99 for StateID in the Author table when 99 does not exist as a value in the State table. Conversely, this means that if we delete a record or row from a parent table, the deletion cannot result in any unmatched foreign key values in the child table.

We have already discussed a common technique to help prevent violation of this rule. However, what are our options when it comes to preventing orphan values? The first solution is to not enable the deletion of records in a parent/child relationship. The second option is to reassign the child records to a new value and then enable the delete. A third option is to cascade the delete, which means that any record in the child table containing the deleted foreign key would also be deleted. There are other options available that are not supported by all RDBMSs. The documentation for your RDBMS is a good source of information on how to utilize keys for maintaining referential integrity.

Relationships

In relational databases, a relationship is established when two tables share common data. This sharing of data is what links or connects the tables. There are three types of relationships:

- One-to-one
- One-to-many
- Many-to-many

During database design, one of the first steps is to determine what is our data and how it fits together. We find it useful to think of tables as an actual person, place, thing, or event. In the case of online bookstore, we might start with a table called Book. We would then determine the information that we need about a book.

A book has an International Standard Book Number (ISBN). It also has a title, a publisher, and an author. We next would look at the data to determine what data each instance of a book has for a single value. We know that a book has one ISBN, one title, and one publisher. This is the data that we would place in the table Book.

Now, what about the author? Some books have one only author, whereas others (like this one) have more then one author. This tells us that we need a table that handles the relationship between authors and books. Although a book has only one publisher, there is additional data that we need about the publisher. The Book table is not the appropriate place for this data because it is related to the Publisher, not the Book; so we would create a Publisher table. By this point, you hopefully have seen that we are trying to identify the data that is unique to each instance of an entity presented by our table; we are trying to avoid data redundancy.

This is the reason we said that additional information about the publisher would not be appropriate for the Book table. This is a point that is worthy of a little bit of discussion. If we decided to enter the publisher's address as part of the Book table and inserted 1000 books published by New Riders in the table, what do you think is the chance that it will be entered all 1000 times without a mistake or difference? If New Riders changes their address, we have to locate and update 1000 records. If we instead create a Publisher table, we only have to enter the address for New Riders one time. If they move to a new location, we only have to update one record. When we query the database, we would still be able to use the relationship between the Publisher and Book table to obtain information about the book and publisher. This demonstrates several of the reasons why relational databases have become so popular. The relational database reduces data redundancy and improves maintainability, all without sacrificing data accessibility.

We have alluded to the relationship between tables on a number of occasions and it is now time to examine the three types of relationships more closely. A publisher can publish many books. A state might have many authors. These are examples of a one-to-many relationship. A one-to-many relationship is defined that each record in Table A can have many related records in Table B, but Table B can have only one related record in Table A. A book can have only one publisher, and an author can live in only one state. This is the most common type of relationship.

The next type of relationship that we can look at is the many-to-many relationship. By definition, a many-to-many relationship exists when a record in Table A can have many related records in Table B, although a record in Table B can have many related records in Table A. The relationship between the Author and Book tables is an excellent example of this type of relationship. A book can have many authors and an author can write many books. This type of relationship is actually two one-to-many relationships and is possible only in a relational database with a third table. This third table is known as a junction or cross-reference table. There are two methods for creating the cross-reference table. The first is to create a table with a primary key that is a composite primary key comprised of the foreign keys from Table A and Table B. The second method consists of creating a table with three columns, the foreign keys from Table A and Table B and a unique primary key, normally a simple ID field.

The third type of relationship is the one-to-one relationship. In a one-to-one relationship, each record in Table A can have only one related record in Table B. Conversely, each record in Table B can have only one related record in Table A. Because of this one-to-one relationship, the data would normally be stored in one table.

There are two primary reasons for creating tables with a one-to-one relationship. The first is for performance reasons and the second is for security. A common use of one-to-one relationship is to protect customer credit card information. The second reason for creating a one-to-one relationship is when only a small portion of the records have the related columns.

Indexes

There are two ways that most databases access data, either by performing what is called a full table scan or by utilizing indexes. A full table scan means that the DBMS starts with the first record in a table and scans through all the rows in a table, extracting the rows that meet the query conditions. An index in a database is very much like the index of a book. It provides the database with a method of knowing where to look for specific information. Indexes can be applied to single fields or multiple fields. A multiple field index might be used where the first field contains information that might not be unique. The fields FirstName and LastName would be a prime example of a situation where the use of multiple field indexing would be appropriate. EmployeeID or any other unique ID would be appropriate for single field indexing. A field such as Gender, which has only two possible values (M and F), would not be appropriate for indexing.

As a general rule, if the following five rules or characteristics apply, then an index should be created for the respective field:

- The field has primary keys.
- Foreign keys or columns are joined to other columns in other tables.
- The field contains many different values.
- You anticipate frequent searching of the column.
- You anticipate frequent sorts of the column.

Here are some situations in which you do not want to index columns:

- The column is seldom referenced in a query as part of the condition statement.
- The column contains few unique values.

Datasources

There are two ways that the term *datasource* is used. The first manner refers to the source to which ColdFusion is connecting to obtain data. ColdFusion can interact with a number of external datasources. In addition to databases, ColdFusion can interact with datasources such as spreadsheets, Lightweight Directory Access Protocol (LDAP) directories, Hypertext Transfer Protocol (HTTP) servers, mail servers, and File Transfer Protocol (FTP) servers. Because this chapter is concerned with databases, the rest of our discussion focuses on ColdFusion using a database as the datasource.

The second definition associated with datasource is the connection ColdFusion uses to communicate with an external source. In previous releases of ColdFusion, there were three types of datasources supported to communicate with databases: open database connectivity (ODBC), OLE-DB, and native drivers. This changed with the release of ColdFusion MX.

ColdFusion MX uses Java Database Connectivity (JDBC) drivers to interact with databases. You can still connect to ODBC datasources using the bundled Merant Type IV database drivers or the SQL Link Type III database drivers.

ODBC

ODBC is a widely accepted application program interface (API) for database access. When applications such as ColdFusion use ODBC, they are not communicating with the database directly. Instead they are communicating with the ODBC datasource. The ODBC API uses drivers to give you an abstract layer with which to communicate. This enables you to create an application without concern about the protocols used by the datasource (such as a database or spreadsheet).

In versions of ColdFusion prior to the release of ColdFusion 5, you could not use a datasource without it registering in the ColdFusion Administrator. This does not mean you have to actually create the datasources in the ColdFusion Administrator. You could create the datasource as a system Data Source Name (DSN) in whatever ODBC datasource manager your operating system (OS) provided; ColdFusion would find it in the Registry. The release of ColdFusion 5 introduced the capability to make a dynamic connection to an unregistered datasource. This is accomplished by setting the `dbtype` attribute of the `CFQUERY` tag to `"DYNAMIC"`. This is not supported in MX, however.

JDBC Drivers

JDBC is a Java API that enables applications to interact with a variety of relational databases. The advantage that JDBC enjoys is that it is neither database- nor platform-specific and unlike ODBC, JDBC drivers do not require that a driver manager and drivers be installed on every client machine. There are four types of JDBC drivers, but only Type 3 and Type 4 drivers are supported by MX.

Type 3 drivers are pure Java code and translate JDBC API calls into a DBMS-independent net protocol that is then translated to a DBMS protocol by a server module (middle tier). Because the Type 3 drivers use a DBMS-neutral protocol to send SQL requests, they offer the advantage of an extremely flexible JDBC solution. The requirement to have the server module translate the SQL call to a DBMS-specific code is a disadvantage though.

Type 4 drivers are also pure Java, but convert the SQL call into DBMS-specific code. This enables a direct call to the DBMS directly from the client. Type 4 drivers often use proprietary protocols and are often provided by the database vendors themselves. Although they lack the flexibility of a Type 3 driver, they are platform-independent and do not rely on a server module. Table 23.2 provides a list of the drivers shipped with ColdFusion MX.

Table 23.2   **ColdFusion MX JDBC Type 4 Drivers**

Driver	Type
Microsoft Access	3
ODBC Socket	3
DB2 UDB for OS/390	4
DB2 Universal Database 6.2 and 7.2	4
Informix 9.x	4
Microsoft SQL Server 7.x and 2000	4
MySQL	4
Oracle R3 (8.1.7) and Oracle 9i	4
Oracle Thin Client	4
PostgreSQL	4
Sybase 11, 11.9.2, and 12	4
Sybase jConnector 5.0	4

The ColdFusion documentation, specifically "Administering ColdFusion MX," provides detailed instruction on the configuration of datasources. We highly recommend you review the configuration instructions even if you are an experienced ColdFusion developer—there are changes from previous releases.

Summary

Relational databases provide a way of storing data in a collection of related and defined tables. Each table contains records or rows that represent a unique instance of an entity. A primary key is used to establish this uniqueness. Relationships between the tables are established when two tables share common data. When the column data in one table matches the primary key of another table, it is know as a foreign key. Table indexes provide the DBMS a way of knowing where to look for specific data, much like the index of a book. One of the strengths of a relational database is the ease with which new table (relationships) can be added. A second strength is the capability to access and present data without having to reorganize the database tables. Let's take a look at how we access data within a relational database.

Working with SQL

We spent the last section discussing some of the key concepts concerned with relational databases and communicating with them. SQL is the standard language for communicating with relational databases. SQL provides us with a programming language that we use to select, insert, update, and delete information from a relational database.

The SQL language was developed by IBM researchers as part of a project to develop a prototype relational database based on the relational database model described by E.F. Codd. The new language—SEQEL (Structured English Query Language)—was first described in a 1976 article of the *IBM Journal of R&D*. The name was later changed to SQL. In 1978, IBM released System R, based on Codd's relational database model. IBM came to market with a product named System/R in 1978. In 1979, Oracle Corporation introduced the first commercially available implementation of SQL.

Pure SQL is an American National Standards Institute (ANSI) standard and is therefore independent of any database product. However, most database products include proprietary extensions to the standard SQL language. Database companies include these proprietary extensions for two reasons: to provide features that support developer's needs and to distinguish their database product from other DBMS products.

Understanding SQL

These nonstandard extensions, although proprietary, often provide solutions to common problems. As you move forward with your development, you should keep in mind that if you use these proprietary extensions, you lose portability. For example, ANSI-SQL does not provide a way to automatically assign a number ID to new records. In Access, this is handled with a data type of AutoNumber. Oracle handles this with special database objects called sequences. The obvious drawback is that code written for an Access database might not be totally compatible with an Oracle database.

The primary advantages of SQL are as follows:

- **English–like structure.** Makes the basic syntax easy to learn.

- **Vendor independence and portability.** For the most part, SQL enables the user to change the underlying brand of database and DBMS without having to rewrite the SQL code. (Variations in the standard and proprietary extensions can complicate the issue.)

- **Standardized.** The standard is established by ANSI, with most vendors now supporting the SQL 92 or SQL 99 version.

- **Dynamic data definition.** SQL offers advanced data processing commands that enable embedded and multilevel database queries.

Queries

We are now to the point were we can roll up our sleeves and look at some code! There are a number of reserved words or keywords that are used by SQL. In our discussion. we look at the commands and keywords that are associated with data manipulation.

There are four major command words in SQL that you use to perform most of your database transactions: SELECT, INSERT, UPDATE, and DELETE. In the following sections, we cover all four using an example database to illustrate their use.

Figure 23.1 shows the relationships that exist between the various tables we are using for the SQL examples.

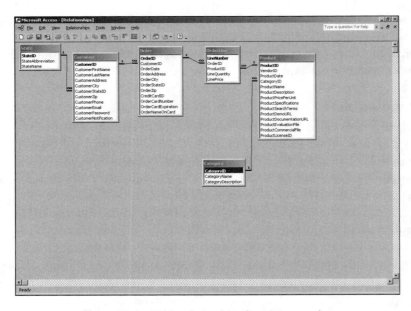

Figure 23.1   Table relationships for SQL examples.

SELECT

The SELECT statement, used to retrieve data from one or more tables, is the most commonly used statement. It requires a minimum of two clauses. The first clause contains the KEYWORD SELECT and identifies the data to be retrieved. The second clause defines the location of the data and is prefaced with the keyword FROM. The following example uses the wildcard character * to retrieve all columns from the table CUSTOMER:

```
SELECT *
FROM CUSTOMER
```

Although there are cases where you need to retrieve all columns, you should refrain from using the wildcard character unless all rows are required. You improve performance by retrieving only the columns that are needed.

Our second example demonstrates retrieval of specific columns. Note that a comma separates the column names:

```
SELECT CustomerID,CustomerFirstName,CustomerLastName
FROM CUSTOMER
```

As you examine more SQL, you'll notice that there a number of methods for formatting the SQL code. The following example shows another way of formatting the same SQL statement in a manner that some feel is easier to edit at a later time:

```
SELECT CustomerID,
       CustomerFirstName,
       CustomerLastName
FROM CUSTOMER
```

There are two additional clauses that can be part of the SELECT query. One is the WHERE clause, which acts as a filter and is discussed in greater detail shortly.

```
SELECT CustomerID, CustomerEmail,
FROM CUSTOMER
WHERE CustomerID = 1234
```

The third clause is the ORDER BY clause, which is used to sort the returned recordset. If more than one column is used to order the sort, the column names are separated by a comma. Sorts can be placed in ascending (ASC) or descending (DESC) order. If neither is specified, the default ASC is assumed. The following example shows the sort done on CustomerLastNames and then CustomerFirstNames in descending order:

```
SELECT CustomerID,CustomerFirstName,CustomerLastName
FROM CUSTOMER
ORDER BY CustomerLastName, CustomerFirstName DESC
```

A technique that is commonly used with SELECT statements is renaming of columns with aliases using the AS keyword. We commonly do this when one of the following conditions applies:

- You are using aggregate functions, such as Count() or Sum().

- You are retrieving multiple columns from multiple tables. This is for clarity and helps reduce the length of the name.

- A condition exists that makes it desirable to rename the column. The condition might be a confusing column name or an illegal character in the column name.

```
SELECT count(CustomerID) AS CustomerCount
FROM CUSTOMER
```

INSERT

The INSERT statement is used to insert or add new records into a table. The first clause of the INSERT statement uses the keywords INSERT INTO followed by the table name and list of column names, again separated by commas. The second clause contains the keyword VALUES followed by a comma–delimited list of values that will be inserted.

```
INSERT INTO CUSTOMER(CustomerID,CustomerFirstName,
    CustomerLastname,CustomerEmail)
VALUES (1234,'Bradford','Haynes',
    'bradford@ekhtech.com')
```

Notice that the value 'Bradford' is surrounded by a single quote although the value 1234 is not. The presence of a single quote indicates that the value is a string.

UPDATE

The UPDATE statement is comprised of at least two clauses and is used to modify existing records. The first clause uses the keyword UPDATE followed by the table to be updated. The second clause uses the keyword SET and lists the column(s) to be updated and the new value.

```
UPDATE CUSTOMER
SET CustomerLastName = 'Smith'
```

The code in the previous example sets the value for CustomerLastName to Smith for all records in the table. Although you might occasionally want to do global updates, you more frequently need to update specific records or sets of records. The UPDATE statement can also use a third clause of WHERE, which acts as a filter to specify the records to be updated.

```
UPDATE CUSTOMER
SET CustomerFirstName = 'Mandi'
WHERE CustomerID = 1234
```

If you be updating more the one column, the column name value pairs are separated by commas.

```
UPDATE CUSTOMER
SET CustomerFirstName = 'Mandi',
    CustomerEmail = 'mandi@ekhtech.com'
WHERE CustomerID = 1234
```

DELETE

The last of our data manipulation statements is the DELETE statement, which is used to remove records from a table. The DELETE statement can be used with a single clause, using the DELETE keyword followed by the table name:

```
DELETE FROM CUSTOMER
```

This is great if you want to delete *all* records in a table, but it is bad if you want delete only one record. To delete a specific record or group of records, you add the WHERE clause to the DELETE statement.

```
DELETE FROM CUSTOMER
WHERE CustomerID = 1234
```

Obviously, a great deal of care has to be exercised when using the DELETE statement. Something that we do prior to executing DELETE statements for the first time is to write the equivalent SELECT statement. This enables you to ensure that the DELETE statement is deleting the record or recordset that you thought it would.

The *WHERE* Clause

The WHERE clause acts as a filter for your queries. As we saw from some of the previous examples, an UPDATE query without a WHERE clause performs a global update and modifies all rows. The same holds true for a DELETE statement; all records will be deleted. If we are looking for the email address of a specific customer, we do not want a query returning several hundred records. The WHERE clause acts as a filter. In our previous examples, we saw the WHERE clause used only with the = condition. Now let's examine some of the other conditions that can be used in the WHERE clause. For instance, not equal (<>) returns all values not equal to the specified value.

```
WHERE CustomerID <> 1234
```

Less than (<) returns all values less than the specified value.

```
WHERE CustomerID < 1234
```

Less than or equal to (<=) returns all values less than or equal to the specified value/

```
WHERE CustomerID <= 1234
```

Greater than (>) returns all values greater than the specified value.

```
WHERE CustomerID > 1234
```

Greater than or equal to (>=) returns all values greater than or equal to the specified value.

```
WHERE CustomerFirstName >= 'H'
```

Now's the time for a couple quick comments on evaluating strings. Remember that strings are evaluated one character at a time and are evaluated as numeric, lowercase, and then uppercase. This means that the previous WHERE clause would return "'Hank'" and "'ROBERT'" but not "'sarah'". BETWEEN returns all values in a given range; this is inclusive of the upper and lower values.

```
WHERE CustomerID BETWEEN 1234 AND 6000
```

The BETWEEN statement is actually a statement that combines a greater than or equal to and a less than or equal to condition.

```
WHERE CustomerID >= 1234 AND WHERE CustomerID <= 6000
```

The LIKE keyword returns any record that contains the specified pattern. Use of the wildcard % indicates that any value can appear.

```
WHERE CustomerLastName LIKE '%nes'
```

The preceding statement returns all CustomerLastNames that end with "nes." The following statement returns all CustomerLastNames that contain "y."

```
WHERE CustomerLastName LIKE '%y%'
```

This statement returns all CustomerLastNames that begin with "Ha."

```
WHERE CustomerLastName LIKE 'Ha%'
```

There is a second type of wildcard that can be used with the LIKE condition. This is used to specify a single character or specific characters.

```
WHERE CustomerFirstName LIKE 'Mand[iy]'
```

This statement returns Mandi or Mandy but not Mandaline.
The IN returns all records that match any of the values in a given list.

```
WHERE CustomerFirstName IN('Bradford','Mandi','EK')
```

The NOT condition negates the rest of the condition. In this example, it would return all CustomerID values that were less than 1234 or greater than 6000.

```
WHERE CustomerID NOT BETWEEN 1234 AND 6000
```

IS NULL returns all records where the column value contains a null value (in other words, the column values are empty).

```
WHERE CustomerFirstName IS NULL
```

IS NOT NULL returns all records that contain a value for the column specified.

```
WHERE CustomerFirstName IS NOT NULL
```

We can also combine conditions. In addition, we can specify whether all the given conditions must be met or just one. If we need to have multiple conditions met, we join the conditions with the keyword AND. In the following example, both conditions must be met.

```
WHERE CustomerFirstName = 'Mandi' AND
      CustomerLastName = 'Haynes'
```

In our next example, we are using the OR keyword. This means that if either condition is met, the record is a match.

```
WHERE CustomerFirstName = 'Mandi' OR
      CustomerLastName = 'Smith'
```

When writing conditions that contain both AND and OR, you need to understand the precedence that is used to evaluate the statement. All AND conditions are evaluated first, and then the OR conditions are evaluated. When we wrote the condition

```
WHERE CustomerFirstName = 'Mandi' AND
      CustomerLastName = 'Haynes' OR
      CustomerLastName = 'Smith'
```

we wanted all records with a CustomerFirstName of Mandi and CustomerLastName of either Haynes or Smith. What we received were records with a CustomerFirstName of Mandi, a CustomerLastName of Haynes, and all records with a CustomerLastName of Smith. Use parentheses to control the evaluation. This returns the recordset that you really wanted.

```
WHERE CustomerFirstName = 'Mandi' AND
      (CustomerLastName = 'Haynes' OR
      CustomerLastName = 'Smith')
```

Summary

SQL is used to access data in a relational database. SQL provides you with a means of both retrieving and manipulating the data. The four command words of SELECT, INSERT, UPDATE, and DELETE are used for data manipulation. The WHERE clause provides the means for filtering or setting conditions for the records that are returned. The ORDER BY clause enables you to sort the recordset to meet your needs. Although SQL is an ANSI standard, many DBMSs include proprietary extensions. Use of these proprietary extensions prevents code from being platform-independent.

Stored Procedures

A stored procedure is defined as a DBMS operation, which is typically a set of SQL statements that is stored on the database server. Stored procedures are a method of encapsulating repetitive tasks and improving performance.

Although a detailed discussion of stored procedures is beyond the scope of this chapter, you should be familiar with the advantages of using stored procedures and how to utilize them with ColdFusion. Stored procedures can do the following:

- **Improve performance.** Provides a single execution plan on the server. A stored procedure is precompiled and residing on the database server.

- **Share application logic between applications.** We recently developed a web site that utilized a web interface that was developed with ColdFusion. The existing application was a Visual Basic application that utilized the same stored procedures. This capability to share code between applications helped to ensure that both applications used the same business logic. In addition, if changes were required to the existing business logic, the changes could be effected in a single place—the stored procedure.

- **Shield users from details of the tables in the database.** The user is not required to know any details about tables to execute the stored procedure, only parameters passed and values returned. Because stored procedures are often used to execute business logic, this enables changes to be made to the business logic, and even the table schemas, without changing the code ColdFusion is using to call the stored procedure.

- **Provide security.** The user can be granted permission to execute a stored procedure without having to be granted access to tables.

- **Reduce network traffic.** Eliminates the need to send complex SQL statements.

There are two ways to execute stored procedures in ColdFusion: the CFSTOREDPROC and CFQUERY tags. The following syntax is used to execute a stored procedure with the CFQUERY tag.

```
<cfquery NAME="TestQuery" DATASOURCE="TestDNS"
(Execute database.sp_testsp
@var1 = '#CustomerFirstName#',
@var2 = '#CustomerLastName#')
</cfquery>
```

When executing a stored procedure using the CFQUERY tag, you face a number of limitations. One of the major limitations is that you have no way to access return codes or output parameters that are created by the stored procedure. To use CFQUERY to execute a stored procedure, you must have a native-drive datasource.

CFSTOREDPROC

The preferred method for executing a stored procedure is the CFSTOREDPROC tag. The CFSTOREDPROC tag executes stored procedures using either an ODBC or native connection to a server database. It specifies database connection information and identifies the stored procedure. The CFSTOREDPROC tag has two required attributes: procedure and datasource.

There are also several optional attributes, many of which you have already encountered with other ColdFusion tags. The one optional attribute that might not be familiar is returncode. When a stored procedure is executed using CFSTOREDPROC, two return values, cfstoredproc.statuscode and cfstoredproc.executiontime, are automatically generated by ColdFusion. When the returncode is Yes, the value of cfstoredproc.statuscode is set to the status code returned by the stored procedures. An example of use of the CFSTOREDPROC tag is shown in the following code:

```
<cfstoredproc PROCEDURE = "sp_test"
DATASOURCE="TestDNS" RETURNCODE = "YES">
```

The CFSTOREDPROC tag simply executes the desired stored procedure; it uses the child tags CFPROCPARAM and CFPROCRESULT to pass parameters and receive result sets.

CFPROCPARAM

The CFPROCPARAM tag is nested within a CFSTOREDPROC tag and is used to pass parameters to the stored procedure. This tag is used to identify parameters and their data types. You need to provide one CFPROCPARAM tag for each parameter. Only one attribute is required in the CFPROCPARAM tag: CFSQLTYPE.

The `CFSQLTYPE` attribute specifies the SQL type to which the parameter is bound. The following list presents the allowable values:

- `CF_SQL_BIGINT`
- `CF_SQL_BIT`
- `CF_SQL_BLOB`
- `CF_SQL_CHAR`
- `CF_SQL_CLOB`
- `CF_SQL_DATE`
- `CF_SQL_DECIMAL`
- `CF_SQL_DOUBLE`
- `CF_SQL_FLOAT`
- `CF_SQL_IDSTAMP`
- `CF_SQL_INTEGER`
- `CF_SQL_LONGVARCHAR`
- `CF_SQL_MONEY`
- `CF_SQL_MONEY4`
- `CF_SQL_NUMERIC`
- `CF_SQL_REAL`
- `CF_SQL_REFCURSOR`
- `CF_SQL_SMALLINT`
- `CF_SQL_TIME`
- `CF_SQL_TIMESTAMP`
- `CF_SQL_TINYINT`
- `CF_SQL_VARCHAR`

The `type` attribute has three options: `"in"`, `"out"`, and `"inout"`. It specifies whether the parameter is being passed in or out. The option of `"inout"` is used when a parameter with the identical name is being passed both in and out.

There are a number of optional attributes that become required and dependent upon the use of other optional attributes. When the attribute `TYPE` is specified as `"in"` or `"inout"`, the attribute `"value"` is required. The `"value"` attribute corresponds to what is passed to the stored procedure. When the `type` attribute is `"out"` or `"inout"`, the attribute `"variable"` is used to represent the data returned by the stored procedure.

```
<cfprocparam TYPE = "in"
      CFSQLType = "CF_SQL_VARCHAR"
 DBVARNAME = "FirstName"
       VALUE = "#CustomerFirstName#">
```

Although the CFPROCPARAM tag offers a way to get data from a stored procedure, the recommended way is with the CFPROCRESULT tag.

CFPROCRESULT

The CFPROCRESULT tag enables you to specify a name for the results set returned by a stored procedure. This enables you to then call the result set with other ColdFusion tags. The only required attribute is the name attribute. If a stored procedure returns more than one result set, you need to use the resultset attribute.

```
<cfprocresult NAME = "CustomerID"
resultSet = "1" >
<cfstoredproc procedure="sp_ProcessOrder" datasource="rits" returncode="yes">
  <cfprocparam type="In" cfsqltype="CF_SQL_INTEGER" dbvarname="@OrderNumber"
value="#FORM.OrderNumber#" null="No">
<cfprocparam type="In" cfsqltype="CF_SQL_VARCHAR" dbvarname="@CustomerID"
value="#FORM.CustomerID#" null="No">
<cfprocparam type="In" cfsqltype="CF_SQL_INTEGER" dbvarname="@ProductID"
value="#FORM.ProductID#" null="No">
<cfprocparam type="In" cfsqltype="CF_SQL_TIMESTAMP" dbvarname="@OrderDate"
value="#FORM.OrderDate#" null="No">
... more code
</cfstoredproc>
<cfquery name="custdetail" datasource="rits">
      SELECT CustomerID, CustomerFirstName, CustomerLastName
      FROM Customer
      WHERE CustomerID = #Form.CustomerID#
<cfoutput>
    <cfif CFSTOREDPROC.STATUSCODE EQ '-1'>
              The order was not processed, the return code for the stored procedure
is: #CFSTOREDPROC.STATUSCODE#
         <cfelse>
              Order number #Form.OrderID# for #custdetail.CustomerFirstName#
#custdetail.CustomerLastName# , Customer ID #custdetail.CustomerID# has been
sucessfully processed.
         </cfif>
</cfoutput>
```

Summary

Stored procedures are a named set of SQL statements that are stored on the database server. They offer a method of encapsulating repetitive tasks. This translates to improved performance, code reuse, reduced network traffic, and security benefits. ColdFusion enables two methods for executing stored procedures: the CFQUERY and CFSTOREDPROC tags. The CFQUERY approach cannot access return codes or output from the stored procedure, and it requires the use of a native driver. The CFSTOREDPROC tag uses the child tags of CFPROCPARAM and CFPROCRESULT. The CFPROCPARAM tag is used to identify stored procedure parameters and their type. A CFPROCPARAM tag is required for each parameter passed to or returned by the stored procedure. The CFPROCRESULT tag provides a name by which other ColdFusion tags can access stored procedure results.

Transactions

The last item that we discuss in this chapter is the concept of transactions and the CFTRANSACTION tag. There are two reasons that transactions are important to us. One reason is that if any one query fails, all the other queries are, in effect, failed by the database server. Transactions can also be used to prevent multiple users from editing the same data at the same time. An application that displays inventory is an example of such a situation. You obviously would not want two users attempting to modify inventory at the same time. What happens if FlyByNite Airlines enables two customers to purchase a ticket for the same seat on Flight 123 at the same time? We could easily have a situation where both customers purchase the same or the last ticket. Maybe FlyByNite Airlines is not a good example because they intentionally oversell flights, but it should demonstrate the concept; you are trying to prevent two users from modifying the data at the same time.

Let's take this example another step. A transaction can be a series of queries that either succeeds in bulk or not at all. We are attempting to purchase a ticket on Flight 123. What are some of the tasks that would have to be accomplished for a customer to purchase a ticket? A couple of simple actions would be adding the customer information, assigning the customer a seat on the flight, and charging his or her credit card.

Assume that Mr. Smith is at work and needs to fly from Los Angles to Chicago on a business trip next week. He has completed the online form, provided his personal information (including credit card number), and has requested seat 5B because it is the only seat left. Just as he is about to click the Submit button, the phone rings and he becomes involved in a five-minute conversation with a friend about plans for this weekend. After he hang ups the phone, he clicks the Submit button, but unfortunately, while he was on the phone, the last seat on Flight 123 was purchased.

If the Submit page were created as a simple series of queries, what would happen? The query to insert his customer information would succeed, but when the query to insert his customer number or flight manifest ran, it would fail because there were no seats left. The next query, which bills his credit card, would then execute. We obviously do not want Mr. Smith to be billed if he cannot purchase the ticket. Initially, you might think the solution is to add a conditional statement around the credit card query so that if the ticket is not issued, the credit card is not billed. However, what happens when a ticket is issued and then it turns out that Mr. Smith has reached his limit on his credit card? You can see where there is a need to be able to treat this series of queries as one so that if one fails, the others are not executed, and any previous updates are rolled back.

CFTRANSACTION

The `CFTRANSACTION` tag enables you to treat all query operations within the open and closing tags as a single transaction. This means that none of the changes to a database are committed until all the queries within the transaction have successfully completed. The `CFTRANSACTION` tag has two optional attributes: `action` and `isolation`. The `action` attribute specifies the transaction `action` to be taken. The supported options are `begin`, `commit`, and `rollback`. We examine these options in detail shortly. The `isolation` attribute specifies the ODBC lock type to be used.

This is good place to discuss the concepts of *locking* and *isolation*. There are two types of locking: exclusive and shared. When exclusive locking is employed, no other user can access the data being locked. With shared locking, other users can read but not modify the data.

ColdFusion cannot declare locks on a database. It can, however, provide the database with a suggestion or plan for locking with use of isolation levels in the `CFTRANSACTION` tag.

There are four levels of isolation that are supported by ColdFusion. Serializable isolation is the highest level and is the equivalent of the exclusive lock. The Repeatable Read isolation level enables other SQL statements to perform inserts. When using this level of isolation, you need to ensure that inserts do not affect your transactions. Read Committed enables both inserts and reads. This means that if a user reads data and then reads the data a second time, it is possible for the data to have changed between the reads. One caveat to this is that the data does not change until a `commit` has been run by the transaction that changed the data. The last level of isolation is the Read Uncommitted. This is similar to the Read Committed level except that users read changes to data as soon as they occur without a `commit`. This means that you are reading "dirty" data, which could actually change once more if the transaction fails and the data is rolled back.

So how does the `CFTRANSACTION` tag work? The transaction starts with the first ColdFusion tag after the `CFTRANSACTION` tag and ends with the `CFTRANSACTION` closing tag. It should be noted that only ColdFusion tags that require a datasource are considered to be part of the transaction. Additionally, all ColdFusion tags must use the same datasource. This is probably the one drawback to the use of the `CFTRANSACTION` tag—it cannot span multiple datasources. When ColdFusion encounters the `CFTRANSACTION` end tag, the transaction is committed. If at any point the database returns an error, the database actions to this point are rolled back and the transaction is ended.

```
<!--- Customer has cancelled order. We want to ensure that when order is deleted from
→ORDER table all associated records from ORDERLINE table are also deleted--->
<cftransaction>
    <!--- Delete order information from ORDER table --->
    <cfquery NAME="DeleteOrder" DATASOURCE="MyTest">
        DELETE FROM ORDER
        WHERE ORDERID = #OrderID#
    </cfquery>
    <!--- Delete associated records from ORDERLINE table--->
    <cfquery  NAME="DeleteOrderLine" DATASOURCE="MyTest">
        DELETE FROM ORDERLINE
        WHERE ORDERID = #OrderID#
    </cfquery>
</cftransaction>
```

There are situations where we might need additional control over the behavior of the `CFTRANSACTION` tag. One application that we worked on had several steps involved in the processing of an order for merchandise. The steps included deducting the item(s) from inventory, processing the credit card charge, and making an entry in the inventory log table. If the credit card processing failed, we wanted the inventory rolled back. Conversely, if the entry to the inventory log table failed, we did not want the entire transaction to rollback.

Another example is that of transactions that involve batch processing a number of individual transactions nested inside a transaction. If we are processing a number of credit card transactions, we would want to roll back an individual failure but not have the rollback affect the credit card transactions that had been successful. We can have more control over the `CFTRANSACTION` tag behavior with use of the `action` attribute of the `CFTRANSACTION` tag. There are three supported values for the `action` attribute:

```
action="begin" (default)
action="commit"
action="rollback"
```

BEGIN

The default action option is BEGIN. This specifies the beginning of the block of code to be executed. If no action attribute is specified, `action=begin` is assumed.

COMMIT

This option is used to commit pending transactions. CFTRANSACTION tags using either `action=commit` or `action=rollback` must be nested inside a `<CFTRANSACTION></CFTRANSACTION>` block.

```
<cftransaction ACTION="COMMIT"/>
```

Let's modify our previous example a bit so that we are deleting a number of orders and have a commit after each order is processed:

```
<!--- A part of our business model we have decided to manually verify each credit card
➥order that specifies a shipping address that is different from the customer's address.
➥At the end of each business day we delete all orders that cannot be verified.  This is
➥accomplished with a batch process.--->
<cftransaction>
        <!--- Obtain list of orders to be deleted--->
        <cfset OrderList = #ordernumbers#>
        <!--- Delete order information from ORDER table --->
        <cfloop LIST="#OrderList#" INDEX="OrderID">
            <cfquery NAME="DeleteOrder" DATASOURCE="MyTest">
                DELETE FROM ORDER
                WHERE ORDERID = #OrderID#
            </CFQUERY>
        <!--- Delete associated records from ORDERLINE table--->
        <cfquery NAME="DeleteOrderLine" DATASOURCE="MyTest">
            DELETE FROM ORDERLINE
            WHERE ORDERID = #OrderID#
        </cfquery>
        <!--- We want to commit with each loop, this way if one
        transaction fails the other are already committed and will not be
        rolled back--->
        <cftransaction ACTION="COMMIT"/>
        </cfloop>
</cftransaction>
```

You might recall that we said one of the drawbacks of the CFTRANSACTION tag is that it cannot work across multiple datasources. That is not entirely true, as we can use the CFTRANSACTION ACTION="commit"/ tag to make this happen. By nesting the CFTRANSACTION ACTION="commit"/ tag, we can commit a transaction and change the datasource.

```
<cftransaction>
    <!---Insert a record and then run select against the record to
    ➥obtain some output--->
    <cfquery NAME="test_test" DATASOURCE="test">
        SET NOCOUNT ON
```

```
        INSERT INTO tbl_news (title,body,dept_id)
        VALUES ('Test Test','testing test and transactions',1)
        SELECT title_id = @@identity
        SET NOCOUNT OFF
    </cfquery>
    <cfquery NAME ="get_test" DATASOURCE ="test">
     SELECT news_id
      FROM tbl_news
      WHERE news_id = #test_test.title_id#
    </cfquery>
    <!---use the ACTION="COMMIT--->
    <cftransaction ACTION="COMMIT"/>
    <cfquery NAME="test_rits" DATASOURCE="rits">
      INSERT INTO auth_users (userid, pwd, lastName, sysadmin,
      createAccounts)
      VALUES ('clearwater','dstm','Gimpy','1','1')
    </cfquery>
    <cfquery NAME="GET_rits" DATASOURCE="rits">
      SELECT userid,pwd
      FROM auth_users
      WHERE userid='clearwater'
    </cfquery>
</cftransaction>
<cfoutput>
news id - #get_test.news_id# <br>
transaction change<br>
userid - #get_rits.userid#<br>
pwd - #get_rits.pwd#
</cfoutput>
```

Figure 23.2 shows the results of the preceding code with CFTRANSACTION
ACTION="commit"/ commented out. Notice the resulting error reads "More
than one datasource used in a CFTRANSACTION."

ROLLBACK

The ROLLBACK option forces a rollback of pending transactions:

```
<cftransaction ACTION="ROLLBACK"/>
```

You should notice the trailing forward slash after the action attribute with
both the COMMIT and ROLLBACK options. This tells ColdFusion that there is no
closing tag. In this next example, we are going to show how to use the CFTRY
and CFCATCH tags in conjunction with CFTRANSACTION:

```
<cfset commitMe="Yes">
<cftransaction>
    <cftry>
      <cfquery NAME="DeleteOrder" DATASOURCE="MyTest">
          DELETE FROM ORDER
          WHERE ORDERID = #OrderID#
      </cfquery>
      <cfcatch TYPE="Database">
```

```
            <cftransaction ACTION="ROLLBACK"/>
            <cfoutput>
            WARNING a database error has occurred<br>
            Message :#CFCATCH.message# <br>
            Type :#CFCATCH.type# <br>
            </cfoutput>
            <cfset commitMe = "No">
        </cfcatch>
        <cfif commitMe EQ 'Yes'>
        <cftransaction ACTION="COMMIT"/>
        <cfelse>
        <cfset commitMe = "Yes">
        </cfif>
    </cftry>
</cftransaction>
```

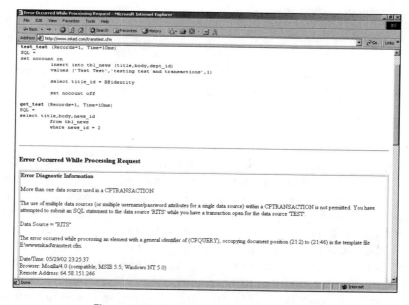

Figure 23.2   Error occurred while processing.

There is one "misconception" related to the CFTRANSACTION tag that we would like to point out. Many developers use the CFTRANSACTION tag to guarantee the retrieval of the ID of the record that was just submitted. The common approach in Microsoft SQL using an ID Column of CustomerID would be something like this:

```
<cftransaction>
    <cfquery NAME="Test" DATASOURCE="MyTest">
        INSERT INTO CUSTOMER (FirstName,LastName)
        VALUES ('#FirstName#','#LastName#')
    </cfquery>
```

```
    <cfquery NAME="getMaxID">
        SELECT Max(CustomerID) AS MaxID FROM CUSTOMER
    </cfquery>
</cftransaction>
```

Although this works a high percentage of the time, it does not guarantee that the correct value is returned. When we are developing with Microsoft SQL, we prefer to use the following method instead:

```
<cfquery NAME="Test" DATASOURCE="MyTest">

    <!--- Set NOCOUNT ON prevents the return of number of rows from the
    insert--->
    SET NOCOUNT ON

    INSERT INTO CUSTOMER (FirstName,LastName)
    VALUES ('#FirstName#','#LastName#')
    SELECT  cust_id = @@identity
    SET NOCOUNT OFF
</cfquery>
```

Of course, only some databases such Microsoft SQL Server 2000 and Sybase ASE 12 support the previous example. With Oracle, you must take another approach involving sequences.

Summary

Transactions provide a way for data manipulation to be processed as a single event. The advantage is that either all SQL statements execute successfully and are committed or all are rolled back. Databases that support transactions provide levels of locking. Although ColdFusion cannot control the level of locking used by the database, the CFTRANSACTION tag can influence the lock with the use of the isolation attribute. The action attribute provides you additional control over the behavior of the CFTRANSACTION tag. It is important to remember that although most commercial databases support transactions, there are some popular open-source databases that do not or did not until recent releases.

Summary

Databases provide us with a structured and organized manner in which to store data. One of the most popular types of database models is the relational database. Relational databases use tables as a way of representing relationships between entities. SQL is the language used to communicate with relational databases. Although you do not need to be a SQL expert to develop ColdFusion applications, you do need a basic understanding of the SQL language.

Our discussion of SQL should get you started; but if you are not familiar or comfortable with SQL, we strongly recommend that you invest in any one of the excellent texts on the market that cover the topic in detail. Keep in mind that most DBMSs have added proprietary extensions to the basic SQL, so it is strongly suggested you purchase a text that focuses on the database system with which you are working.

Stored procedures offer a way to encapsulate repetitive and complex tasks that are normally accomplished with a series of SQL statements. The use of stored procedures offers many advantages, including improved performance. In ColdFusion, we can execute stored procedures using either the CFSTORED-PROC or CFQUERY tags. You normally want to execute stored procedures with the CFSTOREDPROC tag because of the limitations of the CFQUERY tag.

Many databases support the concept of transactions. Transactions enable us to treat a group of queries as one, meaning that if one fails, the results of the preceding queries are rolled back. Transactions also provide a mechanism to prevent multiple users from editing the same data at the same time. We use the CFTRANSACTION tag to identify the queries we desire to treat as a single transaction.

In the Chapter 24, "Advanced Database Interaction," we discuss how to take our database interactions to the next level by writing dynamic SQL statements and queries of queries (CFSQL). We also examine how to improve performance in applications by using query caching.

24

Advanced Database Interaction

In previous chapters, we reviewed some of the basic concepts relating to relational databases as well as the fundamental ways ColdFusion can interact with a database. Our interactions with the database have been based on static structured query language (SQL) statements. Take a look at the code in Listing 24.1. This is a simple `select` statement that returns all records from the database table named `State`, where the state name begins with the letter C. The recordset returned would look something like Figure 24.1.

Listing 24.1 **A Simple Static Select Statement**

```
<cfquery name="GetStates" datasource="MyTest">
    SELECT StateAbbreviation,StateName
    FROM State
    WHERE StateName LIKE 'C%'
</cfquery>
<TABLE WIDTH=50%>
    <TR>
        <TD WIDTH=50%><B>Abbreviation</B></TD>
        <TD WIDTH=50%><B>Name</B></TD>
    </TR>
    <cfoutput query="GetStates">
    <TR>
        <TD>#StateAbbreviation#</TD>
        <TD>#StateName#</TD>
    </TR>
    </cfoutput>
</TABLE>
```

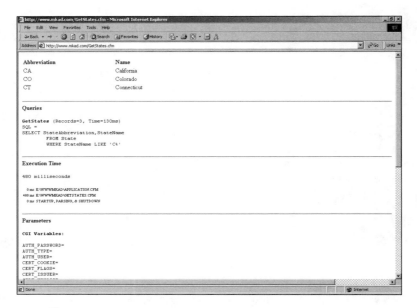

Figure 24.1 Recordset returned by the simple `select` statement.

With a static SQL statement, the exact same query is executed each time the query is called. Let's assume that we are building an application and we need to be able to return a recordset that contains a listing of state names based on the first letter of the state name. Now we could write 26 queries (one for each letter of the alphabet), but that would be a bit cumbersome, particularly if we had similar scenarios that required complex queries. Instead, we could write our `GetStates` query so that it enabled the user to specify the letter(s) to be used in the `WHERE` clause when he or she called the query. Dynamic queries enable the user to specify parameters in the form page. These parameters are then passed to the `CFQUERY` tag on the action page.

Dynamic SQL

Queries of this type are known as dynamic queries because the SQL sent to the database is not known until runtime. Dynamic queries contain both static (common SQL) and dynamic SQL. Let's look at our `GetStates` query, written as dynamic SQL in Listing 24.2.

Listing 24.2 *GetStates* **Query Written as Dynamic SQL**

```
<cfquery name="GetStates" datasource="MyTest">
    SELECT StateAbbreviation,StateName
    FROM State
    WHERE StateName LIKE '#Form.State#%'
</cfquery>
```

If the user entered a value of D in the input form, the SQL statement sent to the database would look like the code in Listing 24.3.

Listing 24.3 **Code Executed in the *GetStates* Query**

```
SELECT StateAbbreviation,StateName
FROM State
WHERE StateName LIKE 'D%'
```

One of the most common uses of dynamic queries is to generate the query based on user inputs. In Listing 24.1, the only portion that is dynamic is the string value used to search for state names. There might be many scenarios in which you would construct dynamic queries that have multiple conditional statements all based on input from the user. In these scenarios, you often would include only the condition if the user provides input. Such a scenario would be a search of a Customer table.

You might want the capability to search for customers based on the customer's ID number, last name, state, or a combination of the three. There are a couple of different methods that can be used to accomplish this task. The first involves using a combination of the CFIF tag and IsDefined() function. In this situation, you would use the IsDefined() function to check for the existence of a parameter value and, if it exists, check the value to ensure that it meets certain conditions. This would be done prior to the submission of the query. The second method, which builds on some of the best practices discussed in previous chapters, employs the CFPARAM tag to ensure that the parameter always exist and then uses the CFIF tag to determine if a value was passed by the user. You likely will encounter both methods, so I want to demonstrate both in Listing 24.4.

Listing 24.4 **Dynamic Query Using *IsDefined()***

```
<cfquery name="FindCustomer" datasource="MyTest">
     SELECT CustomerID, CustomerFirstName, CustomerLastName,
     CustomerEmail
     FROM Customer
     WHERE 0 = 0
     <cfif IsDefined("Form.ID") AND Form.ID IS NOT "">
               AND CustomerID = #Form.ID#
     </cfif>
     <cfif IsDefined("Form.LastName") AND Form. LastName IS NOT "">
               AND CustomerLastName ='#Form.LastName#'
     </cfif>
     <cfif IsDefined("Form.StateID") AND Form.StateID IS NOT "">
               AND CustomerStateID = #Form.StateID#
     </cfif>
</cfquery>
```

If the user input the criteria of LastName = Smith and StateID = 5, the resulting SQL statement would look like Listing 24.5.

Listing 24.5 **Code Executed in the *FindCustomer* Query**

```
SELECT CustomerID, CustomerFirstName, CustomerLastName, CustomerEmail
FROM Customer
WHERE 0 = 0
AND CustomerLastName = 'Smith'
AND CustomerStateID = 5
```

You might encounter similar examples that use a nested CFIF statement rather than the combined CFIF statement that I used. Although it looks a bit different, they both accomplish the same thing:

```
<cfifF IsDefined("Form.ID")>
              <cfif Form.ID IS NOT "">
              AND CustomerID = #Form.ID#
          </cfif>
</cfif>
```

So, what did our code actually do here? We first checked whether the Form field was defined. This check prevents an error if the page has been changed and the field no longer is part of the Form. We then checked whether there was actually a value in the form field. In most circumstances we want the condition to be part of the SQL statement passed to the database only if a value is passed. Keep in mind that if our form page contains three input fields named `ID`, `LastName` and `StateID`, a value of `""` is passed when the form is posted to the action page and the user does not provide a value. To demonstrate the point, let's remove the second part of the `CFIF` statement from our `CFQUERY`.

Listing 24.6 *FindCustomer* **Without Value Check**

```
<cfquery name="FindCustomer" datasource="MyTest">
     SELECT CustomerID, CustomerFirstName, CustomerLastName,
     CustomerEmail
     FROM Customer
     WHERE 0 = 0
     <cfif IsDefined("Form.ID")>
          AND CustomerID = #Form.ID#
     </cfif>
     <cfif IsDefined("Form.LastName")>
          AND CustomerLastName ='#Form.LastName#'
     </cfif>
     <cfif IsDefined("Form.State")>
          AND CustomerStateID = #Form.StateID#
     </cfif>
</cfquery>
```

If the user once again submits the values of `LastName` = `Smith` and `StateID` = 5, the resulting SQL statement would be much different, as shown in Listing 24.7.

Listing 24.7 **SQL Executed by** *FindCustomer* **Without Value Check**

```
SELECT CustomerID, CustomerFirstName, CustomerLastName, CustomerEmail
FROM Customer
WHERE 0 = 0
AND CustomerID =
AND CustomerLastName = 'Smith'
AND CustomerStateID = 5
```

Take a look at Figure 24.2. As you can see, not only is the SQL statement that is passed to the database different, so are the results.

Let's show how we can write our `FindCustomer` query utilizing the `CFPARAM` tag instead of the `IsDefined()` function. Notice in this method that we do not need to check for the existence of the variable as we use the `CFPARAM` tag to ensure it exists. We still check the variable to determine whether the user passed a value. As with our previous example, we still do not want the search criteria to be part of the SQL `WHERE` clause unless, of course, the user provides a value.

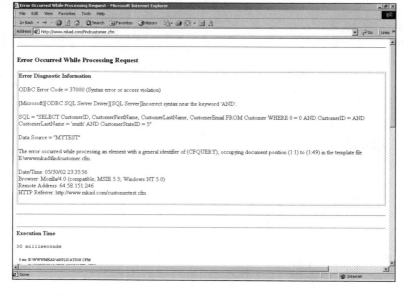

Figure 24.2   FindCustomer without value check throws error.

Listing 24.8   *FindCustomer* Query Using *CFParam*

```
<cfparam name="form.id" default="0">
<cfparam name ="form.lastname" default="">
<cfparam name ="form.stateid" default="0">
<cfquery name="findcustomer" datasource="MyTest">
  SELECT CustomerID,
         CustomerFirstName,
         CustomerLastName,
         CustomerEmail
    FROM Customer
   WHERE 0 = 0
  <cfif NOT Val(Form.ID)>
     AND CustomerID = #Val(Form.ID)#
  </cfif>
  <cfif Len(Trim(Form. LastName))>
     AND CustomerLastName ='#Trim(Form.LastName)#'
  </cfif >
  <cfif Val(Form.StateID)>
     AND CustomerStateID = #Val(Form.StateID)#
  </cfif >
</cfquery>
```

Although one of the most popular uses of dynamic queries is creating user-generated search criteria, there are other ways to use dynamic queries. One of the most common is to specify the datasource dynamically. This enables you to change the datasource, normally set in the `Application.cfm` file, without having to modify additional code.

Listing 24.9 **Dynamic Datasource**

```
<cfquery name="ListStates" datasource="#Request.DSN#">
    SELECT StateID,StateAbbreviation
    FROM State
</cfquery>
```

Query Caching

In Listing 24.9, the code returns a recordset containing the state abbreviation and the state ID from the `State` table. As you might imagine, this query could be used to populate a form select list. By using the results of our `ListStates` query to populate a select list, we remove the need to hard code 50 or more `OPTION` tags. Not only does this save us time, but also it eliminates potential mistakes in our code. Yes, I know that there are only 50 states, but let's not forget about Washington, D.C., Puerto Rico, and the various territories.

I am sure that you can think of a number of templates that could require the use of this `States` select list. Let's assume that we have created a form that new customers use to open new accounts. Each time a customer goes to create a new account, the `ListStates` query is run, and the result set is the same each time. Although this is a simple query and takes only a few milliseconds to execute, it could be called hundreds of times a day as new accounts are created. Because the `ListStates` query could be used in a number of CFM templates, we could realistically have a situation in which this query is executing several thousand times a day. Those "few milliseconds" of execution time start adding up, not to mention the resulting network traffic.

Fortunately, ColdFusion offers the capability to cache in server memory the result sets of specified SQL queries. It does this with two optional attributes of the `CFQUERY` tag: `cacheWithin` and `cacheAfter`. The `cachedWithin` attribute is used to specify a time span for caching the query results. The `CreateTimeSpan` function creates a time span from the present backward. If the original query was executed within the specified time span, the recordset in memory is used. If not, the query is executed and the new recordset is placed in memory.

Listing 24.10 **Query Caching Using the *CACHEDWITHIN* Attribute**

```
<cfquery name="GetStates" datasource="MyTest"
    cachedWithin=#CreateTimeSpan(0,1,0,0)#>
    SELECT StateAbbreviation,StateName
    FROM State
    WHERE StateName LIKE 'C%'
</cfquery>
```

The CACHEDAFTER attribute caches the query based on a particular date and time. When a call for the query is made, ColdFusion verifies whether a recordset of the query exists. If it does, ColdFusion checks the timestamp of the cached recordset and if it is after the time specified in the CACHEDAFTER attribute, it uses the existing recordset. There is one important difference between the CACHEDWITHIN and CACHEDAFTER attributes. The CACHEDWITHIN attribute eventually expires; the CACHEDAFTER attribute does not.

Listing 24.11 **Query Caching Using the *CACHEDAFTER* Attribute**

```
<cfquery name="GetStates" datasource="MyTest"
    cachedAfter="04/25/02 14:32">
    SELECT StateAbbreviation,StateName
    FROM State
    WHERE StateName LIKE 'C%'
</cfquery>
```

At this point, we should point out a few quick tips concerning the "date" for the cachedAfter attribute. The date can be in different formats, including the following:

- 04/25/02
- 26 April 2002
- April 26 2002
- 04-26-02

The time of 00:01 is assumed if a time is not specified. You can use either the 24-hour or a.m./p.m. time formats:

- 14:32 (24-hour format)
- 2:32PM (a.m./p.m format, which assumes a.m. if not specified)

Figure 24.3 shows our query being executed without query caching being utilized. Be sure to note the query execution time in the QUERY debug output.

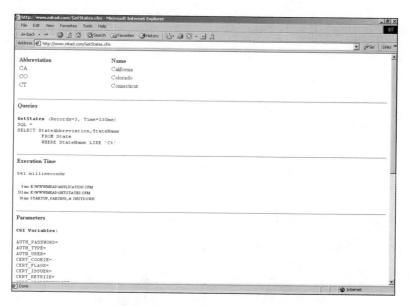

Figure 24.3 GetStates without query caching.

Now look at Figure 24.4, which is our query executed with the cachedWithin attribute. Again, be sure to look at the execution time in the QUERY debug output. You can see that the execution time has changed from 130ms to Cached Query.

Query caching must be enabled in the ColdFusion Administrator for the CACHEDAFTER and CACHEDWITHIN attributes to be functional. You enable caching in the ColdFusion Administrator by setting the value for "Limiting the maximum number of cached queries on the server to" to a value greater than 0 (see Figure 24.5).

Queries are cached on a serverwide basis, not per application. Prior to the release of ColdFusion 4.5, you were limited to a maximum of 100 cached queries. The removal of this limit does not mean you should attempt to cache all the queries in your application. Remember that cached queries are stored in the server memory, so the queries and number of queries that you cache can impact overall server performance.

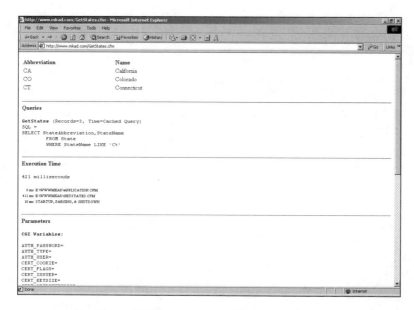

Figure 24.4 GetStates with query caching.

ColdFusion uses the FIFO (First In, First Out) model to manage cached queries when the limit is reached. This means that when the limit for cached queries is reached, the oldest cached query is dropped to make room for the new cached query.

There are a couple things to keep in mind when caching queries. For caching purposes, queries must use same SQL statement, datasource, query name, username, password, and DBTYPE. There are three sample queries. ColdFusion treats all three differently, even though they appear to be identical at first glance.

Listing 24.12 *GetStates* **Examples 1–3**

```
Example 1
<cfquery name="GetStates" datasource="MyTest"
    cachedWithin=#CreateTimeSpan(0,1,0,0)#>
    SELECT StateAbbreviation,StateName
    FROM State
    WHERE StateName LIKE 'C%'
</cfquery>
Example 2
<cfquery name="GetStates" datasource="MyTest2"
    cachedWithin=#CreateTimeSpan(0,1,0,0)#>
```

```
      SELECT StateAbbreviation,StateName
      FROM State
      WHERE StateName LIKE 'C%'
</cfquery>
Example 3
<cfquery name="GetStates" datasource="MyTest"
      cachedWithin=#CreateTimeSpan(0,1,0,0)#>
      SELECT StateAbbreviation, StateName
      FROM State
      WHERE StateName LIKE 'C%'
</cfquery>
```

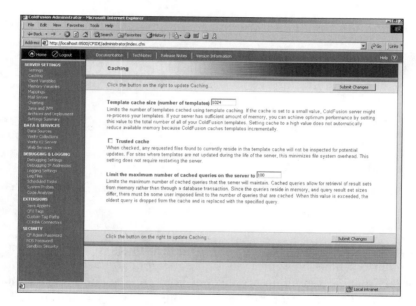

Figure 24.5 ColdFusion MX Administrator caching settings.

Examples 1 and 2 have different datasources, which cause ColdFusion to treat Example 2 as a new query. Still trying to see the difference between Example 1 and 3? Look closely at the select statement in Example 3; notice the space after the comma separating StateAbbreviation and StateName. You must pay particular attention to the SQL statement because something as small as tabbing causes ColdFusion to treat what appear to be identical SQL statements as different SQL statements. Being "doubting developers," we had to prove the tabbing to ourselves when we first worked with query caching in ColdFusion.

Compare the executed SQL statement in Figure 24.3 and Figure 24.4 with Figure 24.6. Notice that there is a space in the SELECT statement in Figure 24.6; that it is the only difference.

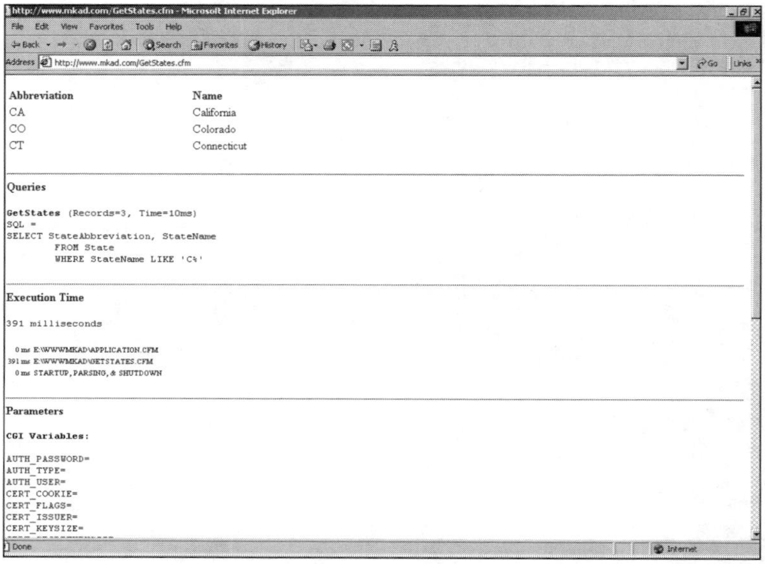

Figure 24.6   SELECT statement with a space.

Up to this point, we have used examples of static queries for our discussion of query caching. Now, what about the use of query caching with dynamic SQL? There is nothing to prevent you from caching queries that contain dynamic SQL, but you should exercise some caution. ColdFusion caches a recordset for each dynamic value. If we modify our ListStates query to cache, we most likely have only one recordset cached unless we have multiple applications on our server using the same query.

Listing 24.13   Caching a Dynamic Query

```
<cfquery name="ListStates" datasource="#DSN#"
    cachedWithin=#CreateTimeSpan(0,1,0,0)#>
        SELECT StateID,StateAbbreviation
        FROM State
</cfquery>
```

If we add the cacheWithin attribute to the GetStates query found in Listing 24.2, we easily could have dozens of cached recordsets. This is not to say that you should not use caching with dynamic SQL queries other than with scenarios similar to Listing 24.13. What we are pointing out is that caution should be used.

Another thing to consider when using caching queries is that cached queries do not reflect changes to the database until the cache interval has expired. In some cases, this is acceptable; in other cases, we need to have changes to the database reflected immediately.

To handle scenarios that require the return of real-time recordsets, we have some options. We can choose not to use query caching, to use short cache time spans if we know when or how frequently updates will occur, or to force updates of the cached queries. In Listing 24.14, we have a query that returns a product list. The cache time span is set for 12 hours because updates are fairly infrequent.

Listing 24.14 **Cached *ProductList* Query**

```
<cfquery name="ProductList" datasource="#DSN#"
    cachedWithin=#CreateTimeSpan(0,12,0,0)#>
        SELECT ProductID, ProductName, ProductDescription,
        ProductPricePerUnit
        FROM Product
        WHERE CategoryID = 10
</cfquery>
```

This is a query that we want to cache, but when products are updated or added, we want the change to be reflected immediately. If we add a new product or change the price of a product, we do not want to run the risk of the change not being reflected for up to 12 hours. To force updates of the cached query, we can have the queries that effect changes followed by a CFQUERY that contains a negative cachedWithin value.

Listing 24.15 **Forcing an Update of a Cached Query**

```
<cfquery name="UpdateProduct" datasource="#DSN#">
    UPDATE Product
    SET ProductPricePerUnit = '#newPrice#'
    WHERE ProductID = #ProductID#
</cfquery>
<cfquery name="ProductList" datasource="#DSN#"
    cachedWithin=#CreateTimeSpan(0,0,0,-1)#>
        SELECT ProductID, ProductName, ProductDescription,
        ProductPricePerUnit
        FROM Product
        WHERE CategoryID = 10
</cfquery>
```

There is one other way to force the update of cached queries. ColdFusion 5 introduced the CFOBJECTCACHE tag. Unlike our example in Listing 24.15, CFOBJECTCACHE tag flushes the *entire* query cache. If you use this tag, exercise caution, particularly in a shared hosting environment. It uses the following syntax:

```
<cfobjectcache action="clear">
```

There is another way to enhance performance that is related to SQL queries. When you create a datasource, one of the options is Maintain Database Connections. When this option is enabled, ColdFusion keeps the connection open after its first connection to the database. This means that ColdFusion is not constantly opening and closing database connections. This concept is outside the scope of this discussion, but is nonetheless important. If you do not fully understand what ColdFusion does when it encounters a SQL statement or how it handles database connections, you should read Macromedia TechNote 22128, "How Are Database Connections Handled in ColdFusion." It is available at www.macromedia.com/v1/handlers/index.cfm?ID=22128. Another excellent article is "ColdFusion Timeouts and Unresponsive Requests," which is available at www.macromedia.com/v1/Handlers/index.cfm?ID=21641&Method=Full.

Query of Queries (CFSQL)

One of the new features introduced with the release of ColdFusion 5 was the query of queries. The query of queries (CFSQL) is actually an extension of the CFQUERY tag that we have already covered. With a basic CFSQL, you begin with a CFQUERY tag just as we have done in previous examples. You then write a second CFQUERY tag with two modifications—you do not use the datasource attribute and you set the DBTYPE attribute to query.

There are a number of advantages offered by the use of a CFSQL. The first potential use is to reduce the interaction with the database.

In Listing 24.16, we are querying our Product table for information about all products that are in category 21. The result set then is cached in memory for one hour. We now can run queries about individual products or groups of products without having to make additional calls to our database. We simply run a query against the in-memory recordset.

Listing 24.16 **Query of a Query**

```
<cfquery name="ProductList" datasource="#Request.DSN#"
    cachedWithin=#CreateTimeSpan(0,1,0,0)#>
        SELECT ProductID, ProductName, ProductDescription,
        ProductPricePerUnit
        FROM Product
        WHERE CategoryID = 10
</cfquery>
<cfquery CFQUERY name="GetProduct" dbtype="query" >
    SELECT *
    FROM ProductList
    WHERE ProductID = #Form.ProductID#
</cfquery>
```

Although it is possible to store large recordsets in memory, we are again in a situation of "just because we can" does not mean that we should. Placing a large number of record sets in memory in this manner makes sense only when a high number of the records are accessed repeatedly or the recordset itself is repeatedly called, such as in a sorting scenario.

Another use of the CFSQL is to create joins or unions across datasources. In Listing 24.17, we have created a union of the recordsets of two queries with different data sources. This is particularly useful if you need to interact with legacy applications. In Listing 24.18, we demonstrate the same principle, but with a join.

Listing 24.17 **Creating a Union with a CFSQL**

```
<cfquery name="SurfProductList" datasource="MyTest">
    SELECT ProductID, ProductName, ProductDescription,
    ProductPricePerUnit
    FROM Product
    WHERE CategoryID = 10
</cfquery>
<cfquery name="SkiProductList" datasource
    ="MyTest2">
    SELECT ProductID, ProductName, ProductDescription,
    ProductPricePerUnit
    FROM Product
    WHERE CategoryID = 11
</cfquery>
<cfquery name="GetProduct" DBTYPE="query">
    SELECT ProductID, ProductName, ProductDescription,
    ProductPricePerUnit
    FROM SurfProductList
    UNION
    SELECT ProductID, ProductName, ProductDescription,
    ProductPricePerUnit
    FROM SkiProductList
</cfquery>
```

Listing 24.18 **Creating a Join with a CFSQL**

```
<cfquery name="NewCustomerList" datasource="MyTest">
    SELECT CustomerID, CustomerFName, CustomerLName, CustomerAddress,
    CustomerCity, CustomerState, CustomerZipCode
    FROM Customer
</cfquery>
<cfquery name="CustomerCCList" datasource
    ="MyTest2">
    SELECT CustomerID, CustomerCCNumber, CustomerCCType,
    CustomerCCExpire
    FROM CustomerCC
</cfquery>
<cfquery name="GetCustomers" DBTYPE="query">
    SELECT *
    FROM NewCustomerList,CustomerCCList
    WHERE  NewCustomerList.CustomerID = CustomerCCList.CustomerID
</cfquery>
```

There are a number of ColdFusion tags, such as CFDIRECTORY, CFFTP, CFPOP, CFSEARCH, CFREGISTRY, CFHTTP, and CFPROCRESULTS, that return query objects. In addition, many CFX and custom tags return query objects that also can be used with CFSQLs. The CFSQLs can be used to query on the result sets or create a join of the result sets of these query objects.

In Listing 24.19, we are using the CFPOP tag to obtain the header information about the first 25 emails on a POP mail server. The result set is returned as a query object, which the code queries, looking for only those emails that are from the well-known ColdFusion mail list, CFGURUS.

Listing 24.19 **Using a CFSQL to Query a Query Object**

```
<cfpop server="www.mypoperver.com" username="myaccount" password="topsecret"
actions="getheaderonly" name="testpop">
<cfquery name="getmail" dbtype="query">
    SELECT testpop.From as Who ,testpop.Subject as What
    FROM testpop
    WHERE testpop.Subject LIKE '%cfgurus%'
</cfquery>
<cfoutput>
Mail Count for Testpop is #testpop.RecordCount#
</cfoutput><BR>
<B>CFDJLIST</B><BR>
<cfoutput QUERY="getmail">
Row: #CurrentRow#  From: #Who#  Subject:#.What# <BR>
</cfoutput>
```

Keep in mind that any ColdFusion tag that returns a query object can be used with a CFSQL. We could have just as easily used a second CFPOP tag to obtain emails from work and then created a union of the two with the CFSQL. We can also use CFSQLs to join database and nondatabase result sets.

As you can see, using the CFSQL is a simple concept that has a lot of potential uses. The CFSQL enables you to query result sets in memory, create cross-data source joins, query nondatabase sources, and join database and nondatabase queries. There are, however, some limitations that we must discuss. The first is that you can perform only SELECTS; keep in mind that you are performing your queries against an existing result set, not the database. CFSQL also does not support comparisons of open database connectivity ODBC dates or nested aggregate functions.

Summary

One of the real strengths of ColdFusion is its capability to interact with a number of types of datasources, including relational databases, to deliver dynamic content. In this chapter, we examined how to use dynamic SQL to take the delivery of the content to the next level. Dynamic SQL gives us the ability to create our SQL statements at runtime, thus enabling us to write one statement that can meet the requirements of many scenarios.

25

Administering the ColdFusion Server

In the section, we begin to explore the ColdFusion Administrator, how it works, and some common settings that you can adjust to complete common administrative tasks or tweak the performance of your server. Although the Administrator itself has changed slightly with the release of ColdFusion MX, the layout is still familiar if you've worked with previous versions of ColdFusion. Figure 25.1 demonstrates the layout of the ColdFusion Administrator as it exists in ColdFusion MX.

As you can see, the Administrator is divided into three main panes. The left pane, used for primary navigation through the Administrator, contains links to all the other settings that can be accessed through the Administrator. The main window is where you actually adjust settings or make changes. Finally, the top pane contains links to the Macromedia Knowledge Base, any documentation you might have chosen to install, and a link to get more information with your server.

We will be looking at all the settings that you can adjust in this section and what effects changes to those settings have on your server.

The ColdFusion Administrator can be found (by default) at `http://servername/cfide/administrator/index.cfm`. After you get there, you be presented with a simple login page. Here you enter the Administrator password that you set up during install, and then you are sent to the Administrator home page. This is the page you see in Figure 25.1.

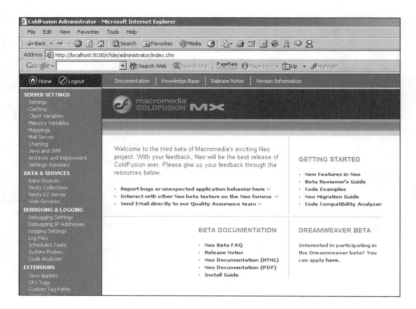

Figure 25.1 Main page of the ColdFusion MX Administrator.

At the home page, you can choose from a variety of other areas that you'd like to examine by using the left navigational menu. The left navigational menu is divided into several distinct categories. The first of these categories is Server Settings.

Server Settings

The first header, Server Settings, contains several items beneath it that control how the ColdFusion Server behaves. We examine each below.

Settings

Beneath the Server Settings header, you have several clickable items from which you can choose. The first of these is, simply enough, Settings. This page enables you to adjust several serverwide settings that have an effect on how the ColdFusion Server performs. Figure 25.2 gives you a look at the Settings page.

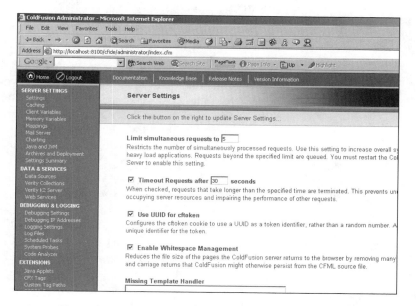

Figure 25.2   Settings page in the ColdFusion Administrator.

On the page shown in Figure 25.2, you can adjust six unique serverwide settings. Table 25.1 provides you an overview of each setting.

Table 25.1   **ColdFusion Administrator Server Settings, Settings Page**

Setting	Description of Setting
Limit simultaneous requests to	This setting enables you to limit the number of requests that ColdFusion Server can process concurrently. After this limit is reached, all other incoming requests are queued. Limiting the number of requests served concurrently can increase the performance of the ColdFusion Server.
Timeout requests after x seconds	By checking this check box, you are essentially telling ColdFusion Server to wait no more than x seconds for a request to complete before timing that request out. By enabling a timeout request value, you help ensure that server resources aren't tied up processing problematic or particularly long running requests.

continues ▶

Table 25.1 **Continued**

Setting	Description of Setting
Use UUID for `cftoken`	When this option is checked, rather than a random number being generated when a **CFTOKEN** is requested, a universal unique identifier (UUID) is generated instead. UUIDs are, by their nature, much less likely to be duplicated (in fact, they are virtually always unique) than a random number.
Enable Whitespace Management	By checking this check box, you are telling ColdFusion to compress carriage returns, spaces, and tabs that are present in raw ColdFusion Markup Language (CFML) templates to help reduce the size of the output. Checking this setting helps to eliminate extraneous whitespace throughout the output of CFML templates, thus reducing the overall size of the output file.
Missing Template Handler	This setting enables you to specify a particular template that you'd like to run whenever ColdFusion encounters a 404 error. By specifying a missing template handler, you are shielding your users from unfriendly "standard" error templates.
State-wide error handler	Much like the missing template handler, the state-wide error handler enables you to specify a template that you'd like to have run in the event that ColdFusion encounters an unhandled error while processing a request. Again, the purpose of this is to create error messages that are more friendly to the end user while shielding critical server information.

Settings—Helpful Hints

A couple of the settings deserver further comment. Here are some helpful hints concerning them.

Limit Simultaneous Requests

This setting can have the most dramatic effect on how the ColdFusion Server performs. When adjusting this setting, your goal is to achieve a balance between the maximum use of your processing power and the total time it takes to process requests. As an example, if you have this setting set to 4, then each request gets 25% of the total processor power dedicated to the servicing of that request. That means that, theoretically, each request completes more quickly than if you had a simultaneous request value of 10, where each request would use only 10% of the processor power. Of course, what this value should be set to is different for each application. If you have a database-intensive application in which most of the time in a given request is spent waiting for results to return from the database, you can afford to have a higher simultaneous request limit.

Timeout Requests After x Seconds

It is important to *always* have a timeout value set. What you set this timeout to is completely up to you, though it is helpful to determine the maximum amount of time that you think your users will wait for a page to return. In our experience, we've seen very few users who are patient enough to wait more than 60 seconds for a page to come back (and in many cases, the patience level is much lower). I don't think it's particularly helpful to have this value set much higher than what you believe your user base will bear. If you do, your users will click Stop or Refresh in their browsers and spawn another request.

If you have a page that you know is going to take a particularly long time to return, it's best to warn your users ahead of time (with some form of message letting them know of the process that they're about to start). Then use things like incremental page delivery (via CFFLUSH) to help speed up the perception of delivery. You can also specify a longer timeout value (for pages that you know run long) by appending a RequestTimeout=x parameter to the uniform resource locator (URL) of the long-running page. The value you insert here supercedes the value that is set in the Administrator, and this is often the better choice for handling a few problematic pages within the application. The syntax of the RequestTimeout parameter would look similar to the following example:

```
http://servername/longRunningTemplate.cfm?RequestTimeout=300
```

Caching

The next place we want to go in our tour of the ColdFusion Administrator is to the Caching page. Figure 25.3 gives you a look at the page inside of Administrator.

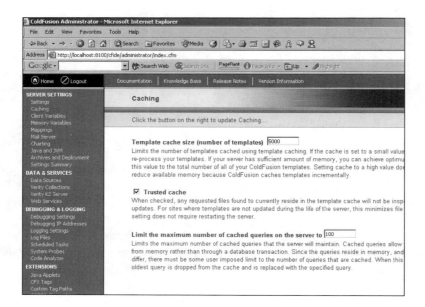

Figure 25.3 Caching page in the ColdFusion Administrator.

On the Caching page shown in Figure 25.3, you can adjust three unique, serverwide settings. Table 25.2 gives you an overview of each.

Table 25.2 **ColdFusion Administrator Server Settings, Caching Page**

Setting	Description of Setting
Template cache size (number of templates)	In ColdFusion MX, this setting has been changed slightly. If you've worked with performance tuning previous versions of ColdFusion, you might remember that the rule of thumb was to set this value to 3–5 times the total size of all of your raw CFML templates. In ColdFusion MX, you simply set this value equal to the total number of templates that you want to remain in cache. It's best to set this value equal to the total number of ColdFusion templates on your server. This eliminates the need to reprocess your templates and compile them to bytecode again if it's already been done once. In ColdFusion MX, this can greatly help with server performance.

Setting	Description of Setting
Trusted cache	Checking this setting tells ColdFusion that the copies of the template it has in memory are the most current, so there is no need to check for updates from the disk. On production servers, where updates to the codebase are closely managed, leaving this setting on can have a positive effect on server performance.
Limit the maximum number of cached queries on the server to x	This setting enables you to put a limit on the number of cached queries that ColdFusion holds onto before dumping the oldest one and replacing it with a new one. Of course, you can have as many cached queries as you'd like, but you need to remember that queries and the subsequent result sets stored in memory increase the overall memory footprint of the ColdFusion Server. Having too many cached queries, or having several that are excessively large (including results), can be a performance drain, especially if you have limited random-access memory (RAM) available.

Caching—Helpful Hints

A few words on the Trusted Cache setting might prove helpful. Before you turn this setting on in production, it's critical that you have a complete understanding of the effect of this setting. When a user requests a ColdFusion template from your server, your web server receives that request. It understands that a ColdFusion file is being requested, and the web server passes the request to the ColdFusion engine. The ColdFusion engine then retrieves the raw CFML file being requested from disk and compiles it to bytecode.

After the template has been compiled to bytecode, it's placed in a template cache. That means that the next time a request comes in for that particular template, ColdFusion won't need to recompile it, provided that the template cache is big enough to accommodate the compiled version. However, even if a template has already been compiled and is in template cache, ColdFusion still compares what is compiled in cache to the copy of the raw template on disk to make sure that no changes have been made. If no changes have been made, the ColdFusion goes ahead and serves back the cached copy. If any changes have been made to the source, the template is recompiled before being sent back to the client.

Turning on "trusted cache" eliminates the comparison of what is in cache to the source templates on disk. You are essentially telling the ColdFusion server to "trust" the copy of the template that is has in cache as the most current copy— hence the name "trusted cache." On servers where the source never changes or changes in a infrequent, managed way, having this setting on improves server performance and response time.

Client Variables

Next, we move to the Client Variables page. Figure 25.4 gives you a look at this page inside the Administrator.

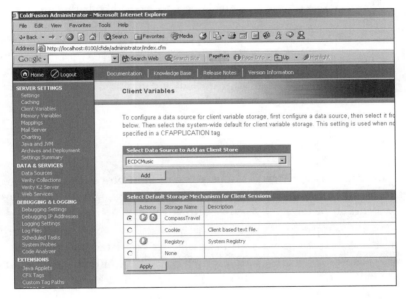

Figure 25.4 Client Variables page in the ColdFusion Administrator.

On the Client Variables page shown in Figure 25.4, you can choose where you'd like to store client variables on your system. Table 25.3 gives you an overview of each choice you have for client variable storage.

Table 25.3   **Choices for Client Variable Storage**

Storage Location	Pros and Cons
Registry	Yes, you can store client variables in the system registry, and there are some people who would tell you that there are actually reasons why you'd want to do so. However, I can't think of any good reason to do this, and all kinds of reasons why you shouldn't. Please don't store client variables in the system registry if you want any modicum of performance on your server.
Cookies	You can store your client-variable information in cookies on the client's browser. This works well as long as the client doesn't have cookies disabled and you don't want to store anything larger than 4K.
Database	This is by far the best choice for storing client-variable information, and it's relatively simple and easy to manage.

Memory Variables

Next we move to the Memory Variables page. Figure 25.5 gives you a look at the page inside the Administrator.

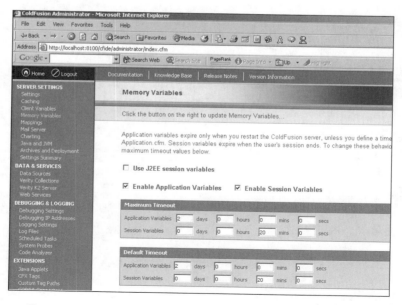

Figure 25.5   Memory Variables page in the ColdFusion Administrator.

By default, when ColdFusion is installed, application and session variables are enabled. If you uncheck either of these items, you no longer can use either application- or session-scoped variables in your ColdFusion applications.

You can also come to this page in the Administrator to specify maximum and default timeout values for application and session variables. You should be aware that the values you enter here override any maximum timeout values that you have set in the `Application.cfm`, so be careful when adjusting these values.

In addition, a new option in ColdFusion MX is the ability to use J2EE session variables. When you check this box, ColdFusion creates an internal identifier for each session that's spawned, and you no longer see `CFID` and `CFTOKEN` values.

Mappings

Next we move to the Mappings page. Figure 25.6 gives you a look at the page inside the Administrator.

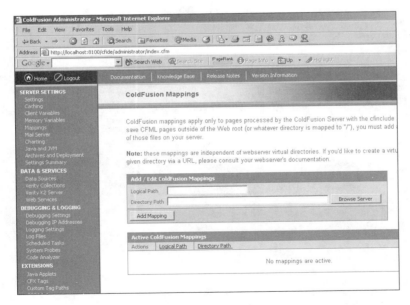

Figure 25.6 Mappings page in the ColdFusion Administrator.

The mappings section of the ColdFusion Administrator is used to created aliases for paths to directories on your server. For example, if you had a directory of images outside the webroot that you need to reference from your CFML templates, you'd create a mapping to that image directory here.

Mail Server

Next we move to the Mail Server page. Figure 25.7 gives you a look at the page inside the Administrator.

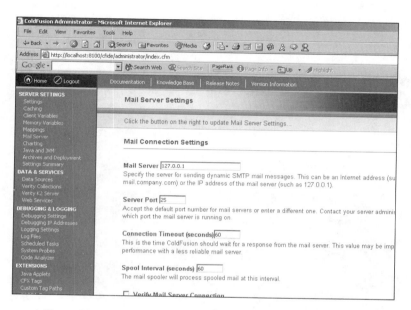

Figure 25.7 Mail Server page in the ColdFusion Administrator.

On this page, you can choose how you'd like to configure the mail server that's going to work with ColdFusion Server.

In the Mail Server field, you can enter the Internet Protocol (IP) address of the mail server that you want ColdFusion to use when you send mail from within an application with the CFMAIL tag. This can be an IP address of a remote server, or it can simply be a loopback address if you're going to use a mail server that's local to the machine on which ColdFusion is running.

Next, you have an option to specify the port that you'd like to send mail on. Typically, this port is 25, so using the default is okay, but you can change the port here should you need to.

You can also elect to set a connection timeout. Essentially, this caps the maximum amount of time that ColdFusion waits for the mail server to respond before timing out the mail process being attempted and moving the message to the Undeliverables folder.

The spool interval can also be adjusted. This setting controls how frequently ColdFusion looks at its spool directory and processes any mail that is waiting there.

The Verify Mail Server Connection check box simply instructs ColdFusion to attempt to connect to the mail server when changes to this page are submitted, to ensure that you've entered everything correctly.

You also have the option, at the bottom of page, to control how mail messages are logged. The settings here are fairly self-explanatory, but it helps to know where to go if you need to make changes.

Charting

Next we move to the Charting page. Figure 25.8 gives you a look at the page inside the Administrator.

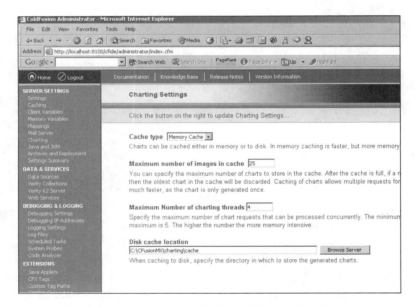

Figure 25.8   Charting page in the ColdFusion Administrator.

On the Charting page shown in Figure 25.8, you can adjust four settings that control how charting is handled within ColdFusion. Table 25.4 gives you an overview of these four settings.

Table 25.4 **Overview of Charting Settings**

Setting	Description of Setting
Cache type	When you create charts, you have the choice of caching them to disk or RAM. Of course, caching them to RAM is faster, but it also increases the overall ColdFusion memory footprint.
Maximum number of images in cache	This setting enables you to control the maximum number of charting images that you want to remain stored in cache at any given time. After your limit is reached, the oldest image is thrown out and replaced with a new one.
Maximum Number of charting threads	This setting enables you to specify the maximum number of charting requests that can be processed concurrently. By default, this value is set to 1. It can be no higher than 5. Keep in mind when adjusting this value that charting is a very memory-intensive activity, so attempting to process a large number of concurrent charting requests at any given time can cause performance degradation.
Disk cache location	When you choose to cache to disk rather than to RAM, this setting enables you to specify the location where you'd like to store the cached image files on your disk.

Java and JVM Settings

Next we move to the Java and JVM page. Figure 25.9 gives you a look at the page inside the Administrator.

On the Java and JVM page shown in Figure 25.9, you can adjust five, serverwide settings that control how Java and the Java Virtual Machine (JVM) are configured for use with ColdFusion. Table 25.5 gives you an overview of these five settings

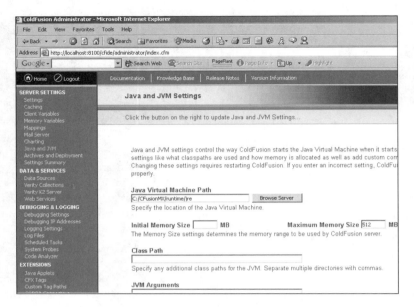

Figure 25.9 Java and JVM page in the ColdFusion Administrator.

Table 25.5 **Overview of Java and JVM Settings**

Setting	Description of Setting
Java Virtual Machine Path	This setting enables you to specify the path of the Java Runtime Environment (JRE) that you want to use with ColdFusion MX. When ColdFusion MX is installed, it installs its own JRE that is mutually exclusive from any other JRE on the system. It is this JRE with which ColdFusion MX is tested, and this is the supported configuration. It is not recommended that you attempt to change the JRE path as the results might be unpredictable.
Initial Memory Size	This setting enables you to specify an initial heap size for the JVM.
Maximum Memory Size	This setting enables you to specify a maximum heap size for the JVM.
Class Path	This setting enables you to specify the file path to the directories that contain any class files that you'd like to use with ColdFusion MX.
JVM Arguments	This setting enables you to specify any arguments that you'd like to be used when running the JVM.

Archives and Deployment

Next, we move to the Archives and Deployment page. Figure 25.10 gives you a look at the page inside the Administrator.

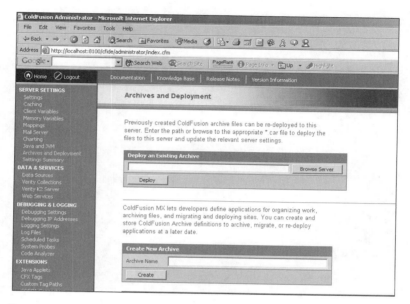

Figure 25.10   Archives and Deployment page in the ColdFusion Administrator.

This page enables you to specify the location of ColdFusion applications, datasources, and configuration information that you'd like to deploy to another location. Working through this page, you can also deploy existing archive files to your server.

Settings Summary

The final item under the Server Settings header is an item that enables you to view a settings summary. This summary runs down all the relevant settings on your ColdFusion Server, providing you a convenient way to determine, at a glance, how a given ColdFusion Server is configured.

Data and Services

Looking at the left navigational bar, the next header we encounter is the Data and Services header. Beneath this header, you find several clickable menu items that control how datasources and other external configurable data components behave. We examine this section in detail in the following sections.

Data Sources

First, let's look at the Data Sources page. Figure 25.11 gives you a look at page inside the Administrator.

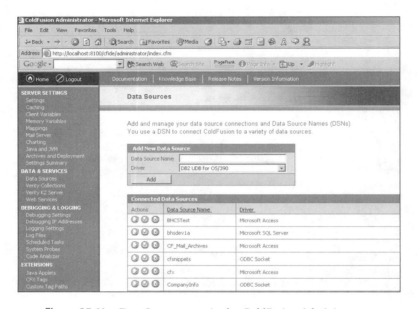

Figure 25.11 Data Sources page in the ColdFusion Administrator.

The Data Sources page enables you to create, edit, configure, and delete external datasources that you'd like to use with your ColdFusion applications. There's nothing particularly tricky about this section of the Administrator. You simply choose the appropriate driver for the database to which you want to connect, enter the appropriate connection information, and begin using your database.

Verity Collections

Next, let's look at the Verity Collections page. Figure 25.12 gives you a look at the page inside the Administrator.

On this page, you can add a new verity collection to the ColdFusion Server by naming the collection you want to create and pointing to an appropriate directory of files on your server. Beyond that, you can also repair, optimize, purge, and delete existing verity collections from this page. Table 25.6 discusses each verity management option.

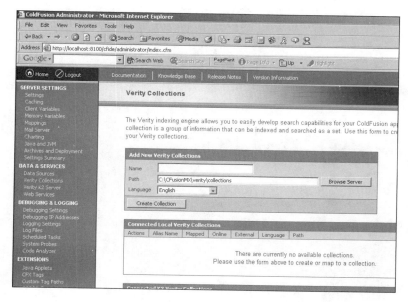

Figure 25.12   Verity Collections page in the ColdFusion Administrator.

Table 25.6   **Verity Management Options**

Action	Effect
Repair	Running a repair on a collection has the same effect as "reindexing" the collection. This eliminates broken or outdated links and includes recent document additions in the collection.
Optimize	Much like a fragmented hard disk, when you delete files that were once in a collection, the index itself gets out of date and fragmented. Running an optimize has the effect of "defragging" the collection, enabling you to save disk space and conduct faster searches against the index.
Purge	When you purge a collection, you are leaving the shell of the collection intact, but deleting all the documents that were a part of that collection.
Delete	Deleting a collection deletes both the shell of the collection and all the associated documents.

Web Services

Now, let's look at the Web Services page. Figure 25.13 gives you a look at the page inside the Administrator.

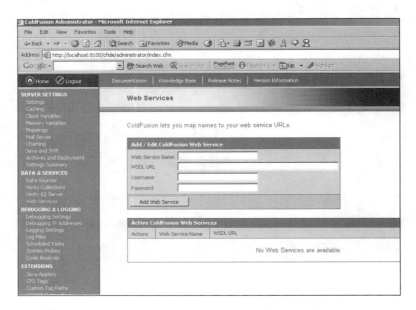

Figure 25.13   Web Services page in the ColdFusion Administrator.

The main purpose of this page of the ColdFusion Administrator is to enable you to register your web services with a name so that when you call them from your code, you do not need to enter the full Web Services Description Language (WSDL) URL. This enables easier and cleaner CFML code.

Debugging and Logging

Looking at the left navigational bar, the next header we encounter is the Debugging and Logging header. Beneath this header, you find several clickable menu items that control how data sources and other external configurable data components behave.

Debugging Settings

First, let's look at the Debugging Settings page. Figure 25.14 gives you a look at the page inside the Administrator.

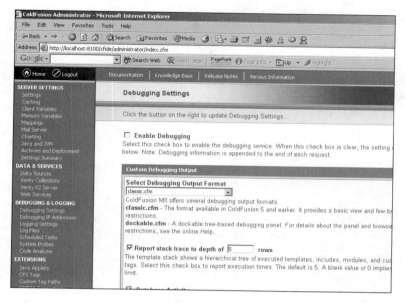

Figure 25.14   Debugging Settings page in the ColdFusion Administrator.

In this part of the Administrator, you can control seven, serverwide debugging options. Table 25.7 covers those seven options and what they do.

Table 25.7   **Debugging Options Available Through the ColdFusion Administrator**

Option	Description of Option
Enable Debugging	The Enable Debugging check box is the key to the debugging engine. Without this box checked, you are unable to retrieve any debugging information. It is good to leave this turned off in production, as there is generally no need to debug code on a production server.
Select Debugging Output Format	In ColdFusion MX, you can now choose from two ways in which to present the debugging information. There is the classic.cfm selection, which present debugging data as you're used to seeing it if you've worked with previous versions of ColdFusion, but there's also now the dockable.cfm selection, which puts all the debugging output into a dockable Dynamic

	Hypertext Markup Language (DHTML) browser window. This enables you to collapse and expand the debugging information and keep it open in a separate window at all times.
Report stack trace to a depth of *x* rows	This selection enables you to tell ColdFusion how much information you want returned when a stack trace is generated on your server. Whatever number you enter into this field, that is the number of CFML tag executions the stack trace records backward from the point of the crash.
Database activity	Checking this box displays the structured query language (SQL) or stored procedure information that was used to execute against the database in whatever template you are currently running.
Exception Information	Leaving this option turned on cause ColdFusion to display any exception information in the debugging output should an exception be encountered while running the current template.
Tracing Information	When this is turned on, tracing information shows up in the debugging output. You need to turn this setting on if you want to use the CFTRACE tag to watch logic flow from within your CFML templates.
Variables	When this setting is turned on, all common gateway interface (CGI), form, session, application, and other variables are displayed in the debugging output.

Debugging IP Addresses

This section, again, is fairly self-explanatory. This is where you enter the IP addresses of any machines that you want the debugging information returned to when debugging is enabled. If debugging is enabled and no IP addresses are present, debugging output is returned to all clients. For this reason, it's usually a good idea to leave the loopback IP address (127.0.0.1) entered here. This way, when you want someone else to view the debugging output, you are forced to add them. This might sound like a pain, but it can keep you from unwittingly exposing your debugging information to someone whom you don't want to see it.

Logging Settings

Next, let's look at the Logging Settings page. Figure 25.15 gives you a look at the page inside the Administrator.

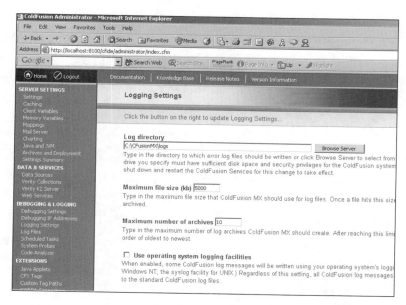

Figure 25.15   Logging Settings page in the ColdFusion Administrator.

From this page, you can control seven, serverwide settings that control how logging is handled on this particular ColdFusion Server. Table 25.8 gives you an overview of each setting available.

Table 25.8   **Options Available on the Logging Settings Page Within the ColdFusion Administrator**

Setting	Description of Setting
Log directory	This setting enables you to specify the directory where you would like all error log files to be written.
Maximum file size (kb)	This setting enables you to control the maximum file size that you want ColdFusion to use for its log files. This setting caps an individual log size at whatever number you enter here. When that file size is reached, the files are deleted in order from oldest to newest.

continues ▶

Table 25.8 **Continued**

Setting	Description of Setting
Maximum number of archives	This setting enables you to control the maximum number of log archives that you want to be created. After reaching this limit, archived log files are deleted in order from oldest to newest.
Use operating system logging facilities	Checking this box sends all logging information to the operating system's internal logging facilities, bypassing the standard ColdFusion logs.
Log slow pages taking longer than x seconds	This setting enables you to specify a maximum time that you want any template to take before an entry is made in the log file telling you that the template is running long.
Log all CORBA calls	Just as it says, this setting log all Common Object Request Broker Architecture (CORBA) calls.
Enable Logging for Scheduled Tasks	This setting logs any task scheduling in your standard logs.

Logging Files

Next, let's look at the Log Files page. From this page, you can manage any log files that have been created by the ColdFusion Server. From this page, you can view, delete, email, or archive any of the existing log files and search specific log files for information.

Scheduled Tasks

Next, let's look at the Scheduled Tasks page. Figure 25.16 gives you a look at the page inside the Administrator.

From this page you can add/edit/delete scheduled tasks to the ColdFusion Administrator. Creating a scheduled tasks works just as it would if you were to call a CFML template manually on a URL—only with scheduled tasks, you can control the specific date and time that these templates are called.

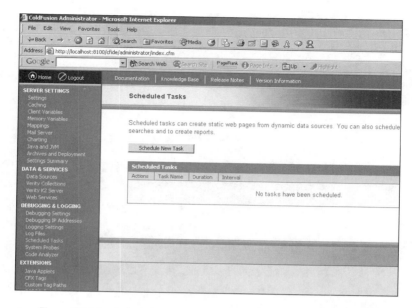

Figure 25.16   Scheduled Task page in the ColdFusion Administrator.

System Probes

Much like scheduled tasks, system probes access a CFML template at a specific time. However, system probes are checking for either the presence or absence of a string at the URL they are calling. These probes enable you to keep a "health-check" on your ColdFusion Server. You are essentially asking the server if it's okay. If the server is okay, it says "yes." Otherwise, notifications are sent as you have specified in the system probes section of the Administrator.

Code Analyzer

The code analyzer enables you to check your existing ColdFusion applications for compatibility with ColdFusion MX. In almost all cases, applications written for previous versions of ColdFusion work fine on ColdFusion MX. In those rare instances where you might encounter problems, the code analyzer has been provided to help you easily highlight those problems before migration so that you can correct them.

Extensions

Looking at the left navigational bar, the next header we encounter is the Extensions header. Beneath this header, you find several clickable menu items that control how extensions are managed. We examine this section now.

Java Applets

First, let's look at the Java Applets page. Figure 25.17 gives you a look at the page inside the Administrator.

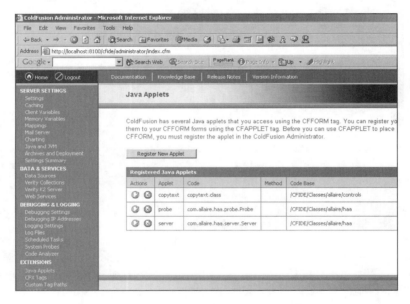

Figure 25.17 Java Applets page of the ColdFusion Administrator.

This page, very simply, enables you to register applets with the ColdFusion Administrator. Before attempting to use Java applets within your ColdFusion pages, you must register these applets with the ColdFusion Administrator, letting ColdFusion know the name of the applet that you want to use, the class file associated with that applet, and the path to the applets code base.

CFX Tags

Next, let's look at the CFX Tags page. Figure 25.18 gives you a look at the page inside the Administrator.

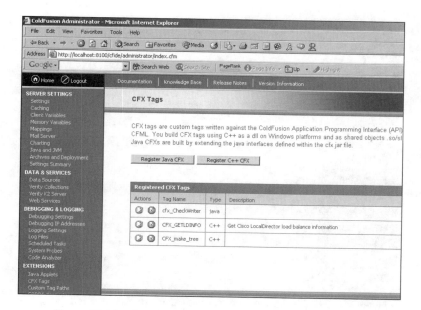

Figure 25.18 CFX Tags page of the ColdFusion Administrator.

Just as with Java applets, before you can use CFX tags within your ColdFusion applications, you must register those CFX tags with the ColdFusion Administrator, letting ColdFusion know the type of CFX tag you are using (Java or C++) and the name of the tag.

Custom Tag Paths

Next, let's look at the Custom Tag Paths page. Figure 25.19 gives you a look at the page inside the Administrator.

When you install ColdFusion MX, you are given a default custom tags directory beneath the CFusionMX folder. This is the default location where you can store all the custom tags that you want to use from within your ColdFusion applications.

Should you want to store your ColdFusion custom tags in another location on the disk, you would come to this section of the Administrator to configure another location for the storage of custom tags. Setting a custom tag path tells ColdFusion to include the directory you've added when it runs its search for installed custom tags after you invoke one from within your code.

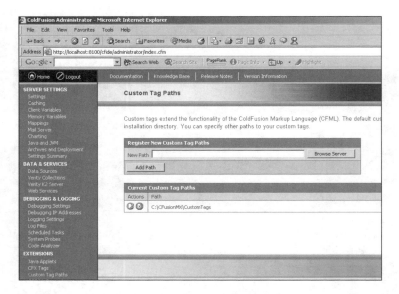

Figure 25.19 Custom Tag Paths page of the ColdFusion Administrator.

CORBA Connectors

Next, let's look at the CORBA Connectors page. Figure 25.20 gives you a look at the page inside the Administrator.

Figure 25.20 CORBA Connectors page of the ColdFusion Administrator.

You use the CORBA Connectors page of the Administrator to add, edit, or delete CORBA connectors to your ColdFusion Server.

A connector for Visibroker is included with ColdFusion Server, but you can use any object request broker you'd like, simply by registering it with the CORBA Connectors section of the ColdFusion Administrator.

Security

Looking at the left navigational bar, the next header we encounter is the Security header. Beneath this header, you find several clickable menu items that control how security is managed on the ColdFusion Server. We examine this section now.

CF Admin Password

First, let's look at the CF Admin Password page. Figure 25.21 gives you a look at the Security Permissions page inside the Administrator.

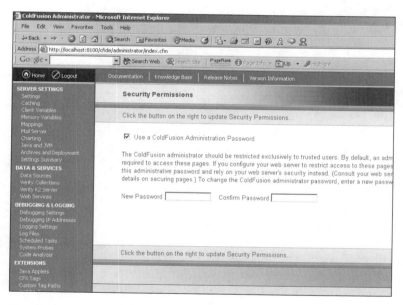

Figure 25.21   CF Admin Password page within the ColdFusion Administrator.

This, of course, is a no-brainer page. It would be advisable to always use a ColdFusion Administrator password. You are also given the option to change the current Administrator password to a new one if you so desire.

RDS Password

Next, let's look at the RDS Password page. Figure 25.22 gives you a look at the page inside the Administrator.

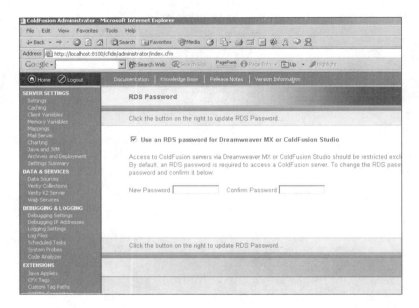

Figure 25.22 RDS Password page within the ColdFusion Administrator.

Just as with the CF Admin Password page, if you're using Remote Development Server (RDS) on the server, it is always advisable to use a password. Once again, you are presented with the option of changing the existing RDS password if you so desire.

Sandbox Security

Next, let's look at the Sandbox Security page. Figure 25.23 gives you a look at the page inside the Administrator.

Life wouldn't be complete without this section in the ColdFusion Administrator. Basically, you want to use security sandboxes any time that you want to control access to some ColdFusion resource. Using sandboxing, you can give specific applications access to certain ColdFusion functionality (CFFILE, CFDIRECTORY, and so on) while keeping the operations that these applications can complete contained within their own area.

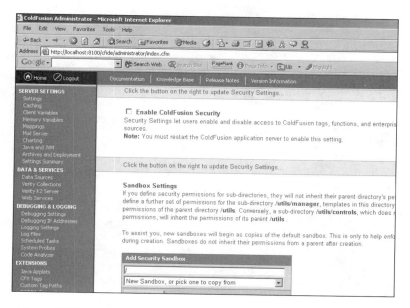

Figure 25.23   Sandbox security page within the ColdFusion Administrator.

This is a necessary thing if you are running a shared server, as you obviously don't want the developer of Application A to go over and delete files (through CFFILE) in the directory of Application B.

Of course, you might wonder how you set up a security sandbox. We knew you'd ask, so, just for you, we're going to step through setting up a security sandbox. Thankfully, the entire process is much less painful with ColdFusion MX than it has been *rumored* to be in the past.

Step 1—Add a New Sandbox

You begin by adding a sandbox. This process is pretty simple; you just name your new sandbox and click the Add button. In this example, we've added the new Tidy Cat Sandbox. After you've added the sandbox, it shows up in the list of available sandboxes, as shown in Figure 25.24.

So, adding a sandbox is easy enough, right? Just a few simple keystrokes and a click of the mouse. But now, the fun part comes in.

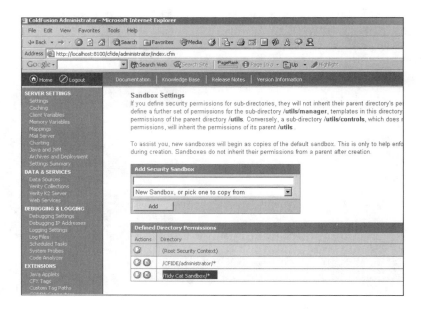

Figure 25.24 Tidy Cat Sandbox added to the list.

Step 2—Configuring Your New Sandbox

To configure our new sandbox, the first thing that we need to do is click the Edit button next to our sandbox name in the Defined Directory Permissions list. The Edit button is the little button that looks like a piece of paper with a pencil on the corner.

After you've clicked this button, you are presented with a tabbed configuration window, like the one shown in Figure 25.25.

As you can see, this tabbed interface includes tabs for data sources, CF Tags, CF Functions, Files and Directories, and Server/Port settings. The important thing to note, and this is very important, is that when a sandbox is created, *everything* is available to it by default. To properly configure the sandbox, you must select the items contained within this sandbox that you want to disable or make unavailable to users.

Of course, the one exception to this rule (and you knew there was going to be an exception) is the Files/Dirs tab. On this tab, you are going to explicitly state the files and directories that you would like to enable for users of this sandbox. By default, the sandbox has access to no files or directories on the server. You have to explicitly spell out where you want this sandbox to be restricted to on your server.

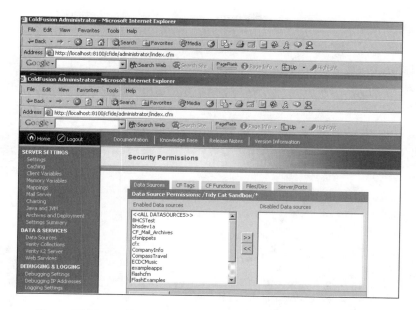

Figure 25.25   Tabbed configuration window for security sandboxing.

In addition, as you make your selections on each tab in this tabbed interface, click the Finish button at the bottom of the tab on which you're working prior to moving on to the next tab. Otherwise, your changes are lost and you have to start again.

Summary

In this chapter, we've examined, in detail, each section of the ColdFusion MX Administrator. After reading through this chapter, you should have a firm grasp on what each element of the ColdFusion Administrator does and how changing the settings within the ColdFusion Administrator affects your server's performance.

Now that you have an understanding, play with the settings on some of your servers to see which changes have the most dramatic performance effect on your ColdFusion applications.

26

Performance Optimization and Scalability Planning

N OW THAT YOU HAVE CONFIGURED COLDFUSION MX and built your first application, let's talk about performance. *Performance* is speed—period. When users are surfing the web, they want the pages to render instantaneously. Whether the pages are static Hypertext Markup Language (HTML) or data-driven templates, users will leave your site if they experience any unreasonable response time. Your job as a web site developer or ColdFusion administrator is to ensure that your application operates at maximum performance for a single request and that your servers and network have the optimum capacity to efficiently handle simultaneous requests.

Measuring Performance

You can measure performance in response time and throughput. Response time is the round-trip time of a single request. This is the period from the initiation of the request in the browser to the web server, through the ColdFusion Server to the backend systems, back to the web server, and to the final page rendering in the browser. Various factors adversely affect ColdFusion application response times:

- Poor application logic
- Bad database design
- Server configuration issues
- ColdFusion Administrator settings
- Network environment

Throughput is the number of transactions (requests) a server processes within a specific period of time. The units used to measure a server's throughput are as follows: the number of requests (Hypertext Transfer Protocol [HTTP] hits), the numbers of kilobytes (KB), and the number of transactions. The number of requests is the most commonly used measurement.

A site or application's ability to deliver content (data and graphics) as traffic or user load increases is called its *scalability*. A site's performance tends to degrade as page requests increase. However, response times of truly scalable sites increase proportionately with increasing user load. Achieving such scalability is your challenge in the successful deployment of high-performance web sites.

How to Test for Performance

To test a site for throughput and performance, you first need to identify a load-testing suite that enables you to adequately test your application.

There are different products on the market that offer a full range of load-testing capabilities. The key attributes that you need to look for in identifying the load-testing software that you will use are as follows:

- **The capability to simulate a high number of virtual users.** This is usually addressed in the licensing of the product that you purchase.

- **The capability to simulate unique client connections.** This is frequently achieved through a mechanism of enabling you to enter an Internet Protocol (IP) address pool from which the load testing software will draw when creating simulated connections to your server.

- **The capability to randomize variables during your testing.** This is an important point, and it is one that can make a difference in your testing results. If each virtual user will need his or her own unique CFID/CFTOKEN to test your application properly, your load-testing software will need to enable you to randomize these types of variables.

After you've identified the load-testing product that you're going to use, you need to begin building your test scripts.

Test scripts generally include a site traversal of your most commonly accessed site paths. You can mine this information from your own web logs, if necessary. What you are trying to do in creating your test script is to mimic what typical users would do when they visit your site. This might include creating an account, logging in, performing some data retrieval, and so on. You want to make sure that the site-traversal script you create is an adequate reflection of what your real-world users are doing when they visit your site.

After you have a site-traversal script in place, you can begin throwing virtual users at your server using this site-traversal script. As load on the server increases, the response times for all the pages should *gradually* increase, rather than spike. This is how you'll measure how scalable your site is.

Enhancing Scalability

Enhancing scalability requires the active monitoring of your production platform and methodical offline load testing of staging or quality assurance (QA) systems. Analysis of the gathered metrics will show you problem areas to address to increase performance.

Promoting reusable resources to minimize system overhead enhances scalability. Caching is your chief weapon in helping your ColdFusion Server scale. Utilizing the ColdFusion caching mechanisms and code optimizations discussed earlier in this book will help improve performance. Your goal in making these enhancements is to achieve perfect scalability, or *linear scalability*.

Linear Scalability Explained

There are two ways to define linear scalability:

- **Relative to load.** An application scales linearly if, with fixed resources, its performance decreases at a constant rate as application load increases.
- **Relative to resources.** A server scales linearly if, with fixed resources, its load capacity increases at a constant rate relative to additional resources (such as processors).

System and resource overhead directly affect an application server's linear scalability. Again, caching enables reuse of previously processed templates and previously allocated resources. This eliminates the system overhead of reprocessing and reallocating the templates and resources to serve subsequent requests.

Resource management involves analyzing the overhead of all the resources that may constrain system performance. This includes processors, random-access memory (RAM), hard drives, network capacity, and so on. It is important to understand the overhead incurred with additional resources. For example, adding an additional processor to a single-processor Windows 2000 server increases processing power at the cost of additional overhead incurred by the operating system to manage the additional processing power. Similarly, adding additional servers to your cluster will not improve performance if your network bandwidth is the bottleneck.

To help you understand what resources are being consumed while you are performing your load testing, you can use two tools that are provided by Macromedia. The first is the built-in performance monitor counters for ColdFusion Server. If you've never loaded these counters, you'll want to do so prior to beginning your load testing so that you can monitor the health of the ColdFusion Server and its resource consumption as you test.

The performance monitor counters can be found in the `CFUSIONMX/BIN` directory on your server. Double-click the `ColdFusionMXServer.pmc` file and the counters will automatically be loaded into the PerfMon window for you.

On a UNIX system, the same information provided through the PerfMon counters can be obtained using the CFSTAT utility. Note that the CFSTAT utility can also be used on Windows systems, although the information is the same as you would obtain through PerfMon.

The `CFSTAT` utility can also be found in the `CFUSIONMX\BIN` directory, and it can be used at the command line with the following syntax:

```
./cfstat n
```

where *n* is the number of seconds you want the utility to wait before refreshing its data.

Both utilities give you insight into how the ColdFusion Server itself is performing while you are doing your load testing.

It is paramount that you understand how the overhead of system resources affects your application's linear scalability. The only way to quantitatively measure the effectiveness of your efforts to enhance scalability relative to system resource overhead is through load testing.

Load Testing

Load testing simulates real-world scenarios on your applications and is the only way to quantitatively measure your application's performance and how mitigating factors—such as network environments, code optimizations, and resource changes—affect scalability. Load testing validates application performance, assists in performance tuning, and determines system load capacity.

Interpretation of Load Test Data

It's important that you understand how to interpret the data that you get from load testing your applications. Although entire books could be written based just on how to interpret load test results, the important thing to understand is that this testing should point out the key weaknesses in your application.

Do you have particular pages or sections of your applications that are bottlenecks, slowing down performance in the rest of the application? If so, this should show up in the results of your load tests.

Are you finding that your application doesn't scale as linearly as you'd expect it to? Perhaps that's due to improper use of shared resources that are staring to cause problems as concurrency increases. These issues make themselves evident as load testing progresses.

Keep your eyes open for any unusual or unexpected application behavior as you test. In a perfect world, you'd expect your application to respond exponentially more slowly as you increase load. There should be no point at which the response time suddenly spikes. If this happens, you have a concurrency issue that you need to investigate further and resolve before you take your application live.

Finding the Sweet Spot

"Finding the sweet spot" is a phrase you might hear used by people who have done load testing on several applications. Essentially, it means making the most of your hardware resources (pushing them to their upper limits) without giving in to unbearable response times from a user's perspective.

Prior to load testing, you need to determine the maximum acceptable response time for *any* page within your application while it is running under peak load. Peak load is defined as the maximum amount of load that your application can handle before it becomes essentially unresponsive and practically inoperable.

When determining that maximum response time, keep in mind that you're trying to push the hardware to the limit of its usefulness. Thus, saying that "three seconds is as long as anyone should have to wait" is a little unreasonable.

In the load testing in which this author has been involved, an acceptable maximum response time under peak load could come in anywhere from 30 to 60 seconds. If it is any longer than this, the vast majority of your users are going to bail out.

Testing Methodology

The key to successful load testing is developing and maintaining a load testing methodology. Load testing should be systematic and focused. It should simulate real-world scenarios that effectively emulate user behaviors, browsers, and connection speeds. Although there are several models from which to choose, this part of the chapter will focus on the following: isolation testing, stress testing, and endurance testing. You should use these at different stages of your application's life cycle.

Isolation testing involves focusing on a particular section or functionality of your application. This may be testing the responsiveness of a search engine or measuring the response times of a shopping cart checkout process. Isolation testing is most useful during early stages of development when you are trying to identify potential bugs in sections of code. It can also be useful during QA before deploying new sections of code.

Stress testing is the application of continuous user loads, at a maximum speed, on your system without any *think times* between transactions or page views. If a *hit* is the actual delivery of a page, then a *view* is the actual scanning or reading of that page. Think times are the time a user spends viewing the rendered page.

Stress testing disables the loading of images and other HTML resources (such as external style sheets) to eliminate the time incurred waiting for these to render. After all, not only are images usually the last items to load on a page, but also they add to the document weight, which increases the response time.

The goal of stress testing is to *stress* the system limits. This determines the maximum number of simultaneous requests the application can handle, and it determines the server's load threshold. Stress testing is most useful when applied to identified paths throughout your completed application.

Recommended periods for stress testing include the following:

- **Deployment.** Stress test in stages before deployment of your application to production.

- **Quarterly.** Stress test periodically during the season or year to ensure stability.

- **Peak season.** Stress test before peak seasons when you anticipate application load spikes. These typically happen around sale seasons (Christmas, Labor Day, and so on), product releases, and accounting and payroll cycles.

Endurance testing applies real-world user load over a period of 24 hours or longer. This helps determine the following facts:

- The length of system stability
- The length of stability of response times
- The stability of resource usage
- Any flaws that may occur over time that jeopardize system stability

Endurance testing is most useful before deployment. Because you are applying a real-world user load over a length of time, this test is useful in determining an optimal server configuration for hosting your application.

The most useful model in determining overall site scalability is stress testing. Isolation tests identify problem areas in code; endurance tests identify problem areas in system stability over time. Stress tests thoroughly assess system resources for pure responsiveness and are useful in determining the correct user load and system settings for your endurance tests.

Just as there are varying load testing models, there are many variations in load testing methodologies. All the major testing tool vendors have their own methodologies that their consultants utilize and that their trainers teach. Similarly, IT department administrators, developers, and Internet service providers (ISPs) also have their own methodology for measuring a server's load capacity. The disparity among these methodologies is as disproportionate as their respective site designs. However, no matter what tool you decide to use or what model you employ, there is a correct way to load test a ColdFusion Server.

The proper way to load test a ColdFusion Server is to test a virtual user path through your application that emulates real users. This probably sounds similar to what you are already doing; however, if you have more than one ColdFusion application on your server, your test script must explore paths along each application and do so simultaneously. This is required because although you may have a virtual site or server for each application, there is only one ColdFusion Server to service CFM requests. That means ColdFusion's pool of simultaneous requests services requests from all these virtual sites in a FIFO (First In, First Out) fashion. If the metrics you gather do not consider data for all these applications, you should consider your data incomplete or "dirty." Thus, load testing and optimizing one application does not buy you much if the other applications on the server perform poorly and you have not considered them in your testing and optimizations.

Other Performance Considerations

When determining the maximum amount of load your application can handle, it can be helpful to look at some of the other ways that you can improve the performance of your application to help achieve the best results possible during your testing. Some of these methods are discussed in the following list:

- Using application-level caching to speed up page delivery
- Making use of query-of-query functionality to eliminate trips to the database

- Using cached queries to reuse commonly accessed result sets
- Avoiding poor coding practices that can slow down the execution of your ColdFusion Markup Language (CFML) code
- Monitoring database activity closely to make sure you're not overusing your database resources
- Monitoring local and Internet bandwidth utilization to ensure your applications are being delivered quickly

Of course, beyond these methods, there's the tried and true "throw hardware at it" method. If you need to be able to serve more users concurrently, but you simply cannot squeeze any more performance out of your application or current hardware, you can always explore clustering your application or database servers to pool horsepower or divide load among several servers.

This strategy is a perfectly acceptable method for increasing application performance, and you'll find that, if your traffic grows for any length of time, it will be a method that you'll have to eventually explore.

There are many methods for calculating the amount of hardware that you'll need to scale to a certain level of load. Although we don't endorse any particular method, you'll find that this is an area where your load-testing data will come in handy. For example, if based on your load testing you know that your current hardware can adequately support 200 concurrent connections, you should be able to extrapolate the fact that if you want to service 1000 users simultaneously, you will need to consider a cluster of 5 similar servers.

Summary

In this chapter, we've examined ways in which you can optimize your ColdFusion applications. We've also talked about how to conduct proper load testing, how to use those test results to interpret the health of your application, and the ways in which you can plan for scalability. It's important to ensure that your application is stable before exploring performance optimization.

The application itself should perform well under normal circumstances, and your error logs should be relatively clean. If they aren't, you've got some areas you need to address prior to looking at optimizing for performance. There can be no scalability without stability.

27

Migration to ColdFusion MX

AFTER YOU'VE HAD AN OPPORTUNITY TO INSTALL ColdFusion MX and learn about its new features and architectural changes, the very next thing you'll most likely to want to do is migrate existing ColdFusion applications to the new ColdFusion MX environment. Although Macromedia has made every attempt to ease the transition from earlier versions of ColdFusion, you still might encounter some minor incompatibilities or inconsistencies between versions.

One of the best ways to ease the transition is to develop a migration plan for your existing applications early on. A structured plan for migrating applications will help you discover very early in the process the types of problems you're likely to encounter with your applications. Although each organization's migration plan will probably be different, there are a few key steps you'll want to take to make sure things go as smoothly as possible.

First and foremost, you'll want to deploy your existing ColdFusion applications on a test server running ColdFusion MX. Next you'll want to aggressively test your application for ColdFusion MX compatibility. This will involve creating structured testing paths and traversing the applications to observe behaviors. This process should closely resemble the QA testing you would do on any new application prior to deployment.

Using the Code Compatibility Analyzer

In addition to the steps in the preceding section, Macromedia has provided a Code Compatibility Analyzer with ColdFusion MX to help you ensure that your existing applications are ready for ColdFusion MX deployment.

You can access the Code Analyzer by clicking the link in the ColdFusion Administrator, as shown in Figure 27.1.

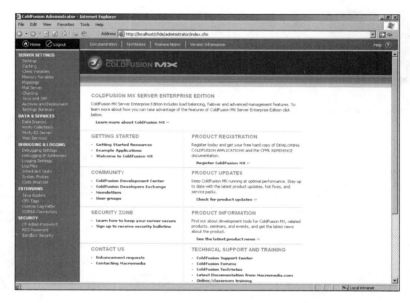

Figure 27.1   Accessing the Code Analyzer in the ColdFusion Administrator.

After you click this link, you'll be taken to another page in the Administrator where you can specify the directory on the server that contains the code you'd like to have analyzed for compatibility. At this point, you can either enter the directory of your code manually or click the Browse Server button to choose the directory containing your code.

Figure 27.2 shows the code selection page. After you've selected the directory on your server that contains the code you'd like to have analyzed, you just need to click the Run Analyzer button to begin the process.

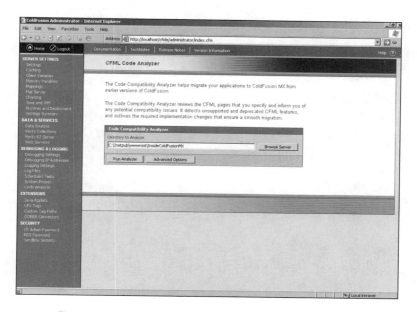

Figure 27.2   The code selection page for the Code Analyzer.

After the analyzer has been started, it will parse all the CFML files in the directories you specify and will present you with a report of suggested implementation changes prior to moving that code to a ColdFusion MX server. The code analyzer will look for deprecated CFML, features that might not behave as expected in ColdFusion MX, and syntactical errors in your code.

After the analyzer has completed parsing the directories specified, you will be presented with a report like the one shown in Figure 27.3.

For more information on any error returned, just click the document name. You will be presented with a pop-up window like the one shown in Figure 27.4.

Using the information provided in this detail window, you should be able to determine the reason why the code was tagged as incompatible. Often you will be given hints by the code analyzer as to what action should be taken to correct the problem.

Using the code analyzer early on in the migration process will help ease the number of problems you encounter as you prepare to move ColdFusion MX into production.

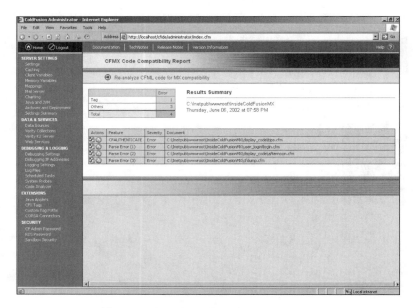

Figure 27.3 The code analysis error report.

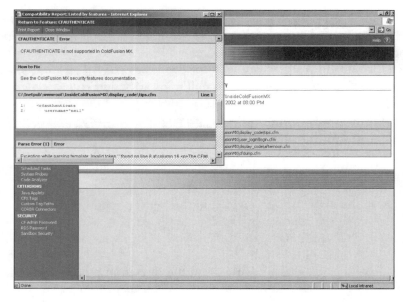

Figure 27.4 Detailed information regarding errors encountered in the code analysis.

Deprecated or Changed CFML Tags

Several CFML changes in ColdFusion MX have caused the expected behavior of certain tags to change and have caused other tags to become deprecated altogether.

Table 27.1 lists the changes to CFML tags in ColdFusion MX.

Table 27.1 **Changed or Deprecated CFML Tags**

Tag	Attribute or Value
CFCACHE	timeout attribute
CFFILE	attributes attribute value archive
	attributes attribute value system
	attributes attribute value temporary
CFGRAPH	All
CFGRAPHDATA	All
CFGRIDUPDATE	connectString attribute
	dbName attribute
	dbServer attribute
	dbType attribute
	provider attribute
	providerDSN attribute
CFINDEX	external attribute
CFINSERT	connectString attribute
	dbName attribute
	dbServer attribute
	dbType attribute
	provider attribute
	providerDSN attribute
CFLDAP	filterConfig attribute
	filterFile attribute
CFLOG	date attribute value "No"
	thread attribute value "No"
	time attribute value "No"
CFQUERY	connectString attribute
	dbName attribute
	dbServer attribute

continues ▶

Table 27.1 **Continued**

Tag	Attribute or Value
	The following `dbType` attribute values:
	`dynamic`
	`ODBC`
	`Oracle73`
	`Oracle80`
	`Sybase11`
	`OLEDB`
	`DB2`
	`provider` attribute
	`providerDSN` attribute
	`sql` attribute
CFREGISTRY	All, on UNIX only
CFSEARCH	`external` attribute
CFSERVLET	All
CFSERVLETPARAM	All
CFSLIDER	`img` attribute
	`imgStyle` attribute
	`grooveColor` attribute
CFSTOREDPROC	`connectString` attribute
	`dbName` attribute
	`dbServer` attribute
	`provider` attribute
	`providerDSN` attribute
CFUPDATE	`connectString` attribute
	`dbName` attribute
	`dbServer` attribut
	`provider` attribute
	`providerDSN` attribute

The CFML tags, attributes, and attribute values listed in Table 27.2 are obsolete. They should not be used in ColdFusion MX applications because they could cause errors.

Table 27.2   **Obsolete CFML Tags and Attributes**

CFML Tag	Attribute or Value
CFAUTHENTICATE	All
CFIMPERSONATE	All
CFINDEX	action attribute value optimize
CFINTERNALADMINSECURITY	All
CFNEWINTERNALADMINSECURITY	All
CFSETTING	catchExceptionsByPattern attribute

Deprecated or Changed CFML Functions

Just as there are changes in CFML tags under ColdFusion MX's new architecture, there are also changes in the way that CFML functions behave. Table 27.3 lists the changes to CFML functions in ColdFusion MX.

Table 27.3   **Changes to CFML Functions in ColdFusion MX**

CFML Function Affected	Parameter or Value
AuthenticatedContext	All
AuthenticatedUser	All
isAuthenticated	All
isAuthorized	All
isProtected	All

Summary

In this chapter, we briefly discussed some of the changes you might encounter when attempting to upgrade your current ColdFusion applications to ColdFusion MX.

Prior to attempting an upgrade, make sure you have planned adequate time for your migration, developed a migration plan, and taken into account the architectural changes in the ColdFusion MX release that might affect your code base.

Planning ahead and making use of the tools Macromedia has provided for smooth migration—including the ColdFusion MX upgrade documentation and the Code Compatibility Analyzer—will ensure that you have an upgrade experience that's as problem-free as possible.

28

ColdFusion Tips and Tricks

I F YOU'VE BEEN AROUND COLDFUSION FOR any length of time, you already know that one of the best resources for information and great ideas is the ColdFusion community.

One of the sections I wanted to include in *Inside ColdFusion MX* was a section covering some tips and tricks that other developers have submitted. These are concepts and ideas that people have found, through their experience, to be helpful in the development of their applications.

In all cases, the original author of the contribution is credited at the beginning of the section.

Design for Reusability

Submitted by Tom Luttrell, tom@luttrellstudios.com

After a ColdFusion programmer learns the basics of how to develop advanced web sites, the one thing he should invest time in is learning to make code modular and reusable. Why? It will save you—and anyone else who uses your code—many headaches. Modular and reusable code not only saves time in doing repeated work, it is easier to maintain and integrates into other projects faster.

One common criticism of ColdFusion is that it is not object-oriented, meaning it does not natively support modularity. ColdFusion already has the features necessary to make code modular, however, by using custom tags or cfmodule.

My advice is to put as much of your code into custom tags or modules as you can. There is one downside to this: Performance might be slightly degraded. Because each module or custom tag has its own memory space, nesting them too deep or using them too many times can cause a page to become heavy or expensive in memory and possibly slower as a result. If you are careful, however, the benefits of making most of your code modular will outweigh the weaknesses.

You can use any flavor of the Fusebox methodology out there, but using *any* method of making your code reusable is far better than using none at all. I happen to use a variation of Fusebox that ensures that most of the files being used are called as a custom tag or `cfmodule`.

When using custom tags, a good programmer tends to restrict calls to a few scopes: attributes and local variables. Attributes are the variables that get passed in to the module when the tag is called.

Use `cfparam` to default all the variables your file will need at the top of your page. Try to restrict calls to one scope during most of your code. If the file will only be called as a custom tag or module (as in some flavors of Fusebox), the only types of variables you should ever call directly within the main part of your files are attributes or local variables. When you do need to access variables in other scopes, default these variables at the top of your file using `cfparam` before "localizing" it. This gives you the flexibility to override this value by explicitly passing in an attribute value. The following code provides an example of this:

```
<CFPARAM NAME="Request.FuseBox.LogicalPath"
DEFAULT="../..">
<CFPARAM name="Attributes.LogicalPath"
DEFAULT="#Request.FuseBox.LogicalPath#">
<CFOUTPUTT>#Attributes.LogicalPath#</CFOUTPUT>
```

Values that might change should never be hard-coded. Instead, they can be set as defaults for attribute parameters so that, if the module is to be reused again and requires different values, they can be overwritten.

Validating Data Received from the Client

Submitted by Jackson Moore, `jackson@devusion.com`

The most important thing you can do at the code level to prevent errors and security breaches is to validate all data received from the client's browser. Validating this data will prevent CFML code errors, HTML display errors, cross-site scripting attacks, unauthorized access to web site content, and unintended server-side operations.

Depending on his skill level (and desire), any user can alter the query string, modify his cookies, or spoof his IP address. A user can also save your form page to his computer, override form fields, and bypass client-side validation before submitting a form. You can't even rely on `CGI.HTTP_REFERER` to verify the origin of a form submission because it can be changed by the user and is often blocked altogether by some privacy software and corporate firewalls.

All URL parameters, form fields, cookies, and browser variables must be validated on the server for both data type and value before you reference them in your code. Ask yourself, "Is `URL.ARTICLE_ID` an integer, and does it correspond with a database record that this user is authorized to access?" Make sure the answer is "yes."

Use *Application.cfm* to Make Your Code Faster and More Portable

Submitted by Dave Hannum, hannum@ohio.edu

Using the `Application.cfm` file in your applications can make them extremely powerful and portable. Think of it as a configuration file. For example, it seems that every system administrator has his own "right" way of configuring and laying out the directory structures of the servers he administers. Utilizing your `Application.cfm` file, you can move from machine to machine relatively painlessly. In the `Application.cfm` script, set the `DATASOURCE`, `URL`, and `PHYSICAL PATH` in `REQUEST` scope variables.

```
<CFSET REQUEST.myURL = "http://www.myapp.com">
<CFSET REQUEST.myPATH = "c:\inetpub\wwwroot\clients\myapp">
<CFSET REQUEST.myDATASOURCE = "myappData">
```

Then, when you want to use the application on a different machine, you only need to change these three variable values in the `Application.cfm` file, and your application will run. Using the `REQUEST` scope makes these values available to any modules, custom tags, and so on. You can also go even more granular with, say, the URL to your start page and so on. Set variables in `Application.cfm` to easily account for time-zone differences. Also, use `SESSION` or `APPLICATION` scope variables in conjunction with the `IsDefined()` functions in `Application.cfm` to set variables that require a call to your database. You can speed up your application significantly by avoiding unnecessary calls to the database if you store values in `SESSION` or `APPLICATION` scope variables to be used in your application.

Using Session Variables with Care

Submitted by Brad J. Gallagher, `bradjgallagher@yahoo.com`

One very powerful tool in the ColdFusion arsenal is the capability to use session variables. As with all other powerful tools, using session variables with care is important. Using proper coding procedures, session variables can speed up code, allow for cleaner application planning, and ease administration. With improper coding practices, using session variables can bring a server to its knees.

Like other variables with persistent scope, session variables need to be protected from simultaneous read/write access. Without such protection, data corruption can occur when several threads have access to the same session variable. In certain cases, improper use of just one session variable can hang the ColdFusion Server!

One tactic when working with a file that has a large number of read/write requests to multiple session variables is to copy data from persistent scope to local scope. After all computation is done, copy the results back into persistent scope. This will drastically reduce the number of CFLOCK tags required and will eliminate the possibility of neglecting to properly protect a session variable. Remember that it takes just one unprotected session variable to kill the server.

All session data is stored into a structure named `session`. To copy this to local scope, a developer could do the following:

```
<cflock scope="SESSION" type="READONLY" timeout="10">
    <cfset local.sessionvars = structNew()>
    <cfset local.sessionvars = duplicate(session)>
</cflock>
```

The developer could then read/write to the local variable `local.sessionvars.foo` as many times as needed in the page without fear of data corruption. After all computation is done, return the results to persistent scope at the end of the file. We can do this by copying our local data back into the structure `session`, like this:

```
<cflock scope="SESSION" type="exclusive" timeout="10">
    <cfset session.foo = duplicate(local.sessionvars.foo)>
</cflock>
```

Protect Yourself

Submitted by Chris Norloff, cnorloff@norloff.com

Protect yourself, your application, and your server. But from what? Protect from users, code errors, database errors, and network errors. This is to keep your application running, to please your users and customer, and to ensure that your application is not unfairly blamed for downtime.

Coding

The most important protection is to code to eliminate errors: Test variables for existence before using them, use CFPARAM for default values, and include code to handle data that is not what it "should" be. Explicitly account for all conditions when using conditionals like CFIF and CFSWITCH. Second most important is to place CFTRY/CFCATCH blocks around all code to catch errors. Use CFERROR for errors not caught by CFCATCH. The ColdFusion server can't be serving up application pages if it's spending time serving up errors.

Make your error messages as specific as possible to inform your users, particularly if there's something they can do (such as making a reduced request if the page has timed out). Nobody likes generic error messages. Provide debug information for programmers: We provide all CFCATCH-scoped or error-scoped information. We use HTML comments <!--   --> in the error page to display programmer-oriented debug information. This way, the user does not see it, but the programmer can use View, Source. This is very handy for machines for which we can't access the code directly. Log all handled errors using CFFILE and review the logs regularly.

Other considerations for the application are to prevent users from pressing submit buttons multiple times, to use CFQUERYPARAM to protect the database from bad data, and to protect the application from commands stored as data. Can your application respond if the database is down? Don't let a database or database-connectivity problem appear to be a ColdFusion problem.

We also place test files in the application so that we can easily determine what services are running, particularly on a production machine for which we might not have administrator access. We use a basic HTML file, a basic CFM file, and a CFML file with a database query.

Testing

We review the logs from the quality assurance server after every new release from development. All errors have a test problem report written. Code should be error-free when it leaves the development server. We use PVCS Tracker to automate the communication and tracking of problem reports.

These ideas and similar approaches will make your application more robust and will give you fewer headaches from downtime and performance problems.

Establishing Standard Prefixes in Your ColdFusion Code

Submitted by Tyson Vanek, tyson.vanek@remotesite.com

Establishing standard naming conventions for variables in your ColdFusion code can help you and other developers identify what is being stored in different variables. Specifically, it will help indicate which data type is stored in the variable (such as string, integer, Boolean, array, structure, or query result set). Table 28.1 includes a list of suggested prefixes. You could always come up with your own replacements or additions to this list.

Table 28.1 **Suggested Prefixes for Various Data Types**

Prefix	Data Type	Example
str	String	strVariableName
int	Integer	intVariableName
num	Numeric	numVariableName
bln	Boolean	blnVariableName
lst	List	lstVariableName
arr	Array	arrVariableName
stc	Structure	stcVariableName
qry	Query	qryVariableName
uuid	UUID	uuidVariableName
w	WDDX packet	wstcVariableName or wqryVariableName

Server–Side Redirections in CFMX

Submitted by Charlie Arehart, carehart@systemanage.com

Did you know that you can now do server-side redirection (a forward) in ColdFusion MX? It's not being mentioned much, and some might not appreciate what doors this opens, but in the right circumstances, it's a big improvement over our prior redirection via CFLOCATION. Though many didn't know it, CFLOCATION did a client-side redirect, meaning a header was sent to the browser to have it request the new URL. One of the big challenges/ drawbacks of this was that no variables set in the caller were available to the called program.

Server-side redirects—or forwards, as they're known in Servlets and JSP— do allow you to share REQUEST scope variables between templates (between ColdFusion and ColdFusion or between ColdFusion and JSP). They also are the key to doing true model-view-controller style design. You can now do it using ColdFusion MX's capability to use the new getPageContext function, which exposes the methods in the underlying Servlet PageContext object. The key for this solution is to use the forward method, as follows:

```
<CFSCRIPT> getPageContext().forward("sometemplate"); </ CFSCRIPT>
```

Again, this does a server-side transfer of control (much like the ASP3 server.transfer did versus the older response.redirect), and it allows any variables set in the request scope of the caller to be available in the called program (via the request scope there). There are some things to consider. The URL shown to the user will still be that of the page that did the forward, not the page to which control was redirected. This has several ramifications: challenges if they bookmark it, possibly unexpected results for you or them if they click the Refresh button. These issues are well discussed in the literature regarding the use of forwards in JSPs and Servlets. Over time, we'll all come to learn the same lessons and find the strengths and weaknesses of this approach.

One last bonus: Even though it's a server-side redirect and distinctly unlike CFLOCATION, any cookies you set before the forward *are* indeed passed to the browser.

Group Totals and Details in One Database Query

Submitted by Rudy Limeback, rudy@rudy.ca

The challenge is to print groups of detail records but also precede each group with a line showing the number of detail records in the group.

To print groups, we are familiar with CFOUTPUT GROUP. We also know we can use RecordCount, but that gives only the total number of detail rows in the entire result set, not in the individual groups.

Your first thought might be to CFLOOP through the groups, build up an array of group detail record counts, CFOUTPUT the detail records, and in the GROUP logic, search through the array of saved counts and match on the group column—but that's messy.

This solution embeds the group counts into the result set, using a "total" record that must sort first in each group. The CFOUTPUT GROUP logic will print the count, but it must skip over the "total" record so that it's not printed along with the "detail" records.

The query uses two subselects to obtain both totals and details, combining them with UNION ALL.

```
SELECT dept.id
     , dept.descr
     , 'T' as rowtype
     , count(*) as staffcount
     , '' as staffid
     , '' as fullname
  FROM dept INNER JOIN staff
    ON dept.id = staff.deptid
 GROUP BY dept.id, dept.descr
UNION ALL
 SELECT dept.id
     , dept.descr
     , 'D'
     , 0
     , staff.id
     , staff.fullname
   FROM dept INNER JOIN staff
     ON dept.id = staff.deptid
 ORDER BY 1, 2, 3 DESC, 5
```

The first subquery obtains the totals for each group. Each "total" record is identified by a 'T' in the rowtype column. The second subquery obtains the "detail" records, identified by 'D' in the rowtype column.

Notice that the ORDER BY is as follows:

1. dept.id

2. dept.descr

3. rowtype DESC

4. staffid

The rowtype is sorted in descending order so that the 'T' record in each group precedes the 'D' records.

UNION ALL is specified instead of UNION to avoid the unnecessary sort to eliminate duplicates. (There cannot be any rows duplicated between subselects because of the rowtype column.)

Table 28.2 shows the raw data that the query produces. This is not what will be printed for the solution; it is shown just to illustrate the interleaving of "total" and "detail" rows.

Table 28.2 **The Raw Output of the Data We'll Be Working With**

Id	Descr	Row-type	Staff-count	Staffid	Fullname
Acctg	Accounting	T	1		
Acctg	Accounting	D	0	JD	John Dough
HR	Human Resources	T	3		
HR	Human Resources	D	0	FJ	Fred Jones
HR	Human Resources	D	0	MS	Mary Smith
HR	Human Resources	D	0	TT	Thom Thumb
IT	Information Technology	T	4		
IT	Information Technology	D	0	BB	Bill Brown
IT	Information Technology	D	0	JC	Jeff Case
IT	Information Technology	D	0	MR	Mike Rophone
IT	Information Technology	D	0	RG	Rudy Green
Mktg	Marketing	T	2		
Mktg	Marketing	D	0	JW	Jane White
Mktg	Marketing	D	0	ME	Mark Etting

Here's the grouped output:

The Accounting department has **1** staff member:

- JD John Dough

The Human Resources department has **3** staff members:

- FJ Fred Jones
- MS Mary Smith
- TT Thom Thumb

The Information Technology department has **4** staff members:

- BB Bill Brown
- JC Jeff Case
- MR Mike Rophone
- RG Rudy Green

The Marketing department has **2** staff members:

- JW Jane White
- ME Mark Etting

Here's the `CFOUTPUT` that produced these results:

```
<cfoutput query="myquery" group="id">
  <cfset firstrec = "y">
  <p>The <b>#myquery.descr#</b> department
      has <strong>#myquery.staffcount#</strong>
    staff member<cfif myquery.staffcount GT 1>s</cfif>:
    <cfoutput>
      <cfif firstrec EQ "y">
        <cfset firstrec = "n">
      <cfelse>
        <br />   #myquery.staffid# #myquery.fullname#
      </cfif>
    </cfoutput>
  </p>
</cfoutput>
```

The `firstrec` variable is set to `"y"` for each new group. This logic is conveniently controlled by the `GROUP` parameter. The nested `CFOUTPUT`, which prints the detail records, contains a `CFIF` test to skip over the first record so that it is not printed along with the details.

Storing and Displaying Hierarchical Data

Submitted by Jeff Howden, `jeff@jeffhowden.com`

Storing and displaying hierarchical data—often called a tree—is not a simple task, but it often is an unfortunate necessity to show the relationship between sets of data. The most common type you'll find is probably nested categories with parent/child relationships for products.

If you've ever worked with hierarchical data before, you know it's not a simple task. There are a number of ways to store the data, but most of them seem to put a lot of extra burden on the ColdFusion Server to retrieve and display for the user in its entirety. If you've never worked with hierarchical data, don't worry; you'll run up against it sooner or later. I'm going to show you what I believe is the simplest way, from a web-based perspective, to store this type of data to make displaying it as efficient as possible.

The important thing on the web is to think about what actions that can be taken against the data will be performed the most and try to structure your data to make the most common action the least hit on the database and the ColdFusion user. If you've guessed that the most common thing you'll do is retrieve data from the database and display it, give yourself 10 points. If you said that adding new data or updating the data is the most common, deduct 10 points.

To make the data as simple as possible to retrieve and display, we'll need to store a couple of small tidbits about each record: parent_id, tree_level, and rank. (see Table 28.3).

Table 28.3 **The Three Columns That Make This Approach Work**

Parent_id	This is a foreign key that tells us what record in the table the current record is a child of.
Tree_level	This is a number that represents how many positions the record is indented.
Rank	This is a number that represents the current record's placement among all the other records, without regard for what's a parent or child of what.

Let's take a look at some sample data. The hierarchical data in Table 28.4 represents a guessing game. I only show three levels of nesting, but this method could handle as many levels as you want. Along with the three columns previously detailed, we'll also need two additional columns at a minimum: id (the primary key column) and name. You can store additional information if the situation warrants.

Table 28.4 **The Raw Data We'll Be Using for This Example from a Table Named** *game*

Id	Name	Parent_Id	Tree_Level	Rank
1	Guessing Game	0	1	1
2	Animal	1	2	2
3	Elephant	2	3	3
4	Aardvark	2	3	4
5	Lemur	2	3	5
6	Mineral	1	2	6
7	Titanium	6	3	7
8	Gold	6	3	8
9	Carbon	6	3	9
10	Vegetable	1	2	10
11	Broccoli	10	3	11
12	Spinach	10	3	12
13	Cauliflower	10	3	13

The simplest thing you can do is query for all child records that are one level in and that match an id that's passed in the URL or by a form post.

```
<cfparam name="url.parent_id" default="0">
<cfquery name="getchildren">
  SELECT id
       , name
    FROM game
   WHERE parent_id = #Val(url.parent_id)#
</cfquery>
```

This would be used in the classic drill-down approach you see often on the web. However, you usually need to be able to display more of the tree at a time. So, let's see how to retrieve the entire tree and display it to the user.

```
<cfquery name="gettree">
  SELECT name
       , tree_level
    FROM game
   ORDER BY rank
</cfquery>
```

To display the results, all we need to is use a simple CFOUTPUT and pad the left side of each record with the appropriate amount of space to indicate a relationship between the records.

```
<cfoutput query="gettree">
#RepeatString("  ", tree_level - 1)##name#<br>
</cfoutput>
```

The preceding code results in the following output:

```
Guessing Game
  Animal
    Elephant
    Aardvark
    Lemur
  Mineral
    Titanium
    Gold
    Carbon
  Vegetable
    Broccoli
    Spinach
    Cauliflower
```

What if you want to grab an entire branch of the tree, including the parent record based on a parent_id that was passed via the query string? All you'd need to do is use the following query. The two subselects keep the database from returning records with a rank and tree_level less than or equal to the selected record. This guarantees that you're only selecting those records that belong to the branch (provided you've taken precautions that the data is all correct in the three integral columns: parent_id, tree_level, and rank).

```
<cfquery name="gettree">
  SELECT name
       , tree_level
    FROM game
   WHERE id = #Val(url.parent_id)#
      OR (rank > (SELECT rank
                    FROM game
                   WHERE id = #Val(url.parent_id)#)
     AND tree_level > (SELECT tree_level
                         FROM game
                        WHERE id = #Val(url.parent_id)#))
   ORDER BY rank
</cfquery>
```

Assuming the value 2 was passed to this query and we're using the simple CFOUTPUT code sample from earlier, here's what the server would return:

```
Animal
  Elephant
  Aardvark
  Lemur
```

There are other ways in which you'll need to query the data to get things like a record's parent record, all the sibling records for a given record, and so on, but I'll leave that for you to figure out. (It's not as tough as it looks. I promise.)

I'll warn you right now, though, that this method of storing the data does not solve the problems of adding new records and updating existing records. You'll still need to come up with ways to move things around and maintain the proper parent_id, tree_level, and rank values. The solutions to these problems can be difficult to solve, but the burdens on the server are few and far between. Thankfully, using this method, you'll be reducing the load on the server for the action that's taken most often, thereby making your application much better performing for the end user.

Summary

The tips and tricks provided in this chapter represent suggestions for improving your ColdFusion applications from some people who are "in the trenches" developing real-world applications each and every day. If you're new to ColdFusion development, you'll soon discover that there's a very powerful and knowledgeable user community out there, and people are always willing to offer suggestions or help.

A
Tag Reference

THIS IS AN ALPHABETICAL LISTING OF COLDFUSION (CF) tags that make up part of the ColdFusion Markup Language (CFML). This list can be helpful to explain exactly what a tag does. It also defines what attributes need to be present. If you are not sure if a particular attribute is required or optional, this is a good place to check.

The format used should be fairly easy to follow. The tags are organized in the following manner: tag name, syntax, tag description, and attribute description. If you need to know what an attribute does, reference the attribute description; but if you are looking for code syntax, check the top listing.

CFABORT

```
<cfabort showError = "error_message">
```

Description

Most often used in conjunction with error handling, this tag stops the processing of a ColdFusion page where the tag is placed. Everything that was processed before the tag is displayed normally on the page.

Attributes

> showError (Optional)
> Error to display on a user defined error page.

CFAPPLET

```
<cfapplet appletSource = "applet_name"
      name = "form_variable_name"
      height = "height in pixels"
      width = "width in pixels"
      vSpace = "space_above_and_below_in_pixels"
      hSpace = "space_on_each_side_in_pixels"
      align = "Left/Right/Bottom/Top/TextTop/Middle/AbsMiddle/ /Baseline/AbsBottom"
      notSupported = "message_to_display_for_nonJava_browser"
      param_1 = "applet_parameter_name"
      param_2 = "applet_parameter_name"
      param_n = "applet_parameter_name">
```

Description

Used to reference a registered custom Java applet. Java applets are registered in the ColdFusion Administrator in the Java Applets section.

Using this tag within a CFFORM tag is optional. If you use it within CFFORM, and the method attribute is defined in the Administrator, the return value is incorporated into the form.

Attributes

> appletSource (Required)
> Name of registered applet.

> name (Required)
> Form variable name for applet.

> height (Optional)
> Height of applet.

> width (Optional)
> Width of applet.

> vSpace (Optional)
> Space above and below applet.

hSpace (Optional)
Space on left and right of applet.

align (Optional)
Alignment: Left, Right, Bottom, Top, TextTop, Middle, AbsMiddle, Baseline, and AbsBottom.

notSupported (Optional)
Text to display if a page that contains a Java applet-based CFFORM control is opened by a browser that does not support Java or has Java support disabled.

param_ n (Optional)
Registered parameter for applet. Specify only to override values for applet in ColdFusion Administrator.

CFAPPLICATION

```
<cfapplication name = "application_name"
        clientManagement = "Yes" or "No"
        clientStorage = "datasource_name" or "Registry" or "Cookie"
        setClientCookies = "Yes" or "No"
        sessionManagement = "Yes" or "No"
        sessionTimeout = #CreateTimeSpan(days, hours, minutes, seconds)#
        applicationTimeout = #CreateTimeSpan(days, hours,minutes, seconds)#
        setDomainCookies = "Yes" or "No">
```

Description

Defines the scope of a ColdFusion application; enables and disables storage of client variables; specifies the client variable storage mechanism; enables session variables; and sets application-variable timeouts.

Server-, session-, and application-scope variables are stored in memory as structures. The user-defined function (UDFs) scope is not accessible as a structure.

Attributes

name (Required for application/session variables; optional for client variables)
Name of application, with a 64-character limit.

clientManagement (Optional)
Default: No. Yes enables client variables.

clientStorage (Optional)

Default: registry

Options: (Where variables are stored)

- datasource_name. In ODBC or native data source.

- registry. In the system registry.

- cookie. On client computer in a cookie. This is a scalable option if you have a large number of clients, but will not work if cookies are disabled in the browser.

setClientCookies (Optional)

Default: Yes enables client cookies. With No, ColdFusion does not automatically send CFID and CFTOKEN cookies to the browser and CFID and CFTOKEN must be manually coded on the URL for every page.

sessionManagement (Optional)

Default: No. Yes enables session variables.

sessionTimeout (Optional)

The lifespan of session variables. This option is also set in the Variables page of the ColdFusion Administrator.

applicationTimeout (Optional)

The lifespan of application variables. This option is also set in the Variables page of the ColdFusion Administrator.

setDomainCookies (Optional)

Default: No. Yes sets CFID and CFTOKEN cookies for a domain. Required for applications running on clusters.

CFARGUMENT

```
<cfargument
        name="argument name"
        type="any"
        required="YES or NO"
        default="default argument value">
```

Description

Used within the CFFUNCTION tag, this creates a parameter definition within a component and defines a function argument. This tag must be the first tag in a page.

Attributes

`name` (Required)
Name for the argument.

`type` (Optional)
This is the data type of the argument which can be anything. Some examples are any, `array`, `binary`, `Boolean`, `date`, `numeric`, `query`, `string`, `struct`, `uuid`, `variableName`, and a component name.

`required` (Optional)
Default: `No`. Determines whether the parameter is required to execute the component method.

`default` (Optional)
If no argument is passed, specifies a default argument value. When using this attribute, the required attribute must be set to `No` or not specified.

CFASSOCIATE

```
<cfassociate
  baseTag = "base_tag_name"
  dataCollection = "collection_name">
```

Description

Used only with customer tags, this enables subtag data to be saved with a base tag.

Attributes

`baseTag` (Required)
Base tag name.

`dataCollection` (Optional)
Structure in which base tag stores subtag data.

CFAUTHENTICATE (Obsolete)

Description

Use the newer security tools.

CFBREAK

```
<cfbreak>
```

Description

Used to break out of a CFLOOP. This tag has no attributes.

CFCACHE

```
<cfcache action = "action"
     username = "username"
     password = "password"
     protocol = "protocol_name"
     directory = "directory_name_for_map_file"
     cacheDirectory = "directory_name_for_cached_pages"
     expireURL = "wildcarded_URL_reference"
     port = "port_number">
```

Description

Used to help improve performance, this tag stores a copy of a page on the server and/or client. Creates temporary files that contain the Hypertext Markup Language (HTML) returned from a ColdFusion page. This tag should only be used if the content of the page does not change very often; otherwise the user receives old data.

Attributes

action (Optional)
Default: cache

- **cache.** Server-side caching.
- **flush.** Refresh cached page. You can also specify directory and expireURL attributes.
- **clientCache.** Browser caching.
- **optimal.** Optimal caching; combination of server-side and browser caching.

username (Optional)
A username if it is required for authentication.

password (Optional)
A password, if it is required for authentication.

protocol (Optional)
Default: http://. Protocol used to create pages from cache.

directory (Optional)
Directory of the current page; this is an absolute directory path
and contains cfcache.map to use if action = "flush".

cacheDirectory (Optional)
Directory of the current page; this is an absolute path of the directory
in which to cache pages.

expireURL (Optional)
Use this to flush all mappings. Used when action = "flush" and takes a
URL reference, including wildcards, that ColdFusion matches against all
mappings in cfcache.map file.

port (Optional)
Default: 80
Port number of the web server from which the page is requested. If the
port is specified correctly in an internal call to CFHTTP, the URL of each
retrieved document is resolved to preserve links.

CFCASE

```
<cfcase action="action">
```

Description

Used with the CFSWITCH and CFDEFAULTCASE tags. For more information, see
CFSWITCH. The action attribute must always be present and is the condition
that enables a particular case to be executed.

CFCATCH

```
<cfcatch>
```

Description

Used with the CFTRY tag. For more information, see CFTRY. This tag has no
attributes.

CFCHART *(New in MX)*

```
<cfchart
        format = "flash, jpg, png"
        chartHeight = "integer number of pixels"
        chartWidth = "integer number of pixels"
        scaleFrom = "integer minimum value"
        scaleTo = "integer maximum value"
        showXGridlines = "yes" or "no"
        showYGridlines = "yes" or "no"
        gridlines = "integer number of lines"
        seriesPlacement = "default,cluster, stacked, percent"
        foregroundColor = "Hex value or Web color"
        dataBackgroundColor = "Hex value or Web color"
        borderBackgroundColor = "Hex value or Web color"
        showBorder = "yes" or "no"
        font = "font name"
        fontSize = "integer font size"
        fontBold = "yes" or "no"
        fontItalic = "yes" or "no"
        labelFormat = "number, currency, percent, date"
        xAxisTitle = "title text"
        yAxisTitle = "title text"
        sortXAxis = "yes/no"
        show3D = "yes" or "no"
        xOffset = "number between -1 and 1"
        yOffset = "number between -1 and 1"
        rotated = "yes/no"
        showLegend = "yes/no"
        tipStyle = "MouseDown, MouseOver, Off"
        tipBGColor = "hex value or web color"
        showMarkers = "yes" or "no"
        markerSize = "integer number of pixels"
        pieSliceStyle = "solid, sliced"
        url = "onClick destination page"
        name = "String"
</cfchart>
```

Description

This tag creates a user-defined graph that is stored as an HTML object or as an image tag, depending on the chosen attribute.

Attributes

format
Default: flash. File format in which to save graph. Format options include flash, jpg, and png.

chartHeight
Default: 240. Chart height in pixels.

chartWidth
Default: 320. Chart width in pixels.

scaleFrom
Determined by data. Y-axis minimum value.

scaleTo
Determined by data. Y-axis maximum value.
showXGridlines
Default: No.

- **Yes.** Displays X-axis gridlines.

- **No.** Hides X-axis gridlines.

showYGridlines
Default: yes.

- **Yes.** Display Y-axis gridlines.

- **No.** Hide Y-axis gridlines.

gridlines
Default: 3 (top, bottom, and zero).
Number of grid lines to display on value axis, including axis; This should be a positive number. 0= hides gridlines.

seriesPlacement
Default: Default
Applies to charts that have more than one data series and is the relative positions of series.
Default: ColdFusion determines relative positions based on graph types. Other options include cluster, stacked, percent.

foregroundColor
Default: Black. Color of text, gridlines, and labels. Hex value or web color.

dataBackgroundColor
Default: White. Color of area around chart data. Hex value or web color.

borderBackgroundColor
Default: White. Color of area between data background and border, around labels, and around legend.

showBorder
Default: No

font
Default: Arial. Name of text font.

fontSize
Default: 11. Font size.

fontBold
Default: No

fontItalic
Default: No

labelFormat
Default: Number. This is the format for Y-axis labels. Other options include number, currency, percent, and date.

xAxisTitle
Title for the X–axis.

yAxisTitle
Title for the Y–axis.

sortXAxis
Default: No. If Yes, displays column labels in alphabetic order along X-axis.

show3D
Default: No. If Yes, displays chart with three-dimensional appearance.

xOffset
Default: 0.1
Only applies if show3D="yes". The number of units by which to horizontally angle the chart when it is displayed. A number in the range –1 to 1, where ·1 specifies 90 degrees left and 1 specifies 90 degrees right.

yOffset
Default: 0.1
Applies if show3D="yes". The number of units by which to vertically angle the chart when it is displayed. A number in the range –1 to 1, where ·1 specifies 90 degrees down, and 1 specifies 90 degrees up.

rotated
Default: No. If Yes, rotate chart 90 degrees. Use this option for a horizontal bar chart.

`showLegend`

Default: `Yes`; the legend is displayed if the chart contains more than one data series.

`tipStyle`

Default: `mouseOver`

- **mouseDown.** This option only works on Flash graphs and displays when the mouse is clicked. For other formats,this option works the same as `mouseOver`.

- **mouseOver.** Displays if the user positions the cursor over the element.

- **off.** Suppresses display.

`tipBGColor`

Default: `White`; applies only to Flash graphs. Hex value or web color.

`showMarkers`

Default: `Yes`, which displays markers at data points.

`markerSize` (Automatic)

Size of data point marker.

`pieSliceStyle`

This attribute only works with pie charts.

Default: `sliced`

- **solid.** Displays pie as if unsliced.

- **sliced.** Displays pie as if sliced.

`url`

The URL to open if an item is clicked. Variables may be specified within the URL, and ColdFusion passes the current values of the variables.

- **$VALUE$.** Value of selected row. If none, the value is an empty string.

- **$ITEMLABEL$.** Label of selected item. If none, the value is an empty string.

- **$SERIESLABEL$.** Label of selected series. If none, the value is an empty string.

CFCHARTDATA

```
<cfchartdata
        item = "text"
        value = "number">
```

Description:

Used with the CFCHART and CFCHARTSERIES tags. This tag defines chart data, which is then passed to the CFCHARTSERIES tag.

Attributes:

item
Name of the data.

value
Value of the data. This should be a number.

CFCHARTSERIES

```
<cfchartseries
        type="type"
        query="queryName"
        itemColumn="queryColumn"
        valueColumn="queryColumn"
        seriesLabel="Label Text"
        seriesColor="Hex value or Web color"
        paintStyle="plain, raise, shade, light"
        markerStyle="style"
        colorlist = "list">
</cfchartseries>
```

Description

Used with the CFCHART tag. This tag defines the way the chart is displayed. Options include bar, line, pie, and so on.

Attributes

type (Required)
Display styles include bar, line, pyramid, area, cone, curve, cylinder, step, scatter, and pie.

query (Optional)

Name of ColdFusion query from which to get data.

itemColumn (Required)

If the query attribute is used, this is the name of a column from the query that contains the item label to graph. If the query attribute is used, this is the name of a column from the query. This column should contain the values to graph.

seriesLabel (Optional)

Text of data series label.

seriesColor (Optional)

Color of the main element (such as the bars) of a chart. For a pie chart this will be the color of the first slice.

Default: plain

- **plain.** Solid color.
- **raise.** The appearance of a button.
- **shade.** Gradient fill (that is darker at the edges).
- **light.** A lighter shade of color.

markerStyle (Optional)

Default: rectangle

Other icon options include triangle, diamond, circle, letterx, mcross, snow, and rcross.

colorlist (Optional)

Applies if chart series type attribute = "pie"; sets the pie slice colors. This should be a comma-delimited list of hex values or web colors.

CFCOL

```
<cfcol
        header = "column_header_text"
        width = "number_indicating_width_of_column"
        align = "Left" or "Right" or "Center"
        text = "column_text">
```

Description

Defines table column header, width, alignment, and text. Used within a CFTABLE tag.

Attributes

> `header` (Required)
> Column header text. To use this attribute, you must also use the `CFTABLE` `colHeaders` attribute.
>
> `width` (Optional)
> Default: `20`. Column width. Data trimmed to fit within this size.
>
> `align` (Optional)
> Default: `left`
> Column alignment: `left`, `right`, and `center`.
>
> `text` (Required)
> The text that is displayed in the column. This should be a double-quotation mark-delimited hyperlink; image references and input controls may be inserted.

CFCOLLECTION

```
<cfcollection
        action = "action"
        collection = "collection_name"
        path = "path_of_verity_directory"
        language = "language"
        name = "queryname">
```

Description

> This tag is used to create a collection that can be searched with the Verity search engine. External collections can be created using a native Verity indexing tool, such as Vspider or MKVDK.

Attributes

> `action` (Optional)
> Default: `list`
>
> - **create.** Creates and maps a directory for a collection, which is made up of the `path` attribute value and the `collection` attribute value.
> - **repair.** Fixes data corruption in a collection. This action must be completed before another action on the collection can begin.
> - **delete.** Deletes a map to a collection.

- **optimize.** Optimizes the structure and contents of a collection for searching.
- **list.** Gets the attributes of one or more collections. The returned value is one row per collection.

collection (Required)
Sets the collection name, which can include spaces.

path (Required if action = "create")
Absolute path to a Verity collection. The value to provide depends on the action attribute. If action=create, supply the directory path to the collection.

language (Optional)
Default: english. Other languages can be used but this requires the appropriate (European or Asian) Verity Locales language pack.

name (Required if action = "list")
Name for the query results returned by the list action.

CFCOMPONENT

```
<cfcomponent>
        extends ...
        output = "yes" or "no"
    <cffunction ...>
        ...
    </cffunction>

</cfcomponent>
```

Description

This is the tag used to create ColdFusion components (CFC) and is saved as a CFC file. It may contain additional functionality that within CFFUNCTION tags that define methods. All code that is not contained within CFFUNCTION tags is executed when the CFC is first called. A component can be invoked in several ways including from a CFINVOKE tag, from a URL, from within CFScript, through a web service, or from Flash code.

Attributes

extends (Optional)
Name of parent component from which to inherit methods and properties. If not used, the component inherits the methods and properties of ColdFusion.

output (Optional)

Yes: Suppresses component method output.

No: Permits component method output.

CFCONTENT

```
<cfcontent
        type = "file_type"
        deleteFile = "Yes" or "No"
        file = "filename"
        reset = "Yes" or "No">
```

Description

Sets the file or Multipurpose Internet Mail Extension (MIME) content type returned by the current page. It can also specify the name of a file to return with the page. Note that this tag must be enabled in the ColdFusion Administrator.

Attributes

type (Required)

File or MIME content type returned by current page.

deleteFile (Optional)

Default: No. Applies only if you specify a file with the file attribute.

Yes: Deletes a file after the download operation.

file (Optional)

Name of the file to get. When using ColdFusion in a distributed configuration, the file attribute must refer to a path on the system on which the web server runs.

reset (Optional)

Default: Yes. The reset and file attributes are mutually exclusive. If you specify a file, this attribute has no effect.

- **Yes.** Discards output that precedes call to CFCONTENT.

- **No.** Preserves output that precedes call to CFCONTENT.

encoding (Optional)

Default: ISO-8859-1. The character encoding of generated output is text/html or any valid character encoding.

CFCOOKIE

```
<cfcookie
        name = "cookie_name"
        value = "text"
        expires = "period"
        secure = "Yes" or "No"
        path = "url"
        domain = ".domain">
```

Description

Defines web browser cookie variables, including expiration and security options.

Attributes

name (Required)
Name of cookie.

value (Optional)
Value assigned to cookie.

expires (Optional)
Handles the expiration of the cookie. Can be a date (for example, 12/20/02) or a number of days (for example, 10 or 100).

- **now.** Deletes cookie from client cookie.txt file.

- **never.** Never deletes cookie from client; writes cookie data to cookie.txt file.

secure (Optional)
The cookie will not be sent if the browser does not support Secure Sockets Layer (SSL). If Yes, variable must be transmitted securely.

path (Optional)
URL to which the cookie applies, or use multiple CFCOOKIE tags to have multiple URLS.

domain (Required)
This attribute is required in conjunction with the path attribute. The domain must start with a period and can be subdomains if desired.

CFDEFAULTCASE

```
<cfdefaultcase>
    ...
</cfdefaultcase>
```

Description

Used with the CFSWITCH and CFCASE tags.

CFDIRECTORY

```
action = "directory action"
        directory = "directory name"
        name = "query name"
        filter = "list filter"
        mode = "permission"
        sort = "sort specification"
        newDirectory = "new directory name">
```

Description

Use this tag to work with directories. This tag must be enabled in the ColdFusion Administrator for it to execute.

Attributes

action (Optional)
Default: list, which returns a query recordset of the files in the specified directory. Other commands include create, delete, and rename.

directory (Required)
Absolute path name of directory against which to perform action.

name (Required if action = "list")
Name for the output recordset.

filter (Optional if action = "list")
Can be used to filter the results by file extensions for one file type.

mode (Optional)
Used with action = "create". This tag only applies to Solaris and HP-UX. Use in conjunction with Octal values of CHMOD command.

- **644.** Assigns read/write permission to owner and read permission to group and other.

- **777.** Assigns read/write/execute permission to all.

sort (Optional)
Used if action = "list" to query column(s) by which to sort directory listings.

newDirectory (Required if action = "rename")
New name for directory.

CFDUMP

```
<cfdump
        var = #variable#
        expand = "Yes or No"
        label = "text">
```

Description

This is used to dump values without regard for formatting and is useful for debugging. For example, you can get a quick output of a structure without the use of CFLOOP. This tag displays the contents of simple and complex variables, objects, and components.

Attributes

var (Required)
Variable to display. Be sure to enclose the variable name in pound signs. Most useful when used with the following types of variables and objects: array, ColdFusion, Java object, query, structure, UDF, WDDX, and XML.

expand (Optional)
Default: Yes, which in Internet Explorer and Netscape automatically closes expanded views. No leaves expanded views expanded.

label (Optional)
A string that serves as a header for the dump output.

CFELSE

```
<cfelse>
```

Description

Used to create conditional logic in conjunction with the CFIF and CFELSEIF tags. This tag has no attributes.

Example

```
<cfif conditon = "condition 1">
   Do action one.
<cfesle>
   Do action two.
</cfif>
```

CFELSEIF

```
<cfelseif>
```

Description

Used to create conditional logic in conjunction with the CFIF and CFELSE tags. You can have as many CFELSEIF tags in a logic block as required. This tag has no attributes.

Example

```
<cfif conditon = "condition 1">
   Do action one.
<cfelseif condition = "condition 2">
Do action two.
<cfesle>
   Do action three.
</cfif>
```

CFERROR

```
<cferror type = "request" or "validation" or "exception"
       template = "template_path"
       mailTo = "email_address"
       exception = "exception_type">
```

Description

Used to create a custom error page and to create a consistent look and feel in an application.

Attributes

type (Required)
Type of error that the custom error page handles. Error types include application, database, template, security, object, missinginclude, expression, lock, custom_type, and any.

template (Required)
Relative path to the custom error page. (A ColdFusion page was formerly called a template.)

mailTo (Optional)
Email address to send errors.

CFEXECUTE

```
<cfexecute name = " ApplicationName "
       arguments = "CommandLine Arguments"
       outputFile = "Output file name"
       timeout = "Timeout interval in seconds">
       ...
</cfexecute>
```

Description

Used to execute a process on the server, such as executing commands from the command line or running programs and scripts.

Attributes

name (Required)
Absolute path of the application to execute. On Windows, you must specify an extension, such as C:\example.exe.

arguments (Optional)
There are command-line variables passed to an application. Generally arguments are processed in these ways:

- **Windows.** Passed to process control subsystem for parsing.
- **UNIX.** Tokenized into an array of arguments. The default token separator is a space.

If passed as an array:

- **Windows.** Elements are concatenated into a string of tokens separated by spaces.
- **UNIX.** Elements are copied into an array of `exec()` arguments.

outputFile (Optional)
A file to have results stored. If not this attribute is not used, the output is displayed directly to the page.

timeout (Optional)
Default: 0. Length of time, measured in seconds, that the ColdFusion will wait for the process.

CFEXIT

```
<cfexit method = "method">
```

Description

Used in conjunction with custom tags, this enables ColdFusion to abort processing the custom tag.

Attributes

method (Optional)
Default: exitTag

- **exittag.** Aborts processing of currently executing tag.
- **exittemplate.** Exits page of currently executing tag.
- **loop.** Reexecutes the code of the current tag.

CFFILE

```
<cffile action = "upload"
        fileField = "formfield"
        destination = "full_path_name"
        nameConflict = "behavior"
        accept = "mime_type/file_type"
        mode = "permission"
        attributes = "file_attribute_or_list">

<cffile action = "move/rename/copy/delete"
        source = "full_path_name"
        destination = "full_path_name"
```

```
        mode = "mode"
        attributes = "file_attributes_list"
        charset = "charset_option">

<cffile action = "read/readBinary"
        file = "full_path_name"
        variable = "var_name"
        encoding = "encoding_option"
        charset = "charset_option">

<cffile action = "write/append"
        file = "full_path_name"
        output = "content"
        mode = "permission"
        addNewLine = "Yes" or "No"
        attributes = "file_attributes_list"
        encoding = "encoding_option"
        charset = "charset_option" >
```

Description

Used to work with files on the server on which ColdFusion is installed. The action performed depends on the action attribute. For this tag to work, it must be enabled in the ColdFusion Administrator.

Attributes

action (Required)
The type of action that the tag performs, including upload, move, rename, copy, read, delete, readBinary, write, and append.

fileField (Required)
Name of form field used to select the file. Do not use pound signs to specify the field name.

destination (Required)
The absolute path name of a directory or file on the web server.

nameConflict (Optional)
Default: error
Action to take if filename is the same as that of a file in the directory.

- **error.** File is not saved. ColdFusion stops processing the page and returns an error.

- **skip.** File is not saved. This option permits custom behavior based on file properties.

- **overwrite.** Replaces file.
- **makeUnique.** Forms a unique filename for the upload.

accept (Optional)
You can limit the types of files that can be uploaded with this attribute. If
you want to allow multiple file types, they should put into a comma-
delimited list.

mode (Optional)
Applies only to Solaris and HP-UX. Enacts permissions and allows use
of the chmod command. For example:

- **644.** Assigns read/write permission to owner and read permission
  to group and other.
- **777.** Assigns read/write/execute permission to all.

attributes (Optional)
This enables you to set file attributes on a file. You can only set one
attribute for Windows files. You can set a list of attributes for other platforms. Options include readOnly, hidden, and normal.

source (Required)
Absolute path name of a file on the web server.

charset (Optional)
Default: ISO-8859-1, which is the Java character set name used for the
file contents.

file (Required)
Absolute path name of a file.

variable (Required)
Name of variable to contain contents of text file.

encoding (Optional)
Default: (ISO-8859)-1, which is the character encoding of generated
output. Any valid character encoding is usable.

output (Required)
Content of the file to be created.

addNewLine (Optional)
Default: Yes, which appends newline character to text.
After a file upload is completed, you can get status information using the
file upload parameters listed next. The status parameters use the cffile

prefix; for example, `cffile.clientDirectory`. Status parameters can be used anywhere other ColdFusion parameters can be used. The upload parameters include the following:

`attemptedServerFile`
Initial name ColdFusion used when attempting to save a file.

`clientDirectory`
Directory location of the file uploaded from the client's system.

`clientFile`
Name of the file uploaded from the client's system.

`clientFileExt`
Extension of the uploaded file on the client system.

`clientFileName`
Name of the uploaded file on the client system.

`contentSubType`
MIME content subtype of the saved file.

`contentType`
MIME content type of the saved file.

`dateLastAccessed`
Date and time the uploaded file was last accessed.

`fileExisted`
Whether the file already existed with the same path.

`fileSize`
Size of the uploaded file.

`fileWasAppended`
Whether ColdFusion appended an uploaded file to a file.

`fileWasOverwritten`
Whether ColdFusion overwrote a file.

`fileWasRenamed`
Whether the uploaded file was renamed to avoid a name conflict.

`fileWasSaved`
Whether ColdFusion saved a file.

`oldFileSize`
Size of the file that was overwritten during the file upload operation.

serverDirectory
Directory of the file saved on the server.

serverFile
Filename of the file saved on the server.

serverFileExt
Extension of the uploaded file on the server.

serverFileName
Name of the uploaded file on the server.

timeCreated
Time the uploaded file was created.

timeLastModified
Date and time of the last modification to the uploaded file.

CFFLUSH

```
<cfflush interval = "integer number of bytes">
```

Description

Use this tag to push data to the browser in increments for pages that take a long time to execute. This tag cannot be used on a page that uses CFLOCA-TION.

Attributes

interval (Optional)
Used to control the amount of data that is sent to the browser, excluding headers and already available data.

CFFORM

```
<cfform name = "name"
        action = "form_action"
        preserveData = "Yes" or "No"
        onSubmit = "javascript"
        target = "window_name"
        encType = "type"
        passThrough = "HTML_attribute(s)"
        codeBase = "URL"
        archive = "URL" >
...
</cfform>
```

Description

Used instead of a normal form tag, when you want to take advantage of built-in ColdFusion functionalities, such as CFINPUT, CFTEXTINPUT, CFSILDER, CFTREE, and CFSELECT.

Attributes

name (Optional)
A name for the form.

action (Optional)
Name of the ColdFusion page to execute when form is submitted.

preserveData (Optional)
Whether to override (preserve the display of) default data entered in controls in the action page display after the user submits the form.

onSubmit (Optional)
Enables the use of JavaScript before the form is submitted for such functionality as client-side validation.

target (Optional)
Window or frame to which form output is sent.

encType (Optional)
Default: application/x-www-form-urlencoded
MIME type to encode data sent by the post method. It is recommended that you use the default.

passThrough (Optional)
For HTML attributes that are not supported by CFFORM. Attributes and values are passed to the HTML code that is generated for the tag.

codeBase (Optional)
This attribute only works with Internet Explorer and gives a URL of a downloadable Java Runtime Environment (JRE) plug-in. Default is /ColdFusionIDE/classes/cf-j2re-win.cab.

archive (Optional)
URL for downloadable Java classes for ColdFusion controls. Default is /ColdFusionIDE/classes/ColdFusionJava2.jar.

CFFTP

The syntax will vary depending on the action attribute used.

```
<cfftp action = "action"
```

Description

Executes File Transfer Protocol (FTP) commands and can be used to implement a connection to an FTP server, for connection caching, or to implement file and directory operations.

Attributes

action (Required)
FTP operation to perform which can be one of the following: open, close, changedir, createDir, listDir, removeDir, getFile, putFile, rename, remove, getCurrentDir, getCurrentURL, existsDir, existsFile, and exists.

username (Required if action = "open")
Username to use during the FTP operation. If not using a cached connection, this tag is also required for directory and file commands.

password (Required if action = "open")
Password for the username. If not using a cached connection, this tag is also required for directory and file commands.

server (Required if action = "open")
FTP server to which to connect, such as www.exampleserver.com.

timeout (Optional)
Default: 30. Value in seconds for the timeout of all operations, including individual data request operations.

port (Optional)
Default: 21. Remote port to connect.

connection (Optional)
Name of the FTP connection. This can be used to cache a new FTP connection or for connection reuse.

proxyServer (Optional)
Name of a proxy server or servers to use if proxy access is necessary.

retryCount (Optional)
Default: 1. Number of retries until failure is reported.

stopOnError (Optional)
Default: No

- **Yes.** Halts processing and displays an appropriate error.
- **No.** Populates these variables:
- **cfftp.succeeded.** yes or no.
- **cfftp.errorCode.** Error number.
- **cfftp.errorText.** Message text, which is the text for the error message.

passive (Optional)
Default: No. The Yes enables passive mode.

name (Required if action = "listDir")
Query name of directory listing.

ASCIIExtensionList (Optional)
Default: txt, htm, html, cfm, cfml, shtm, shtml, css, asp, asa.
Delimited list of file extensions that force ASCII transfer mode if the
transferMode = "auto".

transferMode Optional)
Default: auto. Options include ASCII FTP transfer mode, Binary FTP
transfer mode, and Auto FTP transfer mode.

failIfExists (Optional)
Default: Yes. If a local file with the same name exists, then getFile fails.

directory (Required if action =
"changedir/createDir/listDir/existsDir")
Directory on which to perform an operation.

localFile (Required if action = "getFile/putFile")
Name of the file on the local system.

remoteFile (Required if action = "getFile/putFile/existsFile")
Name of the file on the FTP server.

item (Required if action = "exists/remove")
Object of these actions: file or directory.

existing (Required if action = "rename")
Current name of the file or directory on the remote server.

new (Required if action = "rename")
New name of file or directory on the remote server.

proxyServer (Optional)
Name of the proxy server or servers to use if proxy access is necessary.

passive (Optional)
Default: No. Yes enables passive mode.
The following query objects are returned by CFFTP when
action = "listdir".
Use the syntax *queryname.querycolumn* to access data.

Name
Filename of the current object.

Path
File path of the current object.

URL
Complete URL for the current object.

Length
File size of the current object.

LastModified
Unformatted date/time value of the current object.

Attributes
Attributes of the current object can be normal or directory.

IsDirectory
Whether object is a file or directory.

Mode
Applies only to Solaris and HP-UX. This is the permissions set on the file
as an octal number, such as 644 or 777.

CFFUNCTION

```
<cffunction
        name = "methodName"
        returnType = "dataType"
        roles = "securityRoles"
        access = "methodAccess"
        output = "yes" or "no"
        exceptions = "exception1, exception2, ...">
```

Description

Used to create functionality within a CFC usually written in CFML.

Attributes

name (Required)
Defines the component method that is used within the CFCOMPONENT tag.
The valid types are query, string, numeric, boolean, date, struct, array,
binary, xml, customFunction, object, any, or the name of a component.

returnType (Optional)
The value that is returned by the function.

roles (Optional)
Default: " " (empty), which is a comma-delimited list of ColdFusion security roles that can invoke the method. If this attribute is omitted, all roles
can invoke the method.

access (Optional)
Default: public

- **private.** Available only to the component that declares the method.
- **package.** Available only to the component that declares the method
  or to another component in the same package.
- **public.** Available to a locally executing page or component method.
- **remote.** Available to a locally or remotely executing page or component
  method, or to a remote client through a URL, Flash, or web service.

output (Optional)
Default: Function is processed as standard CFML.

- **Yes.** The function is processed as if it were within a CFOUTPUT tag.
- **No.** The function is processed as if it were within a CFSILENT tag.

exceptions (Optional)
Comma-delimited list of exceptions.

CFGRAPH

Description

This tag is deprecated. Use the CFCHART, CFCHARTDATA, and CFCHARTSERIES
tags instead.

CFGRID

```
<cfgrid name = "name"
        height = "integer"
        width = "integer"
        autoWidth = "Yes" or "No"
        vSpace = "integer"
        hSpace = "integer"
        align = "value"
        query = "query_name"
        insert = "Yes" or "No"
        delete = "Yes" or "No"
        sort = "Yes" or "No"
        font = "column_font"
        fontSize = "size"
        italic = "Yes" or "No"
        bold = "Yes" or "No"
        textColor = "web color"
        href = "URL"
        hrefKey = "column_name"
        target = "URL_target"
        appendKey = "Yes" or "No"
        highlightHref = "Yes" or "No"
        onValidate = "javascript_function"
        onError = "text"
        gridDataAlign = "position"
        gridLines = "Yes" or "No"
        rowHeight = "pixels"
        rowHeaders = "Yes" or "No"
        rowHeaderAlign = "position"
        rowHeaderFont = "font_name"
        rowHeaderFontSize = "size"
        rowHeaderItalic = "Yes" or "No"
        rowHeaderBold = "Yes" or "No"
        rowHeaderTextColor = "web color"
        rowHeaderWidth = "col_width"
        colHeaders = "Yes" or "No"
        colHeaderAlign = "position"
        colHeaderFont = "font_name"
        colHeaderFontSize = "size"
        colHeaderItalic = "Yes" or "No"
        colHeaderBold = "Yes" or "No"
        colHeaderTextColor = "web color"
        bgColor = "web color"
        selectColor = "web color"
        selectMode = "mode"
        maxRows = "number"
        notSupported = "text"
        pictureBar = "Yes" or "No"
        insertButton = "text"
        deleteButton = "text"
        sortAscendingButton = "text"
        sortDescendingButton = "text">
</cfgrid>
```

Description

Used within the CFFORM tag and enable grid control of table data in a form. To specify column data, use the CFGRIDCOLUMN tag. To render a grid, you must specify a value for one of these: CFGRIDCOLUMN width attribute, CFGRID coheaders attribute, CFGRID autowidth attribute.

Attributes

name (Required)
Name of the grid.

height (Optional)
Height of the grid.

width (Optional)
Width of the grid.

autoWidth (Optional)
Default: No

- **Yes.** Sets column widths so that all columns display within grid width.
- **No.** Sets columns to equal widths.

vSpace (Optional)
Vertical space above and below the grid.

hSpace (Optional)
Horizontal space to left and right of the grid.

align (Optional)
Alignment can be any of the following values: Top, Left, Bottom, Baseline, Texttop, Absbottom, Middle, Absmiddle, and Right.

query (Optional)
Name of a query associated with the grid.

insert (Optional)
Default: No. If Yes, user can insert row data in the grid. Only works if selectmode="edit".

delete (Optional)
Default: No. If Yes, user can delete row data from the grid. Only works if selectmode="edit".

sort (Optional)
Default: No. The sort button performs simple text sorts on a column, which allows the user to sort columns by clicking the column title. If Yes, sort buttons display on the grid.

font (Optional)
Sets the font of the data in the grid.

fontSize (Optional)
Size of text in the grid.

italic (Optional)
Default: No. If Yes, displays text in italics.

bold (Optional)
Default: No. If Yes, displays text in bold.

textColor (Optional)
Default: black. Color of text as hex value or web color.

href (Optional)
If a grid is associated with a query, this is the URL to associate with a grid item or query column.

hrefKey (Optional)
If grid uses a query, this sets the name of a query column as a key.

target (Optional)
The name of a fame to open the associated a URL.

appendKey (Optional)
Default: Yes, which appends a query value to the URL and passes it to the page specified in the action of the form.

highlightHref (Optional)
Default: Yes; any associated href links are highlighted.

onValidate (Optional)
Used to call a JavaScript function for input validation.

onError (Optional)
A JavaScript function to use if the validation fails.

gridDataAlignu
Default: Left
Options are Left, Right, or Center.

gridLines (Optional)
Default: Yes, which enables row and column rules in the grid.

`rowHeight` (Optional)
Minimum row height of the grid.

`rowHeaders` (Optional)
Default: `Yes`, which displays a column of numeric row labels in the grid.

`rowHeaderAlign` (Optional)
Default: `Left`
Options are `Left`, `Right`, or `Center`.

`rowHeaderFont` (Optional)
Row label font.

`rowHeaderFontSize` (Optional)
Row label text size.

`rowHeaderItalic` (Optional)
Default: `No`. If `Yes`, displays row label text in italics.

`rowHeaderBold` (Optional)
Default: `No`. If `Yes`, displays row label text in bold.

`rowHeaderTextColor` (Optional)
Default: `black`; text color of row headers.

`colHeaders` (Optional)
Default: `Yes`, which displays column headers in the grid

`colHeaderAlign` (Optional)
Default: `Left`
Options are `Left`, `Right`, or `Center`.

`colHeaderFont` (Optional)
Font of column header.

`colHeaderFontSize` (Optional)
Size of column header text.

`colHeaderItalic` (Optional)
Default: `No`. If `Yes`, displays column headers in italics.

`colHeaderBold` (Optional)
Default: `No`. If `Yes`, displays column headers in bold.

`colHeaderTextColor` (Optional)
Color of column headers.

`bgColor` (Optional)
Background color of the grid.

selectColor (Optional)
Background color for a selected item.

selectMode (Optional)
Default: Browse
Selection mode for items in the grid.

- **Edit.** User can edit grid data. With `Single`, user selections are limited to the selected cell.

- **Row.** User selections automatically extend to the row that contains the selected cell.

- **Column.** User selections automatically extend to the column that contains the selected cell.

- **Browse.** User can only browse grid data.

maxRows (Optional)
Maximum number of rows to display in the grid.

notSupported (Optional)
Text to display if the browser does not support Java or has Java support disabled.

pictureBar (Optional)
Default: No. If Yes, images for Insert, Delete, and Sort buttons.

insertButton (Optional)
Default: insert. Only works if `selectmode = "edit"`.

deleteButton (Optional)
Default: delete. Only works if `selectmode = "edit"`.

sortAscendingButton (Optional)
Default: A -> Z

sortDescendingButton (Optional)
Default: Z -> A

CFGRIDCOLUMN

```
<cfgridcolumn name = "column_name"
        header = "header"
        width = "column_width"
        font = "column_font"
        fontSize = "size"
        italic = "Yes" or "No"
        bold = "Yes" or "No"
        textColor = "web color" or "expression"
```

```
bgColor = "web color" or "expression"
href = "URL"
hrefKey = "column_name"
target = "URL_target"
select = "Yes" or "No"
display = "Yes" or "No"
type = "type"
headerFont = "font_name"
headerFontSize = "size"
headerItalic = "Yes" or "No"
headerBold = "Yes" or "No"
headerTextColor = "web color"
dataAlign = "position"
headerAlign = "position"
numberFormat = "format"
values = "Comma separated strings and/or numeric range"
valuesDisplay = "Comma separated strings and/or numeric range"
valuesDelimiter = "delimiter character">
```

Description

Use this tag to specify column data in a CFGRID. Font and alignment settings created in the CFGRID are overridden by this tag.

Attributes

name (Required)
Name of the grid column element. If the grid uses a query, then the column name must use the name of a query column.

header (Optional)
Default: Yes. Column header text.
Works only if the CFGRID colHeaders = "Yes".

width (Optional)
Column header width.

font (Optional)
Font of data in the column.

fontSize (Optional)
Size of text in the column.

italic (Optional)
Yes: Displays text in italics.

bold (Optional)
Yes: Displays text in bold.

`textColor` (Optional)
Color of text in the column or an expression to manipulate color.

`bgColor` (Optional)
Background color of the column or an expression to manipulate color.

`href` (Optional)
Relative or absolute URL to associate with a grid item.

`hrefKey` (Optional)
If grid uses a query, this sets the name of a query column as a key.

`target` (Optional)
The name of a fame to open the associated a URL.

`select` (Optional)
`Yes`: User can select the column in the grid.
`No`: User cannot edit the column regardless of `CFGRID` insert and delete values. If `CFGRID` `selectMode` = `"Row"` or `"Browse"`, this attribute is ignored.

`display` (Optional)
Default: `Yes`. If `No`, hides column.

`type` (Optional)

- **image.** Grid displays image that corresponds to the value in the column. If the image is larger than the width of the column, it is cropped. Built-in image names are as follows CD, computer, document, element, folder, floppy, fixed, and remote.
- **numeric.** User can sort grid data numerically.
- **boolean.** Column displays as a check box.
- **string_noCase.** User can sort grid data as non-case-insensitive text.

`headerFont` (Optional)
Column header font.

`headerFontSize` (Optional)
Column header text size.

`headerItalic` (Optional)
`Yes` displays column header in italics.

`headerBold` (Optional)
`Yes` displays column header in bold.

headerTextColor (Optional)
Color of column header text. Can be a hex value or a web color.

dataAlign (Optional)
Column data alignment: `Left`, `Right`, or `Center`.

headerAlign (Optional)
Column header text alignment: `Left`, `Right`, or `Center`.

numberFormat (Optional)
Format for displaying numeric data in grid.

values (Optional)
Formats the cells in the column as a drop-down list. Example of syntax used is `values = "grape, apple, orange, 1-10"`.

valuesDisplay (Optional)
Maps elements in the values attribute to display in the drop-down list.

valuesDelimiter (Optional)
Default: `,` (comma), which is the delimiter for the values and `valuesDisplay` attributes.

CGGRIDROW

```
<cfgridrow data = "col1, col2, ...">
```

Description

Populates a grid that does not use a query. This tag does not work if the query attribute is specified in `CFGRID`.

Attributes

data (Required)
A comma-delimited list of values. If a value contains a comma, it must be escaped with another comma.

CGGRIDUPDATE

```
<cfgridupdate
      grid = "gridname"
      dataSource = "data source name"
      tableName = "table name"
      username = "data source username"
      password = "data source password"
```

```
tableOwner = "table owner"
tableQualifier = "qualifier"
keyOnly = "Yes" or "No">
```

Description

This tag enables a direct input with the data source by updating the edited grid data. This tag applies delete row actions first, then insert row actions, and then update row actions. If it encounters an error, it stops processing rows.

Attributes

grid (Required)
Name of the CFGRID that is the source for the update action.

dataSource (Required)
Name of the data source for the update action.

tableName (Required)
Name of the table to update. For ORACLE drivers, entry must be in all uppercase. For Sybase drivers, entry is case-sensitive.

username (Optional)
Overrides username value specified in the ODBC settings.

password (Optional)
Overrides password value specified in the ODBC settings.

tableOwner (Optional)
Table owner, if supported.

tableQualifier (Optional)
Table qualifier, if supported.

keyOnly
Default: No

- **Yes.** The WHERE criteria are limited to the key values.
- **No.** The WHERE criteria include key values and the original values of the changed fields.

CFHEADER

```
<cfheader
        name = "header_name"
        value = "header_value">
or
<cfheader
        statusCode = "status_code"
        statusText = "status_text">
```

Description

Generates custom HTTP response headers to return to the client.

Attributes

name (Required if statusCode not specified)
Header name.

value (Optional)
HTTP header value.

statusCode (Required if name not specified)
HTTP status code.

statusText (Optional)
Explains the status code.

CFHTMLHEAD

```
<cfhtmlhead text = "text">
```

Description

Creates text inside the <head> of an HTML page and is useful to create JavaScript or to embed metadata.

Attributes

text (Required)
Text to add to the <head> area of the HTML page.

CFHTTP

```
<cfhttp
        url = "hostname"
        port = "port_number"
        method = "get_or_post"
        username = "username"
        password = "password"
        name = "queryname"
        columns = "query_columns"
        firstrowasheaders = "yes" or "no"
        path = "path"
        file = "filename"
        delimiter = "character"
        textQualifier = "character"
        resolveURL = "yes" or "no"
        proxyServer = "hostname"
        proxyPort = "port_number"
        userAgent = "user_agent"
        throwOnError = "yes" or "no"
        redirect = "yes" or "no"
        timeout = "timeout_period">
</cfhttp>
```

Description

Executes HTTP POST and GET operations on files. You can execute standard GET operations and create a query object from a text file. POST operations upload MIME file types to a server, or post cookie, formfield, URL, file, or CGI variables directly to a server.

Attributes

url (Required)
Default: http. Absolute URL of a host name or IP address of the server on which the file resides. The URL must include protocol (http or https) and the host name and can contain a port number.

port (Optional)
Default: 80. Port number on the server from which object is requested. Can be overridden by specifying a port in the url attribute.

method (Required)
Default: get

- **get.** Downloads text or binary file or to create a query from the contents of a text file.

- **post.** Sends information to a server and requires a cfhttpparam tag.

`username` (Optional)
Username for authentication when required.

`password` (Optional)
Password for authentication when required.   .

`name` (Optional)
Name to give a query if it is created from a file.

`columns` (Optional)
When using the GET function, this enables the creation of column names. The default uses the first row of the file as the column name; if this is not desired, this attribute overwrites this functionality, but ColdFusion will never use the first row of the file as data.

`firstrowasheaders` (Optional)
Default: Yes

- **Yes.** If the columns attribute is not specified, then the first row is used as column heads. If the columns attribute is specified then this attribute is ignored

- **No.** If the columns attribute is not specified, then it processes the first row as data and creates its own column names, such as `"column_1"`. If the columns attribute is specified, then this attribute is ignored.

`path` (Optional)
Path to directory in which to store the file. If path is not specified in POST or GET, a variable (`cfhttp.fileContent`) is created.

`file` (Required if post and if path is specified)
Name of the file that is accessed. For GET operations, defaults to name specified in the URL.

`delimiter` (Required to create query)
Default: , (comma). Options are tab or comma.

`textQualifier` (Required to create query)
Default: `""` (double quotation mark)
This shows the start and finish of a column.

resolveURL (Optional)
Default: No. For GET and POST.
Yes: So that links remain valid, this resolves internal URLs, including port number in a page reference returned into fileContent. The following HTML tags are resolved: img src, a href, form action, applet code, script src, embed src, embed pluginspace, body background, frame src, bgsound src, object data, object classid, object codebase, and object usemap.

proxyServer (Optional)
Host name or IP address of a proxy server.

proxyPort (Optional)
Default: 80, which is the port number on proxy server from which the object is requested.

userAgent (Optional)
User agent request header.

throwOnError (Optional)
Default: No. If Yes, throws an exception that can be caught with the CFTRY and CFCATCH tags.

redirect (Optional)
Default: Yes. Enables up to four redirects and can be followed by accessing the variable cfhttp.responseHeader[LOCATION].

- **Yes.** Redirect execution.

- **No.** Stop execution.

timeout (Optional)
This setting overrides the timeout setting in the ColdFusion Administrator, but ColdFusion will always make sure that the timeout will occur at the same time as the page timeout.

CFHTTPPARAM

```
< cfhttpparam
      name = "name"
      type = "type"
      value = "transaction type"
      file = "filename">
```

Description

Required for a `CFHTTP POST` operation and specifies the parameters to build the operation.

Attributes

name (Required)
Variable name for the data that is passed.

type (Required)
Transaction type: URL, FormField, Cookie, CGI, File.

value (Optional if `type = "File"`)
Value of URL, FormField, Cookie, File, or CGI variables that are passed.

file (Required if `type = "File"`)
Filename.

CFIF

```
<cfif expression>
        HTML and CFML tags
<cfelseif expression>
        HTML and CFML tags
<cfelse>
        HTML and CFML tags
</cfif>
```

Description

This tag is used to create conditional logic within ColdFusion. It tests a condition such as an expression and then returns `true` or `false`. If `True`, then the code within the tag is executed; if `false`, then the code within the tag is ignored. Can also be used with the `CFELSE` and `CFELSEIF` tags. This tag has no attributes but can include multiple conditions, such as:

```
<cfif "11/23/1998 " GT "11/15/1998">
```

CFIMPORT

```
<cfimport
        taglib = "taglib-location"
        prefix = "custom"
        webservice = "URL"
/>
```

Description

Copies a Java Server Page (JSP) tag library into a CFML page. A JSP tag library is a packaged set of tag handlers that conformS to the JSP 1.1 tag extension API.

Attributes

`taglib` (Required)
Tag library name and location that can be either a URL or a path.

`prefix`
Prefix by which to access imported JSP tags on the CFML page. To import tags directly, specify an empty value, `""` . Use this to create server-side versions of common HTML tags.

`webservice` (Optional)
URL of a WSDL file.

CFINCLUDE

```
<cfinclude template = "template_name">
```

Description

Includes the code from a separate file into the current ColdFusion page. This tag can be used recursively or the included code may also contain a CFINCLUDE.

Attributes

`template` (Required)
A logical path to a ColdFusion page.

CFINDEX

```
<cfindex
        collection = "collection_name"
        action = "action"
        type = "type"
        title = "title"
        key = "ID"
        body = "body"
        custom1 = "custom_value"
```

```
custom2 = "custom_value"
URLpath = "URL"
extensions = "file_extensions"
query = "query_name"
recurse = "Yes" or "No"
language = "language">
```

Description

Used in conjunction with other Verity search engine tags, such as CFCOLLECTION, to create indexed data for a collection. For this tag to work, a collection must exist. To learn more about creating collections, see the CFCOLLECTION tag.

Attributes

collection (Required)
Collection name. For unregistered collections, use an absolute path such as collection = "c:\collections\exampleCollection".

action (Optional)
- **update.** Updates a collection and adds a key to the index.
- **delete.** Deletes data in the entities specified by the type attribute.
- **purge.** Deletes all keys from a collection.
- **refresh.** Purges a collection before updating it.

type (Optional)
- **default.** Custom if the query attribute is specified. If not, then file.
- **file.** Uses filenames or file paths to apply the action using the key attribute value of the query result.
- **path.** Uses filenames or file paths that pass the extension filter to apply the action using the key attribute value of the query result.
- **custom.** If action = "update" or "delete", then it applies the action to custom entities in the query results.

`title` (Required if `type` = `"Custom"`)
Title for the collection.
Enables collections to be searched by title or key.

`key` (Depends on `action` attribute value)
Default: `""`(empty string)
Absolute path if `type` = `"file"`
Absolute path if `type` = `"path"`
A query column name (typically, the primary key column name) if `type` = `"custom"`
Query column name if `type` = any other value.
This attribute is required for the actions listed unless you intend for its value to be an empty string.

`body` (Required if `type` = `"custom"`)
Text to index. This can be a column name if there is a query specified.

`custom1` (Optional)
Custom field that can be used to store data during an indexing operation.

`custom2` (Optional)
Same as `custom1`.

`URLpath` (Optional)
If `type="file"` or `"path"`, specifies the URL path. This path name is prefixed to the filenames when using `CFSEARCH`.

`extensions` (Optional)
Default: HTM, HTML, CFM, CFML, DBM, DBML. Delimited list of file extensions that ColdFusion uses to index files if `type` = `"Path"`.
"★". returns files with no extension.

`query` (Optional)
Query against which collection is generated.

`recurse` (Optional)
Default: `No`. If `Yes` and if `type` = `"path"`, then the directories below the path specified in the key are included in the indexing operation.

`language` (Optional)
Default: `english`. Requires the appropriate (European or Asian) Verity Locales language pack.

cfinput

```
<cfinput type = "input_type"
        name = "name"
        value = "initial_value"
        required = "Yes" or "No"
        range = "min_value, max_value"
        validate = "data_type"
        onValidate = "javascript_function"
        pattern = "regexp"
        message = "validation_msg"
        onError = "text"
        size = "integer"
        maxLength = "integer"
        checked
        passThrough = "HTML_attributes">
```

Description

Used within the CFFORM tag to place radio buttons, check boxes, or text boxes on a form. Can also provide input validation if the validate attribute is specified.

Attributes

type (Optional)
Default: text

- **text.** Creates a text entry box control.
- **radio.** Creates a radio button control.
- **checkbox.** Creates a check box control.
- **password.** Creates a password entry control.

name (Required)
Name for the form element.

value
Initial value for the form element.

required (Optional)
Default: No

range (Optional)
Minimum and maximum value range separated by a comma.
Can only be used with numeric data.

`validate` (Optional)
Verifies a value's format:

- **date.** US date mm/dd/yyyy.
- **eurodate.** European date dd/mm/yyyy.
- **time.** Time hh:mm:ss.
- **float.** Floating point entry.
- **integer.** Integer entry.
- **telephone.** Telephone ###-###-####.
- **separator.** Hyphen or blank. Area code and exchange must begin with a digit 1 - 9.
- **zipcode.** (U.S. formats only) 5-digit ##### or 9-digit #####-####.
- **separator.** Hyphen or blank.
- **creditcard.** Strips blanks and dashes; uses the mod10 algorithm.
- **social_security_number.** ###-##-####.
- **separator.** Hyphen or blank.
- **regular_expression.** Matches input against regular expression specified by the pattern attribute.

`onValidate` (Optional)
Can be used to call a custom JavaScript function to validate the input. If used, the `validate` attribute is ignored.

`pattern` (Required if `validate` = `"regular_expression"`)
A JavaScript regular expression pattern from which to validate the input.

`message` (Optional)
Message text to display if validation fails.

`onError` (Optional)
Custom JavaScript function to execute if validation fails.

`size` (Optional)
Display size of the input. Ignored if `type` = `"radio"` or `"checkbox"`.

`maxLength` (Optional)
Maximum length of text entered if `type` = `"text"` or `" password"`.

`checked` (Optional)
Selects a control. No value is required. Only works for `type` = `"radio"` or `"checkbox"`.

passThrough (Optional)

Ignores HTML attributes that are not supported by CFINPUT and passes them to the generated page.

cfinsert

```
<cfinsert dataSource = "ds_name"
        tableName = "tbl_name"
        tableOwner = "owner"
        tableQualifier = "tbl_qualifier"
        username = "username"
        password = "password"
        formFields = "formfield1, formfield2, ...">
```

Description

Inserts records into a datasource from data in a CF form or form scope without the need for creating a SQL statement.

Attributes

dataSource (Required)
The ColdFusion datasource.

tableName (Required)
Table in which to insert form fields. For Oracle drivers, the name must be in all uppercase. For the Sybase driver, it is case-sensitive.

tableOwner (Optional)
For datasources that support table ownership (such as SQL Server, Oracle, and Sybase SQL Anywhere), use this field to specify the owner of the table.

tableQualifier (Optional)
For datasources that support table qualifiers, use this field to specify the qualifier for table.

username (Optional)
Overrides username specified in ODBC setup.

password (Optional)
Overrides password specified in ODBC setup.

formFields (Optional)
Default: All on form, except keys.

Comma–delimited list of form fields to insert. If not specified, all fields in the form are included. If a form field is not matched by a column name in the database, ColdFusion throws an error. The database table key field must be present in the form.

cfinvoke

```
<cfinvoke
        component = "component name or reference"
        returnVariable = "variable name"
        argumentCollection = "argument collection"
        ...
>
```

Syntax 2

```
<cfinvoke
        method = "method name"
        returnVariable = "variable name"
        argumentCollection = "argument collection"
        ...
>
```

Syntax 3

```
<cfinvoke
        webservice = "taglib-location"
        method = "operation_name"
        input_params ...
        returnVariable = "var_name"
>
```

Description

Invokes component methods from within a ColdFusion page or component. When operating on components, it instantiates a web component and invokes a method on it. It also invokes a method on an instantiated component. When operating on web services, it invokes a method on a web component. This tag can pass parameters to a method in the following ways:

- With the cfinvokeargument tag.
- As named attribute-value pairs, one attribute per parameter.
- As a structure, in the argumentCollection attribute.

Attributes

component (Required if method is not specified)
A reference to a component or a component to instantiate.

method (Required if component is not specified)
Name of a method; for a web service, the name of an operation.

returnVariable (Optional)
Name of a variable for the invocation result.

argumentCollection (Optional)
Name of a structure with arguments to pass to the method.

username (Optional)
Overrides username specified in ODBC setup.

password (Optional)
Overrides password specified in ODBC setup.

webservice
The URL of the WSDL file for the web service.

input_params (Optional)
Input parameters.

cfinvokeargument

```
<cfinvokeargument
        name="argument name"
        value="argument value"
>
```

Description

Passes an argument to a method independently of the cfinvoke tag.

Attributes

name (Required)
Argument name.

value (Required)
Argument value.

cfldap

```
<cfldap server = "server_name"
        port = "port_number"
        username = "name"
        password = "password"
        action = "action"
        name = "name"
        timeout = "seconds"
        maxRows = "number"
        start = "distinguished_name"
        scope = "scope"
        attributes = "attribute, attribute"
        filter = "filter"
        sort = "attribute[, attribute]..."
        sortControl = "nocase" and/or "desc" or "asc"
        dn = "distinguished_name"
        startRow = "row_number"
        modifyType = "REPLACE" or "ADD" or "delete"
        rebind = "Yes" or "No"
        referral = "number_of_allowed_hops"
        secure = "multi_field_security_string"
        separator = "separator_character"
        delimiter = "delimiter_character">
```

Description

Provides an interface to a Lightweight Directory Access Protocol (LDAP) directory server, such as the Netscape Directory Server.

Attributes

server (Required)
Host name or IP address of LDAP server.

port (Optional)
Default: Port 389

username (Required if secure = "CFSSL_BASIC")
User ID.

password (Required if secure = "CFSSL_BASIC")
Password that corresponds to username. If secure = "ColdFusionSSL_BASIC", then the password is encrypted.

`action` (Optional)
Default: `query`

- **query.** Returns LDAP entry information only. Requires `name` and `start` attributes.
- **add.** Adds LDAP entries to the LDAP server.
- **modify.** Modifies LDAP entries, except for the distinguished name (`dn`) attribute on the LDAP server.
- **modifyDN.** Modifies `dn` attribute for LDAP entries on the LDAP server.
- **delete.** Deletes LDAP entries on the LDAP server.

`name` (Required if `action` = `"Query"`)
Name of the LDAP query.

`timeout` (Optional)
Default: `60`. Maximum length of time in seconds to wait for processing to occur.

`maxRows` (Optional)
Maximum number of entries for LDAP queries.

`start` (Required if `action` = `"Query"`)
Distinguished name of an entry to be used to start a search.

`scope` (Optional)
Default: `oneLevel`

- **oneLevel.** Entries one level below starting entry.
- **base.** Only the entry.
- **subtree.** Entry and all levels below it.

`attributes` (Required if `action` = `"Query/Add/ModifyDN/Modify"`)
For queries, this should be a comma-delimited list of attributes to return. For `action` = `"add"` or `"modify"`, you can specify a list of update columns. Separate attributes with a semicolon. For `action` = `"ModifyDN"`, ColdFusion passes attributes to the LDAP server without syntax checking.

`filter` (Optional)
A filter to limit search criteria when `action` = `"query"`.

`sort` (Optional)
Attribute(s) by which to sort query results. Use a comma-delimited list for multiple sort criteria.

sortControl (Optional)
Default: asc. Combinations of sort types are also valid. For example,
sortControl = "nocase, asc".

- **nocase.** Case-insensitive sort.
- **asc.** Ascending (A to Z) case-sensitive sort.
- **desc.** Descending (Z to A) case-sensitive sort.

dn (Required if action = "Add/ModifyDN/Modify/delete")
Distinguished name for an update action.

startRow (Optional)
Default: 1. Used with action = "query". First row of LDAP query
to insert into a ColdFusion query.

modifyType (Optional)
Default: replace. You cannot add an attribute that is already present or that
is empty.

- **add.** Appends it to any attributes.
- **delete.** Deletes it from the set of attributes.
- **replace.** Replaces it with specified attributes.

rebind (Optional)
Default: No

- **Yes.** Attempts to rebind referral callback and reissue query by referred
  address using original credentials.
- **No.** Referred connections are anonymous.

referral (Optional)
Number of hops allowed in a referral. A value of 0 disables referred
addresses for LDAP.

secure (Optional)
Security to employ and required information:

- **CFSSL_BASIC.** certificate_db
- **CFSSL_BASIC.** Provides V2 Secure Socket Layer (SSL) encryption
  and server authentication.
- **certificate_db.** Certificate database file.

separator (Optional)
Default: , (comma). Used by query, add, and modify actions by CFLDAP to output multivalue attributes using the specified delimiter to separate attribute values.

delimiter (Optional)
Separator for attribute name-value pairs.

cflocation

```
<cflocation
        url = "url"
        addToken = "Yes" or "No">
```

Description

Used to redirect to a different ColdFusion or HTML page. When ColdFusion executes this tag, the processing of the current page stops.

Attributes

url (Required)
URL of ColdFusion or HTML page to open.

addToken (Optional)
clientManagement must be enabled. If Yes, appends client variable information to the URL.

cflock

```
<cflock timeout = "timeout in seconds "
        scope = "Application or Server or Session"
        name = "lockname"
        throwOnTimeout = "Yes" or "No"
        type = "readOnly" or "exclusive">
        <!--- CFML to be synchronized --->
</cflock>
```

Description

Ensures the integrity of shared data. Instantiates the following kinds of locks:

- **Exclusive.** Enables single-thread access to the CFML constructs in its body. Can only be executed by one request at a time and no other requests can start executing when the request has an exclusive lock. ColdFusion issues exclusive locks on a first-come, first-served basis.

- **Read-only.** Creates a read-only lock that does not enable data to be modified but enables multiple requests to access data concurrently.

Attributes

timeout (Required)
Maximum length of time to wait to obtain a lock.

scope (Optional)
Mutually exclusive with the name attribute. Options are Application, Server, or Session.

name (Optional)
Lock names are shared among applications and user sessions so that a lock can be used in different parts of an application. Only one request can execute within a given name.

throwOnTimeout (Optional)
Default: Yes

- **Yes.** Exception is generated for the timeout.
- **No.** Execution continues past this tag.

type (Optional)
Default: exclusive

- **read-only.** Lets more than one request read shared data. Note that if performance is an issue, the read-only lock is faster than the exclusive lock.
- **exclusive.** Lets one request read or write shared data.

cflog

```
<cflog text = "text"
       log = "log type"
       file = "filename"
       type = "message type"
       thread = "yes"
       date = "yes"
       time = "yes"
       application = "application name yes or no">
```

Description

Writes a message to a log file.

Attributes

text (Required)
Message text to log.

log (Optional)
If you omit the file attribute, writes messages to standard log files.

- **application.** Writes to Application.log, normally used for application-specific messages.
- **scheduler.** Writes to Scheduler.log, normally used to log the execution of scheduled tasks.

file (Optional)
The message file to write log reports. Specify only the main part of the filename; to log to the Example.log file, specify "Example". The file must be located in the default log directory and will be created if it does not exist.

type (Optional)
Default: Information
Severity of the message: Information, Warning, Error, and Fatal.

thread (Optional)
Default: Yes. A thread ID identifies which internal service thread logged a message. Useful to help identify server activity patterns.

- **Yes.** Log thread ID.
- **No.** Deprecated. This option throws an error.

date (Optional)
Default: yes

- **Yes.** Logs the system date.
- **No.** Deprecated. This option throws an error.

time (Optional)
Default: yes

- **Yes.** Logs the system time.
- **No.** Deprecated. This option throws an error.

application (Optional)

Default: Yes. Logs application name, if it is specified in a CFAPPLICATION tag.

CFLOGIN (New in MX)

```
< cflogin
        <cfloginuser
                name = "name"
                roles = "roles">
>
```

Description

A container for the code that authenticates a user. The body of this tag checks the user-provided ID and password against a datasource, LDAP directory, or other repository of login identification. Must include a CFLOGINUSER tag to work. This tag has no attributes.

CFLOGINUSER (New in MX)

```
<cfloginuser
        name = "name"
        roles = "roles"
>
```

Description

Used within the CFLOGIN tag to identify an authenticated user. Can also be used to specify the user ID and roles tag.

Attributes

name (Required)
User ID.

roles (Optional)
A comma-delimited list of role identifiers. ColdFusion processes spaces in a list element as part of the element.

cflogout (New in MX)

```
<cflogout>
```

Description

Used within CFLOGIN to log out the current user. Additionally, this removes knowledge of the user ID and roles from the server. Alternatively, if the session expires, the user is automatically logged out. This tag has no attributes.

cfloop

Index Loop

```
<cfloop index = "parameter_name"
        from = "beginning_value"
        to = "ending_value"
        step = "increment">
        ...
        HTML or CFML code to execute
...
```

Conditional Loop

```
<cfloop condition = "expression">
```

Query Loop

```
<cfloop query = "query_name"
        startRow = "row_num"
        endRow = "row_num">
```

List/File Loop

```
<cfloop index = "index_name"
        list = "list_items"
        delimiterS = "item_delimiter">
```

COM Collection/Structure Loop

```
<cfloop collection = #variable#
        item = "item">
```

Description

Looping is a programming technique that repeats a set of instructions or displays output repeatedly until one or more conditions are met. An Index loop repeats for a number of times that is determined by a numeric value. An Index loop is also known as a For loop.

Attributes

index (Required)
The current value that the loop is on; it is set by ColdFusion increments or decrements by the step value until it equals to the final value.

from (Required)
Beginning value of index.

to (Required)
Ending value of index.

step (Optional)
Default: 1; the step by which to increment or decrement the index value.

condition (Required for conditional loop)
Condition that controls the loop.

query (Required for query loop)
Query that controls the loop.

startRow (Optional)
First row of the query that looped over.

endRow (Optional)
Last row of the query that is looped over.

index (Required in an index of List/File loop)
In a list loop, the variable to receive next list element.

list (Required in a List/File loop)
A list, variable, or filename that contains a list to loop over.

delimiters (Optional)
Character(s) that separates items in the list.

cfmail

```
<cfmail to = "recipient"
        from = "sender"
        cc = "copy_to"
        bcc = "blind_copy_to"
        subject = "msg_subject"
        type = "msg_type"
        maxRows = "max_msgs"
        MIMEAttach = "path"
        query = "query_name"
        group = "query_column"
        groupCaseSensitive = "Yes" or "No"
        startRow = "query_row"
        server = "servername"
        port = "port_ID"
        mailerID = "headerid"
        timeout = "seconds">
        spoolEnable = "Yes" or "No">
        ...
</cfmail>
```

Description

Sends an email message that can contain query output or that can be hard coded using an Simple Mail Transfer Protocol (SMTP) server. An SMTP server must be specified in the ColdFusion Administrator for this tag to work.

Attributes

to (Required)
Message recipient name.

from (Required)
Email message sender.

cc (Optional)
Address to which to copy the message.

bcc (Optional)
Address to which to send a blind copy of the message. This message recipient is not listed in the message.

subject (Required)
Message subject, which can be set dynamically or hard-coded.

type (Optional)
Used to create a message that is not plain text, such as an HTML formatted message.

maxRows (Optional)
Maximum number of messages to send.

MIMEAttach (Optional)
If you would like to send an attachment with the e-mail, use this attribute to create a path to that file.

query (Optional)
Name of CFQUERY to use data from for the message. Use this attribute to send more than one message or to send query results within a message.

group (Optional)
Default: CurrentRow
Query column to use when you group sets of records to send as a message.

groupCaseSensitive (Optional)
Default: Yes. If there is case-sensitive data, use this attribute or set to No to keep the record intact.

startRow (Optional)
Default: 1. Row in a query from which to start.

server (Optional)
Used to override the value for an SMTP server that is set in the ColdFusion Administrator.

port
Default: -1. TCP/IP port on which SMTP server listens for requests. This is normally port 25.

mailerID (Optional)
Default: ColdFusion Application Server. Mailer ID to be passed in X-Mailer SMTP header, which identifies the mailer application.

timeout (Optional)
Default: -1. Number of seconds to wait before timing out the connection to the SMTP server.

spoolEnable (Optional)
Default: Yes

- **Yes.** Saves a copy of the message until the sending operation is complete.

- **No.** Queues the message for sending, without storing a copy until the operation is complete. Use this option is performance is a concern.

CFMAILPARAM

```
<cfmail>
        <cfmailparam  file = "file-name" >
        or
        <cfmailparam
                name = "header-name"
                value = "header-value" >
        ...
</cfmail>
```

Description

Use as many of these as you want within the CFMAIL tag to attach a file or add a header to the email message.

Attributes

file (Required)
Attaches a file to the email. Cannot be used with the name attribute.

name (Required)
Name of a header to include in the email. Cannot be used with the file attribute.

value (Optional)
Value of header.

cfmodule

```
<cfmodule
        template = "path"
        name = "tag_name"
        attributeCollection = "collection_structure"
        attribute_name1 = "valuea"
        attribute_name2 = "valueb"
...>
```

Description

Calls custom tags for use in applications without the possibility of name conflicts.

Attributes

template (Required unless name attribute is used)
A path to the page that implements the tag.

- **Relative path.** Expanded from the current page.

- **Absolute path.** Expanded using ColdFusion mapping.

name (Required unless template attribute is used)
A custom tag name in the form "Name.Name.Name...".

attributeCollection (Optional)
This creates a structure for collecting value pairs that are generated by the tag.

attribute_name (Optional)
Use this attribute to specify any parameters that the custom tag may need. Use this attribute as many times as necessary.

CFOBJECT

```
<cfobject
      type = "com/component/corba/Java/webservice"
      action = "action/NA/NA/Create"
      class = "program_ID/NA/c:\\myobject.ior/Java class/ "
      name = "text/variable name/GetName/object name/"
      context = "context/NA/IOR/NA/NA"
      server = "server_name"(type = "com")
      component = "component"(type = "compoent")>
```

Description

Used to create and manipulate component object model (COM) objects, CFCs, webservice objects, and Java and Enterprise JavaBeans. This can also be used to call a method on a registered Common Object Request Broker Architecture (CORBA) object.

This tag may be disabled under ColdFusion basic security in the ColdFusion Administrator. On UNIX, this tag does not support COM objects.

Attributes

cfobject type = "com"

`action` (Required)

- **create.** Instantiates a COM object (typically a DLL) before invoking methods or properties.
- **connect.** Connects to a COM object (typically an EXE) running on the server.

`class` (Required)
Component ProgID for the object to invoke.

`name` (Required)
A name for the instantiated component.

`context` (Optional)
InProc/Local/Remote.
On Windows: If not specified, uses Registry setting.
`server` (Required if `context` = `"Remote"`)
Server name, using Universal Naming Convention (UNC) or Domain Name Serve (DNS) convention, in one of these forms: `\\lanserver`, `http://www.servername.com`, or `http://127.0.0.1`.

cfobject type = "component"

`name` (Required)
A name for the instantiated component.

`component` (Required)
Name of component to instantiate.

cfobject type = "corba"

`context` (Required)

- **IOR.** ColdFusion uses Interoperable Object Reference (IOR) to access a CORBA server.
- **NameService.** ColdFusion uses naming service to access a server. This option is valid only with the InitialContext of a VisiBroker Orb.

`class` (Required)
If `context` = `"IOR"`, this is name of file that contains string-formatted version of IOR. ColdFusion must be able to read this file. If `context` = `"NameService"`, this is the period-delimited naming context for the naming service (for example, `IBM.Dept.Doc.empobject`).

`name` (Required)
A name for the instantiated component. An application uses it to reference the CORBA object's methods and attributes.

`locale` (Optional)
Sets arguments for a call to `init_orb`. Use of this attribute is specific to VisiBroker orbs. It is available on C++, Version 3.2. The value must be in the form `locale` = `" -ORBagentAddr 199.99.129.33 -ORBagentPort 19000"`.

cfobject type = "java"

`action` (Required)
`create`: Creates a Java or WebLogic Environment object.

`class` (Required)
Java class.

`name` (Required)
A name for the instantiated component.

cfobject type = "webservice"

`webservice` (Required)
URI of the web service.

`action` (Required)
Action to take with the web service.

`name` (Required)
A name for the web service.

CFOBJECTCACHE

```
<cfobjectcache action = "clear">
```

Description

Flushes the query cache.

Attributes

> `action` (Required)
> `clear`: Clears queries from the cache in the application scope.

cfoutput

```
<cfoutput
        query = "query_name"
        group = "query_column"
        groupCaseSensitive = "Yes" or "No"
        startRow = "start_row"
        maxRows = "max_rows_output">
</cfoutput>
```

Description

> Use this tag to display ColdFusion results of queries and other operations.

Attributes

> `query` (Optional)
> Name of `CFQUERY` from which to get data for output.

> `group` (Optional)
> Use this attribute if you want to group records according to a column in the query. This attribute is useful to eliminate duplicate data.

> `groupCaseSensitive` (Optional)
> Default: `Yes`. Used to group by case, if this is important and a non-case-sensitive query is used to retrieve the data.

> `startRow` (Optional)
> Default: 1. Row from which to start output.

> `maxRows` (Optional)
> Maximum number of rows to display. This can be used to limit the number of records displayed.

cfparam

```
<cfparam name = "param_name"
        type = "data_type"
        default = "value">
```

Description

Use this tag to test whether a parameter exists, to test its data type, and to assign a default value.

Attributes

name (Required)
Name of the parameter to test.

type (Optional)
Uses: any, array, binary, Boolean, date, numeric, query, string, struct, UUID, and variableName.

default (Optional)
Value to set parameter to if it does not exist.

cfpop

```
<cfpop server = "servername"
        port = "port_number"
        username = "username"
        password = "password"
        action = "action"
        name = "queryname"
        messageNumber = "number"
        uid = "number"
        attachmentPath = "path"
        timeout = "seconds"
        maxRows = "number"
        startRow = "number"
        generateUniqueFilenames = "boolean">
```

Description

Retrieves and deletes email messages from a POP mail server.

Attributes

server (Required)
The POP server identifier, as a host name (exampleserver.nowhere.com) or as an IP address (127.0.0.1).

port (Optional)
Default: 110. The POP port.

username (Optional)
Default: anonymous. A username.

password (Optional)
Password that corresponds to a username.

action (Optional)
Default: getHeaderOnly

- **getHeaderOnly.** Returns message header information only.

- **getAll.** Returns message header information, message text, and attachments if attachmentPath is specified.

- **delete.** Deletes messages on POP server.

name (Required if action = "getAll" or "getHeaderOnly")
Name for index query.

MessageNumber (Required if action = "delete")
Enables retrieval of a specific message or a list of messages. If this attribute is not specified, all messages on the server are retrieved.

uid (Required if action = "delete")
Retrieves or deletes a specific UID(s) or a comma-delimited list of UIDs. Invalid UIDs are ignored.

attachmentPath (Optional)
If action = "getAll", enables attachments to be written to a directory. If this value is invalid, no attachment files are written to the server.

timeout (Optional)
Default: 60. Maximum time, in seconds, to wait for mail processing.

maxRows (Optional)
Default: 999999. The maximum number of messages that can be returned starting with the startRow number. If messageNumber is specified, this attribute is ignored.

startRow (Optional)
Default: 1. First row number to get. If messageNumber is specified, this
attribute is ignored.

generateUniqueFilenames (Optional)
Default: No. If Yes, used for avoiding naming conflicts when downloading
attachments by creating unique names for files.

cfprocessingdirective

```
<cfprocessingdirective
        suppressWhiteSpace = "Yes" or "No"
        pageEncoding = "page-encoding literal string">
        CFML tags
</cfprocessingdirective>
```

Description

Use this tag to control the generation of whitespace and the page encoding
by ColdFusion.

Attributes

suppressWhiteSpace (Required)

- **Yes.** Suppress whitespace.

- **No.** Generate whitespace as it is output by ColdFusion.

pageEncoding (Optional)
Use this attribute to control the character encoding of the page for
different languages.

cfprocparam

```
<cfprocparam type = "in" or "out" or "inout"
        variable = "variable name"
        dbVarName = "DB variable name"
        value = "parameter value"
        CFSQLType = "parameter datatype"
        maxLength = "length"
        scale = "decimal places"
        null = "Yes" or "No">
```

Description

Used within the CFSTOREDPROC tag; use this tag to specify variables and parameters for passing information to the stored procedure.

Attributes

type (Optional)
Default: in

- **in.** Passes the parameter by value.
- **out.** Passes parameter as bound variable.
- **inout.** Passes parameter as a bound variable.

variable
A ColdFusion variable name. This is the variable that stores the output and that you can reference after the stored procedure is called.

dbVarName (Required for named notation)
Parameter name that corresponds to the name of the parameter in the stored procedure.

value (Required if type = "out/inout")
Value that corresponds to the value that ColdFusion passes to the stored procedure.

CFSQLType (Required)
SQL type to which the parameter is bound.

maxLength (Optional)
Default: 0. Maximum length of the parameter.

scale (Optional)
Default: 0. Number of decimal places in the parameter.

null (Optional)
Default: No. Whether the parameter is passed as a null value. If Yes, tag ignores the value attribute.

cfprocresult

```
<cfprocresult name = "query_name"
         resultSet = "1-n"
         maxRows = "maxrows">
```

Description

Used with the `CFSTOREDPROC` tag, this tag enables you to specify which result set from the stored procedure to use within `CFOUTPUT` and `CFTABLE` tags.

Attributes

`name` (Required)
Name for the query result set.

`resultSet` (Optional)
Default: 1. Name of one result set if the stored procedure returns more than one.

`maxRows` (Optional)
Default: -1 (All). Maximum number of rows returned in the result set.

cfproperty

```
<cfproperty
         name="..."
         type="..."
         ...
>
```

Description

Used in conjunction with components, this tag creates complex types that can be used with web services. The attributes of this tag are exposed as component metadata and are subject to inheritance rules.

Attributes

`name` (Required)
A property name that must be a static value.

`type` (Optional)
A property type name that must be a static value.

cfquery

```
<cfquery name = "query_name"
        dataSource = "ds_name"
        username = "username"
        password = "password"
        maxRows = "number"
        blockFactor = "blocksize"
        timeout = "seconds"
        cachedAfter = "date"
        cachedWithin = "timespan"
        debug = "Yes" or "No"  or debug>

SQL statement(s)

</cfquery>
```

Description

Use this tag to write structured query language (SQL) queries that are passed on to your database through the datasource name. SQL statements within this tag are executed just as they are written and can be used to select, insert, update, or delete data.

Attributes

name (Required)
Name of the query. This query name will be referenced throughout the application to utilize the data.

dataSource (Required)
Name of datasource from which the query retrieves data.

username (Optional)
Overrides username specified in the ColdFusion Administrator for the datasource.

password (Optional)
Overrides password specified in the ColdFusion Administrator for the datasource.

maxRows (Optional)
Default: -1 (All). Maximum number of rows to return in the recordset.

blockFactor (Optional)
Default: 1. Maximum rows to get at one time from the server. The range is from 1 − 100. This can be used to make the query more efficient.

`timeout`

Maximum number of seconds that each action of a query is permitted to execute before returning an error.

`cachedAfter` (Optional)

If query caching is enabled, then ColdFusion retrieves the data from the cache if the current date is after the specified date. Year values in the range 0-29 are interpreted as 2000-2029; in the range 30-99, they are interpreted as 1930-1999. Values in the range 100 – 9999 are interpreted as absolute A.D. dates.

`cachedWithin` (Optional)

Time span, using the `CreateTimeSpan` function. If original query date falls within the time span, the cached query data is used. `CreateTimeSpan` defines a period from the present back. Takes effect only if query caching is enabled in the Administrator. To use cached data, the current query must use the same SQL statement, datasource, query name, username, password, and `dbType`.

`debug` (Optional); value and equals sign may be omitted

- **Yes.** or if value is omitted. If debugging is enabled, but the Administrator Database Activity option is not enabled, displays SQL submitted to datasource and number of records returned by query.

- **No.** If the Administrator Database Activity option is enabled, suppresses display.

cfqueryparam

```
<cfquery>
        <cfqueryparam value = "parameter value"
                CFSQLType = "parameter type"
                maxLength = "maximum parameter length"
                scale = "number of decimal places"
                null = "Yes" or "No"
                list = "Yes" or "No"
                separator = "separator character">
        AND/OR ...additional criteria of the WHERE clause...
</cfquery>
```

Description

Checks the data type of a query parameter. This tag is nested within a `CFQUERY` tag and embedded in a query SQL statement. If you specify optional parameters, this tag performs data validation.

Attributes

value (Required)
Value that ColdFusion passes to the right of the comparison operator in a
WHERE clause if CFSQLType is a date or time option.

maxLength (Optional)
Length of string in value attribute. Maximum length of parameter.

scale (Optional)
Default: ø. Number of decimal places in parameter. Applies to
CF_SQL_NUMERIC and CF_SQL_DECIMAL.

null (Optional)
Default: No

- **No.** Whether parameter is passed as a null value.
- **Yes.** Tag ignores the value attribute.

list (Optional)
Default: No. If Yes, the value attribute value is a delimited list.

separator (Required if value = "list")
Character that separates values in list in the value attribute.

cfregistry

action = "getAll"

```
<cfregistry action = "getAll"
        branch = "branch"
        type = "data type"
        name = "query name"
        sort = "criteria">
```

action = "get"

```
<cfregistry action = "get"
        branch = "branch"
        entry = "key or value"
        variable = "variable"
        type = "data type">
```

action = "set"

action = "delete"

Description

Reads, writes, and stores values in the system registry. Provides persistent storage of client variables.

Attributes

action (Required)
Options include getall/get/set/delete.

branch (Required)
Name of a registry branch.

type (Optional)
The type of registry setting as a string.

name (Required)
Name of recordset to contain returned keys and values.

sort (Optional)
Default: ASC. A non-case-insensitive sort of query data.

entry (Required)
Registry value to access.

variable (Required)
Variable into which to put value.

cfreport

```
<cfreport report = "report_path"
        dataSource = "ds_name"
        type = "type"
        timeout = "number of seconds"
        orderBy = "result_order"
        username = "username"
        password = "password"
        formula = "formula">

 </cfreport>
```

Description

Use this tag to interface with Crystal Reports through the `CFCRYSTAL.EXE` file. Crystal Reports parameters are set by the attribute values that are set within the tag.

Attributes

`datasource` (Optional)
Name of a registered datasource.

`type` (Optional)
Default: `standard`. Options include `standard`, `netscape`, and `microsoft`.

`timeout` (Optional)
Maximum time in which a connection must be made to a Crystal Report.

`report` (Required)
This sets the path in which to store Crystal Reports files.

`orderBy` (Optional)
Orders results according to your specifications.

`username` (Optional)
If the username is other than the one set in the ColdFusion Administrator, then use this attribute to specify the username.

`password` (Optional)
Password that corresponds to the username.

`formula` (Optional)
One or more named formulas. If you are using more than one formula, use a semicolon to separate the values.

cfrethrow

```
<cfrethrow>
```

Description

Rethrows the currently active exception and preserves the exception's `cfcatch.type` and `cfcatch.tagContext` variable values. This tag has no attributes.

cfreturn

```
<cfreturn expr>
```

Description

Used with CFCOMPONENTS, this tag returns values from a method and contains an expression returned as result of the function.

Attributes

expr (Required)
Function result that can be the value of any type.

CFSAVECONTENT

```
<cfsavecontent variable = "variable name">
      content
</cfsavecontent>
```

Description

Saves everything in the body of the open and closing CFSAVECONTENT tags, including the results of evaluating expressions and executing custom tags.

Attributes

variable (Required)
Name of variable in which to save generated content within the tag.

cfschedule

```
<cfschedule
      action = "update/delete/run"
      task = "taskname"
      operation = "HTTPRequest"
      file = "filename"
      path = "path_to_file"
      startDate = "date"
      startTime = "time"
      url = "URL"
      publish = "Yes" or "No"
      endDate = "date"
      endTime = "time"
```

```
interval = "seconds"
requestTimeOut = "seconds"
username = "username"
password = "password"
resolveURL = "Yes" or "No"
proxyServer = "hostname"
port = "port_number"
proxyPort = "port_number">
```

Description

To help improve application performance where dynamic data is not essential, this tag provides an interface to the scheduling engine and enables pages to be run at set intervals. Information supplied by the user should include the scheduled page to execute, the time and frequency of execution, and whether to publish the task output.

Attributes

action (Required)

- **delete.** Deletes task.

- **update.** Creates task if one does not exist.

- **run.** Executes task.

task (Required)
Name of task.

operation (Required if action = "update")
Task that scheduler performs. For static page generation, the only option is "HTTPRequest".

file (Required if publish = "Yes")
Filename for the published file.

path (Required if publish = "Yes")
Path location for the published file.

startDate (Required if action = "update")
Date when the task scheduling starts.

startTime (Required if action = "update")
Time when scheduling of the task starts.

url (Required if action = "update")
URL to execute.

publish (Optional)
Default: No. If Yes, save the result to a file.

endDate (Optional)
Date when the scheduled task ends.

endTime (Optional)
Time when the scheduled task ends.

interval (Required if action = "update")
Default: One hour. Interval at which the task is scheduled. Options include seconds (minimum is 60), once, daily, weekly, and monthly.

requestTimeOut (Optional)
Customizes requestTimeOut for the task operation.

username (Optional)
Username if the URL is protected.

password (Optional)
Password that corresponds to the username.

proxyServer (Optional)
Host name or IP address of a proxy server.

resolveURL (Optional)
Default: No. If Yes, resolves links in result page to absolute references.

port (Optional)
Default: 80. Server port number from which the task is scheduled. If resolveURL= "yes", retrieved document URLs that specify a port number are automatically resolved to preserve links in the retrieved document.

proxyPort (Optional)
Default: 80. Port number on proxy server from which task is requested.

cfscript

```
<cfscript>
        cfscript code goes here
</cfscript>
```

Description

Use this tag to use ColdFusion's scripting language that is somewhat like JavaScript. In some cases, creating certain functions inside of a CFScript block can increase performance. This tag has no attributes.

cfsearch

```
<cfsearch name = "search_name"
        collection = "collection_name"
        type = "criteria"
        criteria = "search_expression"
        maxRows = "number"
        startRow = "row_number"
        language = "language">
```

Description

For use with the Verity search engine, this tag does a search against data that is indexed in a Verity collection. A collection must exist and be indexed before this tag can return search results.

Attributes

name (Required)
Name of the search query. For a registered collection, specify the collection name. For an unregistered collection, specify an absolute path.

collection (Required)
Path(s) and/or registered collection name(s). Registered names are listed in ColdFusion Administrator, Verity Collections, and Verity Server pages.

type (Optional)
Default: simple

- **simple.** STEM and MANY operators are used.

- **explicit.** Operators must be invoked explicitly.

criteria (Optional)
The search criteria, which follows the syntax rules of the type attribute. If you pass a mixed-case entry in this attribute, the search is case-sensitive. If you pass all uppercase or all lowercase, the search is non-case-sensitive.

maxRows (Optional)
Default: all. The maximum number of rows to return in the query results.

startRow (Optional)
Default: 1. First row number to get.

language (Optional)
Default: english. Languages other than English require the ColdFusion International Search Pack.

CFSELECT

```
<cfselect name = "name"
        required = "Yes" or "No"
        message = "text"
        onError = "text"
        size = "integer"
        multiple = "Yes" or "No"
        query = "queryname"
        selected = "column_value"
        value = "text"
        display = "text"
        passThrough = "HTML_attributes">
</cfselect>
```

Description

In a CFFORM, this tag creates a drop-down list. You can populate the list from a query or by using the HTML option tag. If you use a query to populate the list you can have the data persist by using the preserveData attribute.

Attributes

name (Required)
Name of the form.

size (Optional)
Number of entries in the drop-down list.

required (Optional)
Default: No. If Yes, a list element must be selected before the form is submitted.

message (Optional)
Message to display if required = "Yes" and no selection is made.

onError (Optional)
Custom JavaScript function to execute if validation fails

multiple (Optional)
Default: No. If Yes, enables the selection of multiple elements in the drop-down list

query (Optional)
Name of a query to use to populate data in the drop-down list.

selected (Optional)
The value that is selected in drop-down list when it is created. This attribute can be used only with a query.

value (Optional)
Used with the query attribute, this gives a column name for the values list.

display (Optional)
Value of the value attribute.

passThrough (Optional)
HTML attribute(s) that are not explicitly supported by CFSELECT. If you specify an attribute and its value, they are passed to HTML code that is generated for CFSELECT tag.

CFSERVLET

Description

This tag is deprecated. Do not use it in new applications.

CFSERVLETPARAM

Description

This tag is deprecated. Do not use it in new applications.

CFSET

```
<cfset variable_name = expression>
```

Description

Defines a ColdFusion variable. If the variable exists, this tag sets it to the specified value.

Attributes

> `variable_name` (Required)
> A name for the variable.

CFSETTING

```
<cfsetting enableCFoutputOnly = "Yes" or "No"
        showDebugOutput = "Yes" or "No"
        requestTimeOut = "seconds">
```

Description

> Used to control how ColdFusion processes a page and can override certain settings, such as debugging, that are set in the ColdFusion Administrator.

Attributes

> `EnableCFoutputOnly` (Required)
> `Yes`: Blocks output of HTML that is outside `CFOUTPUT` tags.
>
> `showDebugOutput` (Optional)
> Default: `Yes`. If `No`, suppresses debugging information that would otherwise display at end the page.
>
> `RequestTimeout` (Optional)
> A set amount of time that ColdFusion uses to stop processing a page. Enabling this setting overrides the time set in the ColdFusion Administrator.

CFSILENT

```
<cfsilent>
     ...
</cfsilent>
```

Description:

> Used to suppress the output of any code that is put in between the opening and closing tags. This tag has no attributes.

CFSLIDER

```
<cfslider name = "name"
        label = "text"
        refreshLabel = "Yes" or "No"
        range = "min_value, max_value"
        scale = "uinteger"
        value = "integer"
        onValidate = "script_name"
        message = "text"
        onError = "text"
        height = "integer"
        width = "integer"
        vSpace = "integer"
        hSpace = "integer"
        align = "alignment"
        tickMarkMajor = "Yes" or "No"
        tickMarkMinor = "Yes" or "No"
        tickMarkImages = "URL1, URL2, URLn"
        tickMarkLabels = "Yes" or "No" or or "list"
        lookAndFeel = "motif" or "windows" or "metal"
        vertical = "Yes" or "No"
        bgColor = "color"
        textColor = "color"
        font = "font_name"
        fontSize = "integer"
        italic = "Yes" or "No"
        bold = "Yes" or "No"
        notSupported = "text">
```

Description

Used inside a CFFORM, this creates a slider for selecting a numeric value from a range.

Attributes

name (Required)
Name of the CFSLIDER.

label (Optional)
Label to display with the slider.

refreshLabel (Optional)
Default: yes, which refreshes label when the slider is moved.

range (Optional)
The numeric slider range values. Separate values with a comma.

`scale` (Optional)
Defines the scale of the slider scale for the range of values.

`value` (Optional)
The starting value for the slider setting. This must be set within the slider range.

`onValidate` (Optional)
Enables a custom JavaScript function to be called in order to validate input.

`message` (Optional)
Text to display if the validation fails.

`onError` (Optional)
The custom JavaScript function to call if the validation fails.

`height` (Optional)
Slider control height.

`width` (Optional)
Slider control width.

`vSpace` (Optional)
Vertical spacing above and below the slider.

`hSpace` (Optional)
Horizontal spacing to left and right of the slider.

`align` (Optional)
Alignment of the slider: Options include `top`, `left`, `bottom`, `baseline`, `texttop`, `absbottom`, `middle`, `absmiddle`, and `right`.

`tickMarkMajor` (Optional)
Default: `No`

- **Yes.** Renders major tickmarks in the slider scale.

- **No.** No major tickmarks.

`tickMarkMinor` (Optional)
Default: `No`

- **Yes.** Renders minor tickmarks in the slider scale.

- **No.** No minor tickmarks.

`tickMarkImages` (Optional)

Creates images for tick marks if the `tickmark` attribute is set to `Yes`. This is a comma-delimited list of URLs for the images. If there are not enough images, the last image will be repeated for the remaining tickmarks.

`tickMarkLabels` (Optional)
Default: `No`

- **Yes.** Numeric tickmarks based on the value of the `range` and `scale` attributes.
- **No.** Prevents label text from displaying.

`lookAndFeel` (Optional)
Default: `windows`

- **motif.** Renders slider using Motif style.
- **windows.** Renders slider using Windows style.
- **metal.** Renders slider using Java Swing style.

`vertical` (Optional)
Default: `No`

- **Yes.** Renders the slider vertically.
- **No.** Renders the slider horizontally.

`bgColor` (Optional)

Background color of the slider label. Can be a hex value or web color.

`textColor` (Optional)

Color for the text. Can be a hex value or web color.

`font` (Optional)

Font name for label text.

`fontSize` (Optional)

Font size for label text.

`italic` (Optional)
Default: `No`

- **Yes.** Label text in italics.
- **No.** Normal text.

bold (Optional)
Default: No

- **Yes.** Label text in bold.

- **No.** Medium text.

notSupported (Optional)
Text to display if a page that contains a Java applet-based CFFORM control is opened by a browser that does not support Java or has Java support disabled.

CFSTOREDPROC

```
<cfstoredproc procedure = "procedure name"
        dataSource = "ds_name"
        username = "username"
        password = "password"
        blockFactor = "blocksize"
        debug = "Yes" or "No"
        returnCode = "Yes" or "No">
```

Description

Executes stored procedures by an open database connectivity (ODBC) or native connection to a server database. It specifies database connection information and identifies the stored procedure.

Attributes

procedure (Required)
Name of stored procedure on database server.

dataSource (Required)
Name of ODBC or native datasource that points to database that contains stored procedure.

username (Optional)
Overrides username in datasource setup.

password (Optional)
Overrides password in datasource setup.

blockFactor (Optional)
Default: 1. Maximum number of rows to get at a time from server. Range is 1 to 100. ODBC driver may dynamically reduce block factor at run-time.

debug (Optional)
Default: No. If Yes, lists debug information on each statement.

returnCode (Optional)
Default: No. If Yes, the tag populates cfstoredproc.statusCode with the status code returned by the stored procedure.

cfswitch

```
<cfswitch expression = "expression">
        <cfcase value = "value" delimiters = "delimiters">
          HTML and CFML tags
        </cfcase>
        additional <cfcase></cfcase> tags
        <cfdefaultcase>
          HTML and CFML tags
        </cfdefaultcase>
</cfswitch>
```

Description

Often used with programming methodologies, this tag enables evaluation of an expression and then passes control to the CFCASE tag that matches the expression result. This can also encapsulate a default case, which would execute if the expression does not match.

Attributes

expression (Required)
ColdFusion expression that yields a scalar value. ColdFusion converts integers, real numbers, Booleans, and dates to numeric values. For example, True, 1, and 1.0 are all equal.

value (Required)
One or more constant values that CFSWITCH compares to the expression (non-case-sensitive). If a value matches expression, CFSWITCH executes the code between CFCASE start and end tags. Duplicate value attributes cause a runtime error.

delimiters (Optional)
Default: , (comma). Character that separates entries in a list of values.

cftable

```
<cftable query = "query_name"
        maxRows = "maxrows_table"
        colSpacing = "number_of_spaces"
        headerLines = "number_of_lines"
        HTMLTable
        border
        colHeaders
        startRow = "row_number">
        ...
</cftable>
```

Description

Use this tag to build an HTML table from data from a ColdFusion query. It
or it can also be used to output the table as preformatted text. Preformatted
text (defined in HTML with the <PRE> and </PRE> tags) displays text in a
fixed-width font. It displays whitespace and line breaks exactly as they are
written within the PRE tags.

Attributes

query (Required)
Name of CFQUERY from which to draw data.

maxRows (Optional)
Maximum number of rows to display in the table.

colSpacing (Optional)
Default: 2. Number of spaces between columns

headerLines (Optional)
Default: 2. Number of lines to use for the table header.

HTMLTable (Optional)
Renders data in an HTML 3.0 table.

border (Optional)
Used in conjunction with htmlTable attribute, this adds a border
around the table.

colHeaders (Optional)

Displays column heads. If you use this attribute, you must also use the CFCOL tag header attribute to define them.

startRow (Optional)

Default: 1. The query result row to put in the first table row.

cftextinput

```
<cftextinput
        name = "name"
        value = "text"
        required = "Yes" or "No"
        range = "min_value, max_value"
        validate = "data_type"
        onValidate = "script_name"
        message = "text"
        onError = "text"
        size = "integer"
        font = "font_name"
        fontSize = "integer"
        italic = "Yes" or "No"
        bold = "Yes" or "No"
        height = "integer"
        width = "integer"
        vSpace = "integer"
        hSpace = "integer"
        align = "alignment"
        bgColor = "color"
        textColor = "color"
        maxLength = "integer"
        notSupported = "text">
```

Description

Used with CFFORM, this creates a text input box with added ColdFusion functionality, such as validation.

Attributes

name (Required)
Name for CFTEXTINPUT.

value (Optional)
Initial value to display in the text box.

`required` (Optional)
Default: `No`. If `Yes`, the user must enter or change text.

`range` (Optional)
Minimum to maximum value range, delimited by a comma. Valid only for numeric data.

`validate` (Optional)
Validates to preset criteria embedded into `CFTEXTINPUT`. Options include `date`, `integer`, `telephone`, `time`, and `zipcode`.

`onValidate` (Optional)
Call a custom JavaScript function to validate input.

`pattern` (Required if `validate` = `"regular_expression"`)
JavaScript regular expression pattern to validate input.

`message` (Optional)
Message text to display if validation fails.

`onError` (Optional)
Custom JavaScript function to execute if validation fails.

`size` (Optional)
Controls the display size of the input box.

`font` (Optional)
Font name for text.

`fontSize` (Optional)
Font size for text.

`italic` (Optional)
Default: `No`. Puts text in italics.

`bold` (Optional)
Default: `No`. Puts text in bold.

`height` (Optional)
Default: `40`. Height of the text box.

`width` (Optional)
Width of the text box.

`vSpace` (Optional)
Vertical spacing of the text box.

`hSpace` (Optional)
Horizontal spacing of the text box.

align (Optional)
Alignment of text box: Left, Right, Bottom, Top, TextTop, Middle, AbsMiddle, Baseline, and AbsBottom.

bgColor (Optional)
Background color of the text box.

textColor (Optional)
Text color for the text box.

maxLength (Optional)
The maximum length of text entered.

notSupported (Optional)
Text to display if a page that contains a Java applet-based CFFORM control is opened by a browser that does not support Java or has that Java support disabled.

cfthrow

```
<cfthrow
        type = "exception_type "
        message = "message"
        detail = "detail_description "
        errorCode = "error_code "
        extendedInfo = "additional_information ">
Syntax   2

<cfthrow object = #object_name#>
```

Description

Use this tag for error handling; when an exception is thrown, it can be caught and handled using the CFCATCH tag.

Attributes

type (Optional)
Default: application, a custom type. Do not enter another predefined type; types are not generated by ColdFusion applications. If you specify application, you need not specify a type for CFCATCH.

message (Optional)
Message that describes exception event.

detail (Optional)
Description of the event.

errorCode (Optional)
A custom error code that you supply.

extendedInfo (Optional)
A custom error code that you supply.

object (Optional)
Requires the value of the CFOBJECT tag name attribute. Throws a Java exception from a CFML tag. This attribute is mutually exclusive with all other attributes of this tag.

cftrace

```
<cftrace
        abort = "Yes or No"
        category = "string"
        inline = "Yes or No"
        text = "string"
        type = "format"
        var = "variable_name"
</cftrace>
```

Description

Displays and logs debugging data about the state of an application at the time the CFTRACE tag executes. Tracks runtime logic flow, variable values, and execution time. Displays output on the application page or, in Dreamweaver 5 and later, in a Studio window. ColdFusion logs CFTRACE output to the file logs\cftrace.log in the ColdFusion installation directory.

Attributes

abort (Optional)
Default: No. If Yes, calls CFABORT tag when the tag is executed.

category (Optional)
User-defined string for identifying trace groups.

inline (Optional)
Default: No. If Yes, flushes output to page as the tag executes. Within a CFSILENT tag, this option suppresses message display, but trace summary information is included in the debug output.

text (Optional)

User-defined string or simple variable. Outputs to `CFLOG` text attribute.

type (Optional)

Information output format. Outputs to `CFLOG` type attribute. Includes `Information`, `Warning`, `Error`, and `Fatal Information`.

var (Optional)

The name of one simple or complex variable to display. A complex variable, such as a structure, is displayed in `CFDUMP` format. Useful for displaying a temporary value or a value that does not display on any CFML page.

cftransaction

```
<cftransaction
       action = "begin/commit/rollback"
       isolation = "read_uncommitted/read_committed/repeatable_read" >
queries to execute

</cftransaction>
```

Description

Use this tag when data integrity is essential to the proper execution of your code. This enables the commit and rollback on your database if the transaction is not processed successfully.

Attributes

action (Optional)
Default: begin

- **begin.** The start of the block of code to execute.
- **commit.** Commits a pending transaction.
- **rollback.** Rolls back a pending transaction.

isolation (Optional)
ODBC lock type. Types include `read_uncommitted`, `read_committed`, `repeatable_read`, and `serializable`.

cftree

```
<cftree name = "name"
        required = "Yes" or "No"
        delimiter = "delimiter"
        completePath = "Yes" or "No"
        appendKey = "Yes" or "No"
        highlightHref = "Yes" or "No"
        onValidate = "script_name"
        message = "text"
        onError = "text"
        lookAndFeel = "motif" or "windows" or "metal"
        font = "font"
        fontSize = "size"
        italic = "Yes" or "No"
        bold = "Yes" or "No"
        height = "integer"
        width = "integer"
        vSpace = "integer"
        hSpace = "integer"
        align = "alignment"
        border = "Yes" or "No"
        hScroll = "Yes" or "No"
        vScroll = "Yes" or "No"
        notSupported = "text">

</cftree>
```

Description

Use with the CFFORM tag this tag creates a tree control in a form. A query may be used to supply data, and user input can also be validated.

Attributes

name (Required)
Name for the tree.

required (Optional)
Default: No. If Yes, user must select an item in the tree.

delimiter (Optional)
Default: \\ (double slash). Character to separate elements in the form variable path.

`completePath` (Optional)
Default: No

- Yes: Passes the root part of `treename.path` form variable when CFTREE is submitted.

- No, or omitted: Root level of form variable is not passed and the path value starts with the first node.

`appendKey` (Optional)
Default: Yes, when used with HREF, passes ColdFusion TREEITEMKEY variable with the value of the selected tree item in the URL to the application page specified in the CFFORM action attribute.

`highlightHref` (Optional)
Default: Yes

- **Yes.** Highlights links that are associated with a CFTREE item with a URL value.

- **No.** Disables highlight.

`onValidate` (Optional)
Calls a custom JavaScript function to validate input.

`message` (Optional)
Message to display if validation fails.

`onError` (Optional)
JavaScript function to execute if validation fails.

`lookAndFeel` (Optional)
Default: windows

- **motif.** Renders slider in Motif style.

- **windows.** Renders slider in Windows style.

- **metal.** Renders slider in Java Swing style.

`font` (Optional)
Font name for data in the tree.

`fontSize` (Optional)
Font size for text in the tree.

`italic` (Optional)
Default: No. If Yes, displays the tree text in italics.

bold (Optional)
Default: No. If Yes, displays the tree text in bold.

height (Optional)
Default: 320. Tree height.

width (Optional)
Default: 200. Tree width.

vSpace (Optional)
Vertical margin above and below the tree.

hSpace (Optional)
Horizontal spacing to left and right of the tree.

align (Optional)
Tree alignment. Options are Left, Right, Bottom, Top, TextTop, Middle, AbsMiddle, Baseline, and AbsBottom.

border (Optional)
Default: Yes, which adds a border around the tree.

hScroll (Optional)
Default: Yes, which permits horizontal scrolling.

vScroll (Optional)
Default: Yes, which permits vertical scrolling.

notSupported (Optional)
Message to display if page that contains Java applet-based form control is opened by browser that does not support Java or that has Java support disabled.

cftreeitem

```
<cftreeitem
        value = "text"
        display = "text"
        parent = "parent_name"
        img = "filename"
        imgopen = "filename"
        href = "URL"
        target = "URL_target"
        query = "queryname"
        queryAsRoot = "Yes" or "No"
        expand = "Yes" or "No">
```

Description

Adds data into a CFFORM tree created with the CFTREE tag. To display icons, you can use the image values that ColdFusion provides or reference your own icons.

Attributes

value (Required)
Value passed when CFFORM is submitted. Use a comma-delimited list for multiple values when using a query.

display (Optional)
Tree item label. Use a comma-delimited list for multiple values when using a query.

parent (Optional)
Value for tree item parent.

img (Optional)
Use this attribute to create icons on the tree. If you are using custom icons, specify the path and file extension.

imgopen (Optional)
Icon displayed with open tree item. You can specify icon filename with a relative path or use a ColdFusion predefined image.

href (Optional)
If the tree is populated with a query, this associates a URL tree item.

target (Optional)
Target attribute of HREF URL. When populating a tree with data from a query, specify target in delimited list: target = "FRAME_BODY,_blank".

query (Optional)
Query name to generate data for the tree item.

queryAsRoot (Optional)
Defines query as the root level. This avoids having to create another parent tree item.

expand (Optional)
Default: Yes

- **Yes.** Expands tree to show tree item children.
- **No.** Keeps tree item collapsed.

cftry

```
<cftry>
        Add code here
<cfcatch type = "exceptiontype">
        Exception processing code here
</cfcatch>
Optional: More cfcatch blocks here
</cftry>
```

Description

Used for error handling in conjunction with the CFCATCH tag. When used with each other, this tag set catches exceptions that cause errors that stop the execution of a ColdFusion page. Exceptions can be user-defined events or normal errors, such as missing include files or undefined variables.

Attributes

type (Optional)
Default: any

- **application.** Catches application exceptions.

- **database.** Catches database exceptions.

- **template.** Catches ColdFusion page exceptions.

- **security.** Catches security exceptions.

- **object.** Catches object exceptions.

- **missinginclude.** Catches missing include-file exceptions.

- **expression.** Catches expression exceptions.

- **lock.** Catches lock exceptions.

- **custom_type.** Catches developer-defined exceptions, defined in the CFTHROW tag.

- **searchengine.** Catches Verity search engine exceptions.

- **any.** Catches all exception types.

cfupdate

```
<cfupdate dataSource = "ds_name"
        tableName = "table_name"
        tableOwner = "name"
        tableQualifier = "qualifier"
```

```
username = "username"
password = "password"
formFields = "field_names">
```

Description

Used to update a recordset in a database from a form. This tag eliminates the need for writing a SQL update statement. The table that is updated must have a key and the key must be passed with the form.

Attributes

dataSource (Required)
Name of the datasource that contains the table to be updated.

tableName (Required)
Name of the table to update.

tableOwner (Optional)
For datasources that support table ownership (for example, SQL Server, Oracle, Sybase SQL Anywhere), the table owner.

tableQualifier (Optional)
For datasources that support table qualifiers. Note the following about table qualifiers:

- **SQL Server and Oracle.** Name of database that contains table.
- **Intersolv dBASE driver.** Directory of DBF files.

username (Optional)
Overrides the username the datasource settings.

password (Optional)
Overrides password value specified in the datasource settings.

formFields (Optional)
Comma-delimited list of form fields to update. If a form field is not matched by a column name in the database, ColdFusion throws an error. The database table key field must be present in the form.

cfwddx

```
<cfwddx action = "action"
        input = "inputdata"
        output = "resultvariablename"
        topLevelVariable = "toplevelvariablenameforjavascript"
        useTimeZoneInfo = "Yes" or "No"
        validate = "Yes" or "No" >
```

Description

Creates or decodes a WDDX packet that is a generic way of passing data from different applications or servers. WDDX is an eXtensible Markup Language (XML) schema that is native to ColdFusion and describes complex data structures in a way that is usable by ColdFusion. Using WDDX limits the scope of the XML that is usable by applications other than ColdFusion; if you want to use generic XML, refer to the CFXML tag.

Attributes

action (Required)

- **cfml2wddx.** Serialize ColdFusionML to WDDX.
- **wddx2cfml.** Deserialize WDDX to ColdFusionML.
- **cfml2js.** Serialize CFML to JavaScript.
- **wddx2js.** Deserialize WDDX to JavaScript.

input (Required)
A value to process.

output (Required if action = "wddx2cfml")
Name of variable for output. If action = "WDDX2JS" or "ColdFusionML2JS", and this attribute is omitted, result is output in HTML stream.

TopLevelVariable (Required if action = "wddx2js/cfml2js")
Name of top-level JavaScript object created by deserialization. The object is an instance of the WddxRecordset object.

useTimeZoneInfo (Optional)
Default: Yes. Whether to output time-zone information when serializing CFML to WDDX.

- **Yes.** The hour-minute offset, represented in ISO8601 format.
- **No.** The local time is output.

validate (Optional)
Default: No. Applies if action = "wddx2cfml/wddx2js".

- **Yes.** Validates WDDX input with an XML parser using WDDX DTD. If parser processes input without error, the packet is deserialized; otherwise, an error is thrown.

- **No.** No input validation.

cfxml

```
<cfxml
      variable="xmlVarName"
      caseSensitive="yes" or "no">
```

Description

Creates a ColdFusion XML document object that contains the markup in the tag body. This tag can include XML and CFML tags. ColdFusion processes the CFML code in the tag body and then assigns the resulting text to an XML document object variable.

Attributes

variable
Name of an XML variable

caseSensitive (Optional)
Default: No. If Yes, maintains the case of document elements and attributes.

B

Function Reference

THIS APPENDIX PROVIDES AN ALPHABETIC LISTING of ColdFusion (CF) functions. This reference list explains what each function does and then provides an example of how to use the function.

In some cases, the examples use preexisting files. In these cases, you will have to try to use the function on a file you have on your server. In most of these cases, any generic file of the proper type will be acceptable.

Abs

Abs (*number*)

Description

Use this function to get the absolute value of a number or a number without its sign.

Example

```
The absolute value of -6 is <cfoutput>#Abs(-6)#</cfoutput>
```

ACos

ACos (*number*)

Description

The arccosine is the angle whose cosine is a number in radians. The value must be between −1.0 and 1.0.

Example

```
The arccosine of 0.5 is <cfoutput>#Acos(.05)#</cfoutput>
```

ArrayAppend

ArrayAppend (*array*, *value*)

Description

Appends an array element to the end of an array.

Example

```
<cfset zipcode = ArrayNew(1)>
<cfset zipcode[1] = 80202>
<cfset zipcode[2] = 80203>
<cfset zipcode[3] = 80204>
```

To append **80205** to an array, use the following:

```
<cfset ArrayAppend(zipcode, "80205")>
```

ArrayAvg

ArrayAvg (*array*)

Description

Calculates the average of the values in an array.

Example

```
<cfset zipcode = ArrayNew(1)>
<cfset zipcode[1] = 80202>
<cfset zipcode[2] = 80203>
<cfset zipcode[3] = 80204>
```

```
<cfoutput>
     #ArrayAvg(zipcode)#
</cfoutput>
```

ArrayClear

ArrayClear (*array*)

Description

Deletes the data in an array.

Example

```
<cfset zipcode = ArrayNew(1)>
<cfset zipcode[1] = 80202>
<cfset zipcode[2] = 80203>
<cfset zipcode[3] = 80204>

<cfset ArrayClear(zipcode)>

<cfoutput>
#ArrayIsEmpty(zipcode)#
</cfoutput>
```

ArrayDeleteAt

ArrayDeleteAt (*array, position*)

Description

Deletes an element from an array at a specific index position. ColdFusion then automatically recalculates the array index positions. Therefore, index position 4 becomes position 3 after position 3 gets deleted. This returns a value of True.

Example

```
<cfset zipcode = ArrayNew(1)>
<cfset zipcode[1] = 80202>
<cfset zipcode[2] = 80203>
<cfset zipcode[3] = 80204>

<cfset ArrayDeleteAt(zipcode, 2)>

<cfoutput>
Array index position 2 is now: #zipcode[2]#
</cfoutput>
```

ArrayInsertAt

```
ArrayInsertAt (array, position, value)
```

Description

Inserts a value into an array at a specified position and returns true if successful. Array elements whose indexes are greater than the new position are incremented by one. The array length increases by one.

Example

```
<cfset zipcode = ArrayNew(1)>
<cfset zipcode[1] = 80202>
<cfset zipcode[2] = 80203>
<cfset zipcode[3] = 80205>

<cfset ArrayInsertAt (zipcode, 3, 80204)>

<cfoutput>
Array index position 3 is now: #zipcode[3]#
</cfoutput>
```

ArrayIsEmpty

```
ArrayIsEmpty (array)
```

Description

Determines whether an array is empty of data elements and returns true if empty; otherwise, it returns false.

Example

```
<cfset zipcode = ArrayNew(1)>
<cfset zipcode[1] = 80202>
<cfset zipcode[2] = 80203>
<cfset zipcode[3] = 80205>

<cfoutput>
Is the Array empty? #ArrayIsEmpty(zipcode)#
</cfoutput>
```

ArrayLen

```
ArrayLen (array)
```

Description

Determines the number of elements in an array.

Example

```
<cfset zipcode = ArrayNew(1)>
<cfset zipcode[1] = 80202>
<cfset zipcode[2] = 80203>
<cfset zipcode[3] = 80204>

To find this array's length:
<cfoutput>#ArrayLen(zipcode)#<cfoutput>
```

ArrayMax

```
ArrayMax (array)
```

Description

Gives the largest value in an array. Only use this with numeric values.

Example

```
<cfset zipcode = ArrayNew(1)>
<cfset zipcode[1] = 80202>
<cfset zipcode[2] = 80203>
<cfset zipcode[3] = 80204>

To find the largest numeric value of an array:
<cfoutput>#ArrayMax(zipcode)#<cfoutput>
```

ArrayMin

```
ArrayMin (array)
```

Description

Gives the smallest numeric value in an array. Returns 0 if the array is empty.

Example

```
<cfset zipcode = ArrayNew(1)>
<cfset zipcode[1] = 80202>
<cfset zipcode[2] = 80203>
<cfset zipcode[3] = 80204>
```

To find the smallest numeric value of an array:
```
<cfoutput>#ArrayMin(zipcode)#<cfoutput>
```

ArrayNew

```
ArrayNew (dimension)
```

Description

Creates an array of one to three dimensions. Array elements are indexed with square brackets: [ ]. Arrays expand dynamically as data is added.

Example

```
<cfset zipcode = ArrayNew(1)>
<cfset zipcode[1] = 80202>
<cfset zipcode[2] = 80203>
<cfset zipcode[3] = 80204>
```

ArrayPrepend

```
ArrayPrepend (array, value)
```

Description

Inserts an array element at the beginning of an array.

Example

```
<cfset zipcode = ArrayNew(1)>
<cfset zipcode[1] = 80202>
<cfset zipcode[2] = 80203>
<cfset zipcode[3] = 80204>

<cfoutput>
#ArrayPrepend(zipcode, "80201")#
</cfoutput>
```

ArrayResize

```
ArrayResize (array, minimum_size)
```

Description

Resets an array to a specified minimum number of elements. `ArrayResize` can improve performance if used to size an array to its expected maximum. If you expect to have more than 500 elements, use `ArrayResize` immediately after using the `ArrayNew` tag.

Example

```
<cfset zipcode = ArrayNew(1)>
<cfset ArrayResize(zipcode, 100)>
```

ArraySet

```
ArraySet (array, start_pos, end_pos, value)
```

Description

In a one-dimensional array, this sets the elements in a specified index range to a value. It is useful for initializing an array after a call to `ArrayNew`. This will create a temporary value in that position until it is overwritten.

Example

```
<cfset zipcode = ArrayNew(1)>
<cfset exampleArray = ArraySet(zipcode, 1, 10, "tempValue")>
```

ArraySort

```
ArraySort (array, sort_type [, sort_order ])
```

Description

Sorts array elements numerically or alphanumerically.

Example

```
<cfset zipcode = ArrayNew(1)>
<cfset zipcode[1] = 80203>
<cfset zipcode[2] = 80202>
<cfset zipcode[3] = 80204>

<cfset tempArray = ArraySort(zipcose, "Numeric", "Desc")>
```

ArraySum

```
ArraySum (array)
```

Description

Returns the sum of the values in an array.

Example

```
<cfset zipcode = ArrayNew(1)>
<cfset zipcode[1] = 80203>
<cfset zipcode[2] = 80202>
<cfset zipcode[3] = 80204>
<cfoutput>
The sum of the zipcode array equals #ArraySum(zipcode)#.
</cfoutput>
```

ArraySwap

```
ArraySwap (array, position1, position2)
```

Description

Swaps the values of an array at the given positions. It is faster to use this tag than multiple `cfset` tags.

Example

```
<cfset zipcode = ArrayNew(1)>
<cfset zipcode[1] = 80203>
<cfset zipcode[2] = 80202>
<cfset zipcode[3] = 80204>

<cfset ArraySwap(zipcode, 1, 3)>
```

Array To List

```
ArrayToList (array  [,delimiter])
```

Description

Converts a one-dimensional array to a list. The default delimiter is a comma, although you can set whatever you want as a delimiter.

Example

```
<cfset zipcode = ArrayNew(1)>
<cfset zipcode[1] = 80203>
<cfset zipcode[2] = 80202>
<cfset zipcode[3] = 80204>

<cfset zipcodeList = ArrayToList(zipcode)>
```

Asc

```
Asc (string)
```

Description

Determines the value of the first character in a string.

Example

```
<cfset exampleVariable = "This is an ASCII value">

<cfoutput>
The ASCII value of exampleVariable is #Asc(exampleVariable)#
</cfoutput>
```

ASin

```
ASin (number)
```

Description

Determines the arcsine of a number. The arcsine is the angle whose sine is a number in radians.

Example

```
<cfoutput>
The arcsine of 0.5 is #Asin(0.5)#
</cfoutput>
```

Atn

Atn (*number*)

Description

Shows the arctangent of a number in radians.

Example

```
<cfoutput>
The aarctangent of 0.5 is #Atn(0.5)#
</cfoutput>
```

BitAnd

BitAnd (*number1* , *number2*)

Description

Performs a bitwise logical AND operation.

Example

```
<cfoutput>
The Bitand of  10 and 1 is: #BitAnd(10,1)#
The Bitand of  125 and 125 is: #BitAnd(125,125)#
</cfoutput>
```

BitMaskClear

BitMaskClear (*number, start, length*)

Description

Performs a bitwise mask clear operation.

Example

```
<cfoutput>
The bit mask of 255 is #BitMaskClear(255, 4, 4)#
</cfoutput>
```

BitMaskRead

BitMaskRead (*number*, *start*, *length*)

Description

Performs a bitwise mask read operation.

Example

```
<cfoutput>
The bit mask of 255 is: #BitMaskRead(255, 4, 4)#
</cfoutput>
```

BitMaskSet

BitMaskSet (*number* , *mask* , *start* , *length*)

Description

Performs a bitwise mask set operation.

Example

```
<cfoutput>
To set a bit mask for 255 use: #BitMaskSet(255, 255, 4, 4)#
</cfoutput>
```

BitNot

BitNot (*number*)

Description

Performs a bitwise logical NOT operation.

Example

```
<cfoutput>
The logical not of 255 is: # BitNot(255) #
</cfoutput>
```

BitOr

```
BitOr (number1 ,   number2)
```

Description

Performs a bitwise logical OR operation.

Example

```
<cfoutput>
The logical or of 5 and 255 is: #BitOr(5,255)#
</cfoutput>
```

BitSHLN

```
BitSHLN (number, count)
```

Description

Performs a bitwise shift left. There is no rotation when the bitwise is shifted to the left.

Example

```
<cfoutput>
The BitSHLN of  10 and 1 is: # BitSHLN(10,1)#
The BitSHLN of  125 and 125 is: # BitSHLN(125,125)#
</cfoutput>
```

BitSHRN

```
BitSHRN (number, count)
```

Description

Performs a bitwise shift right. There is no rotation when the bitwise is shifted to the right.

Example

```
<cfoutput>
The BitSHRN of  10 and 1 is: # BitSHRN (10,1)#
The BitSHRN of  125 and 125 is: # BitSHRN (125,125)#
</cfoutput>
```

BitXor

```
BitXor (number1, number2)
```

Description

Performs a bitwise logical XOR operation.

Example

```
<cfoutput>
The BitXOr of  10 and 1 is: #BitXOr(10,1)#
The BitXOr of  125 and 125 is: #BitXOr(125,125)#
</cfoutput>
```

Ceiling

```
Ceiling (number)
```

Description

Determines the closest integer that is greater than a specified number.

Example

```
<cfoutput>
The ceiling of 5 is #ceiling(5)#
The ceiling of 5.4 is #ceiling(5.4)#
</cfoutput>
```

Chr

```
Chr (number)
```

Description

Shows the character represented by an ASCII code. Supports values up to 65536 in the Unicode character set, although 0 to 31 are nonprintable characters.

Example

```
<cfoutput>
 The character represented by 101 is: #Chr(101)#
</cfoutput>
```

Cjustify

Cjustify (*string*, *length*)

Description

Centers a string in a field length. If the length is less than the string, it is returned unchanged.

Example

To set a form string dynamically, you could use something like the following:

```
<cfset examplestring = Cjustify("#FORM.textinput#", 35)>
```

Compare

Compare (*string1* , *string2*)

Description

Performs a case-sensitive comparison of two strings. Returns the following:

- -1, if *string1* is less than *string2*
- 0, if *string1* is equal to *string2*
- 1, if *string1* is greater than *string2*

Example

```
<cfoutput>
 Compare dogs and Dogs: #compare('dogs', 'Dogs')#
 Compare bunnies and bunnies: #compare('bunnies', 'bunnies')#
 Compare dogs and bunnies: #compare('dogs', 'bunnies')#
</cfoutput>
```

CompareNoCase

CompareNoCase (*string1*, *string2*)

Description

Performs a non–case-sensitive comparison of two strings. Returns the following:

- A negative number, if *string1* is less than *string2*
- 0, if *string1* is equal to *string2*
- A positive number, if *string1* is greater than *string2*

Example

```
<cfoutput>
 Compare dogs and Dogs: # CompareNoCase ('dogs', 'Dogs')#
 Compare bunnies and bunnies: # CompareNoCase ('bunnies', 'bunnies')#
 Compare dogs and bunnies: # CompareNoCase ('dogs', 'bunnies')#
</cfoutput>
```

Cos

Cos (*number*)

Description

Shows the cosine of an angle in radians.

Example

```
<cfoutput>
The cosine of 0.5 is: #cos(0.5)#
</cfoutput>
```

CreateDate

CreateDate (*year*, *month*, *day*)

Description

Creates a date/time object.

Example

```
<cfoutput>
 The following code makes a date/time stamp: #CreateDate(1975, 07, 04)#
</cfoutput>
```

CreateDateTime

CreateDateTime (*year*, *month*, *day*, *hour*, *minute*, *second*)

Description

Creates a date/time object. Requires six arguments.

Example

```
<cfoutput>
 The following code makes a date/time stamp:
#CreateDateTime(1975, 07, 04, 20, 0, 0)#
</cfoutput>
```

CreateObject

```
CreateObject("com", class, context, serverName)
CreateObject("CORBA", class, context, locale)
CreateObject("Java", class)
```

Description

Creates ColdFusion components and COM, CORBA, and Java objects. This function can be disabled in the ColdFusion Administrator.

COM Objects

The CreateObject function creates and manipulates component object model (COM) objects. You can invoke an automation server object type that is currently registered on a computer. To create a COM object, you must provide the following information: the object's program ID or filename, methods and properties available to the object through the IDispatch interface, and arguments and return types of the object's methods.

CORBA Objects

The CreateObject function calls methods on CORBA objects. The objects must be defined and registered for use.

Java Object Functions

Functions create and use Java objects and, by extension, EJB objects.

CreateODBCDate

```
CreateODBCDate (date)
```

Description

Creates an ODBC date object.

Example

```
<cfoutput>
 This is what today's date looks like in ODBC format: #CreateODBCDate(now())#
</cfoutput>
```

CreateODBCDateTime

```
CreateODBCDateTime (date)
```

Description

Creates an ODBC date/time object.

Example

```
<cfoutput>
 This is what right now's date and time looks like in ODBC format:
# CreateODBCDateTime (now())#
</cfoutput>
```

CreateODBCTime

```
CreateODBCTime (date)
```

Description

Creates a time in ODBC format.

Example

```
<cfoutput>
 This is what right now's time looks like in ODBC format:
#CreateODBCDateTime (now())#
</cfoutput>
```

CreateTime

```
CreateTime (hour, minute, second)
```

Description

Creates a time object. Requires three arguments.

Example

```
<cfoutput>
 This is what a time stamp looks like: #CreateTime (12, 30, 0)#
</cfoutput>
```

CreateTimeSpan

```
CreateTimeSpan (days, hours, minutes, seconds)
```

Description

Creates a date/time object that defines a time period. You can add or subtract it from other date/time objects and use it with the cachedWithin attribute of cfquery.

Example

```
<cfset exampleTime = now()>
<cfset timetoadd = CreateTimeSpan(0, 1, 12, 0)>

<cfoutput>
 The new time is: #TimeFormat(Evaluate(exampleTime + timetoadd), 'hh:mm')#
</cfoutput>
```

CreateUUID

```
CreateUUID ()
```

Description

Creates a universally unique identifier (UUID). A UUID is a 35-character string representation of a unique 128-bit integer.

Example

```
<cfoutput>
This is your unique ID: #CreateUUID()#
</cfoutput>
```

DateAdd

```
DateAdd ("datepart", number, "date")
```

Description

Adds units of time to a date. `datepart` can be one of the following: yyyy: year, q: quarter, m: month, y: day of year, d: day, w: weekday, ww: week, h: hour, n: minute, s: second.

Example

```
<cfset exampleDate = now()>

<cfoutput>
Add 1 day to our current date:  #DateFormat(DateAdd('d', 1, exampleDate),
'mm/dd/yyyy')#
Subtract 1 day from our current date:  #DateFormat(DateAdd('d', -1, exampleDate),
'mm/dd/yyyy')#
</cfoutput>
```

DateCompare

```
DateCompare ("date1" , "date2"  [, "datePart" ])
```

Description

Performs a full date/time comparison of two dates. Returns the following:

- −1, if *date1* is less than *date2*
- 0, if *date1* is equal to *date2*
- 1, if *date1* is greater than *date2*

Example

```
<cfset exampleDate = now()>

<cfoutput>
Compare the current date with 08/01/2002: #DateCompare(exampleDate, '08/01/2002')#
</cfoutput>
```

DateConvert

```
DateConvert ("conversion-type", "date")
```

Description

Converts local time to universal coordinated time (UTC) or vice versa. If required, it uses the daylight savings settings on the executing computer to integrate daylight savings time. Use conversion types: local2Utc (converts local time to UTC time) or utc2Loca (converts UTC time to local time).

Example

```
<cfset exampleDate = now()>
<cfset utcdate = DateConvert('local2utc', exampleDate)

<cfoutput>
The UTC date looks like this: #utcdate#
</cfoutput>
```

DateDiff

```
DateDiff (" datepart" , " date1" , " date2")
```

Description

Determines the number of units by which date1 is less than date2. datepart can be one of the following; yyyy, year; q, quarter; m, month; y, day of year; d, day; w, weekday; ww, week; h, hour; n, minute; s, second.

Example

```
<cfset exampleDate1 = dateformat(now(), 'mm/dd/yyyy')>
<cfset exampleDate2 = "12/25/2001">

<cfoutput>
How many weeks since Christmas: #DateDiff("ww", exampleDate1, exampleDate2)#
</cfoutput>
```

DateFormat

```
DateFormat ("date" [, "mask" ])
```

Description

Formats a date value. Supports dates in the U.S. date format. For international date support, use LSDateFormat. A mask is optional, and the default is dd-mmm-yy format. Use the following values for the mask:

- **d.** Day of the month as digits (no leading zero for single digits).
- **dd.** Day of the month as digits (leading zero for single digits).
- **ddd.** Day of the week as a three-letter abbreviation.
- **dddd.** Day of the week as its full name.
- **m.** Month as digits (no leading zero for single digits).
- **mm.** Month as digits (leading zero for single digits).
- **mmm.** Month as a three-letter abbreviation.
- **mmmm.** Month as its full name.
- **y.** Year as last two digits (no leading zero for years less than 10).
- **yy.** Year as last two digits (no leading zero for years less than 10).
- **yyyy.** Year represented by four digits.
- **gg.** Period/era string. Ignored, but reserved for future use.

Example

```
<cfset exampleDate = now()>

<cfoutput>
  #DateFormat(exampleDate)#
  #DateFormat(exampleDate, "mm/dd/yyyy")#
  #DateFormat(exampleDate, "mmm-dd-yyyy")#
  #DateFormat(exampleDate, "mmmm d, yyyy")#
  #DateFormat(exampleDate, "d/m/yy")#
</cfoutput>
```

DatePart

```
DatePart ("datepart", "date")
```

Description

This returns part of a date as a number. `datepart` can be one of the following; yyyy, year; q, quarter; m, month; y, day of year; d, day; w, weekday; ww, seek; h, hour; n, minute; s, second.

Example

```
<cfset exampleDate = now()>

<cfoutput>
  year: #DatePart("yyyy", exampleDate)#
  quarter: #DatePart("q", exampleDate)#
  month: #DatePart("m", exampleDate)#
  day of year: #DatePart("y", exampleDate)#
  day: #DatePart("d", exampleDate)#
  weekday: #DatePart("w", exampleDate)#
  week: #DatePart("ww", exampleDate)#
  hour: #DatePart("h", exampleDate)#
  minute: #DatePart("n", exampleDate)#
  second: #DatePart("s", exampleDate)#
</cfoutput>
```

Day

```
Day ("date")
```

Description

Determines the day of the month, in a date.

Example

```
<cfoutput>
#Day(now())#
</cfoutput>
```

DayOfWeek

```
DayOfWeek ("date")
```

Description

Determines the day of the week.

Example

```
<cfoutput>
# DayOfWeek (now())#
</cfoutput>
```

DayOfWeekAsString

```
DayOfWeekAsString (day_of_week)
```

Description

In a date, this function determines the day of the week.

Example

```
<cfoutput>
Thank god it's: # DayofWeekAsString(DayOfWeek(now()))#
</cfoutput>
```

DayOfYear

```
DayOfYear ("date")
```

Description

Determines the day of the year.

Example

```
<cfoutput>
Today is: # DayOfYear(now())#
</cfoutput>
```

DaysInMonth

```
DaysInMonth ("date")
```

Description

Determines the number of days in a month.

Example

```
<cfoutput>
This month has #DaysInMonth (now())# days
</cfoutput>
```

DaysInYear

```
DaysInYear ("date")
```

Description

Determines the number of days in a year.

Example

```
<cfoutput>
This year has # DaysInYear (now())# days
</cfoutput>
```

DE

```
DE (string)
```

Description

Used to delay evaluation of a string as an expression in conjunction with the
IIf or Evaluate functions. Escapes any double quotation marks in the parameter and wraps the result in double quotation marks. This only works with
expressions that are not surrounded by pound signs. Expressions surrounded
by pound signs are always evaluated first.

Example

```
<cfset exampleVariable = "2 + 2">

<cfoutput>
The example variable is #exampleVariable# or if you use
#DE(exampleVariable)# or you can use #Evaluate(DE(exampleVariable))#
</cfoutput>
```

DecimalFormat

```
DecimalFormat (number)
```

Description

Converts a number to two decimal places.

Example

```
<cfoutput>
Pi: #Pi()#
Pi to 2 decimal places: #DecimalFormat(Pi())#
</cfoutput>
```

DecrementValue

```
DecrementValue (number)
```

Description

Decrements the integer part of a number by one.

Example

```
<cfoutput>
The value of a decremened 1 is: #DecrementValue("1")#
The value of a decremened 100 is: #DecrementValue("100")#
</cfoutput>
```

Decrypt

```
Decrypt (encrypted_string, seed)
```

Description

Decrypts a string that is encrypted with the Encrypt function. The seed is the 32-bit key used to encrypt the string.

Example

```
<cfset exampleString = "Welcome to the secret club">
<cfset exampleKey = "44abc">

<cfset secretMessage = Encrypt(exampleString, exampleKey)

<cfoutput>
The unencrypted string is:
#Decrypt(secretMessage, exampleKey)#
</cfoutput>
```

DeleteClientVariable

```
DeleteClientVariable ("name")
```

Description

Deletes a client variable. Returns a value of true if the variable is deleted or if the variable did not exist.

Example

```
<cfset client.exampleVariable = "test">

<cfoutput>
This is the variable: #exampleVariable#
Has the variable been deleted: #DeleteClientVariable("exampleVariable")#
</cfoutput>
```

DirectoryExists

DirectoryExists (*absolute_path*)

Description

Determines whether a directory exists and returns `true` or `false`.

Example

```
<cfset exampleDirectory = "c:\myfictionaldir">

<cfoutput>
Does my directory exist? #DirectoryExists(exampleDirectory)#
</cfoutput>
```

DollarFormat

DollarFormat (*number*)

Description

Formats a string in U.S. dollar format. For non-U.S. currencies, use `LSCurrencyFormat` or `LSEuroCurrencyFormat`. Returns a number with a dollar sign and two decimal places.

Example

```
<cfoutput>
A quarter becomes #DollarFormat(".25")#
The number one hundred looks like: #DollarFormat(100)#
</cfoutput>
```

Duplicate

Duplicate (*variable_name*)

Description

Returns a clone, also known as a deep copy, of a variable. There is no reference to the original variable. This function does not duplicate COM, CORBA, or Java object structures.

Example

```
<cfset exampleStructure = StructNew()>
<cfset exampleStructure.nested  = StructNew()>
<cfset exampleStructure.nested.item = "test">

<cfset exampleDup = Duplicate(exampleStructure)>

<cfoutput>
The duplicate contains the value: # exampleDup.nested.item#
</cfoutput>
```

Encrypt

```
Encrypt (string, seed)
```

Description

Encrypts a string. Uses a symmetric key-based algorithm, in which the same key is used to encrypt and decrypt a string. The security of the encrypted string depends on the key. seed is the key that is used to encrpyt and decrypt the string.

Example

```
<cfset exampleString = "Welcome to the secret club">
<cfset exampleKey = "44abc">

<cfset secretMessage = Encrypt(exampleString, exampleKey)
```

Evaluate

```
Evaluate (string_expression1 [, string_expression2 [, ... ] ])
```

Description

Evaluates one or more string expressions, dynamically from left to right. Returns the result of evaluating the rightmost expression.

Example

```
<cfset a = 2>
<cfset b = 3>
<cfoutput>
#Evaluate(a + b)#
#Evaluate(sqr(a))#
#Evaluate((a + b)* 2)#
#Evaluate(a + b, 2 + 2)#
</cfoutput>
```

Exp

```
Exp (number)
```

Description

Raises the constant e by the power of the number. The constant e equals 2.71828182845904, the base of the natural logarithm. This function is the inverse of Log.

Example

```
<cfoutput>
e to the 4 power is: #exp(4)#
</cfoutput>
```

ExpandPath

```
ExpandPath (relative_path)
```

Description

Creates an absolute, platform-appropriate path that is equivalent to the value of a relative path that is appended to the base path. The base path is the currently executing page's directory path. It is stored in pageContext.getServletContext().

Example

```
<cfoutput>
<cfset examplePath= ExpandPath("*.*") >
</cfoutput>
```

FileExists

```
FileExists (absolute_path)
```

Description

Checks to see if a file exists and returns true or false.

Example

```
<cfoutput>
 Does my example file exist? #FileExists(c:\test\example.doc)#/cfoutput>
```

Find

```
Find (substring ,  string  [,  start  ])
```

Description

Finds the first occurrence of a substring in a string. An optional start point can be provided, and the search is case-sensitive.

Example

```
<cfset exampleString = "This is my example string to Demonstrate the find function.">

<cfoutput>
The position at which Demonstrate starts is #find(exampleString, "Demonstrate")#
</cfoutput>
```

FindNoCase

```
FindNoCase (substring, string [,start])
```

Description

Finds the first occurrence of a substring in a string. An optional start point can be provided, and the search is non-case-sensitive.

Example

```
<cfset exampleString = "This is my example string to Demonstrate the findnocase
function. As you will notice this search is case-insensitive.">

<cfoutput>
The position at which Demonstrate starts is #findnocase(exampleString, "demonstrate")#
</cfoutput>
```

FindOneOf

```
FindOneOf (set, string [, start])
```

Description

Finds the first occurrence of any one of a set of characters in a string, from a specified start position. The search is case-sensitive.

Example

```
<cfset exampleString = "This is my example string to Demonstrate the findoneof
function.">

<cfoutput>
The position at which "is" can be found is: #findoneof(exampleString, "is")#
</cfoutput>
```

FirstDayOfMonth

```
FirstDayOfMonth (date)
```

Description

Returns the number of the day (1–365) that the first day of the month falls on for a given date within the year.

Example

```
<cfoutput>
The first day of the current month is day #FirstDayOfMonth(Now())# of the year.
</cfoutput>
```

Fix

```
Fix (number)
```

Description

Converts a real number to an integer. Returns the closest integer less than the number if it is greater than or equal to 0. If it is less than 0, it returns the closest integer greater than the number.

Example

```
<cfoutput>
The fix of 4 is #fix(4)#
The fix of -4 is #fix(-4)#
</cfoutput>
```

FormatBaseN

```
FormatBaseN (number, radix)
```

Description

Converts a number to a string in the base specified by radix.

Example

```
<cfoutput>
 The BaseN of 10 & 2: #FormatBaseN(10,2)#
 The BaseN of 1024 & 16: #FormatBaseN(1024,16)#
</cfoutput>
```

GetAuthUser

```
GetAuthUser ()
```

Description

Gets the name of an authenticated user.

Example

```
<cfoutput>
 Authenticated User: #GetAuthUser()#
</cfoutput>
```

GetBaseTagData

```
GetBaseTagData (tagname [, instancenumber])
```

Description

Finds the calling tag by name and accesses its data within a custom tag.

Example

```
<cfset exampleData = GetBaseTagData(exCustomTag)>
```

GetBaseTagList

```
GetBaseTagList ()
```

Description

Gets ancestor (calling) tag names, starting with the parent tag. Returns a comma-delimited list of ancestor tag names as a string.

Example

```
<cfset baseList = GetBaseTagList()>
```

GetBaseTemplatePath

```
GetBaseTemplatePath ()
```

Description

Gets the absolute path of an application's base page.

Example

```
<cfoutput>
The current page's template path is #GetBaseTemplatePath()#
</cfoutput>
```

GetClientVariablesList

```
GetClientVariablesList ()
```

Description

Finds the client variables to which a page has write access. Returns a list of client variables in a comma-delimited list as a string.

Example

```
<cfoutput>
Client variable list: #GetClientVariablesList()#
</cfoutput>
```

GetCurrentTemplatePath

GetCurrentTemplatePath ()

Description

Gets the path of the page that calls this function.

Example

```
<cfoutput>
The template path of the current page is #GetCurrentTemplatePath()#
</cfoutput>
```

GetDescriptor_html

GetDescriptor_html (*object*)

Description

Gets metadata (the methods and properties of a component) associated with an object that is deployed on the ColdFusion server in HTML format. This functionality, called introspection, permits applications to dynamically determine how to use a component.

GetDirectoryFromPath

GetDirectoryFromPath (*path*)

Description

Extracts a filename and directory from an absolute path.

Example

```
<cfset exampleDirectory = GetDirectoryFromPath(thisPath)>
```

GetException

GetException (*object*)

Description

Used with the cftry and cfcatch tags. Retrieves a Java exception object from a Java object.

Example

```
<cfset exception = GetException(exampleObj)>
```

GetFileFromPath

```
GetFileFromPath (path)
```

Description

Extracts a filename from an absolute path.

Example

```
<cfoutput>
The path of the current template is: #GetFileFromPath (GetTemplatePath())#
</cfoutput>
```

GetFunctionList

```
GetFunctionList( )
```

Description

Displays a list of the functions available in ColdFusion.

Example

```
<cfset fucntionList =  GetFunctionList()>
```

GetHttpRequestData

```
GetHttpRequestData()
```

Description

Makes HTTP request headers and bodies available to CFML pages. Useful for capturing SOAP request data, which can be delivered in an HTTP header.

Example

```
<cfset x = GetHttpRequestData()>
```

GetHttpTimeString

```
GetHttpTimeString (date_time_object)
```

Description

Gets the current time in the universal time code (UTC).

Example

```
<cfoutput>
#GetHttpTimeString("#Now()#")#
</cfoutput>
```

GetK2ServerCollections

```
GetK2ServerCollections()
```

Description

Gives a list of all the K2 collection aliases available to the K2 server. The list is returned in comma-delimited format, and the K2 server must be on for this function to work.

Example

```
<cfoutput>
#GetK2ServerCollections()#
</cfoutput>
```

GetK2ServerDocCount

```
GetK2ServerDocCount ()
```

Description

Gives the total number of items in all collections for one K2 server.

Example

```
<cfoutput>
There are #GetK2ServerDocCount()# documents being indexed by the K2 Server.
</cfoutput>
```

GetK2ServerDocCountLimit

```
GetK2ServerDocCountLimit ()
```

Description

Gives the maximum number of collection items that the K2 server is permitted to return from a search. This limit is set by the version of the ColdFusion server that is running.

Example

```
<cfoutput>
The document limit for this K2 Server is #GetK2ServerDocCountLimit()#.
</cfoutput>
```

GetLocale

```
GetLocale ()
```

Description

Gets the current geographic/language locale value. This is useful in conjunction with the SetLocale function to set a default local display.

Example

```
<cfoutput>
This systems current locale is #GetLocale()#.
</cfoutput>
```

GetMetaData

```
GetMetaData(object)
```

Description

Gives the metadata (the methods, properties, and parameters of a component) associated with an object that is deployed on the ColdFusion Server. Can also be used in conjunction with the cfdump tag.

Example

```
<cfscript>
<exampleObject=CreateObject("Component", "exampleCFC");>
</cfscript>

<cfdump examplevar ="#GetMetaData(exampleObject)#">
```

GetMetricData

GetMetricData (*mode*)

Description

Gets server performance statistics depending on the mode. This works on all platforms.

Mode

- perf_monitor

  Returns internal data in a structure. Returned data includes: InstanceName, PageHits, ReqQueued, DBHits, ReqRunning, ReqTimedOut, BytesIn, BytesOut, AvgQueueTime, AvgReqTime, AvgDBTime.

- simple_load

  Returns an integer value that is computed from the state of the server's internal queues.

- prev_req_time

  Returns the time, in milliseconds, that it took the server to process the previous request.

- avg_req_time

  Returns the average time, in milliseconds, that it takes the server to process a request.

GetPageContext

GetPageContext ()

Description

This is a wrapper for the Java PageContext object that provides access to page attributes, configuration, and request and response objects.

Example

```
<!--- this example shows using the page context to set a page
➥variable and access the language of the current locale --->
➥<cfset pc = GetPageContext() >
```

```
<cfset pc.setAttribute("name","John Doe")>
<cfoutput>name: #variables.name#</cfoutput>

<cfoutput>Language of the current locale is
#pc.getRequest().getLocale().getDisplayLanguage()#</cfoutput>>.
```

GetProfileSections

GetProfileSections (*iniFile*)

Description

Returns all the sections of an initialization file. Initialiaztion files have an .ini extension and assign initial values to the operating system and applications.

Example

```
<cfoutput>
The current odbc data sources on this machine are:
#GetProfileSections("c:\Windows\odbc.ini")#
</cfoutput>
```

GetProfileString

GetProfileString (*iniPath*, *section*, *entry*)

Description

Gets an initialization file entry. Initialiaztion files have an .ini extension and assign initial values to the operating system and applications.

Example

```
<cfset timeout = GetProfileString(IniPath, Section, "timeout")>
```

GetServiceSettings

GetServiceSettings ()

Description

Accesses service settings available through ColdFusion, such as data stored in the registry.

Example

```
<cfoutput>
The current on this machine are:
#GetServiceSettings()#
</cfoutput>
```

GetTempDirectory

```
GetTempDirectory ()
```

Description

Returns the current directory being used by ColdFusion as its temporary directory.

Example

```
<cfoutput>
CF is currently using #GetTempDirectory()# as the temp directory.
</cfoutput>
```

GetTempFile

```
GetTempFile (dir, prefix)
```

Description

Creates a temporary file in a directory whose name starts with the first three characters of prefix.

Example

```
<cfoutput>#GetTempFile(GetTempDirectory(),"temp")#</cfoutput>
```

GetTickCount

```
GetTickCount ()
```

Description

Determines the differences between the results of GetTickCount at successive points of page processing.

Example

```
<cfset Begin = GetTickCount()>

<cfloop Index = i From = 1 To = 100>
<cfset counter = i>
</cfloop>
<cfset End = GetTickCount()>
<cfset totalTime = evaluate(End - Begin)>

<cfoutput>Total processing time was: #total Time# milliseconds</cfoutput>
```

GetTimeZoneInfo

```
GetTimeZoneInfo ()
```

Description

Gets local time zone information for the computer on which it is called, relative to universal coordinated time (UCT). Returns values in a structure containing the following information: utcTotalOffset, utcHourOffset, utcMinuteOffset, isDSTOn.

Example

```
<cfset timezone =  GetTimeZoneInfo() >
<cfoutput>
<p>Total offset in seconds is #timezone.utcTotalOffset#.</p>
<p>Offset in hours is # timezone.utcHourOffset#.</p>
<p>Offset in minutes minus the offset in hours is #timezone.utcMinuteOffset#.</p>
<p>Is daylight savings turned on: # timezone.isDSTOn#.</p>
</cfoutput>
```

GetToken

```
GetToken (string, index [, delimiters ])
```

Description

Gives the token in a list at the space of the index based on a list of delimiters. If the index number is greater than the number of tokens, an empty string is returned.

Example

```
<cfset teststring = "07/04/1965">

<cfoutput>
#GetToken(teststring, 2, "/")#
</cfoutput>
Returns the value 04.
```

Hash

```
Hash (string)
```

Description

Converts a string into a 32-byte, hexadecimal string, using the MD5 algorithm. There is no way to convert this hash back to the original string. This is often used to encrypt passwords so that they are more secure.

Example

```
<cfset password = Hash('unguessableword')>

<cfoutput>
This is the #password# after hash function.
</cfoutput>
```

Hour

```
Hour (date)
```

Description

Gets the current hour of the day.

Example

```
The hour is currently <cfoutput>#Hour(now())#</cfoutput>.
```

HTMLCodeFormat

```
HTMLCodeFormat (string [, version ])
```

Description

Replaces special characters in a string with their HTML-escaped equivalents and inserts `<pre>` and `</pre>` tags at the beginning and end of the string. To apply the latest version of HTML, use `-1` in the `version` attribute or use `2.0` or `3.2` for their HTML version equivalents.

Example

```
<cfset exampleString = "<h1>Test string</h1>">
<cfoutput>
#HTMLCodeFormat(exampleString)#
</cfoutput>
```

HTMLEditFormat

```
HTMLEditFormat (string [, version ])
```

Description

Removes all carriage returns and replaces special characters in a string with their HTML-escaped equivalents. To apply the latest version of HTML, use `-1` in the `version` attribute or use `2.0` or `3.2` for their HTML version equivalents.

Example

```
<cfset exampleString = "<h1>Test string</h1>">
<cfoutput>
# HTMLEditFormat(exampleString)#
</cfoutput>
```

IIf

IIf (*condition* ,   *string_expression1* ,   *string_expression2*)

Description

Evaluates a Boolean condition expression. Depending on whether the expression is true or false, it dynamically evaluates one of two string expressions and returns the result. This function is convenient for incorporating a cfif tag inline in HTML.

Example

```
<cfoutput>
#IIf(Month(Now())  GTE 6,
 DE("It's not spring"),
  DE("It might be spring"))#
</cfoutput>
```

IncrementValue

IncrementValue (*number*)

Description

Adds one to an integer.

Example

```
<cfoutput>
Using 0 #IncrementValue(0)#
Using 151.05 #IncrementValue(151.05)#
</cfoutput>
```

InputBaseN

InputBaseN (*string* ,   *radix*)

Description

Converts a string, using the base specified by radix, to an integer.

Example

```
<cfoutput>
InputBaseN("1010",2): # InputBaseN("1010",2) #
InputBaseN("3ff",16): # InputBaseN("3ff",16) #
```

```
InputBaseN("125",10): # InputBaseN("125",10) #
InputBaseN(1010,2): # InputBaseN(1010,2) #
</cfoutput>
```

Insert

```
Insert (substring , string , position)
```

Description

Inserts a substring into a string after a specified character position. If position is 0, it prefixes the substring to the string.

Example

```
<cfset examplestring = "Rock and Roll is the best.">

<cfoutput>
#Insert("almost", examplestring, 17)#
</cfoutput>
```

Int

```
Int (number)
```

Description

Calculates the closest integer that is smaller than number.

Example

```
Int(11.7):   <cfoutput>#Int(11.7)#</cfoutput>
Int(-11.7):  <cfoutput>#Int(-11.7)#</cfoutput>
Int(0):      <cfoutput>#Int(0)#</cfoutput>
```

IsArray

```
IsArray (value  [, number ])
```

Description

Determines whether value is an array.

Example

```
<cfset zipcode = ArrayNew(1)>
<cfset zipcode[1] = 80202>
<cfset zipcode[2] = 80203>
<cfset zipcode[1] = 80204>

<cfoutput>
  This is an array: #IsArray(zipcode)#
</cfoutput>
```

IsBinary

```
IsBinary (value)
```

Description

Checks to see if a value is binary and returns true or false.

Example

```
<cfoutput>
567: #IsBinary(567)#
xyz: #IsBinary('xyz')#
</cfoutput>
```

IsBoolean

```
IsBoolean (value)
```

Description

Checks to see if a value can be converted to a Boolean and then returns true or false.

Example

```
<cfoutput>
0: #IsBoolean(0)#
1: #IsBoolean(1)#
567: #IsBoolean(567)#
xyz: #IsBoolean('xyz')#
yes: #IsBoolean('yes')#
no: #IsBoolean('no')#
</cfoutput>
```

IsCustomFunction

```
IsCustomFunction ("name")
```

Description

Checks to see if a function can be called as a user-defined function and also displays information about the function. If the name does not exist, ColdFusion throws an error, so be sure to check for its existence first.

Example

```
<cfscript>
function exampleUDF() {
  return 1;
}
</cfscript>

<CFIF IsDefined("exampleUDF") AND  IsCustomFunction("exampleUDF") >
  exampleUDF is a function.
</CFIF>
```

IsDate

```
IsDate (string)
```

Description

Checks to see if a string can be converted to a date/time value and then returns true or false.

Example

```
<cfset exampleValue = "12/13/75">
<cfif  IsDate(exampleValue) >
   <cfoutput>#DE(exampleValue)#</cfoutput>
   is a valid date.
<cfelse>
   <cfoutput>#DE(exampleValue)#</cfoutput>
   is not a valid date.
</cfif>
```

IsDebugMode

```
IsDebugMode ()
```

Description

Checks to see if debug is turned on or off in the ColdFusion Administrator and returns Yes if debug mode is turned on.

Example

```
<cfoutput>
Debug mode is currently turned on? #IsDebugMode( )#
</cfoutput>
```

IsDefined

```
IsDefined ("variable_name")
```

Description

Checks to see if the variable name currently exists and returns true or false.

Example

```
<cfset exampleVariable = 1>

<cfif  IsDefined("exampleVariable")>
We can use example variable because it is currently set.  Otherwise we could not use
it.
<cfelse>
The example variable has not been set yet.
</cfif>
```

IsK2ServerABroker

```
IsK2ServerABroker ()
```

Description

Checks to see if the K2 server version is a K2 broker. Also checks the GetK2ServerDocCountLimit function for more information.

Example

```
<cfoutput>
Is the K2 Server a Broker: #IsK2ServerABroker()#
</cfoutput>
```

IsK2ServerDocCountExceeded

```
IsK2ServerDocCountExceeded ()
```

Description

Checks whether the limit on indexed items allowed to be stored in verity collections is exceeded. The K2 server platform limit is set by your version of ColdFusion.

Example

```
<cfoutput>
Has the K2 Document limit been exceeded? # IsK2ServerDocCountExceeded()#
</cfoutput>
```

IsK2ServerOnline

```
IsK2ServerOnline ()
```

Description

Checks whether the K2 server is running and available. This function is dependent on using the K2.2 version of the verity server.

Example

```
<cfoutput>
Is K2 Server currently on-line: # IsK2ServerOnline()#
</cfoutput>
```

IsLeapYear

```
IsLeapYear (year)
```

Description

Checks to see if a year is a leap year and returns true or false.

Example

```
<cfoutput>
Is year is a Leap Year?  #IsLeapYear(now())#
</cfoutput>
```

IsNumeric

```
IsNumeric (string)
```

Description

Checks to see if a string can be converted to a numeric value and returns true or false.

Example

```
<cfset exampleVariable = "1">

<cfif IsNumeric(exampleVariable)>
This is a number
<cfelse>
This is not a number.
</cfif>
```

IsNumericDate

```
IsNumericDate (number)
```

Description

Checks for the "real value" of a date/time object and returns true or false.

Example

```
<cfset exampleVariable = "121375">

<cfoutput>
This is a numeric date? #IsNumericDate(exampleVariable)#
</cfoutput>
```

IsObject

IsObject (*value* [, *type* [, ...]])

Description

Checks to see if a value is an object and returns true or false. Types include Component, java, corba, com, webservice, and template. Returns false for query and XML objects.

Example

```
<cfscript>
<exampleObject=CreateObject("Component", "exampleCFC");>
</cfscript>

<cfoutput>
Is the above example a component object: #IsObject(exampleObject, component)#
</cfoutput>
```

IsQuery

IsQuery (*value*)

Description

Checks to see if a value is a query.

Example

```
<cfquery name = "exampleQuery" datasource = "exampleDS">
SELECT *
FROM exampleTable
</cfquery>

<cfif IsQuery(exampleQuery)>
exampleQuery is a query.
</cfif>
```

IsSimpleValue

```
IsSimpleValue (value)
```

Description

Checks the type of a value and returns `true` for string, number, Boolean, or date/time. For everything else, returns `false`.

Example

```
<cfset zipcode = ArrayNew(1)>
<cfset zipcode[1] = 80202>
<cfset zipcode[2] = 80203>
<cfset zipcode[1] = 80204>

<cfoutput>
<p>The number 1 is a simple value: #IsSimpleValue(1)#</p>
<p>The zipcode array is a simple value: #IsSimpleValue(zipcode)# </p>
</cfoutput>
```

IsStruct

```
IsStruct (variable)
```

Description

Checks to see if a variable is a structure and returns `true` if the variable is a ColdFusion structure.

Example

```
<cfscript>
   Products = StructNew();
   StructInsert(Products , "ProductName", "Blizzard Blender");
   StructInsert(Products , "ProductID", 1001);
   StructInsert(Products , "SKU", "555-6582");
</cfscript>

<cfoutput>
Is the Products a structure? #IsStruct(Products)#
</cfoutput>
```

IsUserInRole

```
IsAuthUserInRole ("role_name")
```

Description

> Checks to see if an authenticated user belongs to the specified role and
> returns true or false.

Example

```
<cfif IsAuthUserInRole("Admin") >
<cfoutput>Authenticated user is an administrator</cfoutput>
<cfelse IsAuthUserInRole("User") >
<cfoutput>Authenticated user is a user</cfoutput>
</cfif>
```

IsWDDX

```
IsWDDX (value)
```

Description

> Checks to see if a value is a well-formed WDDX packet and returns
> true or false.

Example

```
<cfset packet="
<wddxPacket version='1.0'>
<header></header>
<data>
  <struct>
  <var name='ARRAY'>
    <array length='3'>
      <string>one</string>
    <string>two</string>
    </array>
  </var>
  <var name='NUMBER'>
    <string>5</string>
  </var>
  <var name='STRING'>
    <string>hello</string>
  </var>
  </struct>
</data>
```

```
</wddxPacket>"
><hr>
<xmp>
<cfoutput>#packet#
</xmp>
<hr>
IsWDDX() returns # iswddx(packet) #
</cfoutput>
<hr>
<cfwddx action="wddx2cfml"  input=#packet#  output="s"  validate="yes"
```

IsXmlDoc

IsXmlDoc (*value*)

> Checks to see if a function parameter is an eXtensible Markup Language (XML) document object and returns true or false.

IsXmlElement

IsXmlElement (*value*)

Description

> Checks to see if a function parameter is an eXtended Markup Language (XML) document object element and returns true or false.

IsXmlRoot

IsXmlRoot (*value*)

Description

> Checks to see if a function parameter is the root element of an eXtended Markup Language (XML) document object and returns true or false.

JavaCast

JavaCast (*type, variable*)

Description

> Converts the data type of a ColdFusion variable to pass as an argument to an overloaded method of a Java object. Use only for scalar and string arguments. Can convert to the following types: Boolean, int, long, double, string.

Example

```
Within ColdFusion, you use the following code: <cfobject
  type = java
  CLASS = fooClass name = obj>
  <!--- ColdFusion may treat this as a string or a real number --->
  <cfset x = 33>
  <!--- Perform an explicit cast to an int. --->
  <cfset myInt = JavaCast("int", x)>
  <cfset void = fooMethod(myInt)>
  <!--- Perform an explicit cast to a string. --->
  <cfset myString = javaCast("String", x)>
  <cfset void = fooMethod(myString)>
</cfobject>
```

JSStringFormat

```
JSStringFormat (string)
```

Description

Escapes special JavaScript characters such as single quotation mark, double quotation mark, and newline.

Example

```
<cfset exampleString="This string contains some characters such as 'single quotes'
➥that normally javascript does not like">
<cfset exampleString = JSStringFormat(#stringValue#)>
```

LCase

```
LCase (string)
```

Description

Converts all the letters in a string to lowercase.

Example

```
<cfset exampleText = "This Sentence Will Be Made Into All Lowercase">

<cfoutput>
#LCase(exampleText)#
</cfoutput>.
```

Left

```
Left (string, count)
```

Description

Counts to the left the number of characters from the beginning of the string parameter to the location specified by the count parameter.

Example

```
<cfoutput>
# Left("This is a test string", 6)#
</cfoutput>
```

Len

```
Len (string or binary object)
```

Description

Determines the length of a string or binary object.

Example

```
<cfset exampleString = "We are not sure of the length of this string of text">

<cfoutput>
My example string is #Len(exampleString)# characters long.
</cfoutput>
```

ListAppend

```
ListAppend (list, value [, delimiters])
```

Description

Adds a value to the end of a list.

Example

```
<cfset exampleList = "Apples, Oranges, Grapes, Pears, Mangoes">

<cfoutput>
# ListAppend (exampleList, 'Cranberry')#
</cfoutput>
```

ListChangeDelims

```
ListChangeDelims (list, new_delimiter [, delimiters])
```

Description

Allows for the change of a list delimiter.

Example

```
<cfset exampleList = "Apples, Oranges, Grapes, Pears, Mangoes">

<cfoutput>
List with new delimiters: #ListChangeDelims(exampleList, '$$', ',')#
</cfoutput>
```

ListContains

```
ListContains (list, substring [, delimiters])
```

Description

Determines the index of the first list element that contains a specific value.

Example

```
<cfset exampleList = "Apples, Oranges, Grapes, Pears, Mangoes">

<cfoutput>
Oranges is the number # ListContains (exampleList, "Oranges")# in this list.
</cfoutput>
```

ListContainsNoCase

```
ListContainsNoCase (list, substring [, delimiters])
```

Description

Searches for a value's index within a list that contains the substring.

Example

```
<cfset exampleList = "Apples, Oranges, Grapes, Pears, Mangoes">

<cfoutput>
Oranges is the number #ListContainsNoCase(exampleList, "oranges")# in this list.
</cfoutput>
```

ListDeleteAt

```
ListDeleteAt (list, position [, delimiters])
```

Description

Deletes an element from a list at the specified index position.

Example

```
<cfset exampleList = "Apples, Oranges, Grapes, Pears, Mangoes">

<cfoutput>
Oranges is gone from the list: #ListDeleteAt(exampleList, 2)#.
</cfoutput>
```

ListFind

```
ListFind (list, value [, delimiters])
```

Description

Determines the index of the first list element in which a specified value occurs. This is a case-sensitive search.

Example

```
<cfset exampleList = "Apples, apples, Oranges, Grapes, Pears, Mangoes">

<cfoutput>
Apples is the number # ListFind(exampleList, "Apples")# element in the list.
</cfoutput>
```

ListFindNoCase

```
ListFindNoCase (list, value [, delimiters])
```

Description

A non-case-sensitive index of the first list element in which a specified value occurs.

Example

```
<cfset exampleList = "apples, Apples, Oranges, Grapes, Pears, Mangoes">

<cfoutput>
Apples is the number: # ListFind(exampleList, "Apples")# element in the list.
</cfoutput>
```

ListFirst

```
ListFirst (list [, delimiters])
```

Description

Gets the first element of a list.

Example

```
<cfset exampleList = "Apples, Oranges, Grapes, Pears, Mangoes">

<cfoutput>
#ListFirst(exampleList)#
</cfoutput>
```

ListGetAt

```
ListGetAt (list, position [, delimiters])
```

Description

Returns a list element at the specified position in the parameters.

Example

```
<cfset exampleList = "Apples, Oranges, Grapes, Pears, Mangoes">

<cfoutput>
#ListGetAt(exampleList, 3)#
</cfoutput>
```

ListInsertAt

```
ListInsertAt (list, position, value [, delimiters])
```

Description

Inserts an element into a list at a specified index position.

Example

```
<cfset exampleList = "Apples, Oranges, Grapes, Pears, Mangoes">

<cfoutput>
#ListInsertAt(exampleList, "3", "Cranberry")#
</cfoutput>
```

ListLast

```
ListLast (list [, delimiters])
```

Description

Gets the last element of a list.

Example

```
<cfset exampleList = "Apples, Oranges, Grapes, Pears, Mangoes">

<cfoutput>
#ListLast(exampleList)#
</cfoutput>
```

ListLen

```
ListLen (list [, delimiters])
```

Description

Gets the length of a list.

Example

```
<cfset exampleList = "Apples, Oranges, Grapes, Pears, Mangoes">

<cfoutput>
#ListLen(exampleList)#
</cfoutput>
```

ListPrepend

```
ListPrepend (list, value [, delimiters])
```

Description

Inserts an element at the beginning of a list.

Example

```
<cfset exampleList = "Apples, Oranges, Grapes, Pears, Mangoes">

<cfoutput>
#ListPrepend(exampleList, "Strawberry")#
</cfoutput>
```

ListQualify

```
ListQualify (list, qualifier [, delimiters] [, elements])
```

Description

Inserts a string at the beginning and end of list elements. The elements parameter can be either all (all elements) or character.

Example

```
<cfset exampleList = "Apples, Oranges, Grapes, Pears, Mangoes">
<cfset qualifiedExample = ListQualify(exampleList, "'", ",", "all")>

<cfoutput>
This is a list with single quotes:
#qualifiedExample#
</cfoutput>
```

ListRest

```
ListRest (list [, delimiters])
```

Description

Returns *list* without its first element. Returns an empty string if list only has one element.

Example

```
<cfset exampleList = "Apples, Oranges, Grapes, Pears, Mangoes">

<cfoutput>
#ListRest (exampleList)#
</cfoutput>
```

ListSetAt

ListSetAt (*list, position, value* [, *delimiters*])

Description

Assigns a value to a list element at the specified position.

Example

```
<cfset exampleList = "Apples, Oranges, Grapes, Pears, Mangoes">

<cfoutput>
# ListSetAt (exampleList, "2", "Strawberry")#
</cfoutput>
```

ListSort

ListSort (*list, sort_type* [, *sort_order*] [, *delimiters*])

Description

Sorts list elements according to a sort type and sort order. Sort types include numeric, text (sort alphabetically), textnocase (non-case-sensitive). Sort orders can be asc (ascending) or desc (descending).

Example

```
<cfset exampleList = "Apples, Oranges, Grapes, Pears, Mangoes">

<cfset sortedList = ListSort(exampleList, "Text")>

<cfoutput>
#sortedList#
</cfoutput>
```

ListToArray

```
ListToArray (list [, delimiters ])
```

Description

Copies the elements of a list to an array.

Example

```
<cfset exampleList = "Apples, Oranges, Grapes, Pears, Mangoes">

<cfset exampleArray = ListToArray(exampleList)>

<cfdump var= #exampleArray#>
```

ListValueCount

```
ListValueCount (list, value [, delimiters])
```

Description

Counts the number of times a value occurs in a list. The search is case-sensitive.

Example

```
<cfset exampleList = "Apples, Apples, Oranges, Grapes, Pears, Mangoes, Apples,
apples,">

<cfoutput>
Apples occurs #ListValueCount(exampleList, Apples)# times in the list.
</cfoutput>
```

ListValueCountNoCase

```
ListValueCountNoCase (list, value [, delimiters])
```

Description

Counts the number of times a value occurs in a list. The search is non-case-sensitive.

Example

```
<cfset exampleList = "Apples, Apples, Oranges, Grapes, Pears, Mangoes, Apples,
apples,">

<cfoutput>
Apples occurs #ListValueCount(exampleList, Apples)# times in the list.
</cfoutput>
```

LJustify

```
LJustify (string, length)
```

Description

Left-justifies characters in a string of a specified length.

Example

```
<cfset examplestring = "left justified" >

<cfoutput>
This is the string: #LJustify(examplesrting, 30)#
</cfoutput>
```

Log

```
Log (number)
```

Description

Calculates the natural logarithm of a number. Natural logarithms are based on the constant e (2.71828182845904).

Example

```
<cfoutput>
The log of 4 is #log(4)#
</cfoutput>
```

Log10

```
Log10 (number)
```

Description

Calculates the logarithm of number to base 10.

Example

```
<cfoutput>
The 4 to log10: #log10(4)#
</cfoutput>
```

LSCurrencyFormat

```
LSCurrencyFormat (number [, type])
```

Description

Formats a number in a specific locale currency format. The format is set by the locale of the server. To find out the current locale setting, use the GetLocale function.

Example

```
<cfoutput>
    Local: #LSCurrencyFormat(100, "local")#
    International: #LSCurrencyFormat(100, "international")#
    None: #LSCurrencyFormat(100, "none")#
</cfoutput>
```

LSDateFormat

```
LSDateFormat (date [, mask ])
```

Description

Formats a date in a specific locale format. The format is set by the locale of the server. To find out the current locale setting, use the GetLocale function.
Use the following values for the mask:

- **d.** Day of the month as digits (no leading 0 for single digits).
- **dd.** Day of the month as digits (leading 0 for single digits).

- **ddd.** Day of the week as a three-letter abbreviation.
- **dddd.** Day of the week as its full name.
- **m.** Month as digits (no leading 0 for single digits).
- **mm.** Month as digits (leading 0 for single digits).
- **mmm.** Month as a three-letter abbreviation.
- **mmmm.** Month as its full name.
- **y.** Year as last two digits (no 0 if less than 10).
- **yy.** Year as last two digits (leading 0 if less than 10).
- **yyyy.** Year represented by four digits.
- **gg.** Period/era string. Ignored, but reserved for future use.

Example

```
<cfoutput>
#LSDateFormat(Now())#
#LSDateFormat(Now(), "mmm-dd-yyyy")#
#LSDateFormat(Now(), "mmmm d, yyyy")#
#LSDateFormat(Now(), "ddd, mmmm dd, yyyy")#
#LSDateFormat(Now(), "d/m/yy")#
</cfoutput>
```

LSEuroCurrencyFormat

```
LSEuroCurrencyFormat (number [, type])
```

Description

Formats a number in a specific locale currency format. The format is set by the locale of the server. To find out the current locale setting, use the GetLocale function.

Example

```
<cfoutput>
  Local: #LSEuroCurrencyFormat(100, "local")#
  International: #LSEuroCurrencyFormat(100, "international")#
  None: #LSEuroCurrencyFormat(100, "none")#
</cfoutput>
```

LSIsCurrency

```
LSIsCurrency (string)
```

Description

Checks whether a string is formatted as a specific locale currency string. Returns true if the current locale is a Eurozone country and the string is a valid currency.

Example

```
<cfloop index="currentLocale" list="#Server.ColdFusion.SupportedLocales#">
<cfset exampleLocale = SetLocale(currentlocale)>
<cfoutput>
 #currentLocale#
Is 60.00 a currency: #LSIsCurrency(60.00)#
Is $60.00 a currency: #LSIsCurrency($60.00)#
Is $1,300 a currency: #LSIsCurrency($1,300.00)#
</cfoutput>
</cfloop>
```

LSIsDate

```
LSIsDate (string)
```

Description

Checks whether a string is a date/time value that can be formatted in a specific locale format. Returns true if the string can be formatted as a date/time.

Example

```
<cfloop index="currentLocale" list="#Server.ColdFusion.SupportedLocales#">
<cfset exampleLocale = SetLocale(currentlocale)>
<cfoutput>
 #currentLocale#
Is 8/15/00 date formattable: # LSIsDate (8/15/00)#
Is August 15 2000 date formattable: # LSIsDate (August 15 2000)#
Is 7:30  time formattable: # LSIsDate (7:30)#
Is seven thirty time formattable: # LSIsDate (seven thirty)#
</cfoutput>
</cfloop>
```

LSIsNumeric

LSIsNumeric (*string*)

Description

Check whether a string can be formatted in a specific locale format. Returns true if the string can be formatted in the current locale.

Example

```
<cfloop index="currentLocale" list="#Server.ColdFusion.SupportedLocales#">
<cfset exampleLocale = SetLocale(currentlocale)>
<cfoutput>
 #currentLocale#
Is 10 numeric: #LSIsNumeric (10)#
Is $10.00 numeric: #LSIsNumeric ($10.00)#
Is yes numeric: #LSIsNumeric (yes)#
Is .99 numeric: #LSIsNumeric (.99)#
</cfoutput>
</cfloop>
```

LSNumberFormat

LSNumberFormat (*number* [, *mask*])

Description

Formats a number in a specific locale format. The following characters can be used for the mask.

- **_ (underscore)**   Digit placeholder.
- **Nine-digit placeholder**   Shows decimal places more clearly than an underscore.
- **.**   Location of a mandatory decimal point (or locale-appropriate symbol).
- **0**   Located to the left or right of a mandatory decimal point. Pads with zeros.
- **( )**   If number is less than zero, puts parentheses around the mask.
- **+**   Puts a plus sign before positive number, a minus sign before negative number.
- **-**   Puts a space before a positive number, a minus sign before a negative number.

- **,**   Separates every third decimal place with a comma.
- **L,C**   Left-justifies or center-justifies the number within the width of the mask column. The first character of mask must be L or C. Default: right-justified.
- **$**   Puts a dollar sign (or locale-appropriate symbol) before formatted number. First character of mask must be the dollar sign ($).
- **^**   Separates left and right formatting.

Example

```
<cfoutput>
  #LSNumberFormat(-1674.872, "_____") #
  #LSNumberFormat(-1674.872, "_____.___")#
  #LSNumberFormat(1674.872, "_____")#
  #LSNumberFormat(1674.872, "_____.___")#
  #LSNumberFormat(1674.872, "$_(_____.___)")#
  #LSNumberFormat(-1674.872, "$_(_____.___)")#
  #LSNumberFormat(1674.872, "+_____.___")#
  #LSNumberFormat(1674.872, "-_____.___")#
</cfoutput>
```

LSParseCurrency

```
LSParseCurrency (string)
```

Description

Formats a specific locale currency string as a number. Attempts conversion through each of the default currency formats (none, local, international).

Example

```
<cfoutput>
  Local: #LSCurrencyFormat(5487, "local")#
  Currency: # LSParseCurrency(LSCurrencyFormat(5487,"local")) #
  International: #LSCurrencyFormat(5487, "international")#
  None: #LSCurrencyFormat(5487, "none")#
</cfoutput>
```

LSParseDateTime

```
LSParseDateTime (date/time-string)
```

Description

Formats a date/time string in a specific locale format.

Example

```
<cfloop index = "exampleLocale"  LIST = "#Server.Coldfusion.SupportedLocales#">
  <cfset currentLocale= SetLocale(exampleLocale)>
  <cfoutput>
    #exampleLocale#
    #LSDateFormat(Now())# #LSTimeFormat(Now())#
    #LSDateFormat(Now(), "mmm-dd-yyyy")#
    #LSDateFormat(Now(), "mmmm d, yyyy")#
    #LSDateFormat(Now(), "mm/dd/yyyy")#
    #LSDateFormat(Now(), "d-mmm-yyyy")#
 </cfoutput>
</cfloop>
```

LSParseEuroCurrency

```
LSParseEuroCurrency (currency)
```

Description

Formats a specific locale currency string that contains the euro symbol € or sign (EUR) as a number.

Example

```
<cfoutput>
  Euro Currency: #LSParseEuroCurrency("EUR548766") #
</cfoutput>
```

LSParseNumber

```
LSParseNumber (string)
```

Description

Formats a specific locale string as a number.

Example

```
<cfoutput>
The number: #LSParseNumber(LSNumberFormat(8745.13, "_____")) #
</cfoutput>
```

LSTimeFormat

```
LSTimeFormat (time [, mask ])
```

Description

Formats the time part of a date/time string in a specific locale format. mask options include:

- **h.** Hours, no leading zero for single-digit hours (12-hour clock)
- **hh.** Hours, leading zero for single-digit hours (12-hour clock)
- **H.** Hours, no leading zero for single-digit hours (24-hour clock)
- **HH.** Hours, leading zero for single-digit hours (24-hour clock)
- **m.** Minutes, no leading zero for single-digit minutes
- **mm.** Minutes, leading zero for single-digit minutes
- **s.** Seconds, no leading zero for single-digit seconds
- **ss.** Seconds, leading zero for single-digit seconds
- **t.** One-character time marker string, such as A or P
- **tt.** Multiple-character time marker string, such as AM or PM

Example

```
<cfoutput>
#LSTimeFormat(Now())#
#LSTimeFormat(Now(), 'hh:mm:ss')#
#LSTimeFormat(Now(), 'hh:mm:sst')#
</cfoutput>
```

LTrim

```
LTrim (string)
```

Description

Deletes leading spaces from a string.

Example

```
<cfset exampleString = "    This is a string with leading spaces.">

<cfoutput>
 Left Trimmed string:  "#Ltrim(exampleString)#"
</cfoutput>
```

Max

```
Max (number1, number2)
```

Description

Returns the greater of two numbers.

Example

```
<cfoutput>
 The larger of 100 and 10 is: #Max(100, 10)#
</cfoutput>
```

Mid

```
Mid (string, start, count)
```

Description

Gives *x* number of characters from a string from the starting point.

Example

```
<cfset exampleString = "(303)445-6790 ext:310"

<cfoutput>
  The extension is: #Mid(exampleString, 19, 3)#
</cfoutput>
```

Min

```
Min (number1, number2)
```

Description

Gives the smaller of two numbers.

Example

```
<cfoutput>
 The smaller of 100 and 10 is: #Max(100, 10)#
</cfoutput>
```

Minute

```
Minute (date)
```

Description

Gives the minute from a date/time object.

Example

```
<cfoutput>
 Currently #Minute(Now())# minutes on the hour.
</cfoutput>
```

Month

```
Month (date)
```

Description

Gives the month from a date/time object.

Example

```
<cfoutput>
Aren't you glad we are #Month(now())# of 12?
</cfoutput>
```

MonthAsString

```
MonthAsString (month_number)
```

Description

Shows the name of the month that corresponds to the number.

Example

```
<cfoutput>
 The 6th month is also known as #MonthAsString(6)#.
</cfoutput>
```

Now

```
Now ()
```

Description

Returns the current date and time of the server running ColdFusion.

Example

```
<cfoutput>
The computer says today is #Now()#, but we want to make it look pretty. So we use the
dateFormat function to find out that today is:
#DateFormat(Now(), 'mm/dd/yy')#
</cfoutput>
```

NumberFormat

```
NumberFormat (number, [, mask ])
```

Description

Creates a custom-formatted number. The following characters can be used for the mask:

- **_ (underscore)**   Digit placeholder.
- **Nine-digit placeholder**   Shows decimal places more clearly than an underscore.
- **.**   Location of a mandatory decimal point (or locale-appropriate symbol).
- **0**   Located to the left or right of a mandatory decimal point. Pads with zeros.
- **( )**   If number is less than zero, puts parentheses around the mask.
- **+**   Puts a plus sign before a positive number, a minus sign before a negative number.
- **-**   Puts a space before positive number, a minus sign before a negative number.

- **,** Separates every third decimal place with a comma.
- **L,C** Left-justifies or center-justifies the number within the width of the `mask` column. The first character of `mask` must be L or C. Default: right-justified.
- **$** Puts a dollar sign (or locale-appropriate symbol) before a formatted number. The first character of `mask` must be the dollar sign ($).
- **^** Separates left and right formatting.

Example

```
<cfloop FROM = 1 TO = 9 INDEX = "examplenumber">
<cfset examplenumber2 = Evaluate(examplenumber * sqr(2))>

<cfoutput>
#NumberFormat(examplenumber2,'_____._ ')#
</cfoutput>
</cfloop>
```

ParagraphFormat

```
ParagraphFormat (string)
```

Description

Gives an HTML format to a string by replacing single newline characters with spaces and double newline with a <p>.

Example

```
<cfset exampleString = "This is my example paragraph. As you can see it has
single new line characters in it as well as double new line characters.

We will use this to demonstrate the usage of the paragraph format function.">

<cfoutput>
#ParagraphFormat(exampleString)#
</cfoutput>
```

ParseDateTime

```
ParseDateTime (date/time-string  [, pop-conversion])
```

Description

Formats a date/time to the U.S. locale convention. If pop is used, it formats to GMT (Greenwich Mean Time).

Example

Pi

```
Pi ()
```

Description

Gives the mathematical constant pi, accurate to 15 digits.

Example

```
<cfoutput>
This is PI to 15 decimal places: #NumberFormat(Pi(), '_._____')#
</cfoutput>
```

PreserveSingleQuotes

```
PreserveSingleQuotes (variable)
```

Description

Prevents ColdFusion from automatically escaping single quotation-mark characters that are contained in a variable. ColdFusion does not evaluate the argument.

Example

```
<cfset exampleList = "'Blender', 'Food Processor', 'Mixer', 'Toaster'">

<cfquery name = "exampleQuery" datasource = "exampleDB">
  SELECT ProductName, SKU, InStock
  FROM Products
  WHERE ProductType IN (#PreserveSingleQuotes(exampleList)#)
</cfquery>
```

Quarter

Quarter (*date*)

Description

Calculates the quarter of the year in which a date falls.

Example

```
<cfoutput>
We are in Quarter #Quarter(Now())# of this year.
</cfoutput>.
```

QueryAddColumn

QueryAddColumn (*query*, *column-name*, *array-name*)

Description

Inserts a column in a query and populates its rows with the contents of a one-dimensional array. If necessary, ensures that all columns have the same number of rows.

Example

```
<cfset exampleCar = ArrayNew(1)>
<cfset exampleCar [1] = "Ford">
<cfset exampleCar [2] = "GM">
<cfset exampleCar [3] = "Chevrolet">
<cfset exampleCar [4] = "Toyota">

<cfset exampleColumn = QueryAddColumn(myQuery, "CarBrand", exampleCar)>
```

QueryAddRow

QueryAddRow (*query* [, *number*])

Description

Adds *x* number of empty rows to a query.

Example

```
<cfquery name = "exampleQuery" datasource = "exampleDB">
  SELECT ProductName, SKU, InStock
  FROM Products
</cfquery>

<cfoutput>
Example query has #exampleQuery.RecordCount# rows.
</cfoutput>

<cfset temp = QueryAddRow(exampleQuery, 5)>

<cfoutput>
Now Example query has #exampleQuery.RecordCount# rows.
</cfoutput>
```

QueryNew

```
QueryNew (columnlist)
```

Description

Creates an empty query.

Example

```
<cfset exampleQuery = QueryNew("ProductID, ProductType, SKU")>
```

QuerySetCell

```
QuerySetCell (query, column_name, value [, row_number])
```

Description

Sets a cell in a query to a value. If no row number is given, the cell in the last row is set.

Example

```
<cfset exampleQuery = QueryNew("ProductID, ProductType, SKU")>

<cfset newQuery = QuerySetCell(exampleQuery, " ProductID", 1001)>
```

QuotedValueList

QuotedValueList (*query.column* [, *delimiter*])

Description

Gets the values of each record returned from an executed query.

Example

```
<cfquery name="exampleQuery" datasource="exampleDSN">
SELECT Name, Email, Company
From Contacts
</cfquery>

<cfoutput>
The companies that are currently in my database are:
#QuotedValueList(exampleQuery.Company)#
</cfoutput>
```

Rand

Rand ()

Description

Generates a random number.

Example

```
<cfoutput>
This is a compeletely random number: #Rand()#
And so is this: #Rand()#
</cfoutput>
```

Randomize

Randomize (*number*)

Description

Seeds the ColdFusion random-number generator with an integer number. Although the number returned by the randomize function is not random, seeding the generator helps ensure that the Rand function generates highly random numbers.

Example

```
<cfset exampleRan = Randomize(23)>

<cfoutput>
This is very random number: #Rand()#
</cfoutput>
```

RandRange

```
RandRange (number1, number2)
```

Description

Creates a random integer between two specified numbers. Using a number greater than 100,000,000 results in nonrandom numbers.

Example

```
<cfoutput>
This is a random number between 1 and 100: #RandRange(1, 100)#
</cfoutput>
```

REFind

```
REFind (reg_expression, string [, start] [, returnsubexpressions])
```

Description

Performs a case-sensitive search for the position and length of the first occurrence of a regular expression (RE) in a string, starting from a specific position.

Example

```
<cfset exampleString = "This is an example that will show how to use the refind
function.">
<cfset exampleVar = Refind("show",exampleString, 1)>

<cfoutput>
The word show starts at position #exampleVar#
</cfoutput>
```

REFindNoCase

REFindNoCase (*reg_expression*, *string* [, *start*][, *returnsubexpressions*])

Description

Performs a non-case-sensitive search for the position and length of the first occurrence of a regular expression (RE) in a string, starting from a specific position.

Example

```
<cfset exampleString = "This is an example that will SHOW how to use the refind
function.">
<cfset exampleVar = Refind("show",exampleString, 1)>

<cfoutput>
The word show starts at position #exampleVar#
</cfoutput>
```

RemoveChars

RemoveChars (*string*, *start*, *count*)

Description

Removes characters from a string.

Example

```
<cfset exampleString = "examasdfple">

<cfoutput>
The modified string:  #RemoveChars(exampleString, 5, 4)#
</cfoutput>
```

RepeatString

RepeatString (*string*, *count*)

Description

Creates a new string that contains *x* number of repetitions of the specified string.

Example

```
<cfoutput>
This is a string of 12 dashes: #RepeatString("-", 12)#
</cfoutput>
```

Replace

```
Replace (string, substring1, substring2 [, scope])
```

Description

A case-sensitive search that replaces substring1 with substring2 in a string. scope can be one, which replaces the first occurrence, or all, which replaces all occurrences.

Example

```
<cfset exampleString = "This is a test of the emergency broadcasting system">
<cfset exampleString2 = "George George George of the Jungle">

<cfoutput>
#Replace(exampleString, "broadcasting", "ColdFusion")#
#Replace(exampleString2, "George", "", all)#
</cfoutput>
```

ReplaceList

```
ReplaceList (string, list1, list2)
```

Description

A case-sensitive replacement of values from a delimited list with corresponding values from another delimited list.

Example

```
<cfset exampleString = "It is a curse to be born in interesting times.">
<cfset exampleList1 = "curse, born, interesting">
<cfset exampleList2 = " blessing, live, boring">

<cfoutput>
This is my original saying: #exampleString#
This is my new saying: # ReplaceList(exampleString, exampleList1, exampleList2)#
</cfoutput>
```

ReplaceNoCase

```
ReplaceNoCase (string, substring1, substring2 [, scope])
```

Description

> A non-case-sensitive search that replaces occurrences of substring1 with substring2.

Example

```
<cfset exampleString = "This is a test of the emergency broadcasting system">
<cfset exampleString2 = "George George George of the Jungle">

<cfoutput>
#Replace(exampleString, "Broadcasting", "ColdFusion")#
#Replace(exampleString2, "george", "", all)#
</cfoutput>
```

REReplace

```
REReplace (string, reg_expression, substring [, scope])
```

Description

> A case-sensitive search using regular expressions (RE) to search a string for a string pattern and replace it with another. scope can be one or all.

Example

```
<cfoutput>
#REReplace("CABARET","C¦B","G","ALL")#
#REReplace("CABARET","[A-Z]","G","ALL")#
#REReplace("I love jelly","jell(y¦ies)","cookies")#
</cfoutput>
```

REReplaceNoCase

```
REReplaceNoCase (string, reg_expression, substring [, scope])
```

Description

> A non-case-sensitive search that uses a regular expression to search a string for a string pattern and replace it with another. Uses one and all for the scope.

Example

```
<cfoutput>
#REReplaceNoCase("cabaret","C|B","G","ALL")#
#REReplaceNoCase("I LOVE JELLIES","jell(y|ies)","cookies")#
#REReplaceNoCase("I LOVE JELLY","jell(y|ies)","cookies")#
</cfoutput>
```

Reverse

```
Reverse (string)
```

Description

Reverses the order of items, such as the characters in a string, the digits in a number, or the elements in an array.

Example

```
<cfoutput>
Using reverse on #Reverse("wow")# does not work well.
On the other hand #Reverse(7 * 3)# does not equal 21.
</cfoutput>
```

Right

```
Right (string, count)
```

Description

Gets a specified number of characters from a string, beginning at the right.

Example

```
<cfset exampleString = "(303)455-5000 ext:310">

<cfoutput>
The extension number is: #Right(exampleString, 3)#
</cfoutput>
```

RJustify

```
RJustify (string, length)
```

Description

Right-justifies characters in a string.

Example

```
<cfset exampleString = "right justified">

<cfoutput>
The example string right justified: #RJustify(exampleString, 30)#
</cfoutput>
```

Round

```
Round (number)
```

Description

Rounds a number to the closest integer following standard mathematical rules.

Example

```
<cfoutput>
10.49 stays at 10: #Round(10.49)#
10.51 goes to 11: #Round(10.51)#
</cfoutput>
```

RTrim

```
RTrim (string)
```

Description

Deletes spaces from the end of a string.

Example

```
<cfset exampleString = "This string has spaces at the end.      ">

<cfoutput>
The trimmed string: "#Rtrim(exampleString)#"
</cfoutput>
```

Second

Second (*date*)

Description

Extracts the seconds from a date/time object.

Example

```
<cfoutput>
 The current second #Second(Now())# of the day.
</cfoutput>
```

SetEncoding

SetEncoding (*scope_name*,*charset*)

Description

For when the locale is anything except English, this sets the character encoding of form scope variable values. Scope name can be either a URL or a form name.

Example

In this example an example form is set and we are assuming that Japanese Shift-JIS characters are being sent to the processing page.

```
<form action="example.cfm" method="post">
Name: <input type="text" name="exampleName">
Address: <input type="text" name="exampleAddress">
City: Name: <input type="text" name="exampleCity">
</form>

<form name="exampleForm" action="example.cfm" method="post">
Name: <input type="text" name="exampleName">
Address: <input type="text" name="exampleAddress">
City: Name: <input type="text" name="exampleCity">
</form>

<cfscript>
 setEncoding("exampleForm", "SHIFT-JIS");
 newName = "#exampleForm.exampleName#";
 newAddress = "#exampleForm.exampleAddress#";
 newCity = "#exampleForm.exampleCity#";
</cfscript>
```

SetLocale

SetLocale (*new_locale*)

Description

Sets a country/language locale option for the current application session. The locale value encapsulates a set of attributes that determines the default display format of date, time, number, and currency values, according to language and regional conventions. Locales include the following:

Chinese (China)	
Chinese (Hong Kong)	
Chinese (Taiwan)	
Dutch (Belgian)	nl_be
Dutch (Standard)	nl_NL
English (Australian)	en_AU
English (Canadian)	en_CA
English (New Zealand)	en_NZ
English (UK)	en_GB
English (US)	en_US
French (Belgian)	fr_BE
French (Canadian)	fr_CA
French (Standard)	fr_FR
French (Swiss)	fr_CH
German (Austrian)	de_AT
German (Standard)	de_DE
German (Swiss)	de_CH
Italian (Standard)	it_IT
Italian (Swiss)	it_CH
Japanese	ja_JP
Korean	ko_KR
Norwegian (Bokmal)	no_NO
Norwegian (Nynorsk)	no_NO_nynorsk
Portuguese (Brazilian)	pt_BR
Portuguese (Standard)	pt_PT
Spanish (Modern)	es_ES
Spanish (Standard)	es_ES
Swedish	sv_SE

Example

```
<cfset tempLocale = SetLocale("Portuguese (Standard)")>

<cfoutput>
The locale is now set to: #GetLocale()#
</cfoutput>
```

SetProfileString

```
SetProfileString (ini Path, section, entry, value)
```

Description

Sets the value of a profile entry in an initialization file.

Example

```
<cfset temp = SetProfileString(IniPath, Section, "timeout", exampleTimeout)>
```

SetVariable

```
SetVariable (name, value)
```

Description

This function is no longer required in well-formed ColdFusion pages.

Sgn

```
Sgn (number)
```

Description

Determines the sign of a number and returns 1 (if the number is positive), 0 (if the number is 0), or -1 (if the number is negative).

Example

```
<cfoutput>
The sign of 10 is: #Sgn(10)#
The sign of -10 is: #Sgn(-10)#
</cfoutput>
```

Sin

Sin (*number*)

Description

Calculates the sine of an angle.

Example

```
<cfoutput>
The sin of 90 is: #Sin(90)#
</cfoutput>
```

SpanExcluding

SpanExcluding (*string*, *set*)

Description

A case-sensitive search that gets characters from a string, from the beginning to a character that is in a specified set of characters.

Example

```
<cfset exampleString = "I like bunnies and big dogs">

<cfoutput>
I don't really like big dogs: #SpanExcluding(exampleString, "a">#
</cfoutput>
```

SpanIncluding

SpanIncluding (*string*, *set*)

Description

A case-sensitive search that gets characters from a string, from the beginning to a character that is not in a specified set of characters.

Example

```
<cfset exampleString = "I like bunnies and big dogs">

<cfoutput>
I don't really like big dogs: # SpanIncluding (exampleString, "I like bunnies">#
</cfoutput>
```

Sqr

```
Sqr (number)
```

Description

Calculates the square root of a number.

Example

```
<cfoutput>
The Square of 4 is #Sqr(4)#
</cfoutput>
```

StripCR

```
StripCR (string)
```

Description

Deletes return characters from a string.

Example

```
<cfset exampleString = "This is a paragraphs that has line
returns.#Chr(10)##Chr(10)#The function will erase them.">

<cfoutput>
<p><pre>#exampleString#</pre></p>

<p>#StripCR(exampleString)#</p>
</cfoutput>
```

StructAppend

```
StructAppend (struct1, struct2, overwriteFlag)
```

Description

Appends one structure to another and returns true if successful. The
overwriteFlag default is Yes and means that data in struct2 will overwrite
corresponding data in struct1. Setting it to No will prevent any overwriting.

Example

```
<cfset newStruct = StructAppend(exampleStruct1, exampleStruct2)>
```

StructClear

```
StructClear (structure)
```

Description

Deletes all data from a structure. Returns true on completion.

Example

```
<cfscript>
   Products = StructNew();
   StructInsert(Products , "ProductName", "Blizzard Blender");
   StructInsert(Products , "ProductID", 1001);
   StructInsert(Products , "SKU", "555-6582");
</cfscript>

<cfscript>
  StructClear(Products);
</cfscript>
```

StructCopy

```
StructCopy (structure)
```

Description

Makes a copy of a structure. Copies top-level keys, values, and arrays in the structure by value. The copy is not by reference, meaning changes to the original structure will not be reflected in the copy. To copy deeply nested structures, use the Duplicate function.

Example

```
<cfscript>
   Products = StructNew();
   StructInsert(Products , "ProductName", "Blizzard Blender");
   StructInsert(Products , "ProductID", 1001);
   StructInsert(Products , "SKU", "555-6582");
</cfscript>

<cfset copyStruct = StructCopy(Products)>
```

```
<cfoutput>
#copyStruct.ProductName#
#copyStruct.ProductID#
#copyStruct.SKU#
</cfoutput>
```

StructCount

```
StructCount (structure)
```

Description

Counts the keys in a structure.

Example

```
<cfscript>
   Products = StructNew();
   StructInsert(Products , "ProductName", "Blizzard Blender");
   StructInsert(Products , "ProductID", 1001);
   StructInsert(Products , "SKU", "555-6582");
</cfscript>

<cfoutput>
There are #StructCount(Products)# values in the struct.
</cfoutput>
```

StructDelete

```
StructDelete (structure, key [, indicatenotexisting])
```

Description

Removes an element from a structure.

Example

```
<cfscript>
   Products = StructNew();
   StructInsert(Products, "ProductName", "Blizzard Blender");
   StructInsert(Products, "ProductID", 1001);
   StructInsert(Products, "SKU", "555-6582");

   StructDelete(Products,SKU);
</cfscript>


<cfoutput>
These are the keys in the struct: #StructKeyList(Products)#.
</cfoutput>
```

StructFind

StructFind (*structure*, *key*)

Description

Gives the value associated with a key in a structure.

Example

```
<cfscript>
   Products = StructNew();
   StructInsert(Products, "ProductName", "Blizzard Blender");
   StructInsert(Products, "ProductID", 1001);
   StructInsert(Products, "SKU", "555-6582");
</cfscript>


<cfoutput>
The product name is # StructFind(Products, "ProductName")#.
</cfoutput>
```

StructFindKey

StructFindKey (*top*, *value*, *scope*)

Description

Performs a recursive search through a substructure of nested arrays, structures, and other elements for structures whose values match the search key in the value parameter. scope can be set as one or all.

Example

```
<cfscript>
   Products = StructNew();
   StructInsert(Products, "ProductName", "Blizzard Blender");
   StructInsert(Products, "ProductID", 1001);
   StructInsert(Products, "SKU", "555-6582");
</cfscript>


<cfoutput>
The product name is #StructFindKey(Products, "SKU")#.
</cfoutput>
```

StructFindValue

```
StructFindValue (top, value [, scope])
```

Description

Searches recursively through a substructure of nested arrays, structures, and other elements for structures with values that match the search key in the value parameter.

Example

```
<cfscript>
   Products = StructNew();
   StructInsert(Products, "ProductName", "Blizzard Blender");
   StructInsert(Products, "ProductID", 1001);
   StructInsert(Products, "SKU", "555-6582");
</cfscript>


<cfoutput>
The product name is #StructFindValue(Products, "SKU")#.
</cfoutput>
```

StructGet

```
StructGet (pathDesired)
```

Description

Creates nested structures without having to use the StructNew function. Automatically creates all the necessary structures and substructures in the path attribute.

Example

```
<cfset exampleStruct = StructGet("Products.Kitchen")>
<cfset exampleStruct.ProductName = "Blender">
<cfset exampleStruct.ProductName = "Toaster">
<cfset exampleStruct.ProductName = "Microwave">

<cfoutput>
The Keys in the above structure are:
#StructKeyList(Products.Kitchen)#
</cfoutput>
```

StructInsert

```
StructInsert (structure, key, value[, allowoverwrite])
```

Description

Inserts a key–value pair into a structure.

Example

```
<cfscript>
   Products = StructNew();
   StructInsert(Products, "ProductName", "Blizzard Blender");
   StructInsert(Products, "ProductID", 1001);
   StructInsert(Products, "SKU", "555-6582");
</cfscript>


<cfoutput>
The values in the structure are #StructKeylist(Products)#.
</cfoutput>
```

StructIsEmpty

```
StructIsEmpty (structure)
```

Description

Checks whether a structure contains data and returns true if it is empty.

Example

```
<cfscript>
   Products = StructNew();
   StructInsert(Products, "ProductName", "Blizzard Blender");
   StructInsert(Products, "ProductID", 1001);
   StructInsert(Products, "SKU", "555-6582");

  StructClear(Products);
</cfscript>


<cfoutput>
Is this struct empty?  # StructIsEmpty(Products)#.
</cfoutput>
```

StructKeyArray

```
StructKeyArray (structure)
```

Description

Creates an array with all the keys in a structure.

Example

```
<cfscript>
   Products = StructNew();
   StructInsert(Products, "ProductName", "Blizzard Blender");
   StructInsert(Products, "ProductID", 1001);
   StructInsert(Products, "SKU", "555-6582");
</cfscript>

<cfset keyarray = StructKeyArray(Products)>
```

StructKeyExists

```
StructKeyExists (structure, " key")
```

Description

Checks whether a key exists in a structure and returns true if the key exists.

Example

```
<cfscript>
   Products = StructNew();
   StructInsert(Products, "ProductName", "Blizzard Blender");
   StructInsert(Products, "ProductID", 1001);
   StructInsert(Products, "SKU", "555-6582");
</cfscript>

<cfoutput>
Does the key SKU exist? #StructKeyExists(SKU)#
</cfoutput>
```

StructKeyList

```
StructKeyList (structure [, delimiter])
```

Description

Gives a list of all the keys in a structure.

Example

```cfscript
<cfscript>
   Products = StructNew();
   StructInsert(Products, "ProductName", "Blizzard Blender");
   StructInsert(Products, "ProductID", 1001);
   StructInsert(Products, "SKU", "555-6582");
</cfscript>
```

```
<cfoutput>
These are the keys in the struct: #StructKeyList(Products)#.
</cfoutput>
```

StructNew

```
StructNew ()
```

Description

Creates a new structure.

Example

```cfscript
<cfscript>
   Products = StructNew();
   StructInsert(Products, "ProductName", "Blizzard Blender");
   StructInsert(Products, "ProductID", 1001);
   StructInsert(Products, "SKU", "555-6582");
</cfscript>
```

StructSort

```
StructSort (base, sortType, sortOrder, pathToSubElement)
```

Description

Finds and sorts structures that contain top-level key names. sortType can be numeric, text, or textnocase, and sortOrder can be asc (ascending) or desc (descending).

Example

```cfscript
<cfscript>
   Products = StructNew();
   StructInsert(Products, "ProductName", "Blizzard Blender");
   StructInsert(Products, "ProductName2", "Nukeit Microwave");
   StructInsert(Products, "ProductName3", "Toastit Toaster");
</cfscript>
```

```
<cfoutput>
#ArraytoList(StructSort(Products, "Text", "Asc"))#
</cfoutput>
```

StructUpdate

```
StructUpdate (structure, key, value)
```

Description

Updates an existing key with a new value.

Example

```
<cfscript>
   Products = StructNew();
   StructInsert(Products, "ProductName", "Blizzard Blender");
   StructInsert(Products, "ProductID", 1001);
   StructInsert(Products, "SKU", "555-6582");

   StructUpdate(Products, "ProductName", "Hardcore Chopper");
   StructUpdate(Products, "ProductID", 1200);
   StructUpdate(Products, "SKU", "666-7892");
</cfscript>
```

```
<cfoutput>
These are the keys in the struct: #StructKeyList(Products)#.
</cfoutput>
```

Tan

```
Tan (number)
```

Description

Calculates the tangent of an angle.

Example

```
<cfoutput>
The tangent of 90 degrees is #Tan(90)#.
</cfoutput>
```

TimeFormat

```
TimeFormat (time [, mask])
```

Description

Formats a time value. If no `mask` is used, it returns the time in the form of `hh:mm tt`.

Use the following values for the `mask`:

- **h.** Hours, no leading zero for single-digit hours (12-hour clock)
- **hh.** Hours, leading zero for single-digit hours (12-hour clock)
- **H.** Hours, no leading zero for single-digit hours (24-hour clock)
- **HH.** Hours, leading zero for single-digit hours (24-hour clock)
- **m.** Minutes, no leading zero for single-digit minutes
- **mm.** Minutes, a leading zero for single-digit minutes
- **s.** Seconds, no leading zero for single-digit seconds
- **ss.** Seconds, leading zero for single-digit seconds
- **t.** One-character time marker string, such as A or P
- **tt.** Multiple-character time marker string, such as AM or PM

Example

```
<cfset exampleDate = now()>

<cfoutput>
  #TimeFormat(exampleDate)#
  #TimeFormat(exampleDate, "hh:mm:ss")#
  #TimeFormat(exampleDate, "hh:mm:sst")#
  #TimeFormat(exampleDate, "hh:mm:sstt")#
  #TimeFormat(exampleDate, "HH:mm:ss")#
</cfoutput>
```

ToBase64

```
ToBase64 (string or binary_object [, encoding])
```

Description

Calculates the Base64 representation of a string or binary object. The Base64 format uses printable characters, allowing binary data to be sent in forms and email and stored in a database or file. Encodings include US-ASCII, ISO-8859-1, UTF-8, and UTF-16.

```
<cffile action="READBINARY" file="D:\CFusionMX\wwwroot\testbinary.jpg"
variable="exampleBin">

<cfoutput>
My Picture in Base64 representation:
#ToBase64(exampleBin)#
</cfoutput>
```

ToBinary

```
ToBinary (string_in_Base64 or binary_value)
```

Description

Calculates the binary representation of Base64-encoded data.

Example

Because this is using an image as the example, the following example Base64 is just a representation of the actual full Base64 because the full text is too long to include. Use a JPG image of your own in conjunction with the ToBase64 function if you are interested in testing the functionality.

```
<cfset exampleBase64 =
"/9j/4AAQSkZJRgABAQAAAAAAAD/2wBDAAMCAgMCAgMDAwMEAwMEBQgFBQQEBQoHBwYIDAoMDAsKCwsNDhIQD
Q4RDgsLEBYQERMUFRUVDA8XGBYUGBIUFRT/2wBDAQMEBAUEBQkFBQkUDQsNFBQUFBQUFBQUFBQUFBQUFBQUFBQ
UFBQUFBQUFBQUFBQUFBQUFBQUFBT/xAGiAAABBQEBAQEBAQAAAAAAAAAQIDBAUGBwgJCgsQA
AIBAwMCBAMFBQQEAAABfQECAwAEEQUSITFBBhNRYQcicRQygZGhCCNCscEVUtHwJDNicoIJChYXGBkaJSYnKCk
qNDU2Nzg5OkNERUZHSElKU1RVVldYWVpjZGVmZ2hpanN0dXZ3eHl6g4SFhoeIiYqSk5SVlpeYmZqio6Slpqeoq
aqys7S1tre4ubrCw8TFxsfIycrS09TV1tfY2drh4uPk5ebn6Onq8fLz9PX29/j5+gEAAwEBAQEBAQEBAQAAAAAA
AAECAwQFBgcICQoLEQACAQIEBAMEBwUEBAABAncAAQIDEQQFITEGEkFRB2FxEyIygQgUQpGhscEJIzNS8BVic
tEKFiQ04SXxFxgZGiYnKC">

<cffile action="WRITE" file="D:\CFusionMX\wwwroot\newBin.jpg"
output="#ToBinary(exampleBase64)#">
```

ToString

```
ToString (any_value [, encoding])
```

Description

Converts a value to a string. Encodings include US-ASCII, ISO-8859-1, UTF-8, and UTF-16.

Example

```
<cfset exampleString = "This is an example">
<cfset exampleBinary = "ToBinary(exampleString)">
<cfset backttoString = "ToString(exampleBinary)">

<cfoutput>
#backttoString#
</cfoutput>
```

Trim

```
Trim (string)
```

Description

Removes leading and trailing spaces from a string.

Example

```
<cfset exampleString = "  This is a string with spaces   ">

<cfoutput>
With the spaces trimed: #Trim(exampleString)#
</cfoutput>
```

UCase

```
UCase (string)
```

Description

Converts a string to all uppercase letters.

Example

```
<cfset exampleText = "this sentence will be made into all uppercase">

<cfoutput>
#UCase(exampleText)#
</cfoutput>.
```

URLDecode

```
URLDecode (urlEncodedString)
```

Description

Decodes a URL-encoded string.

Example

```
<cfset exampleString = "This string will not break a browser">
<cfset exampleEncode = URLEncodedFormat(exampleString)>


<cfoutput>
<p>This is the encoded string:</p>
<p>#exampleEncode#</p>
<p>This is the string after it is decoded:</p>
<p>#URLDecode(exampleEncode)#</p>
</cfoutput>
```

URLEncodedFormat

```
URLEncodedFormat (string)
```

Description

Generates a URL-encoded string. Replaces spaces with + and nonalphanumeric characters with equivalent hexadecimal escape sequences.

Example

```
<cfset exampleString = "This string will not break a browser">
<cfset exampleEncode = URLEncodedFormat(exampleString)>


<cfoutput>
<p>This is the encoded string:</p>
<p>#exampleEncode#</p>
</cfoutput>
```

URLSessionFormat

URLSessionFormat (*request_URL*)

Description

> This is conditional on whether a client computer accepts cookies. If the client does not accept cookies, the function automatically appends all required client identification information to a URL. If the client accepts cookies, it does not append the information.
>
> This function automatically determines which identifiers are required and sends only the required information. It provides a more secure and robust method for supporting client identification than manually encoding the information in each URL. This is because it sends only required information when it is required, and it is easier to code.

Example

```
<cfform method="Post"  action="#URLSessionFormat("ExamplePage.cfm")#>
```

Val

Val (*string*)

Description

> Converts numeric characters that occur at the beginning of a string to a number.

Example

```
<cfif Val(exampleValue) is not 0>
```

ValueList

ValueList (*query.column* [, *delimiter*])

Description

> Inserts a delimiter between each value in an executed query. ColdFusion does not evaluate the arguments.

Example

```
<cfquery name = "exampleQuery1" datasource = "test">
SELECT testID FROM Example
WHERE testID IN ('XZY')
</cfquery>

<cfquery name = " exampleQuery1" datasource = "test">
SELECT *
FROM Test
WHERE testID IN ('#ValueList(exampleQuery1.testID)#')
</cfquery>
```

Week

```
Week (date)
```

Description

Returns the week number within the year for a date/time object.

Example

```
<cfset exampleDate = now()>

<cfoutput>
This is week number #week(exampleDate)# this year.
</cfoutput>
```

WriteOutput

```
WriteOutput (string)
```

Description

Use this tag to write output to the page inside of a `cfscript` block. This function writes to the page-output stream, regardless of conditions established by the `cfsetting` tag.

Example

```
<cfscript>
  employee = StructNew();
  StructInsert(employee, "firstname","Joe");
  StructInsert(employee, "lastname", "Bazooka");
  StructInsert(employee, "email", "joe@bubble.com");
  StructInsert(employee, "phone","970-555-444");
```

```
StructInsert(employee, "department", "cartoon");
WriteOutput("About to add " & firstname &amp; " " &amp;
lastname);
</cfscript>
```

XmlChildPos

XmlChildPos (*elem*, *childName*, *N*)

Description

Gets the position of a child element within an XML document object.

Example

In this example, we use an XML file that is located on the test server. To try using this function, simply point the cffile to an XML file that exists on your server. You will also need to change the dot notation and child element to match your file.

```
<cffile action="read" file="d:\cfusionmx\wwwroot\xml\users.xml" variable="XMLFileText">

<cfset myXMLDocument=XmlParse(XMLFileText)>

<cfdump var = #myXMLDocument#>
<cfoutput>
<p>The xml position is: #XmlChildPos(myXMLDocument.Users.sysuser, "LastName",1)#</p>
</cfoutput>
```

XmlElemNew

XmlElemNew (*elem*, *childName*)

Description

Creates a new XML element inside of an existing XML document at the specified position in the document.

Example

In this example, we use an XML file that is located on the test server. To try using this function, simply point the cffile to an XML file that exists on your server. You will also need to change the dot notation and child element to match your file.

```
<cffile action="read" file="d:\cfusionmx\wwwroot\xml\users.xml" variable="XMLFileText">

<cfset myXMLDocument=XmlParse(XMLFileText)>
```

```
<cfdump var = #myXMLDocument#>

<cfset ArrayAppend(myXMLDocument.Users.sysuser[1].XmlChildren,
XmlElemNew(myXMLDocument,"phoneNumber"))>

<cfdump var = #myXMLDocument#>
```

XmlFormat

XmlFormat (*string*)

Description

Escapes special XML characters in a string so that the string is safe to use
with XML.

Example

```
<?xml version = "1.0"?>
<cfoutput>
<XMLExample>
  <ElementOne Attribute = "#XMLFormat("'a value'")#>
    #XMLFormat("ElementText")#
  </ElementOne>
</XMLExample>
</cfoutput>
```

XmlNew

XmlNew ([*caseSensitive*])

Description

Use this function to create an XML document object. The default setting is
No, meaning thatColdFusion ignores case. Setting it to Yes maintains case and
thus zip.addr and zip.ADDR would be treated as two distinct elements.

Example

```
<cfscript>
  exampleDoc = XmlNew();
</cfscript>
```

XmlParse

XmlParse (*xmlString* [, *caseSensitive*])

Description

Converts an XML document that is represented as a string variable into an XML document object.

Example

In this example we use an XML file that is located on the test server; to try using this function, simply point the cffile to an xml file that exists on your server.

```
<cffile action="read" file="e:\cfusionmx\wwwroot\xml\users.xml" variable="XMLFileText">

<!--- XMLParse function turns our text into a XML document object or ColdFusion
Structure --->

<cfset ExampleDocument=XmlParse(XMLFileText)>

<cfdump var=#ExampleDocument#>
```

XmlSearch

XmlSearch (*xmlDoc*, *xPathString*)

Description

Uses an XPath language expression to search an XML document that is represented as a string variable.

Example

```
<cffile action="read" file="d:\cfusionmx\wwwroot\xml\users.xml" variable="XMLFileText">

<cfset myXMLDocument=XmlParse(XMLFileText)>

<cfdump var = #myXMLDocument#>

<cfset searchterm = XMLsearch(myXMLDocument, "/users")>

<cfdump var = #searchterm#>
```

XmlTransform

```
XmlTransform (xmlString, xslString)
```

Description

Applies an eXtensible Stylesheet Language Transformation (XSLT) to an XML document object that is represented as a string variable. An XSLT converts an XML document to another format or representation by applying an eXtensible Stylesheet Language (XSL) style sheet to it.

Example

In this example, we are joining two preexisting files. To test this function, you will need to have a preexisting XML file and an XSL file to use the transform function on.

```
<cffile action="read"  file="d:\cfusionmx\wwwroot\xml\people.xml"  variable="myxml">

<cffile action="read" file="d:\cfusionmx\wwwroot\xml\people.xsl" variable="xslDoc">

<cfset xslAsString=ToString(xslDoc)>
<cfset mydocAsString=ToString(myxml)>
<cfset transformedXML = XmlTransform(mydocAsString, xslAsString)>

<cffile action="write" file="d:\cfusionmx\wwwroot\xml\resulhtm.html"
output="#transformedXML#">

<cfdump var = #transformedXML#>
```

Year

```
Year (date)
```

Description

Returns the year value from a date.

Example

```
<cfset exampleDate = now()>

<cfoutput>
The current year is #Year(exampleDate)#.
</cfoutput>
```

YesNoFormat

YesNoFormat (*value*)

Description

Evaluates a number or Boolean value and returns Yes for a nonzero; all else returns false.

Example

```
<cfoutput>
  The number 1 in Yes/No format: #YesNoFormat(1)#
  The number 3126 in Yes/No format: #YesNoFormat("3126")#
</cfoutput>
```

Index

Symbols

* (asterisk), in regular expressions, 230

\\ (backslash), in regular expressions, 231

^ (carat), in regular expressions, 231

{ } (curly brackets), in regular expressions, 231

$ (dollar sign), in regular expressions, 231

// (double forward slash), comments in CFScript code, 275

( ) (parentheses), in regular expressions, 231

. (period), in regular expressions, 232

| (pipe), in regular expressions, 232

+ (plus sign), in regular expressions, 232

(pound sign), in variables, 88, 304–305

? (question mark), in regular expressions, 232

2-tier architecture, 38–39

A

Abs( ) function, 691

access levels (CFC security), 157–159

access to content (content management systems), 343–345
   creating content, 345–348
   editing content, 348–350

ACos( ) function, 692

ActionScript, new features of ColdFusion MX, 4

adding
   elements
      to arrays, 179-180
      to structures, 183-184
      to XML documents, 421-424
   rows to query objects, 168

Administrator. *See* ColdFusion Administrator

aggregation, defined, 394

Allaire, history of ColdFusion, 1–2

alnum (POSIX character class), 233

alpha (POSIX character class), 232

AND keyword (SQL), 491

any content (XML), 391

Apache AXIS (web services), 447

Apache Project web site, 414

appending text to files, 258

application architecture. *See* architecture (of application)

Application Deployment Services, new features of ColdFusion MX, 4

application framework (development methodologies), 72

application performance. *See* performance

application planning, 35–36
   architecture of application, 36–37
      tiered architecture, 37-42
   development methodologies, 62, 73–74
      BlackBox, 71
      cfObjects, 67-69
      Fusebox, 62-67
      important components of, 71-73
      SmartObjects, 69
      Switch_box, 70

E

G

M

N

Q

T

U

RELATED NEW RIDERS TITLES

ColdFusion MX: From Static to Dynamic in 10 Steps

Barry Moore

Get the 10 steps you need to convert a static site to a dynamic site using ColdFusion MX. With reusable real-world examples and exercises, this book is easy to use and the concepts are easy to incorporate.

ISBN: 0735712964
US$35.00

Dynamic Publishing with ColdFusion MX

Benjamin Elmore, with Seth Hodgson, Michael Mazzarana, and Jeff Tapper

Learn from examples that are based in a real-world application, addresses the interaction of three key roles in dynamic publishing: developer, architect, and technical manager. The focus on implementation and solutions and the teams involved in the process sets this book apart from all the others.

ISBN: 073571312X
US$45.99

ColdFusion MX Applications with Dreamweaver MX

David Golden

Get everything you need to know to get up-to-speed on creating ColdFusion MX applications in Dreamweaver MX, in a no-frills hands-on approach. This is the only book concentrating on developing ColdFusion MX with the visual tool of choice for creating ColdFusion applications: Dreamweaver MX.

ISBN 0735712719
US $49.99

Joseph Lowery's Beyond Dreamweaver

Joseph Lowery

This book is designed to take web developers to the next level, increasing your productivity and range. It provides detailed solutions for advanced problems, as well as combining real-world deconstructions of techniques by acknowledged master designers. The step-by-step implementations show you how the designers did the work and how you can do it.

ISBN: 0735712778
US$45.00

Dreamweaver MX Magic

Brad Halstead, Josh Cavalier, et al.

Your project-based guide to learning Dreamweaver MX tips, tricks, and best practices.

ISBN: 0735711798
US$39.99

Inside Dreamweaver MX

Laura Gutman, Patty Ayers, Donald S. Booth

A solid mix of in-depth explanation of Dreamweaver MX features and real-world tips and tricks to make Dreamweaver work.

ISBN: 073571181X
US$45.99

HOW TO CONTACT US

VISIT OUR WEB SITE

WWW.NEWRIDERS.COM

On our web site, you'll find information about our other books, authors, tables of contents, and book errata. You will also find information about book registration and how to purchase our books, both domestically and internationally.

EMAIL US

Contact us at: **nrfeedback@newriders.com**

- If you have comments or questions about this book
- To report errors that you have found in this book
- If you have a book proposal to submit or are interested in writing for New Riders
- If you are an expert in a computer topic or technology and are interested in being a technical editor who reviews manuscripts for technical accuracy

Contact us at: **nreducation@newriders.com**

- If you are an instructor from an educational institution who wants to preview New Riders books for classroom use. Email should include your name, title, school, department, address, phone number, office days/hours, text in use, and enrollment, along with your request for desk/examination copies and/or additional information.

Contact us at: **nrmedia@newriders.com**

- If you are a member of the media who is interested in reviewing copies of New Riders books. Send your name, mailing address, and email address, along with the name of the publication or web site you work for.

BULK PURCHASES/CORPORATE SALES

The publisher offers discounts on this book when ordered in quantity for bulk purchases and special sales. For sales within the U.S., please contact: Corporate and Government Sales (800) 382-3419 or **corpsales@pearsontechgroup.com**. Outside of the U.S., please contact: International Sales (317) 581-3793 or **international@pearsontechgroup.com**.

WRITE TO US

New Riders Publishing
201 W. 103rd St.
Indianapolis, IN 46290-1097

CALL/FAX US

Toll-free (800) 571-5840
If outside U.S. (317) 581-3500
Ask for New Riders
FAX: (317) 581-4663

VOICES THAT MATTER

New Riders

WWW.NEWRIDERS.COM

Solutions from experts you know and trust.

www.informit.com

OPERATING SYSTEMS

WEB DEVELOPMENT

PROGRAMMING

NETWORKING

CERTIFICATION

AND MORE...

**Expert Access.
Free Content.**

New Riders has partnered with **InformIT.com** to bring technical information to your desktop. Drawing on New Riders authors and reviewers to provide additional information on topics you're interested in, **InformIT.com** has free, in-depth information you won't find anywhere else.

- **Master the skills you need, when you need them**

- **Call on resources from some of the best minds in the industry**

- **Get answers when you need them, using InformIT's comprehensive library or live experts online**

- **Go above and beyond what you find in New Riders books, extending your knowledge**

As an **InformIT** partner, **New Riders** has shared the wisdom and knowledge of our authors with you online. Visit **InformIT.com** to see what you're missing.

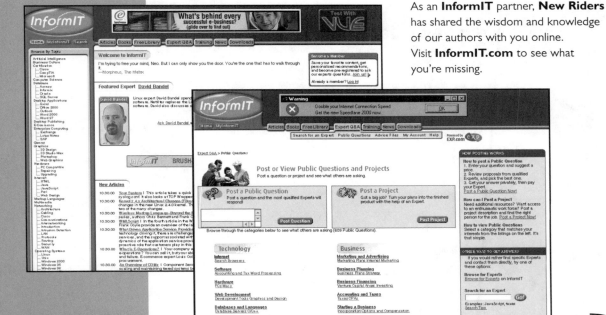

www.informit.com   ■   **www.newriders.com**

New Riders

Publishing the Voices that Matter

OUR AUTHORS

PRESS ROOM

| web development | design | photoshop | new media | 3-D | server technologies |

EDUCATORS

ABOUT US

CONTACT US

You already know that New Riders brings you the **Voices That Matter**. But what does that mean? It means that New Riders brings you the Voices that challenge your assumptions, take your talents to the next level, or simply help you better understand the complex technical world we're all navigating.

Visit **www.newriders.com** to find:

- ▸ **10% discount** and **free shipping** on all book purchases
- ▸ Never before published chapters
- ▸ Sample chapters and excerpts
- ▸ Author bios and interviews
- ▸ Contests and enter-to-wins
- ▸ Up-to-date industry event information
- ▸ Book reviews
- ▸ Special offers from our friends and partners
- ▸ Info on how to join our User Group program
- ▸ Ways to have your Voice heard

New Riders

WWW.NEWRIDERS.COM

Colophon

The image of an evening lightning storm on the cover was captured by award-winning photographer Jeremy Woodhouse (PhotoDisc).

This book was written and edited in Microsoft Word, and laid out in QuarkXPress. The font used for the body text are Bembo and Digital. It was printed on 50# Husky Offset Smooth paper at Edwards Brothers in Anarbor, Michigan. Prepress consisted of PostScript computer-to-plate technology (filmless process). The cover was printed at Moore Langen Printing in Terre Haute, Indiana, on Carolina, coated on one side.